.NET Framework
Solutions

.NET Framework Solutions: In Search *of the* Lost Win32 API

John Paul Mueller

SYBEX

San Francisco · London

Associate Publisher: Joel Fuggazzotto
Acquisitions and Developmental Editor: Denise Santoro Lincoln
Editors: Judy Flynn, William Rodarmor
Production Editor: Kylie Johnston
Technical Editor: Ross Russell Mullen
Graphic Illustrator: Jeff Wilson, Happenstance Type-O-Rama
Electronic Publishing Specialists: Jill Niles, Judy Fung, Scott Benoit
Proofreaders: Laurie O'Connell, Dave Nash, Nancy Riddiough, Monique van den Berg
Indexer: Lynnzee Elze
CD Coordinator: Dan Mummert
CD Technician: Kevin Ly
Cover Designer: Caryl Gorska/Gorska Design
Cover Photographers: Peter Samuels, Tony Stone

Library of Congress Card Number: 2002108076

ISBN: 0-7821-4134-X

Manufactured in the United States of America

10 9 8 7 6 5 4 3 2 1

This book is dedicated to my loving wife—
she is my first, best friend.

Acknowledgments

Thanks to my wife, Rebecca, for working with me to get this book completed during an exceptionally difficult time. I really don't know what I would have done without her help in researching and compiling some of the information that appears in this book (especially the glossary). She also did a fine job of proofreading my rough draft and page-proofing the final result.

Russ Mullen deserves thanks for his technical edit of this book. He greatly added to the accuracy and depth of the material you see here. I really appreciated the time he devoted to checking my code for accuracy—especially the last minute checks of test utilities. Russ also supplied some of the URLs you see in the book and other helpful tips and hints.

Matt Wagner, my agent, deserves credit for helping me get the contract in the first place and taking care of all the details that most authors don't really consider. I always appreciate his help. It's good to know that someone wants to help.

Finally, I would like to thank Denise Santoro Lincoln, Kylie Johnston, Judy Flynn, Dan Mummert, Kevin Ly, Lynnzee Elze, William Rodarmor, and the rest of the production staff at Sybex for their assistance in bringing this book to print. It's always nice to work with such a great group of professionals.

Contents at a Glance

Contents

Introduction

Hey! I needed that!

You might be tempted to yell something like this when you discover that Microsoft has implemented some, but not all, of the Win32 API in the .NET Framework. In some cases, you might find that Microsoft mislaid the feature in an out-of-the-way spot, but more often than not, the feature is simply missing. It's not documented anywhere and Microsoft doesn't give you even one clue as to where the feature might have gone. A visit to the newsgroups will often yield a pathetic claim that the missing feature will appear in the next version of the .NET Framework—so much for developing your application today.

The good news is that there are ways around your problem. In fact, sometimes the method for overcoming the loss of a feature is so simple you have to wonder why Microsoft didn't implement it (or at least document it). In other situations, the road to your missing Win32 function lies along a twisted path strewn with the boulders of incompatibility. This book helps you in both cases. We explore both the easy and the hard fixes. In fact, by the time you complete this book, you'll have discovered that the .NET Framework simply hides much of the functionality that you thought it offered as an open feature.

Hunting for Treasure

In some respects, this book is about the adventure of programming in the .NET Framework. Like any adventure, you need a map to find the treasure at the end, and this book is your map. You'll discover all of the functionality that other developers only dream about listed right in this map, and not only that, the road is marked for easy recovery. I'll also show you all of the hidden traps and how to avoid them. We'll discuss the problems of implementing an application solution that relies on the Win32 API and how you can easily achieve success.

We'll begin simply by looking at the tools you need to go on your adventure. You'll learn about messaging and using callback functions. Together we'll explore the depths of the data structure. In many places, you'll learn about the secret code words required to open the doors of files filled with treasure. For many of you, the path will begin to look familiar. But watch out! Working with the Win32 API from .NET is nothing like working with it from the languages of days gone by.

Once you're an accomplished adventurer, we'll begin delving into the new features found in Windows XP. You'll begin to understand that you don't have to implement security Microsoft's way and that the hardware really hasn't disappeared after all. Adventurers with a thirst for the most exotic treasures will discover the media player, MMC snap-ins, and even DirectX. By the time the journey ends, you'll find that every dream of Windows functionality treasure you might have wanted is answered. In sum, this is the one true map for all .NET developers who need the Win32 API in all of its forms.

Hidden Nuggets

This book is also about finding the hidden nuggets that all adventurers seek. In many of the chapters, you'll learn about tools that you might not have known about and will almost certainly learn new ways to use them. We'll also discuss how to create tools of your own. Finally, you'll receive two special DLLs that will help you overcome the problems of Win32 API access. The first DLL helps you create MMC snap-ins with less effort. The second DLL does the same for DirectX.

Who Should Read This Book?

I've designed this book for Visual Basic .NET and Visual C# .NET developers who need access to the Win32 API. Given the current state of the .NET Framework, I'm betting that most .NET developers will need some type of access to the Win32 API, and this book explores the issue at all levels. All of the examples contain full explanations, and for each, you'll find both the source and the compiled example on the CD that accompanies this book.

You won't find any information on using the language of your choice in this book—I concentrate on the Win32 API and what you need to work with it. Consequently, you won't want to look at this book until you've already learned to use either Visual Basic or Visual C#. We'll begin working with the Win32 API in the examples that appear in the first chapter and you won't stop until you reach the end of the book. Every chapter has at least one detailed example, and most contain several. You'll also find supplementary examples in the \Extras folder of the CD.

Tools Required

There are some assumptions that I've made while writing the application programming examples in this book. While writing this book, I used a Windows 2000 and Windows XP workstation. There's no guarantee that any of the code in the book will work with Windows 9x, although most of it will. You must install the latest service packs for all products before the examples will work properly. Microsoft's .NET product line is new technology and relies on the latest versions of many DLLs and the .NET Framework. In some cases, I'll list other special requirements that you must observe before the example application will run.

NOTE   Most of the concepts you'll learn in this book won't appear in your online documentation. Some of it's so new that it only appears on selected Web sites. Throughout the book you'll find tips and notes alerting you to the location of such information. In addition, Microsoft made some material available only through selected channels like an MSDN subscription. Other pieces of information are simply undocumented, and you won't find them anywhere except within a newsgroup when someone finds the feature accidentally. In a few cases, I'll tell you outright that I learned about the feature through trial and error—the type of research you won't have to perform when using this book.

I tested all of the examples in this book with Visual Studio .NET Enterprise Architect Edition. None of these examples are guaranteed to work with any other programming language products and none of them will work with the educational versions of Visual Studio.

Conventions Used in This Book

It always helps to know what the special text means in a book. In this section we'll cover usage conventions. This book uses the following conventions:

Convention	Explanation
`Inline Code`	Some code will appear in the text of the book to help explain application functionality. The code appears in a special font that makes it easy to see it. This mono-spaced font also makes the code easier to read.
`Inline Variable`	As with source code, variables that appear inline will also appear in a special font that makes them stand out from the rest of the text. When you see monospaced text in an italic typeface, you can be sure it's a variable of some type.
`User Input`	Sometimes I'll ask you to type something. For example, you might need to type a particular value into the field of a dialog box. This special font helps you see what you need to type.
[*`Filename`*]	When you see square brackets around a value, switch, or command, it means that this is an optional component. You don't have to include it as part of the command line or dialog field unless you want the additional functionality that the value, switch, or command provides.
`Filename`	A variable name is a value that you need to replace with something else. For example, you might need to provide the name of your server as part of a command-line argument. Because I don't know the name of your server, I'll provide a variable name instead. The variable name you'll see usually provides a clue as to what kind of information you need to supply. In this case, you'll need to provide a filename.

Continued on next page

Convention	Explanation
File ➢ Open	Menus and the selections on them appear with a special menu arrow symbol. "File ➢ Open" means "Access the File menu and choose Open."
italic	You'll normally see words in italic if they have special meaning or if this is the first use of the term and it is accompanied by a definition. Always pay special attention to words in italic because they're unique in some way.
`monospace`	Some words appear in a monospace font because they're easier to see or require emphasis of some type. For example, all filenames in the book appear in a monospace font to make them easier to read.
`URLs`	URLs will normally appear in a monospace font so that you can see them with greater ease. The URLs in this book provide sources of additional information designed to make your development experience better. URLs often provide sources of interesting information as well.

Icons

This book contains many icons that help you identify certain types of information. The following paragraphs describe the purpose of each icon.

NOTE Notes tell you about interesting facts that don't necessarily affect your ability to use the other information in the book. I use note boxes to give you bits of information that I've picked up while using C#, Windows 9x, Windows 2000, or Windows XP.

TIP Everyone likes tips because they tell you ways of doing things that you might not have thought about before. Tip boxes might also provide an alternative way of doing something; often you might like the alternative better than the first approach I provided.

You'll also find that I use notes and tips to hold amplifying information. For example, many of the URLs in this book appear as part of a note or a tip. The Internet contains a wealth of information, but finding it can be difficult, to say the least. URLs within notes and tips help you find new sources of information on the Internet, information that you can use to improve your programming or learn new techniques. You'll also find newsgroup URLs that tell where you can find other people to talk with about C#. Finally, URLs will help you find utility programs that'll make programming faster and easier than before.

WARNING The warning icon means "Watch out!" Warnings almost always tell you about some kind of system or data damage that'll occur if you perform a certain action (or fail to perform others). Make sure you understand a warning thoroughly before you follow any instructions that come after it.

About the Author

John Mueller is a freelance author and technical editor. He has writing in his blood, having produced 55 books and over 200 articles to date. The topics range from networking to artificial intelligence and from database management to heads-down programming. Some of his current books include a C# developer guide, a small business and home office networking guide, and several Windows XP user guides. His technical editing skills have helped over 29 authors refine the content of their manuscripts. John has provided technical editing services to both *Data Based Advisor* and *Coast Compute* magazines. He's also contributed articles to magazines like *SQL Server Professional*, *Visual C++ Developer*, and *Visual Basic Developer*. He's currently the editor of the .NET electronic newsletter for Pinnacle Publishing.

When John isn't working at the computer, you can find him in his workshop. He's an avid woodworker and candle maker. On any given afternoon, you can find him working at a lathe or putting the finishing touches on a bookcase. One of his newest craft projects is glycerin soap making, which comes in handy for gift baskets. You can reach John on the Internet at `JMueller@mwt.net`. John is also setting up a Web site at `http://www.mwt.net/~jmueller/`. Feel free to look and make suggestions on how he can improve it. One of his current projects is creating book FAQ sheets that should help you find the book information you need much faster.

PART I

An Overview of the Win32 API

CHAPTER 1

Overcoming Holes in the .NET Framework

- Why Access the Win32 API?

- Win32 Access for C# Developers

- Win32 Access for Visual Basic Developers

There are few, if any, perfect programming platforms in the world and .NET is no exception. Developers who spend any time working in the unmanaged environment before they begin working with .NET will notice some distinct problems with functionality in the .NET environment. Some of these holes (such as those in the security area) are apparent and require an immediate fix; others (such as the lack of support for a Beep() function) are subtle and you might never notice them. The point is that the .NET Framework is new technology and there are bound to be some holes in coverage, and you'll notice them with regular frequency.

This chapter provides a quick overview of some major areas of omission in the .NET Framework. I want to say at the outset that I feel the .NET Framework is a big improvement over using unmanaged code, but it's new and lacks some features that most developers will need. Consequently, you'll find that this book discusses "holes" in coverage or augmentation of features. I'm not here to tell you that the .NET Framework is technically flawed. The goal of this chapter is to help you plan your development efforts to make the best use of existing .NET Framework functionality and to access the Win32 API when the .NET Framework proves less than perfect.

NOTE   Visual C++ represents a unique language in .NET because it provides both managed and unmanaged coding environments. Consequently, you can access the Win32 API in its entirety from Visual C++ using the same unmanaged techniques you used before .NET appeared on the horizon. This unique functionality means that Visual C++ developers won't need the special techniques found in this book. It also means that you can use Visual C++ as a language bridge between managed and unmanaged environments.

Why Access the Win32 API?

Many of you have a lot of experience working with the Win32 API are already familiar with the programming requirements for unmanaged code. The idea of working with unmanaged code presents few problems for the seasoned developer. However, the .NET Framework that Microsoft has advertised is supposed to obviate the need to work with unmanaged code, so the first question on most developer's minds is: why they would even need to access the Win32 API? The short answer is that you'll find a lack of functionality in some areas such as DirectX, the Microsoft Management Console (MMC), and direct hardware access when working with the .NET Framework. You can only gain access to this functionality through the Win32 API.

The long answer requires a little more explanation. For example, not all .NET languages have an equal measure of missing functionality. The .NET Framework doesn't include a Beep() function, so you'll find this feature missing in C# as well. However, because Visual Basic includes a Beep() function as part of the language, it doesn't require any special programming to access this Win32 API feature. In sum, the question of missing functionality is a matter of determining if the language you're using provides the feature and then determining the best method to access the feature if it is missing.

You'll find that the question of Win32 API access becomes more complex as you move from simple functions such as Beep() to major programming projects such as creating an MMC Snap-in. The level of Win32 API access varies by language, which is why this book addresses C# and Visual Basic. You'll find that some chapters, including this one, contain separate C# and Visual Basic sections because the two languages provide varying levels of Win32 API access. Consequently, the third issue in Win32 API access is whether the target language provides support for the required feature. It might not, which means you'll need to create wrappers for the missing functionality.

Now that you have a basic overview of the question of why you'd want to access the Win32 API, let's discuss the issues in more detail. The following sections describe needs and requirements for Win32 API access in a generic manner. You can apply this material equally to any language you might want to use with .NET.

A Case of Missing Functionality

As previously mentioned, the .NET Framework lacks functionality for some basic calls such as Beep(). This means that a C# developer who needs to create a sound within an application has to find some other means to do it. There's no doubt that the functionality is missing, but the technique used to create the desired functionality varies by language capability, environment, and flexibility. For example, when working with Visual Basic, you already have access to a basic Beep() function, so no additional coding is required if you require a simple beep. However, as shown in Listing 1.1, there are actually four ways to create a beep in C# and not all of them provide the same features. (You'll find the source code for this example in the \Chapter 01\C#\MakeSound folder of the CD; a Visual Basic version appears in the \Chapter 01\VB\MakeSound folder.)

Listing 1.1   **Creating a Beep in C#**

```
// Import the Windows Beep() API function.
[DllImport("kernel32.dll")]
private static extern bool Beep(int freq, int dur);

// Define some constants for using the PlaySound() function.
public const int SND_FILENAME = 0x00020000;
public const int SND_ASYNC = 0x0001;

// Import the Windows PlaySound() function.
[DllImport("winmm.dll")]
```

```
public static extern bool PlaySound(string pszSound,
                                     int hmod,
                                     int fdwSound);


[STAThread]
static void Main(string[] args)
{
    // Create a sound using an escape character.
    Console.Write("\a");
    Console.WriteLine("Press Any Key When Ready...");
    Console.ReadLine();

    // Create a sound using a Windows API call.
    Beep(800, 200);
    Console.WriteLine("Press Any Key When Ready...");
    Console.ReadLine();

    // Create a sound using a Visual Basic call.
    Microsoft.VisualBasic.Interaction.Beep();
    Console.WriteLine("Press Any Key When Ready...");
    Console.ReadLine();

    // Create a sound using a WAV file.
    PlaySound("BELLS.WAV",
              0,
              SND_FILENAME | SND_ASYNC);
    Console.WriteLine("Press Any Key When Ready...");
    Console.ReadLine();
}
```

It's important to note that using an escape character to produce a sound only works for a console application—you can't use this technique in a GUI application. However, this technique does enable you to circumvent the requirement to access the Win32 API just to create a beep. The technique is important because it provides you with another choice; one that doesn't rely on unmanaged code.

The Win32 API Beep() function has the advantage of providing the greatest flexibility for the smallest cost in resources. To use this technique, you must declare the Win32 API Beep() function as a DLL import using the [DllImport] attribute. In this case, you must use unmanaged code to achieve your objective, but you don't need a wrapper DLL—C# and Visual Basic both provide all the support required. Notice that the Win32 API Beep() function enables you to choose both the tone (frequency) and duration of the beep, which is something you won't get using an escape character or Visual Basic's built-in function.

Some developers might not realize that they are able to access other language features from within the current language by relying on a .NET Framework feature called Interaction. The third method, shown in Listing 1.1, simply calls the Visual Basic Beep() function. You need to include a reference to the `Microsoft.VisualBasic.DLL` to make this portion of the example work. This technique requires a little more effort than making a direct Win32 API call, but it has the advantage of using pure managed code within the C# application.

Sometimes you don't want to use a plain beep within an application, so it's helpful to know how to access WAV files. The fourth technique, shown in Listing 1.1, has the advantage of complete sound source flexibility. However, this technique also has the dubious honor of being the most complicated way to produce a sound. The function call to `PlaySound()` is more complicated than the `Beep()` Win32 API call. You also need to define constants to use it.

The point of this section is that you'll find missing functionality within the .NET Framework, but you don't always have to rely on Win32 API calls to fill the gap. In many situations, you can rely on language interoperability or built-in operating system functionality. When you do need to rely on the Win32 API, you'll find that some functions are easier to use than others. It isn't always necessary to use the most complex method when a simple one will work. In fact, in some cases, you'll find that you can't use the full-featured function because the target language won't support it.

Win32 Function Types

One of the problems in determining if a piece of functionality is missing from the .NET Framework is that the framework is relatively large—not as large as the Win32 API, but large nonetheless. (At the time of this writing, the download size for the .NET Framework was 21 MB.) So it pays to know where you'll find holes in the .NET Framework most often. The following sections discuss the various places where other developers have found holes in the .NET Framework coverage of the Win32 API. You might find other areas when working with special Win32 API features, but these sections provide you with a fairly complete overview.

Hardware

Every time Microsoft releases a new technology, they find a way to add yet more layers of code between the developer and the hardware, and .NET is no exception. Any hope you entertained of direct hardware access will quickly fade as you make your way through a few programming tasks. You'll even find it difficult to access Windows driver and low-level DLL functionality—the access just isn't there. Generally, you'll find that the .NET Framework provides you with objects that indirectly relate to some type of hardware functionality, such as the use of streams for hard drive and printer access.

The lack of direct hardware access isn't always a negative, however. Once you get used to using the .NET Framework objects, you might find that direct hardware access is unnecessary or, at least, a rare event. Common hardware types, such as printers and hard drives, won't present a problem in most cases. Some developers have complained about the level of support provided for common low-level devices like the serial ports.

You'll also run into problems when working with hardware that Microsoft didn't anticipate. For example, accessing many USB devices is a frustrating experience when working with .NET. In most cases, you'll need to use unmanaged code and a third-party library to access new devices. We'll talk more about direct hardware access in Chapter 7.

Security

Microsoft's latest security craze is role-based security. It's true that role-based security is extremely easy to use and requires less effort on the part of the developer. In many cases, role-based security is also more flexible than the security that Microsoft provided in the past. However, role-based security is also less than appropriate if you need low-level control over the security features of your application.

There's a place for tokens, access control lists, and all of the other paraphernalia of Win32 API security in many applications, but you can't gain access to these features within the .NET Framework. To gain access to the low-level details of security within Windows, you still need to use the security calls provided by the Win32 API. We'll discuss security access within Chapter 8.

Operating System

It would seem that the operating system is the first thing you'd need to support as part of development platform, but this isn't necessarily true. Consider two existing types of application that don't rely very heavily on the operating system: browser-based applications and Java applications. Yes, both technologies require basic access to the operating system, but you'll find that for the most part you can't access the operating system as an entity. These development platforms rely on runtime engines that interact with the operating system in a predefined manner.

The .NET Framework is a modern development platform that will hopefully see implementation on other platforms. Consequently, you won't see any operating system support in the core namespaces, but will see some support in the Microsoft-specific namespaces. The separation of .NET functionality from operating system functionality is understandable, given Microsoft's stated goal of platform independence. However, unlike other platforms, the .NET Framework does provide limited operating system interfaces. In fact, there are three levels of operating system support that you need to consider when working with the .NET Framework—and .NET only supports one of them.

Upper-Level Interface   This is the level of operating support that the .NET Framework does support. The support appears in several areas, but the two main namespaces are `System.Windows.Forms` and `Microsoft.Win32`. As the names imply, the first namespace helps you gain access to the GUI features that Windows provides, while the second namespace provides access to features like the registry. The level of support in both areas is extensive, but limited to features that Microsoft felt a developer would need to create business applications.

Low-Level Services   There are a lot of low-level services that the .NET Framework doesn't even touch. For example, if you want to learn about the capabilities of the display, you'll need to use a Win32 API call to do it. Likewise, if you want to learn the status of the services on a remote machine, you'll have to resort to the Win32 API. We'll discuss low-level service access in greater detail in Chapter 10.

Version-Specific Features   Generally, you'll find that any operating system features that the .NET Framework does support are also found in all versions of Windows since Windows NT. In some cases, you'll also find the new features originally found in the Windows 9*x* operating system interface. However, if you want to use the new graphical features found in Windows XP, you'll have to rely on the Win32 API. We'll discuss some of these special features and how to access them in Chapter 9.

Multimedia

Microsoft engineered the .NET Framework for business users. You won't find support for any sound capability and barely any functions for graphics. There isn't any support for devices such as joysticks. In short, if you want to work with multimedia, your only choices are using the Win32 API calls or employing DirectX. Both of these solutions currently require the use of unmanaged code. Microsoft has said they plan to create a managed version of DirectX, but it's not a high priority. We'll discuss multimedia issues in greater detail in Chapter 11. A joystick example appears in Chapter 7 as part of direct hardware access.

Utility

There are a number of utility applications within Windows that require special interfaces. The most prominent of these utility applications is the Microsoft Management Console (MMC), which acts as a container for special components called *snap-ins*. The MMC is a vital tool for network administrators (and even for the common user) because it enables you to perform tasks such as monitor computer performance and manage user security. Unfortunately, the .NET Framework doesn't include support for this necessary utility, despite constant requests from developers during the beta process. You'll find a comprehensive MMC example in Chapter 12, along with tips for working with other utility application types.

DirectX

It wasn't long ago that game developers fought with Microsoft over the need to access hardware directly in a way that would keep Windows in the loop without the performance-robbing penalty of actually using Windows. The result of this conflict is DirectX—an advanced programming technology for working with a wide range of multimedia hardware. Given Microsoft's goal of making the .NET Framework business friendly, it's not too surprising they failed to include any DirectX support.

Unfortunately, some business application developers rely on DirectX to produce complex reports and perform other business-related multimedia tasks. Part of the problem may be that Microsoft viewed the behemoth that is DirectX and decided they needed to implement it at a later date to get the .NET Framework out in a timely manner. Rumors abound that Microsoft plans to release a .NET Framework friendly version of DirectX sometime in the future, but for now, you need to rely on unmanaged programming techniques to work with DirectX.

DirectX is a complex topic—one that many books can't cover in detail. Consequently, we'll discuss DirectX in the chapters found in Part IV of the book. We won't discuss DirectX itself. I'm assuming you already know how to use DirectX (or will find another book to guide you). These chapters show how to make DirectX work with managed applications—no small undertaking, but definitely doable.

Win32 Access Requirements

It's important to know what you need to do in order to access the Win32 API once you decide that the .NET Framework doesn't provide a required level of support. Generally speaking, Win32 API access isn't difficult for general functions. If you look again at the Beep() example in Listing 1.1, you'll notice that gaining access to the required functions doesn't require a lot of code. However, you do need to know something about the function you want to access, including the fact that it exists. The following list details some of the information you need (we'll discuss this information in detail in Chapter 2).

- A knowledge of the function and its purpose
- A complete list of all function arguments and return values
- A description of any constants used with the function
- Complete details about any structures the function requires for data transfer
- The values and order of any enumeration used with the function

Not every function requires all of this information, but you need to at least verify what information the function does require. A simple function may require nothing more than a [DLLImport] entry and a call within your code. Complex functions might require structures, which means converting the data within the structure to match the language you're using within .NET. The most complex functions may have data structure elements such as unions that are impossible to replicate properly within a managed environment, which means creating a wrapper function in an unmanaged language such as Visual C++ (the language we'll use for this purpose throughout the book).

Sometimes what appears to be a single function call actually requires multiple functions. For example, the .NET Framework doesn't offer any way to clear the console screen, so you need to perform this task using a Win32 API call. Unfortunately, clearing the screen means moving the cursor and performing other low-level tasks—a single call won't do. Listing 1.2 shows a typical example of a single task that required multiple function calls. (The source code for this example appears in the \Chapter 01\C#\ClearScreen and the \Chapter 01\VB\ ClearScreen folders of the CD.)

Listing 1.2   Clearing the Screen Requires Multiple Function Calls

```
// This special class contains an enumeration of
// standard handles.
class StdHandleEnum
{
   public const int STD_INPUT_HANDLE   = -10;
   public const int STD_OUTPUT_HANDLE  = -11;
   public const int STD_ERROR_HANDLE   = -12;
};

// This sructure contains a screen coordinate.
[StructLayout(LayoutKind.Sequential, Pack=1)]
   internal struct COORD
{
   public short X;
   public short Y;
}

// This stucture contains information about the
// console screen buffer.
[StructLayout(LayoutKind.Sequential, Pack=1)]
   internal struct CONSOLE_SCREEN_BUFFER_INFO
{
   public COORD     Size;
   public COORD     p1;
   public short     a1;
   public short     w1;
   public short     w2;
   public short     w3;
   public short     w4;
   public COORD     m1;
}

// We need these four functions from kernel32.dll.
// The GetStdHandle() function returns a handle to any
// standard input or output.
```

```csharp
[DllImport("kernel32.dll", SetLastError=true)]
public static extern IntPtr GetStdHandle(int nStdHandle);

// The GetConsoleScreenBufferInfo() returns information
// about the console screen buffer so we know how much to
// clear.
[DllImport("kernel32.dll", SetLastError=true)]
public static extern bool GetConsoleScreenBufferInfo(
    IntPtr hConsoleOutput,
    out CONSOLE_SCREEN_BUFFER_INFO lpConsoleScreenBufferInfo);

// The SetConsoleCursorPosition() places the cursor on the
// console screen.
[DllImport("kernel32.dll", SetLastError=true)]
public static extern bool SetConsoleCursorPosition(
    IntPtr hConsoleOutput,
    COORD dwCursorPosition);

// The FillConsoleOutputCharacter() allows us to place any character
// on the console screen. Using a space clears the display area.
[DllImport("kernel32.dll", SetLastError=true, CharSet=CharSet.Auto)]
public static extern bool FillConsoleOutputCharacter(
    IntPtr hConsoleOutput,
    short cCharacter,
    int nLength,
    COORD WriteCoord,
    out int lpNumberOfCharsWritten);

[STAThread]
static void Main(string[] args)
{
    // Needed ask Windows about the console screen
    // buffer settings.
    CONSOLE_SCREEN_BUFFER_INFO   CSBI;
    // Handle to the otuput device.
    IntPtr                       hOut;
    // Number of characters written to the screen.
    int                          CharOut;
    // Home cursor position.
    COORD                        Home;

    // Write some data to the screen.
    Console.Write("Some Text to Erase!" +
                "\r\nPress any key...");
    Console.ReadLine();

    // Clear the screen.
    // Begin by getting a handle to the console screen.
    hOut = GetStdHandle(StdHandleEnum.STD_OUTPUT_HANDLE);
```

```
    // Get the required console screen buffer information.
    GetConsoleScreenBufferInfo(hOut, out CSBI );

    // Set the home position for the cursor (upper left corner).
    Home.X = 0;
    Home.Y = 0;

    // Fill the console with spaces.
    FillConsoleOutputCharacter(hOut,
                               (short) ' ',
                               CSBI.Size.X * CSBI.Size.Y,
                               Home,
                               out CharOut);

    // Place the cursor in the upper left corner.
    SetConsoleCursorPosition(hOut, Home);

    // Show the screen is clear.
    Console.ReadLine();
}
```

Notice that this example uses more of the elements typical of a Win32 API call, including an enumeration and two structures. The code requires an enumeration for standard output handles. An output handle is simply a pointer to a device such as the screen. The three standard devices are input, output, and error. We also need two structures to fulfill the needs of the Windows API calls used in the example. The code listing describes each structure's task.

The example code relies on four Windows API functions, all of which appear in the KERNEL32 .DLL. All four perform some type of console screen manipulation. The code listing describes each function's task.

The short part of the code is actually demonstrating the console screen clearing process. Main() creates some output on screen. The ReadLine() call merely ensures the code will wait until you see the text. Press Enter and the clearing process begins.

The first thing we need is a handle to the console output. The handle tells Windows what device we want to work with. Once we have a handle to the output device, we need to ask Windows about its dimensions. The dimensions are important because you want to ensure the console screen erases completely. The FillConsoleOutputCharacter() function call fills the screen with spaces—the equivalent of erasing its content. Finally, we place the cursor in the upper left corner—the same place the CLS command would.

Of course, working with Windows means more than just making simple function calls; sometimes you need to work with COM as well. Once you get past simple functions and into the COM environment, development quickly gains a level or two of complexity. For example, if you want to create a COM equivalent component, you'll also need to discover and implement the interfaces supported by the unmanaged component. Sometimes the interfaces can become complex and difficult to re-create, as we'll see in the MMC example in Chapter 12.

Win32 Access for C# Developers

C# developers have a number of advantages over other .NET languages when it comes to Win32 access. The most important is the ability to use unsafe code and pointers. Many developers find that C# is an outstanding choice for the low-level programming tasks required for Win32 access. Of course, there's no free lunch—you pay a price whenever you gain some level of flexibility in the development environment. The following sections provide you with an overview of the pros and cons of using C# as your development language. We'll discuss these issues in greater detail as the book progresses.

Understanding the Effects of Unsafe Code

The term "unsafe code" is somewhat ambiguous because it doesn't really tell you anything about the code. A better way to view unsafe code is unmanaged code that appears within a managed environment. Any code that relies on the use of manual pointers (* symbol) or addresses (& symbol) is unsafe code. Whenever you write code that uses these symbols, you also need to use the unsafe keyword in the method declaration as shown below. (This example appears in the \Chapter 01\C#\Unsafe folder of the CD.)

```
unsafe private void btnTest_Click(object sender, System.EventArgs e)
{
    int   Input = Int32.Parse(txtInput.Text); // Input string.

    // Convert the input value.
    DoTimeIt(&Input);

    // Display the result
    txtOutput.Text = Input.ToString();
}

unsafe private void DoTimeIt(int* Input)
{
    int   Output;  // Output to the caller.

    // Display the current minute.
    txtMinute.Text = System.DateTime.Now.Minute.ToString();
```

```
    // Create the output value.
    Output = *Input;
    Output = Output * System.DateTime.Now.Minute;

    // Output the result.
    *Input = Output;
}
```

This is a simple example that we could have created using other methods, but it demonstrates a principle you'll need to create applications that rely on the Win32 API later. The btnTest_Click() accesses the input value, converts it to an *int*, and supplies the address of the *int* to the DoTimeIt() method. Because we've supplied an address, rather than the value, any change in the supplied value by DoTimeIt() will remain when the call returns.

The DoTimeIt() method accesses the current time, multiplies it by the value of the input string, and then outputs the value. Notice the use of pointers in this method to access the values contained in the Input and Output variables. The reason this code is unsafe is that the compiler can't check it for errors. For example, you could replace the last line with Input = &Output; and the compiler would never complain, but you also wouldn't see the results of the multiplication.

Besides using the unsafe keyword, you also need to set your application to use unsafe code. Right-click the project name in Solution Explorer and choose Properties from the context menu. Select the Configuration Properties\Build folder and you'll see the Allow unsafe code blocks option shown in Figure 1.1. Set this option to True to enable use of unsafe code in your application.

FIGURE 1.1:

Using the Allow unsafe code blocks option to enable use of unsafe code in your application.

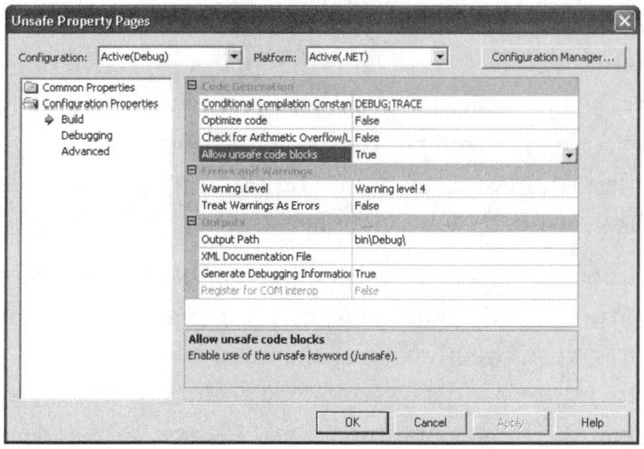

NOTE   You can't use pointers on managed types, but you can use them on values. For example, you can't obtain the address of a string because a string is a managed type. The reason this example works in C# is that int is a value type. If you need to pass a string, then it's important to know other ways to mimic pointers. For example, you can pass a string using the ref or out keywords, or you can marshal it using various techniques.

Generally, you should avoid using unsafe code whenever possible, if only to get as much help as possible from the compiler. The "Understanding the Effects of Pointers" section tells you about managed alternatives that mimic pointers. In short, while unsafe code is a necessity when working with the Win32 API, you should avoid it whenever possible.

Understanding the Effects of Pointers

One of the first issues that you'll face when working with the Win32 API is the use of pointers—the Win32 API uses them by the gross. You'll find pointers as function arguments, within structures, and even nested within each other. The problem with pointers is that they aren't objects; they really aren't anything. A pointer is an abstraction, an address for something real. The pointer to your house is the street address found on letters and packages. The .NET Framework refrains from relying on pointers (from a developer's perspective) and uses the actual object whenever possible. The pointers are still there; CLR simply manages them for you.

As mentioned in the previous section, you can use actual pointers in C# if you're also willing to deal with the problems of unsafe code. Unlike other .NET languages, C# embraces C++ type pointers, which makes it ideal for creating low-level routines and even wrapper DLLs in many situations. However, there are many ways to mimic pointers so that you can gain the benefits of the Win32 API without losing the benefits of the managed environment.

The first thing to consider is that pointers aren't always necessary. For example, the code in Listing 1.1 works fine without pointers because we're passing values to the Win32 API and not expecting anything in return. Avoid pointers whenever possible by verifying the need for them first. In many situations, you can simply pass a value to the Win32 API when a return value isn't needed by your application.

Another issue to consider is the use of pointer substitutes. Look at the FillConsoleOutput-Character() method declaration in Listing 1.2 and you'll notice that it relies on the out keyword to return the number of characters written to the screen. An IntPtr easily handles the console output handle (essentially a pointer to a pointer). In fact, you can place this use of an IntPtr in your rules of thumb book. Generally, you can replace a handle with an IntPtr for all Win32 API calls.

Sometimes you must use a pointer—there simply isn't any way around the issue. For example, you'll often find that COM calls require pointers to pointers, such as when you want to work with an interface. In this situation, you might find it impossible to develop a substitute for pointers. When this problem occurs, try to localize the pointer code to a special function, even if it might not make sense to create a separate function from a program flow perspective. Placing the pointer in its own function makes it simpler to work with the pointer, reduces the probability of missed pointer errors, and makes it easier to debug the application later.

Advantages for the C# Developer

C# developers have certain advantages when using the Win32 API. We've already discussed some of these advantages, but the most important is support for pointers and unsafe code. However, C# has some other advantages and I'd be remiss not to mention them.

C-like Language Structures   Most of the information you'll need to access Win32 API is found in the C header files that come with Visual Studio. In fact, when you research a function in the Visual Studio help files, the information is often presented using C header file entries. While C# isn't C, it does have many of the same features, making conversion a lot easier than other languages.

Direct Language Conversion   It's possible to recreate most C structures using C# without much effort. In fact, several of the examples in the book use the content from the C header files with small changes to account for language differences between C and C#. Because you don't have to interpret the structures, you'll find that writing the code to access the Win32 API from C# is relatively easy. The only time you'll run into problems is when you need to write code for complex COM interfaces and methods.

Less Language Baggage   Generally, you'll find that if the .NET Framework doesn't support a Win32 API feature, then C# doesn't support it either. Knowing this fact saves time because you don't have to research the language to discover if it provides the required support. Of course, this could also be viewed as a negative because C# will require Win32 API function calls more often than languages that do provide robust language support for Windows features.

Better Microsoft Support   It may be a quirk, but every time someone from Microsoft demonstrates a low-level language example for .NET, it appears in C# before it appears in any other language. C# is also the language of choice on newsgroups and on Web sites in many cases. Visual Basic is next on the list. Interestingly enough, the language most capable of handling Win32 API calls is the one that is seldom used—Visual C++.

Win32 Access for Visual Basic Developers

In the past, Advanced Visual Basic developers were used to accessing Win32 API functions because Visual Basic has always had certain holes in its coverage of Windows features. From this perspective, nothing has changed for Visual Basic .NET developers. What has changed is that you now have the additional hurdle of working with managed code when accessing the Win32 API, and this can make a significant difference.

WARNING   Don't get the idea that you can use your old Visual Basic code directly in Visual Basic .NET. Some developers have stated that Microsoft created an entirely new language when they developed Visual Basic .NET. While this view might not be strictly true, it's true that your old code won't run as is—even the Win32 API access code. Your old code does provide a starting point, however, so make sure you use it as a reference as you develop your new Visual Basic .NET code.

Visual Basic still offers ease of use features that C# doesn't have. You can still prototype applications quickly using very little code. Unfortunately, the addition of managed code has put Visual Basic developers at a decided disadvantage in the Win32 API access arena. There are certain types of Win32 API access that you simply can't create using Visual Basic because it lacks support for unsafe code and pointers.

The following sections detail the advantages and disadvantages of using Visual Basic to access the Win32 API. At times you'll consider the disadvantages more important and may even decide to implement the Win32 API access using a wrapper DLL. However, Visual Basic does have features that make it the best language choice, in some cases, and we'll discuss them as well.

NOTE   Throughout the book, you'll see examples in both Visual Basic and C#. If it's possible to perform an access task in both languages, you'll find the example in both languages on the CD, even if the Visual Basic source code doesn't appear in the text. You can create every example in the book using C#, but some examples are beyond the capabilities of Visual Basic .NET. Whenever an example fails in Visual Basic, the book will include an explanation of the problem and provide you with some alternatives whenever possible. There are some examples where you'll have to rely on C# or Visual C++ to perform the task.

Understanding Visual Basic Limitations

The biggest limitations for Visual Basic .NET developers are lack of unsafe code and lack of pointer support. You can get around some of these limitations using the techniques in the "Understanding the Effects of Pointers" section of the chapter. Essentially, you need to be able to provide the input to the Win32 API call using something other than a pointer, which often means a either compromise or not using the call at all.

Visual Basic developers also have language problems to overcome. If you want to use the Win32 API, you also need to know how the C header files work, which means having some knowledge of the C language. Many Visual Basic developers lack this knowledge, making it difficult to create a Visual Basic version of a structure, function call, or other construct originally written in C.

In most cases, Visual Basic developers will find it difficult to re-create complex COM interfaces. For example, the MMC example defies implementation in Visual Basic because it relies heavily on COM interface simulation. In fact, this particular task is barely doable in C# and you still need to create a Visual C++ wrapper for certain MMC function calls. In short, some tasks will defy every effort to complete in Visual Basic because there's no conduit for communication with the Win32 API.

Another problem with Visual Basic is that you can't re-create some of the stranger Win32 API structures. For example, some structures include unions, which is a feature that Visual Basic doesn't support. Unfortunately, there isn't any workaround for this problem other than to emulate the union in some other manner. In many cases, there isn't any way to emulate the union, making it impossible to call the Win32 API function that relies on the structure in question.

One of the advantages of Visual Basic is also a disadvantage. Developers gain a significant development speed boost by using Visual Basic. It enables a developer to prototype applications quickly. Coding and debugging are equally fast in most cases. All of these features come with a price, however, a lack of contact with the lower-level functions of the operating system. Visual Basic hides a lot of the usual operating system plumbing from the developer—a bonus when you don't require such access and a problem when you do.

Advantages for the Visual Basic Developer

Visual Basic .NET does have some limitations when it comes to Win32 API access, but it also has some advantages. Faster development time is just one advantage we've discussed so far and it's an important issue in a world where speed is everything. However, there are other factors in favor of Visual Basic and the following list tells you about them.

Existing Code   Even though you can't use existing Visual Basic code to access the Win32 API, you can use it as a source of information, and that's worth quite a bit to developers on a time schedule. The existing code is well understood, debugged, and ready to use. Simple Win32 API calls present the least number of problems for the Visual Basic developer. For example, the various beep function calls examined in Listing 1.1 present few problems because they require basic input and no output.

Stronger Language Support   Remember that it's only necessary to call the Win32 API if the .NET Framework and the language lack support for a Windows feature. For example, C# lacks support for any type of beep function, so we need to create one. However, Visual Basic doesn't have this lack—it supplies a beep function, so you don't even need to use the Win32 API in this case. Visual Basic provides more built-in features than many other languages, making Win32 API access unnecessary in the first place.

Where Do You Go from Here?

This chapter has introduced you to the needs and requirements for Win32 API access from .NET languages. We've discussed some of the potential problems of working with the Win32 API and why you need to exercise care when making a Win32 call. This chapter has also pointed out some areas where the .NET Framework lacks certain types of support, so the need to use the Win32 API is very real.

Make sure you run the examples in this chapter because they demonstrate some of the essential principles we'll discuss in detail as the book progresses. It's also important to begin learning the rules of thumb presented throughout the chapter. For example, you should only use pointers when necessary in an application; otherwise, you might find it difficult to troubleshoot an errant pointer or figure out why an application misbehaves in some strange way.

As part of the preparation for this book, you'll want to know how to work in the .NET environment using either Visual C# or Visual Basic. It's important to know how the .NET Framework is put together and how you use it within an application. Consequently, you might want to use my previous book, *Visual C# .NET Developer's Handbook* (ISBN 0782140475, Sybex 2002) as an aid to learning C# at the intermediate level.

Chapter 2 begins the process of working with the Win32 API. We'll discuss data in its various forms. You'll learn about everything from simple variables to structures to enumerations. Remember that the Win32 API relies on unmanaged data, so you always need to consider data conversion a part of the calling process. In some cases, CLR will help you with the data conversion; but in many other situations, you'll need to create your own solutions. Chapter 2 is your key to making good data conversion decisions.

CHAPTER 2

Working with Win32 API Data

- A Short View of Data

- Working with Variables

- Working with Data Structures

- Working with Pointers

- Working with Enumerations

- Importing Resources

The goal of most operations in a computer application is data access. The function retrieves, sets, modifies, deletes, creates, or otherwise manipulates the data. With that in mind, this chapter will discuss Win32 API data—the essential part of the Win32 API experience for most developers.

There are four levels of data that the Win32 API manipulates: variables, data structures, pointers, and enumerations. This chapter discusses all four levels of data in separate sections because each type requires a different treatment within a managed application. Even a data structure, which is essentially a collection of variables and pointers, requires special handling because of the way that managed applications work.

We'll also discuss the all-important issue of importing resources from the unmanaged environment into the managed application environment. You need to know how to perform this task to make use of the existing resources that Windows provides instead of taking a "reinvent the wheel" approach merely because the resource is inconveniently placed in a DLL.

A Short View of Data

Microsoft wrote many of the DLLs found in Windows using C, not C++ but straight C. Some of the DLLs use C++ and a very few use other languages (and we're talking a very few). This means that you'll have to work with C libraries to use the Win32 API in most cases. Unlike the unmanaged environment found in Visual Studio 6, Visual Studio .NET provides little in the way of wrappers that you can simply use to access the Win32 API without the frustration of working with C.

Working with C library files means converting data from the managed environment into a form that the library functions will understand. Of course, neither Visual Basic nor C# provides support for an *HRESULT* or a *LPTSTR*, which are the standard fare of C library routines. This means that you need to know the underlying data type for the C library types that you'll encounter. For example, you'll find that an *HRESULT* converts quite easily to a *System.Int32* value. The problem is that you won't know this at first because none of the documentation provided with Visual Studio tells you about conversions between managed and unmanaged types—an issue we'll discuss throughout the book, but especially in this chapter.

In some cases, you can't directly convert an unmanaged type to a managed type. This is always true for structures, but you'll also run into the problem with some variable types. When this problem occurs, the .NET Framework generally provides some way to marshal the data using the [MarshalAs] attribute. You'll find this attribute in the System.Runtime.Interop-Services namespace. Listing 2.1 shows an example of how to use the [MarshalAs] attribute, along with a few new Win32 API techniques we haven't yet discussed. You'll find the source code for this example in the \Chapter 02\C#\ShowMessage and \Chapter 02\VB\ShowMessage folders of the CD.

NOTE The example code in Listing 2.1 shows all of the potential inputs for `MessageBoxEx()`. However, not all of the inputs are available in every version of Windows. In fact, many of the unique features are only available in Windows 2000 and Windows XP. Make sure you check the Platform SDK documentation for potential problems when using these features in other versions of Windows. The example was tested under both Windows 2000 and Windows XP—it doesn't work under most versions of Windows 9x.

Listing 2.1   MessageBoxEx() Example using the [MarshalAs] Attribute

```
// MessageBoxEx() provides features, including a language identifier,
// not found in the .NET Framework version. This function also enables
// you to add special buttons and other features to the message box.
[DllImport("user32.dll", CharSet=CharSet.Auto)]
public static extern int MessageBoxEx(
    IntPtr hWnd,
    [MarshalAs(UnmanagedType.LPTStr)]String Message,
    [MarshalAs(UnmanagedType.LPTStr)]String Header,
    UInt32 Type,
    UInt16 LanguageID);

// Create a list of buttons.
public class MBButton
{
    public const UInt32 MB_OK =                 0x00000000;
    public const UInt32 MB_OKCANCEL =           0x00000001;
    public const UInt32 MB_ABORTRETRYIGNORE =   0x00000002;
    public const UInt32 MB_YESNOCANCEL =        0x00000003;
    public const UInt32 MB_YESNO =              0x00000004;
    public const UInt32 MB_RETRYCANCEL =        0x00000005;
    public const UInt32 MB_CANCELTRYCONTINUE =  0x00000006;
    public const UInt32 MB_HELP =               0x00004000;
}

// Create a list of icon types.
public class MBIcon
{
    public const UInt32 MB_ICONHAND =           0x00000010;
    public const UInt32 MB_ICONQUESTION =       0x00000020;
    public const UInt32 MB_ICONEXCLAMATION =    0x00000030;
    public const UInt32 MB_ICONASTERISK =       0x00000040;
    public const UInt32 MB_USERICON =           0x00000080;
    public const UInt32 MB_ICONWARNING =        MB_ICONEXCLAMATION;
    public const UInt32 MB_ICONERROR =          MB_ICONHAND;
    public const UInt32 MB_ICONINFORMATION =    MB_ICONASTERISK;
    public const UInt32 MB_ICONSTOP =           MB_ICONHAND;
}
```

```
// Create a list of default buttons.
public class MBDefButton
{
   public const UInt32 MB_DEFBUTTON1 =    0x00000000;
   public const UInt32 MB_DEFBUTTON2 =    0x00000100;
   public const UInt32 MB_DEFBUTTON3 =    0x00000200;
   public const UInt32 MB_DEFBUTTON4 =    0x00000300;
}

// Create a list of message box modalities.
public class MBModal
{
   public const UInt32 MB_APPLMODAL =      0x00000000;
   public const UInt32 MB_SYSTEMMODAL =    0x00001000;
   public const UInt32 MB_TASKMODAL =      0x00002000;
}

// Create a list of special message box attributes.
public class MBSpecial
{
   public const UInt32 MB_SETFOREGROUND =               0x00010000;
   public const UInt32 MB_DEFAULT_DESKTOP_ONLY =        0x00020000;
   public const UInt32 MB_SERVICE_NOTIFICATION_NT3X =   0x00040000;
   public const UInt32 MB_TOPMOST =                     0x00040000;
   public const UInt32 MB_RIGHT =                       0x00080000;
   public const UInt32 MB_RTLREADING =                  0x00100000;
   public const UInt32 MB_SERVICE_NOTIFICATION =        0x00200000;
}

// Return values can use an enum in place of a class.
public enum MBReturn
{
   IDOK =         1,
   IDCANCEL =     2,
   IDABORT =      3,
   IDRETRY =      4,
   IDIGNORE =     5,
   IDYES =        6,
   IDNO =         7,
   IDCLOSE =      8,
   IDHELP =       9,
   IDTRYAGAIN =   10,
   IDCONTINUE =   11,
   IDTIMEOUT =    32000
}

private void btnTest_Click(object sender, System.EventArgs e)
{
   MBReturn Result;  // Result of user input.

   // Display a message box.
   Result = (MBReturn)MessageBoxEx(this.Handle,
```

```
        "This is a message box.",
        "Test Message Box",
        MBButton.MB_CANCELTRYCONTINUE | MBButton.MB_HELP |
        MBIcon.MB_ICONEXCLAMATION |
        MBModal.MB_SYSTEMMODAL |
        MBDefButton.MB_DEFBUTTON4 |
        MBSpecial.MB_TOPMOST,
        0);

    // Determine a result.
    switch (Result)
    {
        case MBReturn.IDCANCEL:
            MessageBox.Show("Returned Cancel");
            break;
        case MBReturn.IDTRYAGAIN:
            MessageBox.Show("Returned Try Again");
            break;
        case MBReturn.IDCONTINUE:
            MessageBox.Show("Returned Continue");
            break;
        default:
            MessageBox.Show("Couldn't Determine Return Value");
            break;
    }
}

private void frmMain_HelpRequested(object sender,
    System.Windows.Forms.HelpEventArgs hlpevent)
{
    // Display information about the help request.
    MessageBox.Show("The user requested help:\r\n" +
        "\r\nSender: " + sender.ToString() +
        "\r\nMouse Position: " + hlpevent.MousePos,
        "Help Requested",
        MessageBoxButtons.OK,
        MessageBoxIcon.Information);

    // Tell Windows that the help request was handled.
    hlpevent.Handled = true;
}
```

Yes, this is a lot of code to display a simple message box, but the MessageBoxEx() function provides a lot of functionality that you won't find in the MessageBox.Show() function. Like MessageBox.Show(), you can associate a MessageBoxEx() message box with the current window. In fact, you have to provide the association to make the special features such as the Help button work correctly. If you want a working Help button, you also need to include a HelpRequested() event handler for the main form—see the frmMain_HelpRequested() method in Listing 2.1 for details.

TIP   One of the problems you'll notice with the information provided to the `frmMain_Help-Requested()` method is that C# doesn't tell you who actually called the help routine. The best way to handle this problem is to set a property or field prior to the `MessageBoxEx()` call, and then check that value within the `frmMain_HelpRequested()` method. This technique helps you determine the true source of a help request, making context-sensitive help easier to provide.

The main focus of this section is the use of the `[MarshalAs]` attribute in the `MessageBoxEx()` declaration. Notice that we need to use this attribute for both string inputs. You might see some odd output without the attribute (or the call might simply fail). As previously mentioned, you need to use an `IntPtr` for handles. The *Type* variable can include a number of inputs as shown in the `btnTest_Click()` method. You use it for the buttons, icons, and special features. One special feature affects the modality of the resulting message box. We'll discuss the various enumerations in the "Working with Enumerations" section of the chapter. The *LanguageID* variable doesn't appear to have any use within the current implementation of the `Message-BoxEx()` function—at least not according to the documentation. Given the amount of work Microsoft is doing with language specific features, you should expect to see this variable implemented sometime in the future.

The `btnTest_Click()` shows off a few of the unique features of the `MessageBoxEx()` function. Figure 2.1 shows the output of this code. Notice that the message box has four buttons and that we selected the Continue button as default. The first three buttons appear because of the `MBButton.MB_CANCELTRYCONTINUE` enumeration member, while the help button appears because of the `MBButton.MB_HELP` enumeration member.

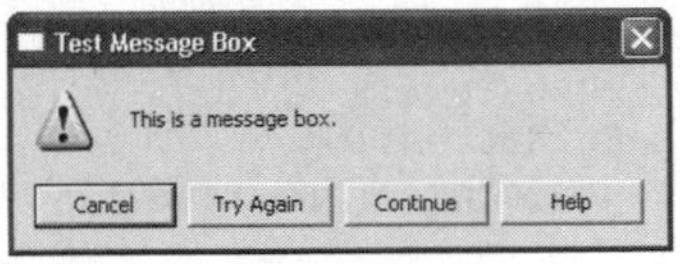

FIGURE 2.1:

The `MessageBoxEx()` function provides features you won't find in `MessageBox.Show()`

One of the special features of this message box is the result of the `MBSpecial.MB_TOPMOST` enumeration member. No matter what you do, this message box will remain on top—you can't hide it. The message box opens with the Help button selected due to the inclusion of the `MBDefButton.MB_DEFBUTTON4` enumeration member. In addition, notice the System menu icon in the upper left corner of the message box. This icon is the result of the `MBModal.MB_SYSTEMMODAL` enumeration member. As you can see in Figure 2.2, you have access to the normal System menu functions within this message box.

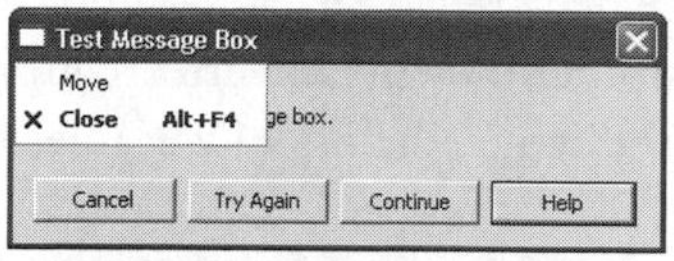

FIGURE 2.2:

The `MessageBoxEx()` function enables you to add a System menu to your message box.

The `btnTest_Click()` method checks the return value of the test message box. Notice that you can check for those special buttons. Replacing the Cancel, Try Again, and Help buttons with Abort, Retry, and Fail resulted in a "Couldn't Determine Return Value" return value. The return values are truly unique. Let's get back to the [`MarshalAs`] attribute. The [`MarshalAs`] attribute tells CLR how to interact with a variable. For example, you can tell CLR that you want to use a *String* variable as a substitute for a *LPSTR*, *LPWSTR*, *LPTSTR*, or *BSTR* variable by specifying the correct `UnmanagedType` enumeration value. You can also include arguments for variable type, array and safearray size, array and safearray subtype, cookies, and a custom marshaler.

Using a custom marshaler means that you can theoretically transform any managed type into an unmanaged equivalent—in practice this task is exceptionally difficult. Not only do you have the normal concerns in writing a marshaler, but you also have to consider the transition from the managed to unmanaged environment (and back in some cases). Fortunately, the need to write a custom marshaler is rare.

One final word of caution when working with the marshaler—don't count on all languages to implement it the same way. The marshaler tends to react differently based on language because each language has different native data types. For example, accessing the `Message-BoxEx()` function requires additional work in Visual Basic because of language differences. Here's the Visual Basic declaration of the same example.

```
<DllImport("user32.dll", _
           EntryPoint:="MessageBoxExW", _
           CharSet:=CharSet.Auto)> _
Public Shared Function MessageBoxEx( _
   ByVal hWnd As IntPtr, _
   <MarshalAs(UnmanagedType.LPTStr)> ByVal Message As String, _
   <MarshalAs(UnmanagedType.LPTStr)> ByVal Header As String, _
   <MarshalAs(UnmanagedType.U4)> ByVal Type As Integer, _
   <MarshalAs(UnmanagedType.U4)> ByVal LanguageID As Integer) _
   As Integer
End Function
```

Notice that in the Visual Basic version of the declaration, you must include a specific entry point or the message text will fail to print properly (you'll see just the first letter). The `<MarshalAs>` attribute now appears for all input parameters except the window handle, because we have to define the input arguments as type `Integer`. Unlike the examples in Chapter 1, this function must be declared as Shared—simply declaring it public won't work. The call to the MessageBoxEx()function will fail with an ambiguous error. In short, Visual Basic tends to require more precise marshaling of variables than C# does.

Unmanaged Resources and the Garbage Collector

There are a number of problems that developers will face when working with Win32 API data in a managed environment—not the least of which is the Garbage Collector. It's essential to remember that the Garbage Collector is designed to work with managed data in a managed environment that the Garbage Collector can monitor. This statement points out two potential problems when working with the Win32 API.

The first problem occurs when a developer creates unmanaged data. For example, you might need to create a pointer to an interface in a COM object or create a handle to an icon that a Win32 API function can use. The Garbage Collector doesn't know about this resource, so it can't automatically release the resource when it goes out of scope. In short, you need to release the resource before the application terminates. Generally, you'll create the resource using a Win32 API function so you'll also free the resource using a Win32 API function.

The second problem occurs when you create a managed resource that you pass to a Win32 API function. The Garbage Collector will collect any resource without a reference, and it doesn't recognize the Win32 API function's use of the resource. Consequently, the Garbage Collector could release the resource before the Win32 API function finishes using it. To prevent this problem, you'll normally need to create a managed reference to the resource at the same scope level as the Win32 API function use of the resource. After you release the resource used by the Win32 API function, you can also release the managed reference to it.

The Garbage Collector can also cause other odd problems with your Win32 API calls. The big problem is that you can't view these problems in the debugger, in many cases, because the debugger creates a reference to the variables and modifies the behavior of the application. In short, troubleshooting an application can become difficult once the Garbage Collector is involved because the problems appear as "ghosts" that you'll have a hard time tracking.

Working with Variables

Understanding the techniques for working with variables is an essential part of gaining access to the Win32 API. For example, as we saw in the "A Short View of Data" section, you can replace the handles required by many Win32 API calls with an IntPtr. However, as with marshaled data, the transition path isn't always clear. In some cases, you have to make decisions on how best to move data from one environment to another.

TIP The easiest way to detect problem variables to is classify them as value or reference types. Value types tend to require little translation and you can usually move them without marshaling in C#. Reference types require some type of translation in most cases. In fact, some reference types won't move between the managed and unmanaged environments, which means you'll need to create a conversion routine that moves the data between object properties and structure elements.

This section of the chapter discusses techniques for working with variables. Most notably, we'll discuss techniques for converting data from managed to unmanaged types and back. While some techniques are the same no matter which language you use, other techniques require language-specific implementations. With this in mind, the following sections discuss data conversion in light of two languages, C# and Visual Basic.

Converting Variables to C# Types

The difference between reference and value types becomes critical when working with C libraries. You can pass most value types such as int directly to a C library routine without any problem. In fact, the example shown in Listing 2.1 passes several value types to the C library. Enumeration also falls into the value category. Unless an enumeration contains both positive and negative values, use the uint type to represent it in your code.

Once you get past basic value types, it's time to convert the C library data type into something C# can understand (and vice versa). Generally, you'll find that pointers convert well to the IntPtr type. We've already discussed handles in several places, but other pointers work well as the IntPtr type. For example, pointers to numeric values such as the LPARAM also convert to the IntPtr with relative ease. Sometimes odd-looking types like MMC_COOKIE are actually long pointers in disguise, so you can use IntPtr to represent them.

TIP   It occasionally helps to create an extremely small example of a Win32 API function call in Visual C++ to determine how to handle the variables in your managed code. Once you have a small working example, you can use the IDE to help you make variable conversion decisions. Hover the mouse over a value in the header file to discover how Visual C++ defines it. In most cases, you'll see a typedef in the balloon that makes the base type of the value clear. For example, the balloon for MMC_COOKIE contains typedef LONG_PTR MMC_COOKIE, which makes it clear that you can use an IntPtr to represent the MMC_COOKIE. If the balloon help isn't as helpful as you'd like, right-click the type (not the variable) and choose Go to Definition or Go to Declaration from the context menu. Generally, you can use this technique to "drill down" into the header file and find useful information for defining the data type in the managed environment.

Variable conversion requires some level of discretion. You can't depend on a one-to-one correspondence between pointer types in the Win32 API call and your managed code. There are some situations when there's less of a need to use an `IntPtr`, even if the function indicates use of a pointer. For example, if a function only requires an integer value as input, you don't need to use an `IntPtr`. Using the `Int` in place of the `IntPtr` will reduce the overhead of your application by a small amount (and those small amounts can really add up). In addition, using an `int` reduces the complexity of the code and makes it easier to debug.

While using an `int` will reduce the overhead of your code, it may leave other developers scratching their heads since the use of an `int` is inconsistent with the use of an `IntPtr` in other cases. If in doubt, always use an `IntPtr`, but be aware that there are some situations when an `int` will work just as well. When you do use an `int` in place of an `IntPtr`, be sure to document the modification and your reasoning as part of the source code.

TIP   The `typedefs` used within C header help make the code easier to read by documenting the data type. Needless to say, when you convert a variety of Win32 API pointers to the `IntPtr` type, some of that documentation is lost. Generally, this means you'll have to provide additional comments in the code. Because you're replicating a documented interface, function, or enumeration, you'll want to avoid changing the variable names. The help file provided with Visual Studio can still help the function user if you maintain the same basic function name and argument names as part of your code.

Converting Variables to Visual Basic Types

Many of the same rules that you observe when converting a variable from the unmanaged environment to C# also apply for Visual Basic. However, the actual details of the conversion will often take a different shape in the two environments. For example, Visual Basic is more sensitive to numeric values than C# in that it uses native numeric formats easier than those supplied in CLR. This sensitivity means that it's easier to use an `Integer` in Visual Basic than it is to use a `UInt32`. The Integer provides a generalized way to handle the data type.

We'll see as the book continues that there are other limitations when working with Visual Basic. For example, you'll find it difficult to use in many COM scenarios (see the section "Special Rules for COM" for details). However, Visual Basic does offer a few features that C# doesn't offer. The most important of these features is that the interface is consistent and simple.

It isn't always easy to tell when to use marshaling with C#. Although you could make the assumption that marshaling is always required, you'll find that making this assumption has certain negative affects, including a performance hit. When working with Visual Basic, marshaling is generally required with all native types, but never required with the `IntPtr` type.

Another problem that Visual Basic developers will learn about is that it doesn't support the UInt types. Unfortunately, the UInt types regularly appear in the Win32 API, so getting around this problem could prove difficult. Generally, try to use an Int type in place of a UInt type if possible. If using an Int type isn't possible, you'll need to write a conversion routine in the wrapper DLL.

Placement of certain variable types is also easier in Visual Basic. Enumerations and data structures always appear at the same level as the class using them in the hierarchy. When working with C#, you have to consider the placement of these elements as a separate issue because they can appear at the same level as the class or as part of the class or even outside the current namespace.

Special Rules for COM

COM hasn't gone away simply because the .NET Framework has appeared on the scene—most developers will continue to use COM. Consequently, you'll find that you need to create bridges between your .NET application and COM. In most cases, the conversion is easy. The only time you'll run into problems is when you want your .NET application to appear as a component with special interfaces, such as those used for an MMC snap-in. When you work in this environment, you need to recreate all of the required interfaces by hand, which includes any required data structures, special variable types, and enumerations. We'll see later in the book that you'll normally place this conversion code in a separate DLL for reuse.

Objects can prove troublesome to convert because of the way that the C language handles classes and structures. Remember that classes and structures are somewhat interchangeable under C and that C views both of them as reference types. .NET (and as a result C# and Visual Basic) views classes as reference types and structures as value types. Consequently, conversion can prove difficult.

As a general rule of thumb, if the C library call defines the argument as an interface or other pure reference type, you can use the Object data type in your code. On the other hand, if the C library defines the object as a structure, you'll need to replicate the structure in your code and then pass the structure to the calling routine. In some cases, you'll need to marshal the object to ensure that the C library views it correctly. For example, if the object is an interface, then you'll need to add the following attribute to your object definition:

```
[MarshalAs(UnmanagedType.Interface)]
```

As part of the data conversion process, you need to consider the direction of data travel between your application and the C library. The C header files commonly mark arguments as [IN], [OUT], or [OUT][IN]. When working with values marked as [OUT], C# developers need to add the out (for uninitialized values) or the ref (for initialized values) keyword to ensure that the application sees the return value. Any argument marked as [OUT][IN] must use the ref keyword. Visual Basic developers will always use the ByRef keyword for [OUT] and [OUT][IN] values. When using a reference value, you must initialize the argument before you pass it to the C library.

For C# developers, it's important to differentiate between ref and out values. Remember that the application must provide an initialized argument for ref values, but can include an uninitialized argument for out values. While C# makes the distinction clear through the use of native keywords, you'll find that other languages such as Visual C++ aren't quite as adept. For example, when working with Visual C++, you'll find that a double pointer will create a ref value, while the [Out] attribute is used to create an out value, as shown here. Notice that out values begin as ref values because they also require a double pointer. Also notice that the [Out] attribute is captialized—using the lowercase [out] attribute will result in errors.

```
// Create a ref value.
MMCHelper::IDataObject **ppDataObject

// Create an out value.
[Out]MMCHelper::IDataObject **ppDataObject
```

One final concern about Windows library calls is that they often use keywords for arguments. For example, the Notify() method shown here normally uses *event* as one of the argument names.

```
virtual /* [helpstring] */ HRESULT Notify(
        /* [in] */ MMCHelper::IDataObject *lpDataObject,
        /* [in] */ MMCHelper::MMC_NOTIFY_TYPE *aevent,
        /* [in] */ IntPtr arg,
        /* [in] */ IntPtr param) = 0;
```

Notice that the source code changes the name to *aevent*. If you don't make this change, the argument name will appear in a decorated form within the managed environment. For example, C# decorates event as *@event*, making the argument difficult to read.

Now we need to look at the bad news for Visual Basic developers. Even though the entire development process is easier when working with Visual Basic, the lack of a distinct ref and out keyword causes problems when working with C library calls. Figure 2.3 shows an imported library that we'll work with later in the book. Notice that this library includes interfaces and that the interfaces have a mix of ref and out keywords associated with them. For example, GetDisplayInfo() includes a ref keyword, while CreateComponent() includes an out keyword.

Figure 2.4 shows the same imported library from the Visual Basic perspective. When Visual Basic imports the library, it assumes that every argument is ByVal, not ByRef. It has problems figuring out the data types, in some cases, and it also lacks the means to detect ref and out keyword conditions. Consequently, you'll find it difficult to make the COM wrapper library work in this situation.

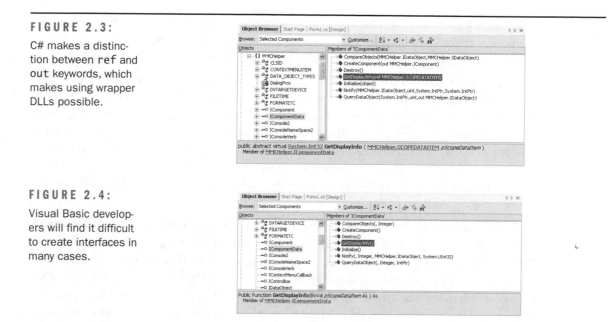

FIGURE 2.3:

C# makes a distinction between ref and out keywords, which makes using wrapper DLLs possible.

FIGURE 2.4:

Visual Basic developers will find it difficult to create interfaces in many cases.

The only way around this fatal scenario, in many cases, is to write the wrapper DLL only in Visual Basic. This means you don't have access to pointers, which means that many types of COM operations are completely inaccessible to the Visual Basic developer. Does this mean you can't use Visual Basic to access the Win32 API? No, we've already seen that Visual Basic is quite capable of using the Win32 API in many situations, but this demonstration shows that it's less capable than C# when performing certain Windows-specific tasks such as COM emulation.

Working with Data Structures

Generally, a data structure provides an organized container approach to transmitting a group of variables between the client application and the Windows API. As with other variables, you normally have to perform some type of data translation to ensure that the data is usable by both the managed environment and Windows. However, you now have other constraints to consider. The most important consideration is the presentation of the data to Windows. While the managed environment accesses the data by variable name, Windows often accesses it by relative position within the data structure, which means the format of the data structure is crucial.

Fortunately, the [StructLayout] attribute provides a way around the problem of structure layout. This attribute enables you to specify a layout for your structure. For example, you can tell Windows that the layout has to be sequential, which means it will appear in precisely the same order you specify as part of the structure definition. However, the [StructLayout] attribute only affects the layout of the structure—you still have to provide the proper variables. Creating a structure with a UInt16 where you need a UInt32 will still result in failure.

Generally, you'll want to create the structures where they fit best. For example, if you need to create a structure for a function in a wrapper DLL, then place the structure in the wrapper DLL, not with the application accessing the function. There are exceptions to every rule, however. You might need to create a special version of a structure for some Windows API function calls when working in Visual Basic. The key is the use of pointers in the structure. Data structures that contain pointers usually present problems for Visual Basic viewers—the result is similar to that shown in Figure 2.4. You'll see the variable name, but Visual Basic will be unable to resolve the data type.

Sometimes you can't easily convert a C library data structure into something that works well within Visual Basic or C#. In this case, use Visual C++ to create a wrapper DLL that contains both the data structure and the associated function call. This technique is especially important when working with data structures that contain a lot of C data types that don't convert well to managed data types. Make sure you create a managed data structure—it's possible to create both managed and unmanaged code in Visual C++, which gives it an advantage when working with this type of code. Ultimately the content of the structure must break down into types that C# and Visual Basic will understand as shown in the following code.

```
[StructLayout(LayoutKind::Sequential)]
public __gc struct DVTARGETDEVICE
{
public:
   UInt32    tdSize;
   short     tdDriverNameOffset;
   short     tdDeviceNameOffset;
   short     tdPortNameOffset;
   short     tdExtDevmodeOffset;
   char      tdData;
};
```

Notice that the structure relies on native Visual C++ types, in many cases, because these types translate well into standard .NET Framework types. However, there are some situations when a native Visual C++ type could cause problems, as in the case of an unsigned integer (UINT). In this case, make sure you use the .NET Framework equivalent type directly (UInt32).

There are other problems to consider when working with structures. For example, a structure must include the [StructLayout] attribute so CLR knows how to work with the data it contains. Generally, you'll use the *LayoutKind::Sequential* argument for Windows function calls. This value ensures that CLR doesn't rearrange or optimize the structure in any way. Note that Visual C++ requires the use of the __gc keyword for managed structures and that you must make all of the data elements public so they appear within the managed environment.

Structures become problematic in some situations. For example, you'll find that some structures contain other structures. The level of nesting can become absurd in some situations. In those cases, you need to determine if the level of nesting is warranted. If not, you can usually provide a substitute value. For example, if the code you create will never pass the structure to Windows (in other words, the structure is always passed as a NULL value), you can normally use an int as a substitute for the structure. Make sure you document any deviations within the DLL source code and as part of the DLL documentation.

NOTE
Don't worry if you don't quite grasp all of the nuances of this next example—we'll spend more time discussing wrapper DLLs in Chapter 3. The sole purpose of this next example is to show you that it's possible to create the structures that Win32 API calls require outside of the base programming environment. This is an especially important technique when the data structure contains unions or other complexities that you can't duplicate in the managed environment.

Finally, there are some extreme cases when you can use the ability of Visual C++ to work with both managed and unmanaged code to your advantage. Create a function within Visual C++ that accepts all of the data required to create the data structure in question, then create that data structure within the Visual C++ code. Make sure you change the Win32 API function call definition to match the new setup. Listing 2.2 is an example of such a construction technique. (You'll find this example in the \Chapter 02\C#\SampleLib folder of the CD.)

Listing 2.2   **A Technique for Creating Data Structures Externally**

```
// Creates a typical data structure.
void CreateDVTargetDevice(IntPtr*  StructOut,
                          Int16    tdDriverNameOffset,
                          Int16    tdDeviceNameOffset,
                          Int16    tdPortNameOffset,
                          Int16    tdExtDevmodeOffset,
                          Char     tdData,
                          Int32    tdSize)

{
    DVTARGETDEVICE *Output;     // Ouput value.
    void*          lpData = malloc(sizeof(DVTARGETDEVICE));

    // Allocate memory for the return data.
    Output = (DVTARGETDEVICE*)lpData;

    // Fill the data structure. Note the use of boxing and
    // data conversion for tdData.
    __box Char* tdDataBoxed = __box(tdData);
    Output->tdData[0] = tdDataBoxed->ToByte(NULL);
    Output->tdDeviceNameOffset = tdDeviceNameOffset;
```

```
Output->tdDriverNameOffset = tdDriverNameOffset;
Output->tdExtDevmodeOffset = tdExtDevmodeOffset;
Output->tdPortNameOffset = tdPortNameOffset;
Output->tdSize = tdSize;

// Return the structure as a pointer.
*StructOut = IntPtr(lpData);
}
```

As you can see, the output of this function is an `IntPtr`, which makes it easy to use with any of the .NET programming languages. The code has to allocate a local pointer in order to provide a place for data output. However, placing data within a `void*` doesn't work particularly well, so you need to assign that memory to a local copy of the data structure in question. Notice that you might have to perform some data conversion. For example, this data structure requires that you box the *tdData* value, convert it to a `Char`, and finally place it within the data structure.

The wrapper DLL also includes a conversion function that accepts the `IntPtr` as input, converts it to a string, and enables the calling application to display the data on screen. You'd never do this in a real application, but it's important to see how the `IntPtr` concept works and this is the easiest way to demonstrate it. You'll find the test application in the \Chapter 02\C#\ SampleLibraryTest and the \Chapter 02\VB\SampleLibraryTest folders. Listing 2.3 shows the important test code.

Listing 2.3   **A Test Program for the External Structure**

```
private void btnTest_Click(object sender, System.EventArgs e)
{
    CreateStructs  NewStruct;  // Create Structure Object.
    IntPtr         ResultPtr;  // IntPtr Containing Structure.
    String         ResultStr;  // String Containing Original Data

    // Initialize the data objects.
    NewStruct = new CreateStructs();
    ResultPtr = new IntPtr(0);

    // Create the new structure.
    NewStruct.CreateDVTargetDevice(ref ResultPtr, 1, 2, 3, 4, 'a', 16);

    // Create a string from the new structure.
    ResultStr = NewStruct.ReturnDVTargetDevice(ResultPtr);

    // Make sure you free the unmanaged memory.
    NewStruct.FreePointer(ResultPtr);

    // Display the application output.
    MessageBox.Show(ResultStr,
```

```
        "Structure Output",
        MessageBoxButtons.OK,
        MessageBoxIcon.Information);
}
```

Notice that the `CreateDVTargetDevice()` function accepts the structure values as single inputs—negating the requirement to work with the data structure within the managed environment. The function returns an `IntPtr` that you can pass to Win32 API functions as needed. As noted in the source code comments, make sure you free the unmanaged memory pointer before the application exits, or the application will have a memory leak. Figure 2.5 shows the output from this example.

FIGURE 2.5:

This example shows that it's possible to create data structures outside the managed environment.

You might wonder how well Visual Basic works with this particular application since it still requires a pointer. A look at the Object Browser (shown in Figure 2.6) shows that this wrapper DLL doesn't present any problems. Visual Basic correctly interprets the pointer as a `ByRef` reference. In short, this technique is the perfect way to get around many of the problems of working with Visual Basic and the Win32 API.

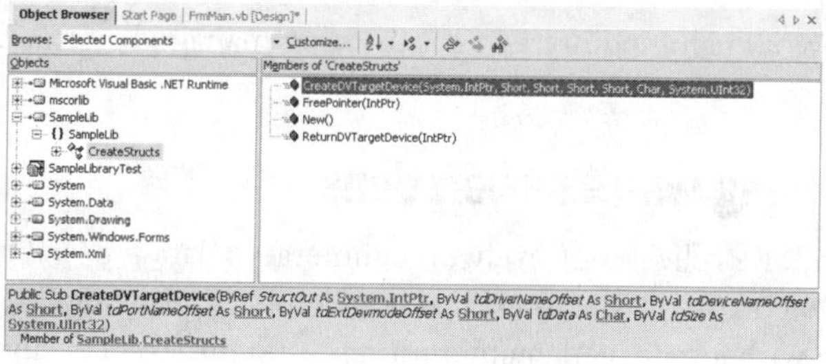

FIGURE 2.6:

The technique shown in this section overcomes many of the problems Visual Basic has with pointers.

Working with Pointers

As you've already seen in other areas of this chapter, pointers can present problems for both Visual Basic and C# developers. However, this is one area where C# developers have a decided advantage and you might find that it's better to use C# whenever you have a lot of pointers to work with. Even if Visual Basic is the main language for your application, you can write a wrapper DLL in C# to meet the requirements of the Win32 API call portion of the code. Generally, anywhere you need to use a UInt value or an odd pointer, you'll also need to use C#.

The IntPtr is the developer's best friend when it comes to pointers. However, remember that an IntPtr contains a void*, not the specialized pointers that Win32 API calls rely on. As shown in Listing 2.2, the use of a void* normally means some type of data conversion later in the process. The whole concept of a void* is to represent a pointer of an unknown type. In sum, an IntPtr enables you to create generic pointers, but not specific pointers.

C# developers also have access to standard C-like pointers. However, to use this feature you must declare the affected method as unsafe. As discussed in the "Understanding the Effects of Unsafe Code" section of Chapter 1, you want to minimize unsafe code sections for a number of reasons. The most important reason is that unsafe code sections don't receive the same level of error checking that normal code sections do, which means that your code is more likely to contain hidden (and difficult to debug) errors. Here are some general rules for using normal pointers.

- Use an IntPtr whenever possible.
- Keep sections with standard pointers small.
- Perform more error checking than normal.
- Include range checks of all data to ensure that it remains within limits.
- Isolate unsafe code sections from the main application whenever possible.
- Consider using Visual C++ for large numbers of pointers.
- Avoid using pointers by substituting managed alternatives.

Working with Enumerations

Windows relies extensively on enumerated data types. These data types normally begin with the enum keyword. However, as you'll notice in Listing 2.1, duplicating a Windows enumerated type with a managed enumeration is difficult. You can always use an enumeration for return values from a Windows API call, but you can't always use it as input. The exception is when the enumerated type will appear singly and not as part of an or-ed or and-ed input.

The MessageBoxEx() function provides a perfect example of the enumerated type problem because you can't use an enumeration to create the input required by the function. In these cases, you need to create a class consisting entirely of constants. Note that there are differences between Visual Basic and C# when working with the class form of an enumeration. When you work with C#, you can declare the type of the constant. For example, in the MessageBoxEx()

example, all of the constants are of the UInt32 type because that's what the function requires. Visual Basic doesn't allow this distinction and it can cause problems. For example, here's the Visual Basic version of the MBButton class.

```
' Create a list of buttons.
Public Class MBButton
    Public Const MB_OK = &H0
    Public Const MB_OKCANCEL = &H1
    Public Const MB_ABORTRETRYIGNORE = &H2
    Public Const MB_YESNOCANCEL = &H3
    Public Const MB_YESNO = &H4
    Public Const MB_RETRYCANCEL = &H5
    Public Const MB_CANCELTRYCONTINUE = &H6
    Public Const MB_HELP = &H4000
End Class
```

TIP Notice the use of hexadecimal numbers in the MBButton class. It's usually easier to present the numbers in this form than use decimal equivalents. The Win32 API documentation normally relies on hexadecimal number input, rather than decimal numbers, so using hexadecimal numbers makes your code easier to debug.

In some cases, working with enumerations and classes becomes so difficult that you might want to define the enumeration as a series of defines or constant values. In fact, the C header files often use this technique when creating an enumeration would prove too complex. Looking into the C header file will often provide you with clues as to the correct enumeration representation in your own code.

Enumerations become even more difficult when working with wrapper DLLs—a topic we'll discuss at length in Chapter 3. The most important reason is that the enum will never appear in the Object Browser and the wrapper DLL user won't be able to access it. Consequently, you need an alternative for creating enumerated types. In most cases, using a class is the best answer because you have good control over how the class will appear to the end user. However, many situations will call for use of defines or constants in wrapper DLLs.

Importing Resources

Resource usage is an important part of any development project. You manage memory, disk space, and other physical resource elements as part of the development project. In addition, most developers are used to finding icons and other graphic resources embedded within DLLs found in the Windows directory. Finally, resources can be code—the embodiment of executable code within an external DLL is a type of resource that most developers are used to having.

We'll discuss resources in a number of places in the book. This section discusses three main issues. First, it tells you how the .NET Framework can help you manage resources located in external files, such as the graphic images located in the Shell32.DLL file. Second, we discuss the issue of using external DLLs from your managed code. Finally, we'll take a quick look at some of the issues involved in using resources with the Win32 API.

Understanding .NET Framework Functionality

While this book isn't about general C# or Visual Basic programming, it's important to remember that the .NET Framework does provide the functionality required to display basic graphics. For example, you can embed a bitmap within your application and display it on screen as needed. You'll find such an application in the \Chapter 02\C#\NETBitmap and the \Chapter 02\ VB\NETBitmap folders of the CD. Here's the basic code needed to perform the task.

```
private void btnTest_Click(object sender, System.EventArgs e)
{
   // Retrieve an embedded bitmap from the current assembly.
   Assembly Asm = Assembly.GetExecutingAssembly();
   Stream   Strm = Asm.GetManifestResourceStream("NETBitmap.Main.bmp");
   Bitmap   Temp = new Bitmap(Strm);

   // Display the bitmap on screen.
   pbMain.Image = (Image)Temp;
}
```

As you can see, this example relies on reflection to get the job done. You must set the Build Action property of the bitmap or other resource to Embedded Resource to use this technique. Figure 2.7 shows the output from this example.

FIGURE 2.7:

Displaying an embedded bitmap within your .NET application is fine for the managed environment.

The resulting bitmap works fine within the managed environment but won't work within the Win32 API, which means you have to use a different technique when making a Win32 API call. The Win32 API doesn't understand the managed resources created by reflection. Fortunately, you can use the special GetHbitmap() call to answer many Win32 API call needs.

The `hBitmap` this call returns is Windows compatible. You must make a call to the Win32 API `DeleteObject()` function to deallocate the handle when you finish using it. Here's the declaration for the `DeleteObject()` function.

```
[DllImport("gdi32.dll")]
public static extern int DeleteObject(IntPtr hObject);
```

Using the IDE Features

You'll find that you need to use wrapper DLLs regularly when creating connections between the .NET Framework and the Win32 API. Using wrapper DLLs enhances code reuse and enables you to use other languages as needed. Of course, this means adding a reference to the external DLL so that you can access the code it contains from within your application. The following steps tell how to add such a reference (the same procedure works whether you use Visual Basic or C#).

1. Right-click the References folder in Solution Explorer and choose Add Reference from the context menu. You'll see an Add Reference dialog box similar to the one shown in Figure 2.8. Notice that there are separate tabs for .NET, COM, and Project related references. Generally, you won't find custom DLLs on any of these tabs, but it always pays to look.

FIGURE 2.8:

The Add Reference dialog box enables you to add custom references to your application.

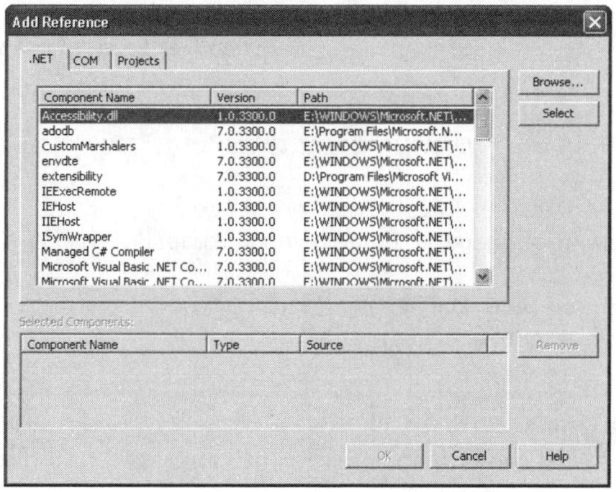

2. Locate and select the reference you want to add to your application. Add the reference to the Selected Components list by highlighting it and clicking Select. If you don't see the DLL, you'll need to add it manually as described in Step 3. Otherwise, you can skip Step 3 and proceed to Step 4.

3. Click Browse and you'll see a Select Component dialog box. Use this dialog box as you would any file open dialog box to locate the file containing the executable code. Once you locate the file, highlight it and click Open.

4. Click OK. You should see the new reference added to the Reference folder.

5. Add a statement to use the new reference to your application. For C# developers this means adding a `using` statement to the beginning of the file. For Visual Basic developers this means adding an `Imports` statement to the beginning of the file.

Working with the Win32 API

Working directly with the Win32 API means locating the various functions you need—they're not all in the same DLL. In many cases, you'll need to perform esoteric tasks such as gaining access to the current application instance using the `Marshal.GetHINSTANCE()` method. You'll also need to know how to gain access to the current application handle using *this .Handle*. However, in many cases, it's a matter of performing straight coding as shown here.

```
[DllImport("user32.dll")]
public static extern IntPtr LoadBitmap(IntPtr hInstance,
    [MarshalAs(UnmanagedType.LPStr)]String lpBitmapName);

[DllImport("gdi32.dll")]
public static extern int DeleteObject(IntPtr hObject);

private void btnTest_Click(object sender, System.EventArgs e)
{
    IntPtr   HBitmap;     // A handle to a bitmap.

    // Load the bitmap using a Windows call.
    HBitmap = LoadBitmap(IntPtr.Zero, "D:\\Main.bmp");

    // Display the bitmap on screen.
    pbMain.Image = Image.FromHbitmap(HBitmap);

    // Delete the hBitmap.
    DeleteObject(HBitmap);
}
```

This code represents an alternative way to load a bitmap from disk. Essentially all you need to do is load the bitmap, convert it to an image, and then release memory used by the bitmap. The tricky part is setting everything up so that Windows understands what you want to do. Once you have the required function calls in place, using the Win32 API calls is about as difficult as using their .NET Framework equivalents. We'll explore the various elements of working with graphics as the book progresses—especially when it comes time to create the MMC snap-in example.

Where Do You Go from Here?

This chapter has demonstrated one of the basic principles of using the Win32 API from the managed environment—data translation. The managed and unmanaged environments only work together when the data they share is formatted correctly. In some situations, you can perform a direct data transfer; but, in other cases, you have to marshal the data or get creative and construct the data using other techniques.

At this point, you have seen enough examples to begin writing some code yourself. You should try creating a few examples that translate data that you need to work with to and from the unmanaged environment. It's important to start small, as we did with the `MessageBoxEx()` example. You'll find that the debugger is lacking when it comes to this type of application programming, so you have to know how a data translation will affect your application and the Win32 API calls that it makes.

In Chapter 3, we'll move on to more complex topics. We'll discuss various types of Win32 API access. For example, that chapter is the first place you'll learn about using wrapper DLLs to access some Win32 API functions. You'll also learn how to access and interpret Win32 API function call return values. Finally, this chapter looks at some important tools that you'll need to develop robust applications. Some tools like Spy++ are indispensable when researching the actual behavior of some poorly documented Win32 API functions or diagnosing errors in a function call.

CHAPTER 3

Accessing the Win32 API

- An Overview of the DLLs

- Types of Win32 Access

- A Direct DLL Access Example

- A C LIB Wrappers Access Example

- A C LIB Substitute Functions Example

- Interpreting Error and Result Values

- Helpful Win32 Programming Tools

So far we've discussed the perimeter of Win32 API development. You've learned about some of the functionality that the Win32 API can provide, and we've considered various aspects of data manipulation. However, we haven't really discussed access techniques for the Win32 API. That's what you'll learn in this chapter.

There are four topics of interest for developers in this chapter. First, you need to know where to find the Win32 API calls because they don't all reside in the same DLL and some don't reside properly in DLLs at all—they appear as part of C LIB files. Second, you need to know what you're giving up by using the Win32 API calls. We've already talked about a few of these issues in previous chapters. Third, you need to know which tools are available to help you locate and observe the effects of Win32 API calls. Finally, you need to know how to obtain error information when working with Win32 API calls and how to interpret the error codes.

Consider this chapter your doorway to the technology-specific chapters that begin with Chapter 6. This chapter contains the generic techniques that we'll use in later chapters to answer specific technology needs—the holes left in the .NET Framework's coverage of the Win32 API. When you complete this chapter, you'll have the basic skills for locating functions, analyzing how they work, and calling them from your managed application. However, anyone who's worked with the Win32 API directly in the past knows that it's anything but consistent, which is why these technology-specific chapters are so important. This chapter tells you the basic rules—the remaining chapters tell you how Microsoft broke them. They'll also show you techniques for getting around some of the anomalies in the Win32 API when viewed from the managed environment.

An Overview of the DLLs

The Windows operating system is composed of more than a few DLLs. If you look in the System32 folder of any Windows installation, you'll see a wealth of DLLs, many with strange-looking names. Most of these DLLs perform special tasks, and you won't need to worry about them unless you need to perform that special task in your application. For example, my System32 folder contains a VJOY.DLL file that I'd only need to use when working with a joystick—something I'm probably not going to do any time soon. Some of the DLLs are also device specific, so you don't need to do anything with them unless you want to work with that device in a very specific way (which usually isn't a good idea).

This excess of DLLs leaves the question of which DLLs you need to consider open to interpretation. There are some DLLs that you'll never use simply because you don't write applications that require their services or the services they provide are found somewhere in the .NET Framework. It's important to know which DLLs to look for in your search of a specific function.

The help file provided with Visual Studio .NET lacks some of the documentation you'll need to understand the Win32 API. Unfortunately, this means you'll need to download a copy of the Platform SDK to gain access to the required help files. Fortunately, Visual Studio .NET does include a complete set of C header files and all of the tools you need to work with the Win32 API. You can obtain a copy of the latest Platform SDK at http://msdn.microsoft.com/library/default.asp?url=/library/en-us/sdkintro/sdkmainportal_71ut.asp. You can also obtain the required information from the help files that are provided with an MSDN subscription.

There are three main DLLs you'll need to use for general functions: USER32.DLL, KERNEL32.DLL, and GDI32.DLL. In general, USER32.DLL contains user-specific functions such as message boxes. You'll find low-level functions such as those used for memory allocation and thread management in KERNEL32.DLL. Most graphics functions appear in GDI32.DLL. Unfortunately, Microsoft didn't strictly adhere to these boundaries. For example, you'll find the Beep() function in KERNEL32.DLL, not USER32.DLL as you might expect. Because the Platform SDK documentation is written with C/C++ developers in mind, it doesn't always list the DLL where you can find a particular function—making the search akin to an egg hunt.

Some DLLs fall into the common category, but the .NET Framework already provides good coverage of the functionality they provide. For example, the COMCTL32.DLL and COMDLG32.DLL files contain functions that developers use frequently, but most of these functions have .NET Framework equivalents. The question for most developers will be whether the .NET Framework equivalents are robust enough to meet application development needs. As shown in the MessageBoxEx() example in Chapter 2, Microsoft tends to leave out special features in .NET Framework equivalents. For example, the MessageBox.Show() function doesn't include the Help button. Likewise, you might find some special feature COMCTL32.DLL and COMDLG32.DLL files that the .NET Framework doesn't implement.

Many of the DLLs you'll use fall into the esoteric category. For example, you'll find the BATMETER.DLL and POWRPROF.DLL files helpful when writing power management code. While the .NET Framework provides access to common needs such as power events, you might find some of the DLL functions useful for power monitoring needs. Of course, most applications that do provide power management support do so by monitoring the events and leaving the grunt work to the operating system, so these functions, while useful, are also esoteric.

We'll discuss many other DLLs as the book progresses. The purpose of this section is to help you understand where these Win32 API functions are coming from—they don't appear out of the air as some developers might suspect. Even if you restrict your programming efforts to the functions found in the three main DLLs, you'll find that you can patch quite a few of the obvious support holes in the .NET Framework.

Types of Win32 Access

There are two ways to access the Win32 API functions. All of the examples we've looked at so far in the book use a single type of access, the direct DLL approach. In most cases, you'll want to use this approach because it's the simplest method to use. However, in other situations, you'll need to use the C LIB file approach due to a lack of documentation of other factors. Sometimes even C# can't bridge the gap between the managed and unmanaged environments, making Visual C++ the language of choice. The following sections describe these two methods of Win32 API access in more detail.

TIP   Working with the Win32 API often means you'll need to access low-level details about your application such as the window handle or the device context. Visual Basic hides this information by default. To see low-level details about your application within the development environment, use the Tools ➤ Options command to display the Options dialog box. Select the Text Editor\Basic folder. Clear the Hide Advanced Members option and click OK. You'll now see features such as `Me.Handle` (the handle for the current window). The C# text editor also has the Hide Advanced Members option, but it's usually cleared by default.

Direct DLL Access

As previously mentioned, you'll generally want to use direct DLL access when using Win32 API functions. This technique enjoys the greatest level of support from the .NET Framework. For example, you can use the `[DllImport]` attribute to gain access to the required function. We haven't looked at all of the features of the `[DllImport]` attribute yet, so you'll gain a better appreciation of just how valuable this attribute is as the book progresses. We've also looked at other attributes, such as the `[StructLayout]` attribute, that helps make DLL access easy.

Of course, the use of DLL access assumes that you know which DLL to access and have documentation about function arguments. The arguments could be anything from pointers to data structures. Learning the names of functions within a DLL isn't hard (we'll see how this works in the "Dependency Walker" section of the chapter), but learning the details can prove frustrating.

There's a hidden problem with the DLL access method. Every time your application makes a transition from the managed to unmanaged environment, CLR has to marshal the variables in the background (this is in addition to any marshaling you perform manually within the application). Consequently, there's a performance hit your application will experience when using the Win32 API. Sometimes it's more efficient to use a wrapper DLL or a function substitute, rather than incur the performance penalty.

Direct DLL access can present other problems as well. For example, some of the structures used to access Win32 API functions include unions, odd variable types, and other data translation problems. Because C# and Visual Basic don't understand these concepts, you'll end up ripping your hair out trying to replicate the data structure. In these cases, it's often easier to bypass the data translation problem by using a C/C++ wrapper DLL. Since managed Visual C++ .NET understands the unmanaged environment completely, you'll experience less frustration in the data translation process. Be warned, though, that Visual C++ presents other challenges such as a more complex programming environment.

Even if you can replicate a data structure, it often bears little resemblance to the original. For example, consider the following unmanaged data structure.

```
struct MyStruct
{
    int data[16];
}
```

This looks like an easy structure to replicate, and in some ways it is. However, the resulting data structure doesn't look like the original and could cause problems for other developers trying to learn about your code. Here's the C# equivalent of the data structure in question.

```
[StructLayout(LayoutKind.Sequential)]
public struct MyStruct
{
    [MarshalAs(UnmanagedType.ByValArray, SizeConst=64)]
    public int[] myField;
}
```

While the two data structures are equivalent, the C# version requires two attributes to accomplish the same task that the Visual C++ version does without any attributes at all. In short, the C# version is actually more complicated. When you consider that this structure is actually very simple, it's not too hard to image how some of the complex data structures will appear within managed code. The realities of developing Win32 API code in a managed environment include added complexity because the managed environment makes assumptions that the Win32 API environment doesn't make.

A final direct DLL access concern is the problem of error handling. You must also import and use the rather strange error-handling functions employed by the Win32 API if you want to provide error feedback to the user. While you still have to figure out which method of error handling to use with working with Visual C++, the actual process of retrieving the error information is easier. Fortunately, error handling isn't so difficult that it prevents you from using the direct DLL method.

C LIB Access

For some developers, the concept of DLL versus LIB function access might prove confusing at first, but the differences between the two methods are distinct and easy to understand. A C/C++ library is a set of precompiled routines that are only accessible from a C/C++ environment. As such, the files have a LIB extension and usually reside in a separate LIB folder on the hard drive.

When you view the documentation for the Win32 API and see a reference for a LIB rather than a DLL file, you're seeing Microsoft's choice of C/C++ as the base language for Windows. The presence of a LIB file reference in the documentation doesn't necessarily mean there's no access from a DLL, but you'll have to do some research to find the name of the associated DLL (when there's a single DLL that implements the required function). In some cases, the answer to the question of which DLL to use is quite simple. For example, the MessageBoxEx() function we used in Chapter 2 relies on User32.LIB in the documentation and User32.DLL in the example.

The following sections discuss two forms of C library access. You'll find examples of these two techniques in the "A C LIB Wrappers Access Example" and "A C LIB Substitute Functions Example" sections of the chapter. You'll rely on both forms of C library access from time to time. Of the two, the wrapper technique is the most common, so we discuss it first. The substitute technique is actually better when you can implement it without loss of functionality.

Using Wrappers

The most common use of a wrapper is when a managed application can't fully duplicate the inputs required by a C library routine or when the output from such a routine contains elements the managed application can't understand. A common example of this problem is when a data structure contains unions or other elements that are difficult to recreate in the managed environment. In some cases, it's possible to create the data structure but not locate the required call within a DLL. If a function exists only within a C library, then you must use a wrapper to access it.

It's important to use a wrapper DLL with care for several reasons. The most important reason is that you're adding another layer to the calling mechanism, which increases the probability of error and increases the complexity of debugging the resulting application. Another good reason to avoid using wrapper DLLs is the complexity of using multiple languages within the application. Low-level programming with Visual C++ requires a good understanding of both C++ and the Win32 API. Many developers will want to use C# or Visual Basic as their main programming language—using Visual C++ to create a wrapper DLL might require more time than a project allows.

A few developers have also complained of language compatibility problems when working with Visual C++. In many cases, the problem is one of not understanding how the interfaces should work, rather than an actual flaw in the interface. However, these errors only serve to point out the complexity of the problem—many of these developers are seasoned programmers who have worked with Visual C++ for several years. We'll discuss some of these interoperability problems as the book progresses, especially when we discuss the MMC snap-in example.

For all of the problems of using the wrapper DLL technique, there are quite a few advantages. The best advantage is that you're working with the Win32 API using a language that's designed to interact with it. All of the documentation Microsoft provides assumes that you're going to use Visual C++ for this type of coding.

Another advantage is speed. Performing all Win32 API calls in an unmanaged black box and simply sending the result to the managed application results in fewer housekeeping tasks such as marshaling data. In addition, Visual C++ tends to provide an efficient coding environment—one where you can closely monitor the use of resources and decrease the number of steps required to perform any given task. While you might not always notice the speed difference in a small application, using a wrapper DLL does include a performance advantage in most cases.

Using Substitute Functions

It isn't very often that you can find a substitute for a Win32 API call if that substitute doesn't appear within the .NET Framework. However, there are times when it's possible to duplicate a behavior if you're willing to accept a few compromises. For example, there's a way to add the Windows XP theme appearance to your application without making special Win32 API calls. However, the substitute technique leaves some vestiges of older programming techniques in place, such as any owner-drawn icons. The only way to make your application completely compatible with Windows XP is to use Win32 API calls.

Of course, the biggest problem with the substitute function technique is finding it. A substitute function is normally a non-obvious way of performing a task. These are the types of techniques that developers share only with friends. In some cases, you'll find the techniques on the pages of higher-end magazines that only expert developers would attempt to read. In short, the substitute function technique is of limited help. Yes, you should always look for a way to avoid using a wrapper DLL, but it simply isn't possible to do so in all situations.

Hidden Functions

Sometimes a function that's relatively easy to learn about for the Win32 API is hidden within the .NET Framework. One such example is the GetDC() function, which retrieves the device context for the current window. This call is used fairly often in the unmanaged world because it represents the only way to draw something on screen. Visual Studio .NET provides rudimentary graphics in an easy-to-use package that doesn't rely on the developer to provide a device context, so knowing how to obtain the device context would seem superfluous until you need it to make a Win32 API call. Here's what you need to do to obtain the device context using managed code.

```
IntPtr   hDC;   // A handle for the device context.
Graphics g;     // A graphics object.

// Create a graphic object from the form.
g = this.CreateGraphics();

// Obtain the device context from the graphics object.
hDC = g.GetHdc();
```

As you can see, this technique isn't nearly as easy as making a simple GetDC() function call from the Win32 API. However, it does avoid some of the performance penalties of making the GetDC() call. The right choice of technique for your application depends on how you plan to use the device context once you have it. If you plan to make calls using the Win32 API anyway, it might be just as easy to pass the window handle to the Win32 API call routine and ask it to grab the device context. However, if you're planning on staying mainly in the managed environment, then the technique shown here will work best.

A Direct DLL Access Example

We've already viewed a number of direct DLL examples in the book. All of the examples so far are for function calls that stand alone—they produce some final result on their own. However, there are a number of useful Win32 API functions that aren't really stand-alone—they're an intermediary for some other task. For example, the SendMessage() function found in User32 .DLL falls into this category. You use SendMessage() to ask some other part of the system (including other parts of your application) to do something. We'll cover this topic in a lot more detail in Chapter 4, so consider the example in this section a taste of things to come.

NOTE When working with most Win32 API structures and COM interfaces, you need to consider the level of exposure. All structure and interface elements are public by default. Consequently, attempting to create a private structure or interface element can have strange side effects—if the code works at all.

Every part of Windows relies on messages. In fact, the message forms the basis of all communication and your application must know how to both send and receive messages. For the most part, the mechanics of sending and receiving messages are hidden within various event handlers. The message processing occurs at a lower level.

The screensaver also relies on messages to perform various tasks. For example, you can create an application that outputs a message to the screensaver and tells it to start hiding the screen. While the .NET Framework provides access to the screensaver settings through the `Microsoft.Win32.UserPreferenceCategory` enumeration, it doesn't provide any means for turning the screensaver on or off. The example in this section shows how to perform that task. You'll find the source code for this example in the `\Chapter 03\C#\ScreenSaver` and `\Chapter 03\VB\ScreenSaver` folders of the CD. Listing 3.1 shows the code you'll need.

Listing 3.1   **Use SendMessage() to Turn the Screensaver On or Off**

```
// Used to send a message that starts the screen saver.
[DllImport("User32.DLL")]
public static extern int SendMessage(IntPtr hWnd,
                                     UInt32 Msg,
                                     Int32 wParam,
                                     Int32 lParam);

// Two constants we need to activate the screensaver:
// message type and message content.
public const Int32 WM_SYSCOMMAND = 0x112;
public const Int32 SC_SCREENSAVE = 0xF140;

private void btnTest_Click(object sender, System.EventArgs e)
{
   // Start the screen saver.
   SendMessage(this.Handle, WM_SYSCOMMAND, SC_SCREENSAVE, 0);
}
```

The example code relies on the `SendMessage()` function to send a system command to the screensaver. As shown in the call, you need to provide a handle to the current application as part of the input. The *WM_SYSCOMMAND* constant is the message—it tells Windows that you're sending a system command. The *SC_SCREENSAVE* constant is the act that you want the system to perform—turn on the screensaver.

Some of you might wonder how the Visual Basic application handles the UInt32 *Msg* argument. If you'll remember from previous discussions that unsigned integers aren't part of the specification, the requirement to use a UInt32 in this case could cause problems. Fortunately, you can get around this problem by using the System.Convert.ToUInt32() method. Here's the Visual Basic version of the SendMessage() call.

```
SendMessage(Me.Handle,
            Convert.ToUInt32(WM_SYSCOMMAND),
            SC_SCREENSAVE,
            0)
```

While this technique does work, it's still better to use integers whenever possible to eliminate the overhead of the conversion. The use of the System.Convert.ToUInt32() method depends on whether the purity of the call or performance requirements takes precedence. In many cases, you'll find that you can use an integer without ill effect.

TIP You can avoid a myriad of .NET to unmanaged DLL memory problems by writing the DLL in such a way that it allocates and frees its own memory whenever possible. In some cases, this means writing a separate function to free the unmanaged memory. If you can't avoid allocating memory within the managed client, make sure you marshal the affected variables properly so that the unmanaged DLL receives a pointer to the managed memory. Otherwise, the call will fail with odd error messages (when the failure allows you to access the error message—sometimes it will simply cause Windows to stop application execution).

A C LIB Wrappers Access Example

There are many times when you'll need to write a wrapper DLL to gain access to a Win32 API call. We've discussed many of the scenarios for using this technique earlier in the chapter, so let's look at the example.

You'll run into more than a few situations when you must gain access to one or more types of security information that the .NET Framework doesn't provide. For example, you might need to know the security information for the local user. Unfortunately, the functions required to access those security features reside in one or more C libraries such as ADVAPI32.LIB. This file is only accessible from within a C application.

The example application shows how to get around this problem. You need to build a separate managed Visual C++ DLL that handles access to the library in question, then access the DLL function from within your application. The first step is to create the required projects. Make sure you add a reference to the Visual C++ DLL in your C# or Visual Basic project's References folder. You'll also need to add a using statement for the Visual C++ DLL at the beginning of your C# or Visual Basic application. The example found in the `\Chapter 03\` `C#\AccessToken` and `\Chapter 03\VB\AccessToken` folders of the source code CD will provide you with the details of this setup.

> **NOTE** The examples in this section assume a familiarity with underlying security concepts such as the use of the Security Access Control List (SACL) and Discretionary Access Control List (DACL). We'll discuss issues regarding the Access Control Entries (ACEs) and you'll learn how to manage access tokens. If you aren't familiar with these topics, make sure you read the security theory sections of the help files starting with "Windows NT Security in Theory and Practice" (`ms-help://MS.VSCC/MS.MSDNVS/dnwbgen/html/msdn_seccpp` `.htm`). The help file has a four-part theory section that will tell you everything you need to understand the examples.

There are a number of ways to create a connection between a C library and your C# application. In some cases, you can create a one-for-one set of function calls. For example, this works well when you want to call the console library routines because they don't exchange pointers—just data. However, the security API calls are a little more complicated, so you'll find that you need to perform a little more work to create the interface. Listing 3.2 shows the Visual C++ DLL code. Remember, this is a managed DLL, so you have access to both managed and unmanaged functionality—a real plus in this situation. You'll find the source code for the wrapper DLL in the `\Chapter 03\C#\AccessToken\SecurityAPI` of the CD.

Listing 3.2   **The Visual C++ DLL Code for User Security Access**

```
// Obtain the size of the data structure for a particular
// token information class.
int GetTokenSize(TOKEN_INFORMATION_CLASS TIC,
                 IntPtr *ReturnLength)
{
   HANDLE  TokenHandle = NULL; // Handle to the process token.
   DWORD   RL = 0;             // Return Length.
   HRESULT hr = 0;             // Operation Result Value.

   // Obtain a handle for the current process token.
   hr = OpenProcessToken(GetCurrentProcess(),
                   TOKEN_QUERY,
                   &TokenHandle);

   // Obtain the size of the token for the desired
   // token information class.
   hr = GetTokenInformation(TokenHandle,
                   TIC,
                   NULL,
                   0,
                   &RL);
```

```
    // Return the size of the token information.
    *ReturnLength = IntPtr((int)RL);

    // Free the token handle.
    CloseHandle(TokenHandle);

    return hr;
}

// Obtain the date for a particular token information
// class. The calling application must provide a properly
// sized buffer.
int GetTokenData(TOKEN_INFORMATION_CLASS TIC,
                 IntPtr *TokenData,
                 IntPtr TokenDataLength,
                 IntPtr *ReturnLength)
{
    HANDLE  TokenHandle = NULL;  // Handle to the process token.
    DWORD   RL = 0;              // Return Length.
    HRESULT hr = 0;             // Operation Result Value.
    VOID*   lpTokenData;        // Token Data Holder.

    // Obtain a handle for the current process token.
    hr = OpenProcessToken(GetCurrentProcess(),
                          TOKEN_QUERY,
                          &TokenHandle);

    // Allocate memory for the return data.
    lpTokenData = malloc(TokenDataLength.ToInt32());

    // Obtain the size of the token for the desired
    // token information class.
    hr = GetTokenInformation(TokenHandle,
                             TIC,
                             lpTokenData,
                             (DWORD)TokenDataLength.ToInt32(),
                             &RL);

    // Return the size of the token information.
    *ReturnLength = IntPtr((int)RL);

    // Return the token data.
    *TokenData = IntPtr(lpTokenData);

    // Free the data holder.
    //free(lpTokenData);

    // Free the token handle.
    CloseHandle(TokenHandle);

    return hr;
}
```

```
// Convert the TOKEN_USER structure to a SID string.
int ConvertTokenUserToSidString(IntPtr TokenData,
                                String **SIDString)
{
    HRESULT      hr = 0;       // Operation Result Value.
    TOKEN_USER  *TU;           // Token user data structure.
    LPTSTR       SIDValue;     // The string version of the SID.
    VOID        *Temp;         // A temporary pointer.

    // Convert the IntPtr to a TOKEN_USER structure.
    Temp = TokenData.ToPointer();
    TU = (TOKEN_USER*)Temp;

    // Convert the SID to a string.
    hr = ConvertSidToStringSid(TU->User.Sid, &SIDValue);

    // Return the string value of the SID.
    *SIDString = new String(SIDValue);

    // Free the memory used by SIDValue.
    LocalFree(SIDValue);

    return hr;
}

// Convert a TOKEN_USER structure to user account information.
int ConvertTokenUserToUserData(IntPtr TokenData,
                               String **UserName,
                               String **Domain)
{
    HRESULT        hr = 0;       // Operation Result Value.
    TOKEN_USER    *TU;           // Token user data structure.
    VOID          *Temp;         // A temporary pointer.
    LPTSTR         lpUserName;   // The user name value.
    LPTSTR         lpDomain;     // The user's domain.
    SID_NAME_USE   SNU;          // Use of the SID Name.

    // Length of the data return values.
    DWORD          UserNameLength = 40;
    DWORD          DomainLength = 40;

    // Convert the IntPtr to a TOKEN_USER structure.
    Temp = TokenData.ToPointer();
    TU = (TOKEN_USER*)Temp;

    // Allocate memory for the return values.
    lpUserName = (LPTSTR)malloc(40);
    lpDomain = (LPTSTR)malloc(40);
```

```
    // Find the user account information.
    hr = LookupAccountSid(NULL,
                             TU->User.Sid,
                             lpUserName,
                             &UserNameLength,
                             lpDomain,
                             &DomainLength,
                             &SNU);

    // Return the user account information.
    *UserName = new String(lpUserName);
    *Domain = new String(lpDomain);

    // Free the local variables.
    free(lpUserName);
    free(lpDomain);

    return hr;
}

// Free unmanaged memory used by the application.
void FreePointer(IntPtr Pointer)
{
    free(Pointer.ToPointer());
}
```

One of the features of this example is that it uses as many generic function calls as possible to reduce the amount of Visual C++ code required to handle any given task. The GetTokenSize() and GetTokenData() both fall into this category. You can use them to obtain any of a number of token types. The example concentrates on the user token—the one that contains security information for the current user, but you can use these two functions to gain access to any other supported token as well.

The GetTokenSize() function begins by using the OpenProcessToken() function to retrieve the token for the current process. Every process the user opens contains a copy of the user's token. However, the system and other external processes can also open processes, so the only certain way to retrieve a copy of the user's token is to look at the current process. Notice that we've opened the token for query purposes only and that we obtain a handle to the current process using the GetCurrentProcess() function.

Once the code obtains a token handle, it can retrieve information about the token. The purpose of the GetTokenSize() function is to tell the caller how much memory to allocate for the token information, not to actually retrieve the information. The caller must provide one of several *TOKEN_INFORMATION_CLASS* enumeration values as input to the GetTokenSize() function. We'll visit these values later. For now, the enumeration is used as input to the GetTokenInformation() function, which also requires the token handle and a variable to return the length. If this were an information retrieval call, the code would also need to supply a pointer to a buffer to receive the information and the length of that buffer.

WARNING   Always close all handles and free all allocated memory when working with unmanaged code. Every call you make to the Win32 API, including the security API, is a call to unmanaged code. Notice the call to `CloseHandle()` in the example code. This call frees the token handle before the `GetTokenSize()` function returns.

The `GetTokenData()` function works much like the `GetTokenSize()`. In this case, the caller must provide a pointer to a buffer used to store the data. However, you need to consider how the `GetTokenInformation()` function works before you proceed. The `GetTokenInformation()` is general purpose—it returns more than one type of data depending on the kind of token you request. As a result, it returns a *VOID** that the application must typecast to another kind of information. We'll see how this works later. The point, for now, is that `GetTokenData()` must allocate the memory for the `GetTokenInformation()` call and that you can't free this memory within the function as you would normally (notice the commented `free(lpTokenData)` call within the code that shows where you'd normally free the buffer).

The data buffer returned by `GetTokenInformation()` contains a *TOKEN_USER* data structure. This data structure contains a security identifier (SID) that we'll use to obtain three pieces of information about the user. The `ConvertTokenUserToSidString()` function accepts the buffer as input, typecasts it to a *TOKEN_USER* data structure, then uses the data structure to make a `ConvertSidToStringSid()` call. The resulting *LPTSTR*, *SIDValue*, is used to create a String value (*SIDString*). Notice that the code requires a double pointer (**) to *SIDString* to create a reference to it. This is an idiosyncrasy of Visual C++ that you need to consider when creating wrapper functions such as this one. Also notice that the function uses `LocalFree()` to free the memory used by *SIDValue*. That's because the memory for *SIDValue* is actually allocated by the `ConvertSidToStringSid()` function. We'll see later that locally allocated memory is freed using the `free()` function.

The final wrapper function, `ConvertTokenUserToUserData()`, retrieves the user name and domain using the SID. In this case, the code relies on the `LookupAccountSid()` function, which requires two locally allocated buffers. Notice the use of the `malloc()` function with appropriate typecasting and the use of the `free()` function calls to free the memory later.

The example does show one instance where there's a direct correlation between a Win32 API function and the wrapper function. The `FreePointer()` function simply calls the `free()` function used earlier to free memory signified by a pointer.

The C# and Visual Basic code required to use all of these wrapper functions is almost mundane compared to the wrapper code. The code calls the various wrappers to obtain a user token, use it to access the user's SID, name, and domain, and then display that information in a message box. Listing 3.3 shows the code to perform these tasks.

Listing 3.3   Obtaining the User SID, Domain, and Name

```
public enum TOKEN_INFORMATION_CLASS
{
    TokenUser = 1,
    TokenGroups,
    TokenPrivileges,
    TokenOwner,
    TokenPrimaryGroup,
    TokenDefaultDacl,
    TokenSource,
    TokenType,
    TokenImpersonationLevel,
    TokenStatistics,
    TokenRestrictedSids,
    TokenSessionId,
    TokenGroupsAndPrivileges,
    TokenSessionReference,
    TokenSandBoxInert
}

private void btnTest_Click(object sender, System.EventArgs e)
{
    int             Result;
    SecurityWrapper SW = new SecurityWrapper();
    IntPtr          TokenSize = new IntPtr(0);
    IntPtr          TokenData = new IntPtr(0);
    String          SIDString = null;
    String          UserName = null;
    String          Domain = null;

    // Get the size of the data structure. The return value of
    // this call is always 0. The call has actually failed because
    // it didn't retrieve the user information token.
    Result = SW.GetTokenSize((int)TOKEN_INFORMATION_CLASS.TokenUser,
                    ref TokenSize);

    // Get the token data. The return value of this call should always
    // be 1. The call has succeeded in returning the user token.
    Result = SW.GetTokenData((int)TOKEN_INFORMATION_CLASS.TokenUser,
                    ref TokenData,
                    TokenSize,
                    ref TokenSize);

    // Obtain the SID String.
    Result = SW.ConvertTokenUserToSidString(TokenData, ref SIDString);
```

```
// Obtain the user account information.
Result = SW.ConvertTokenUserToUserData(TokenData,
                                       ref UserName,
                                       ref Domain);

// Free the memory used by the token data.
SW.FreePointer(TokenData);

// Display the output.
MessageBox.Show("User Name:\t" + UserName +
               "\r\nDomain:\t\t" + Domain +
               "\r\nSID:\t\t" + SIDString,
               "Local Account Information",
               MessageBoxButtons.OK,
               MessageBoxIcon.Information);
}
```

The TOKEN_INFORMATION_CLASS enumeration shows the types of data you can request using the GetTokenSize() and GetTokenData() methods. The example code uses *TokenUser*. However, you can also gain access to the process privileges, owner, group association, statistics, and other kind of information. In short, the technique shown in this section is the tip of a much larger iceberg.

The btnTest_Click() method is straightforward. The GetTokenSize() and GetTokenData() methods work together to obtain the *TokenData* pointer—which is a pointer to the *TOKEN_USER* data structure discussed earlier. However, as far as C# is concerned, *TokenData* is simply a pointer to some data. It could point to any of the data structures used by any of the *TOKEN_INFORMATION_CLASS* enumeration members. It's only during the call to the ConvertTokenUser-ToSidString() and ConvertTokenUserToUserData() functions that the code becomes specific to the TOKEN_USER data structure. Figure 3.1 shows the output of this example.

WARNING The code must free the memory the *TokenData* variable points to before it exits. Otherwise, the application will leak memory. The Visual C++ DLL contains a special function, FreePointer(), for this purpose. Any DLL you create should contain a special function that accomplishes this same task.

FIGURE 3.1:

The output of the example program is simple, but demonstrates token access.

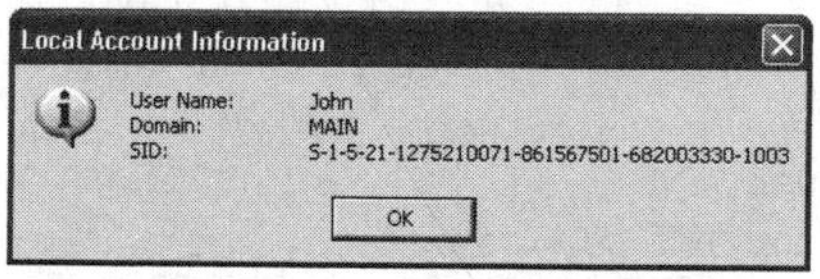

A C LIB Substitute Functions Example

There are times when you can get around using the Win32 API by using a substitute of some type. For example, many developers will want to add Windows XP programming effects to their application so that application uses the themes that Windows XP supports. Normally, this would mean writing code that changes the owner draw functions for the associated application. However, if you're willing to get most but not all of the Windows XP look, you can get around using the Win32 API.

<table>
<tr>
<td>

NOTE

</td>
<td>

The technique shown in this section relies on a relatively new Windows feature called *side-by-side DLLs*. This new technology enables two versions of the same DLL to exist on the same machine. That's how Windows XP keeps an older version of the common controls DLL and the new 6.0 version on the same machine. You'll find the side-by-side files in the \WINDOWS\WinSxS folder of the affected system. In fact, you can use this information to determine if the client machine supports side-by-side functionality. Windows uses the default DLL for applications that don't request special functionality. In the case of this example, the manifest requests the special functionality found in the 6.0 version of the common controls.

</td>
</tr>
</table>

This technique involves making a minor change to the design of your application and creating a special manifest. The minor change won't affect application operation under other versions of Windows, yet will allow you to see the themes supported by Windows XP. The source code for this example appears in the \Chapter 03\C#\ShowMessage and the \Chapter 03\VB\Show-Message folders of the CD. This is the same example from Chapter 2 with one difference—the *FlatStyle* property for all of the controls is set to System, rather than Flat as usual.

Simply changing the *FlatStyle* property won't change the appearance of the application. You also need to create a manifest file that tells Windows XP to use the 6.0 version of the common controls DLL. The following code shows the XML file you'll need to create. Note that the important part of this file is the content of the <dependentAssembly> tag.

```xml
<?xml version="1.0" encoding="UTF-8" standalone="yes"?>
<assembly xmlns="urn:schemas-microsoft-com:asm.v1" manifestVersion="1.0">
  <assemblyIdentity type="win32"
                    name="ShowMessage"
                    version="1.0.0.0"
                    processorArchitecture="x86"
  />
  <dependency>
    <dependentAssembly>
      <assemblyIdentity type="win32"
                        name="Microsoft.Windows.Common-Controls"
                        version="6.0.0.0"
```

```
                             processorArchitecture="X86"
                             publicKeyToken="6595b64144ccf1df"
                             language="*"
            />
        </dependentAssembly>
      </dependency>
    </assembly>
```

The 6.0 version of the common controls DLL includes support for the themes used by Windows XP. If you don't include the manifest, then the application will continue using the older version of the common controls DLL. The interesting part about this solution is that the application will now use the Windows XP themes when running under Windows XP, but act normally under other versions of Windows. Figure 3.2 shows the output of the application (on the right) and contrasts it to the normal appearance of the dialog box without changes (on the left).

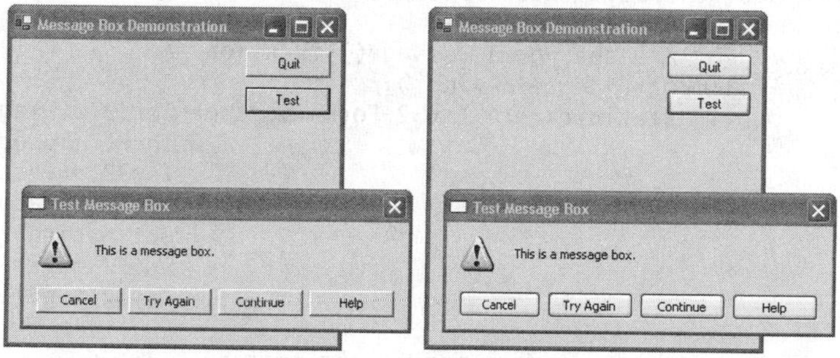

FIGURE 3.2:

A simple change makes Windows XP theme support available to your application.

As you can see from the figure, the application on the right now uses the rounded buttons found in Windows XP applications. You'll find that all of the other common controls work the same way. In fact, this technique also works for all other common elements including dialog boxes. The one compromise you'll need to make is that Windows XP won't change the appearance of owner-drawn controls. For example, the icon displayed in the modified application still reflects its non-Windows XP origin. This is actually a small price to pay for everything you do get without a single line of additional code. The "Working with Theme Support Example" section of Chapter 9 shows how to fix this problem.

Interpreting Error and Result Values

Sometimes your best efforts can't keep the user from making a mistake or prevent the system from befouling perfectly good code. In those situations, you need to trap and report the error so the user has some idea of what's going on with the application. That's why you need to include some type of error reporting in your application. The actual error reporting process is relatively easy—not as easy as within .NET, but certainly easier than some developers think. Listing 3.4 shows the code you'll need to make this example work.

Listing 3.4   **Reporting Win32 API Errors Is Relatively Easy Using This Code.**

```
// Declare the LoadLibraryEx() function.
[DllImport("Kernel32.DLL")]
public static extern IntPtr LoadLibraryEx(String lpFileName,
                                          IntPtr hFile,
                                          Int32 dwFlags);


// Tell Windows to load the DLL as a data file.
public const Int32 LOAD_LIBRARY_AS_DATAFILE = 0x00000002;

// Declare the GetLastError() function.
[DllImport("Kernel32.DLL")]
public static extern Int32 GetLastError();

// Declare the FormatMessage() function.
[DllImport("Kernel32.DLL")]
public static extern Int32 FormatMessage(Int32 dwFlags,
                                         IntPtr lpSource,
                                         Int32 dwMessageID,
                                         Int32 dwLanguageID,
                                         out String lpBuffer,
                                         Int32 nSize,
                                         Int32 Arguments);


// Constants used to format the message.
public const Int32 FORMAT_MESSAGE_ALLOCATE_BUFFER = 0x00000100;
public const Int32 FORMAT_MESSAGE_IGNORE_INSERTS  = 0x00000200;
public const Int32 FORMAT_MESSAGE_FROM_STRING     = 0x00000400;
public const Int32 FORMAT_MESSAGE_FROM_HMODULE    = 0x00000800;
public const Int32 FORMAT_MESSAGE_FROM_SYSTEM     = 0x00001000;
public const Int32 FORMAT_MESSAGE_ARGUMENT_ARRAY  = 0x00002000;
public const Int32 FORMAT_MESSAGE_MAX_WIDTH_MASK  = 0x000000FF;


private void btnTest_Click(object sender, System.EventArgs e)
{
    IntPtr   hLib;     // Handle of the library we want to load.
    Int32    ErrNum;   // Error number.
    String   ErrStr;   // Error message.

    // Attempt to load a non-existent library.
    hLib = LoadLibraryEx("Nothing.DLL",
                         IntPtr.Zero,
                         LOAD_LIBRARY_AS_DATAFILE);
```

```
// Determine there is an error.
if (hLib == IntPtr.Zero)
{

    // Retrieve the error.
    ErrNum = GetLastError();

    // Change it into a string.
    FormatMessage(FORMAT_MESSAGE_ALLOCATE_BUFFER |
                  FORMAT_MESSAGE_FROM_SYSTEM |
                  FORMAT_MESSAGE_IGNORE_INSERTS,
                  IntPtr.Zero,
                  ErrNum,
                  0,
                  out ErrStr,
                  0,
                  0);

    // Display the message on screen.
    MessageBox.Show("Error Number: " + ErrNum.ToString() +
                    "\r\n" + ErrStr,
                    "Library Load Error",
                    MessageBoxButtons.OK,
                    MessageBoxIcon.Error);
}
}
```

I've included the LoadLibrary() function in this example because it comes in handy for a number of purposes. For example, you'll use the LoadLibrary() function to read icons embedded in existing DLLs such as Shell32.DLL. However, in this case, we need to create an error condition, so I've asked LoadLibrary() to read a non-existent DLL file. This code will produce a simple error message.

You have to read the Win32 API documentation carefully when checking for error conditions. In this case, a return value of 0 represents an error. Any other return value is a handle to the library. All that the code needs to do is verify that *hLib* contains a 0 in this example. It will, so the code that follows will execute.

Getting an error message is a two-step process. First, you have to retrieve the error number using GetLastError(). Of course, a number isn't particularly helpful to the end user, so you need to change the error number into a string using the FormatMessage() function. The FormatMessage() function is used for a variety of tasks, so it looks overly complex. However, when you create error message strings, the code shown in Listing 3.4 is generally all you need to provide. You have to tell FormatMessage() how to format the message using a number of flags. The arguments have to include the error number, and you need to provide a buffer to store the error string. Figure 3.3 shows the output from this example.

FIGURE 3.3:

An example of a
system error message
retrieved using
`FormatMessage()`

Helpful Win32 Programming Tools

Visual Studio .NET comes with a variety of tools as part of the package. In many cases, developers will already know about these tools because they'll use them to debug and validate existing applications. However, many of the tools take on special meaning when you develop applications that rely upon the Win32 API. These tools can help you discover some of the behaviors of the Win32 API and information that might not appear in the Visual Studio documentation.

We'll work with several of these tools as the book progresses. However, three tools are exceptionally important when you begin working with the Win32 API from the managed environment.

Dependency Walker   This utility helps you learn about the contents of unmanaged DLLs on your system—both imports and exports. In addition, it helps you understand the relationship between various DLLs.

Error Lookup   This utility enables you to decipher the error numbers returned by many of the Win32 API functions. The error numbers usually don't provide much information, but Error Lookup helps them make sense.

Spy++   This utility makes it possible to spy on your application—to see what the application is doing while running. While Spy++ doesn't provide the detailed information that a debugger would provide, it does help you see the application from the Windows perspective. This view often helps reduce the complexity of learning about the Win32 API.

Now that you know a little more about the utilities, let's look at them in depth. The following sections discuss each of the three utilities. We'll pay special attention to how the utilities can make it easier to work with the Win32 API. Of course, you'll also learn some general usage tips as the section progresses.

Dependency Walker

The Dependency Walker (also called Depends for the name of the executable file) enables you to view the dependencies between various DLLs. For example, you might know that User32.DLL contains the `MessageBoxEx()` function, but may not realize that User32.DLL also relies on other DLLs to make the function work. The interdependencies between DLLs are the cause of a number of problems with older, unmanaged applications, which is why Microsoft is now promoting the .NET Framework. However, whenever you work with the Win32 API, you also need to know about these dependencies to avoid problems with your application.

Now that you know how the Dependency Viewer is used normally, it's helpful to know how you'll use it for Win32 API application development. The Dependency Walker also displays a list of inputs and outputs for a DLL. For example, it shows that the User32.DLL file exports the MessageBoxEx() function. However, the Dependency Walker shows more—it shows that that there are actually two versions of this function, one for Unicode character use and a second for plain American National Standards Institute (ANSI) use. When you work with the C header files, they automatically convert MessageBoxExA() (ANSI) or MessageBoxExW() (Unicode) to MessageBoxEx() for the desired platform. In some cases, you'll have to perform this task manually by specifying an entry point as shown here. (Visual Basic developers will need to perform this task more often than C# developers.)

```
[DllImport("user32.dll",
           CharSet=CharSet.Auto,
           EntryPoint="MessageBoxExA")]
public static extern int MessageBoxEx(
   IntPtr hWnd,
   [MarshalAs(UnmanagedType.LPTStr)]String Message,
   [MarshalAs(UnmanagedType.LPTStr)]String Header,
   UInt32 Type,
   UInt16 LanguageID);
```

Notice that the *EntryPoint* argument specifies which version of the MessageBoxEx() function to use—the ANSI version in this case. Note that you can also use a numeric entry point if desired, but the text version is usually more readable and less susceptible to changes in the DLL's organization. Unfortunately, Windows 2000 and Windows XP both rely on the Unicode version of the MessageBoxEx() function, so you get some odd results as shown in Figure 3.4 when using this form of the DllImport attribute.

FIGURE 3.4:

Choosing the wrong entry point for a DLL can have unanticipated results.

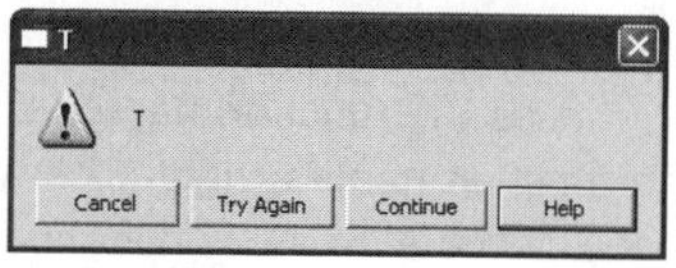

Changing the DllImport attribute to [DllImport("user32.dll", CharSet=CharSet.Auto, EntryPoint="MessageBoxExW")] returns the output to normal. This modification demonstrates that both Visual Basic and C# will choose an appropriate version of a function if the selection is clear. The only time you'll need to specify an *EntryPoint* value is when the entry point is unclear or if you're compiling an application for a platform other than the current platform. For example, you'll need to use the `MessageBoxExA()` entry point when compiling an application for the Windows *9x* platform. You'll also need to provide a specific entry point if you set the *ExactSpelling* argument to true (the default is false). Setting *ExactSpelling* to true ensures that you access only the function you need for a particular application, rather than allow .NET to locate something "close" for you.

TIP   To obtain help on any of the common Windows API functions listed in the Dependency Walker, highlight the function in question and press Enter. Dependency Walker will open the help file currently associated with Visual Studio. Unfortunately, not all of the functions are documented in the help provided with Visual Studio .NET. To obtain full documentation, you'll need a copy of the Platform SDK or MSDN.

Viewing the Dependencies

Dependency Walker (or Depends, as it's listed on the Microsoft Visual Studio 6.0 Tools menu) helps you prevent the problem of the missing file. It lists every file that an application, DLL, or other executable file depends on to execute. You can use the output of this application to create a list of required files for your application or to discover the inner workings of DLLs. Both of these functions are actually important when you use the Win32 API in your application, because you now need to consider the problems of providing the user with the correct version of any DLL that you use.

Loading a file for examination is as easy as using the File ➤ Open command to open the executable file that you want to examine. Figure 3.5 shows an example of the output generated for the `User32.DLL` file. As you can see, `User32.DLL` contains a wealth of functions. Notice that the figure shows the `MessageBoxExA()` function highlighted—the Unicode version, `MessageBoxExW()` function appears directly below this function. The figure also shows that each function entry includes both a function name and an ordinal number—either will work as an entry point.

NOTE   DLLs created with Visual C++ often have what's termed *decoration* in the function names. The decoration makes the function names almost unreadable to the average human. To undecorate the function names, right-click within the appropriate function-listing pane, and then choose Undecorate C++ Functions from the context menu.

FIGURE 3.5:

FIGURE 3.5:

Dependency Walker can help you determine what external files your component needs to operate.

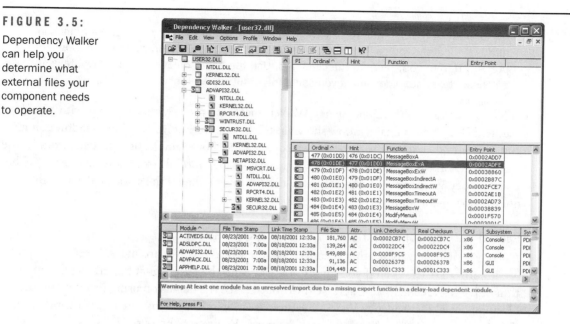

As you can see, this DLL provides you with a lot of information about the dependencies of your file. In the upper-left corner is a hierarchical view of dependencies, starting with the executable file that you want to check. The hierarchy shows the files that each preceding file requires to run. So, while the User32.DLL file itself relies on NTDLL.DLL, KERNEL32.DLL, and GDI32.DLL (along with other files), each of the support DLLs rely on other DLLs, such as the RPCRT4.DLL used by the ADVAPI32.DLL.

To the right of the hierarchical view are two lists. The upper list tells you the functions the parent executable imports from the current file. The lower list tells you the functions the highlighted executable exports for other executables to use. You'll typically see a blank export list for applications. Most DLLs export functions, but some don't import anything. The presentation will vary depending on the type of file you view.

At the bottom, you'll see an alphabetical list of all of the files along with pertinent information, such as the executable file's version number and whether the DLL or other files relies on a debug version of that file. This list comes in handy when debugging an application. It helps you to check for problems that might occur when using an older version of the DLL or to detect potential corruption in a support file. You'll also find it handy when you want to check that final release build before you release it for public use. Many applications have tested poorly because they still had "hidden" debug code in them.

TIP   It's interesting to note that Dependency Walker doesn't include any kind of print function-ality. Fortunately, you can highlight a list of items you want to print, and click Copy (or press Ctrl-C) to copy them to the clipboard. Use the Paste function in your favorite word processor to create a document you can print for future reference.

Newer versions of the Dependency Walker (including the version that ships with Visual Studio .NET) have a final window shown at the bottom of Figure 3.5. This window contains any messages that affect the display of the opened file. For example, User32.DLL or one of the imported DLLs in the hierarchy relies on a delay-loaded module (some executable file). The Dependency Walker might not be able to display this module if the associated executable doesn't document it properly.

Special Viewing Considerations for Managed Applications

As far as a managed application is concerned, the world revolves around MSCOREE.DLL—there are no other DLLs. Even if you import a DLL using the [DllImport] attribute, the applica-tion only sees MSCOREE.DLL—at least at the outset (see the details on using profiling in the "Using Special Dependency Viewer Features" section). To demonstrate this principle, open the ShowMessage.EXE application from Chapter 2. Figure 3.6 shows the C# version of this application, but the Visual Basic version behaves in a similar manner.

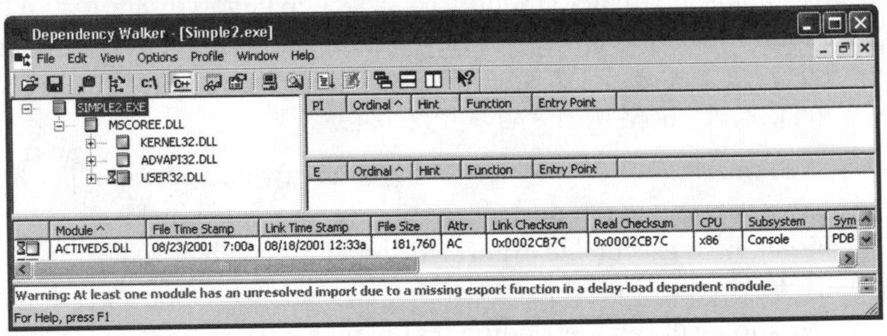

FIGURE 3.6:

Managed applications only see the MSCOREE.DLL file and rely on it for everything.

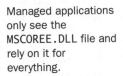

The really odd part of the display is that you won't see any imported or exported functions for the application. The managed environment doesn't expose its requirements for outside sources the same way as the unmanaged environment does. If you want to see which DLLs a managed application requires to work, you'll need to use ILDASM to view the application manifest. Figure 3.7 shows the example from the ShowMessage application. Notice that the imported function appears as any other function, which means that you might spend a con-siderable amount of time looking for imported functions in a complex application.

FIGURE 3.7:

To see the imported functions for a managed application, you must view the application in ILDASM.

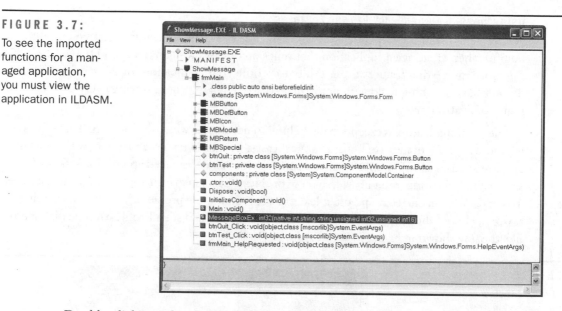

Double-clicking a function is the only way to make sure it's actually imported from an external DLL. Figure 3.8 shows the code for the MessageBoxEx() function. Notice that this function relies on PInvoke—a sure sign that the function appears in another DLL. In fact, the code tells you which DLL is used and all of the implementation details for the function. However, having to dig for this information does make things inconvenient for the developer.

FIGURE 3.8:

ILDASM will tell you which DLL the application uses, as well as any implementation details.

```
frmMain::MessageBoxEx : int32(native int,string,string,unsigned int32,unsigned int16)
.method public hidebysig static pinvokeimpl("user32.dll" autochar winapi)
        int32  MessageBoxEx(native int hWnd,
                            string  marshal( lptstr) Message,
                            string  marshal( lptstr) Header,
                            unsigned int32 Type,
                            unsigned int16 LanguageID) cil managed preservesig
{
}
```

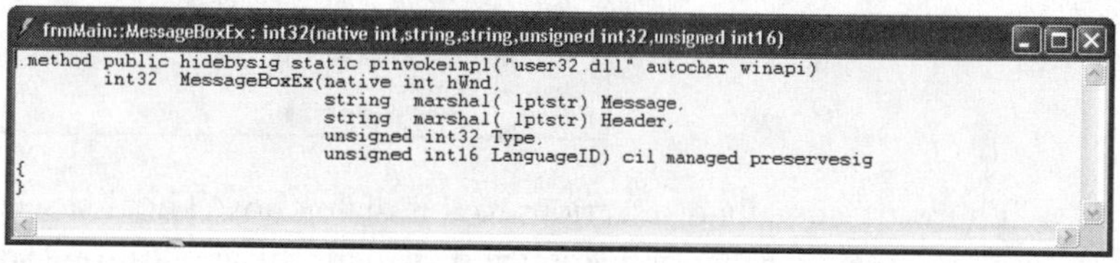

The Visual Basic version of the code looks similar to the code in Figure 3.8. The differences are minor but notable. For example, because we can't use a UInt in Visual Basic, you'll see the *Type* and *Language* arguments listed as Int32 and marshaled as UInt32. The Visual Basic implementation also relies upon the *EntryPoint* argument for [DllImport], so the PInvoke information looks different from the C# implementation, but both act the same. In short, even though there are small differences between languages, the functionality of the PInvoke call is the same.

Using Special Dependency Viewer Features

Newer versions of the Dependency Walker include some special features that you might find helpful when creating an application that relies on one or more unmanaged DLLs. One of the more interesting features is the ability to profile your application. In this case, profiling doesn't have anything to do with performance; we're talking about tracing every call that your application makes.

The profiling feature is exceptionally helpful to developers who use Win32 API calls because it exposes the use of imported DLLs in most cases. In addition, you can track how the managed application uses the Win32 API call and compare it to an unmanaged application's use of the same call. This comparison provides you with clues when a managed application refuses to use a Win32 API call correctly and often leads to a solution to the problem. To start the profiling process, choose the Profile ➢ Start Profiling command. You'll see a Profile Module dialog box like the one shown in Figure 3.9.

FIGURE 3.9:

The Profile Module dialog box configures the profiling feature of the Dependency Walker.

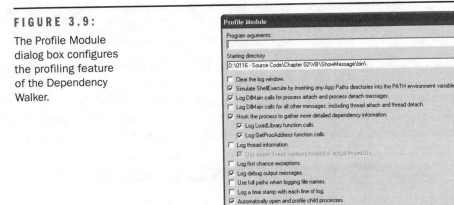

There are actually two sections to this dialog box. The first section provides a command-line argument for the application and changes the application's starting path. In most cases, you won't need to change either entry. You can also choose whether Depends clears the Log window before it begins the profiling process. The Simulate ShellExecute option determines how the application is started. Normally, you'll keep this checked to ensure that the application path information is provided to the application when it starts. The only exception is when you're troubleshooting problems related to the application path. If you uncheck this option, then Dependency Walker will start the application using the `CreateProcess()` API call rather than using `ShellExecute()`.

The second section contains a list of items that you will want to monitor. For example, you might only be interested in profiling the libraries that your application loads and when it loads them. In this case, you'd select the Log LoadLibrary function calls option. The number of entries in the Log window can build very quickly, so it helps to decide what you really need to monitor at the outset, rather than wading through a lot of useless information that you don't really want. Figure 3.9 shows the default information that Depends will collect about your application. This setup is useful in determining how an application uses the various libraries that it requires to operate. It's interesting to note that you can even use Depends to monitor debug output messages that you've placed within an application, making it a handy tool for monitoring application activity outside of a programming language's IDE.

Once you've decided how to start the application and what you want to monitor, click OK. Depends will load the application and start displaying profile information. In many cases, you'll need to clear the log entries shown in the bottom pane of the window before you proceed to test Win32 API calls; otherwise, there's simply too much material to check. Figure 3.10 shows the Log window entries for the ShowMessage.EXE application we looked at earlier. Notice the trapped call to the MessageBoxExW() function. Also notice that User32.DLL is now listed as one of the DLLs used by the application.

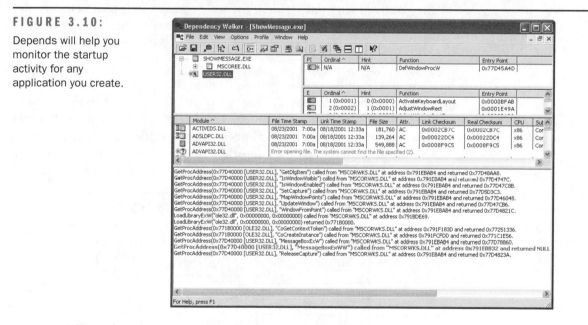

FIGURE 3.10:

Depends will help you monitor the startup activity for any application you create.

Even though you can't see it in the book, the Log window shows a problem with a call made by the application after I clicked Test. This call is highlighted in red in the Log window. In addition, the affected modules are highlighted in red in both the module list and the hierarchical display. What this means to you, as a developer, is that Depends has gone from being a simple analysis aid to an application that can help you diagnose application problems.

In this case, the errant call is caused by the method that .NET uses to locate a function accessed by the [DllImport] attribute. Looking at the C# version of the ShowMessage application, you'll notice that MSCORWKS.DLL first makes a call to User32.DLL for the MessageBoxEx() function. When that fails, it makes a call to the MessageBoxExW() function and succeeds. Now if you look at the Visual Basic version of the ShowMessage application, you'll notice that MSCORWKS.DLL begins by making a request for the MessageBoxExW() function, which succeeds. It then makes a request for the MessageBoxExWW() function, which fails. Observing these behaviors can tell you a lot about how .NET works with Win32 API calls.

Depends returns control of the application to you as soon as the application finishes loading. You can work with the application just as you normally would and monitor the results in the Log window. When you finish working with an application, you can stop the logging process using the Depends Profile ➢ Stop Profiling command.

There are quite a few other new features provided with Depends, but the ability to profile your application is probably the highlight of the list. One of the new capabilities allows you to save a Dependency Walker Image (DWI) file. This option creates a file on disk that allows you to restore your setup as needed. Depends provides so many new features when it comes to configuring the application environment—the previous versions didn't require this useful feature.

The View menu contains three options that you really need to know about. The first is a System Information command that displays a dialog similar to the one shown in Figure 3.11. This short summary provides a quick view of your current system configuration, which could be important if you want to stress the application under a set of specific conditions like low memory. There are also options to display the full paths for all files and to undecorate those really weird function names that you'll normally find within C++ generated DLLs.

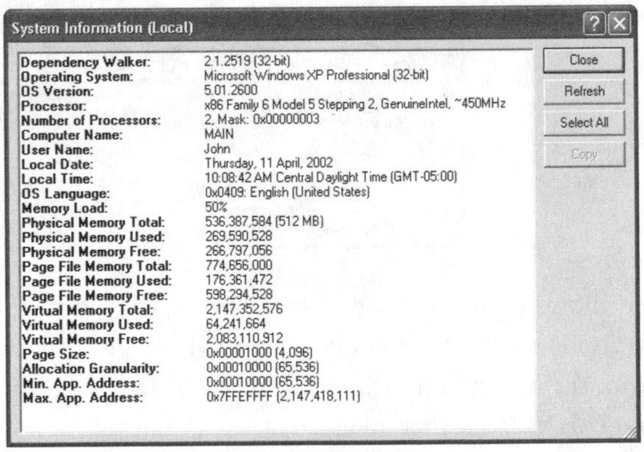

FIGURE 3.11:

The System Information dialog box gives you a quick overview of your system.

One final feature that improves the usability of Depends is the ability to search for specific information. For example, you can highlight a module of interest and use View menu options to search for other occurrences of the same module within the hierarchical view. This allows you to better see where specific modules are used and by whom. Another search feature, this one found on the Edit menu, allows you to search the Log window for words, just as you would with a text editor. You could use this feature to help find errors (the logs do get very long very fast) or to find instances where a specific module is used for tasks like application initialization.

Error Lookup

The Error Lookup program is one of those simple utilities that are simple in design and an obvious addition to the developer's toolbox once you think about it. This tool is important to the managed application developer because you don't have as many resources for locating error information—at least not without specifically adding them to your application. Generally, you'll receive error information as a number from the Win32 API. You must either locate the error number in the help file (an impossible task) or add code to locate the text version of the error message to your code. Fortunately, Error Lookup presents a third solution.

All you need to do to use Error Lookup is start the utility from within the IDE. Type the number into the Value field and click Look Up to see the associated text. Figure 3.12 shows an example of an error message output.

FIGURE 3.12:

Use Error Lookup to find the text associated with an error number.

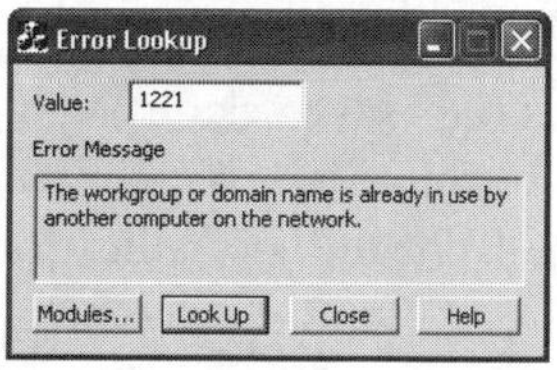

Error Lookup will locate all general Win32 API error messages as configured when you start it. However, you won't always work with generic modules. Sometimes, as in the MMC example later in the book, you'll need to work with specialized DLLs. In this case, you'll want to add that module to the list of modules that Error Lookup uses as a resource. All you need to do is click Modules, add the name of the DLL with the DLL extension to the Module Name field (include path information when necessary), click Add, and then click OK. Error Lookup will also look in the added modules when it can't find an error number in the general message list.

Spy++

Spy++ is a complex utility that can give you more information about your application than you might have thought possible. This section is going to give you a very brief overview of this utility. What I'll do is point out some of the more interesting features that will make working with the applications in this book easier. Make sure you take time to work with this utility further once you've learned the basics. We'll also spend more time with it as the book progresses.

The first thing you'll see when you start Spy++ is a list of windows. A window can be any number of object types, but the most familiar is the application window. Figure 3.13 shows an example of what you might see when you start Spy++ with the ShowMessage sample application running.

FIGURE 3.13:

Spy++ allows you to take your application apart and see it from the Windows perspective.

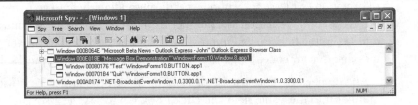

Notice that Spy++ shows two windows that belong to the main application window—all of which are components on the dialog box. In this case, the Test and Quit buttons are both considered windows. The buttons are all objects derived from the `WindowsForms10` class, which means that Spy++ is right on track displaying the information as it has. Note that the class will vary by language, version of the .NET Framework, and even by the type of application. For example, unmanaged Visual C++ applications derive their windows from the `CWindow` class.

> **TIP**   Spy++ often displays more windows than you think are open on the client machine. Some of these windows are hidden from view; others appear in areas such as the Taskbar Tray (Notification Area for Windows XP developers). You can always ask Spy++ to show you where a window resides by right-clicking the window entry and choosing Highlight from the context menu. This menu also contains a Refresh option to update the Spy++ display (it's static) and a Messages option that opens a new window to track messages for the selected window.

Working with Window Properties

Windows are a central part of working with Spy++. They represent the method you'll normally use to begin deciphering how an application works and how well it runs. It makes sense, then, that you can access every aspect of an application, its child windows, processes, and threads through the Window Properties dialog box shown in Figure 3.14.

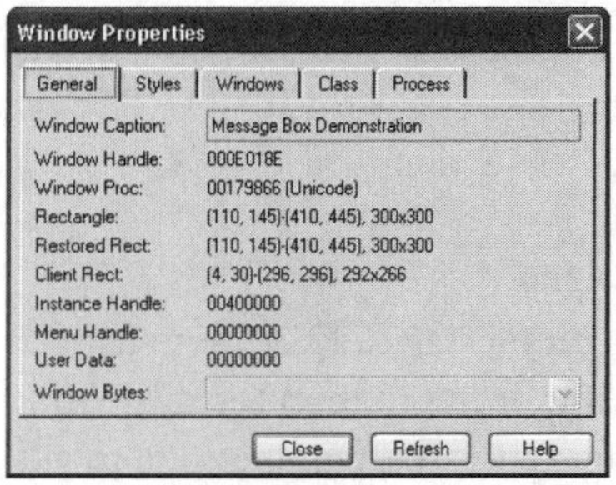

FIGURE 3.14:

The Window Properties
dialog box enables you
to learn more about
the structure of your
application.

Accessing this dialog box is easy: All you need to do is right-click the window you want to view, then choose Properties from the context menu. You can also access this dialog box using the View ➤ Properties command.

The General tab of the Window Properties dialog box tells you about the window as a whole. It includes the window's display name, the window handle, the virtual address of the window procedure, the size of the rectangle used to display the window (both present and restored sizes), and various other pieces of general application information.

The Styles tab contains a list of the window style constants used to create the window. For example, you'll commonly find WS_VISIBLE as one of the items in the list unless you're dealing with an invisible window. This same tab contains extended styles for the window like WS_EX_APPWINDOW. These constants should be familiar to someone with C/C++ programming experience since you need them to display windows in most cases.

The Windows tab contains five entries. You can move between windows at the same level by clicking the links in the Next Window and Previous Window fields. The Parent Window field will contain a link if this is a child window or (None) if this is a main window. If the window contains child windows (like the components for the ShowMessage program), you'll see an entry in the First Child field. Clicking this link will take you down one level in the hierarchy so that you can examine any child windows that belong to the current window. Finally, the Owner Window field will contain a link if another window owns the current window—except for the Desktop, in which case the field displays a value of (None).

The Class tab tells you about the class used to create the window. For example, the main window for the ShowMessage program uses the `WindowsForms10.Window.8.app1` class, while the components are all listed as being part of component-specific classes like the `BUTTON` class (actually the `WindowsForms10.BUTTON.app1` class) used for the Quit button. You'll also find class-specific information such as class style codes, number of data bytes used by this class instance, a window instance handle, number of bytes used by the window, and window details like the name of any associated menus.

The Process tab provides a list of process IDs and thread IDs associated with the current window. Clicking the links associated with each field will display the properties dialog associated with the process or thread ID. We'll look at this properties dialog in more detail in the Viewing Processes section that follows.

Viewing Messages

Windows runs on messages. Every activity that the user engages in generates a message of some sort. It's important to monitor those messages and see how your application reacts. For example, if you expect a certain message to get generated when the user clicks a button, you can monitor the message stream to see if it really does get sent.

There are a number of ways to display the Messages window for a window that you're debugging. You could right-click on the window and choose Messages from the context menu. However, in this particular case, the best way to start the message monitoring process is to use the Spy ➤ Log Messages command. (You won't see the Message Options dialog box when you use the context menu method of displaying the Messages window.) Using this command will display the Message Options dialog box shown in Figure 3.15.

FIGURE 3.15:

The Message Options dialog box enables you to configure Spy++ for message snooping.

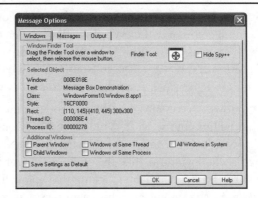

Notice that Selected Object frame on the right side of the dialog box. This frame provides you with information about the object that you've selected. This additional information enables you to determine if this is the window that you want to monitor. The Finder Tool on the left side of the dialog box is interesting as well. Drag this tool to any displayed window, then release the mouse button, and the information on the right side will change to match the data for that window. (Spy++ highlights the windows as you drag the mouse cursor over them so that you can see which one is being selected.) The Windows tab also helps you to choose additional windows. For example, you may want to monitor the child windows as well as the parent window for a specific kind of message.

There are 1,009 different messages that Spy++ can track for the average window. The Messages tab shown in Figure 3.16 gives you some idea of just how extensive the message coverage is.

FIGURE 3.16:

The Messages tab helps you select the messages that you want to track for a window.

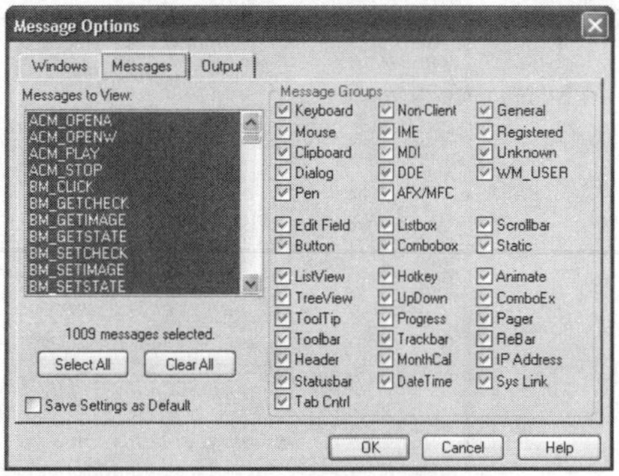

Needless to say, you could end up with a lot of useless tracking information if you don't trim the number of messages down to a more reasonable selection. That's why the Messages tab is so important. This tab helps you choose which messages Spy++ tracks in the Messages window. You can choose messages singularly or by group. A Select All button chooses all of the messages, while a Clear All button clears the current selections. Make sure you tune these settings before you display the Messages window or your chances of getting the input you need are very small indeed.

It's also important to determine how you want information displayed in the Messages window. In most cases, the default options on the Output tab will work just fine. Spy++ assumes that you want to display only decoded information and only on screen. However, there are options for displaying raw message information. You can also choose to send the output to a file as well as to the screen.

Once you have the options set for your Messages window, you can click OK and Spy++ will display it for you. Figure 3.17 shows an example of what a Messages window would look like if you choose to monitor a subset of button and mouse events. As you can see, just selecting these two message groups generates a lot of message traffic.

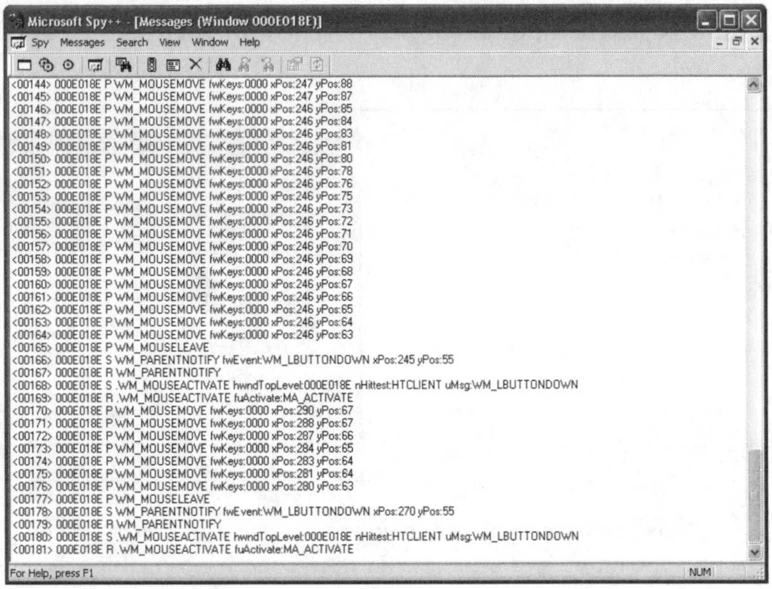

FIGURE 3.17:

The Messages
window will display the
messages that you
choose to monitor for
an application.

FIGURE 3.17:

The Messages
window will display the
messages that you
choose to monitor for
an application.

In this case, I clicked the Test button several times and moved the mouse around on screen. Notice that the log entries contain the handle of the window where the action occurred, the action performed (mouse button up or down, mouse move, or set cursor), and the position where the action occurred. Obviously, this is a simple test case, but it's also easy to see that monitoring messages can provide you with very important debugging clues for your application.

Viewing Processes and Threads

Every application you create will have at least one process and one thread. Consider a process as the overall application identifier, while a thread consists of a particular set of actions taking place within that process. In a multi-threaded application, each thread of execution is performing a single task that affects the application (the process) as a whole.

Spy++ provides methods for monitoring both processes and threads. All you need to do is use the Spy ➤ Processes or Spy ➤ Threads command to display the appropriate window. Figure 3.18 shows an example of the Processes window.

It's interesting to note that the Processes window also contains a list of any threads owned by the process in a hierarchical format. For this reason, you'll normally want to use the Processes window over the Threads window. You get more information in an easier-to-use format using the Processes window. We'll discuss the Processes and Threads windows in more detail as the book progresses.

Spy++ will allow you to monitor both threads and processes.

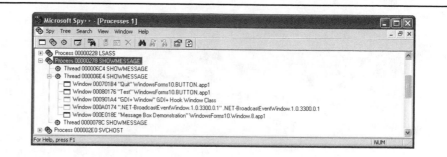

Where Do You Go from Here?

This chapter has provided you with the general information you need to access any Win32 API call. We haven't delved into the nuances of specific technologies, but you now know about the tools to locate and call Win32 API functions in general. You also have some idea of when you need to use a C library instead of a direct Win32 API call and when you need to use Visual C++ to provide glue code for some types of Win32 API calls.

One of the focal points of this chapter is the utilities that Microsoft provides with Visual Studio .NET. These utilities still have their traditional uses, but they also have special uses for Win32 API developers. It pays to know what resources you have at your disposal when you work with something as complex as Win32 API access. Learning about these utilities now will save you considerable time and effort later.

Chapter 4 will help you understand another type of Win32 API call, the Windows message. Sometimes you don't need a Win32 API function to produce a certain effect under Windows— what you need is a message sent to another application or to Windows itself to perform a given task. Consequently, it's essential to know how Windows messages work so that you can make these calls as needed. Interestingly enough, sometimes you have to call your own application to produce an event needed to perform tasks such as shutting the application down in an emergency.

CHAPTER 4

Processing Windows Messages

- Understanding the Windows Message Types

- Windows Message Handlers Found in the .NET Framework

- An Overview of Windows Message Functions

- Creating a Windows Message Handler Example

As part of its effort to hide some of the mundane details of how Windows works from developers, Microsoft has actually hidden a few too many facts. One of the issues you need to know about is how Windows uses and processes messages. For that matter, you need to know how to create your own messages at times. While the built-in message handling provided by Microsoft for the .NET Framework environment works most of the time, there are a few situations where you might want to have more control than the environment provides.

This chapter discusses all of the aspects of Windows message processing, handling, and generation. You'll learn about the message pump and some of the other low-level details that the .NET Framework normally hides. In addition, we'll look at some of the messages that the .NET Framework handles for you. For example, you have access to the WM_HELP message—it's just hidden by a form event handler (more on this topic in the "Windows Message Handlers Found in the .NET Framework" section of the chapter).

The important bit of information to get from this chapter is that Windows uses a messaging system to communicate with applications that's remained essentially unchanged from the days of Windows 3.*x*. The applications can also communicate with Windows and other applications using messages. In short, understanding the messaging system is essential if you want to build robust applications.

Understanding the Windows Message Types

Windows is literally packed with messages. There are thousands of messages to which your application can respond. Even the user interface messages number over a thousand. There are messages for mouse movement, keyboard clicks, system messages, user messages, all kinds of messages. One of the best places to view these messages in action is Spy++. Figure 4.1 shows the Messages tab of the Message Options dialog box. As you can see, there are a number of ways to group just the messages that appear in the user interface portion of Windows. (You can learn more about Spy++ in the "Spy++" section of Chapter 4—messages appear in the "Viewing Messages" subsection.)

User interface messages don't exist in a vacuum—you aren't going to find many messages that exist in isolation. Consider the simple act of clicking a button. When a user clicks the button, it generates a WM_LBUTTONDOWN message, and then a WM_LBUTTONUP message. If the user presses and releases the mouse button within the time limits of a click, the act also generates a BN_CLICKED message, which Windows sends to the button's parent. This action generates a BM_CLICK message, which is where event handlers normally act on the button click (both managed and unmanaged).

However, the presence of a WM_LBUTTONDOWN message doesn't necessarily signify a button click—it also occurs for radio button selections and other control events, so Windows has to know which control is the focus of the action. In addition, the WM_LBUTTONDOWN message can begin a drag-and-drop action. The user might not want to actually select the item; they may simply want to move it. (Of course, dragging and dropping one or more objects normally entails some form of selection—it may simply mean the object isn't activated.)

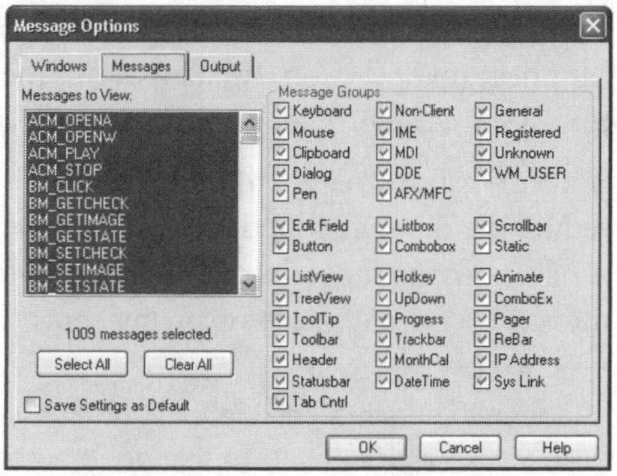

FIGURE 4.1:

Spy++ provides one of the best ways to graphically see the effects of messages.

Something I haven't covered in all of this is the appearance of ancillary messages when a user performs most tasks. For example, looking at the same button click from the previous paragraph, the user doesn't just click a button; the mouse cursor has to appear in the right place to perform the click. This means generating a wealth of WM_MOUSEMOVE messages as the user moves the mouse to the correct position in the dialog box. If the user moves the mouse outside the dialog area, then the dialog will also receive a WM_MOUSELEAVE message. There's no WM_MOUSEENTER message because the WM_MOUSEMOVE message serves to tell the application of the mouse entry into the dialog area.

Fortunately, even in unmanaged applications, a developer only has to track the messages of interest and can ignore everything else. The developer doesn't have to track every message and suffer the repercussions of message overload. The .NET Framework further reduces the need to track messages—as we'll see in the "Windows Message Handlers Found in the .NET Framework" section that follows.

In many cases, a user interface message doesn't affect the user interface directly—it acts in the background as a notification of change. For example, Windows issues the WM_SYSCOLOR-CHANGE message to all top-level windows whenever the user changes the system colors. This notification helps the application maintain the appearance of controls and data so that the reader can still see the screen, no matter how garish the color selection.

There's a group of messages that affect the application as a whole, including the user interface, but act in the background instead of the foreground. For example, Windows issues a WM_POWER message every time the machine is about to enter the suspended mode. An application can track the WM_POWER message to determine when the system is about to suspend operations. It can use this message as a way to determine when to save application status information or open data files.

System-level messages often provide two-way communication for applications. An application can receive a system-level notification such as the WM_POWER message. It can also issue a system-level request using the WM_SYSCOMMAND message. In this last case, the command often has nothing to do with the user interface of an application at all, but does affect system or individual application operation. In many cases, the request is for background services that the operating system can provide anonymously in an asynchronous fashion.

If you haven't noticed already, all of the messages we've discussed have a two-letter identifier followed by the message function, task, or type. The two-letter identifier provides the best means of classifying most (but not all) messages. Table 4.1 provides a list of the most common message types with accompanying short description.

NOTE   Table 4.1 doesn't contain a complete list of all prefixes. It includes a list of common prefixes that the developer is likely to use or care about. For example, the list doesn't contain the NM prefix because these messages are normally used at a low level for parent control notification of events handled at a higher level by application code.

TABLE 4.1: Common Prefixes for Win32 API Messages

Prefix	Description
BCM	A button control message that changes the resource usage or other inner workings of a button or a button-like control.
BCN	A button control notification that notifies the control of a change in status.
BM	A button message that obtains status information about the button or its appearance. This is a general prefix used for all button-like controls.
BN	A button notification that specifies a change in the button status, such as a user click. This is a general prefix used for all button-like controls.
CB	A control box specific status, resource, or setup message. Note that these entries tend to be unique and you'll need to watch button and edit box messages as well.
CBEM	An extended control box specific status, resource, or setup message.
CDM	A common dialog box message that obtains status information about the dialog box or its appearance.
CDN	A common dialog box message that specifies a change in dialog box status, such as the user clicking the OK button.
DBT	A device specific message generally used to signal a device status change, such as a configuration change or when a user plugs in a new device.
DTM	A date/time picker message that obtains status information about the control or its appearance.

Continued on next page

TABLE 4.1 CONTINUED: Common Prefixes for Win32 API Messages

Prefix	Description
DTN	A date/time picker message that specifies a change in control status, such as a change in the date or time format.
EM	An edit box message that obtains status information about the edit box or its appearance. This is a general prefix used for all edit box–like controls.
EN	An edit box notification that specifies a change in the edit box status, such as a change in the text content. This is a general prefix used for all edit box–like controls.
LB	A list box specific status, resource, or setup message.
LBN	A list box message that specifies a change in list box status, such as the user double-clicking an item. These items tend to be very specialized, so you'll need to watch standard button messages (BN) as well. Depending on the configuration of the list box, you'll want to consider the EN and CB messages as well.
LBS	A list box message that specifies a change in the list box style, such as a change in the technique used to sort list box entries.
LVM	A list view message that obtains status information about the control or its appearance.
LVN	A list view message that specifies a change in control status, such as an item change or selection.
LVS	A list view message that specifies a change in the list view style, such as a change in the technique used to sort list view entries. The styles are a lot more comprehensive than those used for LBS messages. For example, there are separate styles for sorting in ascending and descending order.
MM	A multimedia message—usually hardware or media specific. For example, this group includes messages that affect the joystick. It also includes messages that denote multimedia events such as opening a waveform file.
SC	A system control message such as a request to turn on the screensaver or shut the system down.
TB	A toolbar specific status, resource, or setup message.
TBM	A trackbar specific status, resource, or setup message.
TVM	A tree-view specific status, resource, or setup message.
UDM	An up-down control specific status, resource, or setup message.
WM	A generic Windows message used for a variety of purposes including system requests. In some cases, the message will contain service information. For example, you'll find a series of WM_ADS messages that reflect changes in Active Directory Service status.

Notice that most of these message categories are user interface specific. That's because many of the messages that Windows handles are user-generated—a user does something and generates a message as a result. In addition, some controls have specific status and notification classes (such as BM and BN) while others don't (such as CB). Windows will often classify a control as having button-like behavior. It uses the button-related messages to handle user events and programmatic changes to those controls.

Applications can also create messages, and you'll find custom messages for certain classes of applications. For example, many database managers (DBMSs) use the DB message prefix to signal database events such as a new record. In many cases, such as the DB example, you'll find common application messages documented in the Platform SDK help (but not in the Visual Studio .NET help).

A few Win32 API messages are application specific and you'll generally need to consider them only when using Visual C++ (some can be helpful in other situations). For example, the DT prefix is used for text drawing messages. Most of these messages do appear in the Visual Studio .NET documentation because the current version of Visual C++ .NET uses them.

Windows Message Handlers Found in the .NET Framework

The previous section might leave you feeling hopelessly mired in messages you don't know about and aren't sure that you want to know about. However, we'll see as the book progresses that you need to know about messages because that's the only form of communication Windows actually recognizes. In addition, Spy++ can be the most valuable tool in your Win32 API toolbox. However, you don't need to memorize all of these messages and you'll find that you don't have to worry about every message that Windows can process. You'll find that the .NET Framework implements the most common messages for you as event handlers. For example, the Click() event handler is a response to the BN_CLICKED notification. The Spy++ display in Figure 4.2 shows the messages generated for the ShowMessage application from Chapter 3 when you click the Test button.

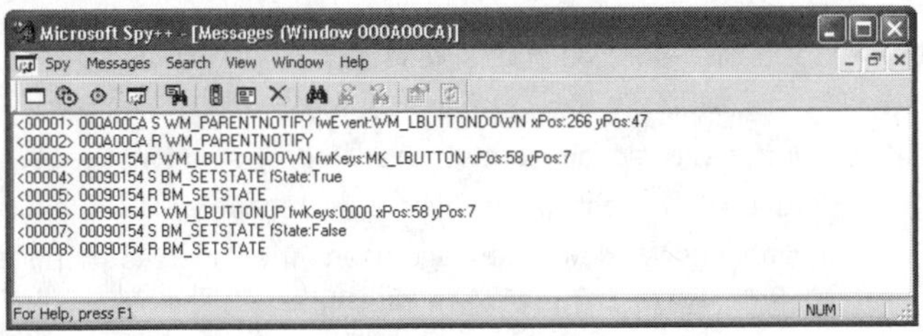

FIGURE 4.2:

Spy++ can provide clues on which messages you need to implement.

As you can see, the parent window receives a message that the user has clicked the left button (WM_PARENTNOTIFY with the WM_LBUTTONDOWN message as data). This message is passed to the child window (a button, in this case), which registers the WM_LBUTTONDOWN message and takes control of the message stream. The button also sets its state to true. The user releases the left mouse button, which generates a WM_LBUTTONUP message and the requisite setting changes for the button. This set of events ends a BN_CLICKED event (not shown).

The same messages occur no matter what type of application you create—managed or unmanaged. Figure 4.3 shows an example of a simple unmanaged Visual C++ application (located in the \Chapter 04\SayHello folder of the CD). The MFC application has a few additional bells and whistles, such as the selection of a default button, but otherwise the message sequence is the same.

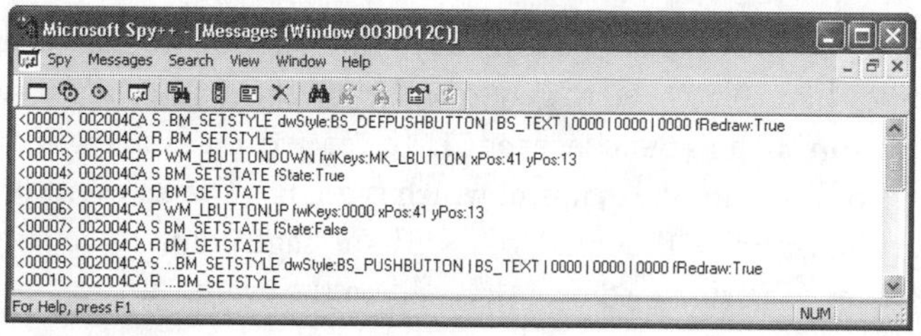

FIGURE 4.3:

Managed and unmanaged applications both generate the same sequence of messages.

TIP

Sometimes it's difficult to correlate a .NET Framework event handler with a Win32 API message. In fact, you might not know whether the .NET Framework even provides support for a given message. In many cases, you can create a test application that uses what you suspect is a Win32 API message, and then see if Spy++ reports that the message is active in the test application. If the message isn't active, then you've at least eliminated some of the .NET Framework functionality that could support the message. Because Microsoft hasn't provided any documentation that shows the correlation between .NET Framework event handlers and Win32 API messages, you'll occasionally need to perform this type of interactive research—making Spy++ one of your best friends.

As previously mentioned, Microsoft hasn't created a list that shows the correlation between Win32 API messages and the event handlers found in the .NET Framework, so you need to test as you go along. However, in general, you can count on the .NET Framework handling all general control messages, as well as many system-related messages. For example, you'll find that the .NET Framework handles all of the button messages you'll ever need, so there shouldn't ever be a need to implement a message handler for a button. The same holds true for edit and list boxes.

The .NET Framework doesn't handle some system messages such as turning the screensaver on or off, or changing the display settings. The .NET Framework doesn't implement any of the Windows XP–specific messages. For example, you won't find any support for the Fast User Switching feature. All of these messages will require some type of application support.

You'll also find a lack of low-level device support in the .NET Framework. For example, general printer commands are handled, but anything going to the parallel port (such as LPT1) isn't. Newer devices such as USB (Universal Serial Bus) drives are handled by the operating system for the most part, and you can access the data they contain using standard .NET file handling calls. However, if you need to access the drive itself, you'll need to create special message handlers (as well as a wealth of other device handling code).

An Overview of Windows Message Functions

Windows messages don't suddenly jump out of your application and appear in a message queue somewhere. You need to generate the messages you want to send to another application using a function such as SendMessage(). To receive a message, your application must provide some type of listening mechanism, which is going to be an event in most cases. The application will need to override the standard .NET message pump to generate the event and provide an event handler to perform some task based on the event.

This section of the chapter discusses some of the Win32 API message functions you'll use to send and receive Windows messages. It's important to note that sending messages requires a complete Win32 API call setup, while receiving messages requires hooks into the existing .NET Framework classes. In short, the information below is a starting point—it's the Win32 API portion of the picture. We'll look at how all of the pieces fit within the .NET Framework in the various examples in this chapter.

> **NOTE**   You might also want to look at the ScreenSaver example in Chapter 3, which demonstrates the simplest way to send a message to Windows that results in a system action. The examples in this chapter are a little more complex, so the Chapter 3 example is a good place to start.

SendMessage()

SendMessage() is the simplest function you can use to send messages to Windows or to other applications. One of the best ways to test this function is to work with the system commands. You'll find a complete test program for the system commands in the \Chapter 04\ C#\SysCommand and \Chapter 04\VB\SysCommand folders of the CD. This example shows the full set of SC commands in action (at least those that are documented). Figure 4.4 shows the dialog for this example, which includes a list of the SC commands, along with one long string for testing the vertical scroll command (SC_VSCROLL).

> **NOTE**   Some commands in the list will only work if you trigger the Test button with the Enter key, instead of clicking Test with the mouse. The reason is that the action takes place immediately—the mouse cursor changes to the double-pointed or other arrow type. Unfortunately, because the mouse is already in use, the command fails. The only way to get around this problem for testing is to use the keyboard in place of the mouse.

FIGURE 4.4:

The SysCommand example shows how the various system commands work.

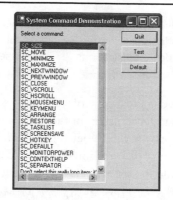

Some of the system commands require special handling. For example, the SC_MONITORPOWER command requires input in the *lParam* argument. The standard value of 0 doesn't accomplish anything. If you input 1, then the display will go to a low power state, while a value of 2 turns the display off. The example uses a value of 2 to ensure that most systems will see at least a momentary power down of the screen. In some cases, you might have to modify the display settings to get this system command to work properly. Here's the modified code.

```
DoSysCommand = (Int32)SystemCommand.SC_MONITORPOWER;
SendMessage(this.Handle, WM_SYSCOMMAND, DoSysCommand, 2);
return;
```

Notice that we're still using the handle for the main window. Figure 4.5 shows another view from Spy++. Notice that each of the major controls in the application is also a window. The window-like quality of the controls enables you to access them by sending them messages. Of course, the control has to have some means of responding to the messages—there's no magic involved.

FIGURE 4.5:

Every visible control in an application is very likely a window as well.

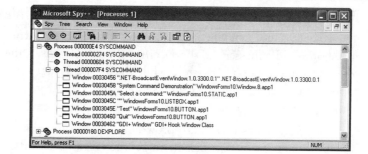

Figure 4.5 also shows two hidden windows—those with a grayed outline. The first is for .NET broadcasts, while the second is for GDI+, as opposed to the plain GDI used by standard Windows applications. In most cases, you won't want to modify these windows or send messages to them—you might see unpredictable results.

To send a message to a control, you need to provide both a handle for the control's window and an event handler to listen for the message. In some cases, such as moving a window, the .NET Framework provides a default handler. You can also add your own handler that CLR will call when the .NET portion of the call completes. The following code shows how to obtain the handle for lbCommandSel and use it to move the list box around.

```
IntPtr   Temp = IntPtr.Zero;   // A temporary handle.

// Load the proper system command.
DoSysCommand = (Int32)SystemCommand.SC_MOVE;

// Obtain the handle to the list box.
Temp = lbCommandSel.Handle;

// Move the list box instead of the main window.
SendMessage(Temp, WM_SYSCOMMAND, DoSysCommand, 0);
return;
```

You must highlight the SC_MOVE (List Box) entry in the list, tab twice to highlight the Test button, and then press Enter. Clicking Test will cause the code to fail because the mouse is already engaged in clicking. You'll see the mouse cursor change to a quad-ended move cursor. Moving the mouse will move the list box. Press Enter again and you'll see the ending message found in the lbCommandSel_Move() method. Normally, you'd place any code required to end the move command in this method, but the example uses a simple message box.

PostMessage(), PostThreadMessage, and PostQuitMessage()

The PostMessage() and the SendMessage() functions perform essentially the same task—they both send a message to the specified thread. However, the PostMessage() function returns from the call immediately, while the SendMessage() function waits for the recipient to respond. Both functions accept essentially the same arguments, so anything you can do with a SendMessage() call, you can do with a PostMessage() call.

You might wonder why Microsoft would include two calls with essentially the same functionality. There's a distinct disadvantage when using the PostMessage() call—you don't know if anyone received the message. It's best to use PostMessage() when you don't care if anyone receives or acts upon the call.

NOTE There are a number of superceded message functions that you'll still find in the Platform SDK help and in the C/C++ header files. Never use these functions within an application because Microsoft doesn't support them and you don't know if they'll work in future versions of Windows. For example, the PostAppMessage() function has been replaced by the PostThreadMessage() function. Unfortunately, examples of these old functions prevail online and you even see them in the help files. Refer to the "Obsolete Windows Programming Elements" topic in the Platform SDK help file for a list of old functions and their replacements. This list isn't complete, but it's good place to start.

Both the PostMessage() and SendMessage() functions can accept special handles. However, one of these special handles works better with PostMessage() because it doesn't incur the delay that using SendMessage() would incur. You can use the *HWND_BROADCAST* handle to tell Windows to send a particular message to every accessible window. For example, you might use such a call to restore all of the windows as shown in Listing 4.1. (The example code appears in the \Chapter 04\C#\MinimizeAll and \Chapter 04\VB\MinimizeAll folders of the CD.)

Listing 4.1   Using the HWND_BROADCAST Handle to Call All Windows

```
// Used to send a system command message.
[DllImport("User32.DLL")]
public static extern int PostMessage(IntPtr hWnd,
                                     UInt32 Msg,
                                     Int32 wParam,
                                     Int32 lParam);

// The WM_SYSCOMMAND constant used to access the SC constants.
public const Int32 WM_SYSCOMMAND = 0x112;

// The HWND_BROADCAST handle sends the message to all windows.
public IntPtr HWND_BROADCAST = new IntPtr(0xFFFF);

// A list of SC constants used for all types of system
// command access.
public enum SystemCommand
{
    SC_SIZE         = 0xF000,
    SC_MOVE         = 0xF010,
    SC_MINIMIZE     = 0xF020,
    SC_MAXIMIZE     = 0xF030,
    SC_NEXTWINDOW   = 0xF040,
    SC_PREVWINDOW   = 0xF050,
    SC_CLOSE        = 0xF060,
    SC_VSCROLL      = 0xF070,
    SC_HSCROLL      = 0xF080,
    SC_MOUSEMENU    = 0xF090,
    SC_KEYMENU      = 0xF100,
```

```
    SC_ARRANGE      = 0xF110,
    SC_RESTORE      = 0xF120,
    SC_TASKLIST     = 0xF130,
    SC_SCREENSAVE   = 0xF140,
    SC_HOTKEY       = 0xF150,
    SC_DEFAULT      = 0xF160,
    SC_MONITORPOWER = 0xF170,
    SC_CONTEXTHELP  = 0xF180,
    SC_SEPARATOR    = 0xF00F
}

private void btnTest_Click(object sender, System.EventArgs e)
{
    // Minimize all of the windows.
    PostMessage(HWND_BROADCAST,
                WM_SYSCOMMAND,
                (Int32)SystemCommand.SC_RESTORE,
                0);
}
```

As you can see, using `PostMessage()` with the broadcast handle is essentially the same as using `SendMessage()`—the main difference is that the function returns immediately. If you try using this code with `SendMessage()` in place of `PostMessage()`, you'll see a definite delay as `SendMessage()` waits for all of the windows to return a response.

This code has an interesting side effect. Not only does it restore all of the visible windows, but it restores all of the hidden windows as well. The resulting chaos might look unappealing, but I've actually learned about a few windows that don't appear in the Spy++ list, but do appear on screen after using this call. Log off and back on your machine to restore the screen—a reboot isn't necessary to hide the hidden windows again.

A second special handle accesses the Desktop. The *HWND_DESKTOP* handle enables you to send messages to the Desktop using either `PostMessage()` or `SendMessage()`. Here's the definition for *HWND_DESKTOP*.

```
// The HWND_DESKTOP handle sends message only to the Desktop.
public IntPtr HWND_DESKTOP = new IntPtr(0);
```

The `AddFontFile()` method replicates the functionality of the `AddFontResource()` function of the Win32 API. Both enable you to add private fonts to your application without registering them within Windows first. Either form of the function works fine if you want to share your registered font with every other application running in Windows. However, what happens if you want to keep your special font truly secret? You need to use the `AddFontResourceEx()` function. This Win32 API function includes flags that keep your font secret and prevent other applications from enumerating the font. However, no matter which function you use to load a font, you still have to tell everyone that there was a change to the font table, which means sending a message. The code in Listing 4.2 shows how to load the VisualUI.TTF font that appears on most hard drives with Visual Studio .NET (among other applications) installed.

> **NOTE**
> For best viewing results, run this example application outside of the debugger. If you load the font while within the debugger, it tends to stay in memory until you exit the Visual Studio IDE. You can still follow code execution within the debugger to see how the various calls work—the only problem is that the font won't unload. That's because Windows associates the font with the Visual Studio IDE instead of the application since the application is executing within the debugger environment.

Listing 4.2   Use the AddFontFileEx() Function to Load Fonts Privately.

```
// The function required to add a private font resource.
[DllImport("GDI32.DLL")]
public static extern int AddFontResourceEx(String lpszFilename,
                                           Int32 fl,
                                           IntPtr pdv);

// The function required to remove a private font resource.
[DllImport("GDI32.DLL")]
public static extern bool RemoveFontResourceEx(String lpszFilename,
                                               Int32 fl,
                                               IntPtr pdv);

// Flags used to define how the private font resource is loaded.
public const Int32 FR_PRIVATE    = 0x10;
public const Int32 FR_NOT_ENUM   = 0x20;

// Used to send a system command message.
[DllImport("User32.DLL")]
public static extern int PostMessage(IntPtr hWnd,
                                     UInt32 Msg,
                                     Int32 wParam,
                                     Int32 lParam);

// The WM_SYSCOMMAND constant used to access the SC constants.
public const Int32 WM_FONTCHANGE = 0x001D;

// The HWND_BROADCAST handle sends the message to all windows.
public IntPtr HWND_BROADCAST = new IntPtr(0xFFFF);

System.Drawing.Text.PrivateFontCollection PFC;

private void btnLoadFont_Click(object sender, System.EventArgs e)
{
    // Determine which action to take.
```

```
    if (btnLoadFont.Text == "Load Font")
    {
        int   Result = 0; // Results of loading the font.

        // Load the desired font.
        Result = AddFontResourceEx(
            "D:\\Program Files\\Microsoft Visual Studio
    .NET\\Common7\\IDE\\VisualUI.TTF",
            FR_PRIVATE,
            IntPtr.Zero);

        // Check the results.
        if (Result == 0)

            // Display an error message if necessary.
            MessageBox.Show("The font failed to load for some reason.",
                        "Load Failure",
                        MessageBoxButtons.OK,
                        MessageBoxIcon.Error);
        else
        {
            // Change the button caption.
            btnLoadFont.Text = "Unload Font";

            // Tell everyone we've loaded a new font.
            PostMessage(HWND_BROADCAST, WM_FONTCHANGE, 0, 0);
        }
    }
    else
    {
        bool  Result;  // Results of loading the font.

        // Load the desired font.
        Result = RemoveFontResourceEx(
            "D:\\Program Files\\Microsoft Visual Studio
    .NET\\Common7\\IDE\\VisualUI.TTF",
            FR_PRIVATE,
            IntPtr.Zero);

        // Check the results.
        if (!Result)

            // Display an error message if necessary.
            MessageBox.Show("The font failed to unload for some reason.",
                        "Unload Failure",
                        MessageBoxButtons.OK,
                        MessageBoxIcon.Error);
        else
        {
            // Change the button caption.
            btnLoadFont.Text = "Load Font";
```

```
        // Tell everyone we've loaded a new font.
        PostMessage(HWND_BROADCAST, WM_FONTCHANGE, 0, 0);
      }
    }
  }

  private void btnDisplayDialog_Click(object sender, System.EventArgs e)
  {
    // Display the font dialog.
    dlgFont.ShowDialog(this);
  }
```

As you can see, the sample code can load and unload the VisualUI.TTF font. The AddFont-ResourceEx() and RemoveFontResourceEx() function calls load the font publicly if you don't specify any flags or privately if you specify the FR_PRIVATE flag shown. Notice the use of PostMessage() in this example. You must tell other windows about the new font or they won't recognize it (this includes other windows in the current application). The WM_FONTCHANGE message doesn't require any parameters—the other windows will create a fresh enumeration of the font list if necessary.

If you click Display Fonts immediately after loading the example application, you'll notice that the VisualUI is missing from the list. Load the font with the code shown in Listing 4.2 and you'll see the VisualUI font in the list as shown in Figure 4.6.

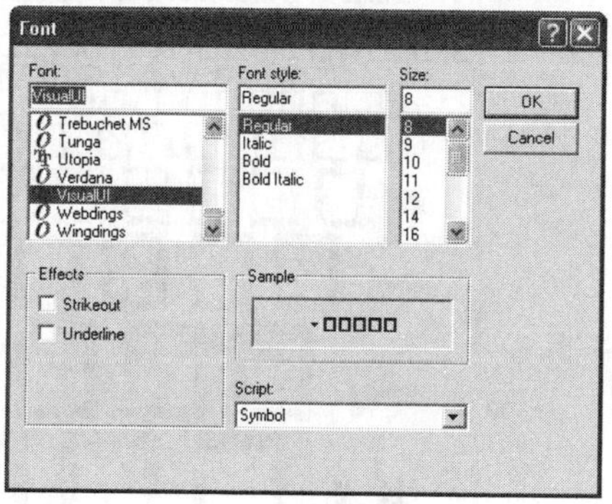

FIGURE 4.6:

Loading the VisualUI font using the default code displays it in the Font dialog box.

There are some interesting changes you can make to the code in Listing 4.2. For example, try the example with a SendMessage() in place of a PostMessage() call and you'll see that the time differential can be significant. Try running the call without sending the WM_FONTCHANGE message at all and you'll notice that not even the local application will notice it in some cases (the change becomes intermittent). Try loading the font publicly (without any flags). Other applications such as Word will contain the font in their font list. Reboot the machine after a public load to ensure that the font is removed from memory. Now, try using the *FR_NOT_ENUM* flag when loading the font and you'll notice that only the test application displays the font.

> **NOTE** The AddFontResourceEx() function, like many of the special functions in the book, isn't supported by Windows 9x systems, including Windows Me. In addition, the fonts you add using this function are only accessible for the current session—they're unloaded as soon as the user reboots the machine. As you can see, it's essential to check the Platform SDK documentation for limitations on using Win32 API functions directly.

The VisualUI.TTF font is interesting for developers, but almost useless for users, so it makes a perfect private font. Figure 4.7 shows what this font looks like. As you can see, it contains the special font Microsoft uses for drawing the VCR-like controls on screen. It also contains some unique graphics such as the pushpin used in some areas of the Visual Studio IDE. Having access to these special graphics can save development time.

FIGURE 4.7:

The VisualUI font may not have much to offer users, but it can save some drawing time for developers.

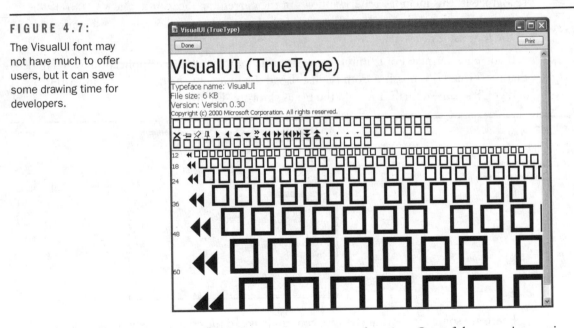

There are several variations on the PostMessage() function. One of the more interesting messages is PostThreadMessage(). This form of the function enables you to post a message to the threads of the current application. You still provide *Msg*, *lParam*, and *wParam* arguments. However, instead of a window handle, you need to provide a thread identifier. The Post-ThreadMessage() function has several constraints, including a special constraint under Windows 2000 and Windows XP—the thread identifier must belong to the same desktop as the calling thread or to a process with the same Locally Unique Identifier (LUID).

You'll almost never need to use the `PostQuitMessage()` function. All .NET languages have a built-in method to perform this task and you're better off using it whenever possible. The `PostQuitMessage()` tells Windows that your application is going to exit. It includes an exit code that an external application can use to determine the exit status of your application (generally 0 for a successful exit). It's important to know about this function because it does come in handy in certain rare circumstances—mainly within wrapper DLLs. You can use this message to force an application exit when catastrophic events occur. The only time you should consider using this message is if the application is hopelessly frozen and you still want to provide some means of exit (so the user doesn't have to perform the task manually). In short, for the .NET developer, this is the message of last resort.

SendNotifyMessage()

Sometimes you need a message whose behavior depends on the circumstance in which it's used. The `SendNotifyMessage()` function combines aspects of the `SendMessage()` and the `PostMessage()` functions we discussed earlier. When you use `SendNotifyMessage()` to send a message to the window process in the same thread, it waits for a response. On the other hand, if you send the message to a window in another thread, `SendNotifyMessage()` returns immediately. This duality of function ensures that you gain reliable message transfer for the local thread, without the performance delay of waiting for other threads to complete their work.

> **WARNING** Avoid using pointers in any asynchronous message function, including `SendNotify-Message()`, `PostMessage()`, `SendMessageCallback()`, because the function will likely fail. The message call will return before the recipient can look at the data pointed at by the pointer, which means the recipient may not have access to the data required to complete the call. For example, the caller could deallocate the memory used by the data immediately upon return from the call. If you need to send a pointer as part of a message, then use the `SendMessage()` function to ensure that the recipient is done using the pointer before the message returns. While this technique does incur a performance penalty, it also ensures that the message will complete as anticipated.

The `SendNotifyMessage()` function requires the same input as both `SendMessage()` and `PostMessage()`. You can use it to send both single-window and broadcast messages.

SendMessageCallback()

The `SendMessageCallback()` function has two main purposes. First, it sends a message to another process—just like the other message-related functions we've discussed so far. Second, it registers a callback function with the message recipient. A callback function is a special function used by the message recipient to return message results to the message sender. In short, this is the first function to provide a two-way communication path for messages.

The first four arguments for the SendMessageCallback() function are the same as any other message function. You need to provide an *hWnd*, *msg*, *lParam*, and *wParam* values. The fifth argument, *lpCallBack*, is a pointer to a callback function. This requirement means you need to use a delegate to pass the address pointer. We'll see how this works in Chapter 5, which concentrates on callback functions. The sixth argument, *dwData*, is a value that you can pass from your application, through the message recipient, and back to the callback function. This application-defined value can provide input to the callback function that determines how it processes the message return data.

You'll normally use the SendMessageCallback() function to retrieve data from a device, system service, or other data source that the .NET framework doesn't support directly. For example, you could use this technique to obtain an enumeration of the devices located on a USB.

GetMessage() and PeekMessage()

We've discussed the Windows message pump and several of the messages that can appear within the message queue. You know that whenever an application sends a message, Windows will place the message in the recipient's message queue, which is essentially an "In Box" for Windows messages. However, we haven't discussed how the recipient actually receives the message so it can act on it. The GetMessage() and the PeekMessage() functions provide the means for retrieving a message from the Windows message queue so the application can act on it. Use the GetMessage() function to remove the message from the queue and the PeekMessage() function to see if the message exists without removing it.

In most cases, you'll never need to use the GetMessage() or the PeekMessage() functions because CLR handles these requirements for you. However, these functions do come in handy for special messages (see the RegisterWindowMessage() section that follows) or within wrapper DLLs. What's most important is to understand the mechanism used to retrieve the messages once they arrive in the queue.

The GetMessage() function requires four inputs. The *lpMsg* argument is the most important because it contains a pointer to the Msg data structure used to hold the message information. When the call returns, the Msg data structure contains the information needed to process the message. The *hWnd* argument contains a handle to a window. However, you can set *hWnd* to null if you want to retrieve a given message for all windows associated with the current process. The *wMsgFilterMin* and *wMsgFilterMax* arguments contain a range of messages that you want to retrieve based on the value for each message (see the C header files for a complete list—the various examples in the chapter have already shown you the values of specific messages). If you want to retrieve a single message, then you set the *wMsgFilterMin* and *wMsgFilterMax* arguments to the same value. There are also predefined range values such as WM_MOUSEFIRST and WM_MOUSELAST that obtain specific input values.

The PeekMessage() function requires all of the arguments used by the GetMessage() function. You also need to provide a *wRemoveMsg* argument value. A value of PM_REMOVE will remove the message from the queue, while a value of PM_NOREMOVE will keep the message on the queue. Given the reason for using PeekMessage(), you'll probably use PM_NOREMOVE in most cases.

RegisterWindowMessage()

You'd think that with all of the messages that Windows supports natively, you'd never need to create a message of your own. Actually, applications commonly create custom messages for intra-application communication. Sometimes an application will spawn other processes and need to communicate with those processes using a special set of messages. Because the messages are sent publicly with SendMessage() or PostMessage(), Windows needs to know about them and you need to provide a unique name for them. The purpose of the RegisterWindow-Message() function is to register a unique name for your custom message. All you need to supply is a string containing the message name.

Creating a Windows Message Handler Example

This chapter already contains several examples that show how to send a message to Windows. Given an application need, you can send a request to Windows to answer that need. In fact, you can affect the operation of all of the applications running under Windows in some circumstances (as was shown with the MinimizeAll example). However, there are times when you want to create an environment where Windows can send a message to your application. Of course, this already happens all the time when users click buttons and enter text, but you might have some special message that you want Windows to send to your application that the .NET Framework doesn't handle by default.

The example in this section shows how to create a message handler that will react when Windows sends a specific message. To do this, we have to override the default .NET functionality for the Windows message pump, create an event that the message pump will fire when it receives the message in question, and create an event handler that does something when it receives an event notification. The following example is a prototype of sorts for handling all kinds of Windows messages. You'll see more advanced examples of this technique in Chapter 9 when we tackle advanced Windows XP features such as Fast User Switching. You'll find the code for this example in the \Chapter 04\C#\ReceiveMessage and \Chapter 04\VB\Receive-Message folders of the CD.

Creating the Event

The event portion of the code generates an event when requested. It will send the event to any number of handlers—all of which must register to receive the event notification. The event portion of the code doesn't do anything with the event notification; it merely reacts to the event and generates the notification. This is an extremely important distinction to consider. Listing 4.3 shows the event code for this example.

Listing 4.3	The Event Code for a Message Handler

```
// Create an event for the message handler to fire. We also
// have to handle this event or nothing will happen.
public delegate void DoSDCheck(object sender, System.EventArgs e);
public static event DoSDCheck ThisSDCheck;

// Provide a means for firing the event.
public static void Fire_ThisSDCheck(object sender, System.EventArgs e)
{
   // If there is an event handler, call it.
   if (ThisSDCheck != null)
      ThisSDCheck(sender, e);
}
```

As you can see, you need a delegate to define the appearance of the event handler. DoSD-Check() isn't an event handler; it merely acts as a prototype for the event handler. The event is an instance of the delegate. You must make the event static or no one will be able to call it.

Once you have an event defined, you need a way to fire it. Microsoft doesn't define the name of the method for firing an event in any concrete terms, but standard practice is to preface the event name with the word "Fire" followed by an underscore, so the name of this method is Fire_ThisSDCheck(). Firing an event can require a lot of work; but generally all you need to do is verify that the event has at least one handler, and then call the event. This step will call every assigned event handler in turn to process the event notification.

Creating the Windows Message Loop Override

The most important tip you can remember about processing messages is that the .NET Framework will only handle the messages that applications commonly use. If you need any other functionality in your application, then you need to add it. Common functionality includes messages associated with the mouse and the keyboard—it doesn't include messages associated with a shutdown.

TIP

Sometimes the Platform SDK documentation is simply wrong. For instance, the documentation for the WM_QUERYENDSESSION message used in this example tells you that it's sent in response to an ExitWindows() function call. Unfortunately, Windows XP doesn't support the ExitWindows() function, so there's no hope of making this function work properly given the documentation. You need to use the ExitWindowsEx() function instead. The best way to find this information is to use the Dependency Walker to view User32.DLL and see if it supports the ExitWindows() function. The answer becomes obvious during the few seconds it takes to check the DLL.

With this in mind, you have to rewrite the message pump to do something with the messages that you want to handle. This means overriding the default message pump, and then calling the base message pump to handle any messages that your code doesn't handle. The two-step process is important. If you don't call the base function, then any messages your code doesn't handle will go unanswered. Of course, you can always use this technique to force an application to handle just a few messages and ignore everything else—a somewhat dangerous proposition unless you know exactly what you're doing. Listing 4.4 shows the message pump override required for this example.

Listing 4.4   Always Override the Message Pump to Handle Custom Messages

```csharp
// We need to know which message to monitor.
public const Int32 WM_QUERYENDSESSION = 0x0011;
public const Int32 WM_ENDSESSION = 0x0016;

protected override void WndProc(ref Message ThisMsg)
{
    // See which message Windows has passed.
    if ((ThisMsg.Msg == WM_QUERYENDSESSION) ||
        (ThisMsg.Msg == WM_ENDSESSION))
    {
        // Fire the event.
        Fire_ThisSDCheck(this, null);

        // No more processing needed.
        return;
    }

    // If this isn't a session end message, then pass the
    // data onto the base WndProc() method. You must do this
    // or your application won't do anything.
    base.WndProc(ref ThisMsg);
}
```

The code for the message pump is relatively straightforward. All you need to do is check for the session ending messages, and then fire the event. Notice that we return from this function without providing a positive response to Windows. This omission enables the application to cancel the shutdown. If you want to allow the system to shut down, you must set the *ThisMsg.Result* value to true.

Creating the Event Handler

The event handler for this example doesn't do much—it displays a message box saying it received a notification. However, it's important to realize that the message handler could do anything within reason. Windows sets a time limit for responding to a shutdown message. If your event handler is code heavy, your application won't respond in time and Windows will try to shut it down manually. Listing 4.5 shows the event handler for this example.

Listing 4.5   **The Event Handler for the Example Is Simple and Fast**

```
public frmMain()
{
    // Required for Windows Form Designer support
    InitializeComponent();

    // Add an event handler for the shutdown check.
    ThisSDCheck += new DoSDCheck(OnShutDownCheck);
}

// Create an event handler for the shutdown event.
private void OnShutDownCheck(object sender, System.EventArgs e)
{
    // Display a message showing that we received the message.
    MessageBox.Show("Windows sent an end session message",
                "End Session Message",
                MessageBoxButtons.OK,
                MessageBoxIcon.Information);
}
```

Notice that you must register the event handler. Otherwise, it won't receive event notifications. In this case, the example registers the event handler in the constructor, which is a good place for the registration for most applications. If an event handler is important enough to monitor messages from Windows, you'll want to register it during the application startup process.

Demonstrating the Windows Message Handler

In older versions of Windows you simply told the operating system that you wanted to shut down, and that was the end of the process. Newer versions of Windows require a little more information, and Windows XP makes it downright impossible to shut down unless you have a good reason. For this reason, the code for initiating a Windows shutdown is a bit long. Listing 4.6 provides you with the essentials.

Listing 4.6   Using the ExitWindowsEx() Function to Shut Windows Down

```
// Used to send a message that starts the screen saver.
[DllImport("User32.DLL")]
public static extern int ExitWindowsEx(UInt32 uFlags,
                                       UInt32 dwReason);

// A list of flags that determine how the system is shut down.
public enum ShutdownFlag
{
    EWX_LOGOFF          = 0,
    EWX_SHUTDOWN        = 0x00000001,
    EWX_REBOOT          = 0x00000002,
    EWX_FORCE           = 0x00000004,
    EWX_POWEROFF        = 0x00000008,
    EWX_FORCEIFHUNG     = 0x00000010
}

// A list of major reasons to shut the system down.
public enum ReasonMajor
{
    SHTDN_REASON_MAJOR_OTHER            = 0x00000000,
    SHTDN_REASON_MAJOR_NONE             = 0x00000000,
    SHTDN_REASON_MAJOR_HARDWARE         = 0x00010000,
    SHTDN_REASON_MAJOR_OPERATINGSYSTEM  = 0x00020000,
    SHTDN_REASON_MAJOR_SOFTWARE         = 0x00030000,
    SHTDN_REASON_MAJOR_APPLICATION      = 0x00040000,
    SHTDN_REASON_MAJOR_SYSTEM           = 0x00050000,
    SHTDN_REASON_MAJOR_POWER            = 0x00060000
}

// A list of minor reasons to shut the system down. Combine
// these reasons with the major reasons to provide better
// information to the system.
public enum ReasonMinor
{
    SHTDN_REASON_MINOR_OTHER            = 0x00000000,
    SHTDN_REASON_MINOR_NONE             = 0x000000ff,
    SHTDN_REASON_MINOR_MAINTENANCE      = 0x00000001,
    SHTDN_REASON_MINOR_INSTALLATION     = 0x00000002,
    SHTDN_REASON_MINOR_UPGRADE          = 0x00000003,
    SHTDN_REASON_MINOR_RECONFIG         = 0x00000004,
    SHTDN_REASON_MINOR_HUNG             = 0x00000005,
    SHTDN_REASON_MINOR_UNSTABLE         = 0x00000006,
    SHTDN_REASON_MINOR_DISK             = 0x00000007,
    SHTDN_REASON_MINOR_PROCESSOR        = 0x00000008,
```

```
    SHTDN_REASON_MINOR_NETWORKCARD              = 0x00000009,
    SHTDN_REASON_MINOR_POWER_SUPPLY             = 0x0000000a,
    SHTDN_REASON_MINOR_CORDUNPLUGGED            = 0x0000000b,
    SHTDN_REASON_MINOR_ENVIRONMENT              = 0x0000000c,
    SHTDN_REASON_MINOR_HARDWARE_DRIVER          = 0x0000000d,
    SHTDN_REASON_MINOR_OTHERDRIVER              = 0x0000000e,
    SHTDN_REASON_MINOR_BLUESCREEN               = 0x0000000F,
    SHTDN_REASON_UNKNOWN                        = SHTDN_REASON_MINOR_NONE
}

// A list of reason flags that provide additional information about the
// cause of shutdown. Combine these flags with the major and minor reason
// values.
public enum ReasonFlag : uint
{
    SHTDN_REASON_FLAG_USER_DEFINED              = 0x40000000,
    SHTDN_REASON_FLAG_PLANNED                   = 0x80000000
}

private void btnTest_Click(object sender, System.EventArgs e)
{
    // Exit Windows.
    ExitWindowsEx((UInt32)ShutdownFlag.EWX_LOGOFF,
        (UInt32)ReasonMajor.SHTDN_REASON_MAJOR_APPLICATION &
        (UInt32)ReasonMinor.SHTDN_REASON_MINOR_MAINTENANCE &
        (UInt32)ReasonFlag.SHTDN_REASON_FLAG_PLANNED);
}
```

There are a lot of predefined reasons for shutting the system down and you should choose one of them within your application. Generally, you'll choose the appropriate *ShutdownFlag* value for the first argument. Notice that there are options for logging off, performing a normal reboot, and forcing a shutdown for a hung application. This last option should be used with care, but it's a valuable option if an application detects that it has frozen and the system is in an unstable state. (Of course, recovering from the condition is even better.)

I decided to split the second argument into three enumerations because each enumeration performs a different task. You should always include a *ReasonMajor* value as part of the shutdown. The *ReasonMinor* value further defines the reason for the shutdown but isn't essential. Finally, you can pass a *ReasonFlag* value if one of the values happens to meet your needs.

Developing for Thread Safety

You might think that all of the convoluted code in this example could be straightened out and made simpler. The fact is that the technique shown in this example becomes more important as the complexity of your code increases. The moment you introduce a second thread into the application, the need for all of the convoluted code becomes essential. Using events as we have here keeps the message handling in the main thread.

One of the Visual Studio IDE windows that you need to look at is the Threads window. Unfortunately, the Visual Studio IDE hides this window by default and most developers don't find it because it's hidden on the Debug menu instead of the View menu. To display the Threads window, use the Debug ➢ Windows ➢ Threads command. Figure 4.8 shows an example of the Threads window for the current application.

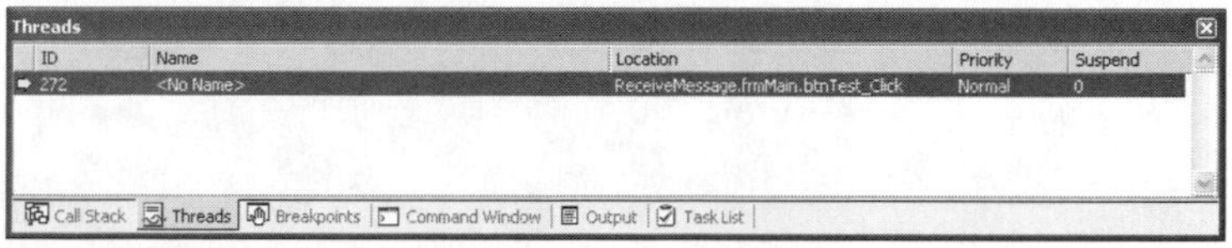

FIGURE 4.8:

The Threads window can be helpful in diagnosing problems with a Win32 API message handler.

Any code that changes the appearance of a Windows Form must execute from the main thread of the application. This is why you want to use an event handler for your message handling code. Using an event handler means that no matter which thread intercepts the message you want to process, the main thread will perform the actual processing.

Where Do You Go from Here?

This chapter has demonstrated various uses for Windows messages in managed applications. Like unmanaged Windows applications, managed applications use messaging to communicate between applications and the operating system. Knowing which Windows messages the .NET Framework supports natively can help you determine when you need to create a handler for non-standard messages.

We've discussed the correlation between some .NET Framework event handlers and the Win32 API messages. Create a small test application and use Spy++ to verify the messages that it responds to. Add objects such as menus to see the effect on the output messages. Remember to limit the message selections in Spy++ so that you can actually see the messages of interest— some messages (especially those for mouse handling) appear with such regularity that it's hard to see the messages that appear only when specific events occur.

Make sure you try out all of the examples on the CD. There are places in the chapter where I mention an example but don't go completely through the code, because most of it has appeared in other chapters. It's still important to check the example out because you'll learn techniques for working with messages by using them. Especially important are some of the system commands that aren't handled very well by the .NET Framework.

Now that you know about messages, it's time to look at the last generic feature for Win32 API programming—the callback function. Chapter 5 tells you how Windows uses callback functions for various tasks and when you'll need to use them for your Win32 API call. Callback functions are important because they provide a mechanism for Windows to interact with an application. Essentially, the application makes a request and Windows answers it through the callback function. This asynchronous handling of application requests enables Windows to run more efficiently, but does add to the developer's workload.

CHAPTER 5

Using Callback Functions

C hapter 4 provided you with a glimpse of some of the internals of the Win32 API. Message processing is a cornerstone of application development with the Win32 API, but it's only part of the equation. When an application sends a message, it hopes that another application will respond. Likewise, when an external application sends a message to your application, it's looking for a response. The problem is that this approach isn't two-way—it's a one-way communication from one application to another.

Callback functions provide the potential for two-way communication. When you make some calls to the Win32 API, you have to supply a pointer to a function that receives the response. This technique enables the Win32 API to provide two-way communication. A request from your application results in a response from the Win32 API to a specific point in your application. Two-way communication has important implications for the developer, as we'll discuss in this chapter.

After you gain an understanding of how callback functions work, we'll look at a callback function example. As you might imagine, getting callback functions to work under .NET is considerably more difficult than working in a pure unmanaged environment because you now have the managed environment to consider. It's not an impossible task, but there are certain restrictions you have to consider and a few programming techniques you'll want to learn.

TIP   Sometimes it's helpful to chat with other developers about questions you have in working with complex code. The VB World site at http://www.vbforums.com/ offers both general and specific topic messaging areas. This site also offers general areas for discussions about other languages such as C#. VB World is exceptionally nice for those developers who prefer a Web interface to the usual newsgroup reader.

What Is a Callback Function?

As previously mentioned, callback functions provide two-way communication. However, a callback function is more than a messaging technique—it's the Win32 API version of the asynchronous call. Your application makes a request and supplies the address of a callback function within your application. Windows will use this address as a communication point for the responses for your request. In many cases, Windows will call this function more than once— some callback functions are called once for each response that the Windows API provides.

Callback functions are important because they allow Windows to provide multiple responses for a single query. For example, when you want to scan the current directory on a hard drive, you actually need one response for each object in that directory. The same holds true for other response types. In this regard, you can view a callback function as a primitive form of collection. However, instead of gaining access to a single object that you have to parse one element at a time, the callback function provides individual elements from the outset.

TIP   We'll create more than a few callback functions as the book progresses. However, you might also want to view callback functions created by other developers. The Code Project includes a few examples of callback function coding on its site at `http://www` `.codeproject.com/win32/` and `http://www.codeproject.com/staticctrl/`. As mentioned on the page, many of these examples are unedited. Another interesting discussion appears on the C# Corner site at `http://www.c-sharpcorner.com/3/` `ExploringDelegatesFB002.asp`. I found this example a little convoluted, but some people may find it useful. The 4GuysFromRolla.com site at `http://4guysfromrolla.411asp` `.net/home/tutorial/specific/system/delegate?cob=4guysfromrolla` contains a number of interesting examples of both delegates and callback functions. Unfortunately, some of the code is also based on Beta 1 of Visual Studio .NET, so you'll need to select examples with care.

Most callback functions have a specific format because you need to know specifics about the object, such as the object type. The use of a specific format also provides a standard communication format between the Win32 API and the requesting application. The message format provides a means of passing information in a specific manner between the Win32 API and the calling application.

In many cases, a callback function can also provide feedback to the message sender. For example, you might not want to know the names of all of the files in a directory—you might only need one file. Once the application finds what it needs, it can tell the Win32 API to stop sending information. We'll see this particular feature in many applications in the book, even the MMC snap-in example in Chapter 12.

Like messages, the .NET Framework also has to provide support for callback functions. However, in this case you can't interact with the callback function directly. What you see instead is a collection that contains the requested data. In most cases, this loss of intermediate result control is a non-issue. There are a few situations, such as a file search, when you can gain a slight performance boost using an actual callback function. In general though, you should only rely on callback functions when the .NET Framework doesn't provide the desired functionality.

Using Callback Functions

Now that you have a better idea of what a callback function is and how you'd use it, let's look at some practical issues for using callback functions. The following sections describe the callback function prototypes and essential design techniques. You'll learn about callback function design using a simple example.

The point of this section is to provide you with a template that you can use in developing other types of callback functions for your applications. The essential task list remains the same, even when the callback function you use changes. For example, you'll always use a delegate to provide a callback address for the Win32 API function—no matter how complex the Win32 API function is or what task it ultimately performs.

An Overview of Callback Function Prototypes

Callback functions are unique, in some respects, because they provide a feedback method from Windows to the application. To ensure that Windows and the callback function use the same calling syntax (a requirement for communication), the Platform SDK documentation provides a set of callback function prototypes—essentially a description of the callback function argument list.

NOTE　This chapter doesn't discuss the special callback function prototypes for DirectX. For a discussion of DirectX callback function prototypes, see the DirectX Callback Function Prototypes section of Chapter 14. In many ways, the DirectX callback prototypes look and act the same as the prototypes in this chapter. However, the calling syntax is quite specific, so you need to know more about them before working with DirectX in applications.

When you make a system request that includes a callback function, you need to supply the address of the callback function matching the function prototype for that call. For example, the `EnumWindows()` and `EnumDesktopWindows()` functions both use the same function prototype in the form of the `EnumWindowsProc()` shown in the following code.

```
BOOL CALLBACK EnumWindowsProc
(
    HWND      hwnd,    // handle to parent window
    LPARAM    lParam   // application-defined value
);
```

In order to use either the `EnumWindows()` or the `EnumDesktopWindows()` function, you must provide the address of a prototype function that includes the handle to a parent window and an application-defined value. The prototypes for other callback functions are all standardized, but vary according to the Win32 API call that you make. It's important to research the callback function to ensure you supply one with the proper arguments in the right order.

TIP　Arguments for callback functions follow the same rules as function and message calls. For example, you'll still use an `IntPtr` for a handle. It pays to check the argument list carefully so that you can avoid defining application-supplied and -reserved arguments incorrectly.

Unfortunately, the prototype description won't tell you about the purpose of the application-defined value. To learn about the application-defined value, you need to look at the documentation for the individual functions. In the case of EnumWindows() and EnumDesktopWindows(), you don't receive any additional information from the application-defined value unless that information is passed as part of the original call.

The only piece of information your callback function will receive from the EnumWindows() function is a handle to the window. The function will continue to call your callback function with one window handle at a time until your callback function returns false (indicating you don't need any more data) or the function runs out of handles to return. You can use the window handle in a number of ways. For example, you could send the window a message as we did in Chapter 4. However, there are a number of other window-related functions that have nothing to do with messaging—you could simply learn more about the window using the GetWindowText() or GetWindowInfo() functions.

Implementing a Callback from the Managed Environment

It's time to look at the first callback example. This example is designed to break the callback creation process down into several discrete steps. In this case, we'll discuss what you need to do to enumerate the current windows. Enumerating the windows is the first step in discovering windows that you might want to communicate with—an important part of the messaging process. The source code for the example appears in the \Chapter 05\C#\EnumWindows and \Chapter 05\VB\EnumWindows folders of the CD.

Creating a Delegate

The first task you need to perform in creating a callback function is to define a delegate to represent the function. You can't pass the address of a managed function to the unmanaged environment and expect it to work. The delegate provides the means for creating a pointer that CLR can marshal. We'll see as the example progresses that the delegate is easy to use but important in effect.

> **TIP**
>
> In general, you'll use an event setup (as shown in Chapter 4) to handle Windows messages. However, you'll use delegates to enable use of callbacks. The main reason you want to use events to handle Windows messages is to allow someone inheriting from your code to access the message without worrying about the details of the Windows message. In addition, this technique works better where multiple threads are involved. Make sure you check thread safety when handling both Windows messages and callbacks. Normally, thread safety is less of a concern when handling callbacks, so the delegate technique shown in this chapter works fine.

The delegate you create must match the callback function prototype. In fact, giving the delegate the same name as the prototype helps document your code for other developers. Notice that the delegate shown in the following requires an IntPtr for the window handle and an Int32 for the lParam.

```
// Create the delegate used as an address for the callback
// function.
public delegate bool EnumWindowProc(IntPtr hWnd, Int32 lParam);
```

Creating the Callback Function

The callback function performs the actual processing of the data returned by the call to the Win32 API function. The main thread of your application will go on to perform other tasks while the callback function waits for data. Listing 5.1 shows the callback function used for this example.

Listing 5.1   **Creating the Callback Function**

```
// Define a function for retrieving the window title.
[DllImport("User32.DLL")]
public static extern Int32 GetWindowText(IntPtr hWnd,
                                         StringBuilder lpString,
                                         Int32 nMaxCount);

// Create the callback function using the EnumWindowProc()
// delegate.
public bool WindowCallback(IntPtr hWnd, Int32 lParam)
{
    // Name of the window.
    StringBuilder  TitleText = new StringBuilder(256);

    // Result string.
    String         ResultText;

    try
    {
        // Get the window title.
        GetWindowText(hWnd, TitleText, 256);
    }
    catch (Exception e)
    {
        MessageBox.Show("GetWindowText() Error:\r\n" +
                        "\r\nMessage: " + e.Message +
                        "\r\nSource: " + e.Source +
                        "\r\nTarget Site: " + e.TargetSite +
                        "\r\nStack Trace: " + e.StackTrace,
                        "Application Error",
                        MessageBoxButtons.OK,
                        MessageBoxIcon.Error);

    }
```

```
    // See if the window has a title.
    if (TitleText.ToString() == "")
        ResultText = "No Window Title";
    else
        ResultText = TitleText.ToString();

    // Add the window title to the listbox.
    txtWindows.Text += ResultText + "\r\n";

    // Tell Windows we want more window titles.
    return true;
}
```

As you can see, the WindowCallback() relies on the GetWindowText() function to display the name of the window in a textbox on the dialog. The use of an IntPtr as one of the inputs is hardly surprising, because it contains the handle to the window pass to WindowCallback() by Windows. Remember that in the past we always used a String to pass text data to the Win32 API function. The GetWindowText() function requires a different technique, however, because it actually creates the string—it allocates the memory for the string and places the data in it. Using a StringBuilder object enables the GetWindowText() function to behave as normal. If you try to use a standard String in this case (even one passed with the out or ref keyword) the function call will fail and the user will see an error on screen.

Notice that the use of a StringBuilder object becomes clearer in the WindowCallback() function. The code allocates a StringBuilder object of a specific size. It then passes this size to the GetWindowText() function in the third argument, *nMaxCount*.

WARNING   Depending on how you set up your callback function, it's possible that the callback function will operate in a different thread from the main form. When the callback function operates in a separate thread, it can't change the content of the main form; otherwise, you might run into thread-related problems with the applications (see the "Developing for Thread Safety" section of Chapter 4 for details). It pays to validate your application for thread safety by viewing the callback function in the debugger using the Threads window. If you see that the application creates a new thread, then you'll need to use an event to trigger changes to the display area.

Always place the GetWindowText() and other string manipulation functions within a try...catch block as shown in the code. These functions tend to fail, at times, even if your code is correct. Unfortunately, there isn't any documented reason for the failure and it occurs intermittently—making the cause exceptionally difficult to track down. The example code shows the minimum error message you should provide as output if the GetWindowText() call fails. You might consider checking the inner error messages as well as using the GetLastError() function to return any Windows-specific information about the error.

A successful call to GetWindowText() is no guarantee that *TitleText* will contain any data on return from the call. In fact, you'll find that many of the hidden windows have no title bar text at all, which means that GetWindowText() will return an empty string. With this in mind, you'll want to create a standard string and place either a default value or the contents of *TitleText* within it. *ResultText* contains the string that we'll actually display on screen. The display code is straightforward—you simply add to the text already found in the textbox.

Notice that GetWindowText() always returns a value of *true*. Because we want the name of every window on the desktop, you have to keep returning *true*. However, not every callback function will require all of the data that Windows has to provide. If this is the case, you'll want to add an end of data check and return *false* if the function has all of the data it needs.

Demonstrating the EnumWindows() and EnumDesktopWindows() Callback Functions

At this point, you have a delegate to provide a pointer to the callback function and a callback function to process the data. All you need is some way to call the Win32 API function with the callback function as one of the arguments. Listing 5.2 shows how to accomplish this task.

Listing 5.2   **Code for Enumerating all Windows or a Single Desktop**

```
// Create the prototype for the EnumDesktopWindows() function.
[DllImport("User32.DLL")]
public static extern void EnumDesktopWindows(IntPtr hDesktop,
                                             EnumWindowProc EWP,
                                             Int32 lParam);


// Create the prototype for the EnumWindows() function.
[DllImport("User32.DLL")]
public static extern void EnumWindows(EnumWindowProc EWP,
                                      Int32 lParam);

private void btnTest_Click(object sender, System.EventArgs e)
{
    // Create an instance of the callback.
    EnumWindowProc PWC = new EnumWindowProc(WindowCallback);

    // Clear the text window.
    txtWindows.Clear();

    // Call the EnumWindows() function.
    EnumWindows(PWC, 0);
}

private void btnTest2_Click(object sender, System.EventArgs e)
{
    // Create an instance of the callback.
    EnumWindowProc PWC = new EnumWindowProc(WindowCallback);
```

```
      // Clear the text window.
      txtWindows.Clear();

      // Call the EnumDesktopWindows() function.
      EnumDesktopWindows(IntPtr.Zero, PWC, 0);
   }
```

The example provides both a general and a desktop-specific version of the windows enumeration functions, EnumDesktopWindows() and EnumWindows(). Notice that the EnumDesktop-Windows() function prototype uses an IntPtr for the window handle as usual. However, the callback function pointer is marked as the EnumWindowsProc delegate. This isn't an error—you actually pass the delegate as a pointer in the code. The final argument is the *lParam* that you can use for application-specific data (we won't for this example).

Look at the btnTest_Click() and btnTest2_Click() methods. The first method is used for general windows enumeration, while the second is used for desktop-specific enumeration. Both follow the same sequence of steps to gain access to the appropriate Win32 API function.

The code begins by creating an instance of the EnumWindowProc delegate with the Window-CallBack() function as a pointer. The code clears the textbox so you don't see the previous data. It then calls the appropriate windows enumeration function. When you run this code, you'll see that the Win32 API begins sending the callback function data almost immediately. Figure 5.1 shows the results.

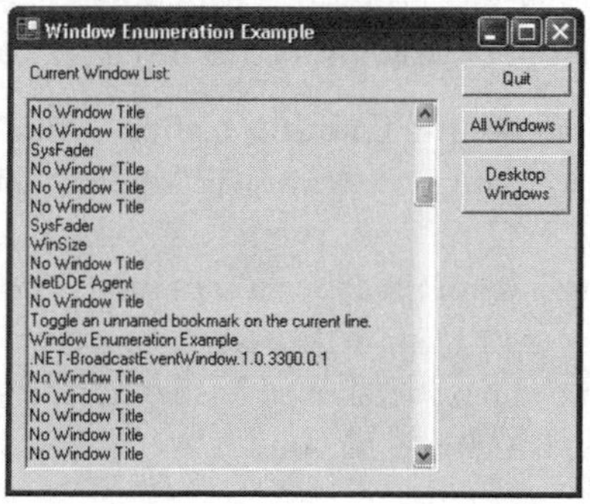

FIGURE 5.1:

The test application shows a complete list of windows for the system.

It shouldn't be too surprising that there are a lot of unnamed windows listed in the example. Windows constantly creates hidden windows that perform tasks silently in the background. However, looking through the list of windows that do have names can prove interesting. For example, the example detected a previously unknown ".NET-BroadcastEventWindow.1.0 .3300.0.1" window.

The point is that you can list the windows as needed. Other functions, such as the GetTitle-Bar() function provide more information about each window, including the presence and use of various common buttons. For example, you'd use the GetTitleBar() function to determine if the window in question has a functional Minimize button. The more generic GetWindow-Info() function tells you about the window's features and setup. For example, you can determine the location and size of the window, as well as its style information.

Implementing a Callback from a Wrapper DLL

There are going to be times when you use a callback function so often that placing it into each of your applications individually doesn't make sense. However, creating a lot of duplicate code isn't the only reason to use the wrapper DLL. The following list provides some additional reasons you should use this technique in your next application.

Packaging Issues   Using a wrapper DLL enables you to package the calling details in a way that you can't do normally. Using a DLL becomes a matter of convenience because the developer sees a package, not lines of code. In addition, when you work with a team of developers, you might want to hide the details of the Win32 API call to make the function easier to use.

Team Development Issues   The biggest advantage for a team is that one group of developers can work on Win32 API calls while other groups work on application code. The use of a DLL detaches one effort from the other and allows both groups to work independently. In addition, because everyone's using the same DLL, you can ensure better consistency among developers, making the resulting code easier to read.

Learning Curve and Training Issues   Another advantage is learning curve. Many of the developers working on a team will know their base language well, but won't know much about the Win32 API, so trying to get them up to speed represents a significant training cost. Having a team that specializes in making the Win32 API fully accessible to other members on your team makes sense because Microsoft will almost certainly fill many of the holes in the next version of Visual Studio. (It's unlikely that Microsoft will ever fill all of the holes, which means you'll always need someone who can work with the Win32 API.)

The example in this section duplicates the functionality of the EnumWindows example presented earlier in the chapter. However, instead of placing all of the Win32 API code within the dialog-based application, it will appear within a wrapper DLL. The dialog-based application will see a collection in place of the Windows-specific data. The example serves to demonstrate two elements of using a wrapper DLL.

- The initial development effort is harder because you need to write more code and the wrapper DLL code has to interact with the application.

- Using the DLL in subsequent development efforts is easier than including the Win32 API code, because the developer need not understand the Win32 API to make the required call.

Creating the Library DLL

The first step in creating this example is to create the wrapper DLL. For the purposes of the example, the wrapper DLL and dialog-based application appear in the same folder on the CD, but you could easily place each element in a separate folder. Listing 5.3 contains the DLL code for the example. You'll find the source code for this example in the \Chapter 05\C#\Library-Access and the \Chapter 05\VB\LibraryAccess folders of the CD.

NOTE   Listing 5.3 contains only the code for the EnumWindows() function. The EnumDesktop-Windows() function code is essentially the same. You can see the minor differences by looking at the source code on the CD.

Listing 5.3   **The DLL Contains All the Win32 API Calls and Returns a Collection**

```
public class AllWindowCollection : CollectionBase
{
    // We could place the code for calling the windows enumerator
    // in the constructor, but using the Fill() function adds more
    // control and becomes important in the DesktopWindowCollection
    // class.
    public AllWindowCollection()
    {
    }

    // Create the delegate used as an address for the callback
    // function.
    private delegate bool EnumWindowProc(IntPtr hWnd, Int32 lParam);

    // Create the prototype for the EnumWindows() function.
    [DllImport("User32.DLL")]
    private static extern void EnumWindows(EnumWindowProc EWP,
                                           Int32 lParam);

    // Fills the collection with data you can access using the
    // Item() function.
    public void Fill()
    {
        // Create an instance of the callback.
        EnumWindowProc PWC = new EnumWindowProc(WindowCallback);

        // Call the EnumWindows() function.
        EnumWindows(PWC, 0);
    }
```

```csharp
// Obtains a specific window title string from the collection
// and returns it to the caller.
public string Item(int Index)
{
    return (string)List[Index];
}

// Define a function for retrieving the window title.
[DllImport("User32.DLL")]
private static extern Int32 GetWindowText(IntPtr hWnd,
                                          StringBuilder lpString,
                                          Int32 nMaxCount);

// Create the callback function using the EnumWindowProc()
// delegate.
private bool WindowCallback(IntPtr hWnd, Int32 lParam)
{
    // Name of the window.
    StringBuilder  TitleText = new StringBuilder(256);

    try
    {
        // Get the window title.
        GetWindowText(hWnd, TitleText, 256);
    }
    catch (Exception e)
    {
        // Throw an exception when required.
        throw new Exception("Error Accessing Window Titles", e);
    }

    // See if the window has a title.
    if (TitleText.ToString() == "")
        List.Add("No Window Title");
    else
        List.Add(TitleText.ToString());

    // Tell Windows we want more window titles.
    return true;
}
}
```

Listing 5.3 shows that there are some differences between a wrapper DLL version of a Win32 API call and the application version. (There are also many similarities between the two implementations—you still need to perform the same set of tasks as before.) Notice that all of the Win32 API calls are declared private, to hide them from view and protect their functionality. In addition, this class inherits from the CollectionBase class, so it already has much of the functionality required for a collection.

The Fill() function is new. It takes the place of the btnTest_Click() function in the previous example. However, notice that this function never touches the form objects, so you don't have to worry about thread concerns. The Fill() function is also simpler than the btnTest_Click() function—not that complexity was a problem with the previous example.

You also have to include an Item() function with the collection so that the user can gain access to the collection elements. You can make this function as simple or complex as you like. The example shows a basic implementation that returns the requested element from the List object inherited from the CollectionBase class. One of the additions you might want to make is a range check to ensure the input isn't out of range.

The WindowCallback() has changed from the previous example. For one thing, the try...catch block throws an exception now instead of displaying an error message. Using this approach ensures that the developer using your library has full access to all of the error information from the call. Another change is that we're adding items to the List object now instead of creating the output directly. Again, this change ensures there are no threading problems with the application because the callback function isn't touching any of the form objects.

The biggest change is simplicity for the developer using the new library. Figure 5.2 shows the Object Browser view of the library. Notice that the interface is exceptionally simple— most of the functionality appears within the CollectionBase class and isn't even implemented in your code. Any developer who's worked with collections in the past will understand how your collection works as well. A simple interface combined with common usage techniques makes the library approach hard to beat in this case. Of course, you do have to perform additional work at the outset, which can be viewed as a disadvantage.

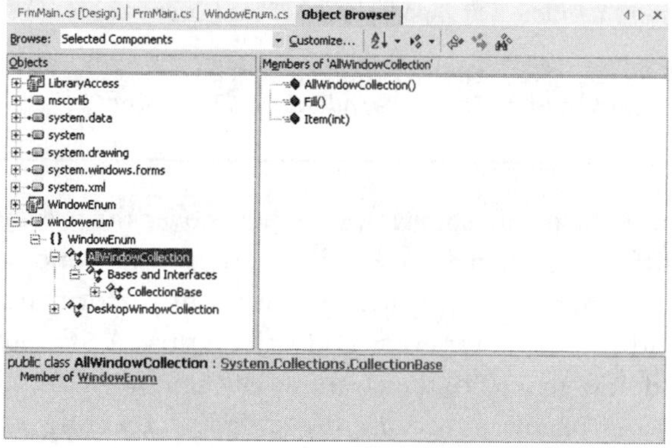

FIGURE 5.2:

The Object Browser view says it all— libraries make Win32 API calls easy to use.

Creating the Dialog-Based Application

Once you create a wrapper DLL for the Win32 API calls, creating the application to use the functionality that the wrapper DLL provides is relatively simple. The example uses a collection to hold the information gathered by the Win32 API call, so you'll create a function to access the collection as shown in Listing 5.4.

NOTE   Listing 5.4 contains only the code for the btnTest_Click() function. The btnTest2_Click() function code is essentially the same. You can see the minor differences by looking at the source code on the CD.

Listing 5.4   **The Dialog-Based Application Code Looks Like Any C# Code**

```
private void btnTest_Click(object sender, System.EventArgs e)
{
   // Create a StringBuilder object to hold the window strings.
   StringBuilder        WindowList = new StringBuilder();

   // Create an instance of the collection.
   AllWindowCollection  AWC = new AllWindowCollection();

   // Fill the collection with data.
   AWC.Fill();

   // Clear the textbox contents.
   txtWindows.Clear();

   // Create a single string with the contents of the collection.
   for (int Counter = 0; Counter < AWC.Count; Counter++)
      WindowList.Append(AWC.Item(Counter) + "\r\n");

   // Display the string on screen.
   txtWindows.Text = WindowList.ToString();
}
```

This code makes some improvements over the previous example and you'll likely notice the difference when you use this function with a lot of windows open. The StringBuilder object, WindowList, provides a significant performance boost because you don't have to rebuild the string for every collection entry. A StringBuilder uses the Append() function to add new strings to the contents of the object. You'll find that using a StringBuilder also saves resources because the code isn't creating a new string for every iteration of the for loop.

Instead of worrying about Win32 API functions, the example creates the AllWindow-Collection object. If you look at the functions provided by this object, you'll see a list that combines the custom functions we created with a list of generalized collection functions. For example, you can use the `Clear()` function to empty the collection, even though that function isn't implemented in the custom code.

The code calls the `Fill()` function to fill the collection object, `AWC`, with data. This function is all that the developer using the wrapper DLL needs to know in order to make the Win32 API calls discussed earlier. When the call returns, `AWC` contains a complete list of the window titles for the current machine.

The next step is to place the formatted string into `WindowList`. The example uses all of the strings, but you can easily filter the strings because we're using a collection. For that matter, you can also sort the strings and perform other tasks that the initial example code can't do with any ease. Notice that AWC has a `Count` property that makes iterating through the items in the collection easy.

The final step is to place the string into the textbox. Notice that we have to use the `ToString()` function because C# views the `StringBuilder` object as something other than a string reference. The output of this example is precisely the same as the output of the first example. You'll see a display that looks like the one shown in Figure 5.1.

Enumerating Calendar Information Example

The .NET Framework provides a vast array of classes for handling international information. You'll find them in the `System.Globalization` namespace. There's so much functionality that sometimes it's hard to find precisely what you need. However, even given the rich array of functions that the .NET Framework provides, there are still times when you need a simple way to list information about a culture. For example, what does a particular culture call the days of the week or the months of the year? The example in this section of the chapter is meant to augment what the .NET Framework already provides. (The fact is that the .NET Framework provides far better functionality overall than the Win32 API in this case.)

This example also brings up a new topic: what do you do with macros? Visual C++ developers have long been familiar with the functionality provided by macros, something that other languages don't support very well without a lot of work. There are two ways to handle the macros. You can create a Visual C++ wrapper and call the macro directly, or you can simulate the macro using managed code. Generally, you'll find that the Visual C++ wrapper method is easier and less error prone, so that's the method we'll use in this example.

> **TIP** Microsoft has a made a wealth of .NET training information available through the Microsoft Developer Network (MSDN) Academic Alliance (MSDNAA) site (`http://www .msdnaa.net/technologies/dotnet.asp`). Make sure you spend some time at this site looking through the offerings—including those that relate to delegates and callback functions.

Now that you have some idea of what this example will show, let's look at some source code. The following sections tackle the various problems of enumerating calendar values using a Win32 API function with callback. You'll find the source code for this example in the `\Chapter 05\C#\CalendarCheck` and `\Chapter 05\VB\CalendarCheck` folders of the CD. The macro wrapper DLL source code is located in the `\Chapter 05\C#\CalendarCheck\Locale-Macros` folder—you can use the same DLL for both versions of the example.

Creating the Macro Wrapper DLL

Visual C++ includes a number of macros used to convert one type of input into another type of input. In many cases, the macro converts two values into a single long value. For example, the macro might convert two WORD values into a single DWORD value with the first WORD located in the high WORD of the DWORD and the second WORD loaded in the low WORD of the DWORD. Modern code doesn't use this technique, but it was quite common when Windows first arrived on the scene, so we still have to contend with this method of transferring data today.

> **WARNING** You must include `Windows.H` as part of `STDAFX.H` to make most Visual C++ wrapper DLLs work correctly. In addition, you must include certain `#defines` to ensure that the compiler will enable advanced Windows features. The `STDAFX.H` entries provided with the example code show the most common additions. We'll see later in the book that this is a baseline configuration. For example, if you want to create an MMC Snap-in, you also need to include `MMC.H` in `STDAFX.H`. The order of the `#includes` is important—placing an `#include` in the wrong place can cause the code to compile incorrectly or not at all.

Listing 5.5 shows the code you'll need to use the `MAKELANGID()` and `MAKELCID()` macros. Don't confuse macros with functions—they're not interchangeable. You'll always need to create a Visual C++ wrapper DLL to use a macro, but most functions are easily accessible from within the .NET host language.

Listing 5.5 **Macro Wrapper for Locale Conversion**

```
// Create a language ID to use with the DoMAKELCID() function.
static Int16 DoMAKELANGID(Int16 usPrimaryLanguage, Int16 usSubLanguage)
{
    return MAKELANGID(usPrimaryLanguage, usSubLanguage);
}
```

```
// Create a LCID to use with functions like EnumCalendarInfoEx().
static Int32 DoMAKELCID(Int16 wLanguageID, Int16 wSortID)
{
    return MAKELCID(wLanguageID, wSortID);
}

// Convenient way to obtain the LOCALE_SYSTEM_DEFAULT value.
static Int32 GetLocaleSystemDefault()
{
    return LOCALE_SYSTEM_DEFAULT;
}

// Convenient way to obtain the LOCALE_USER_DEFAULT value.
static Int32 GetLocaleUserDefault()
{
    return LOCALE_USER_DEFAULT;
}
```

As you can see, the DoMAKELANGID() and DoMAKELCID() functions simply transfer the incoming data to the macros and then return the result. Some macros require data conversion and a few can get quite complex. However, this code represents the vast majority of the macro conversions that you'll perform. The only reason you need to use Visual C++ at all is to access the macro.

NOTE   The source code found in this section of the chapter is smaller than what you'll find on the CD. The macros and the EnumCalendarInfoEx() function both require enumerations to ensure the data input is correct. Because there isn't anything interesting about the enumerations (other than their presence), the code in the book only contains the actual methods.

There are many situations where you'll see default values listed in the Platform SDK documentation that are actually macro results. In many cases, you can duplicate the default values in your code, but it's just as easy to request the default value from Visual C++. Never assign a constant value to a default value derived from a macro because the macro inputs could change. The GetLocaleSystemDefault() and GetLocaleUserDefault() obtain the two default values for this example from Visual C++. We'll see in the "Demonstrating the Calendar Enumeration" section how to perform this same task using the in code method.

TIP   If you're finding the new Visual C++ .NET Managed Extensions difficult to figure out, Microsoft provides an instructor-led course (2558) that covers this particular part of the product in detail. You can learn more at http://www.microsoft.com/TRAINCERT/SYLLABI/2558APRELIM.ASP.

One of the issues you need to work around is the oddity of working with Visual C++ in the managed environment. This often means changing your coding style or becoming aware of a new code word. In the case of enumerations, you need to add a __value keyword as shown here.

```
__value enum SortID
    {
        SI_DEFAULT         = 0x0,     // sorting default
    // Some skipped values here...
        SI_GEORGIAN_MODERN = 0x1      // Georgian Modern order
    };
```

Adding the __value keyword will change the presentation of the enumeration within Visual C++. The symbol will change to show that this is a managed enumeration as shown in Figure 5.3. Notice that the enumeration is also part of the class and doesn't simply exist in the namespace. The code will compile if you place the enumeration in the namespace without a class, but you won't be able to see it when you import the DLL into another language (as we will for the example). Another point of interest is that the Object Viewer will display your comments as long as you're looking at the Visual C++ view of the enumeration.

FIGURE 5.3:

Using the __value keyword changes the presentation of the enumeration in Visual C++.

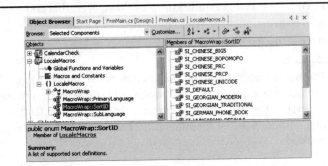

Figure 5.4 show the imported view of the same DLL shown in Figure 5.3. The first thing you should notice is that the enumeration now uses the standard symbol, as if we hadn't done anything special in Visual C++. This is an important piece of information to remember, because it demonstrates that the viewing DLLs in the Object Viewer will tell you about the content of the DLL but not necessarily about the tricks used to produce that content.

You should also notice the lack of comments in Figure 5.4. Even though you can see the comments in the Visual C++ presentation, you won't see them when the DLL is imported into another language. Unfortunately, there isn't a fix for this problem unless you want to resort to some truly interesting coding in the CLR intermediate language (IL). The best way around this problem for now is to ensure that your Visual C++ function names are clear, conform to any Windows documentation the user might already know, and follow any documentation you create for the DLL.

Creating the EnumCalendarInfoEx() Function Code

As in the previous examples, one of the first steps in using a callback function is to create a delegate and a callback function to handle the input. The delegate and callback functions for this example rely on the EnumCalendarInfoProcEx() prototype found in the Platform SDK documentation. Listing 5.6 shows both of these elements.

Listing 5.6   **Creating a Delegate and Callback Function for EnumCalendarInfoEx()**

```
// Create the delegate used as an address for the callback
// function.
public delegate bool EnumCalendarInfoProcEx(
   String lpCalendarInfoString,
   CALID Calendar);

// Create the callback function.
public bool CalendarCallback(String lpCalendarInfoString,
                 CALID Calendar)
{
   // Create the output string.
   txtCalOutput.Text = txtCalOutput.Text +
                 Calendar + "\r\n" +
                 lpCalendarInfoString + "\r\n\r\n";

   // Make sure we return all of the values.
   return true;
}
```

Notice that that callback function receives two inputs. The first is the information string that the caller requested. The second is a calendar identifier that tells which calendar reference the string is using. By using an enumerated type as input, rather than an Int32, the code saves a little work. You can place the returned enumerated value directly in the output string and C# won't complain. We'll see later how this works.

Demonstrating the Calendar Enumeration

One of the most important things to remember about the EnumCalendarInfoEx() function is that it's machine specific. You can only list information for the languages actually installed on the machine. If you don't know which languages the machine has installed, then it's usually safer to ask for an enumeration of all languages. Enumerating all of the languages when there's only one language installed won't produce a different result from asking for the specific language—it simply frees you from finding out which language is installed on the machine.

This example can return quite a few different types of data and it's interesting to view them all. Consequently, the example provides a drop-down list box you can use to select information of interest. Clicking Test will display the data. Listing 5.7 shows the source code for demonstrating the EnumCalendarInfoEx() function.

Listing 5.7   **Demonstrating the EnumCalendarInfoEx() Function**

```
// Retrieves the requested calendar values.
[DllImport("Kernel32.DLL")]
public static extern void EnumCalendarInfoEx(
    EnumCalendarInfoProcEx pCalInfoEnumProcEx,
    Int32 Locale,
    CALID Calendar,
    CALTYPE CalType);

private void btnTest_Click(object sender, System.EventArgs e)
{
    // Create the callback pointer.
    EnumCalendarInfoProcEx  ECIPE = new EnumCalendarInfoProcEx(CalendarCallback);

    // Create the language ID.
    Int16 LANG_SYSTEM_DEFAULT = MacroWrap.DoMAKELANGID(
        (Int16)MacroWrap.PrimaryLanguage.PL_NEUTRAL,
        (Int16)MacroWrap.SubLanguage.SL_SYS_DEFAULT);

    // Create the LCID.
    Int32 Locale = MacroWrap.DoMAKELCID(
        LANG_SYSTEM_DEFAULT,
        (Int16)MacroWrap.SortID.SI_DEFAULT);

    // Clear the textbox.
    txtCalOutput.Clear();

    // Call the calendar enumeration.
    EnumCalendarInfoEx(ECIPE,
                       Locale,
                       CALID.ENUM_ALL_CALENDARS,
                       (CALTYPE)cbCalSelect.SelectedIndex+1);
}
```

The example begins by creating a callback pointer. You can consider this the first step in working with any callback function. Make sure you always use the delegate to create the pointer or the code won't work.

The next two calls create the locale identifier (LCID). The first, DoMAKELANGID(), accepts a primary and secondary language as input. The numbers for these inputs are provided as part of enumerations in the source code. You'll want to do the same thing, whenever possible, to ensure the input to the macros is always correct. (They won't ever report an error, so debugging this kind of problem is frustrating, to say the least.)

The second call, DoMAKELCID() accepts the language identifier created in the first step, along with a sort order. Again, this is an enumeration based on the contents of the C/C++ header files provided with Visual Studio .NET. The return value of this second step is the LCID that you need for the EnumCalendarInfoEx() call.

The final two steps are to clear the contents of the textbox (txtCalOutput) and call the enumerator EnumCalendarInfoEx(). One of the essentials here is to ensure any data conversions are correct, which is why one of the arguments, (CALTYPE)cbCalSelect.SelectedIndex+1, contains a typecast and I've increased it by one. Figure 5.5 shows the output of this example.

FIGURE 5.5:

The example provides information about the language installed on the current machine.

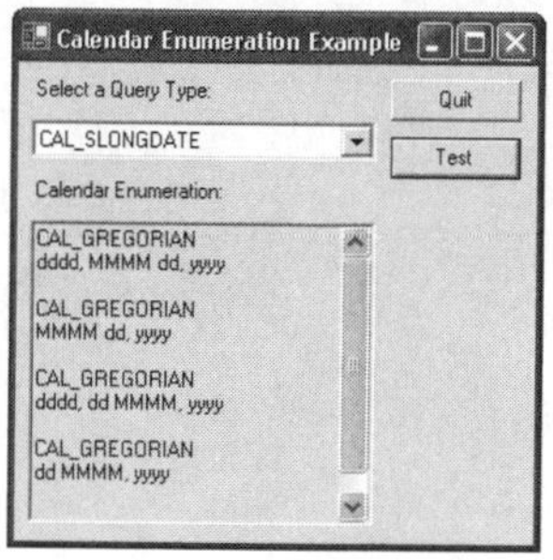

Where Do You Go from Here?

Callback functions are an essential part of using the Win32 API. You won't need to use them as often as other tricks of the trade under .NET, but you'll need them just the same. This chapter has helped you understand what a callback function is, how and when to use it, and demonstrated the kinds of applications you can create using a callback function. However, there are still many issues to discuss for callback functions, so we'll look at this topic again as the book progresses.

Now that you have some idea of what a callback function is and where you'll commonly use it, it's time to look at some .NET code. Look for places where you suspect a collection is really standing in for a callback function found in the Win32 API. You might be surprised at the amount of overlap that you see. Make sure you check out some of the example sites listed in the chapter as well. It's always interesting to see how someone else would tackle the problems of working with callback functions.

It's also important to consider how you might use callback functions in combination with wrapper DLLs. In some cases, you'll want to handle most of a call using unmanaged code to prevent the performance-robbing cost of switching between the managed and unmanaged environment. Using a callback function could help you gain a modicum of flexibility over a function that normally returns more than one result, while reducing the performance overhead of interacting with the DLL.

Chapter 6 begins a new phase of this book. Rather than look at the technologies involved in working with the Win32 API, we'll start seeing how you can put the information learned so far to work. One of the common places to use the Win32 API is at the console screen. The .NET Framework lacks functionality in this area now because it's not one of the areas that Microsoft targeted during development. Chapter 6 will show you some ways to enhance your console applications and provide the user with a better experience—while you gain the benefits of using .NET for your application development.

PART II

Fixing Holes in Standard Applications

CHAPTER 6

Gaining Support for the Console Application

- What Does the .NET Framework Provide?

- Clearing the Screen Example

- Getting Console Information Example

- Changing the Environment Example

S ome people think that console applications are archaic remnants from a past time that are best located in the bit bucket. However, console applications do have an important role to fulfill in current Windows development. For example, utility applications often come in a console format to ensure that the administrator can script them for required maintenance.

Of course, one of the problems with console applications is that the basic console application is devoid of the bells and whistles that people have come to expect. The simple act of clearing the screen is impossible in .NET, much less using some of the techniques developers have used in the past to dress up the display. In many respects, the console applications of today are less capable than the DOS applications of yesterday and there is no reason that they should be.

This chapter will tell you about the functionality that the .NET Framework does provide to make your console application work well. In addition, we'll begin looking at specific holes in the application development environment and you'll learn ways to get around those holes. For example, you'll learn how to perform the simple task of clearing the screen and we'll discuss ways to present the graphical characters on screen (among other things).

What Does the .NET Framework Provide?

The .NET Framework provides you with many essentials for working with the console screen. For example, there are functions to read and write both individual characters and entire lines of data. You can use any of the data-oriented functions provided with the .NET Framework— an impressive array compared to previous environments that you might have used. Any perceptions that you might have at the outset that console applications are completely unsupported by the .NET Framework are untrue—the .NET Framework has a lot to offer. Unfortunately, finding the right call can be daunting at times—Microsoft organized the .NET Framework namespace for use with business applications.

TIP   Most developers like to see as many coding examples as possible, so it's always good to know where you can fine more. You'll find two excellent console application examples at Lutz Roeder's Programming .NET site at `http://www.aisto.com/roeder/dotnet/`. The first is a demonstration of advanced math concepts using .NET (Mapack for .NET). The second is called Managed IL Reader for .NET. Both examples include lightly commented source. The first namespace you'll want to know about is `System.Console`. This namespace enables you to perform common console tasks such as opening the standard error, input, and output streams. You can also read and write text to the console (the standard output stream) without actually opening a stream.

Another good namespace to know about is `System.Diagnostics`. Yes, you'll find the debugger classes here, but you'll also find a wealth of other interesting classes to work with. For example, the `System.Diagnostics` namespace contains the `FileVersionInfo` class—a real aid when you need to know something about the file you're working with. It's also the namespace that contains many of the performance counter classes such as CounterCreationData and Performance-Counter. The Process class is exceptionally useful for console applications that need to manage other processes on a local or remote machine—a task often performed by console applications.

> **TIP**   Some people think that the System namespace is actually a container for all of the other namespaces generally provided by the .NET Framework, so they miss opportunities to use some of the interesting classes that it contains. The System namespace contains classes that you can expect to use on a regular basis. It often helps to type "System." (including the period) in the Visual Studio .NET help index and browse the list of classes—you might be surprised at what you find.

There are many classes and namespaces that don't fall directly within the console application domain, but you'll still find them useful for building applications. For example, the System namespace contains the OperatingSystem class, which tells you about operating system statistics such a version number and platform. There's also an ObsoleteAttribute class that you can assign to functions that appear in an application or DLL, but are no longer supported. One class that anyone using the Win32 API should know about is the Buffer class. This class helps you work with an unmanaged array of bytes.

The BitConverter class is useful for converting those bits you receive from a Win32 API call into something you can actually use within a .NET application. In fact, this is the class you'd use to create simulations of some of the Visual C++ macros that you have to contend with when working with the C/C++ header files. You can use this class to combine to Int16 values into an Int32 value with one value in the high word and the second value in the low word. This is one of the more common macro conversions used in Visual C++ to comply with Win32 API call requirements. The GetBytes() function is especially useful when you need to break one of these combined values apart. In some cases, you need to break them apart in order to know what the Win32 API sent as a return value.

The System.Configuration namespace is the last one we'll look at in this section. This namespace contains classes that enable you to manage the .CONFIG files for the .NET Framework. For example, if you want to read specific values from the configuration files, you'll need the AppSettingsReader class. You'll read individual configuration settings using the ConfigurationSettings class. This class can also return an AppSettings object that enables you to view particular elements within the XML structure of the .CONFIG file.

As you can see, the .NET Framework does have a lot to offer you as a developer. As to why Microsoft chose to leave out such seemingly simple, yet essential, features as clearing the console screen—there doesn't seem to be an answer. Fortunately, you can still access all of these missing elements using the code found in the rest of the chapter.

Clearing the Screen Example

As previously mentioned, the .NET Framework doesn't provide the means to perform the simple act of clearing the console screen. The only way to clear the screen is to rely on Win32 API calls. Unfortunately, this isn't one of those situations where a single call to the Win32 API will do the job. You'll actually need to make several calls, as shown in Listing 6.1. (The source code appears in the \Chapter 06\C#\ClearScreen and \Chapter 06\VB\ClearScreen folders on the CD.)

Listing 6.1   **An Example of How to Clear the Console Screen**

```
// This special class contains an enumeration of
// standard handles.
class StdHandleEnum
{
   public const int STD_INPUT_HANDLE   = -10;
   public const int STD_OUTPUT_HANDLE  = -11;
   public const int STD_ERROR_HANDLE   = -12;
};

// This structure contains a screen coordinate.
[StructLayout(LayoutKind.Sequential, Pack=1)]
   internal struct COORD
{
   public short X;
   public short Y;
}

// This stucture contains information about the
// console screen buffer.
[StructLayout(LayoutKind.Sequential, Pack=1)]
   internal struct CONSOLE_SCREEN_BUFFER_INFO
{
   public COORD     Size;
   public COORD     p1;
   public short     a1;
   public short     w1;
   public short     w2;
   public short     w3;
   public short     w4;
   public COORD     m1;
}

// We need these four functions from kernel32.dll.
// The GetStdHandle() function returns a handle to any
// standard input or output.
[DllImport("kernel32.dll", SetLastError=true)]
public static extern IntPtr GetStdHandle(int nStdHandle);
```

```csharp
// The GetConsoleScreenBufferInfo() returns information
// about the console screen buffer so we know how much to
// clear.
[DllImport("kernel32.dll", SetLastError=true)]
public static extern bool GetConsoleScreenBufferInfo(
    IntPtr hConsoleOutput,
    out CONSOLE_SCREEN_BUFFER_INFO lpConsoleScreenBufferInfo);

// The SetConsoleCursorPosition() places the cursor on the
// console screen.
[DllImport("kernel32.dll", SetLastError=true)]
public static extern bool SetConsoleCursorPosition(
    IntPtr hConsoleOutput,
    COORD dwCursorPosition);

// The FillConsoleOutputCharacter() allows us to place any character
// on the console screen. Using a space clears the display area.
[DllImport("kernel32.dll", SetLastError=true, CharSet=CharSet.Auto)]
public static extern bool FillConsoleOutputCharacter(
    IntPtr hConsoleOutput,
    short cCharacter,
    int nLength, COORD WriteCoord,
    out int lpNumberOfCharsWritten);

[STAThread]
static void Main(string[] args)
{
    // Needed ask Windows about the console screen
    // buffer settings.
    CONSOLE_SCREEN_BUFFER_INFO   CSBI;
    // Handle to the otuput device.
    IntPtr                       hOut;
    // Number of characters written to the screen.
    int                          CharOut;
    // Home cursor position.
    COORD                        Home;

    // Write some data to the screen.
    Console.Write("Some Text to Erase!" +
                "\r\nPress any key...");
    Console.ReadLine();

    // Clear the screen.
    // Begin by getting a handle to the console screen.
    hOut = GetStdHandle(StdHandleEnum.STD_OUTPUT_HANDLE);

    // Get the required console screen buffer information.
    GetConsoleScreenBufferInfo(hOut, out CSBI );

    // Set the home position for the cursor (upper left corner).
    Home.X = 0;
```

```
    Home.Y = 0;

    // Fill the console with spaces.
    FillConsoleOutputCharacter(hOut,
                               (short) ' ',
                               CSBI.Size.X * CSBI.Size.Y,
                               Home,
                               out CharOut);

    // Place the cursor in the upper left corner.
    SetConsoleCursorPosition(hOut, Home);

    // Show the screen is clear.
    Console.ReadLine();
}
```

This looks like a lot of code to clear the console screen, but the process is relatively simple. The code requires an enumeration for standard output handles. An output handle is simply a pointer to a device such as the screen. The three standard devices are input, output, and error. We also need two structures to fulfill the needs of the Windows API calls used in the example. The code listing describes each structure's task.

The example code relies on four Windows API functions, GetStdHandle(), GetConsole-ScreenBufferInfo(), FillConsoleOutputCharacter(), and SetConsoleCursorPosition(). All of these functions appear in the KERNEL32.DLL. All four perform some type of console screen manipulation. The code listing describes each function's task.

The short part of the code is actually demonstrating the console screen-clearing process. Main() creates some output on screen. The ReadLine() call merely ensures that the code will wait until you see the text. Press Enter and the clearing process begins. The following steps tell how the code clears the screen.

1. The first thing we need is a handle to the console output using the GetStdHandle() function. The handle tells Windows what device we want to work with.

2. The next step is to ask Windows about the dimensions of the console window using the GetConsoleScreenBufferInfo() function. The dimensions are important because you want to ensure the console screen erases completely.

3. At this point, you need to fill the screen with spaces using the FillConsoleOutput-Character() function. Filling the screen with spaces is the equivalent of erasing its content.

4. Finally, we place the cursor in the upper-left corner using the SetConsoleCursorPosition() function—the same place the CLS (clear screen) command would.

The ability to clear the screen might not matter when you work with a console application using a script, but it does matter when you want to use the console application in interactive mode. All too often, a console application will continue to scroll data on screen until it becomes so filled with useless characters that it's hard to see the data for the clutter. If you're building a library of essential screen routines in a DLL, this should be one of your first additions.

Getting Console Information Examples

Sometimes you need to know information about the console or the underlying operating system. For example, you might need to know about code pages that the console supports when working in a multiple language environment or the number of processes in use when creating a complex console application. All of these items fall within the console information category. Every time you need data in order to make the console application work, you have to obtain it either from the .NET Framework (as in the operating system version) or from the Win32 API. Generally, you'll find that the Win32 API has a lot more to offer than the .NET Framework in this case.

The following sections show how to make some simple calls using the Win32 API to obtain console information. You saw part of that environmental information in the previous example when we used the GetConsoleScreenBufferInfo() function to obtain the current screen size. However, the Win32 API has a lot more to offer than screen size information. For example, the first application shows how to work with code pages (the character codes mapped to individual characters) when working with the console.

TIP   You can use the FillConsoleOutputCharacter() function to display repetitive characters on screen. However, there are several ways to perform this same task using the .NET Framework methods, so you should determine which method is more appropriate. In most cases, you'll want to use the .NET Framework calls whenever possible.

Working with Code Pages

As previously mentioned, code pages are the character codes mapped to individual characters in the standard 256-character set. Code pages enable a developer to represent information in a variety of languages. The four code page–specific functions include GetConsoleCP(), SetConsoleCP(), GetConsoleOutputCP(), and SetConsoleOutputCP(). Listing 6.2 shows how to use these four functions. (The example code appears in the \Chapter 06\C#\CodePage and \Chapter 06\VB\CodePage folders on the CD.)

Listing 6.2   **Using the Code Page Functions in a Console Application**

```
// The function used to check the current code page.
[DllImport("Kernel32.DLL")]
```

```
public static extern UInt32 GetConsoleCP();

// The function used to check the output code page.
[DllImport("Kernel32.DLL")]
public static extern UInt32 GetConsoleOutputCP();

// The function used to set the current code page.
[DllImport("Kernel32.DLL")]
public static extern bool SetConsoleCP(UInt32 wCodePageID);

// The function used to set the output code page.
[DllImport("Kernel32.DLL")]
public static extern bool SetConsoleOutputCP(UInt32 wCodePageID);

[STAThread]
static void Main(string[] args)
{
   UInt32   CurrentCP;  // The current code page.
   UInt32   OutputCP;   // The output code page.
   UInt32   NewCP;      // The new current code page.
   UInt32   NewOutCP;   // The new output code page.
   char     Special = '\xA5';

   // Obtain the current and output code pages.
   CurrentCP = GetConsoleCP();
   OutputCP = GetConsoleOutputCP();

   // Display the two values on a console screen.
   Console.WriteLine("Checking the current code page.\r\n");
   Console.WriteLine("The current code page is: " +
      CurrentCP.ToString());
   Console.WriteLine("The ouptut code page is: " +
      OutputCP.ToString());

   // Set the console to the Russian code page.
   if (!SetConsoleCP(866))
      Console.WriteLine("Couldn't change the current code page.");
   if (!SetConsoleOutputCP(866))
      Console.WriteLine("Couldn't change the output code page.");

   // Display some text.
   NewCP = GetConsoleCP();
   NewOutCP = GetConsoleOutputCP();
   Console.WriteLine("\r\nUsing new current code page " +
      NewCP.ToString());
   Console.WriteLine("Using new output code page " +
      NewOutCP.ToString());

   // Return the code page to the original value.
   SetConsoleCP(CurrentCP);
```

```
        SetConsoleOutputCP(OutputCP);
        Console.WriteLine("\r\nUsing the original code pages.");

        // Wait until the user is done viewing the information.
        Console.Write("\r\nPress any key when ready...");
        Console.Read();
    }
```

As you can see, the code for working with the code page information is extremely simple. The two functions for obtaining a code page require no input and provide a *UInt32* value as output. The two functions used to change the code page require a *UInt32* value as input and return a *bool* that tells whether the call is successful. Figure 6.1 shows the output from this example.

FIGURE 6.1:

Changing code pages
is relatively easy using
Win32 API calls.

Of course, before the call will actually change the appearance of the screen, you need to load the appropriate code pages, which means modifying the Config.NT file located in the \WINDOWS\system32 of the hard drive. Another item to note is that the default code page for many Windows installations is 1252 (Windows ANSI). The code page functions may still return a value of 437, even if Windows is using code page 1252 because Microsoft wanted to ensure maximum compatibility with older applications. The bottom line is that you must load the code pages you want to use separately from the support provided by Windows.

Gaining Access to Console Mode Information

There are a number of environmental considerations when working with the console. The most important considerations are the mode in which the console is operating at any given time. For example, you might want to display data differently when the console is in full screen mode, than when it operates as a window. The two console mode–specific functions are GetConsoleDisplayMode() and GetConsoleMode(). You might need GetLargestConsole-WindowSize() function on occasion, to learn how big you can make the console window. If you want to change the current console mode, use the SetConsoleMode() function. Listing 6.3 shows several of these functions in action. You'll find the source code for the example in the \Chapter 06\C#\ConsoleMode and \Chapter 06\VB\ConsoleMode folders on the CD.

NOTE   Listing 6.3 omits some of the code we've already discussed as part of Listing 6.1. Please refer to the ClearScreen example for explanations of the GetStdHandle() function and associated enumerations. The ClearScreen example also shows how to use the COORD structure.

Listing 6.3   **Methods Used to Access Console Mode Information**

```
// Obtains the current display mode—fullscreen or fullscreen hardware.
[DllImport("Kernel32.DLL")]
public static extern bool GetConsoleDisplayMode(ref UInt32 lpModeFlags);

// An enumeration used to determine the current display mode.
public enum ConsoleDispMode
{
   CONSOLE_WINDOWED              = 0, // Only implied by function.
   CONSOLE_FULLSCREEN            = 1, // The console is fullscreen.
   CONSOLE_FULLSCREEN_HARDWARE = 2  // The console owns the hardware.
}

// Obtains the size of the largest console window possible.
[DllImport("Kernel32.DLL")]
public static extern COORD
   GetLargestConsoleWindowSize(IntPtr hConsoleOutput);

// Returns the console mode information.
[DllImport("Kernel32.DLL")]
public static extern bool GetConsoleMode(IntPtr hConsoleHandle,
                                         ref UInt32 lpMode);

public enum ModeFlags
{
   // Input mode flags
   ENABLE_PROCESSED_INPUT      = 0x0001,
   ENABLE_LINE_INPUT           = 0x0002,
   ENABLE_ECHO_INPUT           = 0x0004,
   ENABLE_WINDOW_INPUT         = 0x0008,
   ENABLE_MOUSE_INPUT          = 0x0010,

   // Output mode flags
   ENABLE_PROCESSED_OUTPUT     = 0x0001,
```

```csharp
        ENABLE_WRAP_AT_EOL_OUTPUT    = 0x0002
    }

    [STAThread]
    static void Main(string[] args)
    {
        UInt32   DisplayMode = 0;   // The current display mode.
        IntPtr   hOut;              // Handle to the output device.
        IntPtr   hIn;               // Handle to the input device.
        COORD    ScreenSize;        // Maximum screen size.
        UInt32   ConsoleMode = 0;   // The console mode information.

        // Get the current display mode.
        if (GetConsoleDisplayMode(ref DisplayMode))

            // Determine if the console is in windowed mode.
            if (DisplayMode == (UInt32)ConsoleDispMode.CONSOLE_WINDOWED)
                Console.WriteLine("Console is in windowed mode.");
            else
            {

                // If the console is fullscreen mode, determine which
                // of the potential conditions are true.
                switch (DisplayMode)
                {
                    case (UInt32)ConsoleDispMode.CONSOLE_FULLSCREEN:
                        Console.WriteLine("Console is in fullscreen mode.");
                        break;
                    case (UInt32)ConsoleDispMode.CONSOLE_FULLSCREEN_HARDWARE:
                        Console.WriteLine("Console has hardware access.");
                        break;
                    case (UInt32)ConsoleDispMode.CONSOLE_FULLSCREEN +
                         (UInt32)ConsoleDispMode.CONSOLE_FULLSCREEN_HARDWARE:
                        Console.WriteLine("Console is in fullscreen mode and " +
                                          "has access to the hardware.");
                        break;
                }
            }
        else

            // If the call failed, register an error.
            Console.WriteLine("No Display Mode Information Available");

        // Obtain a handle to the console screen and console input.
        hIn = GetStdHandle(StdHandleEnum.STD_INPUT_HANDLE);
        hOut = GetStdHandle(StdHandleEnum.STD_OUTPUT_HANDLE);

        // Determine the largest screen size possible.
        ScreenSize = GetLargestConsoleWindowSize(hOut);
```

```
        // Display the information.
        Console.WriteLine("\r\nThe largest console window size is:" +
                          "\r\n   Columns: " + ScreenSize.X.ToString() +
                          "\r\n   Rows: " + ScreenSize.Y.ToString());

        // Get the console mode information.
        Console.WriteLine("\r\nConsole Mode Information:");

        // Retrieve the input information.
        if (GetConsoleMode(hIn, ref ConsoleMode))
        {
           if ((ConsoleMode & (UInt32)ModeFlags.ENABLE_ECHO_INPUT) ==
              (UInt32)ModeFlags.ENABLE_ECHO_INPUT)
              Console.WriteLine("   Echo Input Enabled");

           if ((ConsoleMode & (UInt32)ModeFlags.ENABLE_LINE_INPUT) ==
              (UInt32)ModeFlags.ENABLE_LINE_INPUT)
              Console.WriteLine("   Line Input Enabled");

           if ((ConsoleMode & (UInt32)ModeFlags.ENABLE_MOUSE_INPUT) ==
              (UInt32)ModeFlags.ENABLE_MOUSE_INPUT)
              Console.WriteLine("   Mouse Input Enabled");

           if ((ConsoleMode & (UInt32)ModeFlags.ENABLE_PROCESSED_INPUT) ==
              (UInt32)ModeFlags.ENABLE_PROCESSED_INPUT)
              Console.WriteLine("   Processed Input Enabled");

           if ((ConsoleMode & (UInt32)ModeFlags.ENABLE_WINDOW_INPUT) ==
              (UInt32)ModeFlags.ENABLE_WINDOW_INPUT)
              Console.WriteLine("   Window Input Enabled");
        }

        // Retrieve the output information.
        if (GetConsoleMode(hOut, ref ConsoleMode))
        {
           if ((ConsoleMode & (UInt32)ModeFlags.ENABLE_PROCESSED_OUTPUT) ==
              (UInt32)ModeFlags.ENABLE_PROCESSED_OUTPUT)
              Console.WriteLine("   Processed Output Enabled");

           if ((ConsoleMode & (UInt32)ModeFlags.ENABLE_WRAP_AT_EOL_OUTPUT)
              == (UInt32)ModeFlags.ENABLE_WRAP_AT_EOL_OUTPUT)
              Console.WriteLine("   Wrap at End of Line Enabled");
        }

        // Wait until the user is done viewing the information.
        Console.Write("\r\nPress any key when ready...");
        Console.Read();
     }
```

This example shows some of the anomalies you'll need to consider when working with the Win32 API. Several of the previous examples have shows API functions that return an HRESULT—essentially an error code. The GetConsoleDisplayMode() and GetConsoleMode() in this example return a bool, which is a simple pass/fail indicator for the function call. On the other hand, the GetLargestConsoleWindowSize() function returns a COORD structure, which means you have neither an error result nor a pass/fail indicator until you attempt to use the data contained within the structure.

The code begins with a call to the GetConsoleDisplayMode() function. If you read the Platform SDK documentation for this function, you'll notice that it only refers to two return values: CONSOLE_FULLSCREEN_HARDWARE and CONSOLE_FULLSCREEN. The problem is that there's an actual third value of CONSOLE_WINDOWED. The code reflects this fact and you'll find that the need for the undocumented value is practical as well. The one important issue to consider is that a windowed console application will never use the CONSOLE_FULLSCREEN_HARDWARE value, so the code reflects this fact too. The GetConsoleDisplayMode() function requires that you pass a *UInt32* variable by reference, not as an out variable. In other words, you must initialize the variable before you pass it or you might receive unpredictable results.

The GetLargestConsoleWindowSize() function call comes next. Notice that you must supply a standard output handle for this function. We'll find with the GetConsoleMode() function that this isn't necessarily true for all Win32 API calls. The GetLargestConsoleWindowSize() function returns a COORD structure containing the largest window you can create for the console referenced by the handle you provide. The screen buffer might not provide the required amount of memory for a full-sized screen, so you need to keep what's possible separate from what the console can support. You can use the SetConsoleScreenBufferSize() function to resize the window to maximum using the results from this call.

Using the GetLargestConsoleWindowSize() function in full-screen mode will yield different results from windowed mode. The reason is that the full-screen mode is controlled by a different set of settings from the windowed mode. To change the full-screen mode settings, you can right-click the title bar of the console window and choose Properties from the context menu. The Options tab contains settings to switch from windowed for full-screen operation. The Layout tab shown in Figure 6.2 enables you to change the screen buffer settings, which also determines the output from the GetLargestConsoleWindowSize() function. However, if the user uses the MODE command to change the size of the window, it doesn't affect the output from the GetLargestConsoleWindowSize() function because the output is based upon the screen buffer size, not the window size.

FIGURE 6.2:

Use the settings on the Layout tab to change the output from the GetLargest-ConsoleWindowSize() function.

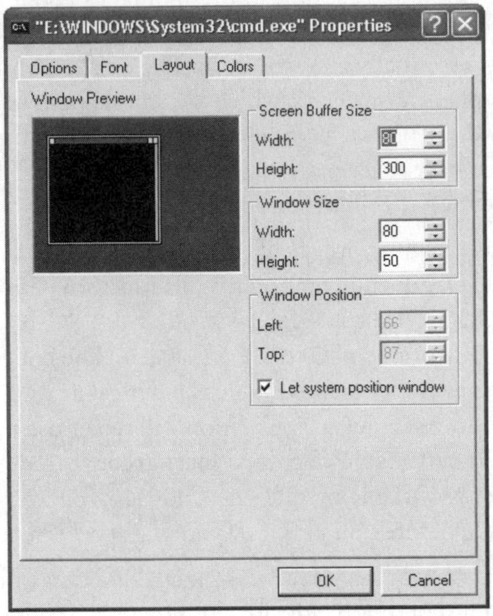

The GetConsoleMode() function is next on the list. It's important to note that you can provide either a screen buffer (standard output) or an input handle for this function. However, the results you obtain will directly reflect the kind of handle you pass to the function. Consequently, the example code shows what happens for both an input and an output handle. The handle tells you the mode settings for both input and output as determined by the handle provided. All of the mode settings except window input are enabled by default. The Platform SDK documentation explains the various settings in detail.

Now that you have some idea of what the console mode functions do, let's look at the example in action. Figure 6.3 shows the windowed output from the example. The full-screen output is different, so you'll want to test both modes. As you can see, the example correctly detects the windowed state of the console window, the largest size the console window will allow, and which mode settings the console window has enabled.

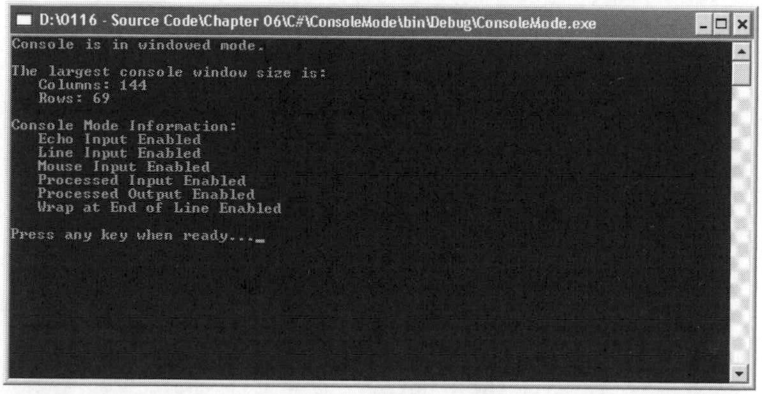

FIGURE 6.3:

The example application demonstrates the usefulness of the console mode information.

Working with Processes

Each console window normally contains one, and only one, process. However, you might create an application that spawns other processes to perform tasks in the background. In this case, you'll want to know about the other processes running in the console window so that you don't close it while another process is still running. The GetConsoleProcessList() function can help you perform this task.

You might think that this function is custom designed for a callback function (see Chapter 5 for details). However, you'll find that the GetConsoleProcessList() function relies on an array to store the retrieved data. This means you have to call the function twice. The first call retrieves the number of elements the array will require, while the second call actually retrieves the data. Listing 6.4 shows an example of how to use this function. You'll find the source code in the \Chapter 06\C#\GetProcess and \Chapter 06\VB\GetProcess folders on the CD.

Listing 6.4   One Method for Obtaining a List of Current Processes

```csharp
// This function obtains the current list of processes.
[DllImport("Kernel32.DLL")]
public static extern Int32 GetConsoleProcessList(
    ref UInt32 []lpdwProcessList,
    Int32 dwProcessCount);

[STAThread]
static void Main(string[] args)
{
    Int32    NumProcesses;              // The number of processes.
    UInt32   []ProcessIDs;              // The array of process IDs.

    // Determine how big to make the array.
```

```
ProcessIDs = new UInt32[1]{0};
NumProcesses = GetConsoleProcessList(ref ProcessIDs, 0);

// Determine if there are any other processes.
if (NumProcesses == 0)
   Console.WriteLine("No other processes to list.");
else
{
   // Create an array capable of holding the data.
   ProcessIDs = new UInt32[NumProcesses];

   // Initialize the array.
   for (int Counter = 0; Counter < NumProcesses; Counter++)
      ProcessIDs[Counter] = 0;

   // Call the function again with the appropriate arguments.
   GetConsoleProcessList(ref ProcessIDs, NumProcesses);

   // Display the output.
   for (int Counter = 0; Counter < NumProcesses; Counter++)
      Console.WriteLine("Process ID {0} is {1}",
         Counter,
         ProcessIDs[Counter]);
}

// Wait until the user is done viewing the information.
Console.Write("\r\nPress any key when ready...");
Console.Read();
}
```

As you can see, using the `GetConsoleProcessList()` function is a bit convoluted. You need to determine the number of array elements first; then create the array; and, finally, make the real call to the function. There are a number of other Win32 API calls that work in a similar fashion, so it's important to realize when a call is actually requesting this type of information exchange.

NOTE   Theoretically, you won't need to access process information for a console application very often, so the convoluted process shown here is an exception to the rule. Only complex console applications spawn other processes. Using processes is a good feature to know about.

The `GetConsoleProcessList()` function is only a partial solution to the problem of determining which processes are running on the machine. What you receive is a process identifier (PID)—a number that uniquely identifies the process in question. To determine anything else about the process, you need to use the PID with other .NET functions to retrieve other process information—including the name of the application running within the process. However, the PID is your key to additional information, so having it as a starting point make sense.

Changing the Environment Examples

In the previous section of the chapter, we discussed how to obtain and manipulate information provided to the console application. Knowing how the console is configured and what the user expects from the console application enable the developer to create flexible, yet powerful applications. However, the console application is also a product of its environment. For example, a console application begins with a default font that may or may not meet the needs of the application.

The following sections discuss the console environment. The purpose of these sections is to help you add emphasis to your applications by changing the environment in which they operate. With this in mind, I also decided to provide a very short section on environmental strings. This section is one of the few non–Win32 API discussions in the book and you can skip it if desired. The reason this section is included is that some developers might not know how to access the environmental strings and this knowledge is essential for some Win32 API calls.

All of the other sections will help you create a friendlier environment for the end user and gain more control over the output of your application. Console applications don't have to look kludged together or provide a bulking or unusable interface. The following sections show you how to overcome some of the perceptions that developers have concerning the console application and its environment.

Accessing the Environmental Strings

Console applications have access to two sets of input in the form of environmental strings—information that controls how the application reacts, locates files, executables, or data, or determines current system status. The first is the command-line arguments passed to the application. These strings are application specific and you'll normally want to provide a means for handling them. The second is the environmental strings provided as part of `AutoExec.NT` or the Environmental Variables dialog box shown in Figure 6.4 for Windows XP. (Windows NT and Windows 2000 also provide the Environmental Variables dialog box, but it looks slightly different than the one shown in the figure.) All of these sources of input for the console application are completely accessible using standard .NET Framework functions. As previously mentioned, the main reason for discussing the environmental strings is so you know how to access them from your application—many Win32 API functions require information provided by these environmental strings.

FIGURE 6.4:

The Environmental
Variables dialog box
contains a set of
system and user
strings.

The command-line arguments are passed to the Main() function of a console application using the *args* variable. You'll need to use the Environment class to retrieve the environmental strings, among other items of information. Listing 6.5 shows how to work with both the command-line arguments and the environmental strings. You'll find the source code for this example in the \Chapter 06\C#\Environment and \Chapter 06\VB\Environment folders on the CD.

Listing 6.5 **Methods of Accessing the Command-line Arguments and Environmental Strings**

```
[STAThread]
static void Main(string[] args)
{
    // Display each of the command line arguments in turn.
    Console.WriteLine("The Command Line Arguments:\r\n");
    for (int Counter = 0; Counter < args.Length; Counter++)
        Console.WriteLine(args[Counter]);

    // Obtain the environmental strings.
    Console.WriteLine("\r\nThe Environmental Strings:");
    foreach (DictionaryEntry DE in
        System.Environment.GetEnvironmentVariables())
    {
        // Display the key/value pairs.
        Console.WriteLine(DE.Key.ToString());
        Console.WriteLine(DE.Value.ToString() + "\r\n");
    }
```

```
    // Obtain a single environmental string.
    Console.WriteLine("\r\nSingle Environmental String (Path):");
    Console.WriteLine(System.Environment.GetEnvironmentVariable("Path"));

    // Wait until the user is done viewing the information.
    Console.Write("\r\nPress any key when ready...");
    Console.Read();
}
```

As you can see, the command-line arguments appear as an array. Simply parsing the array will help you locate the information you need. The example application provides an automatic command line when you start the application in the debugger. You can change this setting in the Configuration Properties\Debugging folder of the Environment Property Pages dialog box. The Command Line Arguments property contains the value you'll need to change.

> **TIP**   You can also retrieve the command-line arguments for an application using the Get-CommandLineArgs() function found in the Environment class. This function enables you to send command-line arguments to a specific function within an application—the application doesn't have to pass the argument around until it reaches the right place.

There are several functions for retrieving the environmental strings—the code shows the two most commonly used techniques. The GetEnvironmentVariables() function returns an IDictionary, which is made up of DictionaryEntry object key/value pairs. The foreach loop provides the perfect method for examining each of these entries in turn. You can also use the GetEnvironmentVariable() function to retrieve a single environmental string. Of course, this implies that you know the name of the environmental string that you want to retrieve. Generally, the GetEnvironmentVariable() function is easier to use because you get one response and don't need to parse through all of the other potential entries. Figure 6.5 shows the output from this example.

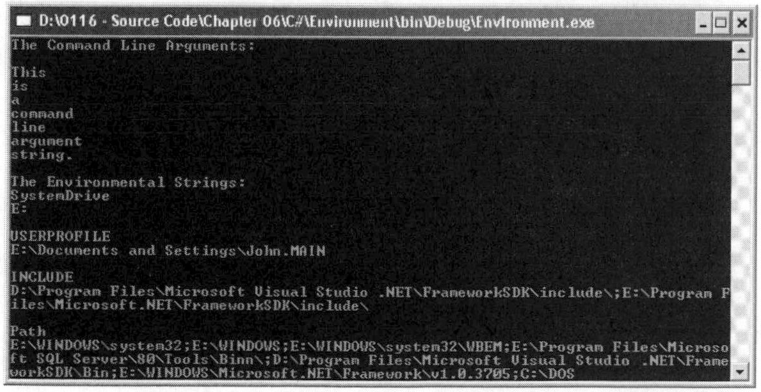

FIGURE 6.5:

Retrieving command-line arguments and environment strings is relatively easy with .NET.

TIP Some environmental variables strings contain environment variables that can prove difficult to work with. For example, the *Path* environmental string could contain a reference to %WinBase%, which doesn't make much sense. You can use the ExpandEnvironment-Variables() function in this situation to expand the variable to something you can use within an application.

You should be wondering, at this point, how you can add new environmental strings or change existing environmental strings. Unfortunately, the .NET Framework falls short of providing this functionality, so you have to rely on a Win32 API call to do it. (You knew I was going to get a Win32 API call in here—didn't you?) To perform this task, you'll need the help of the SetEnvironmentVariable() function as shown in Listing 6.6. You'll find the source code for this example in the \Chapter 06\C#\SetEnvironment and \Chapter 06\VB\ SetEnvironment folders on the CD.

Listing 6.6   **Setting and Changing an Environmental String**

```
// The function required to set or change environmental strings.
[DllImport("Kernel32.DLL")]
public static extern bool SetEnvironmentVariable(String lpName,
                                                 String lpValue);

[STAThread]
static void Main(string[] args)
{
    // Set the new environmental string.
    SetEnvironmentVariable("MyEnvironment", "This is a value.");

    // Obtain the new environmental string.
    Console.WriteLine("\r\nMyEnvironment Environmental String:");
    Console.WriteLine(
        System.Environment.GetEnvironmentVariable("MyEnvironment"));

    // Change the new environmental string.
    SetEnvironmentVariable("MyEnvironment", "A new display value.");

    // Obtain the updated environmental string.
    Console.WriteLine("\r\nUpdated MyEnvironment Environmental String:");
    Console.WriteLine(
        System.Environment.GetEnvironmentVariable("MyEnvironment"));

    // Wait until the user is done viewing the information.
    Console.Write("\r\nPress any key when ready...");
    Console.Read();
}
```

The code for the `SetEnvironmentVariable()` function is surprisingly simple, which is why it's a wonder that Microsoft didn't add it to the .NET Framework. As you can see, the function requires a key/value pair input. The first string contains the key, while the second string contains the value. Figure 6.6 shows the output from this example.

FIGURE 6.6:

Setting environmental strings is easy—just supply a key and a value.

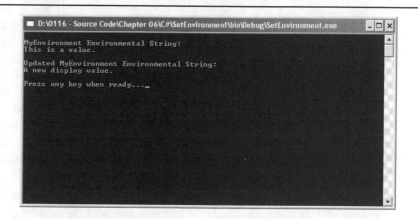

Using Cursors and Fonts

Many people think that they're stuck with the cursor and font originally presented in the console window—others simply don't think too much about the option of changing either item. However, it pays to know about both cursor and font manipulation for those times when you want to emphasize something on screen. The `GetConsoleCursorInfo()` and `SetConsoleCursorInfo()` functions help you with the console cursor.

The `GetConsoleFontSize()` function enables you to work with the font. You can specify the index of the current font or ask for the dimensions of any font supported by the console window. This function can help you perform tasks like size the console window for a specific font. When you only want to know about the current font, you can use the `GetCurrentConsoleFont()` function. You also need to use the `GetCurrentConsoleFont()` function to obtain a font index number for the `GetConsoleFontSize()` function. The `GetCurrentConsoleFont()` function can retrieve the current console font or the font for the maximum window supported by the current window settings and the machine. If you feel that the console needs a bit of color, you can use the `FillConsoleOutputAttribute()` or the `SetConsoleTextAttribute()` functions.

You'll use the cursor-related functions relatively often because the console offers little in the way of console control otherwise. The example in Listing 6.1 shows you how to move the cursor around. The example in this section will show you how to obtain and change the cursor characteristics. Console applications can use these functions to modify the appearance of the cursor for emphasis, such as when the application goes from insert to overwrite mode.

NOTE Unlike a GUI window, you can't change the size of the font within a console window directly because the console window has specific limits placed on it. For example, the console window uses a monospaced font. You can learn more about the criteria for console fonts at `http://support.microsoft.com/default.aspx?scid=kb;en-us;Q247815`. The window size and the number of rows and columns of text determine the size of the console font. If you want to change the size of the font, then you need to change one of the associated font factors. For example, retaining the current number of rows and columns, while increasing the size of the window, will also increase the size of the font.

Modifying font characteristics also presents an opportunity for emphasizing information. For example, you can present the text using a different color—red for danger or green for success. If the font is large enough, you can also add features such as underline (the underline still works with small fonts, but you can't really see it). Listing 6.7 demonstrates the various font and cursor functions discussed in this section. You can find the example code in the \Chapter 06\C#\CursorAndFont and \Chapter 06\VB\CursorAndFont folders on the CD. (The source listing in Listing 6.7 is incomplete—check the source code on the CD for functions and structures discussed in previous sections of the chapter.)

Listing 6.7   Examples of How to Use the Cursor and Font Functions

```
// Obtains the current cursor settings.
[DllImport("kernel32.dll", SetLastError=true)]
public static extern bool GetConsoleCursorInfo(
    IntPtr hConsoleOutput,
    ref CONSOLE_CURSOR_INFO lpConsoleCursorInfo);

// Modifies the cursor settings.
[DllImport("kernel32.dll", SetLastError=true)]
public static extern bool SetConsoleCursorInfo(
    IntPtr hConsoleOutput,
    ref CONSOLE_CURSOR_INFO lpConsoleCursorInfo);

// The data structure used to get or set the cursor information.
public struct CONSOLE_CURSOR_INFO
{
    public UInt32   dwSize;    // Percentage of character cell.
    public bool     bVisible;  // Is it visible?
}

// Function for obtaining the current console font. The font
// can represent either the current window size or the maximum
// window size for the machine.
[DllImport("kernel32.dll", SetLastError=true)]
public static extern bool GetCurrentConsoleFont(
    IntPtr hConsoleOutput,
```

```
        bool bMaximumWindow,
        ref CONSOLE_FONT_INFO lpConsoleCurrentFont);

    // This structure contains the console font information.
    public struct CONSOLE_FONT_INFO
    {
        public UInt32  nFont;      // The font number.
        public COORD   dwFontSize; // The font size.
    }

    // This function obtains the font size specified by the font
    // index (not necessarily the current font).
    [DllImport("kernel32.dll", SetLastError=true)]
    public static extern COORD GetConsoleFontSize(
        IntPtr hConsoleOutput,
        UInt32 nFont);

    // This function changes the text attributes.
    [DllImport("kernel32.dll", SetLastError=true)]
    public static extern bool SetConsoleTextAttribute(
        IntPtr hConsoleOutput,
        CharacterAttributes wAttributes);

    // This enumeration lists all of the character attributes. You
    // can combine attributes to achieve specific effects.
    public enum CharacterAttributes
    {
        FOREGROUND_BLUE            = 0x0001,
        FOREGROUND_GREEN           = 0x0002,
        FOREGROUND_RED             = 0x0004,
        FOREGROUND_INTENSITY       = 0x0008,
        BACKGROUND_BLUE            = 0x0010,
        BACKGROUND_GREEN           = 0x0020,
        BACKGROUND_RED             = 0x0040,
        BACKGROUND_INTENSITY       = 0x0080,
        COMMON_LVB_LEADING_BYTE    = 0x0100,
        COMMON_LVB_TRAILING_BYTE   = 0x0200,
        COMMON_LVB_GRID_HORIZONTAL = 0x0400,
        COMMON_LVB_GRID_LVERTICAL  = 0x0800,
        COMMON_LVB_GRID_RVERTICAL  = 0x1000,
        COMMON_LVB_REVERSE_VIDEO   = 0x4000,
        COMMON_LVB_UNDERSCORE      = 0x8000
    }

[STAThread]
static void Main(string[] args)
{
    IntPtr               hOut;    // Handle to the output device.
    CONSOLE_CURSOR_INFO  CCI;     // The current cursor information.
    CONSOLE_CURSOR_INFO  NewCCI;  // The new cursor information.
```

```
CONSOLE_FONT_INFO      CFI;        // The console font information.
COORD                  FontSize;   // The size of the requested font.

// Obtain a handle to the console screen.
hOut = GetStdHandle(StdHandleEnum.STD_OUTPUT_HANDLE);

// Get the cursor information.
CCI.bVisible = false;
CCI.dwSize = 0;
GetConsoleCursorInfo(hOut, ref CCI);

// Display the results.
if (CCI.bVisible)
   Console.WriteLine("The cursor is displayed at {0}% of the" +
                     " cell height.", CCI.dwSize);
else
   Console.WriteLine("The cursor is invisible.");

// Modify the cursor appearance.
NewCCI.bVisible = true;
NewCCI.dwSize = 100;
if (SetConsoleCursorInfo(hOut, ref NewCCI))
{
   Console.WriteLine("\r\nThe new cursor settings are in effect.");
   Console.Write("Press any key when ready...");
   Console.ReadLine();

   // Reset the cursor to its original size.
   Console.WriteLine("Returning the cursor to normal.");
   SetConsoleCursorInfo(hOut, ref CCI);
}
else
   // The call failed, normally due to an out of range value.
   Console.WriteLine("The cursor settings couldn't be changed.");

// Obtain the current font information.
CFI.nFont = 0;
CFI.dwFontSize.X = 0;
CFI.dwFontSize.Y = 0;
FontSize.X = 0;
FontSize.Y = 0;
GetCurrentConsoleFont(hOut, false, ref CFI);
FontSize = GetConsoleFontSize(hOut, CFI.nFont);
Console.WriteLine("\r\nThe Current Font Information:");
Console.WriteLine("   Font Number: {0}\r\n   FontSize: {1} X {2}",
                  CFI.nFont,
                  FontSize.X,
                  FontSize.Y);

// Display the list of available font sizes.
Console.WriteLine("\r\nThe List of Fonts Includes:");
```

```
GetCurrentConsoleFont(hOut, true, ref CFI);
for (UInt32 Counter = 0; Counter <= CFI.nFont; Counter++)
{
   FontSize = GetConsoleFontSize(hOut, Counter);
   Console.WriteLine("   {0} X {1}", FontSize.X, FontSize.Y);
}

// Display the text using various colors and attributes.
Console.WriteLine("\r\nTesting Character Attributes:");
SetConsoleTextAttribute(hOut, CharacterAttributes.FOREGROUND_BLUE |
                        CharacterAttributes.FOREGROUND_GREEN |
                        CharacterAttributes.FOREGROUND_INTENSITY);
Console.WriteLine("This text is in turquoise.");
SetConsoleTextAttribute(hOut, CharacterAttributes.BACKGROUND_BLUE |
                        CharacterAttributes.BACKGROUND_GREEN |
                        CharacterAttributes.BACKGROUND_RED);
Console.WriteLine("This text is reverse video.");
SetConsoleTextAttribute(hOut, CharacterAttributes.FOREGROUND_BLUE |
                        CharacterAttributes.FOREGROUND_GREEN |
                        CharacterAttributes.FOREGROUND_RED);

// Wait until the user is done viewing the information.
Console.Write("\r\nPress any key when ready...");
Console.Read();
}
```

As you can see from the source listing, most of the Win32 API functions in this example return a bool value indicating success. The exception is GetConsoleFontSize(), which returns a COORD value containing the size of the font. The use of a bool return value makes it easy to perform a quick check of call success.

The code begins by displaying the current cursor information. If the *bVisible* variable is true, then the cursor is visible and the code displays the cursor size. Note that *dwSize* contains the size of the cursor as a percentage of the character size. The code then uses the SetConsole-CursorInfo() function to change the size of the cursor. Again, you need to specify the size of the cursor as a percentage of the character size. The example stops at this point so you can see the new cursor size. When you press Enter, the code returns the cursor to normal.

The font information write-up in the Platform SDK documentation is unclear because it leads you to believe that the GetCurrentConsoleFont() function returns the font size in the *dwFont-Size* variable of the CONSOLE_FONT_INFO structure. What you actually receive in the *dwFontSize* variable is the number of characters on screen. The default character settings allow for 80 characters across by 25 characters down. Consequently, you still need to use the GetConsole-FontSize() function to retrieve the actual size of the characters in pixels.

Another problem with the documentation is that it tells you that you can retrieve the font values for the maximum window size using the GetCurrentConsoleFont(), without defining the term "maximum window size." As shown by the example, the maximum window size is determined by the current window size as well as machine limitations. Increase the current window size and the font index returned by this function will almost certainly increase. In short, the list returned by the code only reflects those fonts available in the current window, not the fonts available to Windows as a whole. In addition, the returned sizes only apply to the selected font, which is the raster font set in most cases. Windows also comes with a Lucida font for console windows, which changes the output from the example quite a bit.

The character attributes work much as you think they might. However, you must provide a complete set of attributes for every call to SetConsoleTextAttribute(). Any value you don't supply is automatically reset to nothing (black when working with colors). Therefore, if you want both foreground and background colors, you must supply both background and foreground attributes as part of the call. In addition, the attributes that begin with COMMON_LVB only apply to a double-byte character set (DBCS). If you want to see underlined text on screen, you need to use a DBCS font. Unfortunately, the standard version of Windows sold in English-speaking countries doesn't include a DBCS font. Figure 6.7 shows the output from this example.

FIGURE 6.7:

The cursor and font example shows just some of what you can do in a console application.

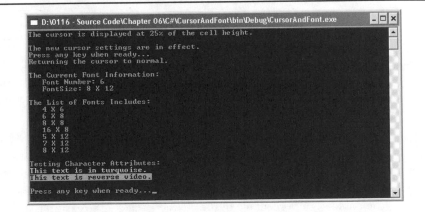

Determining the Console Window Title

Windows will assign a default title to the console window when you create it—normally the name of the execution including path information. In some cases, the default title works just fine. However, there are times when you might want to personalize the window title to reflect the current application. To check the current title you'll use the GetConsoleTitle() function—the SetConsoleTitle() function enables you to change the current title into something more appropriate. Listing 6.8 shows how to use these two functions. You'll find the example code in the \Chapter 06\C#\WindowTitle and the \Chapter 06\VB\WindowTitle folders on the CD.

Listing 6.8   **Changing and Restoring the Console Window Title**

```
// This function retrieves the current window title.
[DllImport("kernel32.dll", SetLastError=true)]
public static extern Int32 GetConsoleTitle(StringBuilder lpConsoleTitle,
                                           Int32 nSize);

// This function sets a new window title.
[DllImport("kernel32.dll", SetLastError=true)]
public static extern bool SetConsoleTitle(String lpConsoleTitle);

[STAThread]
static void Main(string[] args)
{
    StringBuilder  WindowTitle;   // The current window title.
    Int32          TitleSize;     // The size of the buffer.

    // Obtain the current window title.
    WindowTitle = new StringBuilder(256);
    TitleSize = GetConsoleTitle(WindowTitle, 256);
    Console.WriteLine("The Old Window Title Is: \r\n" +
                    WindowTitle.ToString());

    // Create a new console window title.
    Console.WriteLine("\r\nSetting a new console window title.");
    SetConsoleTitle("A New Window Title");
    Console.Write("Press any key to restore the old title...");
    Console.ReadLine();

    // Restore the old console window title.
    SetConsoleTitle(WindowTitle.ToString());

    // Wait until the user is done viewing the information.
    Console.Write("\r\nPress any key when ready...");
    Console.Read();
}
```

Like other examples of Win32 API functions that modify a string buffer, the GetConsole-Title() function relies on a *StringBuilder* variable to hold the returned string value. Of course, you have to allocate the buffer—something you can do when declaring the variable or as a separate step for clarity. You must also provide the size of the buffer as part of the call.

The code could have used a *StringBuilder* variable for the SetConsoleTitle() function as well, but a *String* works fine in this case. Changing the title produces the result shown in Figure 6.8. The only inconvenient aspect of using a string for the SetConsoleTitle() function is that you need to convert the *StringBuilder* variable to a string—something that's easily done.

Changing the console window title is easy using the Win32 API functions.

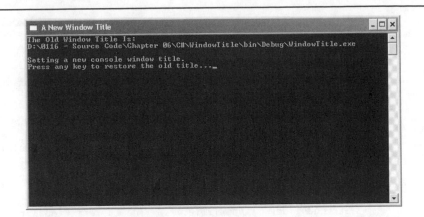

Manipulating the Console Screen Buffer

What precisely is a screen buffer? It's the area of memory set aside to represent the contents of the screen. Windows applications don't write directly to video memory, so they require some area of regular memory in which to place their data. When Windows updates that actual video memory, it considers the content of the screen buffer for each application. Consequently, knowing something about the console screen buffer can help you create a better user environment for your application.

Sometimes you need to move some text around on screen. The easiest way to do this is to use the ScrollConsoleScreenBuffer() function to move the text. You can move any part of the screen buffer to any other part of the screen buffer, making this function exceptionally useful when displaying text on screen. Of course, the movement of text is limited by the clipping rectangle for the window. If part of the text will appear in an off-screen area as a result of the move, then the function merely clips the text to fit. You need to validate that any text movement you perform will stay on screen (unless you actually want to clip the text to fit within certain confines).

An application isn't limited to one screen buffer, but it must have at least one screen buffer to write any text to the console. You create a new screen buffer using the CreateConsole-ScreenBuffer() function. The interesting part about creating a new screen buffer is that you can select a level of sharing for the buffer, which means two processes could potentially work with the same buffer. Use the SetConsoleActiveScreenBuffer() function to set the screen buffer that Windows uses for display purposes. This function also enables you to draw the content of the console screen in the background, and then display it in the foreground—creating a type of animation for the console.

Finally, you can use the SetConsoleScreenBufferSize() function to change the number of rows and columns displayed by the console. This function is especially handy when the default console window is too small or large for the task at hand. Listing 6.9 demonstrates some of the functions described in this section. You can find the source code in the \Chapter 06\C#\ ScreenBuffer and \Chapter 06\VB\ScreenBuffer folders on the CD. (The source listing in Listing 6.9 is incomplete—check the source code on the CD for functions and structures discussed in previous sections of the chapter.)

Listing 6.9   Methods for Working with the Console Screen Buffer

```
// This function enables you to move part of the screen buffer
// to another location.
[DllImport("kernel32.dll", SetLastError=true)]
public static extern bool ScrollConsoleScreenBuffer(
    IntPtr hConsoleOutput,
    ref SMALL_RECT lpScrollRectangle,
    ref SMALL_RECT lpClipRectangle,
    COORD dwDestinationOrigin,
    ref CHAR_INFO lpFill);

// This function enables you to move part of the screen buffer
// to another location.
[DllImport("kernel32.dll", SetLastError=true)]
public static extern bool ScrollConsoleScreenBuffer(
    IntPtr hConsoleOutput,
    ref SMALL_RECT lpScrollRectangle,
    IntPtr NoClipRectangle,
    COORD dwDestinationOrigin,
    ref CHAR_INFO lpFill);

// This structure defines a rectangular area on the screen
// consisting of an upper left and a lower right corner.
[StructLayout(LayoutKind.Sequential)]
public struct SMALL_RECT
{
    public Int16   Left;
    public Int16   Top;
    public Int16   Right;
    public Int16   Bottom;
}

[StructLayout(LayoutKind.Sequential)]
public struct CHAR_INFO
{
    public Char                 Character;
    public CharacterAttributes Attributes;
}
```

```
[STAThread]
static void Main(string[] args)
{
    IntPtr       hOut;        // Handle to the output device.
    SMALL_RECT   ScrollRect;  // The area to scroll on screen.
    COORD        Dest;        // The scrolled area destination.
    CHAR_INFO    FillData;    // The data to put in the scrolled area.

    // Obtain a handle to the console screen.
    hOut = GetStdHandle(StdHandleEnum.STD_OUTPUT_HANDLE);

    // Display some data on screen.
    Console.WriteLine("This is some data to scroll.");
    Console.Write("Press any key to scroll...");
    Console.ReadLine();

    // Initialize the variables.
    ScrollRect.Top = 0;
    ScrollRect.Left = 0;
    ScrollRect.Right = 15;
    ScrollRect.Bottom = 5;

    Dest.X = 20;
    Dest.Y = 10;

    FillData.Attributes = CharacterAttributes.FOREGROUND_BLUE |
                          CharacterAttributes.FOREGROUND_RED |
                          CharacterAttributes.FOREGROUND_INTENSITY;
    FillData.Character = 'A';

    // Scroll an area of the screen.
    if (!ScrollConsoleScreenBuffer(hOut,
                                   ref ScrollRect,
                                   IntPtr.Zero,
                                   Dest,
                                   ref FillData))
        Console.WriteLine("Couldn't scroll the screen buffer.");

    // Wait until the user is done viewing the information.
    Console.Write("\r\nPress any key when ready...");
    Console.Read();
}
```

This example shows you a couple of new tricks to use when working with Win32 API calls. The first problem you need to overcome is allowing the clipping rectangle to contain a null value. Unfortunately, neither C# nor Visual Basic will allow you to assign a null value (Nothing) to a structure, so you need to devise another way to overcome the problem. There are a number of ways to do this, but the example code shows the most convenient way. Simply create two declarations of the function. The first contains a place for the clipping rectangle, while the second doesn't.

The second problem is one that doesn't even appear in the code, but could cause a problem if you don't look for it in the Platform SDK documentation. The CHAR_INFO structure contains a union as shown in the following code:

```
typedef struct _CHAR_INFO {
  union {
      WCHAR UnicodeChar;
      CHAR AsciiChar;
  } Char;
  WORD Attributes;
} CHAR_INFO, *PCHAR_INFO;
```

A union is a special class type for C++ that says you must supply one of the data types to fill the structure, but only one of the data types. The CHAR_INFO structure can accept either an ASCII character or a Unicode character as its first data member. In this case, we don't need to worry about the union because the .NET language takes care of this concern automatically. However, in cases where the language doesn't resolve the problem for you, you'll need to come up with a creative solution. In many cases, the best solution is to create multiple versions of the data structure—one for each of the types listed in the union.

The actual mechanics of the ScrollConsoleScreenBuffer() function are straightforward. The code shows how to fill out the data structures. The example moves some text that originally appears at the top of the screen to a location around the middle of the screen as shown in Figure 6.9. The addition of a clipping rectangle makes it easy to move text within a certain area of the display. Any text that appears outside of the clipping rectangle at the time of the scroll remains untouched. Any text that would appear outside of the clipping rectangle after the scroll is clipped.

FIGURE 6.9:

Moving text around on screen is easy when using the Scroll-ConsoleScreenBuffer() function.

Where Do You Go from Here?

This chapter has shown you some of the things you can do to make your next console application a little easier to use and more functional. Of course, a console application will never have the same level of user interface functionality that you'll find in a GUI application, but the fact remains that most console applications today are decidedly Spartan. Fortunately, you can still access the Win32 API to fill the holes in coverage left by the .NET Framework.

One of the things you should do now that you know how to accomplish the tasks presented in this chapter is look at some of your current applications. Ask yourself whether some of the dialog-based utilities that you currently provide as part of your application would work better as a console-based application. Remember that the main reason to use a console-based application is to provide an easy method for administrators to script the application and to reduce the dependence of the application on the GUI. You'll also want to spruce up your existing console applications. Make sure the applications provide a reliable and useful appearance. Even console applications should work well and keep the user's needs in mind.

It's important to begin creating toolkits of missing Win32 API functions—essentially DLLs that contain functions you can call quickly from managed code and know that the function will work immediately without an understanding of the underlying Win32 API calls. Console applications present a great opportunity for building such DLLs because the number of functions is limited and working with the console screen is somewhat easier than working with the GUI. Of course, you'll want to create toolkits for your GUI applications too, but now might be a good time to experiment with some of the console functions presented in this chapter.

Chapter 7 continues the search for ways to plug the holes in the .NET Framework coverage of the Win32 API. In this next chapter we'll discuss easy access to hardware—especially lower-level hardware such as the serial and parallel ports. The chapter concentrates on fairly generic hardware—you won't find instructions for creating an interface to specific hardware such as a certain model of camera. It's also important to note that this chapter will concentrate on standardized access using existing technology—you won't learn how to create a device driver with .NET (something that .NET is ill-equipped to handle in any event).

CHAPTER 7

Accessing the Hardware Directly

- When is Direct Access Required?

- Serial Port Access Examples

- Parallel Port Access Examples

Hardware, the underlying physical element of the computing world, is also the most difficult part of an application to develop in many cases. It seems as though every piece of hardware has a different interface from every other piece of hardware. For example, you can find hard drives that use SCSI, IDE, EIDE, USB, FireWire, and a host of other interfaces—all of which require different programming techniques. In fact, developing applications that work with all kinds of hardware used to be a major undertaking in the world of DOS because every vendor had to start from scratch.

Fortunately, you don't have to worry about touching the hardware directly in Windows—device drivers and other pieces of software shield the application developer from the strange inner workings of the hardware and present a reasonably simple interface. However, the .NET developer will find that hardware is the one area where .NET support is lacking in a big way. Sure, you can access common devices like the hard drive using objects such as streams, but once you get past the truly common hardware, you'll find that access becomes significantly more difficult.

NOTE   Some developers will attempt the impossible with the .NET Framework. While Microsoft might have some future plans to create a low-level programming environment for the .NET Framework, the basic goal for the .NET Framework today is application development. In essence, this means you shouldn't attempt to write a device driver in .NET; it's unlikely to work at all. Not only do the files required to run CLR load well after the device drivers under Windows, but there's simply no way to create the required low-level access. The point is that you should use the techniques in this chapter to extend your grasp of hardware essentials for applications, not attempt to write code that will certainly fail. If you do decide there's some low-level code in your future, check out Visual C++, Platform SDK, and the Driver Development Kit (DDK).

The main purpose of this chapter is to help you overcome some of the major holes in hardware support currently found in the .NET Framework. We'll discuss common, but lower-level hardware such as the parallel and serial ports. You'll also learn how to access an add-on device—the joystick, in this case, and a bus, USB for this chapter. These four examples will help you understand the requirements for accessing many of the pieces of hardware that the .NET Framework doesn't support. The examples will provide the information you need to interact with other pieces of hardware on the system. Of course, the one overriding assumption in this chapter is that you already have a device driver to provide standardized access to the device; I'm not going into the details of device driver development.

When is Direct Access Required?

It would be easy to say that Microsoft was negligent in leaving out hardware access in the .NET Framework. However, given the goal of providing basic functionality for business users, Microsoft actually did a great job with this first version of .NET. The problem is figuring out where .NET falls down on the job so that you can make a reasonable choice about using the Win32 API to provide the hardware access that your application needs. Here's a list of the three questions you should ask yourself.

1. Can I provide the required access using some other technique?   The .NET Framework provides a lot of hidden functionality that Microsoft markets for one reason, but you can use for another. For example, data streams are an extremely powerful .NET Framework feature and will work fine in many situations. For example, if you need to send output to the printer, you can use a data stream and associated printer objects to do it. However, if you need to ascertain that the paper holder is empty, then a data stream isn't going to perform the task and you'll need to rely on direct hardware access in most cases.

2. Will a technology such a DirectX solve the problem?   DirectX is a powerful technology that Microsoft supports fully—even more fully than the Win32 API in many cases. You still have to use the Win32 API to use DirectX (as explained in Part IV of the book), but DirectX provides certain safeguards and efficiencies you might not find the general Win32 API functions. In addition, Microsoft may release .NET Framework support for DirectX sooner than it will for older Win32 API functions. This means that you can develop the application to use DirectX today and will find it easier to convert to a pure .NET Framework implementation tomorrow. Of course, DirectX is a multimedia-specific solution—you won't find it very useful for creating a utility to enumerate the devices on your USB.

3. Is there a COM object that can provide the support that I need for my application? Using a COM object is always easier than trying to create a new library from scratch. Remember that you can import COM objects into the .NET environment and the Visual Studio IDE will perform all (or at least most) of the transformation for you. While this approach still means that you're accessing unmanaged code, at some point, all of the details of the access are hidden from view. As far as the application is concerned, the access is transparent. In addition, you'll save yourself quite a few hours of work trying to create library routines to perform the direct access. One of the most common devices that supports COM object is the serial port, but you'll also find COM libraries suitable for use with parallel ports, RS-422 port, common scientific equipment, and many types of medical equipment.

There are a number of places that you should consider looking for ready-made components and hardware access information. Of course, the best place to look for information
on accessing your hardware is the vendor Web site, but sometimes that's a lost cause
and you need to look elsewhere. There are many good places to look for components and
controls on the Internet. One of the more interesting places is the HalloGram Publishing
site at http://www.hallogram.com/menus/Controls_Creation_Utilities.html. This
particular page is interesting because they include a lot of control creation tools you
might not find elsewhere. Another interesting place to look is Active-X.COM
(http://www.active-x.com/). The only problem with this site is that you'll end up getting sidetracked by the sheer volume of controls they have available. If you don't find what
you want at these two sites, try the 4Developers link page at http://www.4developers
.com/links/. This site contains a number of links for ActiveX control vendors, as well as
other developer resources. Finally, WinSite has a number of programmer categories on
their site at http://www.winsite.com/winnt/. Many of the components on this site
work just fine with .NET applications. Of course, you'll need to ensure that any component
you download will work with the hardware you want to use.

Sometimes there's no way around the direct access question—you must use the Win32 API
to accomplish the task. For example, any application requirement to request status information
from the hardware isn't supported by the .NET Framework. If you want to know whether the
serial port is configured to use 8-bit data transfers, you'll need to use a Win32 API function to
do it. Likewise, requesting parallel, router, bus, or any other hardware status information will
require a Win32 API (or sometimes a third-party library) call. Fortunately, this gap in support
doesn't extend to virtual devices, such as the display or desktop, which are fully accessible using
.NET Framework calls.

All esoteric devices will require complete support by the Win32 API or a third-party library.
For example, if you attach a camera to the USB or FireWire port on your computer and want
to access it with a custom application, you'll need to write code that accesses it using the Win32
API or a third-party library. Fortunately, you can overcome some of the problems of this
approach by placing the routines in a DLL and using it as a wrapper. Using this technique
means you'll only have to write a set of generic routines one time to gain permanent access to
the device in question.

Serial Port Access Examples

The serial port represents one of the oldest methods for accessing external peripherals on the
PC. It's undergone several transformations over the years, but the basic operation of the serial
port remains the same. Even though the serial port is slow relative to faster options present in
today's computers (such as the USB port), the serial port is still the data transfer method of

choice for many peripherals and applications. The only problem is that the .NET Framework doesn't provide any direct support for the serial port and there isn't any way to determine information such as port status outside of the Win32 API.

TIP It's possible to use existing COM controls to access the serial port for data transfer. For example, the Microsoft Communication Control works well for this task. However, you might run into problems when working with some controls supplied with Visual Studio 6.0 under .NET. The Microsoft Knowledge Base article at `http://support.microsoft` `.com/default.aspx?scid=kb;en-us;Q318597` explains this problem and how to fix it. If you do decide to use Visual Studio 6.0 controls in your .NET application, you'll need to copy the controls from the Visual Studio 6.0 disks to your hard drive and register them using RegSvr32. These controls are licensed, so you'll also need to add the licensing information to the registry. The README.TXT file located in the \Extras\VB6 Controls folder of Disk 4 of the Visual Studio .NET Enterprise Edition distribution disks tells how to apply the required licensing entries. There's an excellent article on using the Microsoft Communication Control under .NET (including instructions for creating a null modem) at `http://www.devhood.com/tutorials/tutorial_details.aspx?tutorial_id=320`. While this technique does work, it doesn't provide the same level of access as the Win32 API functions found in this chapter.

The following sections will explore several serial port examples. The main purpose of these examples is to help you gain full access to the serial port using a combination of the .NET Framework and the Win32 API. I won't discuss a full-fledged communication program because that topic is discussed in better detail in other books. What you'll walk away with is the tools required to create any type of serial access, not just the access used of data exchange.

Creating a Serial Stream

For those of us who've worked with the Win32 API for a while, the idea of needing to use the Win32 API to do something as simple as open the serial port might seem a bit strange. In fact, the .NET framework did provide a means to open the serial port using a `FileStream` object during the beta. You should be able to use something as simple as the following code to open the serial port:

```
FileStream  FS = new FileStream("COM1:", FileMode.Open);
```

Unfortunately, support for this particular call disappeared into the abyss during the beta process, never to return in the released product. In fact, if you attempt to use this code today, you'll receive an error message like the one shown in Figure 7.1. The message is cryptic—what is the `CreateFile()` function? It doesn't exist in the .NET Framework. In fact, this message is Microsoft's way of telling you that you need to use the Win32 API to perform the desired task—a tacit admission that the .NET Framework is far from complete. This is one of many situations when an exception message will tell you which Win32 API function to use. Of course, most of them have the clarity of the example shown in Figure 7.1 (or worse).

FIGURE 7.1:
Using a FileStream object incorrectly yields error messages.

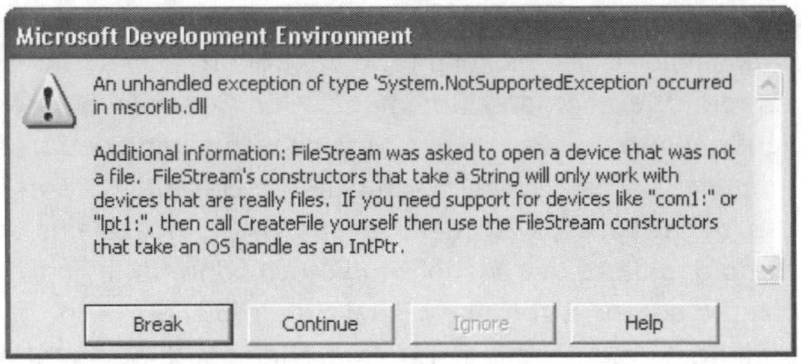

The fact remains that you need to create a serial stream in order to send or receive data using the serial port. However, the method for creating this stream is a little more complex than you might have imagined. Listing 7.1 shows the code to send a simple message to the serial port. Of course, this code doesn't include any status checking code, which is a requirement when using the serial port to connect with another computer. However, the listing does show a simple communication with the modem attached to COM3: on the example machine. You'll find the source code for this example in the \Chapter 07\C#\Serial1 and \Chapter 07\ VB\Serial1 folders on the CD.

The CreateFile() function has several arguments that could be NULL or set to zero. The example code shows only one implementation of CreateFile(), but theoretically you'd need three additional overrides for a complete implementation. A complete set of arguments would include both a template file and a set of security attributes. You could also create overrides that include just the template file or just the security attributes. The example doesn't require any of these overrides and you won't need them to perform direct hardware access. Consequently, the example only includes the version of CreateFile() shown in Listing 7.1.

Listing 7.1   **Use the Win32 API CreateFile() Function to Open the Serial Port**

```
// Function used to create or open a file or other object including
// ports, consoles, mailslots, pipes, and disk devices. It returns a
// handle you can use to create a file stream. Make sure you always
// use the FileStream object whenever possible because this function
// is more complex.
[DllImport("Kernel32.DLL")]
public static extern IntPtr CreateFile(
    String                  lpFileName,
    DesiredAccess           dwDesiredAccess,
    ShareMode               dwShareMode,
    IntPtr                  NoSecurityAttributes,
```

```
        CreationDisposition   dwCreationDisposition,
        FlagsAndAttributes    dwFlagsAndAttributes,
        IntPtr                NoTemplateFile);

// This enumeration defines the level of desired access. The
// enumeration contains a special member for querying the
// device without accessing it.
public enum DesiredAccess : uint
{
    QueryDeviceOnly             = 0,
    GENERIC_READ                = 0x80000000,
    GENERIC_WRITE               = 0x40000000,
    GENERIC_EXECUTE             = 0x20000000,
    GENERIC_ALL                 = 0x10000000,
    DELETE                      = 0x00010000,
    READ_CONTROL                = 0x00020000,
    WRITE_DAC                   = 0x00040000,
    WRITE_OWNER                 = 0x00080000,
    SYNCHRONIZE                 = 0x00100000,
    STANDARD_RIGHTS_REQUIRED    = 0x000F0000,
    STANDARD_RIGHTS_READ        = READ_CONTROL,
    STANDARD_RIGHTS_WRITE       = READ_CONTROL,
    STANDARD_RIGHTS_EXECUTE     = READ_CONTROL,
    STANDARD_RIGHTS_ALL         = 0x001F0000,
    SPECIFIC_RIGHTS_ALL         = 0x0000FFFF,
    ACCESS_SYSTEM_SECURITY      = 0x01000000,
    MAXIMUM_ALLOWED             = 0x02000000
}

// This enumeration defines the type of sharing to support. It
// includes a special member for no sharing at all.
public enum ShareMode
{
    NotShared          = 0,
    FILE_SHARE_READ    = 0x00000001,
    FILE_SHARE_WRITE   = 0x00000002,
    FILE_SHARE_DELETE  = 0x00000004
}

// This enumeration defines how the call will treat files or
// other objects that already exist. You must provide one of
// these values as input.
public enum CreationDisposition
{
    CREATE_NEW          = 1,
    CREATE_ALWAYS       = 2,
    OPEN_EXISTING       = 3,
    OPEN_ALWAYS         = 4,
    TRUNCATE_EXISTING   = 5
}
```

```csharp
// This enumeration defines additional flags and attributes the
// call will use when opening an object. This enumeration contains
// a special value for no flags or attributes.
public enum FlagsAndAttributes : uint
{
    None                                = 0,
    FILE_ATTRIBUTE_READONLY             = 0x00000001,
    FILE_ATTRIBUTE_HIDDEN               = 0x00000002,
    FILE_ATTRIBUTE_SYSTEM               = 0x00000004,
    FILE_ATTRIBUTE_ARCHIVE              = 0x00000020,
    FILE_ATTRIBUTE_NORMAL               = 0x00000080,
    FILE_ATTRIBUTE_TEMPORARY            = 0x00000100,
    FILE_ATTRIBUTE_OFFLINE              = 0x00001000,
    FILE_ATTRIBUTE_NOT_CONTENT_INDEXED  = 0x00002000,
    FILE_ATTRIBUTE_ENCRYPTED            = 0x00004000,
    FILE_FLAG_WRITE_THROUGH             = 0x80000000,
    FILE_FLAG_OVERLAPPED                = 0x40000000,
    FILE_FLAG_NO_BUFFERING              = 0x20000000,
    FILE_FLAG_RANDOM_ACCESS             = 0x10000000,
    FILE_FLAG_SEQUENTIAL_SCAN           = 0x08000000,
    FILE_FLAG_DELETE_ON_CLOSE           = 0x04000000,
    FILE_FLAG_BACKUP_SEMANTICS          = 0x02000000,
    FILE_FLAG_POSIX_SEMANTICS           = 0x01000000,
    FILE_FLAG_OPEN_REPARSE_POINT        = 0x00200000,
    FILE_FLAG_OPEN_NO_RECALL            = 0x00100000,
    SECURITY_ANONYMOUS                  = 0x00000000,
    SECURITY_IDENTIFICATION             = 0x00010000,
    SECURITY_IMPERSONATION              = 0x00020000,
    SECURITY_DELEGATION                 = 0x00030000,
    SECURITY_CONTEXT_TRACKING           = 0x00040000,
    SECURITY_EFFECTIVE_ONLY             = 0x00080000
}

// This constant value helps check for a bad handle.
public const int INVALID_HANDLE_VALUE = -1;

// This function closes most Windows handles, including
// all of the handles returned by the CreateFile() function.
[DllImport("Kernel32.DLL")]
public static extern bool CloseHandle(IntPtr hObject);

// The handle obtained using CreateFile().
IntPtr      FileHandle;

// The object used to access the serial port.
FileStream  FS;

private void btnTest_Click(object sender, System.EventArgs e)
{
    if (btnTest.Text == "Open")
    {
        // Open the serial port for use.
```

```
        FileHandle = CreateFile(
           cbModemSelect.Text,
           DesiredAccess.GENERIC_READ | DesiredAccess.GENERIC_WRITE,
           ShareMode.NotShared,
           IntPtr.Zero,
           CreationDisposition.OPEN_EXISTING,
           FlagsAndAttributes.None,
           IntPtr.Zero);

        // Verify we have a good handle.
        if (FileHandle.ToInt32() == INVALID_HANDLE_VALUE)
        {
           MessageBox.Show("Can't open the serial port, " +
              "make sure it's installed and not in use.",
              "Serial Port Error",
              MessageBoxButtons.OK,
              MessageBoxIcon.Error);
           return;
        }

        // Open a stream based on the serial port.
        FS = new FileStream(FileHandle, FileAccess.ReadWrite);

        // Display a success message.
        MessageBox.Show("Serial port is open!",
                        "Serial Port Success",
                        MessageBoxButtons.OK,
                        MessageBoxIcon.Information);

        // Change the test button caption.
        btnTest.Text = "Close";

        // Enable the Test Modem button.
        btnTestModem.Enabled = true;
     }
     else
     {
        // Close the serial port handle.
        if (CloseHandle(FileHandle))
           MessageBox.Show("Serial port is closed.",
                           "Serial Port Success",
                           MessageBoxButtons.OK,
                           MessageBoxIcon.Information);

        // Change the test button caption.
        btnTest.Text = "Open";

        // Disable the Test Modem button.
        btnTestModem.Enabled = false;
     }
  }
```

```csharp
private void btnTestModem_Click(object sender, System.EventArgs e)
{
    byte  []Input;      // The input byte array.
    byte  []Output;     // The output byte array.
    char  []Temp;       // A temporary character array.
    int   Counter;      // Loop counter.

    // Place the input string into the temporary char array.
    Temp = txtInput.Text.ToCharArray();

    // Size the Input and Output byte arrays.
    Input = new byte[txtInput.Text.Length + 2];
    Output = new byte[4096];

    // Convert the temporary char array to a byte array.
    for (Counter = 0; Counter < txtInput.Text.Length; Counter++)
       Input[Counter] = Convert.ToByte(Temp[Counter]);

    // Add a return to the output.
    Input[Counter] = 10;
    Input[Counter + 1] = 13;

    // Write the data to the file stream.
    FS.Write(Input, 0, Input.Length);

    // Read the result from the file stream.
    FS.Read(Output, 0, Output.Length);

    // Convert the byte array to a temporary char array.
    Counter = 2;
    Temp = new char[4096];
    while ((Output[Counter] != 0) && Counter < 4095)
    {
       Temp[Counter - 2] = Convert.ToChar(Output[Counter]);
       Counter++;
    }

    // Display the result on screen.
    txtOutput.Text = new String(Temp);
}
```

The CreateFile() function is somewhat unforgiving, complicated to use, and prone to providing esoteric feedback. The example code reduces the complexity of the CreateFile() function by using as many enumerations as possible as input. The use of enumerations at least guarantees the input arguments are valid. However, notice the number of exceptions made for .NET within the enumerations. For example, the DesiredAccess enumeration contains a special value for querying the device—a value not provided with the C/C++ headers. If you use enumerations, make sure you also include the special documented values for the argument.

Some of the enumerations for this example get rather lengthy. Adding to the complexity of using the `CreateFile()` function is the fact that not every enumerated value works with every type of object. For example, you wouldn't want to use the `CreationDisposition.CREATE_NEW` value when working with a device because you can't create a new device. The `Creation-Disposition.CREATE_NEW` value is normally used with files. It's tempting to remove enumerated values that you think you'll never use, but this could lead to problems down the road as other developers use your code. The enumerated values you never use might be the ones the other developer requires for a special purpose.

It's essential that you rely on a combination of the Platform SDK documentation and the C/C++ header files when creating your Win32 API calls (as well as some intuition on how the .NET application environment will react). The C/C++ header files define other `FILE_ATTRIBUTE` values, in this case, but they're not safe to use because they don't appear within the Platform SDK documentation and there's no overriding reason to experiment with them. Even though the C/C++ header contains the following `FILE_ATTRIBUTE` values, you won't find them in the example code.

```
#define FILE_ATTRIBUTE_DIRECTORY        0x00000010
#define FILE_ATTRIBUTE_DEVICE           0x00000040
#define FILE_ATTRIBUTE_SPARSE_FILE      0x00000200
#define FILE_ATTRIBUTE_REPARSE_POINT    0x00000400
#define FILE_ATTRIBUTE_COMPRESSED       0x00000800
```

We also have another Visual C++ macro problem in this example. Four of the values are actual macros, not defines. There are situations when you'll have to make a choice between precise accuracy and the needs of your application. Consequently, the four macro values shown in the following code are transformed into actual values.

```
#define SECURITY_ANONYMOUS       ( SecurityAnonymous      << 16 )
#define SECURITY_IDENTIFICATION  ( SecurityIdentification << 16 )
#define SECURITY_IMPERSONATION   ( SecurityImpersonation  << 16 )
#define SECURITY_DELEGATION      ( SecurityDelegation     << 16 )
```

This is one case where there's a minimum potential for problems in converting from a macro value. The other `SECURITY` values are included as actual values and the converted forms follow in sequence as you might expect. However, you need to exercise care in handling macros to ensure you don't end up with something that won't work later—Microsoft has a habit of changing its mind. The `btnTest_Click()` function is the first one that the user will access. It either opens or closes the selected serial port based on the current button caption. Opening a device requires the name of the device and the level of access (read, write, or both). Generally, you won't want to share a device with another application, so one of the special enumerations tells Windows not to allow sharing. Finally, the code must specify `CreationDisposition.OPEN_EXISTING` because an application can't create a new device.

The next step is to check the handle returned by CreateFile(). If the handle is set to INVALID_HANDLE_VALUE, you can't use it. You'll normally receive a bad handle if the serial port doesn't exist or another application is using it. Don't attempt to open a file stream if you receive a bad handle.

Finally, the code opens the file stream using the handle returned by CreateFile(). Notice that you still have to specify a FileAccess value. The FileAccess value must match the level of access you requested from CreateFile() or the application will report strange (and non-reproducible) errors.

Closing the serial port once you've finished using it is easy. Simply use the CloseHandle() function. This Win32 API function works with a number of handle types, including all of the handles that CreateFile() can return. It's important to verify that the serial port is actually closed. There are situations when the device driver is waiting for status or other information and won't close immediately. If your application shuts down without closing the port, the user will have to reboot, in most cases, to close it. The example displays a simple success message, but generally you'll want to provide some level of error trapping as well in a production application.

The btnTestModem_Click() method is only active when the serial port is open. The FileStream object only accepts a byte array as input (or a reasonable facsimile). Unfortunately, the TextBox controls used by the example only handle strings. They also provide conversions for char arrays, which won't work with the FileStream object either. The example shows one of several ways you can convert text to a byte array and back. The biggest issue, in this case, is to ensure the buffers you use are large enough. Otherwise, the application might fail due to a buffer overflow. Figure 7.2 shows typical output from this application. You can use any of the AT commands supported by your modem for testing (although the ATI commands provide informational output that's easy to validate).

FIGURE 7.2:

The example application enables you to check the status of your modem using AT commands.

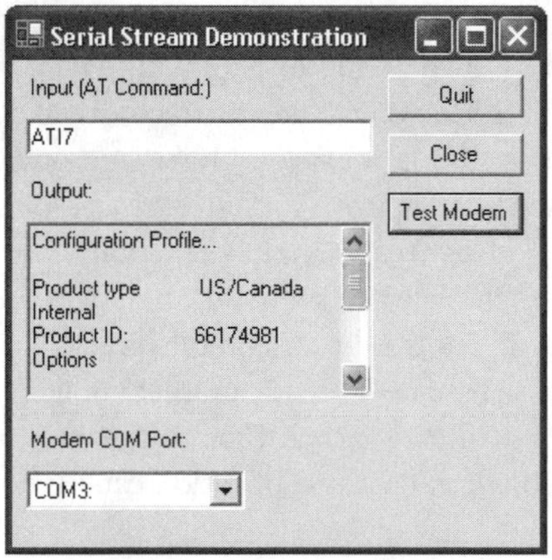

Determining the Port Status

The Win32 API provides a wealth of functions that help you determine the current serial port and modem status. For example, you can use the GetCommConfig() function to determine the modem provider status as well as obtain device control block (DCB) information about the attached device. Each of the functions uses a special structure you need to include with the function call. In some cases, you'll find there are structures within structures. The COMMCONFIG data structure used with the GetCommConfig() function includes a DCB structure that's also used with the GetCommState() function.

This example shows how to obtain the current port status and display the information on screen. You'll need this information to determine facts about the serial port in question, such as the availability of a modem (some functions return more information when a modem is attached to the serial port). Listing 7.2 shows the code for this example. You'll find the source code for this example in the \Chapter 07\C#\Serial2 and \Chapter 07\VB\Serial2 folders on the CD. Note that this code isn't complete—I've used code from the preceding example to open and close the port. The complete code appears on the CD.

Listing 7.2   A Common Port Status Function is GetCommState()

```
// This function returns the current control settings for the
// specified communications device.
[DllImport("Kernel32.DLL")]
public static extern bool GetCommState(IntPtr hFile,
                                       ref DCB dcb);

// This structure contains the control settings.
[StructLayout(LayoutKind.Sequential, Pack=1)]
public struct DCB
{
    public Int32    DCBlength;
    public Int32    BaudRate;

    // This entire section consists of flags. Each flag
    // consumes a specific number of bits. The entire
    // flag is a UInt32 value.
    // public UInt32   fBinary;              // 1 bit
    // public UInt32   fParity;              // 1 bit
    // public UInt32   fOutxCtsFlow;         // 1 bit
    // public UInt32   fOutxDsrFlow;         // 1 bit
    // public UInt32   fDtrControl;          // 2 bits
    // public UInt32   fDsrSensitivity;      // 1 bit
    // public UInt32   fTXContinueOnXoff;    // 1 bit
    // public UInt32   fOutX;                // 1 bit
    // public UInt32   fInX;                 // 1 bit
    // public UInt32   fErrorChar;           // 1 bit
    // public UInt32   fNull;                // 1 bit
```

```
    // public UInt32    fRtsControl;        // 2 bits
    // public UInt32    fAbortOnError;      // 1 bit
    // public UInt32    fDummy2;            // 17 bits
    public UInt32  Flags;

    public Int16   wReserved;
    public Int16   XonLim;
    public Int16   XoffLim;
    public Byte    ByteSize;
    public Byte    Parity;
    public Byte    StopBits;
    public Char    XonChar;
    public Char    XoffChar;
    public Char    ErrorChar;
    public Char    EofChar;
    public Char    EvtChar;
    public Int16   wReserved1;
}

// This enumeration helps determine the flag
// values returned in the DCB structure.
public enum SeeFlags
{
    Binary           = 0x0001,    // 1 bit
    Parity           = 0x0002,    // 1 bit
    OutxCtsFlow      = 0x0004,    // 1 bit
    OutxDsrFlow      = 0x0008,    // 1 bit
    DtrControl       = 0x0010,    // 2 bits
    DsrSensitivity   = 0x0040,    // 1 bit
    TXContinueOnXoff = 0x0080,    // 1 bit
    OutX             = 0x0100,    // 1 bit
    InX              = 0x0200,    // 1 bit
    ErrorChar        = 0x0400,    // 1 bit
    Null             = 0x0800,    // 1 bit
    RtsControl       = 0x1000,    // 2 bits
    AbortOnError     = 0x4000,    // 1 bit
    Dummy2           = 0x8000,    // 17 bits

    // These special flag values handle the
    // two bit flags.
    DTR_CONTROL_DISABLE    = 0x0000, // 0x00 in C header
    DTR_CONTROL_ENABLE     = 0x0010, // 0x01 in C header
    DTR_CONTROL_HANDSHAKE  = 0x0020, // 0x02 in C header
    RTS_CONTROL_DISABLE    = 0x0000, // 0x00 in C header
    RTS_CONTROL_ENABLE     = 0x1000, // 0x01 in C header
    RTS_CONTROL_HANDSHAKE  = 0x2000, // 0x02 in C header
    RTS_CONTROL_TOGGLE     = 0x3000  // 0x03 in C header
}

// This enumeration determines the parity type.
public enum CommParity
```

```
{
   NOPARITY          = 0,
   ODDPARITY         = 1,
   EVENPARITY        = 2,
   MARKPARITY        = 3,
   SPACEPARITY       = 4
}

// This enumeration determines the number of stop bits.
public enum CommStopBits
{
   ONESTOPBIT        = 0,
   ONE5STOPBITS      = 1,
   TWOSTOPBITS       = 2
}

private void btnTest_Click(object sender, System.EventArgs e)
{
   DCB             DevInfo; // The device status information.
   StringBuilder   SB;      // Converted status data.
   Int32           SpecChr; // The special character conversion.

   // Open the communications port.
   if (!CommOpen())
   {
      MessageBox.Show("Can't open the serial port, " +
                    "make sure it's installed and not in use.",
                    "Serial Port Error",
                    MessageBoxButtons.OK,
                    MessageBoxIcon.Error);
      return;
   }

   // Initialize the DCB.
   DevInfo = new DCB();

   // Get the current control status.
   if (!GetCommState(FileHandle, ref DevInfo))
      MessageBox.Show("Couldn't retrieve the device control block.",
                    "Status Error",
                    MessageBoxButtons.OK,
                    MessageBoxIcon.Error);

   // Fill the StringBuilder with data.
   SB = new StringBuilder();
   SB.Append("Baud Rate = " + DevInfo.BaudRate.ToString());

   // The single bit flags require special handling.
   if ((DevInfo.Flags & (UInt32)SeeFlags.Binary)
      == (UInt32)SeeFlags.Binary)
      SB.Append("\r\nBinary Transfer Enabled");
```

```
if ((DevInfo.Flags & (UInt32)SeeFlags.Parity)
   == (UInt32)SeeFlags.Parity)
   SB.Append("\r\nParity Checking Enabled");
if ((DevInfo.Flags & (UInt32)SeeFlags.OutxCtsFlow)
   == (UInt32)SeeFlags.OutxCtsFlow)
   SB.Append("\r\nClear to Send (CTS) Signal is Monitored");
if ((DevInfo.Flags & (UInt32)SeeFlags.OutxDsrFlow)
   == (UInt32)SeeFlags.OutxDsrFlow)
   SB.Append("\r\nData Set Ready (DSR) Signal is Monitored");
if ((DevInfo.Flags & (UInt32)SeeFlags.DsrSensitivity)
   == (UInt32)SeeFlags.DsrSensitivity)
   SB.Append("\r\nCommunications Driver DSR Sensitive");
if ((DevInfo.Flags & (UInt32)SeeFlags.TXContinueOnXoff)
   == (UInt32)SeeFlags.TXContinueOnXoff)
   SB.Append("\r\nData Transfer Continues With Full Input Buffer");
if ((DevInfo.Flags & (UInt32)SeeFlags.OutX)
   == (UInt32)SeeFlags.OutX)
   SB.Append("\r\nXON/XOFF Enabled During Transmission");
if ((DevInfo.Flags & (UInt32)SeeFlags.InX)
   == (UInt32)SeeFlags.InX)
   SB.Append("\r\nXON/XOFF Enabled During Reception");
if ((DevInfo.Flags & (UInt32)SeeFlags.ErrorChar)
   == (UInt32)SeeFlags.ErrorChar)
   SB.Append("\r\nBytes with Errors Replaced with Error Character");
if ((DevInfo.Flags & (UInt32)SeeFlags.Null)
   == (UInt32)SeeFlags.Null)
   SB.Append("\r\nNULL Bytes Discarded When Received");
if ((DevInfo.Flags & (UInt32)SeeFlags.AbortOnError)
   == (UInt32)SeeFlags.AbortOnError)
   SB.Append("\r\nRead/Write Operation Aborted After an Error");

// Process the DTR two-bit flag
if ((DevInfo.Flags & (UInt32)SeeFlags.DTR_CONTROL_ENABLE)
   == (UInt32)SeeFlags.DTR_CONTROL_ENABLE)
   SB.Append("\r\nData Terminal Ready (DTR) Handling Enabled");
else
   if ((DevInfo.Flags & (UInt32)SeeFlags.DTR_CONTROL_HANDSHAKE)
   == (UInt32)SeeFlags.DTR_CONTROL_HANDSHAKE)
   SB.Append("\r\nData Terminal Ready (DTR) Hand Shaking Enabled");
else
   SB.Append("\r\nData Terminal Ready (DTR) Handling Disabled");

// Process the RTS two-bit flag.
if ((DevInfo.Flags & (UInt32)SeeFlags.RTS_CONTROL_ENABLE)
   == (UInt32)SeeFlags.RTS_CONTROL_ENABLE)
   SB.Append("\r\nReady to Send (RTS) Handling Enabled");
else
   if ((DevInfo.Flags & (UInt32)SeeFlags.RTS_CONTROL_HANDSHAKE)
   == (UInt32)SeeFlags.RTS_CONTROL_HANDSHAKE)
   SB.Append("\r\nReady to Send (RTS) Hand Shaking Enabled");
else
```

```csharp
    if ((DevInfo.Flags & (UInt32)SeeFlags.RTS_CONTROL_TOGGLE)
    == (UInt32)SeeFlags.RTS_CONTROL_TOGGLE)
    SB.Append("\r\nReady to Send (RTS) High When Data Available");
else
    SB.Append("\r\nReady to Send (RTS) Handling Disabled");

// Process the remaining data fields.
SB.Append("\r\nXON Character Limit: " +
    DevInfo.XonLim.ToString());
SB.Append("\r\nXOFF Character Limit: " +
    DevInfo.XoffLim.ToString());
SB.Append("\r\nByte Size: " +
    DevInfo.ByteSize.ToString());

// Determine the parity type.
switch (DevInfo.Parity)
{
    case (byte)CommParity.EVENPARITY:
        SB.Append("\r\nUsing Even Parity");
        break;
    case (byte)CommParity.MARKPARITY:
        SB.Append("\r\nUsing Mark Parity");
        break;
    case (byte)CommParity.NOPARITY:
        SB.Append("\r\nUsing No Parity");
        break;
    case (byte)CommParity.ODDPARITY:
        SB.Append("\r\nUsing Odd Parity");
        break;
    case (byte)CommParity.SPACEPARITY:
        SB.Append("\r\nUsing Space Parity");
        break;
    default:
        SB.Append("\r\nCouldn't Determine the Parity");
        break;
}

// Determine the number of stop bits.
switch (DevInfo.StopBits)
{
    case (byte)CommStopBits.ONESTOPBIT:
        SB.Append("\r\nUsing 1 Stop Bit");
        break;
    case (byte)CommStopBits.ONE5STOPBITS:
        SB.Append("\r\nUsing 1.5 Stop Bits");
        break;
    case (byte)CommStopBits.TWOSTOPBITS:
        SB.Append("\r\nUsing 2 Stop Bits");
        break;
    default:
        SB.Append("\r\nCouldn't Determine the Number of Stop Bits");
```

```
        break;
    }

    // List the special characters.
    SpecChr = Convert.ToInt32(DevInfo.XonChar);
    SB.Append("\r\nThe XON Character is: " +
        SpecChr.ToString());
    SpecChr = Convert.ToInt32(DevInfo.XoffChar);
    SB.Append("\r\nThe XOFF Character is: " +
        SpecChr.ToString());
    SpecChr = Convert.ToInt32(DevInfo.ErrorChar);
    SB.Append("\r\nThe Error Character is: " +
        SpecChr.ToString());
    SpecChr = Convert.ToInt32(DevInfo.EofChar);
    SB.Append("\r\nThe End of Data Character is: " +
        SpecChr.ToString());
    SpecChr = Convert.ToInt32(DevInfo.EvtChar);
    SB.Append("\r\nThe Event Character is: " +
        SpecChr.ToString());

    // Display the information on screen.
    txtOutput.Text = SB.ToString();

    // Close the communications port.
    if (!CommClose())
        MessageBox.Show("Can't close the serial port, " +
                        "make sure it's not in use.",
                        "Serial Port Error",
                        MessageBoxButtons.OK,
                        MessageBoxIcon.Error);

}
```

There are some interesting new concepts to learn in this example. For example, the Get-CommState() function declaration is deceptively simple. All you have to supply are two arguments—what could be simpler? However, the reality is that the complexity of this call is hidden in the DCB structure. Hidden complexity is a common theme throughout the Win32 API calls. Many of the really interesting functions require construction of complex data structures that might contain information derived from other calls, which makes the supposedly simple call quite complicated.

The DCB structure has a feature we haven't really had to work with in the past—a flag data element. The commented text shows the various flag values. However, it's important to note that they appear as DWORD values in the Platform SDK documentation. Your only clue that these values are all part of a single DWORD value is the "f" in front of each value. Fortunately, the majority of the flags consume a single bit, which makes them easier to interpret than multiple-bit flags. All you need to perform is a simple comparison (as we'll see later in this example).

Single-bit flags are problematic, but easily handled with special enumerations that you compare to the flag value individually. The two-bit flag values for RTS and DTR present special problems. If you look in the C/C++ header files, you'll notice that these values are defined as shown here.

```
//
// DTR Control Flow Values.
//
#define DTR_CONTROL_DISABLE    0x00
#define DTR_CONTROL_ENABLE     0x01
#define DTR_CONTROL_HANDSHAKE  0x02

//
// RTS Control Flow Values
//
#define RTS_CONTROL_DISABLE    0x00
#define RTS_CONTROL_ENABLE     0x01
#define RTS_CONTROL_HANDSHAKE  0x02
#define RTS_CONTROL_TOGGLE     0x03
```

The problem with these values is that they assume you have isolated the two-bit values and are looking at them as individual values. Unfortunately, our flag is a single 32-bit value that contains the values in bit positions other than the starting bits, so we have to offset the values. That's where the special two-bit field values come from in the code. These values represent that DTR and RTS values as they actually appear to C#, rather than to a Visual C++ application. The SeeFlags enumeration contains the translated values so you can see how to put them together. Unfortunately, you'll have to put these flag enumerations together yourself—the Platform SDK won't offer any help in this area.

TIP   There are times when an enumeration is actually superfluous. For example, the Platform SDK documentation provides a listing of indexes for the *BaudRate* field of the DCB structure. However, the enumerated values are the same as the baud rate. Unless you have some reason to include the enumeration, using the *BaudRate* field as returned from the GetCommConfig() function will work best.

The code begins with a call to CommOpen() and ends with a call to CommClose(). These functions aren't special Win32 API calls that I forgot to document—they're special implementations of the code found in Listing 7.1. The CommOpen() function opens the serial port selected on the dialog box, while the CommClose() function closes the serial port. These two functions represent a partial generalization of the code and you could easily place it within a DLL for use with any application you might create.

In past examples, the code set the individual values of the data structures—a perfectly valid method for making a Win32 API call. In this example the *DevInfo* variable is set to a new instance of the DCB structure. This second method for initializing a structure assumes a default value for each structure member (such as 0 for numeric values). This second method works better in cases where you plan to call a function to obtain default values because you don't need to worry about setting each structure member individually.

TIP   The code uses a StringBuilder object, *SB*, to hold the port status information. You'll find that this technique uses fewer system resources and gives your application a performance boost.

Many of the *DevInfo* structure members are easy to display. All you have to do is convert the member to a string. However, this technique only works for the integer members of the structure, we also have flag, byte, and char members to consider in this case, so the code uses a variety of techniques for conversion purposes.

As you can see, the single bit flags require a simple comparison. You and the flag bit with the appropriate SeeFlags enumeration member, and then verify the setting of that bit. A value of 1 indicates a true value in most cases. The code then adds a new string element to *SB* that shows the enabled status of the flag.

Checking the status of the two-bit flags requires several comparisons. One of the key techniques is to perform all of the comparisons that include at least one set bit. This makes the comparison code easier to create. If you perform all of the comparisons with at least one bit set and none of them match, it's usually safe to assume that none of the bits are set and act accordingly.

The *DevInfo.Parity* and *DevInfo.StopBits* members are both byte values. As shown in the code, you can use a simple enumeration combined with a switch structure to determine their value. The only caveat is that you must translate the enumerated value to a byte value.

The final set of values in *DevInfo* is the special characters used to signify special events in the data stream. All five of these values are of type char, which means you'll need to convert them into something you can display on screen. The problem is that the default value for the special characters is a 0, which also signifies an end of string character. The best approach, in this case, is to perform a two-step conversion. Change the char into an Int32, and then convert the resulting number into a string. Figure 7.3 shows the output from this example.

Port Status Demonstration

Port Status Information:

```
Baud Rate = 115200
Binary Transfer Enabled
Clear to Send (CTS) Signal is Monitored
Data Terminal Ready (DTR) Handling Enabled
Ready to Send (RTS) Hand Shaking Enabled
XON Character Limit: 2048
XOFF Character Limit: 512
Byte Size: 8
Using No Parity
Using 1 Stop Bit
The XON Character is: 17
```

Quit

Test

Modem COM Port:

COM3:

Parallel Port Access Examples

One of the problems with working with the Win32 API is that it's like an onion—there are several layers of code between the developer and the device. At the lowest level is a device driver that relies on IOCTL (input/output control) functions and direct hardware manipulation. Generally, it's a good idea to leave the device driver writing to vendors who have the required expertise.

Unfortunately, as you move up the layers of code, Microsoft makes assumptions about the hardware that might not match the realities of your system. That's what happens in the case of the parallel port—Microsoft assumes that you'll want to attach a printer to it and doesn't provide much functionality in Windows to do anything else with the parallel port. Consequently, if you want to do something special with the parallel port, you'll either have to rely on low-level commands or use a third-party library to gain the required access. Of course, some parallel port peripherals are just like other types of devices that you normally find within the PC and you can therefore access them using the same technique. For example, you access a tape drive the same way whether it's connected internally or relies on a parallel port connection.

Interestingly enough, the printer is one of the devices that don't have a specific DLL in the \System32 folder. The functions used to access a printer appear in the WinSpool.LIB file, which means you must write a wrapper DLL in Visual C++ to use the printer-specific functions. This fact opens some possibilities for creating special functions that are easy to use, but it also increases the complexity of the application as a whole.

Many developers are interested in the problems of accessing hardware using .NET. You can find some interesting examples online in some cases. For example, you'll find an interesting example of how to interact with an X.10 (home automation) network at `http://www.gotdotnet.com/userfiles/gbrinkmann/X10%20Firecracker%20Interface.zip`. Another place to look for good example code is Lutz Roeder's Programming .NET site at `http://www.aisto.com/roeder/dotnet/`.

The two examples in this section show how to work with a printer connected to the parallel port. While the .NET Framework provides a wealth of functions for sending data to the printer, it doesn't provide anything to obtain printer status information. Consequently, your application could experience an error and you wouldn't know that the printer was simply out of paper.

There are a number of functions you can use to obtain printer status information. For example, you can use the `GetPrinterDataEx()` function to retrieve a single specific bit of information such as the default spool directory. The main function is `GetPrinter()`, which relies on a host of data structures to tell you everything from the printer name, to the provider setup, to the current printer status, including the condition of the paper tray. Of course, the printer has to provide the information you need. Most laser printers provide a wealth of information about their status, but you might find other types of printers lacking in some areas.

Creating the Wrapper DLL

The wrapper DLL does most of the work of retrieving the printer information from the Win32 API in this case. There are times when you'll need to write much of your Win32 API access code with the wrapper, instead of the application, in mind. In this case, the functionality needed to access the printer appears in a library, so it makes sense to create a function that will perform a specific sequence of steps. Listing 7.3 shows the code to access the first-level printer information. The second-level printer access is about the same, so Listing 7.3 shows only the first level (we'll discuss the second-level data structure in the "Viewing the Second Level of Printer Information" section of the chapter). You'll find the source code for this portion of the example in the `\Chapter 07\PrinterAccess` folder on the CD.

Listing 7.3   **The Wrapper Code Performs Most of the Work in this Example**

```
// This is the Level1 data structure.
__gc struct PrinterInfo1
{
    UInt32   Flags;
    String   *pDescription;
    String   *pName;
```

```
    String    *pComment;
};

static bool GetPrinterLevel1Data(String* PrinterName,
                                 PrinterInfo1 **PI1)
{
    LPTSTR          Name;               // The printer name.
    HANDLE          hPrinter = NULL;    // Open printer handle.
    PRINTER_INFO_1  *PrnInfo;           // Printer information buffer.
    DWORD           dwSize = 0;         // Actual buffer size.
    bool            ReturnVal = true;   // Determines the return value.

    // Convert the string.
    Name =
        (LPTSTR)Marshal::StringToHGlobalAnsi(PrinterName).ToPointer();

    // Attempt to open the printer without any special defaults.
    if (!OpenPrinter(Name, &hPrinter, NULL))
    {
        // An error has occured.
        // Free the memory allocated for the local pointer.
        Marshal::FreeHGlobal(Name);

        // Return a failure value.
        return false;
    }

    // Determine how big to make the data structure. If the printer
    // doesn't exist, the function will return 0.
    GetPrinter(hPrinter, 1, 0, 0, &dwSize);
    if (dwSize == 0)
    {
        ClosePrinter(hPrinter);
        return false;
    }

    // Allocate the required memory.  If we can't allocate the
    // memory, return a failure value.
    PrnInfo = (PRINTER_INFO_1 *)GlobalAlloc(GPTR, dwSize);
    if (!PrnInfo)
    {
        ClosePrinter(hPrinter);
        return false;
    }

    // Get the printer information.
    if (!GetPrinter(hPrinter,
                    1,
                    (LPBYTE)PrnInfo,
                    dwSize,
```

```
                        &dwSize))
        ReturnVal = false;

    // Transfer the data to the managed structure.
    PrinterInfo1 *Local = new PrinterInfo1();
    Local->Flags = PrnInfo->Flags;
    Local->pComment = new String(PrnInfo->pComment);
    Local->pDescription = new String(PrnInfo->pDescription);
    Local->pName = new String(PrnInfo->pName);
    *PI1 = Local;

    // Attempt to close the printer.
    if (!ClosePrinter(hPrinter))

        // If the attempt fails, return a failure value.
        ReturnVal = false;

    // Return a success value.
    return ReturnVal;
}
```

The first new element you'll notice is that the data structure appears in the wrapper code, rather than the Visual Basic or C# code in this case. It's easier to marshal the data from the unmanaged to the managed environment if you keep the structure in the wrapper code. In addition, using this method means you only have to write the wrapper code once—you can inherit it within the Visual Basic or C# code later.

This example shows how to convert a string into an unmanaged equivalent. The Marshal::StringToHGlobalAnsi() function produces an ANSI string. If you want a Unicode string, you'll need to use the Marshal::StringToHGlobalUni() function. In either case, you must free the global memory allocated by the function using the Marshal::FreeHGlobal() function. Because the garbage collector doesn't know about this memory, it won't free the memory for you.

The next point of interest is the two-step process used to allocate memory for the PRINTER_INFO_1 data structure, *PrnInfo*. The *PrnInfo* variable won't be the right size unless you allocate memory for it. However, the only way to find out how much memory to allocate is to call GetPrinter() without any buffer values. The *dwSize* variable returns with the amount of memory needed to store the printer information. You can then allocate the memory using GlobalAlloc(). Make sure you typecast the pointer returned by this function properly.

The second call to GetPrinter() returns the information you requested, but the information is in unmanaged variables. The code shows one technique for transferring the data from the unmanaged environment to the managed data structure passed by the calling function.

Notice the use of the *Local* intermediate variable. Using this technique will save you a lot of debugging time later because you can check the result of every data translation.

It may appear that the code is checking for trouble every step of the way. The fact is that the example code shows the minimum number of checks that your code should perform. Working with unsafe code means that a lot more can go wrong, and you need to verify that every step works as anticipated. In most cases, you'll want to add code for raising an exception (this is a managed DLL, after all) and provide the caller with detailed error information.

Viewing the First Level of Printer Information

The reason that so many developers use the GetPrinter() function is that it's very versatile, and you choose how much information to retrieve. The Platform SDK documentation specifies nine levels of information retrieval for this function—each of which requires a unique data structure. For the .NET developer this means that you'll need a minimum of nine overrides for the GetPrinter() function to create a full implementation. The example code shown in Listing 7.4 isn't quite that ambitious. It shows you the first level of the GetPrinter() function information. You'll find the source code for the first level of this example in the \Chapter 07\C#\Parallel1 and \Chapter 07\VB\Parallel1 folders on the CD.

Listing 7.4   **Obtaining the Printer Status is a Matter of Choosing an Information Level**

```
public enum PrintFlags
{
    PRINTER_ENUM_EXPAND      = 0x00004000,
    PRINTER_ENUM_CONTAINER   = 0x00008000,
    PRINTER_ENUM_ICON1       = 0x00010000,
    PRINTER_ENUM_ICON2       = 0x00020000,
    PRINTER_ENUM_ICON3       = 0x00040000,
    PRINTER_ENUM_ICON4       = 0x00080000,
    PRINTER_ENUM_ICON5       = 0x00100000,
    PRINTER_ENUM_ICON6       = 0x00200000,
    PRINTER_ENUM_ICON7       = 0x00400000,
    PRINTER_ENUM_ICON8       = 0x00800000
}

private void btnTest_Click(object sender, System.EventArgs e)
{
    // Create a structure to hold the printer data.
    Printer.PrinterInfo1 PI1 = new Printer.PrinterInfo1();

    // Create a StringBuilder to hold the results.
    StringBuilder      SB = new StringBuilder();

    // Query the printer.
    if (!Printer.GetPrinterLevel1Data(txtPrinterName.Text, ref PI1))
```

```
    {
        // If the printer query doesn't work, display an error.
        MessageBox.Show("Printer query failed.  It could" +
                    " be in use by another application.  Make sure" +
                    " the printer actually exists.",
                    "Printer Error",
                    MessageBoxButtons.OK,
                    MessageBoxIcon.Error);

        return;
    }

    // Interpret the string data.
    SB.Append("Name: " + PI1.pName);
    SB.Append("\r\nDescription: " + PI1.pDescription);
    SB.Append("\r\nComment: " + PI1.pComment);

    // Interpret the flags.
    if ((PI1.Flags & (UInt32)PrintFlags.PRINTER_ENUM_EXPAND)
        == (UInt32)PrintFlags.PRINTER_ENUM_EXPAND)
        SB.Append("\r\nThe provider has other objects to enumerate.");
    if ((PI1.Flags & (UInt32)PrintFlags.PRINTER_ENUM_CONTAINER)
        == (UInt32)PrintFlags.PRINTER_ENUM_CONTAINER)
        SB.Append("\r\nThis object contains other enumerable objects.");
    if ((PI1.Flags & (UInt32)PrintFlags.PRINTER_ENUM_ICON1)
        == (UInt32)PrintFlags.PRINTER_ENUM_ICON1)
        SB.Append("\r\nDisplay this object as a top level net name.");
    if ((PI1.Flags & (UInt32)PrintFlags.PRINTER_ENUM_ICON2)
        == (UInt32)PrintFlags.PRINTER_ENUM_ICON2)
        SB.Append("\r\nDisplay this object as a network domain.");
    if ((PI1.Flags & (UInt32)PrintFlags.PRINTER_ENUM_ICON3)
        == (UInt32)PrintFlags.PRINTER_ENUM_ICON3)
        SB.Append("\r\nDisplay this object as a printer server.");
    if ((PI1.Flags & (UInt32)PrintFlags.PRINTER_ENUM_ICON8)
        == (UInt32)PrintFlags.PRINTER_ENUM_ICON8)
        SB.Append("\r\nDisplay this object as a printer.");

    // Display the data on screen.
    txtOutput.Text = SB.ToString();
}
```

As you can see, the majority of this code is dedicated to displaying the data obtained with the wrapper DLL. The data structure is relatively simple, so there isn't much data to display. However, the level 1 data structure does provide the basic elements displayed by Explorer as shown in Figure 7.4. You should also notice that this code works with both local and network printers—there are times when the Win32 API requires separate handling of local and remote requests.

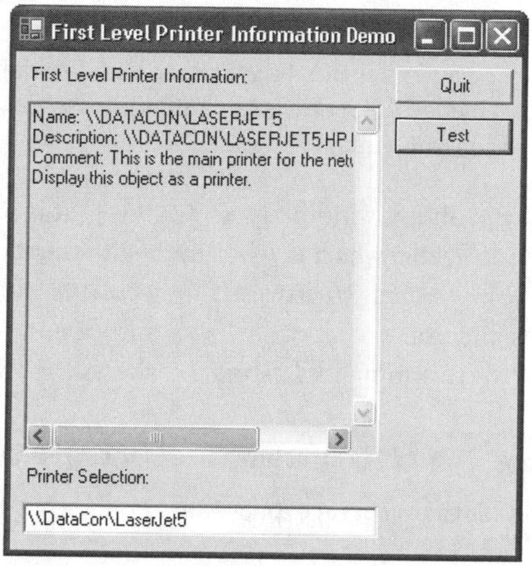

FIGURE 7.4:

The level 1 data
provides enough
feedback for a basic
Explorer display.

First Level Printer Information Demo

First Level Printer Information:

```
Name: \\DATACON\LASERJET5
Description: \\DATACON\LASERJET5,HP |
Comment: This is the main printer for the net
Display this object as a printer.
```

Quit

Test

Printer Selection:

\\DataCon\LaserJet5

NOTE　Many of the `GetPrinter()` function levels apply to specific versions of Windows. For example, levels 3 and 4 apply only to Windows NT, Windows 2000, and Windows XP. You can only use levels 7, 8, and 9 on a Windows 2000 or a Windows XP machine. The version specific nature of these levels means that you need to determine which version of Windows the user has installed before making the call or the application could crash. In addition, there's an undocumented level 6 that some developers have documented online, but a cautious developer would consider unsafe to use.

This data structure, like many other data structures in the book, contains a flag field. However, notice that the code doesn't check all of the flag values—it misses several of the icon flags. These flags are currently undocumented, even though the function sometimes returns a value for them. Rather than return what could be bad information to the user, it's often best to ignore flags marked reserved for future use.

Viewing the Second Level of Printer Information

If you thought the level 1 printer information was sparse, you'll be pleased by the level 2 information. You can find out almost every piece of information about the printer using the level 2 version of `GetPrinter()`. In fact, it's easy to go into information overload because this level provides everything from the printer name, to its security settings, to the printer statistics. For example, you can find out the current form type and the size of the paper use, as well as the number of pages the printer can output per minute.

NOTE   You'll find the source code for the second level of this example in the \Chapter 07\C#\
Parallel2 and \Chapter 07\VB\Parallel2 folders on the CD. Make sure you also view
the second-level wrapper DLL function and associated structures in the \Chapter 07\
PrinterAccess folder on the CD.

The only problem with the level 2 call is that it provides too much information for some
development needs, which is why Microsoft created the other levels. This level requires a
minimum of two data structures. The security information isn't required for most output
operations and you can ignore it as an output unless you intend to modify the security of the
printer. With this in mind, Listing 7.5 shows the two data structures used by the example.

Listing 7.5   **Data Structures Used for Level 2 GetPrinter() Calls**

```
// This data structure provide all of the device mode
// information.
__gc struct DeviceMode
{
    // There are no size declarations in a managed
    // structure. This entry is 32 chars long.
    //BCHAR    dmDeviceName[CCHDEVICENAME];
    Char      dmDeviceName[];

    UInt16    dmSpecVersion;
    UInt16    dmDriverVersion;
    UInt16    dmSize;
    UInt16    dmDriverExtra;
    UInt32    dmFields;

    // You can't include embedded unions and
    // structs within a managed struct. In addition,
    // the POINTL structure is useless because we're
    // working with printers. The following code
    // translates into four Int16 values.
    // union {
    //     struct {
    //         Int16 dmOrientation;
    //         Int16 dmPaperSize;
    //         Int16 dmPaperLength;
    //         Int16 dmPaperWidth;
    //     };
    //     POINTL dmPosition;
    // };
    Int16     dmOrientation;
    Int16     dmPaperSize;
    Int16     dmPaperLength;
    Int16     dmPaperWidth;
```

```
    Int16     dmScale;
    Int16     dmCopies;
    Int16     dmDefaultSource;
    Int16     dmPrintQuality;
    Int16     dmColor;
    Int16     dmDuplex;
    Int16     dmYResolution;
    Int16     dmTTOption;
    Int16     dmCollate;

    // This entry is 32 chars long.
    // BCHAR     dmFormName[CCHFORMNAME];
    Char      dmFormName[];

    UInt16    dmLogPixels;
    UInt32    dmBitsPerPel;
    UInt32    dmPelsWidth;
    UInt32    dmPelsHeight;

    // This was originally a union. It is replaced
    // with a single value.
    //union {
    //    UInt32  dmDisplayFlags;
    //    UInt32  dmNup;
    //}
    UInt32    dmDisplayFlagsOrdmNup;

    UInt32    dmDisplayFrequency;
    UInt32    dmICMMethod;
    UInt32    dmICMIntent;
    UInt32    dmMediaType;
    UInt32    dmDitherType;
    UInt32    dmReserved1;
    UInt32    dmReserved2;
    UInt32    dmPanningWidth;
    UInt32    dmPanningHeight;
};

// This is the level 2 data structure.
__gc struct PrinterInfo2
{
    String*     pServerName;
    String*     pPrinterName;
    String*     pShareName;
    String*     pPortName;
    String*     pDriverName;
    String*     pComment;
    String*     pLocation;
    DeviceMode* pDevMode;
    String*     pSepFile;
    String*     pPrintProcessor;
```

```
   String*      pDatatype;
   String*      pParameters;
   IntPtr       pSecurityDescriptor;
   UInt32       Attributes;
   UInt32       Priority;
   UInt32       DefaultPriority;
   UInt32       StartTime;
   UInt32       UntilTime;
   UInt32       Status;
   UInt32       cJobs;
   UInt32       AveragePPM;
};
```

As you can see, the data structures are somewhat large and complex. Adding the security descriptor information would easily double the amount of information you need to handle with this call. It's interesting to note that there are many Win32 API calls that fall into this category—translating the data structures becomes an exercise in typing.

The PrinterInfo2 data structure is the main data structure—it's the one you submit with the GetPrinter() function call. This data structure contains essentials such as the name of the printer and simple statistics such as the name of the separator page file. Except for the pointers to the DeviceMode and security descriptor data structures, this data structure is relatively straightforward.

The DeviceMode data structure contains detailed information about the printer. It's also a complex data structure that needs to be converted into something that .NET will understand. The first problem you run into is that a BCHAR isn't described anywhere in the Platform SDK documentation. It appears as part of several data structure descriptions, but Microsoft never tells you what a BCHAR is, so creating a .NET equivalent could prove cumbersome. This problem actually occurs more often than you might think, so it's important to know how to work around it. If you right click the BCHAR entry while in Visual C++, there's an option to Go to Definition in the context menu. Use this option to see how Microsoft has defined the BCHAR and you'll see that it's defined as a WCHAR, which is a documented type. Knowing this information tells you what a BCHAR is and how to present it as a .NET data type. In this case, I chose a Char array (make sure you use the .NET type, not the char C/C++ type).

TIP Remember that you can't define an array size in a managed array. If you see array elements that define a size in an unmanaged array, you must remove the size declaration.

During the translation of the DEVMODE data structure into a managed format, you'll be confronted with two unions and an embedded structure. The second union isn't much of a problem—all you need to do is translate it into a single value and code your application to check the flags for the correct value. However, the first union looks like this:

```
union {
    struct {
        short dmOrientation;
        short dmPaperSize;
        short dmPaperLength;
        short dmPaperWidth;
    };
    POINTL dmPosition;
};
```

When confronted with a structure as this, you need to remember the onion-like structure of Windows. Start from the outside and work your way in. The union enables the code to choose between an unnamed structure and a POINTL structure. It's important to remember that we're working with printers. The POINTL structure is designed for use with displays, not printers, so you can simply remove it and the associated union (now that there isn't any choice to make). The unnamed structure is also useless now because its original purpose was to keep the four data elements together. You end up with four *short* variables as shown in Listing 7.5.

At this point, you've converted the two essential data structures. Creating the GetPrinter-Level2Data() function is very similar to the GetPrinterLevel1Data() function described in the previous section. The string and numeric data transfers work the same as before, so I won't show the code here. The problem, in this case, is the BCHAR. You still need to transfer the BCHAR data from the PRINTER_INFO_2 data structure to the managed data structure. Unfortunately, the messages you receive from Visual C++ when working with this data type would lead you to believe that BCHAR is actually a BYTE data type, not a WCHAR data type. Here's the correct way to transfer the data from the unmanaged to the managed data structure.

```
// The BCHAR values require special handling.
Local->pDevMode->dmDeviceName = new Char[CCHDEVICENAME];
for (int Counter = 0; Counter < CCHDEVICENAME; Counter++)
    Local->pDevMode->dmDeviceName[Counter] =
    PrnInfo->pDevMode->dmDeviceName[Counter];

Local->pDevMode->dmFormName = new Char[CCHFORMNAME];
for (int Counter = 0; Counter < CCHFORMNAME; Counter++)
    Local->pDevMode->dmFormName[Counter] =
    PrnInfo->pDevMode->dmFormName[Counter];
```

As you can see, you need to size the char arrays before you use them. The constants that you couldn't use in the data structure come in handy for sizing the char arrays outside the data structure. You can also use the constants as part of the for loop used to transfer data between the two data structures. Using the constants as shown in the example ensures that any changes that Microsoft makes to the Win32 API won't affect your code—your code will automatically adjust. Figure 7.5 shows the output from this example.

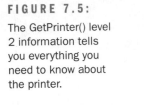

FIGURE 7.5:

The GetPrinter() level 2 information tells you everything you need to know about the printer.

Where Do You Go from Here?

This chapter has shown you some basic techniques for accessing your hardware from a .NET application. The examples in this chapter show various types of hardware access; they're not all the same. However, it's important to remember that this represents the worst-case scenario and you should always look for another way to perform the hardware access task. For example, you can use existing .NET Framework calls in a new way, rely on DirectX, or locate a COM component to perform the task. Still, there are times when you'll need to perform direct hardware access because no other method for accomplishing the task exists.

One of the first things you should do after reading this chapter is to begin assessing the hardware access needs for your development environment. If you're in a larger company, consider putting one or more programmers on a "hardware access" development team. This group should create wrapper DLLs to ensure you have the right access to your hardware when building .NET applications.

I consider hardware support one of the more glaring .NET Framework omissions. If you have a unique piece of hardware and would like to share your .NET access story with me, send me email at JMueller@mwt.net. If your story will help other developers, I'll publish it in

the .NET Developer eXTRA electronic newsletter that I write for Pinnacle (see `http://www`
`.freeenewsletters.com/` for details). If you need help with a unique device, I'll be more than
happy to do what I can to help.

Make sure you visit the Web sites I've provided in this chapter. You'll be surprised at the
number of hardware support sites that are available on the Internet. In some cases, you'll find
just the perfect component or the right access information to create a DLL of your own. It's
always worth your effort to pursue these leads because they can help reduce the total cost of
creating hardware access for your application when working with .NET.

Chapter 8 is one of the most important chapters in the book given the current development
environment. Securing your application is no longer a luxury—it's a requirement in a world
where crackers want to exercise control over your application and hopefully create havoc with
it. However, good security is helpful for another reason. A security audit of your application
also tends to show places where the application falls short in the reliability department. Learning to look at security from both a low and a high level can help you make your application
run better, faster, and longer than ever before. In short, Chapter 8 is your gateway to gaining
full access to the security features that Windows provides and could help you write better
applications in more ways than one.

CHAPTER 8

Overcoming Security Issues

- An Overview of Windows Security

- Using the Access Control Editor

- Using the Security Configuration Editor

- Understanding How .NET Role-Based Security Differs

- Looking Up an Account SID Example

- Using the `GetFileSecurity()` Function Example

- Working with ACEs Example

Security is an increasingly important issue for most developers because the developer is being made responsible for ensuring the safety of data produced by an application. The .NET Framework comes complete with some good security features that are easier to use than security features in the past. However, the security emphasized by the .NET Framework is role based—it emphasizes the role an object or user occupies when requesting data to a system resource. Some development scenarios work well with this new technology; others don't. For example, I can't imagine trying to create a massive Web application using token-based security—that type of project works best when you can define the roles that the users will fulfill.

Many developers are used to using the token-based security originally implemented in Windows NT. The token-based security uses a lock and key view of application security. In some cases, this view is actually easier to use and implement. For example, if you want to check the locks on an individual file or the keys owned by an individual user, then you'll need to use the older style of security.

This chapter doesn't answer the question of which security strategy is best for a given situation. However, it does provide you with the techniques for accessing both strategies from within a managed application. (We actually started this discussion with the AccessToken example found in Chapter 3.) We'll take a quick tour of the two security strategies and then look at several examples of how you can implement the older token-based security strategy in a .NET application.

NOTE   This chapter provides a quick overview of the .NET role-based security model for comparison purposes. It doesn't provide any complete role-based security examples because you can create them using standard .NET language calls. You'll find a few code snippets that demonstrate differences between token-based and role-based security. You'll find examples of the standard .NET language calls in my book *Visual C# .NET Developer's Handbook* (Sybex, 2002).

An Overview of Windows Security

The Windows security API is vast and performs many functions within the operating system and the applications it supports. Unfortunately, understanding the security portion of the Win32 API is about as easy learning a new language while performing a handstand. It's not that the concept is so difficult to understand. The difficulty most developers have is getting the essentials they need from the vast supply of documentation that Microsoft provides—much of which is written in securityspeak. The most important purpose of this section of the chapter is to provide you with Win32 API–based security information without all of the mumbo jumbo.

We're going to talk about two essential topics in this portion of the chapter. The first is the security API, which we'll discuss in detail from a programmer's perspective. While the user may be faintly aware that there's a security API, they're unlikely to use it or even care that it exists. As a programmer, you need to be very aware of this part of Windows 2000 and Windows XP and know how to use the various API calls to make your applications secure.

TIP   One security API to consider relies on biometrics, the use of human body parts such as the iris and fingerprints for identification purposes. The Biometrics API (BAPI) helps programmers embed biometric technology into applications. A consortium of vendors—including IBM, Compaq, IO Software, Microsoft, Sony, Toshiba, and Novell—originated BAPI. Learn more about BAPI at the IO Software Web Site (`http://www.iosoftware.com/products/licensing/bapi/`). You can download an overview, general information, technical information, and the BAPI software development kit (SDK). Lest you think that all of these APIs are vendor specific, you can also find biometrics standards at the Biometrics Consortium Web site (`http://www.biometrics.org/`). This site contains helpful information about seminars, standards progress, and public information such as periodicals. Another interesting place to look for information is the National Institute of Standards and Technology (`http://www.itl.nist.gov/div895/isis/projects/biometrics-project.html`). The main interests at this site are the publications, conferences, products, and success stories.

The second important topic is the use of security functions. This section provides an overview of some of the security-related Win32 API functions you need to know about. As previously mentioned, there are many security-related functions, so knowing where to start is essential. We'll discuss some functions that will help you gain the access you need quickly. Of course, there are many esoteric functions you'll learn about as you delve more deeply into the security functions.

Why Worry About Token-Based Security?

Some developers are under the misconception that the .NET Framework is a complete solution or that it will answer every need. The problem is that the .NET Framework is new technology that extends what developers used in the past—you can't count on it to answer many of the old problems you have. In many cases, you'll find that a particular level of functionality is completely missing. The examples in this chapter demonstrate those lost security features.

However, the problem isn't limited to just missing functionality. The .NET Framework also presents situations where you could assume one level of functionality when the .NET Framework provides another. Consider the `System.IO.FileStream.Lock()` method. In theory, you should use this method to lock a file. In fact, it will lock the file if no one else is using it at the time.

Continued on next page

Unfortunately, the Lock() method uses the LockFile() function found in KERNEL32.DLL, not the more functional LockFileEx() function. This means you don't have the option to ask Lock() to wait until it can lock the file—the method always returns immediately. In addition, you can't differentiate between a shared and an exclusive lock. Your only choices to get around this problem are to create a loop and continually poll the file until it locks or use PInvoke to execute the LockFileEx() function. In short, the .NET Framework is incomplete and you'll need to know how to work with the Windows API to overcome those limitations.

A Detailed View of the Windows Security API

The security portion of the Win32 API is large and cumbersome. However, the actual theory behind Windows security is simple. Every object has a lock and every object requestor has a key. If the requestor's key fits the lock, then the requestor gains access to the object and the resources it provides. This is token-based security. The user's token is their key to resources on the local machine, the network and intranet, and even the Internet.

It's important to understand that the user's access is limited to the combination of groups and individual rights that the administrator assigns. However, most of the configuration options available to the administrator affect Windows as a whole. If you want the administrator to set user-level access for your application, then you must provide a feature to set user access for each object or task your application provides.

User-level access depends on a security ID (SID). When the user first logs into the system, Windows assigns an access token to the user and places the user's SID (stored on the domain controller or other security database) within it. The user object carries both the access token and the SID around for the duration of the session. An access token also contains both a Discretionary Access Control List (DACL) and a Security Access Control List (SACL). The combination of access control lists (ACLs) and SIDs within the access token is a key that allows the user access to certain system resources.

A key is no good without a lock to open. The lock placed on Windows resources is called a security descriptor. In essence, a security descriptor tells what rights the user needs to access the resource. If the rights within the ACLs meet or exceed the rights in the security descriptor, then the lock opens and the resource becomes available. Figure 8.1 shows the content of the ACL and the security descriptor used for token-based security. The following sections provide more details about how token-based security actually works. We'll use Figure 8.1 as the point of discussion.

Token-based security
relies on ACLs and
security descriptors.

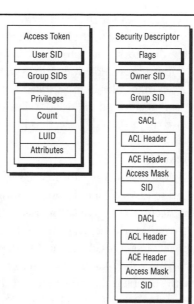

Understanding Access Tokens

There are two ways of looking at a user's rights under Windows: individual access and group access. Remember previously that we talked about the user's SID—the account number that Windows assigns to the user during login. The access token that holds the SID also contains other structures that identify the groups the user belongs to and what privileges the user has. Each group entry also has a SID. This SID points to other structures that tell what rights the group has. To understand what rights the user has, you need to know both the user's individual rights and the rights of the groups that the user belongs to. You'd normally use the Local Users and Groups or the Active Directory Users and Computers Microsoft Management Console (MMC) snap-in to change the contents of this access token.

Let's talk about the "privileges" section of the access token shown in Figure 8.1. It begins with a count of the number of privileges that the user has—the number of special privilege entries in the access token. This section also contains an array of privilege entries. Each privilege entry contains a locally unique identifier (LUID)—essentially a pointer to the entry object—and an attribute mask. The attribute mask tells what rights the user has to the object. Group SID entries are essentially the same. They contain a privilege count and an array of privilege entries.

One of the things that you need to know as part of working with some kinds of objects is that object rights flow down to the lowest possible node unless overridden by another SID.

For example, if you give a user read and write rights to the \Temp directory on a hard drive, those rights would also apply to the \Temp\Stuff directory unless you assigned the user specific rights to that directory. The same holds true for containers. Assigning a user rights to a container object like a Word document gives the user the right to look at everything within that container, even other files in most cases. It's important to track a user's exact rights to objects on your server through the use of security surveys, because you could inadvertently give the user more rights than they need to perform a certain task.

Using Access Tokens

Let's talk briefly about the token calls in the security API, because they are the first stepping-stones you'll need to know about. To do anything with a user's account—even if you want to find out who has access to a particular workstation—you need to know about tokens. As previously stated, tokens are the central part of the user side of the security equation. You'll usually begin a user account access with a call to OpenProcessToken(). Notice the name of this call—it deals with any kind of a process, user or otherwise. The purpose of this call is to get a token handle with specific rights attached to it. For example, if you want to query the user account, you need the TOKEN_QUERY privilege. (Your access token must contain the rights that you request from the system, which is why an administrator can access a token but other users can't.) Any changes to the user's account require the TOKEN_ADJUST_PRIVILEGES privilege. There are quite a few of these access rights, so we won't go through them all here.

NOTE   We've already looked at a simple example of how to use access tokens in the AccessToken example found in Chapter 3. Even though this example is simple, it does explain how security works in reference to this discussion. You might want to look at the example again to see the relationship between the theory in this section and the code in the example.

Once you have an access token handle, you need to decide what to do with it. For example, you can change a user's privilege to do something by accessing the LUID for the privilege you want to change. All of these appear in the WINNT.H file with an SE_. For example, the SE_SYSTEM_PROFILE_NAME privilege enables the application to gather profiling information for the entire system. Some SE values don't relate to users (for example, the SE_LOCK_MEMORY_NAME privilege that allows a process to lock system memory). You get the LUID for a privilege using the LookupPrivilegeValue() call. Now you can combine the information you've gotten so far to change the privilege. In general, you'll use the AdjustTokenPrivileges() call to make the required change.

Querying the user's account (or other token information) is straightforward. You use the GetTokenInformation() call to retrieve any information you need. This call requires a token class parameter, which tells Windows the type of information required. For example, you'd use the TokenUser class to learn about a specific user. You'll also supply an appropriate structure that Windows can use for storing the information you request—which differs by token class.

Understanding Security Descriptors

At this point, you have a better idea of how the access token (the key) works. Now let's look at the security descriptor (the lock). Figure 8.1 shows that each security descriptor contains five main sections. The following list describes each section.

Flags   The header consists of version information and a list of control flags. The flags tell you the descriptor status. For example, the SE_DACL_PRESENT flag indicates the presence of a DACL. If the DACL is missing or if it's NULL, then Windows allows everyone to use the object. Knowing the security descriptor status can greatly reduce the work you need to perform when determining security descriptor specifics.

Owner SID   The owner SID tells who owns the object. This doesn't have to be an individual user; Windows allows you to use a group SID here as well. The limiting factor is that the group SID must appear in the token of the person changing the entry.

Group SID   The group SID tells which group owns the object. This entry only contains the main group responsible for the object and won't contain a list of all groups with access to the object.

NOTE   Of the two security descriptor SIDs, the owner SID is important only under Windows. The Macintosh and POSIX security environments use the group SID. According to the Platform SDK documentation, Windows 2000 and above ignores the contents of the group SID.

SACL   This section controls the Windows auditing feature. Every time a user or group accesses an object when the auditing feature for that object is on, Windows makes an entry in the audit log. There's more than one entry in this section in most cases, so Windows stores the information in an array. The SACL is often left as a NULL value or not included in the security descriptor at all.

DACL   This section controls object use. You can assign groups and users to a specific object. There's more than one entry in this section in most cases, so Windows stores the information in an array. A DACL can contain a custom value, a default value, or a NULL value or not appear in the security descriptor at all (this last option is rare and dangerous). You'll normally find more objects with default values than any other DACL type.

Understanding the Security Descriptor Types

There are two types of security descriptors: absolute and self-relative. Absolute security descriptors contain a copy of each ACL within its structure. Use this type of security descriptor for objects that require special handling. For example, the root directory of a disk drive often uses an absolute security descriptor.

The self-relative security descriptor only contains a pointer to the SACL and DACL. This type of descriptor saves memory and reduces the time required to change rights for a group of objects. You'd use it when all objects in a particular group require the same level of security. For example, you could use this method to secure all threads within a single application.

Windows requires that you convert self-relative security descriptors to absolute format before you save them or transfer them to another process. Every descriptor you retrieve using API calls are of the self-relative type. You can convert a security descriptor from one type to another using the `MakeAbsoluteSD()` and `MakeSelfRelativeSD()` API calls.

Understanding ACLs

As previously mentioned, a security descriptor relies on a SACL and a DACL to control the security of an object. Both of these elements use the same basic ACL data structure, but for different purposes. An ACL consists of two entry types. The first is a header that lists the number of access control entries (ACEs) in the ACL. Windows uses this number to determine when it's reached the end of the ACE list. (There isn't any of end-of-structure record or other way to determine the size of each ACE in the structure.) The second entry is an array of ACEs.

WARNING   Never directly manipulate the contents of an ACL or SID—Microsoft may change its structure in future versions of Windows. The Windows API provides functions such as `Get-SecurityDescriptorDacl()` and `SetSecurityDescriptorDacl()` to change the contents of these structures. (Of course, you have to create the security descriptor structure using the `InitializeSecurityDescriptor()` function—you'll learn more about security descriptor construction as the chapter progresses.) Always use an API call to perform any task with either structure type to reduce the impact of changes in structure on your application.

An ACE defines the object rights for a single user or group. Every ACE has a header that defines the type, size, and flags for the ACE. It includes an access mask that defines rights a user or group has to the object. Finally, there's an entry for the user or group SID.

There are four main ACE header types. Windows currently uses three out of the four main ACE header types. The following list tells you about each of the main header types:

General Access   This header type appears in the DACL and grants object rights to a user. Use it to add to the rights a user already has to an object on an instance-by-instance basis. For example, you might want to prevent the user from changing the system time so that you can keep the machines on the network synchronized. However, there might be one situation—such as daylight savings time—when the user would need this right. You could use an access-allowed ACE to allow the user to change the time in this one instance.

NOTE   Windows divides each of the access header types into two subtypes: allowed and denied. For example, there's both an ACCESS_ALLOWED_ACE_TYPE and an ACCESS_DENIED_ACE_TYPE header type.

Object Access   This is a special header type for Windows 2000 and Windows XP. It enables you to assign specific security to software objects and subobjects. For example, you could use this type of ACE to assign security to the property of a COM object. To use this type of ACE, you need to obtain or create a globally unique identifier (GUID) for the object in question.

System Audit   This ACE header type works with the SACL. It defines which events to audit for a particular user or group. There are system audit header types for both general and object use. Only Windows 2000 and Windows XP systems can use the object-related system audit ACE header type.

System Alarm   This is the currently unused ACE type. It enables either the SACL or the DACL to set an alarm when specific events happen.

Using Security Descriptors

Understanding what a security descriptor is and how the various structures it contains interact is only one part of the picture. You also need to know how to access and use security descriptors to write a program. Windows doesn't generalize security descriptors as it does tokens. You can't use a standard set of calls to access them.

NOTE   Only NTFS provides full security, while VFAT provides it to a lesser degree. You can't assign or obtain security descriptors for either HPFS or FAT/FAT32 file systems. The FAT/FAT32 file system doesn't provide any extended attribute space, one requirement for adding security. The HPFS file system provides extended attributes, but they don't include any security features. Of all the file systems described, NTFS is the most secure. However, never assume that any file system is completely secure.

Windows includes five classes of security descriptors, each of which uses a different set of descriptor calls to access the object initially. (You must have the SE_SECURITY_NAME privilege to use any of these functions.) The five classes of security descriptors are as follows:

Files, Directories, Pipes, and Mail Slots   Use GetFileSecurity() and SetFileSecurity().

Processes, Threads, Access Tokens, and Synchronization Objects   Use GetKernel-ObjectSecurity() and SetKernelObjectSecurity(). All these objects, even access tokens, are kernel objects. As such, they also have their own security descriptor.

Window Stations, Desktops, Windows, and Menus   Use GetUserObjectSecurity() and SetUserObjectSecurity(). A window station is a combination of keyboard, mouse, and screen. Desktops contain windows and menus. These four objects inherit rights from each other in the order shown. In other words, a desktop will inherit the rights of the window station.

System Registry Keys   Use RegGetKeySecurity() and RegSetKeySecurity(). Notice that these two calls start with *Reg*, just like the other registry-specific calls Windows supports.

TIP   You can set some types of permissions using the .NET Framework System.Security.Permissions namespace. For example, the RegistryPermission class provides access to the registry security values. However, you won't gain access to the same level of information using the .NET Framework and you might find that some functionality is lacking.

Executable Service Objects   Use QueryServiceObjectSecurity() and SetService-ObjectSecurity(). For some strange reason, neither call appears with the other security calls in the Windows API help file. An executable service is a background task such as the UPS monitoring function.

Once you do gain access to the object, you can perform a variety of tasks using generic API calls. For example, the GetSecurityDescriptorDACL() retrieves a copy of the DACL from any descriptor type. The descriptors for all of these objects follow roughly the same format—although the lengths of most of the components differ. One reason for the differences in size is that each object will contain a different number of ACEs. The SIDs size differs as well.

The next step to query or modify security descriptor content is to disassemble the components. For example, you could view the ACEs within a DACL or a SACL using GetACE(). You could also use the owner and group SIDs for a variety of SID-related calls. In essence, any security descriptor access will always consist of the same three steps:

1. Get the descriptor.

2. Remove a specific component.

3. Modify the contents of that component.

To change the security descriptor, you reverse the process. Use a call like `AddACE()` to add a new ACE to an ACL, use `SetSecurityDescriptorSACL()` to change SACL within a descriptor, and finally, save the descriptor using a call like `SetFileSecurity()`.

The Importance of Order for Security

Once you know how Windows evaluates the ACEs in the DACL, you'll discover a few problem areas—problems that the Windows utilities address automatically. Order is an important consideration when working with Windows security because Windows uses a very basic method for determining how to evaluate the security elements. You'll need to program around these problems to derive the result found in the various Windows utilities. The SACL has the same problem, but it only affects auditing, so the effect is less severe from the system security standpoint.

Windows evaluates the ACEs in an ACL in the order in which they appear. At first, this might not seem like a very big deal. However, it could become a problem in some situations. For example, what if you want to revoke all of a user's rights in one area but their list of ACEs includes membership in a group that allows access to that area? If you place the access-allowed ACE before the access-denied ACE in the list, the user would get access to the area. The bottom line is that you should place all your access-denied ACEs in the list first to prevent any potential breach in security.

Also, use care in the ordering of group SIDs. Rights that a user acquires from different groups are cumulative. This means a user who's part of two groups, one that has access to a file and another that doesn't, will have access to the file if the group granting the right appears first on the list. In addition, if one ACE grants read rights and another write rights to a file and the user is asking for read and write rights, Windows will grant the request.

Obviously, you could spend all your time trying to figure out the best arrangement of groups. As the number of groups and individual rights that a user possesses increases, the potential for an unintended security breach does as well. That's why it's important to create groups carefully and limit a user's individual rights.

An Overview of the Functions

Now that you have a better idea of how token-based security works, let's look at some of the functions we'll use later in the chapter to create example applications. Table 8.1 contains a list of the various API functions that you'll commonly use to change the user's access token. This list provides only an overview, not a detailed description, of each API function.

TABLE 8.1: Common User Access Token Function Overview

Function Name	Description
AdjustTokenGroups	Allows you to adjust one or more group flags that control group usage within the access token. For example, you can use this function to replace the group's owner.
AdjustTokenPrivileges	Allows you to adjust one or more privileges within the access token. This function enables or disables an existing privilege; you can't add or delete privileges from the access token.
AllocateLocallyUniqueId	Creates a new LUID. The LUID is unique only for the current computer session on a particular computer. Unlike a GUID, a LUID is temporary.
BuildExplicitAccessWithName	Creates an EXPLICIT_ACCESS data structure for the named trustee. This data structure defines the trustee's ACL information. Use this data structure with API functions like SetEntriesInAcl() to define a trustee's access level to objects. The EXPLICIT_ACCESS data structure can affect either the SACL or DACL, depending on the access mode you set for it.
BuildTrusteeWithName	Creates a TRUSTEE data structure used to identify a specific trustee. You supply a trustee name and Windows fills the other data structure elements with default values. You'll need to modify the data structure before using it.
BuildTrusteeWithSid	Creates a TRUSTEE data structure that relies on a SID rather than a trustee name. Windows modifies the default data structure values appropriately.
CheckTokenMembership	Determines whether a SID appears within an access token. This can help you to determine if a user or process belongs to a particular group.
CreateRestrictedToken	Creates a duplicate of an existing token. The new token will have only a subset of the rights within the existing token. You can't use this function to add new rights to the resulting token.
DuplicateToken	Creates a copy of an existing token. Using this technique allows you to create a new token that varies from an existing token by one or two privileges.
DuplicateTokenEx	Creates a duplicate of a token. This function allows you to create either a primary or impersonation token. You can set access rights to the new token as part of the duplication call.
GetAuditedPermissionsFromAcl	Returns a list of ACL entries that result in an audit log entry for the specified trustee. This includes ACL entries that affect the trustee as well as groups to which the trustee belongs. You get a complete list of all audit-generating access events, not just those associated with the trustee. Windows returns the audited access in an ACCESS_MASK data structure.

Continued on next page

TABLE 8.1 CONTINUED: Common User Access Token Function Overview

Function Name	Description
GetEffectiveRightsFromAcl	Returns a list of ACL entries that list the effective rights for the specified trustee. Windows returns the effective rights in an ACCESS_MASK data structure.
GetExplicitEntriesFromAcl	Returns an array of EXPLICIT_ACCESS data structures that define the level of access each ACE within an ACL grants the trustee. The data structure provides information like the access mode, access rights, and inheritance setting for each ACE.
GetTokenInformation	Returns a data structure containing complete information about the access token. This includes the token's user, groups that appear within the token, the owner of the token, the impersonation level, and statistics associated with the token.
GetTrusteeForm	Returns a constant from one of the TRUSTEE_FORM enumeration values for a trustee. In most cases, the constants indicate whether the trustee is a name, SID, or object.
GetTrusteeName	Returns the name associated with a name trustee. If the TRUSTEE data structure that you provide is for a SID or object, Windows returns a NULL value.
GetTrusteeType	Returns a constant from one of the TRUSTEE_TYPE enumeration values for a trustee. In most cases, the constants indicate whether the trustee is a user, group, domain, or alias. There are also values to show deleted or invalid trustees.
IsTokenRestricted	Detects whether the access token contains one or more restricting SIDs.
LookupPrivilegeDisplayName	Converts a privilege name listed in WINNT.H to human-readable form. For example, SE_REMOTE_SHUTDOWN_NAME might convert to "Force shutdown from a remote system."
LookupPrivilegeName	Allows you to convert a privilege name specified by a LUID to one of the constant forms listed in WINNT.H.
LookupPrivilegeValue	Allows you to convert a privilege name as listed in WINNT.H to a LUID.
OpenProcessToken	Opens a token associated with a process (application). As with file tokens, you need to specify level of access to process the token. For example, the TOKEN_ALL_ACCESS constant gives you complete access to the token.
OpenThreadToken	Opens a token that's associated with a thread within an application. As with a process token, you need to request a specific level of access when making the request.
SetEntriesInAcl	Creates a new ACL by merging new access control or audit control information into an existing ACL. You can use this function to create an entirely new ACL using the ACL creation function, BuildExplicitAccessWithName().

Continued on next page

TABLE 8.1 CONTINUED: Common User Access Token Function Overview

Function Name	Description
SetThreadToken	Used mainly to implement impersonation within a thread. Use this function to give different rights to a single thread within an application. This allows the thread to perform tasks that the user may not have the rights to perform.
SetTokenInformation	Sets the information contained within an access token. Before you can set the information within the token, you have to have the required access rights. The three data structures associated with this function allow you to adjust owner, primary group, and DACL information.

Normally, you'll never work with SIDs directly. The reason is that you can address a user by their login name and make your code both easier to debug and understand. However, there are certain situations in which you'll want to work with SIDs. The most important of these situations is when you're dealing with common SIDs like the one for the World, which has a SID of S-1-1-0. The SID for the World always remains the same, but the name for the World could change from country to country. Always refer to common, universal SIDs by their SID rather than a common name. With this in mind, you'll want to know about the SID-related functions, so you'll be familiar with them when you want to work with common SIDs. Table 8.2 contains a list of SID-related functions.

TABLE 8.2: Common SID-Related Function Overview

Function Name	Description
AllocateAndInitializeSid	Creates and initializes a SID with up to eight subauthorities.
ConvertSidToStringSid	Converts a SID to a string in human-readable format. This format consists of values in the form *S-R-I-SA*, where *S* designates the string as a SID, *R* is the revision level, *I* is the identifier authority value, and *SA* is one or more subauthority values. Note that the dashes between SID values are always part of the SID string.
ConvertStringSidToSid	Converts a specially formatted string into a SID.
CopySid	Creates a duplicate of an existing SID.
EqualPrefixSid	Compares two SID prefixes for equality. A SID prefix is the SID value minus the last sub-authority value. This test is useful for detecting two SIDs in the same domain.
EqualSid	Compares two SIDs for equality in their entirety.
FreeSid	Deallocates the memory used by a SID previously created using the AllocateAndInitializeSid() function.

Continued on next page

TABLE 8.2 CONTINUED: Common SID-Related Function Overview

Function Name	Description
GetLengthSid	Returns the length of a SID in bytes.
GetSidIdentifierAuthority	Returns a pointer to a SID_IDENTIFIER_AUTHORITY data structure. This data structure contains an array of six bytes that specify the SID's top-level authority. Predefined authorities include NULL (0), local (1), world (2), creator (3), and Windows NT/Windows 2000/Windows XP (5).
GetSidLengthRequired	Returns the length of a buffer required to hold a SID structure with a specified number of sub-authorities.
GetSidSubAuthority	Returns the address of a specific sub-authority within a SID structure. The sub-authority is a relative identifier (RID).
GetSidSubAuthorityCount	Returns the address of a field used to hold the number of sub-authorities within the SID. Use this address to determine the number of sub-authorities within the SID.
InitializeSid	Sets the identifier authority of a SID structure to a known value using a SID_IDENTIFIER_AUTHORITY data structure. Sub-authority values aren't set using this function. Use the AllocateAndInitializeSid() function to initialize a SID completely.
IsValidSid	Determines the validity of a SID structure's contents. This function checks the revision number and ensures that the number of sub-authorities doesn't exceed the maximum value.
LookupAccountName	Retrieves the SID (and accompanying data) for a specific account. You must supply an account and system name.
LookupAccountSid	Retrieves the name and machine associated with a given SID. It also returns the name of the SID's first domain.

Security isn't this one sided. Once Windows determines the rights a user or other object has, it must match those rights to the access requirements of the system resource. This means working with security descriptors. A security descriptor is a lock on the object or other system resource. Either the key (access token) fits the lock or it doesn't. Windows grants or denies access when the key fits the lock. Table 8.3 is an overview of the security descriptor API functions.

By now, you should have some idea of how to work within the security portion of the Win32 API. The divisions I set up within the tables are artificial; they're for description purposes to make the functions easier to comprehend and use. In a real-world application, you'll combine elements of all three tables to create a complete security picture.

TABLE 8.3: Security Descriptor Function Overview

Function Name	Description
ConvertSecurity-DescriptorToString-SecurityDescriptor	Converts a security descriptor to string format. Flags determine the level of information returned in the string. A complete string contains the owner SID, the group SID, a DACL flag list using coded letters, a SACL flag list using coded letters, and a series of ACE entries.
ConvertStringSecurity-DescriptorToSecurity-Descriptor	Converts a specially formatted string into a security descriptor.
GetNamedSecurityInfo	Returns the security descriptor for the named object provided as input. Flags determine what kind of information to retrieve.
GetSecurityDescriptor-Control	Returns the security descriptor control information and revision number for the security descriptor structure provided as input.
GetSecurityInfo	Returns the security descriptor for an object that is specified using an object handle. Windows provides flags that determine which security descriptor entries to retrieve.
SetNamedSecurityInfo	Modifies the security descriptor information for an object specified by name.
SetSecurityDescriptor-Control	Modifies the control bits of a security descriptor. Functions related to this one include SetSecurityDescriptorDacl, which allows you to set other control bits of the security descriptor.
SetSecurityInfo	Modifies the owner, group, SACL, or DACL within the security descriptor for an object. Each information type requires a separate data structure, which includes flags to tell Windows which elements to change. A handle and object type descriptor identifies the object.

Using the Access Control Editor

The Access Control Editor is a COM control that helps you to add a standard interface to your application—allowing administrators to set application security as needed. These are the same property pages that Microsoft uses within Windows 2000 and Windows XP to set security. The Access Control Editor uses two sets of property pages. The user will normally see the simple property page dialog shown in Figure 8.2.

The Access Control
Editor is a generally
accessible component.

I chose this particular example so that you'd see the dialog in action. The content of the dialog changes to meet object requirements. The Administrator will normally use the advanced property page shown in Figure 8.3.

As you can see, both property pages allow the administrator to work with the security settings for an application with relative ease. Notice that the advanced dialog provides complete controls for setting every security aspect for this particular object. The Permissions tab sets the DACL, the Auditing tab the SACL, and the Owner tab the owner information. The only missing element is the group information, which isn't important at the user level in many cases.

You can easily implement the Access Control Editor in a .NET application by creating the proper interfaces. The ISecurityInformation interface is the essential component of this implementation. I won't go into the programming details in this section. However, it's important to know that you can add the Access Control Editor to your applications by adding the appropriate COM interfaces and implementing the required functions the interfaces describe.

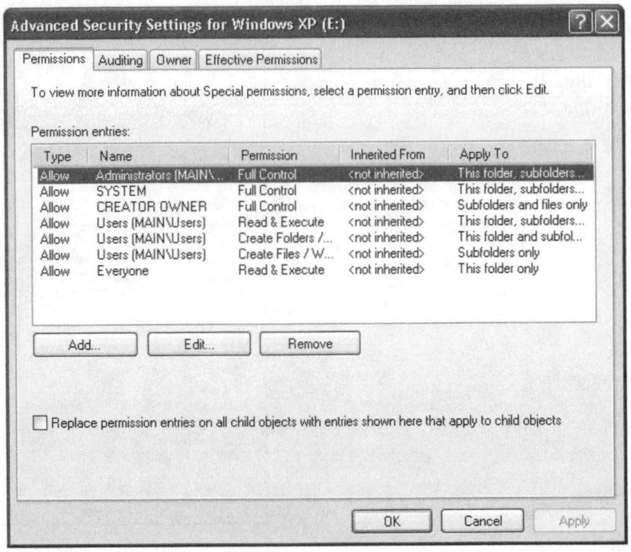

FIGURE 8.3:

The advanced features of the Access Control Editor provide the administrator with full access control.

For the Win32 API developer, the Access Control Editor fulfills another purpose. We'll use this operating system feature to verify changes made by the sample applications. Security is one of those difficult changes to verify unless you want to build a lot of test applications. The Access Control Editor is one of many tools that enable you to check the output of your application, but this particular tool is one of the easiest to use and the most reliable. In general, you'll want to use this tool before you use anything else.

It's also easy to use the Access Control Editor to set up test cases for your applications. For example, you might want to ensure that your application detects certain types of security changes. (This behavior often occurs when a virus is at work, so the ability of your application to detect odd changes is important.) The Access Control Editor enables you to make changes on a test object quickly. You can then test your application to see how the change affects its operation. Generally, your applications need to at least detect changes within certain ranges of approved behavior. For example, an application would want to detect files that have security turned off if the information they contain is sensitive.

Using the Security Configuration Editor

The Microsoft Security Configuration Editor is an administration tool that reduces both security management and analysis time. Initially you'll use this tool to configure the operating system security parameters. Once these parameters are in place, you can use the Security Configuration Editor to schedule periodic tests.

NOTE   Windows NT provides one MMC snap-in for the Security Configuration Editor; it's called the System Configuration Manager. You can use the System Configuration Manager to work with the security database (SDB) and security configuration (INF) files you create using the Security Configuration Editor. Windows 2000 and Windows XP divide the Security Configuration Editor into two parts. The Security Configuration and Analysis MMC snap-in helps you configure the security database. The Security Templates MMC snap-in helps you work with the security configuration files. All of these operating systems provide similar functionality. Windows 2000 and Windows XP do provide some advanced features. All screen shots in this section of the chapter depict the Windows XP setup.

The overall goal of the Security Configuration Editor is to provide a single place to manage all of the security concerns for a network. However, it doesn't actually replace all of the tools you used in the past—the Security Configuration Editor augments other security tools. The Security Configuration Editor also provides auditing tools that Windows has lacked in the past.

One of the unique ideas behind the Security Configuration Editor is that it's a macro-based tool. You'll create a set of instructions for the Security Configuration Editor to perform and then allow it to perform those instructions in the background. Obviously, this saves a lot of developer time because the developer doesn't have to wait for one set of instructions to complete before going to the next set. You can also group tasks, which saves input time.

At this point, you may wonder why a developer should care about this tool at all. After all, configuring network security is a network administrator task. That idea used to be true—a network administrator was responsible for all security on the network. However, as computer networks become more complex and the technologies used with them more flexible, part of the responsibility for network security has shifted to the developer. As a developer, you need to know how this tool works so that you can test the applications you create. This is especially true for token-based applications because the .NET Framework provides nothing in the way of internal checks for your application. For the Win32 API developer, this is an essential test tool.

Creating a security setup begins when you choose an existing template or create a new one using the Security Templates MMC snap-in. If you want to use an existing template as a basis for creating a new one, you can right-click on the desired template and use the Save As command found on the context menu. Microsoft supplies a variety of templates designed to get you started in creating this security database, as shown in Figure 8.4.

Each of the security templates is designed for a different purpose (which is indicated by the name). The one I'll use in this section is the compatibility workstation template (compatws), but all of the other templates work about the same as this one. All of the templates contain the same basic elements shown in Figure 8.5.

As you can see from the figure, each template defines a number of security elements. The following list describes each of these elements for you:

Account Policies Defines the password, account lockout, and Kerberos policies for the machine. Password policies include items like the minimum password length and the maximum time the user can use a single password. The account lockout policy includes the number of times a user can enter the wrong password without initiating a system lockout. Kerberos policies feature elements like the maximum user ticket lifetime.

Local Policies   Defines the audit policy, user rights assignment, and security options. Audit policies determine the types of data you collect. For example, you could audit each failed user logon attempt. User rights assignments are of special interest because this policy affects the rights you can assign to a user (the access token). The security options policy contains the elements that determine how the security system will react given a set of circumstances. For example, one policy will log a user off when their usage hours expire.

Event Log   Defines how the event log stores data and for how long. These policies also determine maximize event log size and event log viewing rights.

Restricted Groups   Defines groups that can't access the workstation or server at all, or restricts the amount of access they can obtain.

System Services   Displays a list of the system services on the target machine. Double-clicking a service displays a dialog that allows you to set the policy for that service and adjust its startup mode. Normally, you'll leave the icons in this policy alone. However, you can safely change any system service DLLs you create.

Registry   Contains all of the major registry hives. Double-clicking a branch displays a dialog you use to set the security for that branch. In addition, you can choose the method of security inheritance by children of this branch.

File System   Contains protected file system entries. You can add new files to the list or modify exiting entries. Double-clicking a file system entry displays a dialog you use to set the security level for that file system member. In addition, you can choose the method of security inheritance by children of this file system entity (applies only to folders).

Active Directory Objects   This entry is only available if you have Active Directory enabled (which means you must have a domain controller set up). It allows you to edit the security settings for any Active Directory objects, including users and groups.

Understanding How .NET Role-Based Security Differs

Even though this chapter is about using token-based security, it's important to realize that the .NET Framework does provide a substantial set of security classes. The big difference is that the .NET Framework uses role-based, not token-based, security in most cases. This section helps you understand how role-based security compares. I've provided it as an optional overview of role-based security and you can easily skip the section if desired.

Most of the security features we'll discuss in this section appear in the `System.Security` namespace. However, it's important to realize that Microsoft attempted to order the .NET Framework for convenience. Despite the fact that most security features appear in the security-related namespaces, you'll find a few in odd places. For example, if you want to lock a file, you'll use the `System.IO.FileStream.Lock()` method. Likewise, if you want to ensure that your Web pages synchronize properly, you'll want to use the `System.Web.HttpApplicationState.Lock()` method. There's even a `System.Drawing.Design.ToolboxItem.Lock()` method you can use to lock individual properties in a toolbox item. In short, if Microsoft felt that a developer would have better access to a security method within the affected object's class, the method appears in that location.

The .NET Framework provides several levels of security. However, you can easily divide security into application and role-based security. Application security defends the code elements used to create an application. In addition, it protects the system from code elements that originate outside the system (such as code downloaded from a Web site) by assigning such code a lower security level. In short, the code receives a trust value based on its origin. Role-based security defines the actions a user (or other entity) is allowed to perform based on their organizational role. This differs from the older individual and group token access because a user can "change hats" (roles) based on current environmental and access conditions. Together, the two levels of security enable you to protect applications without worrying too much about low-level functionality. Of course, these features only work if you've already defined the various security elements.

NOTE   Many of the security features that the .NET Framework provides only affect managed code. If your application uses a combination of managed and unmanaged code, you'll need to implement security that works in both arenas, namely the security portion of the Win32 API we discussed earlier.

Another way to look at .NET security is to consider the method of code implementation. You can programmatically define a security feature using declarative or imperative syntax. Some security features require that you use a specific method, while others allow implementation using either method.

Declarative syntax relies on attributes. The attributes can appear at the assembly, class, or member levels and they can request, demand, or override the security options currently in place. Applications use requests to change their current security settings. A request can ask for more or less access to objects. Demand and overrides appear within library code. A demand protects the object from caller access. On the other hand, an override changes the default security settings. Here's an example of declarative syntax in action (you can also find this example in the \Chapter 08\C#\Declarative and \Chapter 08\VB\Declarative folders of the CD—make sure you change the file location to match your system):

```
[System.Security.Permissions.FileIOPermission(SecurityAction.Deny,
                                              All="E:\\Temp.txt")]
private void btnDeny_Click(object sender, System.EventArgs e)
{
    Stream  FS = null;  // A test file stream.

    // Try to access the file.
    try
    {
        FS = new FileStream("E:\\Temp.txt",
                            FileMode.Open,
                            FileAccess.Read);
    }
    catch(SecurityException SE)
    {
        MessageBox.Show("Access Denied\r\n" +
                        SE.Message,
                        "File IO Error",
                        MessageBoxButtons.OK,
                        MessageBoxIcon.Error);
        return;
    }

    // Display a success message.
    MessageBox.Show("File is open!",
                    "File IO Success",
                    MessageBoxButtons.OK,
                    MessageBoxIcon.Information);

    // Close the file if opened.
    FS.Close();
}
```

The btnAllow_Click() will always fail because the FileIOPermission attribute is set to deny all access to the file. The Assert() or Demand() methods would allow access to the same file (the example uses the Assert() method). As you can see, the result of this code is that the TEMP.TXT file is protected, even if the user would normally have access to it.

Imperative syntax relies on security objects. An application creates a security object and then uses the object to set permissions or perform other tasks. You can use imperative syntax to perform demands and overrides, but not requests. Here's an example of imperative syntax in action (you can also find this example in the \Chapter 08\C#\Imperative and \Chapter 08\VB\ Imperative folders on the CD—make sure you change the file location to match your system):

```
private void btnDeny_Click(object sender, System.EventArgs e)
{
   FileIOPermission  FIOP;         // Permission object.
   Stream            FS = null;  // A test file stream.

   // Create the permission object.
   FIOP = new FileIOPermission(FileIOPermissionAccess.Read,
            "E:\\Temp.txt");

   // Deny access to the resource.
   FIOP.Deny();

   // Try to access the object.
   try
   {
      FS = new FileStream("E:\\Temp.txt",
                        FileMode.Open,
                        FileAccess.Read);
   }
   catch(SecurityException SE)
   {
      MessageBox.Show("Access Denied\r\n" +
                     SE.Message,
                     "File IO Error",
                     MessageBoxButtons.OK,
                     MessageBoxIcon.Error);
      return;
   }

   // Display a success message.
   MessageBox.Show("File is open!",
                   "File IO Success",
                   MessageBoxButtons.OK,
                   MessageBoxIcon.Information);

   // Close the file if opened.
   FS.Close();
}
```

The btnDeny_Click() method will always fail because the imperative security call, FIOP .Deny(), denies access to the file. Notice how the code initializes the *FileIOPermission* object before using it. The code requires a full path to the file in question. As with the declarative syntax, you can use the Assert() or Demand() methods to allow access to an object.

Looking Up an Account SID Example

Sometimes you know the name of a well-known account, such as Administrators, but you don't know anything else about it. The Win32 API provides an answer to this dilemma. You can create a SID for the account without knowing anything about it and then look up the information for that account. This technique proves handy for a number of uses. For example, if you know that you want to create a new user that has starting rights that are the same as those used for a well-known account, you can begin by obtaining information about the well-known account SID. Listing 8.1 shows the code you'll need for this example. You'll find the source code for this example in the \Chapter 08\C#\LookUpSID and \Chapter 08\VB\LookUpSID folders of the CD. (Note that the list of well-known SIDs shown in Listing 8.1 is incomplete—you'll find a complete list on the CD.)

Listing 8.1   **Converting a SID to Human-Readable Form**

```
// This function returns a SID for a well-known account.
[DllImport("AdvAPI32.DLL", CharSet=CharSet.Auto, SetLastError=true )]
public static extern bool CreateWellKnownSid(
    WELL_KNOWN_SID_TYPE WellKnownSidType,
    IntPtr DomainSid,
    IntPtr pSid,
    ref Int32 cbSid);

// This enumeration contains a list of the well-known SIDs.
public enum WELL_KNOWN_SID_TYPE
{
    WinNullSid                              = 0,

    // Lots of other well-known SIDs appear in the source code.

    WinAccountRasAndIasServersSid           = 50,
};

// This define is normally calculated by a macro, but it's
// unlikely to change for either Windows 2000 or Windows XP.
public const int SECURITY_MAX_SID_SIZE = 68;

// This function accepts a SID as input and obtains human
// readable data about it.
[DllImport("AdvAPI32.DLL", CharSet=CharSet.Auto, SetLastError=true )]
public static extern bool LookupAccountSid(
    String lpSystemName,
    IntPtr Sid,
    StringBuilder Name,
    ref Int32 cbName,
    StringBuilder DomainName,
    ref Int32 cbDomainName,
    ref SID_NAME_USE peUse);
```

```csharp
// This enumeration determines the use of the account.
public enum SID_NAME_USE
{
   SidTypeUser = 1,
   SidTypeGroup,
   SidTypeDomain,
   SidTypeAlias,
   SidTypeWellKnownGroup,
   SidTypeDeletedAccount,
   SidTypeInvalid,
   SidTypeUnknown,
   SidTypeComputer
};


private void btnTest_Click(object sender, System.EventArgs e)
{
   Int32          SIDSize;     // Size of the returned SID.
   IntPtr         GuestSID;    // SID of the Guest account.
   int            LastError;   // Last error produced by an API call.
   Int32          NameSize;    // Size of the account name.
   Int32          DomainSize;  // Size of the domain name.
   StringBuilder  Name;        // Account name.
   StringBuilder  Domain;      // Domain name.
   SID_NAME_USE   Use;         // Account use.

   // Allocate memory for the SID.
   GuestSID = Marshal.AllocHGlobal(SECURITY_MAX_SID_SIZE);

   // Create the SID.
   SIDSize = SECURITY_MAX_SID_SIZE;
   if (!CreateWellKnownSid((WELL_KNOWN_SID_TYPE)cbSelect.SelectedIndex,
                  IntPtr.Zero,
                  GuestSID,
                  ref SIDSize))
   {
      // Get the last error.
      LastError = Marshal.GetLastWin32Error();

      // Display an error message and exit if not successful.
      MessageBox.Show("Error creating the account SID." +
                  "\r\nLast Error: " + LastError.ToString(),
                  "Application Error",
                  MessageBoxButtons.OK,
                  MessageBoxIcon.Error);

      // Free the memory we allocated.
      Marshal.FreeHGlobal(GuestSID);

      // Exit the routine.
      return;
   }
```

```
            // Obtain the size of the Name and Domain strings.
            NameSize = 0;
            DomainSize = 0;
            Use = SID_NAME_USE.SidTypeAlias;
            LookupAccountSid(null,
                             GuestSID,
                             null,
                             ref NameSize,
                             null,
                             ref DomainSize,
                             ref Use);

            // Allocate memory for the strings.
            Name = new StringBuilder(NameSize);
            Domain = new StringBuilder(DomainSize);

            // Obtain the SID information.
            if (!LookupAccountSid(null,
                             GuestSID,
                             Name,
                             ref NameSize,
                             Domain,
                             ref DomainSize,
                             ref Use))
            {
                // Get the last error.
                LastError = Marshal.GetLastWin32Error();

                // Display an error message and exit if not successful.
                MessageBox.Show("Error obtaining the account SID data." +
                             "\r\nLast Error: " + LastError.ToString(),
                             "Application Error",
                             MessageBoxButtons.OK,
                             MessageBoxIcon.Error);
            }
            else
            {
                // Display the account information.
                MessageBox.Show("Obtained the SID Account Information" +
                             "\r\nName: " + Name.ToString() +
                             "\r\nDomain: " + Domain.ToString() +
                             "\r\nUse: " + Use.ToString(),
                             "Application Output",
                             MessageBoxButtons.OK,
                             MessageBoxIcon.Information);
            }

            // Free the memory we allocated.
            Marshal.FreeHGlobal(GuestSID);
        }
```

Windows provides a wealth of well-known SIDs—predefined SIDs that every machine can use. The CreateWellKnownSid() function will create a SID for a well-known value such as the World. All you need to supply is an enumerated SID type, a pointer to a buffer to hold the SID, and the size of the SID buffer. The domain SID is optional. However, supplying this value will enable you to look up SIDs on other machines. There are 51 enumerated SID types to choose from and the example application lets you test them all. (Some of the well-known SIDs might not work on your machine if you don't have the required support installed.)

The LookupAccountSid() function accepts a SID as input. It doesn't matter where you get the SID as long as the SID is valid. If the call to this function fails, you can assume the SID was invalid—even if it's a well-known SID. In some cases, this function can tell you which operating system features are installed because some security accounts are only installed when you install the appropriate operating system feature. The LookupAccountSid() function returns the name and domain information for the SID along with the SID usage as indicated by the SID_NAME_USE enumeration.

One of the first tasks the code has to perform is allocating memory for the SID. In many cases, the code could allocate local memory as shown in the Platform SDK documentation. However, when working with a .NET application, it's best to use the Marshal.AllocHGlobal() function. This function returns an IntPtr to the allocated memory, which you must deallocate later using the Marshal.FreeHGlobal() function. The SECURITY_MAX_SID_SIZE constant defines the maximum size of the SID. This is yet another instance where you can convert a Visual C++ macro into a constant with the caveat that Microsoft could change the size of a SID at some later date. The alternative, in this case, is to write a small wrapper DLL to calculate the value for you. Using this technique is more expensive in development time, but it does protect you from future changes.

We've used a number of techniques for gaining access to error information. This example uses the Microsoft-recommended technique of setting the *SetLastError* argument of the [DllImport] attribute true and then using the Marshal.GetLastWin32Error() function to return the error number. Note that the .NET Framework doesn't provide any means for converting this number into a human-readable form. You still need to use the Win32 API FormatMessage() function to perform the conversion. (See the section "Interpreting Error and Result Values" in Chapter 3 for details.)

Once the code obtains the desired SID, it uses the LookupAccountSid() function to determine the SID information. However, the code requires two calls to the LookupAccountSid() function to perform this task. The first call returns the size of the strings used to contain the account name and domain information. The code uses this information to allocate two String-Builder variables. The second call returns the actual information. Figure 8.6 shows typical output from this example for the *WinAnonymousSid* enumerated value.

FIGURE 8.6:

The example
application outputs
the name, domain,
and use for a
well-known SID.

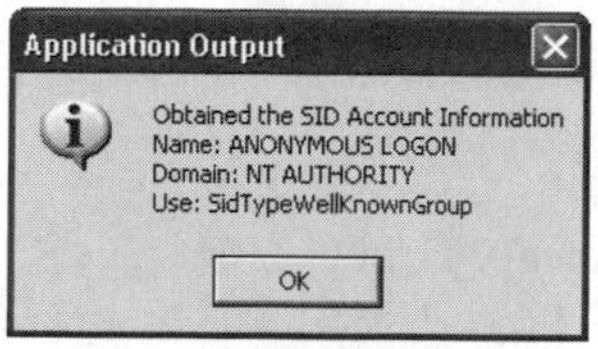

Application Output

Obtained the SID Account Information
Name: ANONYMOUS LOGON
Domain: NT AUTHORITY
Use: SidTypeWellKnownGroup

OK

Using the *GetFileSecurity()* Function Example

One of the problems that many developers have noted with the .NET Framework security is
a lack of access to file (and other object) security information. For example, it's hard to tell
who owns a file without using the Win32 API calls. That's where the GetFileSecurity()
function comes into play. It enables you to retrieve file security information in the form of a
security descriptor. From the theoretical discussion earlier in the chapter, you know that
the security descriptor contains just about every piece of security information that Windows
can supply. The example shown in Listing 8.2 shows how to obtain the owner identification
for a file. However, the same techniques can help you obtain the SACL, DACL, and other
security elements. The source in Listing 8.2 isn't complete—it contains only the material we
haven't discussed in other areas. See the source code in the \Chapter 08\C#\FileSecurity
and \Chapter 08\VB\FileSecurity folders of the CD for details.

Listing 8.2   **One Technique for Accessing File Security Information**

```csharp
// This function retrieves the security information for a file.
[DllImport("AdvAPI32.DLL", CharSet=CharSet.Auto, SetLastError=true )]
public static extern bool GetFileSecurity(
    String lpFileName,
    SECURITY_INFORMATION RequestedInformation,
    IntPtr pSecurityDescriptor,
    Int32 nLength,
    ref Int32 lpnLengthNeeded);

// This enumeration tells what type of information we want to retrieve
// about the file's security.
public enum SECURITY_INFORMATION : uint
{
    OWNER_SECURITY_INFORMATION             = 0x00000001,
    GROUP_SECURITY_INFORMATION             = 0x00000002,
    DACL_SECURITY_INFORMATION              = 0x00000004,
    SACL_SECURITY_INFORMATION              = 0x00000008,
    PROTECTED_DACL_SECURITY_INFORMATION    = 0x80000000,
    PROTECTED_SACL_SECURITY_INFORMATION    = 0x40000000,
    UNPROTECTED_DACL_SECURITY_INFORMATION  = 0x20000000,
```

```
    UNPROTECTED_SACL_SECURITY_INFORMATION      = 0x10000000
};

// This function retrieves the security descriptor for the
// file owner.
[DllImport("AdvAPI32.DLL", CharSet=CharSet.Auto, SetLastError=true )]
public static extern bool GetSecurityDescriptorOwner(
    IntPtr pSecurityDescriptor,
    out IntPtr pOwner,
    ref Boolean lpbOwnerDefaulted);

private void btnTest_Click(object sender, System.EventArgs e)
{
    IntPtr        SecurityDescriptor;   // File security information.
    Int32         SDSize;               // Security descriptor size.
    Int32         SDSizeNeeded;         // Required security desc. size.
    int           LastError;            // Last Win32 API error.
    IntPtr        OwnerSID;             // SID of the owner account.
    Boolean       IsDefault;            // Is this a defaulted account?
    Int32         NameSize;             // Size of the account name.
    Int32         DomainSize;           // Size of the domain name.
    StringBuilder Name;                 // Account name.
    StringBuilder Domain;               // Domain name.
    SID_NAME_USE  Use;                  // Account use.

    // Determine the size of the security descriptor.
    SecurityDescriptor = new IntPtr(0);
    SDSizeNeeded = 0;
    GetFileSecurity(@txtFile.Text,
                    SECURITY_INFORMATION.OWNER_SECURITY_INFORMATION,
                    SecurityDescriptor,
                    0,
                    ref SDSizeNeeded);

    // Allocate the memory required for the security descriptor.
    SecurityDescriptor = Marshal.AllocHGlobal(SDSizeNeeded);
    SDSize = SDSizeNeeded;

    // Get the security descriptor.
    if (!GetFileSecurity(@txtFile.Text,
                    SECURITY_INFORMATION.OWNER_SECURITY_INFORMATION,
                    SecurityDescriptor,
                    SDSize,
                    ref SDSizeNeeded))
    {
        // Get the last error.
        LastError = Marshal.GetLastWin32Error();

        // Display an error message and exit if not successful.
        MessageBox.Show("Error obtaining the security descriptor." +
                    "\r\nLast Error: " + LastError.ToString(),
```

```
                    "Application Error",
                    MessageBoxButtons.OK,
                    MessageBoxIcon.Error);

        // Free the memory we allocated.
        Marshal.FreeHGlobal(SecurityDescriptor);

        // Exit the routine.
        return;
    }

    // Obtain the owner SID for the file.
    IsDefault = false;
    if (!GetSecurityDescriptorOwner(SecurityDescriptor,
                            out OwnerSID,
                            ref IsDefault))
    {
        // Get the last error.
        LastError = Marshal.GetLastWin32Error();

        // Display an error message and exit if not successful.
        MessageBox.Show("Error obtaining the owner SID." +
                    "\r\nLast Error: " + LastError.ToString(),
                    "Application Error",
                    MessageBoxButtons.OK,
                    MessageBoxIcon.Error);

        // Free the memory we allocated.
        Marshal.FreeHGlobal(SecurityDescriptor);

        // Exit the routine.
        return;
    }

    // Code to obtain the user information from the SID and some display
    // code appears in this area.

}
```

The GetFileSecurity() function retrieves a security descriptor for the file requested by *lpFileName*. However, the function doesn't retrieve a complete security descriptor. It instead asks you to supply a SECURITY_INFORMATION enumeration value that chooses one of several pieces of a standard security descriptor. This means that the call must match the data you want to work with later. Notice that the SECURITY_INFORMATION enumeration contains all of the elements we discussed in the theoretical portion of the chapter. You must also provide a buffer pointer and the buffer length. The GetFileSecurity() function returns the security descriptor that you requested and the amount of buffer space needed to store the information.

Remember that we discussed the fact that you should never work with the security descriptor directly, but instead use the Win32 API–supplied functions. The `GetSecurityDescriptorOwner()` function will retrieve owner information from a security descriptor if such information exists. There are also other functions, such as `GetSecurityDescriptorDacl()` and `GetSecurityDescriptorGroup()`, for retrieving other elements of the security descriptor. The `GetSecurityDescriptorOwner()` function accepts a security descriptor as input and returns a SID containing the owner information.

The code actually calls the `GetFileSecurity()` function twice. The first call is used to determine the size of the buffer needed to hold the security descriptor. The second call retrieves the security descriptor if the buffer is large enough to hold the data. Notice that this code uses the `Marshal.AllocHGlobal()` function to allocate the buffer for the *SecurityDescriptor* buffer.

Once the code obtains a security descriptor, it uses the `GetSecurityDescriptorOwner()` function to retrieve the SID. Notice that this second function accepts the uninitialized *OwnerSID* as an out value. If you try to initialize *OwnerSID* and send it as we did for the `GetFileSecurity()` function, the function will fail with an invalid parameter error. The `GetSecurityDescriptorOwner()` function points out that you won't always interact with the Win32 API functions in the same way. Be prepared to send an initialized variable in one case and an uninitialized in other cases. At this point, we have a SID and can use the `LookupAccountSid()` function to retrieve the applicable information. Figure 8.7 shows the output from this example.

FIGURE 8.7:

The example application will tell you who owns a particular file on the hard drive.

Working with ACEs Example

So far, we've looked at examples of how to work with the access token and the security descriptor and the vagaries of working with specific objects such as files. This example completes the tour of security support for the Win32 API by looking at the ACEs that make up the SACL and the DACL. Because you're most likely to work with the DACL, this example emphasizes access over auditing. However, working with the ACEs in either structure is about the same. Listing 8.3 shows how you'd access the ACEs for a file. The listing is incomplete—it doesn't include the functions used in previous examples. Make sure you check the source code in the `\Chapter 08\C#\GetGroupAccess` and `\Chapter 08\VB\GetGroupAccess` folders of the CD for details. This source code includes an encapsulated version of the code used to gain access to the security descriptor in the form of the GetFileSD() function.

Listing 8.3   **Gaining Access to the ACEs Means Reading the ACL**

```
public const Int32 ERROR_SUCCESS = 0;

// This function uses the DACL to retrieve an array of explicit
// entries, each of which contains information about individual ACEs
// within the DACL.
[DllImport("AdvAPI32.DLL", CharSet=CharSet.Auto, SetLastError=true )]
public static extern Int32 GetExplicitEntriesFromAcl(
    IntPtr pacl,
    ref UInt32 pcCountOfExplicitEntries,
    out EXPLICIT_ACCESS []pListOfExplicitEntries);

// This data structure is used to create the explicit entry array.
[StructLayout(LayoutKind.Sequential, Pack=1)]
public struct EXPLICIT_ACCESS
{
    public UInt32        grfAccessPermissions;
    public ACCESS_MODE   grfAccessMode;
    public UInt32        grfInheritance;
    public TRUSTEE       Trustee;
}

// The ACCESS_MODE enumeration tells what type of ACE entry we're
// working with.
public enum ACCESS_MODE
{
    NOT_USED_ACCESS = 0,
    GRANT_ACCESS,
    SET_ACCESS,
    DENY_ACCESS,
    REVOKE_ACCESS,
    SET_AUDIT_SUCCESS,
    SET_AUDIT_FAILURE
}

// This structure contains the trustee information for the ACE.
[StructLayout(LayoutKind.Sequential, Pack=1)]
public struct TRUSTEE
{
    public IntPtr                       pMultipleTrustee;
    public MULTIPLE_TRUSTEE_OPERATION   MultipleTrusteeOperation;
    public TRUSTEE_FORM                 TrusteeForm;
    public TRUSTEE_TYPE                 TrusteeType;
    public String                       ptstrName;
}
```

```csharp
// The MULTIPLE_TRUSTEE_OPERATION enumeration determines if this
// is a single or a multiple trustee.
public enum MULTIPLE_TRUSTEE_OPERATION
{
    NO_MULTIPLE_TRUSTEE,
    TRUSTEE_IS_IMPERSONATE,
}

// The TRUSTEE_FORM enumeration determines what form the ACE trustee
// takes.
public enum TRUSTEE_FORM
{
    TRUSTEE_IS_SID,
    TRUSTEE_IS_NAME,
    TRUSTEE_BAD_FORM,
    TRUSTEE_IS_OBJECTS_AND_SID,
    TRUSTEE_IS_OBJECTS_AND_NAME
}

// The TRUSTEE_TYPE enumeration determines the type of the trustee.
public enum TRUSTEE_TYPE
{
    TRUSTEE_IS_UNKNOWN,
    TRUSTEE_IS_USER,
    TRUSTEE_IS_GROUP,
    TRUSTEE_IS_DOMAIN,
    TRUSTEE_IS_ALIAS,
    TRUSTEE_IS_WELL_KNOWN_GROUP,
    TRUSTEE_IS_DELETED,
    TRUSTEE_IS_INVALID,
    TRUSTEE_IS_COMPUTER
}

// This function retrieves the DACL from the file's security
// descriptor.
[DllImport("AdvAPI32.DLL", CharSet=CharSet.Auto, SetLastError=true )]
public static extern bool GetSecurityDescriptorDacl(
    IntPtr pSecurityDescriptor,
    ref Boolean lpbDaclPresent,
    out IntPtr pDacl,
    ref Boolean lpbDaclDefaulted);

private void btnTest_Click(object sender, System.EventArgs e)
{
    Boolean          DACLPresent;    // Is the DACL present?
    Boolean          Defaulted;      // Is the DACL defaulted?
    IntPtr           DACL;           // Pointer to the DACL.
    Int32            Result;         // Result of a call.
    UInt32           ACECount;       // Number of ACEs in DACL.
    EXPLICIT_ACCESS  []ACEList;      // An array of ACE entries.
```

```
// Obtain a security descriptor containing the DACL.
if (!GetFileSD(txtFile.Text,
    SECURITY_INFORMATION.DACL_SECURITY_INFORMATION))
    return;

// Obtain the DACL.
DACLPresent = false;
Defaulted = false;
if (!GetSecurityDescriptorDacl(SecurityDescriptor,
                               ref DACLPresent,
                               out DACL,
                               ref Defaulted))
{
    // Display an error message.
    MessageBox.Show("Unable to retrieve the DACL.",
                "Application Error",
                MessageBoxButtons.OK,
                MessageBoxIcon.Error);

    // Free the memory we allocated.
    Marshal.FreeHGlobal(SecurityDescriptor);

    return;
}

// Make sure there is a DACL to display.
if (!DACLPresent)
{
    // If not, tell the user there is no DACL.
    MessageBox.Show("There is no DACL.",
                "Processing Report",
                MessageBoxButtons.OK,
                MessageBoxIcon.Information);

    // Free the memory we allocated.
    Marshal.FreeHGlobal(SecurityDescriptor);

    return;
}

// Obtain the array of ACEs from the DACL.
ACECount = 0;
Result = GetExplicitEntriesFromAcl(DACL,
                                ref ACECount,
                                out ACEList);

// Check the results.
if (Result != ERROR_SUCCESS)
{
    // Display an error message.
```

```
        MessageBox.Show("Unable to retrieve the ACEs.",
                        "Application Error",
                        MessageBoxButtons.OK,
                        MessageBoxIcon.Error);

        // Free the memory we allocated.
        Marshal.FreeHGlobal(SecurityDescriptor);

        return;
    }

    // Display the number of ACEs.
    MessageBox.Show("The file has " + ACECount.ToString() +
                    " ACEs attached to it.",
                    "Number of ACEs",
                    MessageBoxButtons.OK,
                    MessageBoxIcon.Information);

    // Free the memory we allocated.
    Marshal.FreeHGlobal(SecurityDescriptor);
}
```

The code begins with a simple define—a reminder that the various Win32 API functions return different values. In this case, the GetExplicitEntriesFromAcl() function returns a value of ERROR_SUCCESS if successful or an error value if unsuccessful. You compare the return value with constants to determine the cause of error.

Notice that the GetExplicitEntriesFromAcl() function is also unique in that it's the only function so far that requires an array as input. You don't define a specific number of array elements—just the fact that the return value is an array. The call will still work, in this case, whether you provide an IntPtr or a single EXPLICIT_ACCESS structure value. The difference is that you won't actually be able to use the return value if you don't use an array.

WARNING   Microsoft acknowledges problems with the various functions used to work with ACEs. For example, the GetExplicitEntriesFromAcl() function can return the incorrect number of ACEs in some cases. (See Microsoft Knowledge Base Article Q260307 for details.) The suggested alternatives of working with the GetAclInformation(), GetAce(), and LookupAccountSid() functions doesn't really replace the missing functionality, so you might need to get creative at times in using the Win32 API. Make sure you check for appropriate Microsoft Knowledge Base articles at http://search.support.microsoft.com/search/default.aspx when you run into problems with any of the Win32 API functions.

The EXPLICIT_ACCESS structure is relatively complex. It includes both an enumerated value and another structure, TRUSTEE. The other two values are flags, which means you have to go through the complicated comparison routine we've used in other examples to determine what the flag values mean.

While the TRUSTEE structure looks relatively simple, it can become complex because it also includes enumerated values that determine what each of the fields in the structure means. For example, the *ptstrName* variable has meaning only if the *TRUSTEE_FORM* enumeration value is TRUSTEE_IS_NAME. Matters are further complicated by hidden rules. The *MULTIPLE_TRUSTEE_OPERATION* should always equal NO_MULTIPLE_TRUSTEE because Microsoft hasn't implemented this feature yet, or at least its developers haven't documented it.

The GetSecurityDescriptorDacl() is another of the functions we talked about earlier for working with the security descriptor. Remember that you should never change the security descriptor directly because other applications might try to access it at the same time. This function has an odd return value until you consider that most parts of the security descriptor are optional. The *lpbDaclPresent* tells you if the DACL is present in the security descriptor. The call can succeed even if the security descriptor doesn't contain a DACL, so you need to know this additional information.

In general, the btnTest_Click() method doesn't contain too many surprises. Of course, the first major call is to GetSecurityDescriptorDacl() because the code has to check the security descriptor created with the GetFileSD() function for a DACL. If there's no DACL, the application hasn't actually experienced an error—it's simply found an unprotected file. Consequently, you need to handle the return as a type of legitimate return value. It simply might not be the return value you were expecting.

The next call is to GetExplicitEntriesFromAcl(). Theoretically, the *ACECount* variable could contain a 0 on return, so you should check it. Again, it's not an actual application error—the DACL could simply be empty. It's unlikely that you'll ever see this happen unless the Get-ExplicitEntriesFromAcl() function experiences some type of error (see the previous warning for details).

At this point, we're ready to test the code. Figure 8.8 shows that the example file contains four ACE entries. When you run the code, you'll find that it reports the same number.

The example
application will
output the number
of ACEs associated
with the test file, as
shown here.

Where Do You Go from Here?

This chapter has provided you with the tools you need to begin using the Win32 API token-based security calls in your code. The Win32 API is huge in this area, so we didn't cover every nuance of the security system. In addition, some tasks such as encrypting and decrypting data are better performed using the .NET Framework calls, so they aren't discussed at all. However, you do know how to check the keys and locks used by the token-based security system, and that's the basis of most of the calls you'll need to make given the good security coverage provided by the .NET Framework.

You now have a decision to make. Which type of security is best for your application? It's an important question that you should answer before you write the first line of code for an application. Most security professionals know (and the crackers agree) that security has to be part of the application design, not added on at the last moment. This statement means that you need to consider what type of security to use now, not later. In some cases, you might want to combine the best elements of both role-based and token-based security to give your application an edge in an increasingly hostile application environment.

It's helpful to get as many opinions as possible when making security decisions. In many cases, security is a matter of perception—viewing things from the angle of the person who will attack your applications. The various URLs in this chapter help you gain the insights needed to write great security for your application. Make sure you spend some time researching your topic and then trying out some example applications. For example, it's often helpful to build a token-based and a role-based version of the same application to see which type of security is easiest to use, fastest to develop, easiest to understand, and least likely to fail.

If you're interested in another security example, check out the effective rights example found in the \Extras\EffectiveRights folder on the CD. This is a short example that shows how to determine the effective rights of a specific individual or group. The example is helpful in that it shows how you might check the credentials of a user in any application.

Chapter 9 begins a discussion of the operating system. We'll begin with an exploration of Windows XP–specific features you can add to your managed application. As you know from the ShowMessage example in Chapter 3, it's possible to add a level of Windows XP look and feel to your application without any programming at all. However, if you want to use the full range of features that Windows XP has to offer, then you'll need to write application code. Chapter 9 shows you how to create an application that uses the full range of features that Windows XP has to offer.

PART III

Fixing Advanced Win32 API Problems

CHAPTER 9

Accessing Windows XP Special Features

- What's New in Windows XP?

- Determining the Operating System Version Example

- Working with Theme Support Example

- Balloon Help Example

- Using NUnit for Automated Testing

Windows XP is the latest version of Windows that Microsoft has produced at the time of this writing. It uses the same core feature set as Windows 2000 but includes a new interface and many compatibility features. Of course, Windows XP includes the latest security features and updates of all utilities and supports the latest hardware. The intent behind Windows XP is to provide an operating system that can run older applications in a new and safer environment. For the most part, Windows XP succeeds in its given task.

Unfortunately, the .NET Framework doesn't contain any support at all for these new features, making your job as a developer much harder. On the one hand, you have users who want to use the new features found in Windows XP; on the other hand, you have management who wants to maximize compatibility and reduce training costs. In short, you know the features exist and it would be nice to use them, but you can't access them easily. This chapter helps by showing which features are easy to implement and will make a large impact on the user experience, yet keep training costs to a minimum and produce only a small effect on compatibility.

TIP   We've already looked at one way to use Windows XP functionality in your application. The example found in the section entitled "A C LIB Substitute Functions Example" in Chapter 3 shows how to create an application that has a Windows XP interface without any new coding.

Of course, sometimes a feature is so new that compatibility isn't a problem—the feature didn't exist in previous versions of Windows, so you have nothing to maintain compatibility with. The chapter also looks at a few examples of new features. These are the features that users are most likely to request in their next application and management is most likely to approve because they fix existing problems and make the user more productive. However, even these new features require a measure of care, so we'll discuss what you gain and what it will cost. As usual, we'll discuss everything in light of the example code.

What's New in Windows XP?

Some industry pundits have stated that Windows XP is only a slight upgrade to Windows 2000. In some respects, that viewpoint is true. Windows XP does use the same operating system core as Windows 2000 does. In addition, many of the utilities provide the same functionality as before, and you'll even find that some new features are available as separate downloads from Windows Update for Windows 2000. However, this viewpoint is also shortsighted in many ways. The new interface and compatibility features make Windows XP a different experience for the user. These new features also provide opportunities for the developer by helping you differentiate your application.

This section of the chapter will acquaint you with some of the most interesting new features that Window XP has to offer. In some cases, these new features are also available to Windows 2000 users in the form of a Windows Update or other Microsoft download. We won't cover every Windows XP feature because some are implemented automatically and others are in the esoteric category. For example, we won't discuss either the new search engine or the Remote Assistance feature, even though these features are unique to Windows XP. Windows XP comes in two versions, and we'll look at both in the sections that follow. You can obtain a list of Home Edition features at `http://www.microsoft.com/windowsxp/home/evaluation/features.asp` and Professional Edition features at `http://www.microsoft.com/windowsxp/pro/evaluation/features.asp`.

Common Features

Some new features are common to both Home Edition and Professional Edition. In some cases, the Home Edition provides a limited version of the Professional Edition feature, but in many situations, the loss of functionality relates to corporate use. The following sections provide details about the most important features.

User Interface Features

Windows XP comes packed with new user interface features. These features help improve user productivity and reduce training time dramatically. Microsoft's major emphasis on the interface is to hide features that user's don't need very often but to make commonly used features instantly available. This type of user interface feature works automatically and you'll never need to worry about it as part of your application. However, you do need to consider it as part of the help for your application. Some users will think your application didn't install correctly if they don't see it on the Start menu.

Some of the new user interface features come in the form of conveniences. For example, the new interface will allow user switching with a minimum of problems. One of the problems with the user switching feature is that, while it makes it easier to switch between users, fast user switching also keeps the account open once the user has made the change. Most organizations will view this as a security risk because a novice user could access a power user's account given the current setup. Part of the answer is good administration practices, but you can also make things easier by adding code for Fast User Switching to your application.

Reduced Need for Reboots

From the user's perspective, rebooting the computer is a waste of time. In some cases, it's also inconvenient. For example, rebooting a server means lost time for everyone who relies on the server for data storage and other services. Windows 2000 began a trend in which Microsoft asked developers to write applications that require fewer reboots. Windows XP continues this trend. In fact, Microsoft made the reboot issue part of the logo program for Windows XP. While this particular feature doesn't require any special operating system code, it could mean rewriting current applications to comply with Microsoft's reboot requirements.

Installation

Windows XP contains many features designed to make application installation easier. For example, a user can use the migration tool to move settings from one machine to another. This was originally an unsupported tool in the Windows 2000 Resource Kit. The savings in setup time can be substantial, especially if the machine supports more than one user.

From a developer's perspective, a Windows XP installation means using Microsoft Installer (MSI) files for installation. It also means adding new features to the installation, such as the support link found in the Add or Remove Programs applet. You might also want to add functionality such as on-demand installation to larger applications. In short, a process that began as copying files from a source directory to a target directory has become an application in its own right.

Balloon Help

You've seen the small balloon help that appears when the mouse hovers over a control or other object. In addition to the small balloon help, Windows XP also offers a new feature that displays a large balloon. For example, whenever Windows Update detects an update online, it displays a large balloon that describes the update and helps the user download it. The balloon help isn't an application dialog—it's more of a quick note for an application executing in the background. This is such an important feature that you'll see an example of it later in the chapter.

Background Intelligent Transfer Service (BITS)

The Background Intelligent Transfer Service (BITS) feature enables an application to transfer data in the background without any user interaction. Windows has had the ability to transfer files from day one, so this ability is nothing new. However, BITS transfers can survive disconnects and even reboots. The transfer continues wherever it left off before the disruption. This is an especially important feature if you have to support users on the road because connections can be intermittent.

Enhanced Hardware Support

Windows XP provides support for a wealth of modern hardware, including Universal Plug and Play (UPnP). The feature that makes UPnP unique is that it supports any intelligent device using any network connection. Theoretically, you could write an application that enables the user's furnace to send a message to the user stating that the temperature has dropped below prescribed limits.

Professional Edition Exclusive Features

The Professional Edition of Windows XP costs quite a bit more than the Home Edition because it contains more features. As previously mentioned, this is the version of Windows you'll want to use if you use your machine mainly in a professional setting. For example, most business users will want this edition to gain full access to important security features.

The following sections discuss unique Professional Edition features. Some of these features already appear in Windows 2000 Professional, but they don't appear at all in Windows 9x or in the Home Edition of Windows XP. Each section tells you when a feature also appears in Windows 2000 Professional.

Scalability

From a developer perspective, Windows XP means having more resources available to run applications. If the user has Windows XP Professional installed, there's a possibility of multiple processor support. You could run threads on a specific processor to help spread the application load evenly.

The scalability features of Windows XP Professional also include the ability to use 4GB of RAM. While Windows 2000 Professional also supports this feature, this is a new addition for users upgrading from Windows 9x, which only supports 512MB. The extra memory that Windows XP supports will enable you to develop more robust applications in the future.

Full NTFS-Based Security

Windows XP supports many of the same file security features that Windows 2000 Professional does. For example, you have full access to the benefits provided by Kerberos. In addition, you can encrypt individual files to protect their content. However, this new version also adds some new benefits.

One change you'll notice is that you can encrypt a file with multiple user accessibility. Windows 2000 Professional only allows single user encryption, which means that you have an option of securing or sharing a file. With Windows XP, you can encrypt the file and still share it with a select group of users.

We've already discussed many security issues in Chapter 8. However, it's important to realize that Windows XP offers far more than previous versions of Windows offered when it comes to security. Imagine creating an application that provides support for multiple user encryption.

File Management

Some of the new Windows XP file management features will require a little time to get used to if you've worked with other versions of Windows. For example, this version of Windows offers improved handling of file associations. If you download a file from the Internet and don't have an application that can access that file, Windows XP can often provide an application suggestion for you. The applications you create can include support for advance file management using this Windows XP feature.

The Web Distributed Authoring and Versioning (WebDAV) protocol allows you to publish files or folders to any Web service that provides the required support. This protocol provides automatic encryption and decryption to keep your data secure, which also makes the data transfer process transparent.

Networking

Windows XP supports all of the features that you'll find in Windows 2000. In addition to standard Windows 2000 features, you'll find a wealth of new features such as wireless support. Microsoft recognizes that most organizations will have to create hybrid networks that contain a mix of desktop and wireless devices in the near future.

Another feature is network awareness. This feature allows the operating system to determine when a machine has changed locations. The operating system and some applications may require configuration changes to access another domain controller or to access resources on the network when a location change occurs. In the past, the network administrator would need to make these changes manually. Windows XP tries to make any required changes automatically.

NOTE   There are some Windows XP features that you don't have to access using Windows API calls, but they fall into the "distributed with the .NET Framework" category. One of these features is GDI+. This updated drawing technology enables you to create graphics easier and faster. One of the more interesting GDI+ features is the ClearType technology that's supposed to make text easier to read on a liquid crystal display (LCD), such as those used for laptops and personal digital assistants (PDAs). In some cases, people have reported headaches when using ClearType on a standard monitor because of the way it displays the fonts. ClearType relies on addressing the LCD at the sub-pixel level to make it appear that the display has higher resolution than it actually provides. You can access the ClearType display technology using the `ClearTypeGridFit` member of the `TextRenderingHint` enumeration.

Determining the Operating System Version Example

It's important to know which version of Windows an application is running on if you plan to use special operating system features. The `GetVersionEx()` function is easy enough to understand—it might seem as if you could use it directly within the .NET Framework application using PInvoke. However, it's not as easy you might think to make this function work.

There are several problems to overcome when using the GetVersionEx() function. The first is that the GetVersionEx() function can use one of two data structures as input: OSVERSIONINFO and OSVERSIONINFOEX. The GetVersionEx() function was originally designed to use the OSVERSIONINFO data structure exclusively. In fact, using the OSVERSIONINFOEX data structure on an older version of Windows will fail, and it's one of the tests you need to run to determine which version of Windows the host system is using.

NOTE   The .NET Framework provides the OperatingSystem class as part of the System namespace. It's possible to perform some level of version checking using the methods in this namespace, but it appears that the OperatingSystem class relies on the GetVersion() Win32 API call instead of the GetVersionEx() Win32 API call to obtain the version information. At the very least, the OperatingSystem class methods use the OSVERSIONINFO structure instead of the OSVERSIONINFOEX structure, which provides additional information. While you can use the OperatingSystem class methods in many situations, it's helpful to remember that the Win32 API call does provide additional information. The additional information includes service pack major and minor revision numbers, a suite mask, and product type. Consequently, you can use the OperatingSystem class methods to determine if you're using Windows XP or Windows .NET Server. However, you can't differentiate between the Home and Professional editions and Windows .NET Server—all three versions look the same.

The second problem is with the OSVERSIONINFOEX data structure. In the C/C++ header definition of the data structure, you'll find the normal DWORD values (among others). However, there's also a TCHAR array like the one shown here:

```
typedef struct _OSVERSIONINFOEX {
   DWORD dwOSVersionInfoSize;
   DWORD dwMajorVersion;
   DWORD dwMinorVersion;
   DWORD dwBuildNumber;
   DWORD dwPlatformId;
   TCHAR szCSDVersion[ 128 ];
   WORD wServicePackMajor;
   WORD wServicePackMinor;
   WORD wSuiteMask;
   BYTE wProductType;
   BYTE wReserved;
} OSVERSIONINFOEX, *POSVERSIONINFOEX, *LPOSVERSIONINFOEX;
```

The problem with this array is that it causes problems in the managed environment. You can define a data structure that contains a suitable replacement for the TCHAR, but when you try to create an instance of the data structure, C# will balk. You can only use it in unsafe mode. If you'll remember from previous discussions, Visual Basic won't even touch this data structure because it doesn't provide the means to work with unsafe code. Consequently, you'll need to create a wrapper DLL for this example. Listing 9.1 shows the wrapper DLL code. You'll find the Visual C++ source code for this part of the example in the \Chapter 09\OSVersion folder of the CD.

Listing 9.1 **The OSVersion Wrapper DLL Performs a Simple Calling Mechanism**

```
// This is the data structure that contains all of the available
// operating system version information.
public __gc struct OSVERSIONINFOEX2
{
public:
    Int32    dwOSVersionInfoSize;
    Int32    dwMajorVersion;
    Int32    dwMinorVersion;
    Int32    dwBuildNumber;
    Int32    dwPlatformId;
    Char     szCSDVersion[];
    Int16    wServicePackMajor;
    Int16    wServicePackMinor;
    Int16    wSuiteMask;
    Byte     wProductType;
    Byte     wReserved;
};

public __gc class OSVer
{
public:
    static bool GetOSVersion(OSVERSIONINFOEX2** VerInfo)
    {
        OSVERSIONINFOEX   OSVer;      // Unmanaged version info.
        OSVERSIONINFOEX2* LocalVer;   // Local version info.

        // Set some memory aside.
        memset(&OSVer, 0, sizeof(OSVERSIONINFOEX));
        OSVer.dwOSVersionInfoSize = sizeof(OSVERSIONINFOEX);

        // Get the version information.
        if (!GetVersionEx((OSVERSIONINFO *)&OSVer))
        {
            // Return a failure value if unsuccessful.
            return false;
        }

        // Transfer the data to the input structure.
        LocalVer = new OSVERSIONINFOEX2();
        LocalVer->dwBuildNumber = OSVer.dwBuildNumber;
        LocalVer->dwMajorVersion = OSVer.dwMajorVersion;
        LocalVer->dwMinorVersion = OSVer.dwMinorVersion;
        LocalVer->dwOSVersionInfoSize = OSVer.dwOSVersionInfoSize;
```

```
LocalVer->dwPlatformId = OSVer.dwPlatformId;
LocalVer->wProductType = OSVer.wProductType;
LocalVer->wServicePackMajor = OSVer.wServicePackMajor;
LocalVer->wServicePackMinor = OSVer.wServicePackMinor;
LocalVer->wSuiteMask = OSVer.wSuiteMask;

// The char array requires special handling. The Platform
// SDK documentation gives the char array a specific size
// in this case.
LocalVer->szCSDVersion = new Char[128];
for (int Counter = 0; Counter < 128; Counter++)
   LocalVer->szCSDVersion[Counter] = OSVer.szCSDVersion[Counter];

// Transfer the data to the client.
*VerInfo = LocalVer;

return true;
   }
};
```

As you can see, the OSVERSIONINFOEX2 data structure is a direct match for the OSVERSIONINFOEX data structure. The only difference is in the use of managed data types. Because Visual C++ works equally well with managed and unmanaged code, using the OSVERSIONINFOEX2 data structure doesn't present any problems.

The call to GetVersionEx() isn't difficult. All we do is create an unmanaged OSVERSION-INFOEX data structure, set memory aside for it, and set the size of the data structure in the *OSVer.dwOSVersionInfoSize* variable. Notice the use of a type cast to pass the data structure to GetVersionEx(). If the function fails, then we return false. Otherwise, the function proceeds to transfer the data to a local copy of the OSVERSIONINFOEX2 data structure.

Most of the data transfers as you might expect. The only problem area is the TCHAR array. We need to use a for loop to transfer the data one TCHAR at a time. Of course, you need to size the managed array first. Because the C/C++ header doesn't use a constant for this particular array, you can simply use a number to size it. The final step is to place a pointer to the local version of the data structure in the reference passed by the application. The wrapper DLL returns true in this case.

The client code is a little more complex because it has to do something with the data contained within the OSVERSIONINFOEX2 data structure. Listing 9.2 shows the code you'll need to determine the host operating system for a client machine. The same type of process could detect a server operating system. You'll find the source for this part of the example in the \Chapter 09\C#\CheckVersion and \Chapter 09\VB\CheckVersion folders of the CD.

Listing 9.2   **The Client Application Detects the Operating System Type**

```csharp
// This enumeration determines the platform ID type.
public enum PlatformID
{
    VER_PLATFORM_WIN32s            = 0,
    VER_PLATFORM_WIN32_WINDOWS     = 1,
    VER_PLATFORM_WIN32_NT          = 2
}

// This enumeration determines the main product type.
public enum ProductType
{
    VER_NT_WORKSTATION             = 0x0000001,
    VER_NT_DOMAIN_CONTROLLER       = 0x0000002,
    VER_NT_SERVER                  = 0x0000003
}

// This enumeration contains the suite flags.
public enum SuiteMask : uint
{
    VER_SERVER_NT                      = 0x80000000,
    VER_WORKSTATION_NT                 = 0x40000000,
    VER_SUITE_SMALLBUSINESS            = 0x00000001,
    VER_SUITE_ENTERPRISE               = 0x00000002,
    VER_SUITE_BACKOFFICE               = 0x00000004,
    VER_SUITE_COMMUNICATIONS           = 0x00000008,
    VER_SUITE_TERMINAL                 = 0x00000010,
    VER_SUITE_SMALLBUSINESS_RESTRICTED = 0x00000020,
    VER_SUITE_EMBEDDEDNT               = 0x00000040,
    VER_SUITE_DATACENTER               = 0x00000080,
    VER_SUITE_SINGLEUSERTS             = 0x00000100,
    VER_SUITE_PERSONAL                 = 0x00000200,
    VER_SUITE_BLADE                    = 0x00000400
}

private void btnTest_Click(object sender, System.EventArgs e)
{
    OSVERSIONINFOEX2  OSVerInfo;  // Version information.

    // Initialize the data structure.
    OSVerInfo = new OSVERSIONINFOEX2();

    // Determine the extended version information.
    if (!OSVer.GetOSVersion(ref OSVerInfo))
    {
        // If not successful, the host system is using an older
        // version of Windows.
        MessageBox.Show("Version older than Windows NT 4 SP6.",
                        "Version Information",
```

```
                    MessageBoxButtons.OK,
                    MessageBoxIcon.Information);

      return;
   }

   // See if this is a Windows 9x system.
   if (OSVerInfo.dwPlatformId !=
      (Int32)PlatformID.VER_PLATFORM_WIN32_NT)
   {
      MessageBox.Show("Using Windows 9x.",
                    "Version Information",
                    MessageBoxButtons.OK,
                    MessageBoxIcon.Information);

      return;
   }

   // Determine if this is a workstation or server.
   if (OSVerInfo.wProductType == (Int32)ProductType.VER_NT_WORKSTATION)
   {
      // Determine if this is Windows XP.
      if ((OSVerInfo.dwMajorVersion == 5) &&
         (OSVerInfo.dwMinorVersion == 1))

         // Determine if this is the Personal Edition.
         if (OSVerInfo.wSuiteMask ==
            (Int32)SuiteMask.VER_SUITE_PERSONAL)
         {
            MessageBox.Show("Using Windows XP Personal.",
                        "Version Information",
                        MessageBoxButtons.OK,
                        MessageBoxIcon.Information);

            return;
         }

         // Must be the Professional Edition.
         else
         {
            MessageBox.Show("Using Windows XP Professional.",
                        "Version Information",
                        MessageBoxButtons.OK,
                        MessageBoxIcon.Information);

            return;
         }

      // Check for Windows 2000 Professional.
      if ((OSVerInfo.dwMajorVersion == 5) &&
         (OSVerInfo.dwMinorVersion == 0))
```

```
      {
         MessageBox.Show("Using Windows 2000 Professional.",
                    "Version Information",
                    MessageBoxButtons.OK,
                    MessageBoxIcon.Information);

         return;
      }

      // Must be Windows NT 4 Workstation.
      else
      {
         MessageBox.Show("Using Windows NT 4 Workstation.",
                    "Version Information",
                    MessageBoxButtons.OK,
                    MessageBoxIcon.Information);

         return;
      }
   }

   // It's probably a server, but it's a good idea to check
   // anyway.
   else if (OSVerInfo.wProductType ==
         (Int32)ProductType.VER_NT_SERVER || OSVerInfo.wProductType
          == (Int32)ProductType.VER_NT_DOMAIN_CONTROLLER)
   {
      MessageBox.Show("Using one of the server versions.",
                    "Version Information",
                    MessageBoxButtons.OK,
                    MessageBoxIcon.Information);

      return;
   }

   // We can't determine the Windows version type.
      MessageBox.Show("Unable to determine Windows version.",
                    "Version Information Error",
                    MessageBoxButtons.OK,
                    MessageBoxIcon.Error);

}
```

This example relies on three enumerations. The `PlatformID` enumeration indicates the major platform: Win32s running on a Windows 3x system, Win32 running on a Windows 9x system, or a Windows NT/2000/XP system. The `ProductType` enumeration determines if the target system is a workstation, server, or domain controller. The `GetVersionEx()` function will actually differentiate between a regular server and a domain controller, which comes in handy for some types of applications. Finally, the `SuiteMask` enumeration contains a list of platform subtypes. For example, this is the enumeration that tells you if the host system is a Windows 2000 Small Business server or a Windows XP Personal system. You can even use this enumeration to detect embedded systems.

The client code begins by creating an OSVERSIONINFOEX2 data structure and instantiating it. It calls the GetOSVersion() function found in the wrapper DLL. A call failure doesn't indicate that the call actually failed—it indicates that the system is using a version of Windows older than Windows NT 4 Service Pack 6.

The code proceeds by using a series of checks to determine the platform type. For example, if the OSVerInfo.dwPlatformId field doesn't contain the platform ID for a Windows NT system, then we know that the system is using Windows 9*x* or Windows 3*x*. Because the .NET Framework won't run on Windows 3*x*, we know for certain that it's a Windows 9*x* system.

The next series of checks begins by verifying that the host system is a workstation rather than a server. The code then uses the version number to detect the specific version of Windows. For example, Windows XP is version 5.1, while Windows 2000 is version 5.0. You can find a complete list of version numbers in the Platform SDK documentation. The remaining check for a Windows XP system is to differentiate between the Home Edition and the Professional Edition. All the code needs to do is check the *OSVerInfo.wSuiteMask* field because a Home Edition system will have the VER_SUITE_PERSONAL value. The checks continue through the series of systems that I decided to check for this example.

Working with Theme Support Example

Themes are one of the more innovation additions to Windows XP. While Windows XP does support the older themes used in previous versions of Windows, it also provides support for a new class of themes. This new theme class enables the user to configure the operating system environment in ways not possible in the past. This technology is loosely based on the "skins" technology used for Microsoft utilities such as the Media Player, but there are differences that make the two technologies incompatible. The main theme files reside in the \WINDOWS\ Resources\Themes folder, but each user has at least one custom theme as well. The themes define the appearance of operating system elements such as push buttons and windows. Support isn't limited to controls but applies equally to all visual elements.

You learned in Chapter 3 that adding a manifest to your application forces Windows to draw the standard controls using the Windows XP themes. However, the manifest doesn't affect owner-drawn controls. If you want owner-drawn display elements to have a Windows XP theme appearance, then you need to draw them manually using special functions such as DrawThemeBackground() and DrawThemeText().

Of course, the first step in using custom operating system function calls is to determine the version of the operating system as we did in the previous example. The example in this section assumes you've already taken that step and want to begin using the theme support that Windows XP provides. Listing 9.3 shows the code for this example. You'll find the source code in the \Chapter 09\C#\WinTheme and \Chapter 09\VB\WinTheme folders of the CD.

Listing 9.3   Using Windows XP Theme Support in an Application

```
// This function verifies that theme support is available.
[DllImport("UXTheme.DLL", CharSet=CharSet.Auto, SetLastError=true )]
public static extern bool IsThemeActive();

// This function opens a handle to the theme support. We need a
// handle in order to access theme features.
[DllImport("UXTheme.DLL", CharSet=CharSet.Auto, SetLastError=true )]
public static extern IntPtr OpenThemeData(IntPtr hWnd,
                                          String pszClassList);

// Use this function to close the handle to the theme support
// when you finish using it.
[DllImport("UXTheme.DLL", CharSet=CharSet.Auto, SetLastError=true )]
public static extern Int32 CloseThemeData(IntPtr hTheme);

// The purpose of this function is to retrieve a device context;
// essentially a drawing area for the application.
[DllImport("User32.DLL", CharSet=CharSet.Auto, SetLastError=true )]
public static extern IntPtr GetDC(IntPtr hWnd);

// Use this function to release the device context.
[DllImport("User32.DLL", CharSet=CharSet.Auto, SetLastError=true )]
public static extern Int32 ReleaseDC(IntPtr hWnd, IntPtr hDC);

// The GetClientRect() function obtains the current client drawing
// area on screen.
[DllImport("User32.DLL", CharSet=CharSet.Auto, SetLastError=true )]
public static extern bool GetClientRect(IntPtr hWnd, ref RECT lpRect);

// The RECT structure is used for many drawing functions.
public struct RECT
{
    public Int32    left;
    public Int32    top;
    public Int32    right;
    public Int32    bottom;
}

// This is the function that enables the application to draw user
// controls using the current theme. You need a minimum of two forms
// of this function. The first requires use of a clipping rectangle,
```

```
// while the second doesn't.
[DllImport("UXTheme.DLL", CharSet=CharSet.Auto, SetLastError=true )]
public static extern Int32 DrawThemeBackground(IntPtr hTheme,
                                     IntPtr hDC,
                                     Int32 iPartId,
                                     Int32 iStateId,
                                     ref RECT pRect,
                                     ref RECT pClipRect);

[DllImport("UXTheme.DLL", CharSet=CharSet.Auto, SetLastError=true )]
public static extern Int32 DrawThemeBackground(IntPtr hTheme,
                                     IntPtr hDC,
                                     Int32 iPartId,
                                     Int32 iStateId,
                                     ref RECT pRect,
                                     IntPtr NoClipRect);

// This function enables the application to draw theme specific text.
[DllImport("UXTheme.DLL", CharSet=CharSet.Auto, SetLastError=true )]
public static extern Int32 DrawThemeText (IntPtr hTheme,
                                     IntPtr hDC,
                                     Int32 iPartId,
                                     Int32 iStateId,
                                     String pszText,
                                     Int32 iCharCount,
                                     UInt32 dwTextFlags,
                                     UInt32 dwTextFlags2,
                                     ref RECT pRect);

// This is an enumeration for the dwTextFlags argument.
public enum TextFlags
{
    DT_TOP                 = 0x00000000,
    DT_LEFT                = 0x00000000,
    DT_CENTER              = 0x00000001,
    DT_RIGHT               = 0x00000002,
    DT_VCENTER             = 0x00000004,
    DT_BOTTOM              = 0x00000008,
    DT_WORDBREAK           = 0x00000010,
    DT_SINGLELINE          = 0x00000020,
    DT_EXPANDTABS          = 0x00000040,
    DT_TABSTOP             = 0x00000080,
    DT_NOCLIP              = 0x00000100,
    DT_EXTERNALLEADING     = 0x00000200,
    DT_CALCRECT            = 0x00000400,
    DT_NOPREFIX            = 0x00000800,

    // This next value is undocumented and might not work.
    //DT_INTERNAL          = 0x00001000,
```

```
    DT_EDITCONTROL              = 0x00002000,
    DT_PATH_ELLIPSIS            = 0x00004000,
    DT_END_ELLIPSIS             = 0x00008000,
    DT_MODIFYSTRING             = 0x00010000,
    DT_RTLREADING               = 0x00020000,
    DT_WORD_ELLIPSIS            = 0x00040000,
    DT_NOFULLWIDTHCHARBREAK     = 0x00080000,
    DT_HIDEPREFIX               = 0x00100000,
    DT_PREFIXONLY               = 0x00200000


// This is the only value for the dwTextFlags2 argument.
public const int DTT_GRAYED = 0x1;

// This function enables the application to draw icons.
[DllImport("UXTheme.DLL", CharSet=CharSet.Auto, SetLastError=true )]
public static extern Int32 DrawThemeIcon(IntPtr hTheme,
                                         IntPtr hDC,
                                         Int32 iPartId,
                                         Int32 iStateId,
                                         ref RECT pRect,
                                         int himl,
                                         Int32 iImageIndex);


// Defines used for the parts and status.
public const int BP_PUSHBUTTON = 1;
public const int PBS_NORMAL = 1;

private void btnTest_Click(object sender, System.EventArgs e)
{
    IntPtr    hTheme;  // Handle to the theme support.
    Int32     Result;  // Result of an operation.
    IntPtr    hDC;     // Handle to the device context.
    RECT      Rect;    // Client drawing area.
    RECT      DrwRect; // Drawing area within the client area.

    // Verify the theme is active.
    if (!IsThemeActive())
    {
        // Display an error message.
        MessageBox.Show("Theme support isn't active!",
                        "Application Error",
                        MessageBoxButtons.OK,
                        MessageBoxIcon.Error);

        return;
    }

    // Obtain a handle to the theme support.
    hTheme = OpenThemeData(lblTestArea.Handle, "Button");
```

```
// Check for errors.
if (hTheme == IntPtr.Zero)
{
    // Display an error message.
    MessageBox.Show("Couldn't open theme data!",
                    "Application Error",
                    MessageBoxButtons.OK,
                    MessageBoxIcon.Error);

    return;
}

// Obtain a device context for the current application.
hDC = GetDC(lblTestArea.Handle);

// Check for errors.
if (hDC == IntPtr.Zero)
{
    // Display an error message.
    MessageBox.Show("Couldn't obtain device context!",
                    "Application Error",
                    MessageBoxButtons.OK,
                    MessageBoxIcon.Error);

    // Close the theme handle.
    CloseThemeData(hTheme);

    return;
}

// Determine the client drawing area.
Rect = new RECT();
if (!GetClientRect(lblTestArea.Handle, ref Rect))
{
    // Display an error message.
    MessageBox.Show("Couldn't obtain client drawing area!",
                    "Application Error",
                    MessageBoxButtons.OK,
                    MessageBoxIcon.Error);

    return;
}

// Draw the theme background and validate the results.
Result = DrawThemeBackground(hTheme,
                             hDC,
                             BP_PUSHBUTTON,
                             PBS_NORMAL,
                             ref Rect,
                             IntPtr.Zero);
```

```
if (Result != S_OK)
   MessageBox.Show("Couldn't draw the theme background!",
                   "Application Error",
                   MessageBoxButtons.OK,
                   MessageBoxIcon.Error);

// Create a drawing area 5 pixels from the top, left, and right.
DrwRect = Rect;
DrwRect.top += 5;
DrwRect.left += 5;
DrwRect.right -= 5;

// Draw the theme text for the window.
Result = DrawThemeText(hTheme,
                       hDC,
                       BP_PUSHBUTTON,
                       PBS_NORMAL,
                       "Left",
                       4,
                       0,
                       0,
                       ref DrwRect);

DrwRect.top += 15;
Result = DrawThemeText(hTheme,
                       hDC,
                       BP_PUSHBUTTON,
                       PBS_NORMAL,
                       "Centered",
                       8,
                       (UInt32)TextFlags.DT_CENTER,
                       0,
                       ref DrwRect);

DrwRect.top += 15;
Result = DrawThemeText(hTheme,
                       hDC,
                       BP_PUSHBUTTON,
                       PBS_NORMAL,
                       "Right",
                       5,
                       (UInt32)TextFlags.DT_RIGHT,
                       DTT_GRAYED,
                       ref DrwRect);

// Draw the theme icon for the window.
DrwRect.top += 15;
DrwRect.bottom = DrwRect.top + 32;
DrwRect.right = DrwRect.left + 32;
Result = DrawThemeIcon(hTheme,
                       hDC,
                       BP_PUSHBUTTON,
```

```
                 PBS_NORMAL,
                 ref DrwRect,
                 ilDraw.hImageList,
                 cbSelect.SelectedIndex);

   // Release the device context when finished drawing.
   Result = ReleaseDC(lblTestArea.Handle, hDC);

   // Close the theme handle when we're finished.
   Result = CloseThemeData(hTheme);
}
```

If you're thinking that this is a lot of code, consider the fact that this is a simple example—the code only gets longer as you add features. However, the code does show the major function declarations you'll need and a few of the enumerations for a full implementation. As you can see, all of the theme-specific functions reside in the UXTheme.DLL file and this file only appears on machines with Windows XP installed.

Notice that most of the function calls return either a handle to a resource or a result value. The result value is always equal to S_OK (defined in the code, but not shown in the listing) except for the ReleaseDC() function. The ReleaseDC() function returns 0 if Windows couldn't release the device context for some reason and 1 if the function succeeds. The application won't actually check for the ReleaseDC() return code because it would be unusual for the function to fail and there isn't any way to recover if it does.

This example relies on a combination of old and new functions. For example, the GetClient-Rect() appears in every version of Windows currently in existence. This function returns the drawing area of the selected object. It uses a RECT structure as shown in the code to return the results. Many Win32 API functions rely on GetClientRect(), so this is one of the functions you should consider placing in a DLL for future use.

Most of the theme drawing functions rely on a part and state identifier. The only problem is that the part and state information is calculated as part of a complex macro located in the tmschema.h header file and that the Platform SDK documentation doesn't tell you that you need this header, even when working with Visual C++. As a result, developers (even Visual C++ developers) need to learn about this header by trial and error. The tmschema.h header file won't tell you anything about the enumerated values, so you'll need to build a Visual C++ wrapper DLL to handle the enumerated values, create a managed enumeration, or rely on constants as we have in the example.

TIP Drawing the theme background means knowing which controls you want to draw and how you want them drawn. The Microsoft documentation uses the term *parts* to refer to controls used within a theme environment. Themes support a number of parts, so it's important to be specific when you call the DrawThemeBackground() function. With this in mind, Microsoft has provided an entire Win32 API help subject on the theme parts and the state of those parts. You'll find this write-up at ms-help://MS.VSCC/MS.MSDNVS/ shellcc/platform/CommCtls/UserEx/reference/topics/PartsAndStates.htm.

The DrawThemeText() function also relies on two enumerations that determine how it draws text on screen. The Visual C++ header file contains all of the values shown for the TextFlags enumeration. However, one of the values in the header file isn't listed in the Platform SDK documentation. That's why DT_INTERNAL is commented out in the example code. This is a use-at-your-own-risk value.

The example code begins by checking for active theme support. Even though Windows XP supports themes, the user can turn the support off. You must use standard drawing technique if the user has turned theme support off. Microsoft recommends that you only make this check once when the application starts. Afterward, you can monitor the WM_THEMECHANGED message. Monitoring this message also tells you when to update the display if the user changes themes during the session. We discussed various messaging techniques in Chapter 4.

Once the code checks for theme support, it needs to open two handles. The first handle is for the theme support. You can't use the theme functions without a handle to the theme support. The second handle is for the device context. Think of the device context as a virtual drawing area for the selected object. Because Windows has to coordinate the drawing commands for every object on the system, it requires the use of a device context so that one drawing doesn't overwrite another in the actual display area.

Notice that the part argument is set to BP_PUSHBUTTON for all of the drawing calls. This means that all of the drawing will take place using the pushbutton characteristics in the theme. In addition, the pushbutton is in the PBS_NORMAL state. A theme normally has entries for several part states. The state that you select will affect the appearance of the application output.

At this point, the application is ready to draw something on screen. The example includes three DrawThemeText() calls so that you can see the effects of various flags. The flags affect the appearance of the text as well as its placement within the drawing area.

The DrawThemeIcon() function requires some unusual input. You must supply the theme and device context flags as usual, along with the part and state identifications. However, notice that the DrawThemeIcon() function also requires an image list and an image index within the image list. Unfortunately, you can't use the managed ImageList control that comes with Visual Studio .NET because the DrawThemeIcon() function won't know what to do with the code. You must use the Visual Basic ImageList control instead by selecting it in the Customize Toolbox dialog. Figure 9.1 shows this dialog box and the option you'll need to check.

FIGURE 9.1:

The example uses a COM version of the ImageList control in place of the managed version.

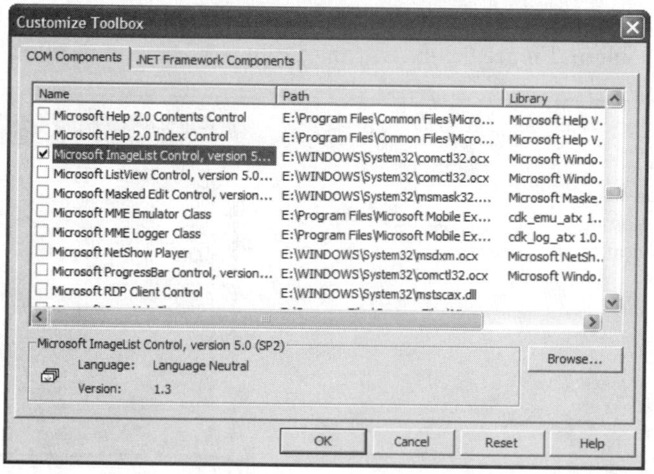

NOTE The icons for this example were created using IconForge. While you could use any good drawing tool to create icons, IconForge has features that make it one of the better options. We'll discuss IconForge in detail in the section "Using IconForge" in Chapter 11.

Configuring this control is relatively easy. All you need to do is right-click the control and choose Properties from the context menu. Select the Images tab and you'll see buttons for adding and removing images. Figure 9.2 shows a typical example of the Properties dialog box for this control. Notice that the index for the control is 1 based instead of 0 based. You'll still need to access the images using a 0 reference.

FIGURE 9.2:

You'll add images to the ImageList control using the Properties dialog box.

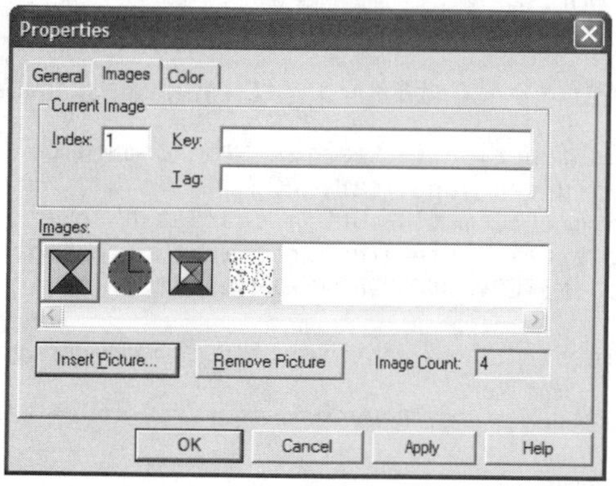

Upon completion of drawing, the code releases both the device context and the theme handles. This is an essential step. Failure to release both handles will result in an application memory and resource leak. In addition, you'll find that the system will experience a slight performance hit because of the open handles. Windows normally requires a reboot to fix this problem. Figure 9.3 shows the output from this application.

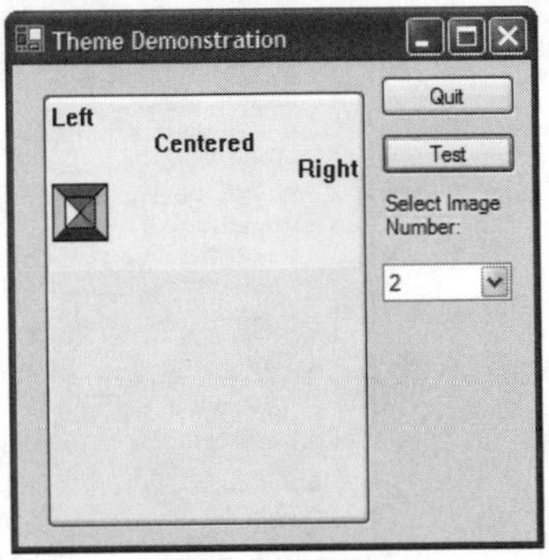

FIGURE 9.3:

The example application draws a background, some text, and an icon of your choice.

Balloon Help Example

Balloon ToolTips are relatively new. They're the ToolTips that you see when Windows wants you to visit the Windows Update site or the modem connects or when Windows needs to provide some other informational message. Balloon ToolTips have rounded edges and accommodate a little more text than a standard ToolTip. The .NET Framework provides good support for most types of ToolTips. However, if you want to create a balloon ToolTip, the Win32 API is the only option. The reason you need to use the Win32 API is that the ToolTip class is sealed—you can't modify it in any way. Listing 9.4 shows the code you'll need to create a balloon ToolTip.

Listing 9.4   One Method for Creating a Balloon ToolTip

```
// This function initializes the common controls for
// the current application.
[DllImport("ComCtl32.DLL", CharSet=CharSet.Auto, SetLastError=true )]
public static extern Boolean InitCommonControlsEx(
    ref INITCOMMONCONTROLSEX lpInitCtrls);

// This structure contains the common control initialization
// information.
public struct INITCOMMONCONTROLSEX
```

```
{
   public Int32 dwSize;
   public Int32 dwICC;
}

// This constant defines the common controls we want to load.
public const int ICC_WIN95_CLASSES = 0x000000FF;

// This function creates a new window. It's a general function,
// but we're using it in a very specific way to create a special
// type of ToolTip window.
[DllImport("User32.DLL", CharSet=CharSet.Auto, SetLastError=true )]
public static extern IntPtr CreateWindowEx(UInt32 dwExStyle,
                                    String lpClassName,
                                    String lpWindowName,
                                    UInt32 dwStyle,
                                    UInt32 x,
                                    UInt32 y,
                                    UInt32 nWidth,
                                    UInt32 nHeight,
                                    IntPtr hWndParent,
                                    IntPtr hMenu,
                                    IntPtr hInstance,
                                    IntPtr lpParam);

// We'll need these defines to set the window up for use.
public const int WS_EX_TOPMOST = 0x00000008;
public const String TOOLTIPS_CLASS = "tooltips_class32";
public const UInt32 WS_POPUP = 0x80000000;
public const UInt32 TTS_ALWAYSTIP = 0x01;
public const UInt32 TTS_NOPREFIX = 0x02;
public const UInt32 TTS_BALLOON = 0x40;
public const UInt32 CW_USEDEFAULT = 0x80000000;

// This function sets the ToolTip position in relation to the
// application window.
[DllImport("User32.DLL", CharSet=CharSet.Auto, SetLastError=true )]
public static extern Boolean SetWindowPos(IntPtr hWnd,
                                    IntPtr hWndInsertAfter,
                                    Int32 X,
                                    Int32 Y,
                                    Int32 cx,
                                    Int32 cy,
                                    UInt32 uFlags);

// These defines help set the window position.
public IntPtr HWND_TOPMOST = new IntPtr(-1);
public const UInt32 SWP_NOSIZE = 0x0001;
public const UInt32 SWP_NOMOVE = 0x0002;
public const UInt32 SWP_NOACTIVATE = 0x0010;
```

```
// This data structure defines elements of the ToolTip.
public struct TOOLINFO
{
    public Int32    cbSize;
    public UInt32   uFlags;
    public IntPtr   hwnd;
    public UInt32   uId;
    public RECT     rect;
    public IntPtr   hinst;
    public String   lpszText;
    public Int32    lParam;
}

// These constants are used with the TOOLINFO data structure.
public const UInt32 TTF_SUBCLASS = 0x0010;
public const UInt32 TTF_TRANSPARENT = 0x0100;
public const UInt32 TTF_CENTERTIP = 0x0002;

// This constant tells the application which message it's
// recieving.
public const Int32 TTM_ADDTOOL = 0x0400 + 50;

private void btnTest_Click(object sender, System.EventArgs e)
{
    INITCOMMONCONTROLSEX ComCtrls;    // Common control data.
    IntPtr               WinHandle;   // Handle to the ToolTip window.
    RECT                 Rect;        // Client drawing area.
    TOOLINFO             TI;          // ToolTip information.
    IntPtr               TIAddr;      // Address of the ToolTip info.
    Assembly             Asm;         // Executing assembly.
    IntPtr               hInstance;   // Handle to the assembly instance.
    Int32                Result;      // Result of the operation.

    // Initialize the common controls.
    ComCtrls = new INITCOMMONCONTROLSEX();
    ComCtrls.dwSize = Marshal.SizeOf(ComCtrls);
    ComCtrls.dwICC = ICC_WIN95_CLASSES;
    if (!InitCommonControlsEx(ref ComCtrls))
    {
        // Show an error message.
        MessageBox.Show("Can't initialize environment.",
                        "Application Error",
                        MessageBoxButtons.OK,
                        MessageBoxIcon.Error);
        return;
    }

    // Create an instance handle.
    Asm = Assembly.GetExecutingAssembly();
    hInstance = Marshal.GetHINSTANCE(Asm.GetModules()[0]);
```

```
// Create the ToolTip window.
WinHandle = CreateWindowEx(
   WS_EX_TOPMOST,
   TOOLTIPS_CLASS,
   "Balloon Help Message",
   WS_POPUP | TTS_NOPREFIX | TTS_BALLOON,
   0,
   0,
   0,
   0,
   IntPtr.Zero,
   IntPtr.Zero,
   hInstance,
   IntPtr.Zero);

// Set the window position on screen.
SetWindowPos(WinHandle,
             HWND_TOPMOST,
             0,
             0,
             0,
             0,
             SWP_NOSIZE | SWP_NOMOVE | SWP_NOACTIVATE);

// Determine the client drawing area.
Rect = new RECT();
GetClientRect(this.Handle, ref Rect);

// Build a toolinfo data structure.
TI = new TOOLINFO();
TI.cbSize = Marshal.SizeOf(TI);
TI.uFlags = TTF_CENTERTIP | TTF_TRANSPARENT;
TI.hwnd = this.Handle;
TI.lpszText = "This is a sample tooltip.";
TI.hinst = IntPtr.Zero;
TI.rect = Rect;

// Create a pointer to the ToolTip information.
TIAddr = Marshal.AllocHGlobal(Marshal.SizeOf(TI));
Marshal.StructureToPtr(TI, TIAddr, true);

// Send the ToolTip message.
Result = SendMessage(WinHandle, TTM_ADDTOOL, 0, TIAddr.ToInt32());
if (!Convert.ToBoolean(Result))
   MessageBox.Show("Error sending the tooltip message.",
                   "Application Error",
                   MessageBoxButtons.OK,
                   MessageBoxIcon.Error);

// Make sure you free the unmanaged memory.
Marshal.FreeHGlobal(TIAddr);
}
```

The InitCommonControlsEx() function is somewhat unique in that you can normally assume that the controls you need are available. When working with ToolTips, you need to ensure that the required controls from ComCtl32.DLL are loaded into the current environment. Because .NET applications use managed controls for the most part, you can't assume that the unmanaged controls are available.

A ToolTip is essentially a special-purpose window. Microsoft provides examples that use both the CreateWindow() and the CreateWindowEx() functions. The CreateWindowEx() function worked more reliably during testing, so that's what the examples uses. Anyone who's worked with CreateWindowEx() knows there are many classes and other features you can add to a window creation call. However, the example is only interesting in ToolTip creation, so it skips the usual enumerations for the sake of simplicity. The constants used in the example are the minimum you can use to create the window.

The application also relies on calls to other functions that we'll discuss as part of the application code (some of which doesn't appear in Listing 9.4). The last item of interest in the declaration area of the example is the TOOLINFO structure. This structure defines the functionality of the ToolTip. It's also the piece of information sent to the ToolTip window as a message. We'll see how this works during the code discussion.

The code begins by initializing the common controls. If the application can't load the controls for some reason, it must exit. There's little point in creating the window if the required controls are unavailable.

The next step is to create an instance handle. You can create the instance handle in a number of ways, but the example uses the two-step process shown. First, you gain access to the assembly using the GetExecutingAssembly() function. The assembly variable, *Asm*, contains a list of all of the modules within the assembly. The second step is to access the module and use the module with the GetHINSTANCE() method. The output is the instance handle needed for the rest of the example.

Creating the window comes next. The essential elements, in this case, are specifying TOOLTIPS_CLASS, one or more of the TTS_ options, and the instance handle. The example code shows the options needed to create a balloon ToolTip. You need other options to create standard and tracking ToolTips. The "Balloon Help Message" string is only supplied for the example—you don't normally supply a window title because Windows won't display it. We'll use Spy++ to see how Windows works with ToolTip windows.

Setting the window position is a good idea, but not essential. The example code sets the position so you can see the message traffic between Windows and the ToolTip window. In addition, setting the position does make it easier to find the ToolTip on screen.

The window is ready to go, but we can't display it yet because the window doesn't have the information needed to display itself. The code creates this information in the form of a TOOLINFO structure. One of the structure entries is a RECT structure that contains the position of the window. The example allows the ToolTip to use as much of the client area as needed for information. The other TOOLINFO structure entries are typical for a balloon ToolTip.

Finally, the code sends a message to the ToolTip window. This message contains the information required to display the window on screen. We can't pass a managed structure to the window because it's essentially operating in an unmanaged environment. The application uses AllocHGlobal() to allocate unmanaged memory and then places the contents of the data structure into that memory using the StructureToPtr() call. One last note here is to ensure that you release any memory used for the unmanaged structure data.

Spy++ can tell you a lot about this particular application. Begin with the Windows display. Locate the Balloon Help Message window. Figure 9.4 shows a typical example of what you'll see. Notice that the window relies on the tooltips_class32 class for support.

Right-click the window entry and choose Properties. The Styles tab will show the TTS_BALLOON style—the essential element for a balloon ToolTip. It's informative to look at the other information provided on the various tabs. For example, you'll find out that Windows automatically adds some style information, such as WS_CLIPSIBLINGS.

Close the Properties window. Open a Messages window by right-clicking the window entry and choosing Messages from the context menu. Figure 9.5 shows the message sequence you can expect to see for the window. Notice that the window received the TTM_ADDTOOL message as anticipated. You'll also see the message that repositions the window on screen.

The message trail tells you what has happened to the window since it was created.

```
Microsoft Spy++ - [Messages (Window 000C0528)]
Spy   Messages   Search   View   Window   Help

<00001> 000C0528 S WM_WINDOWPOSCHANGING lpwp:0012F1C0
<00002> 000C0528 R WM_WINDOWPOSCHANGING
<00003> 000C0528 S WM_WINDOWPOSCHANGED lpwp:0012F1C0
<00004> 000C0528 R WM_WINDOWPOSCHANGED
<00005> 000C0528 S TTM_ADDTOOLW lpti:0017BEE8
<00006> 000C0528 R TTM_ADDTOOLW fSucceeded:True
<00007> 000C0528 P WM_DEVICECHANGE Event:0007 dwData:00000000
<00008> 000C0528 P WM_DEVICECHANGE Event:0007 dwData:00000000
<00009> 000C0528 P WM_DEVICECHANGE Event:0007 dwData:00000000
<00010> 000C0528 S WM_ACTIVATEAPP fActive:False dwThreadID:00000740
<00011> 000C0528 R WM_ACTIVATEAPP
<00012> 000C0528 S WM_ACTIVATEAPP fActive:True dwThreadID:00000140
<00013> 000C0528 R WM_ACTIVATEAPP
<00014> 000C0528 S WM_ACTIVATEAPP fActive:False dwThreadID:00000740
<00015> 000C0528 R WM_ACTIVATEAPP

For Help, press F1                                              NUM
```

Using NUnit for Automated Testing

As you create more application code and the code becomes more complex, it becomes important to have a good testing tool. Microsoft does provide some rudimentary testing tools with Visual Studio .NET, but most of these tools appear with the Enterprise Architect Edition and don't provide much in the way of automation. Consequently, third-party developers have filled in the gaps by creating automated tools for the developer. NUnit represents one of the tools that fill this gap. You'll find this product in the \NUnit folder of the CD.

NUnit provides two forms of testing application. The GUI version is accessible from the NUnit folder of the Start menu. The GUI version enables you to run the application test immediately after adding new code and provides a neater presentation of the logged errors. You'll also find a command-line version of the program called NUnitConsole in the \Program Files\NUnit\ folder of your hard drive. The console version lets you place several testing scenarios in a single batch file and perform automated testing on more than one application at a time. You can also schedule testing using the Task Scheduler.

The product works by examining test cases that you create for your application. A test case is essentially a script that compares the result from your code to an anticipated result (what you expected the code to do). The test case can also check the truth-value of a return value. The author, Philip Craig, recommends creating a section of code and then creating a test case for that code. For example, you'll want to create a minimum of one test case for each method within a class. In this way, you build layers of code and tests that help locate problems quickly and tell you when a piece of code that previously worked is broken by a new addition to the application.

NUnit provides the means to perform individual tests based on a single test case or to create a test suite based on multiple test cases. The use of a special function, `Assert()` or `Assert-Equals()`, enables NUnit to test for the required condition. When NUnit sees a failure condition, it logs the event so you can see it at the end of the test. The point is that you don't have to create test conditions yourself—each test is performed automatically. Of course, the test cases still need to address every failure condition to provide complete application testing.

Let's look at a simple example. (You'll find the source code for this example in the \Chapter 09\NUnitDemo folder of the CD.) The example code performs simple math operations, but the code could perform any task. The `DoAdd()` and `DoMultiply()` methods both work as written. However, there's an error in the `DoSubtract()` method as shown here:

```
public static string DoSubtract(string Input1, string Input2)
{
    int    Value1;
    int    Value2;
    int    Result;

    // Convert the strings.
    Value1 = Int32.Parse(Input1);
    Value2 = Int32.Parse(Input2);

    // Perform the addition.
    Result = Value2 - Value1;

    // Output the result.
    return Result.ToString();
}
```

Obviously, most developers would catch this error just by looking at the code, but it isn't always easy to find this type of error in complex code. That's why it's important to write a test routine as part of your application (or in a separate DLL). Creating the test routine consists of five steps:

1. Include the `NUnitCore.DLL` (located in the `\Program Files\NUnit\bin` folder) as a reference to your application.

2. Create a class that relies on the `NUnit.Framework.TestCase` class as a base class.

3. Add a constructor that includes a string input and passes the string to the base class, such as `public MathCheckTest(String name) : base(name)`.

4. Add a test suite property to your code, formatted as `public static ITest Suite`.

5. Create one or more public test scenarios.

There are a number of ways to create the test suite for your application. The two main methods are dynamic and static, with the dynamic method presenting the fewest problems for the developer. Here's an example of the dynamic test suite declaration:

```
// You must define a suite of tests to perform.
public static ITest Suite
{
   get
   {
      return new TestSuite(typeof (MathCheckTest));
   }
}
```

As you can see, it's a simple read-only property. The property returns the type of the test. In this case, it's the `MathCheckTest` class. The example actually includes two classes, so you can see how the classes appear in the test engine. If you don't include this property, the test engine will claim that there aren't any tests—even if you've defined everything else correctly.

The test can be as complex or simple as you need to verify the functionality of the application. The simpler you can make the test, the better. You don't want errors in the test suite to hide errors in your code (or worse yet, tell you there are errors when it's obvious the code is working as anticipated). Here's an example of a simple test method:

```
// Test the add function using a simple example.
public void TestAdd()
{
   string   Expected = "5";
   string   Result = MathCheck.DoAdd("2", "3");
   Assert(Expected.Equals(Result));
}
```

Sometimes you need two or more test methods to fully examine a method. For example, the `DoDivide()` method requires two tests as a minimum. First, you must examine the code for proper operation. Second, you must verify that the code can handle divide-by-zero scenarios. It's never a good idea to include both tests in one test method—use a single method for each test as shown in the example code.

Now that you know what the code looks like, let's see the code in action. When you first start the NUnitGUI application, you'll see a dialog containing fields for the Assembly File and the Test Fixture. Select an assembly file using the Browse button and you'll see the test suites the assembly contains in the Test Fixture field. Each test suite is a separate class and the name of the class appears in the field, as shown in Figure 9.6.

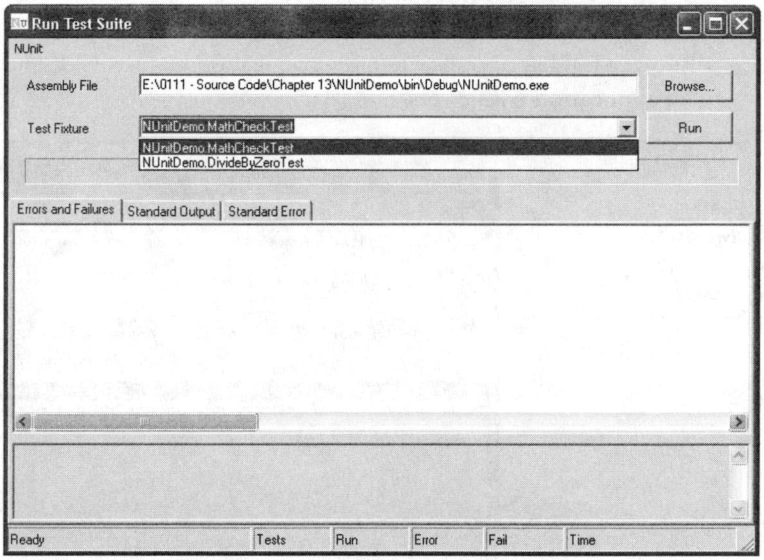

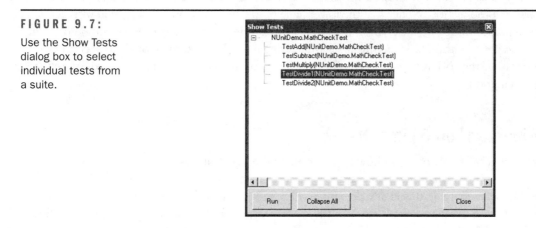

FIGURE 9.6:

An application can contain more than one test suite, but each suite must appear in a separate class.

If you select a test suite and click Run, NUnitGUI will run all of the tests in that suite. However, you might only want to run one test in the suite. In this case, use the NUnit ➤ Show Test Browser command to display the Show Tests dialog box shown in Figure 9.7. Highlight the individual test you want to run and click Run. The results of the individual test will appear in the main window as usual.

FIGURE 9.7:

Use the Show Tests dialog box to select individual tests from a suite.

So, what happens when you run the tests? As the tests run, a bar will move across the window to show the test progress. If the tests run without error, you'll see a green bar on the main window; a red bar appears when the application has errors. Figure 9.8 shows a typical example of an application with errors.

FIGURE 9.8:

This application contains two errors that the test suite found with ease using simple tests.

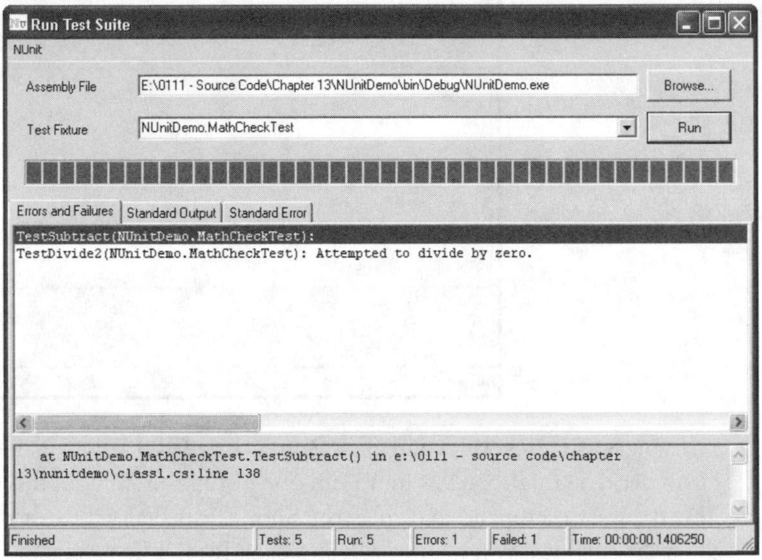

As you can see, the test found two errors. The first is the subtraction error that I mentioned earlier in the section. Notice that the lower pane of the main window provides you with enough information to locate the error in the source code. The second error is one of omission. The DoDivide() method lacks any means for detecting a divide-by-zero error. This second error points out that NUnit can help you find errors of commission, as well as errors of omission, given a good test suite.

Where Do You Go from Here?

This chapter has shown you how to use some of the new features found in Windows XP. We've explored what these new features will mean to the user, how they affect the bottom line, and what they mean to you as a developer. Hopefully, you've found that Windows XP fixes more than it breaks—that it's a step in the right direction for both usability and compatibility. Of course, nothing's perfect and Windows XP does have its share of flaws.

One of the things you should have learned while reading this chapter is that Microsoft has given up on some old functionality in order to provide new functionality that better fits today's computing environment. The problem for you as a developer is all of those lines of existing code that you'll have to rewrite should you decide to use a new Windows XP feature. Most of us like to tinker with our code, so the coding part of the equation isn't a problem so long as you can get the time approved to create the new code. The problem is the cost—how much will the new feature contribute and how much will the company have to pay in terms of development time, user training, and lost investment in existing code. Unfortunately, this is where your work begins—I can't guess how Windows XP will affect your company.

Chapter 10 will explore yet more in the way of unique Windows functionality. In this chapter, you'll learn about the features that exist in some versions of Windows but not in others. It's important to know about these functions. A new function used properly can improve performance, increase reliability, reduce development and debugging time, and even improve the user experience. Consider Chapter 10 the next logical step after reading this chapter. It helps you understand how the history of Windows will affect your coding experience in the Win32 API arena.

CHAPTER 10

Using Operating System Special Functions

- Accessing Status and Other Information

- Creating an Application Shortcut Example

- Shutting the System Down Remotely Example

- Obtaining Device Capabilities Example

- File Compression

- Using PC-Lint for C++ Development

As mentioned in previous chapters, the first release of the .NET Framework targets business development and also targets the operating system features that Microsoft felt developers would use most often. Admittedly, the Win32 API is huge and a significant undertaking, even for Microsoft, so a staged implementation of Win32 API features in the .NET Framework is reasonable from a certain perspective. However, this orientation of the .NET Framework means that you won't have access to anything that Microsoft deemed nontypical. This chapter will help you obtain access to some of these special operating system features and provide pointers on how to access other features lurking in the dark recesses of the Win32 API.

There are two important considerations in working with special operating system features. The first consideration is that your application won't run across all versions of Windows. This might be a moot point since the .NET Framework won't load on all versions of Windows. For example, you can't use the .NET Framework on a Windows 95 machine.

The second consideration is that the special feature might appear in a different form in the next version of the .NET Framework. It's important to realize that Microsoft will continue adding features to the .NET Framework, making some features you add today using the Win32 API irrelevant tomorrow. Of course, this consideration applies to the examples found in other chapters of the book to varying degrees, but it's an especially important consideration for this chapter.

Once you decide to add a special operating system feature, you need to perform system version checks. This chapter will help you understand the nuances of performing this check. Fortunately, the Platform SDK documentation and the C/C++ header files can help you in this regard. You'll learn how to look for this information as you build your application. The clues you find, especially in the header files, will make it easier for you to develop checks that will allow your application to either circumvent version compatibility problems or, at least, fail gracefully for the function that uses the special operating system feature. The important point is that your application should run under all versions of Windows but provide some indicator that a particular version is preferable to provide full application functionality.

NOTE   This chapter builds on some of the information learned in Chapter 9, "Accessing Windows XP Special Features." For example, you need to know which version of Windows is running on your system in order to use unique operating system features. The code found in the section "Determining the Operating System Version Example" tells you how to check the operating system version. Of course, you'll need to modify the code to meet specific application requirements. In some cases, you might need to determine the server operating system with a little more detail than shown in the example, something you can do with ease with the data provided. It's also important to know that all of the checks we made in Chapter 9 also apply to this chapter—the fact that you might use a special Windows 2000 operating system feature instead of one found in Windows XP makes little difference.

Accessing Status and Other Information

Knowing the status of objects on the platform on which your application is running is essential. For example, if you require the output of a service within your application, it's important to verify that the service is actually running. Otherwise, the application will wait forever for information that will never arrive. Unlike some types of calls, a service that is installed and functioning, yet stopped, doesn't generate an error message, so your application will remain in blissful ignorance until it actually determines the status of the service.

When an application executes on more than one machine, the need for status information becomes even more important. Doubling the number of machines also doubles the number of application failure points and reduces reliability. An application that doesn't provide proactive status monitoring is simply a failure waiting to happen. In short, if you want to create robust, reliable applications, you also need to incorporate some level of status monitoring in your application. Any resource that could fail without providing error information is a candidate for monitoring.

There are a number of resources that applications commonly monitor. For example, if your application has critical power requirements, it might monitor the power system to ensure that it isn't ready to shut down due to an error. Many of these resources use services as the means for reporting status information. In other cases, they'll use common API calls. For example, you'll find that the Media Player provides status information through the Win32 API. When you need status information, it's important to determine which technique to use to gather the information. Generally, the use of services is obvious by looking through the Services console (MMC snap-in).

Unfortunately, the .NET Framework doesn't provide full service status reporting (although it does provide a level of service support). For example, the `System.ServiceProcess.Service-Base` namespace contains functions for handling certain types of power-related events, and you can determine what types of events the system can generate. However, there isn't any way to determine the current power system status—the information you'd normally receive using the `GetSystemPowerStatus()` Win32 API function. You'll learn how to gain power status information in this section.

Access to a status function doesn't necessarily guarantee host system support. We also discuss some of the problems with version support under Windows. You might be surprised to learn that backward compatibility often takes a backseat to the requirements of the operating system. For example, in a few cases, Windows XP provides an updated version of a function and leaves the original version of the function out of the picture.

Using the C/C++ Header Files to Your Advantage

Digging through the C/C++ header files that come with Visual Studio .NET may seem unnecessary and cumbersome, but sometimes you don't have much choice if you want to learn the true implementation of a Win32 API function. We've used many techniques in the book to uncover the true implementation of the functions that we've used. However, there's one class of function that requires more—the function that doesn't actually exist.

The Platform SDK documentation discusses a function named `RtlCopyMemory()`. You'll notice that the documentation doesn't include the usual DLL location information, but as far as the documentation is concerned, this function exists. However, if you were to try to find this function in the Windows DLLs, you'd be disappointed—it doesn't actually exist. Look at the `Kernel32.DLL` file and you'll find several `Rtl` functions, but no `RtlCopyMemory()` function. This function is actually implemented as a macro within the `WinNT.H` file. (It also helps to look at the code in the `WinBase.H` file.)

So, how do you replicate the functionality of the `RtlCopyMemory()` function? It turns out that `Kernel32.DLL` does contain the `RtlMoveMemory()` function. Unlike the `RtlCopyMemory()` function, the `RtlMoveMemory()` function is real, so you can implement the `RtlMoveMemory()` function within your .NET application. Viewing the code within the header files will help you replicate the functionality of the alias function.

This problem does point out the need to review problem functions in the C/C++ headers. In many cases, functions that you assume exist in the DLL files actually exist only as macros or are aliases of existing functions. The fastest way to determine if a function actually exists is to open the associated DLL with the Dependency Walker and see if the DLL actually exports the function in question. In many cases, you'll find an associated function that's the true source of the Win32 API call in question.

Learning How to Avoid Version Compatibility Problems

One of the problems with Windows is that every version provides updates to existing features and incompatible new features while removing some features found in older versions. For example, Windows XP provides several new API calls while making an effort to get rid of older API calls that might not perform as well as anticipated in the new Windows environment. In most cases, Microsoft has warned about the loss of these functions for several Windows versions, so no one uses them anymore and the number of incompatibilities are reduced. In a few cases, Windows XP actually provides a function stub that calls the new function for older applications. This is one of the purposes behind the compatibility environment found in Windows XP—to provide the means for older applications to run in the new environment by redirecting some outdated calls.

TIP   It's interesting to note that the Win32 API has many hidden compatibility problems that are often made worse by inaccurate documentation and flawed header files. Unfortunately, many developers don't realize how bad the situation can get with new Windows features and will spend hours (sometime days) trying to fix their code when there's no fix to apply. In many cases, the developers found on the `microsoft.public.dotnet.framework` `.interop` newsgroup have already run across the problem and can provide an answer that you might not find on a Web site. In a few cases, you'll want to ask your question on a Windows-specific newsgroup. For example, you'll find some great version-specific help on the `microsoft.public.windowsxp.device_driver.dev` newsgroup. The developers that frequent this newsgroup tend to be different from the ones who frequent the `microsoft` `.public.dotnet` newsgroups.

The problem for developers is that not every user has upgraded to Windows 2000 or Windows XP. Some users are still using Windows 9x and a few might even use Windows 3x. Interestingly enough, this is a point of discussion on all of the Microsoft developer newsgroups and beyond. Developers don't know how to handle mutually incompatible environments. While Microsoft does an excellent job of providing a transition path for common function calls, older function calls often disappear without a trace, leaving developers wondering what to do next.

Of course, one of the first tasks a developer needs to perform is to determine how common a function is. In at least some cases, there isn't any compatibility problem to consider because the call is so common that Microsoft must support it. For example, developers will always need a way to obtain the current device context, so it's unlikely the GetDC() function will go away anytime soon. However, even with this common function, incompatibilities exist. A newer GetDCEx() function enables the developer to determine how clipping takes place, but the function appears to work inconsistently on some platforms. The following knowledge base articles demonstrate these compatibility issues (the list includes the URL at which you can find the complete story):

Q174511   Access Violation in Win32K When Calling GetDCEx (`http://support` `.microsoft.com/default.aspx?scid=kb;en-us;Q174511`)

Q118472   PRB: SelectClipRgn() Cannot Grow Clip Region in WM_PAINT (`http://` `support.microsoft.com/default.aspx?scid=kb;en-us;Q118472`)

Q149289   BUG: GDI Leaks Memory When Font Selected In MM_ISOTROPIC and MM_ANISOTROPIC Mode (`http://support.microsoft.com/default.aspx?scid=kb;` `en-us;Q149289`)

Q255744   HOWTO: Obtain a Device Context Handle for a Print Device (`http://` `support.microsoft.com/default.aspx?scid=kb;en-us;Q255744`)

Notice that this list contains Microsoft Knowledge Base articles. If the folks at Microsoft receive enough reports of a verifiable error, they'll create a Knowledge Base article for it. Unfortunately, they aren't always very good at telling anyone about these articles, so you have to "discover" them on your own as the need arises. The Microsoft Knowledge Base URL is `http://search.support.microsoft.com/search/default.aspx`. If you can't find what you need, Google Advanced Search (`http://www.google.com/advanced_search`) often provides better answers and in less time. However, the problem with Google Advanced Search is that the results aren't limited to problems—you obtain information on every aspect of the Win32 API call.

TIP   Many other developers are struggling with the same problems that you face in working with the .NET Framework. In a few cases, you'll find examples of their work online. For example, the 15 Seconds site (`http://www.15seconds.com/`) contains a wealth of code in various languages. This site also provides articles that look at the .NET Framework in depth, providing you with the insights needed to create useful code. Another great place to look for coding examples is Programmer's Heaven (`http://www.programmers-heaven.com/`). This site specializes in coding examples, but it isn't .NET specific—you'll find everything from assembler to Perl beside the .NET examples. A great place to look for tutorial-type examples is .NET Extreme (`http://www.dotnetextreme.com/`). Make sure you also revisit The Code Project site mentioned in Chapter 5 and the GotDotNet site mentioned in Chapter 7. Both sites contain a wealth of code that demonstrates how to use special operating system features.

Once you determine there's a possibility of compatibility problems with a certain function, you need establish the host operating system version. We've already discussed that issue as part of the section "Determining the Operating System Version Example" in Chapter 9. This example shows you how to detect the operating system version based on the output of the `GetVersionEx()` function. Knowing the host operating system version enables you to use the correct call based on the application environment. Of course, there's often no way to overcome limitations in the application environment. If the version of Windows in use on the host system doesn't support a particular feature, you'll need to report the loss of functionality to the user or create an alternative application feature with similar functionality.

Avoiding compatibility problems means more than just knowing the contents of the Microsoft Knowledge Base and the version of Windows installed on the host system. The final piece in the version compatibility puzzle is to know when a feature won't work as anticipated despite what Microsoft might say. Watch the newsgroups and you'll find almost daily reports to Microsoft of problems. In many cases, Microsoft will admit that the problem exists, but a Knowledge Base article is a long time in coming because there's either no fix for the problem or the Microsoft developers will determine that they actually meant a feature to work in a certain way all of the time. The developers on these newsgroups aren't always correct, but they're dedicated and can usually provide you with tips on how to avoid or fix a compatibility problem using techniques that are often undocumented and not supported by Microsoft. Of course, the choice is yours. You can choose to ignore the error, work around it using an undocumented fix, or create your own workaround using documented techniques.

Determining System Power Status Example

The example in this section shows how to use the GetSystemPowerStatus() function. Remember that the purpose of this function is to retrieve power system information. If you want to interact with the power system, such as when the system is about ready to shut down due to a power failure, then you need to use the events found in the System.ServiceProcess.ServiceBase class. In addition, don't confuse the GetSystemPowerStatus() function with the GetSystemPowerStatusEx() or GetSystemPowerStatus2() functions. The latter two functions only work with the Windows CE operating system. Listing 10.1 shows how to use the GetSystemPowerStatus() function. The source code for the example appears in the \Chapter 10\C#\PowerStat and \Chapter 10\VB\PowerStat folders of the CD.

Listing 10.1   Monitoring the Power Status of a System

```
// This is the function that will retrieve the power status
// information.
[DllImport("Kernel32.DLL", CharSet=CharSet.Auto, SetLastError=true )]
public static extern bool GetSystemPowerStatus(
    ref SYSTEM_POWER_STATUS lpSystemPowerStatus);

// This data structure contains the power system status on return
// from the GetSystemPowerStatus() call.
public struct SYSTEM_POWER_STATUS
{
    public Byte   ACLineStatus;
    public Byte   BatteryFlag;
    public Byte   BatteryLifePercent;
    public Byte   Reserved1;
    public Int32  BatteryLifeTime;
    public Int32  BatteryFullLifeTime;
}

// The BatteryStatus enumeration enables the application to detect
// the current battery status.
public enum BatteryStatus
{
    High      = 1,
    Low       = 2,
    Critical  = 4,
    Charging  = 8,
```

```
        NoBattery   = 128,
        Unknown     = 255
}

private void btnTest_Click(object sender, System.EventArgs e)
{
    SYSTEM_POWER_STATUS  SPS;      // The power status.
    StringBuilder        Stats;    // Power status display string.

    // Initialize the data structure.
    SPS = new SYSTEM_POWER_STATUS();

    // Determine the power status.
    if (!GetSystemPowerStatus(ref SPS))
    {
        // Display an error message.
        MessageBox.Show("Couldn't determine the power status!",
                        "Application Error",
                        MessageBoxButtons.OK,
                        MessageBoxIcon.Error);

        return;
    }

    // Create the power system information display string.
    Stats = new StringBuilder();

    // Determine the AC Line status.
    switch(SPS.ACLineStatus)
    {
        case 0:
            Stats.Append("On Battery\r\n");
            break;
        case 1:
            Stats.Append("On AC Line\r\n");
            break;
        case 255:
            Stats.Append("AC Line Status Unknown\r\n");
            break;
    }

    // Determine the battery status.
    if (SPS.BatteryFlag == (Byte)BatteryStatus.Unknown)
        Stats.Append("Battery Status Unknown\r\n");
    else
        if (SPS.BatteryFlag == (Byte)BatteryStatus.NoBattery)
            Stats.Append("No Battery Installed\r\n");
        else
        {
            // The battery status is known and there is a
            // battery installed.
```

```
        if ((SPS.BatteryFlag & (Byte)BatteryStatus.Charging)
            == (Byte)BatteryStatus.Charging)
            Stats.Append("Battery is Charging\r\n");
        if ((SPS.BatteryFlag & (Byte)BatteryStatus.Critical)
            == (Byte)BatteryStatus.Critical)
            Stats.Append("Battery Power is Critical\r\n");
        if ((SPS.BatteryFlag & (Byte)BatteryStatus.High)
            == (Byte)BatteryStatus.High)
            Stats.Append("Battery Power is High\r\n");
        if ((SPS.BatteryFlag & (Byte)BatteryStatus.Low)
            == (Byte)BatteryStatus.Low)
            Stats.Append("Battery Power is Low\r\n");
    }

    // Determine the percentage of battery charge.
    if (SPS.BatteryLifePercent == 255)
        Stats.Append("Cannot Determine Battery Charge\r\n");
    else
        Stats.Append("Battery Life in Percent: " +
                SPS.BatteryLifePercent.ToString() + "%\r\n");

    // Determine the remaining battery life.
    if (SPS.BatteryLifeTime == -1)
        Stats.Append("Cannot Determine Remaining Time\r\n");
    else
        Stats.Append("Remaining Battery Time (Seconds): " +
                SPS.BatteryLifeTime.ToString() + "\r\n");

    // Determine the full charge rundown time.
    if (SPS.BatteryFullLifeTime == -1)
        Stats.Append("Cannot Determine the Full Charge Time");
    else
        Stats.Append("Full Charge Rundown Time (Seconds): " +
                SPS.BatteryFullLifeTime.ToString());

    // Transfer the data to the display.
    txtOutput.Text = Stats.ToString();
}
```

The GetSystemPowerStatus() function declaration includes a reference to the SYSTEM_POWER_STATUS data structure, which contains the power status information. Notice that the example uses Byte values for many of the SYSTEM_POWER_STATUS data structure elements. It's important to use an unsigned integer value when working with these elements because of the way that the Platform SDK documentation describes the data structure. The *BatteryLifeTime* and *BatteryFullLifeTime* fields are of type Int32 because the documentation actually describes them using unsigned values. This seeming dichotomy in the same data structure is actually quite common for the Win32 API.

The btnTest_Click() method begins by creating and initializing the data structure. It also creates a StringBuilder object that we'll use to create the output string. Remember that the StringBuilder provides optimal string handling when you plan to manipulate and add to the string value several times in the same method. However, the StringBuilder also requires more memory than a standard String, so you need to use it with care.

The code makes the GetSystemPowerStatus() call and tests the return value. If the call returns false, it likely failed because the Uninterruptible Power Supply (UPS) service isn't started. Make sure you check the Uninterruptible Power Supply service and start it if necessary, as shown in Figure 10.1. The GetSystemPowerStatus() function actually returns other values if the host system doesn't support a UPS.

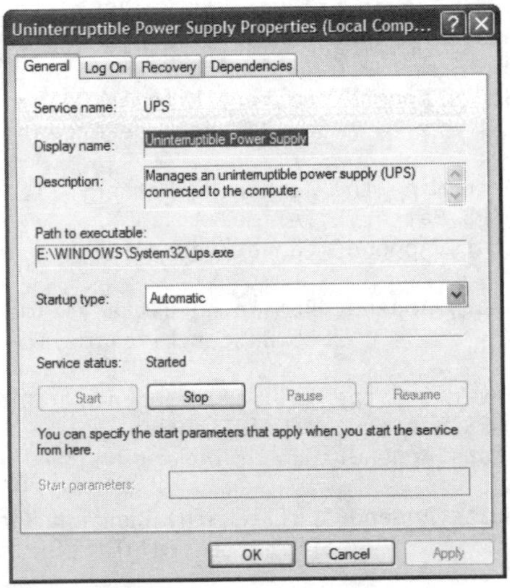

FIGURE 10.1:

The Uninterruptible Power Supply service must be running before this application will work.

Once the code knows that the Uninterruptible Power Supply service is installed and running, it begins checking the power status information. The first check is to determine the AC line status, which is found in the *SPS.ACLineStatus* field. A return value of 255 for this field usually means that the Uninterruptible Power Supply service is configured incorrectly (or perhaps not at all). The Power applet found in the Control Panel helps configure the UPS if there are no third-party utilities installed on the host machine. Figure 10.2 shows the UPS tab of the Power Options Properties dialog box, which is used to install and configure a UPS for the system. Notice that the default Windows drivers don't supply very much information. You can normally see more information when using a third-party driver specifically designed for the UPS.

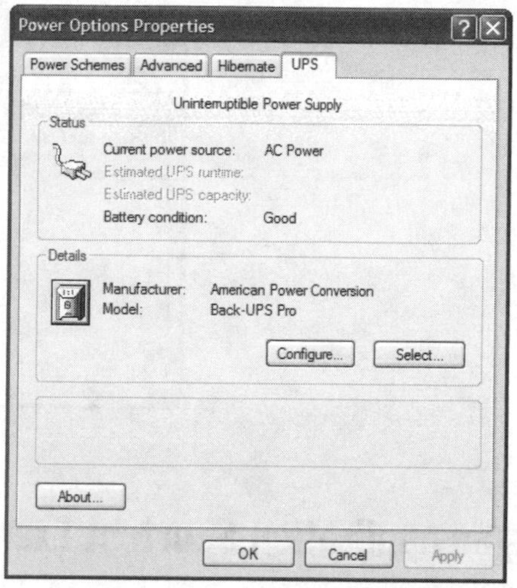

FIGURE 10.2:

An incorrectly
configured UPS will
return odd AC line
status information.

The next step in the process is to determine the battery status using the *SPS.BatteryFlag*
field. This flag is somewhat odd in that you don't work with it as a flag until you make two
checks with it first. If the flag returns a value of 255, then the system couldn't determine the
battery status. This usually means that the system lacks a UPS, that the cable between the
system and the UPS is faulty, or that some other condition has caused a loss of communication between the UPS and the system.

The second check determines the battery status when communication is enabled. A simple
UPS will usually say that there's no battery installed (at least according to the Platform SDK),
which doesn't make sense if there's a UPS attached to the system. In many cases, a return value
of 128 simply means that the UPS is incapable of reporting the battery status. Many companies
are unwilling to spend the extra money required to buy a UPS that includes reporting hardware.

If the code determines that the UPS can communicate and that there's a battery installed (or
at least the hardware to monitor the battery), it can begin using the *SPS.BatteryFlag* field as
a flag. The battery monitoring hardware in the UPS can return any of the condition codes
shown in the example. For example, the battery could be both low on power and charging.

The remaining fields in the SPS structure contain numeric information. However, notice
that the code must treat the *SPS.BatteryLifePercent* field differently from the *SPS.Battery-
LifeTime* field. In the first case, a return value of 255 means that the code couldn't determine
the percentage of battery charge, while in the second case, a return value of -1 means the
code couldn't determine the amount of battery time left. Both fields report a numeric value,
but the first is a `Byte` value instead of an `Int32` value. Figure 10.3 shows the output from the
example application.

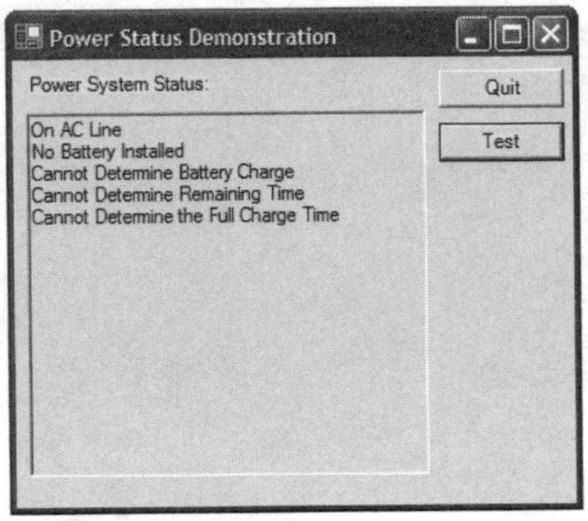

FIGURE 10.3:

FIGURE 10.3:

The example
application will tell
you the status of the
power system.

Creating an Application Shortcut Example

For some developers, creating new types of code is the goal rather than a necessity for creating
an application. Code reuse is something they'd rather avoid because reusing code deprives
them of a new coding experience. However, it's not always necessary to have a coding adventure
unless you need some special functionality that existing applications can't provide. One such
example is the application shortcut. You can't create an application shortcut using the .NET
Framework. Consequently, the first solution some developers will attempt to use is the long
and arduous implementation of complex COM interfaces within the managed environment.
This section of the chapter demonstrations that you don't always have to reinvent the wheel to
obtain an objective—sometimes other solutions present themselves.

> **TIP**   In some cases, you have to take the COM coding route because you can't gain access to
> the functionality you need from other sources. In fact, implementing COM interfaces is the
> rule rather than the exception shown in this section of the chapter. To see an application
> shortcut example implemented using C#, see http://www.msjogren.net/dotnet/eng/
> samples/dotnet_shelllink.asp. This example has many features to recommend it, so
> it's something that you should consider. However, the example in this section of the chapter
> has the advantage of being quick and easy to implement.

The Windows Scripting Host (WSH) already provides the functionality we need and in
an easy-to-use package. The IWshRuntimeLibrary interface contains the CreateShortcut()
method described at ms-help://MS.VSCC/MS.MSDNVS/script56/html/wsMthCreateShortcut
.htm. The CreateShortcut() method contains all of the functionality that most developers
will need to create an application (or any other) shortcut. The advantage of using this technique is that you don't need to consider COM interfaces in your application. The disadvantages include being unable to use this technique if the user disables scripting and experiencing

problems in implementing the required functionality in situations that WSH isn't designed to handle.

The first thing you'll need to do is add WSH support to your application. This is easier said than done because the Microsoft documentation isn't very clear about the COM element used to implement WSH. You'll need to add a reference to the Windows Script Host Object Model as shown in Figure 10.4. Notice that this support appears in wshom.ocx on my machine. After you add the reference, you'll notice that the name in the References folder changes to the IWshRuntimeLibrary interface.

FIGURE 10.4:

Adding WSH support to your application is easy after you figure out where it's stored.

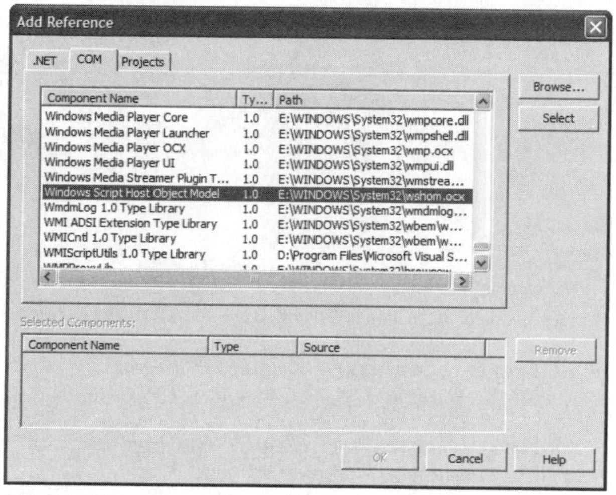

After you add the WSH support, it pays to look through the features this COM object provides. Figure 10.5 provides a view of just some of the features you can access through WSH. It often pays to look at WSH first if you need operating-system-level functionality that you can't obtain using a standard Win32 API call. While WSH doesn't answer every need, it's a good alternative.

Now that you have an idea of how we're going to pursue this problem, let's look at an example. Listing 10.2 shows a simple example of using WSH to create a shortcut on the Desktop. Of course, you could place the shortcut anywhere, but a good starting place is on the Desktop, where it's easily seen. You'll find the source code for this example in the \Chapter 10\C#\AppLink and \Chapter 10\VB\AppLink folders of the CD.

The Object Browser shows that WSH has a lot to offer as an alternative to the Win32 API.

Listing 10.2   **Creating a Shortcut with WSH**

```csharp
private void btnCreateShortcut_Click(object sender, System.EventArgs e)
{
   // Create a new copy of the WSHShell.
   WshShell WSHShell = new WshShell();

   // Determine the location of the Desktop.
   Object ItemName = "Desktop";
   Object Desktop = WSHShell.SpecialFolders.Item(ref ItemName);

   // Create a link on the desktop.
   IWshShortcut Link =
      (IWshShortcut)WSHShell.CreateShortcut(Desktop.ToString() +
                                            @txtLinkName.Text);

   // Fill in the details.
   Link.TargetPath = @txtFilename.Text;
   Link.Description = txtDescription.Text;

   // Save the link to the desktop.
   Link.Save();
}
```

The code begins by creating a new WshShell object. You don't need to do anything special to instantiate the object—it works like many other COM objects in this regard. Notice that we also don't need any arguments for this call.

Once the code has access to WSH, it can begin making calls. The first call determines the location of the Desktop. Notice that you must create an object to store the item name string and that the call returns an object that you'll need to convert to a string. One of the problems with using WSH seems to be a heavy reliance on objects that you have to convert to every other type—including strings.

The code creates a shortcut object (*Link*). You must supply the full path to the eventual shortcut LNK file. The code converts the *Desktop* to a string and then adds the input from the form to create the *Link* output.

We haven't actually created a shortcut yet, just a shortcut object. The next step is to fill in the shortcut details. The example includes only the *TargetPath* and *Description* property values. WSH also provides access to the following shortcut properties:

- *Arguments*
- *FullName*
- *Hotkey*
- *IconLocation*
- *RelativePath*
- *WindowStyle*
- *WorkingDirectory*

After the code fills out the shortcut information, it uses the Save() method to create a permanent copy of the shortcut. Note that there's also a Load() method you can use to load the data from an existing shortcut. This feature enables the developer to modify existing shortcuts as needed. Figure 10.6 shows the output of this example.

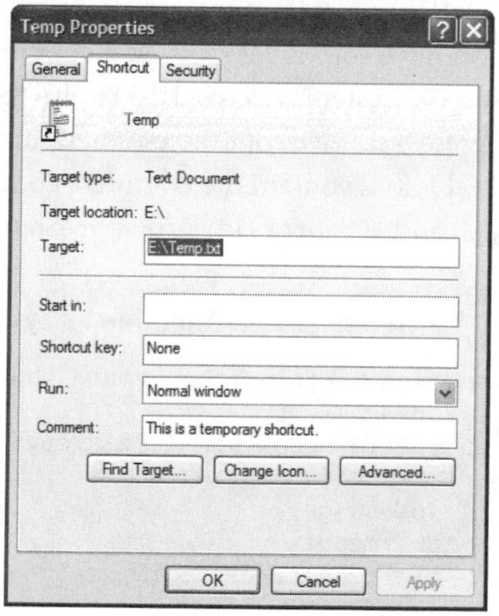

FIGURE 10.6:

The example application creates a shortcut on the Desktop with the requested comment.

Shutting the System Down Remotely Example

You'll run into situations in which you need to shut a system down from a remote location. Most people associate this action with servers; the server might reside in a closet and not even include a monitor and keyboard. However, remote shutdown becomes more important for desktop computers on a daily basis. For example, when a user logs in from a remote location, part of the login process could turn the user's desktop computer on and prepare it for use. When the user session ends, it's good practice to shut the computer back down. This action could also occur when a maintenance action takes place. In sum, the uses for a remote shutdown are numerous.

NOTE This chapter doesn't tell how to shut a system down locally because we've already discussed this issue as part of the message processing information in Chapter 4. See the section "Demonstrating the Windows Message Handler" in Chapter 4 for an example of how you can shut down your system locally. This chapter also shows how to trap and handle shutdown messages—an essential feature for many applications.

From the discussion in Chapter 4, you know that the ExitWindows() and ExitWindowsEx() functions only work on the local computer. If you want to shut down a remote computer, you need to use the InitiateSystemShutdown() or the InitiateSystemShutdownEx() function. The main difference between the latter two functions is that the InitiateSystemShutdownEx() function allows the developer to log a reason for the shutdown in the system log. Before either of these functions will work, however, the remote system has to allow remote shutdowns. In addition, there are a number of Windows bugs that appear in the Platform SDK documentation that will prevent a remote shutdown. For example, Windows 9x will often refuse to shut down after a remote request if the system is locked for some other reason (such as when the screensaver is active).

Now that you have some idea of what the example will do, let's look at the code required to shut down a remote system. Listing 10.3 shows the code we'll use for this example. This source code is incomplete—it leaves out the enumerations we used for the example in Chapter 4. The source on the CD does contain the complete code. You'll find the code in the \Chapter 10\C#\ RemoteShutdown and \Chapter 10\VB\RemoteShutdown folders of the source code CD.

Listing 10.3   A Technique to Shut Down a System Remotely

```
// This function performs the remote shutdown.
[DllImport("AdvAPI32.DLL")]
public static extern Boolean InitiateSystemShutdownEx(
    String    lpMachineName,
    String    lpMessage,
    Int32     dwTimeout,
    Boolean   bForceAppsClosed,
```

```
    Boolean   bRebootAfterShutdown,
    UInt32    dwReason);

private void btnShutdown_Click(object sender, System.EventArgs e)
{
    // Shut the remote system down.
    if (!InitiateSystemShutdownEx(
            txtMachine.Text,
            txtMessage.Text,
            Int32.Parse(txtTimeout.Text),
            ckAppClose.Checked,
            ckReboot.Checked,
            (UInt32)ReasonMajor.SHTDN_REASON_MAJOR_OTHER |
            (UInt32)ReasonMinor.SHTDN_REASON_MINOR_MAINTENANCE |
            (UInt32)ReasonFlag.SHTDN_REASON_FLAG_PLANNED))

        // Display an error if not successful.
        MessageBox.Show("Couldn't Shut Remote System Down",
                        "Shutdown Error",
                        MessageBoxButtons.OK,
                        MessageBoxIcon.Error);
    else
        // Display a success message.
        MessageBox.Show("Remote System Shutting Down",
                        "Shutdown Success",
                        MessageBoxButtons.OK,
                        MessageBoxIcon.Information);
}
```

As you can see, the InitiateSystemShutdownEx() function code isn't complex and you don't need to perform a lot of setup to use it. However, this example does point out some additional inconsistencies of the Win32 API. Compare this example to the ExitWindowsEx() function in Chapter 4 and you'll see that it's actually easier to use, in some ways, because it doesn't require as many flags and enumerations. Figure 10.7 shows the input dialog box for this example. Notice that it includes options for setting the forced application close and the automatic reboot options.

FIGURE 10.7:

The example application provides inputs for most of the InitiateSystem-ShutdownEx() features.

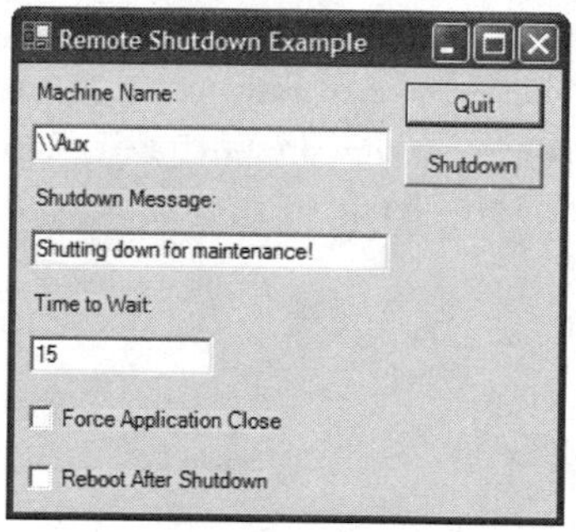

If you set the *lpMachineName* argument to null, the InitiateSystemShutdownEx() function will shut down the local machine instead of a remote machine. However, the only way to do this with a .NET application is to provide an override that includes an IntPtr as the first argument. Using a value of IntPtr.Zero will set the first value to null. Generally, however, you'll want to use ExitWindowsEx() whenever possible for local shutdown because it exits cleanly.

The *lpMessage* argument displays a message on screen. It's usually a good idea to tell the user why you want to shut the system down. On the other hand, there's no reason to include a message for a server in a closet, so you can set this argument to null.

A final consideration for this example is the *bForceAppsClosed*. Setting this value to true means that Windows will close without allowing the user to save their data. In the case of a frozen machine or a server, this could actually make it possible for the machine to reboot, albeit with some loss of data. However, you'll normally set this argument to false when rebooting a user machine on the network so the user has time to save their data. Figure 10.8 shows the remote message that the InitiateSystemShutdownEx() function creates.

FIGURE 10.8:
The Initiate-
SystemShutdown-
Ex() function creates
a remote message for
the user.

Obtaining Device Capabilities Example

It's important to know the capabilities of the devices installed on your system. Of course, Windows provides a myriad of ways to find this information. For example, in Chapter 7 you learned the techniques for discovering the capabilities of the parallel and serial devices attached to a system. However, one function stands out from the rest as providing a little more in the way of generic information, the GetDeviceCaps() function. This function helps you obtain information about any device with a device context, which includes printers and even cameras.

TIP

A number of Web sites now offer small Win32 API examples. One of the better places to find short examples on using the Windows Management Interface (WMI) is the VB*net* Visual Basic Developers Resource Centre (http://www.mvps.org/vbnet/). This site also offers a number of other interesting examples. For instance, it includes a couple of short examples on performing security tasks and simple data routines (such as converting temperatures from one unit of measure to another). Most of the examples on this site are oriented toward a specific task, so you'll often find interesting nuggets of code buried in a task normally associated with another call.

The GetDeviceCaps() function requires two arguments. The first is a handle to a device context—the IntPtr that we've used in several other examples. The second is an index into the data for that device context. We'll use an enumeration for this example. The actual C header contains a set of #define entries, but an enumeration normally works better in the managed environment. Unlike other functions we've used, you can return only one value at a time when using the GetDeviceCaps() function. This function doesn't accept a structure that returns all of the required values because the values you can request vary by device type.

NOTE

It pays to look through the enumerations for the GetDeviceCaps() function because not all of the functions appear in the Platform SDK documentation. In some cases, such as NUMMARKERS, the value is device specific. In other cases, the value is operating system version specific—several of the values only work with Windows 2000 and Windows XP. Make sure you understand the purpose of an undocumented value before you use it.

Now that you have a better idea of how the GetDeviceCaps() function works, let's look at some code. Listing 10.4 contains the working code for this example. The enumerated values are quite long, so I left them out of the listing in this case. Be sure to check the enumerated values in the source code found in the \Chapter 10\C#\DevCaps and \Chapter 10\VB\DevCaps folders of the CD.

Listing 10.4   Using the GetDeviceCaps() Function

```
// This function returns the device capability value specified
// by the requested index value.
[DllImport("GDI32.DLL", CharSet=CharSet.Auto, SetLastError=true )]
public static extern Int32 GetDeviceCaps(IntPtr hdc, Int32 nIndex);

private void btnTest_Click(object sender, System.EventArgs e)
{
   IntPtr        hDC;      // Device context for current window.
   Int32         Result;   // The result of the call.
   StringBuilder Output;   // The output for the method.
```

```
    // Obtain a device context for the current application.
    hDC = GetDC(this.Handle);

    // Check for errors.
    if (hDC == IntPtr.Zero)
    {
        // Display an error message.
        MessageBox.Show("Couldn't obtain device context!",
                        "Application Error",
                        MessageBoxButtons.OK,
                        MessageBoxIcon.Error);

        return;
    }

    // Obtain the current display capability.
    Output = new StringBuilder();
    Result = GetDeviceCaps(hDC, (Int32)DevCapParm.DESKTOPHORZRES);
    Output.Append("The horizontal resolution: " + Result.ToString());
    Result = GetDeviceCaps(hDC, (Int32)DevCapParm.DESKTOPVERTRES);
    Output.Append("\r\nThe vertical resolution: " + Result.ToString());
    Result = GetDeviceCaps(hDC, (Int32)DevCapParm.BITSPIXEL);
    Output.Append("\r\nThe bits/pixel value: " + Result.ToString());

    // Display the results.
    MessageBox.Show(Output.ToString(),
                    "Current Display Capabilities",
                    MessageBoxButtons.OK,
                    MessageBoxIcon.Information);

    // Release the device context when finished.
    ReleaseDC(this.Handle, hDC);
}
```

The application begins by obtaining the device context for the display. It's essential that you obtain the device context for whatever drawing device you want to learn about. This might mean creating a managed object of the right type and using it to obtain the correct device context. In a few cases, you'll need to use additional Win32 API calls to access the device because the .NET Framework doesn't provide the correct support.

After the code obtains the device context handle, it can begin calling GetDeviceCaps(). The output value is always returned as a number that you can convert to something the user will understand or a value your application can use for drawing or other tasks. The application obtains three common values that you can check using the Display Properties dialog box: horizontal resolution, vertical resolution, and the number of bits per pixel. Figure 10.9 shows the output from the application.

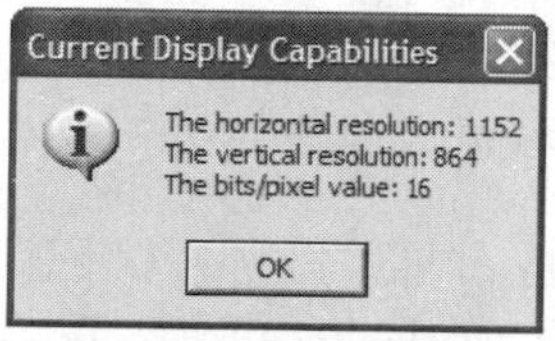

FIGURE 10.9:

The application
displays
common display
characteristics.

It's important to remember to release the device context before the application exits or it will have a memory leak. The last act of the application is to use the `ReleaseDC()` function discussed in other chapters to release the handle and associated resources obtained using the `GetDC()` function.

File Compression

Microsoft doesn't provide an easy method for compressing files as part of the documented Win32 API. In fact, compressing a file is so difficult under Windows that most developers turn to third-party libraries to perform the task. However, it's possible to decompress files and this support isn't found in the .NET Framework.

TIP   There are a number of good third-party libraries available for compressing and decompressing files in the ZIP format. One of the better libraries is The Zip/GZip Implementation For .NET at `http://www.icsharpcode.net/OpenSource/NZipLib/default.asp`. The author provides both a compiled version of the library (it's an assembly rather than a DLL) and the accompanying source code. A short look at the source code will help you appreciate just how much work went into this library. A second library is the ZZIPlib Library found at `http://zziplib.sourceforge.net/`. This second product is also free for the price of a download. It relies on another third-party library for some functionality. However, this product also seems to have more usage documentation and therefore might be easier to learn.

One of the older methods for compressing Windows files relies on the Lempel-Ziv algorithm. Consequently, most of the function names associated with this compression method begin with *LZ*. The problem with the LZ functions is that they've been around for a long time and Microsoft has made many of them obsolete. While the names of the functions still float around the Internet (with example code no less) and the function names still appear in the Platform SDK documentation, the older functions themselves are obsolete and you should avoid using them. See the Obsolete Windows Programming Elements help topic at `ms-help://MS.VSCC/MS.MSDNVS/win32/obsol_044z.htm` for additional information.

You should remember one LZ function and that's LZCopy(). This function accepts two arguments as input—the source and the destination filenames. If the source file is compressed, LZCopy() will decompress it and copy it to the destination file. Otherwise, LZCopy() performs a straight copy of the file. To obtain the handles required for the LZCopy() function, you can use any of a number of file-opening functions, including LZOpen(), which is the recommended function for the source file because it allocates resources required by the LZCopy() function. If you open a file using LZOpen(), you must close it using the LZClose() function. Microsoft completes the LZ series of functions with two functions for working with pieces of a file rather than the file as a whole, LZRead() and LZSeek(). The two functions perform tasks that you'd expect, given their names. These functions appear in LZ32.DLL.

Microsoft doesn't use just the Lempel-Ziv algorithm anymore, so you might not be able to use the LZ functions. There are new functions that handle both the Lempel-Ziv algorithm and the newer MSZIP format. The first two functions are SetupGetFileCompressionInfo() and SetupGetFileCompressionInfoEx(). These functions help you determine the status of the file, including the type of compression used to create it. Once you know a little more about the file, you can use the SetupDecompressOrCopyFile() function to decompress it. You'll find these functions in SetupAPI.DLL.

Windows XP users might wonder how Microsoft displays ZIP files in Explorer and optionally allows you to add files to them. This functionality resides in ZIPFldr.DLL, which is found in the \System32 folder along with the rest of the system DLLs. The undocumented RouteThe-Call() function aids in performing the magic Windows XP users see in Explorer. Unfortunately, everything about this DLL is undocumented and no amount of coaxing seems to help. Generally, you'll find it a lot easier to work with a third-party product than to decipher the inner workings of ZIPFldr.DLL. In fact, some industry pundits have found the ZIP file support so slow in Windows XP that they advocate turning it off. (See sites such as ZDNet Australia at http://www.zdnet.com.au/reviews/software/os/story/0,2000023564,20261492,00.htm for details.)

Using PC-Lint for C++ Development

We've looked at more than a few wrapper DLLs so far in the book. None of them involve heavy-duty Visual C++ programming, but there's enough code involved that it would be nice to get a little help—especially if you aren't as familiar with Visual C++ as you are with other languages. PC-Lint is a source code analysis tool. It helps you find programming errors that the compiler won't find. There are a number of Visual C++ analysis tools on the market, but many look just as complex as Visual C++ itself. These tools are designed to help a developer perform the tasks for which Visual C++ is known—low-level programming. PC-Lint is more of a tool designed for everyone—it can help you find problems in your code no matter how experienced or inexperienced you might be.

As unfortunate as it might seem, I was unable to obtain an evaluation version of PC-Lint to include on the CD. However, the vendor does provide a fact-filled Web site and you can always call or write for additional information. The Gimpel contact information is as follows:

Gimpel Software
3207 Hogarth Lane
Collegeville, PA 19426
(610) 584-4261 (voice)
(610) 584-4266 (fax)
`http://www.gimpel.com`

One of the things that impressed me from the outset about this tool is the ease of installation. If every application I had to install were this easy, there would never be a need for technical support line. In addition, PC-Lint appears to support every version of Visual C++ in existence, not to mention the C/C++ compilers from a wealth of other vendors, including Borland, Datalight, IBM, Intel, Lattice, Symantec, Texas Instruments, Top Speed, Turbo, and Watcom (there are still more). Most important for .NET developers is that this is one of the first products to fully support Visual C++ .NET.

The installation program leads directly into a configuration program. The configuration program sets application defaults. For example, you can configure PC-Lint to support a specific memory model that includes the new 64-bit environment. Configuration includes the addition of default libraries, including libraries from other vendors if you use them. One of the more interesting configuration options enables you to select a specific book author's recommendations for setup. The author-recommended settings often result in an analysis that includes more details than many developers would like. Unless you agree completely with a particular author's way of writing code, you might want to avoid this option. One of the final configuration options asks where the header files are for your C/C++ installation. Once you complete this step, the configuration file is complete. However, you don't have to stop at one configuration—PC-Lint automatically asks if you want to create additional configuration files. Each configuration file will automatically configure PC-Lint for a particular environment, which can save a substantial amount of time.

If you think you're done when the configuration is set up, you'd be only partially correct. PC-Lint also provides the means for suppressing unwanted messages. This information is stored in a separate file, not with the configuration information. Essentially, the message suppression feature provides a method for telling PC-Lint just how much help you want it to provide. I wish more products offered this option because some do help me more than I'd like. The questions ask how you'd like to format your code and what tests you'd like PC-Lint to perform. For the purposes of this section, I decided not to suppress any of the messages— I was curious to see just how much help PC-Lint can provide.

Gimpel Software provides the PC-Lint documentation in PDF format, along with the latest version of Adobe Acrobat to read it. Overall, the documentation is organized like most developer products. However, it does include some perks, such as a clearly written set of usage instructions and a short tutorial. The test files all worked as explained in the text. Figure 10.10 shows an example of the output from one of these test files after I ran it through PC-Lint. Note that this output uses the default configuration information. PC-Lint includes a large number of command-line switches that affect its operation—everything from the way it processes the file to the level of output verbosity. Appendix A of the PDF manual contains a complete list of these command-line switches.

FIGURE 10.10:

Typical output from PC-Lint showing application error information

The output appears on screen and within the _LINT.TMP file. Each entry includes a line number so you can find the affected code quickly. The entries also include an error number, an error message, and a code snippet as needed. Of course, you have to decipher the meanings of the error codes by looking at Chapter 17 of the PDF supplied with the product. Overall, the explanations are a little short, but they're understandable to anyone who's worked with C or C++ code for very long. The point is that this code normally compiles without error—PC-Lint locates errors that would normally cost you debug time.

NOTE   For those who don't own an IDE that produces line numbers, Gimpel Software provides the PR utility, which prints out the source code with line numbers included. The PR utility provides all of the switches needed to produce formatted code output that you can mark up as you go through the errors in the _LINT.TMP file. It even provides a special switch that determines the placement of the last form within the printer (just in case you haven't retired that dot-matrix yet).

After working with the test files for a while, I tried a few test files of my own. PC-Lint worked flawlessly on every unmanaged file that I tried. However, there are a few things that you should consider when using PC-Lint. This tool will find errors that the IDE might miss, but it doesn't necessarily find every error in your code. For example, a test application that I created used an LPTSTR without first allocating memory for it. The result is that the application crashes. Neither the IDE nor PC-Lint found the problem because neither tool is designed to find problems of that sort. However, PC-Lint did find a structure error that the IDE missed in the same test program. In sum, don't rely on any tool to fix poor programming technique. The best you can hope to achieve is reduced debugging, not an elimination of application debugging.

I also noticed a few irregularities when working with managed code. The biggest problem is that PC-Lint will stumble on the legitimate using and namespace keywords. Figure 10.11 shows the output from the OSVersion.DLL source code found in Chapter 9. Notice that the using and namespace keywords are the only errors found in this example, so it's safe to say that PC-Lint didn't find any errors. The point is that the product might locate other "errors" in managed code that aren't really errors at all.

FIGURE 10.11:

PC-Lint doesn't handle managed code as well as it could.

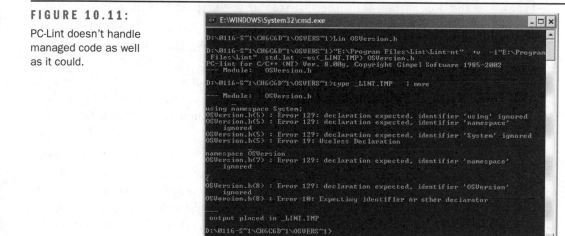

Generally, PC-Lint is an invaluable tool if you plan on writing much code in Visual C++. Given the number of places we use Visual C++ in this book, using PC-Lint if your first language is Visual Basic or C# could save considerable time. The best way to view PC-Lint is as a tool that saves the developer time in locating little nagging errors—the kind that require hours to locate because you've viewed the code once too often.

Where Do You Go from Here?

This chapter has shown you some of the special features that newer versions of Windows can provide. It's also helped you understand the need to exercise care when using these functions, how to create your applications to use alternatives when possible, and how to allow specific application functions to fail gracefully when necessary. Of course, creating applications that use advanced operating system features creates compatibility problems, but it also enables you to enhance the functionality of your applications.

Microsoft spent a great deal of time working on .NET Framework features that would appeal to business users and work on the greatest number of Windows versions. Your job as a developer is to ensure that your applications ship with the maximum functionality possible for the operating system on which they will run. Of course, this means spending some time as a detective ferreting out the operating system features you need. In many cases, this time-consuming process is made easier by simply checking the Microsoft Web sites to learn what new versions of Windows add to the capabilities of their predecessors. One of the things you might want to do today to save work tomorrow is begin keeping a list of new operating system features you'd like to use. Newsgroups, magazines, Web sites, and other sources usually tell you about the latest Windows features—make sure you keep track of these features for future use.

Make sure you check at least a few of the Web sites listed in this chapter. In many cases, they can save you time by providing example code or at least ideas on which Win32 API functions make most sense for .NET developers. When you do learn about a new function, try testing it out on the members of one of the newsgroups listed in this and previous chapters. Generally, you'll find that someone in the newsgroup has at least tried the function and knows some of the problems that you'll run into.

Chapter 11 looks at one of the add-on features of Windows—the Media Player. This utility is shipped as part of Windows, but it resides as a separate part of the operating system. The fact that you can find this utility in every Windows installation means that you can rely on it to play certain types of media files. Because the .NET Framework ships with less than stellar support for the Media Player, you need to access it using the Win32 API for the most part. Chapter 11 will provide everything you need to get started adding media pizzazz to your applications.

CHAPTER 11

Accessing the Media Player

- A Quick Overview of the Media Player

- Displaying a Configuration Dialog Example

- Playing Sound Files Example

- Using IconForge

The Windows Media Player began as a simple utility for playing wave and musical instrument digital interface (MIDI) sound files. Its capabilities were distinctly limited to playing simple sounds and the few pieces of music designed to go with it. Of course, when the Windows Media Player arrived on the scene, being able to play sounds at all was considered quite novel. Even the noise produced by early computers was a welcome change from complete silence.

Today, however, video games and other multimedia presentations have taken both sound and video well beyond the realm of simple noises. Users today demand more from their applications because the systems they use are capable of doing much more than in any time in the past. The computers of today can create presentation-quality graphics and sound that are almost as good as the best product Hollywood can produce.

This chapter won't turn you into a budding movie director. However, it will acquaint you with the features of the Windows Media Player, or simply Media Player for short. We'll discuss what the Media Player can do as an introduction because many developers are unaware of just where Microsoft has taken the Media Player. Afterward, we'll look at several ways in which your applications can interact with the Media Player to produce effects you might not have considered in the past.

A Quick Overview of the Media Player

Some developers haven't ever tried the Media Player, probably because it looked drab and uninteresting at the outset. Even the version of the Media Player that originally shipped with Windows 2000 lacked appeal. Microsoft has added so many improvements to the Media Player that you'll hardly recognize it the first time you see it. Figure 11.1 shows a typical example of this utility with a CD loaded. Notice that the Media Player automatically identifies the CD and provides track information. The following sections describe how to use the Windows Media Player.

NOTE   For those of you who were looking for the venerable CD Player with its interesting quirks, this particular utility was not included with Windows XP. You'll find that the Windows Media Player does a far better job than the CD Player could ever do. However, if you absolutely must have the CD Player to feel comfortable, the version from Windows 2000 works just fine under Windows XP.

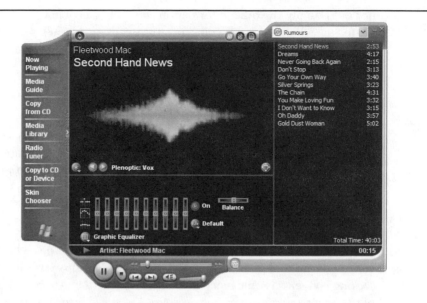

FIGURE 11.1:

The Windows Media Player sports both new looks and updated features.

This section of the chapter provides you with a general overview of the capabilities of the Media Player. You'll learn about general operation and some of the special features that it provides, including Internet Support. However, given that this is a programming book, I'll leave it up to you to learn about some of the more interesting features that it would be hard to use in development. For example, the Media Player supports audio CD creation—a feature we won't discuss in this chapter. Once you complete this section, you might find that you want to give the Media Player a second look as a new source of entertainment for your system as well as a means to make your applications more usable.

The purpose of this section is to show you the capabilities of the Media Player from a user perspective so that you can appreciate the opportunities it provides to you as a developer. If you're already familiar with the Media Player, you can probably skip this section and get right into the programming examples. All of the sections that follow do have developer-oriented counterparts and we won't spend a lot of time on this overview. Consider this section one of the fun parts of the book.

Windows Media Player General Operation

You can adjust every aspect of your Media Player experience. For example, you can adjust the graphic in the center of the display. Click Select Visualization or Album Art (the button with the asterisk in the lower-left corner of the display area). You'll see a list of visualizations, plus an Album Art option. Interestingly enough, Media Player was able to display the album art from quite a few of my CDs, even though I didn't supply this information to the computer, nor did I supply any other information about the CD. Choose the visualization you want to see (or the album cover). If you choose a visualization, you'll see two arrow buttons next to the visualization button. Click these arrows to see different versions of that visualization. If you want to see your visualization full screen, click View Full Screen in the lower right corner of the display area. This is the button with a window in the center and four arrows pointing outward from the edges of the window.

> **TIP**   If you choose the album art visualization and then click on the album art, a copy of Internet Explorer will open. You'll go to the `http://windowsmedia.com/` site where you'll see a list of all the albums available by the same group. The site will help you explore these other options. For example, you can play samples from many of the albums to determine if you'd like to hear more. You can buy the albums directly online if desired with a few additional clicks. (The site links to CD-NOW.)

At the bottom of the screen, you'll see a set of 10 controls. These controls allow you to control the current position in the CD using pause, stop, next song, previous song, a position-seeking pointer, a rewind function, and a fast forward function. You can also control the volume of the music and mute it when necessary. The final button, Switch to Skin Mode, changes the appearance of the Windows Media Player to the selected skin. Figure 11.2 shows just one of many skins you can choose.

FIGURE 11.2:
Select the skin that suits your personal preferences.

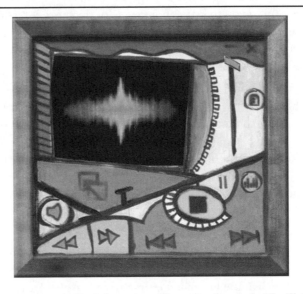

Yes, that's a Picasso-like picture and all of the painted buttons do work. You'll find quite a few skins for your Media Player, and I anticipate that people will want to create their own. In fact, one of the examples in this chapter will demonstrate how you can create skins for users of your applications. This feature has a lot of uses, including marketing your company. A well-designed skin could advertise your services or simply act as a means for people to remember your company name.

Three of the four buttons at the top of the display control the window display. The Show/Hide Menu Bar button controls the window surrounding the Windows Media Player. Normally, this window is invisible so you can see the effect of the skin. The Show/Hide Equalizer and Settings in Now Playing button displays a window immediately below the visualization window shown in Figure 11.1. This new window can display SRS WOW effect, graphic equalizer settings, video settings, media information, captions, and lyrics. The Show/Hide Playlist in Now Playing button shows a list of the songs you plan to play. Double-clicking a song in this list automatically changes the player to that song. The fourth button at the top, Turn Shuffle On/Off, automatically selects tracks at random when set to on. This means the CD won't play end-to-end; it will continuously play random selections.

The playlist has a lot more to offer than allowing you to select the tracks on the CD and add lyrics. The context menu contains options to play the selected song, enable sections, and disable selections. The Media Player will skip a selection that you have disabled when playing the CD in random or sequential order. The Edit option allows you to change the name of the song in the playlist. You can also change the order of songs in the list using the Move Up and Move Down options. The context menu contains several other options that we'll discuss as part of performing other tasks.

Internet Content

We haven't discussed many of the buttons on the left side of the Windows Media Player yet. You'll find that several of them enable you to find media on the Internet. The main Internet button is Media Guide. Click this and you'll go to WindowsMedia.com. This is Microsoft's main site for all things media.

The Radio Tuner feature also relies on the Internet. You click this option and after a few seconds, Windows Media Player displays the radio station page of WindowsMedia.com. Select a radio station and Windows Media Player will begin streaming content from it.

The Internet content functionality provided by the Media Player also has potential for developers. For example, this option could help you create better tutorials that wouldn't suffer from the problem of being out of date with patches for your application. Because the user would download the tutorial from the Web site each time it was needed, the content would always provide the latest information about your application. The same approach works for help desk and other support needs. You could even add to the application media features that would change over time to meet specific user needs or even provide a mood. For example, consider an application that would automatically dress itself up for Christmas or New Years.

Using the Media Library

The Media Library helps you organize all your media. The first time you select it, you'll see a dialog box that asks if you want to search your hard drive for media. Click Yes and Windows Media Player will begin the search. Of course, you can always conduct the search later using the Tools ➤ Search for Media Files option (you can also press F3). After you click Yes, Windows Media Player will ask where to search for media on your system. However, unless you click Advanced, you won't see the additional options shown in Figure 11.3.

FIGURE 11.3:

The Windows Media Player helps you find media on your system.

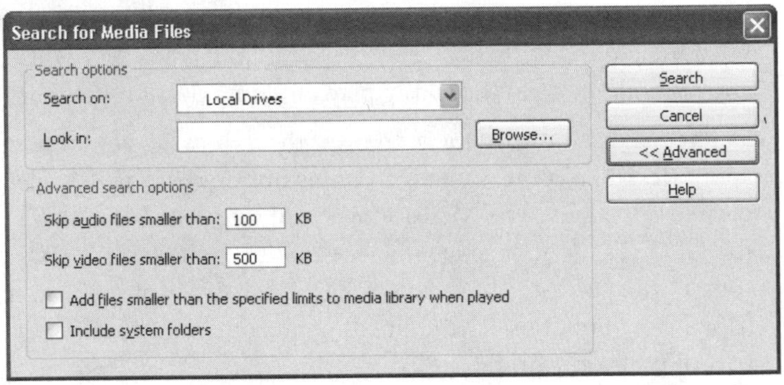

Select the search criteria you want to use for searching. The default settings may not work in all cases. For example, you may want to keep track of your sound bites in the library. The size options may prevent this by excluding files that are too small yet fit within the sound bite category.

Notice that the default search criteria doesn't include system folders. If you want to include Microsoft-supplied media in your list, you'll want to check the Include System Folders option. In some cases, you might want to add files that you play to the media library even if they're smaller than the limits you set. The Search for Media Files dialog box also includes an option to address this concern. Once you're happy with the search settings, click Search and Windows Media Player will begin searching your system for media. After the Windows Media Player finds all of your media, you'll need to click Cancel to exit the Search for Media Files dialog box.

The Media Library will categorize your audio and video data using a hierarchical format like the one shown in Figure 11.4. Notice that this library shows the video clips by author. The other category selections present the data in other ways.

FIGURE 11.4:

Use the Media Library to organize your media selections.

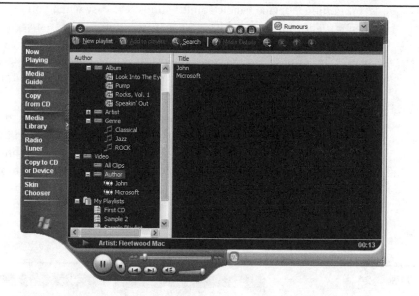

Creating a database of your media selections makes it easier to see what you have and to work with the data. You can play everything in your library. The Windows Media Player also allows you to copy the data to an audio CD or work with it in other ways. For example, you can use this screen to create and manage playlists.

NOTE   Some of the elements on the left side of the hierarchical list don't support a context menu. The choices for the selection normally appear at the top of the window, so you need to highlight the element before you can do anything with it. For example, if you want to create a new playlist, you have to highlight My Playlists and then click New Playlist at the top of the window.

Displaying a Configuration Dialog Example

Many of the multimedia devices on your system have configuration dialogs. The configuration data affects the quality of the device output, as well as its capabilities in many situations. In some cases, you might want the user to configure a device before using it to play a sound or perform some other multimedia task. The configuration is important because you want to provide the user with the best possible multimedia experience. When you want to perform this type of task, you need to work with the driver directly, which means opening a driver handle using the OpenDriver() function.

Obtaining a device handle sounds almost too easy when you first consider it. You use the `OpenDriver()` function, which accepts three inputs. The first argument is mandatory. It's the device driver name. The second argument is optional and usually unnecessary for modern drivers. It defines the location of the driver information in the registry. The third argument is device-driver specific. Only supply this information if the vendor documentation for the driver requires it.

The main problem with the `OpenDriver()` function is finding the required device driver name, especially if you aren't privy to the vendor documentation (which few of us are). The Platform SDK documentation provides a hint, but only a small hint when it tells you that the default location is the `Drivers32` key. The actual location of this information is the `HKEY_LOCAL_MACHINE\SOFTWARE\Microsoft\Windows NT\CurrentVersion\Drivers32` key in most cases. Figure 11.5 shows that there are two wave devices in this case: wave and wave1. To determine which device to use, you'd need to match the driver to a specific piece of hardware using the entries in the Device Manager.

FIGURE 11.5:

The registry provides the device names you need to use with the `OpenDriver()` function.

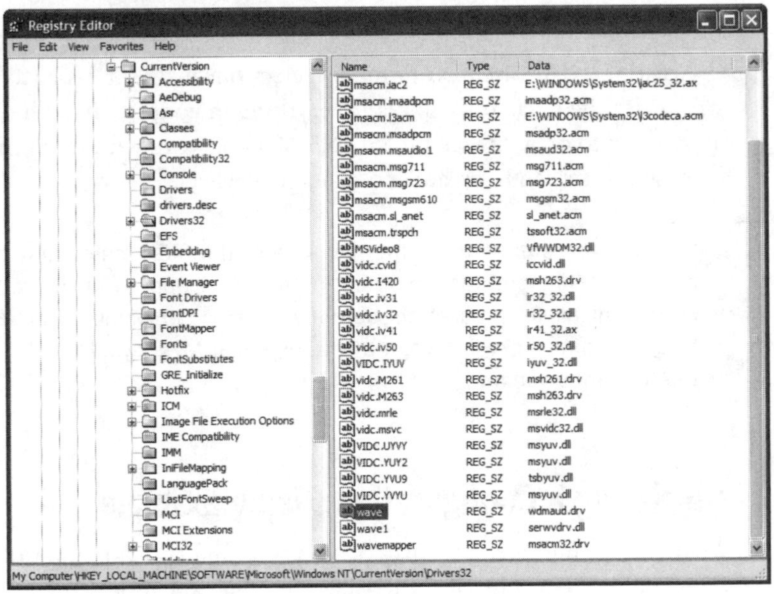

The example application shows how to open a device, display the associated configuration dialog, and then close the device so another application can access it. Listing 11.1 shows the code that you'll need. You'll find the source code for this example in the `\Chapter 11\C#\ConfigDlg` and `\Chapter 11\VB\ConfigDlg` folders of the CD.

Listing 11.1   Displaying a Device Configuration Dialog

```
// This function opens a device for use. There are two forms this
// function can take. The first form should only include the driver
// name. Set the IntPtr value to IntPtr.Zero and the lParam to 0. The
// second form can include just a section name or both a section name
// and an lParam.
[DllImport("WinMM.DLL", CharSet=CharSet.Auto, SetLastError=true )]
public static extern IntPtr OpenDriver(String lpDriverName,
                                       IntPtr NoSectionName,
                                       Int32 NoParam);

[DllImport("WinMM.DLL", CharSet=CharSet.Auto, SetLastError=true )]
public static extern IntPtr OpenDriver(String lpDriverName,
                                       String lpSectionName,
                                       Int32 lParam);

// This function sends a message to the driver. The message will
// normally require one or two lParam values.
[DllImport("WinMM.DLL", CharSet=CharSet.Auto, SetLastError=true )]
public static extern Int32 SendDriverMessage(IntPtr hdrvr,
                                             UInt32 msg,
                                             Int32 lParam1,
                                             Int32 lParam2);

// Use this enumeration to define which driver message to send.
public enum DrvMsg : uint
{
    DRV_LOAD              = 0x0001,
    DRV_ENABLE            = 0x0002,
    DRV_OPEN              = 0x0003,
    DRV_CLOSE             = 0x0004,
    DRV_DISABLE           = 0x0005,
    DRV_FREE              = 0x0006,
    DRV_CONFIGURE         = 0x0007,
    DRV_QUERYCONFIGURE    = 0x0008,
    DRV_INSTALL           = 0x0009,
    DRV_REMOVE            = 0x000A,
    DRV_EXITSESSION       = 0x000B,
    DRV_POWER             = 0x000F,
    DRV_RESERVED          = 0x0800,
    DRV_USER              = 0x4000
}

// This structure is used with DRV_CONFIGURE the message.
public struct DRVCONFIGINFO
{
    public Int32    dwDCISize;
    public String   lpszDCISectionName;
```

```csharp
    public String    lpszDCIAliasName;
}


// This function closes a driver handle previously opened using the
// OpenDriver() function. Don't pass anything for the lParam values
// unless the driver documentation requests it.
[DllImport("WinMM.DLL", CharSet=CharSet.Auto, SetLastError=true )]
public static extern Int32 CloseDriver(IntPtr hdrvr,
                                       Int32 lParam1,
                                       Int32 lParam2);

private void btnTest_Click(object sender, System.EventArgs e)
{
    IntPtr          hDriver; // Handle to the driver.
    Int32           Result;  // Results of a call.
    DRVCONFIGINFO   DCI;     // The driver configuration data.
    IntPtr          DCIPtr;  // Pointer to the DCI

    // Open the driver handle.
    hDriver = OpenDriver(txtDevice.Text, IntPtr.Zero, 0);

    // Check for errors.
    if (hDriver == IntPtr.Zero)
    {
        MessageBox.Show("Couldn't obtain driver handle!",
                        "Application Error",
                        MessageBoxButtons.OK,
                        MessageBoxIcon.Error);
        return;
    }

    // Determine whether the device supports a capabilities
    // dialog box.
    Result = SendDriverMessage(hDriver,
                               (UInt32)DrvMsg.DRV_QUERYCONFIGURE,
                               0,
                               0);

    // Check for a configuration dialog.
    if (Result == 0)
    {
        MessageBox.Show("No configuration dialog available!",
                        "Application Result",
                        MessageBoxButtons.OK,
                        MessageBoxIcon.Information);
        CloseDriver(hDriver,0,0);
        return;
    }
```

```
        // Display the configuration dialog.
        DCI = new DRVCONFIGINFO();
        DCI.dwDCISize = Marshal.SizeOf(DCI);
        DCIPtr = Marshal.AllocHGlobal(DCI.dwDCISize);
        Marshal.StructureToPtr(DCI, DCIPtr, true);
        Result = SendDriverMessage(hDriver,
                        (UInt32)DrvMsg.DRV_CONFIGURE,
                        0,
                        DCIPtr.ToInt32());

        // Free the allocated memory.
        Marshal.FreeHGlobal(DCIPtr);

        // Close the driver handle.
        CloseDriver(hDriver, 0, 0);
    }
```

As you can see, the example provides for two forms of the OpenDriver() function—the form you use depends on the needs of the device driver. However, the first form works, in most cases, because the driver names are stored in the Drivers32 key and most drivers don't require any additional input.

The SendDriverMessage() function requires at least two pieces of input: the handle of the device and a message value. The SendDriverMessage() function can also accept one or two *lParam* values to send as part of the message. We'll see later in the code that these two values are often optional and that you must pay attention to the placement of values that are required. The DrvMsg enumeration contains all of the messages that you can send to a device driver. Generally, it's better to create a single enumeration that covers all possibilities than to create a specific enumeration for each potential use. The SendDriverMessage() function only works with the following messages:

- DRV_CONFIGURE

- DRV_QUERYCONFIGURE

- DRV_INSTALL

- DRV_REMOVE

One of the messages we'll work with in this example does require additional information in the form of the DRVCONFIGINFO structure. The DRV_CONFIGURE message tells the device driver to display its configuration dialog. The requestor must provide the size of the data structure as a minimum. The data structure also contains entries for a custom section of the registry (if the driver isn't in the Drivers32 section) and an alias name for the driver. Neither of these two entries is required, even if you supply the structure.

As with all other forms of handle access, you must close the driver before the application exits. The effects of not doing so, in this case, are especially noteworthy because they're so severe. In most cases, the user will lose access to the device. In addition, the application will lose access to the handle memory, causing a small memory leak within Windows. Finally, in several cases, the loss of device access could result in system failure. Closing the handle isn't an option or something to forget in this situation. Unfortunately, the .NET Framework can't recover for you, so it's up to the developer to ensure proper application execution.

The code for this example begins by opening the driver. It examines the handle for a null value. If the value is null, it's more than likely that the system or another application has already opened the device. Of course, you could have supplied a nonexistent device name as well, so it's important to check spelling and capitalization if you receive the same error more than once. The application will display an error message and exit the method when it receives a null value.

Not every device provides a configuration dialog, so the code uses the SendDriverMessage() function to output a DRV_QUERYCONFIGURE message to the driver. In this case, we don't need to supply any additional information. If the driver returns 0, then it doesn't provide support for a configuration dialog and the method exits. Notice that you must free the device handle before the method exits.

The code can finally display the configuration dialog. However, to do this, it must provide a pointer to a DRVCONFIGINFO data structure, even if the structure is blank. Of course, this brings up the question of how to pass the data structure to a message when the message only accepts an integer as input. The code shows one technique for accomplishing this task. It creates the data structure and fills in the one required field that contains the size of the structure. The code then allocates an IntPtr that points to unmanaged memory of the same size of the data structure. At this point, the Marshal.StructureToPtr() method can convert the managed memory into a pointer to unmanaged memory. Finally, during the SendDriverMessage() call, the code converts the pointer to an Int32 value. At this point, the device driver will display a configuration dialog box similar to the one shown in Figure 11.6.

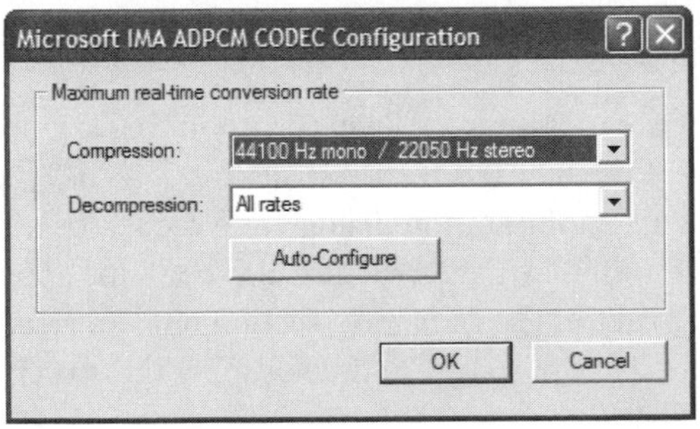

FIGURE 11.6:
The device driver will display its configuration dialog box after it receives the DRV_CONFIGURE message.

In this case, I chose the msacm.imaadpcm device to display the Microsoft IMA ADPCM CODEC Configuration dialog box, which adjusts the Interactive Multimedia Association (IMA) Adaptive Differential Pulse Code Modulation (ADPCM) compression/decompression (CODEC) module. The Microsoft Audio Compression Manager (MSACM) actually includes several device entries in the Drivers32 section of the registry and you'll find the associated code in the MSACM32.DLL file. You might wonder why anyone would adjust this feature. In this case, it's a matter of performance versus resource usage. A higher compression rate requires fewer resources and transfers better over slow media such as a modem connection. On the other hand, a lower compression rate performs better on slower machines with connections to a high-speed local network.

The final two steps of the example include freeing the unmanaged memory and freeing the device handle. Both steps are essential to free resources that the Garbage Collector can't work with. We've covered these two steps quite a few times in the book already, so there's no need to go into detail again.

Playing Sound Files Example

It's interesting to play a sound stored in a wave (WAV) file on your machine. Of course, if you use the PlaySound() or the associated sndPlaySound() function, there's little control over the sound. You can play it, but that's about it. Even the flags for these two functions are mundane and allow only minimal control over the sound presentation. In short, if the sound file isn't defined well, you won't be able to make any changes to the presentation using application-programming techniques.

> **NOTE**   The example in this section assumes some knowledge of the Media Player sound capability. We've already looked at one such example as part of the MakeSound example in Chapter 1. Be sure to look at that example before you begin working with the example in this section.

There are two other sound-related functions that you need to know about. The first set begins with *aux* and the second set begins with *wave*. As the names suggest, the functions work with the auxiliary or the wave device. The wave functions provide far better control than the aux functions, so we'll discuss the wave functions in this section of the chapter.

The wave functions are divided into input and output devices. In fact, some functions are repeated for both input and output devices. For example, you need to use the waveInGet-DevCaps() function to get the device capabilities of an input device and the waveOutGetDev-Caps() function to get the device capabilities of an output device. The two functions aren't interchangeable, so you need to use the correct function for the type of device you want to query.

A single system might have more than one wave device, so the wave functions make an allowance for this issue as well. You need to provide a device identifier of some sort as input to the wave functions. The function will accept an actual identifier or the handle of an open wave device of the correct type. The handle option can prove tricky because some devices can act as both input and output devices. In addition, the system automatically opens the handles for common devices. Sound cards fall into this category—they're used for input and output and also provide common services so the operating system opens them automatically in most cases. It's essential to provide the correct handle for the wave function call that you want to make.

Determining Device Capabilities

Before we make a sound, let's look at a simpler example. Listing 11.2 shows the technique you can use to determine the characteristics of the wave devices. The example doesn't go through the usual flag machinations because we've seen that technique in many examples in the past. Rather, this example exposes you to some new techniques that we haven't explored. You'll find the flag definitions in the MMSystem.H file and the manufacturer and product identifiers in the MMReg.H file. The source code for this example appears in the \Chapter 11\C#\ WaveCaps and \Chapter 11\VB\WaveCaps folders of the CD.

Listing 11.2   **A Technique for Detecting Wave Device Capabilities**

```
// This function obtains the number of wave output devices.
[DllImport("WinMM.DLL", CharSet=CharSet.Auto, SetLastError=true )]
public static extern UInt32 waveOutGetNumDevs();

// This function determins the capabilities of the specified
// wave output device.
[DllImport("WinMM.DLL", CharSet=CharSet.Auto, SetLastError=true )]
public static extern Int32 waveOutGetDevCaps(IntPtr uDeviceID,
                                             ref WAVEOUTCAPS pwoc,
                                             UInt32 cbwoc);

// Use this structure to hold the device capabilities data.
[StructLayout(LayoutKind.Explicit, CharSet=CharSet.Unicode)]
public struct WAVEOUTCAPS
{
    [FieldOffset(0)]    public Int16          wMid;
    [FieldOffset(2)]    public Int16          wPid;
    [FieldOffset(4)]    public MMVERSION      vDriverVersion;
    [MarshalAs(UnmanagedType.ByValTStr, SizeConst=MAXPNAMELEN)]
    [FieldOffset(8)]    public String         szPname;
    [FieldOffset(72)]   public Int32          dwFormats;
    [FieldOffset(76)]   public Int16          wChannels;
    [FieldOffset(78)]   public Int16          wReserved1;
```

```
    [FieldOffset(80)] public Int32          dwSupport;
};

// This is the maximum size of the path name data.
public const Int32 MAXPNAMELEN = 32;

// This data structure contains the version information.
public struct MMVERSION
{
    public Byte bMinor;
    public Byte bMajor;
    public Int16 Reserved;
}

private void btnTest_Click(object sender, System.EventArgs e)
{
    UInt32        NumDevs;      // The number of output devices.
    WAVEOUTCAPS   WaveData;     // Wave Device Capabilities
    UInt32        CapsSize;     // Wave data structure size.
    Int32         Counter;      // Loop counter variable.
    StringBuilder Output;       // Output string.

    // Obtain the number of output devices.
    NumDevs = waveOutGetNumDevs();

    // Check the capabilties of each device.
    for (Counter = 0; Counter < NumDevs; Counter ++)
    {
        // Determine the device capabilities information.
        WaveData = new WAVEOUTCAPS();
        CapsSize = (UInt32)Marshal.SizeOf(WaveData);
        waveOutGetDevCaps(new IntPtr(Counter),
                    ref WaveData,
                    CapsSize);

        // Display the information on screen.
        Output = new StringBuilder();
        Output.Append("Device Number: " + Counter.ToString());
        Output.Append("\r\nName: " + WaveData.szPname);
        Output.Append("\r\nVersion: " +
                WaveData.vDriverVersion.bMajor.ToString() + "." +
                WaveData.vDriverVersion.bMinor.ToString());

        // Show the information on screen.
        MessageBox.Show(Output.ToString(),
                    "Device Information",
                    MessageBoxButtons.OK,
                    MessageBoxIcon.Information);
    }
}
```

The function calls in this example follow the standard procedure. We use [DllImport] as usual and define the function arguments. Theoretically, we could make the return type for waveOutGetNumDevs() an Int32 instead of a UInt32, but this could lead to problems when working with large numbers of devices. Generally, you should use whatever data types the Platform SDK documentation defines.

The WAVEOUTCAPS data structure looks like something from Mars compared to the other examples in the book. You'll find that the data structures for multimedia are exceptionally picky and this is one of them. Notice that we're using LayoutKind.Explicit instead of LayoutKind.Sequential in this case. In general, you want to avoid using LayoutKind.Explicit because it requires a lot more work and the potential for error is very high. However, LayoutKind.Explicit also gives you precise control over the layout of the data structure and we need that control in this situation. The character set is specifically set to CharSet.Unicode instead of CharSet.Auto. The structure could experience data corruption in some environments if you don't make this change.

The WAVEOUTCAPS data structure fields also look quite strange. Whenever you use the LayoutKind.Explicit option, you must also use the [FieldOffset] attribute for every field in the structure. The [FieldOffset] attribute defines the precise position of every data field within the structure. Using the [FieldOffset] attribute also means exercising extreme care in determining the data element sizes.

Notice that we've defined MMVERSION as a data structure. The MMSystem.H file defines this value as a UINT. However, the Platform SDK documentation is quite confusing on the topic because it references the value as two BYTES. The MMVERSION data structure adds clarity to the situation by making the use of the various data clear.

There's one additional surprise in the WAVEOUTCAPS data structure. Notice that the *szPname* field is defined as type string. However, if you look at both the documentation and the C/C++ headers, you'll notice that this field is actually a TCHAR array. In some cases, you can use the [MarshalAs] attribute, as shown in the listing, to make the Win32 API think you've sent a TCHAR array and not a regular string. Notice the use of the UnmanagedType.ByValTStr option. This option is a requirement to make this solution work. You must also provide a SizeConst that matches the C/C++ header values.

NOTE   You can't combine the <FieldOffset> attribute with the <MarshalAs(UnmanagedType. ByValTStr, SizeConst:=MAXPNAMELEN)> attribute in Visual Basic. The lack of this support makes this example more error prone. In this particular case, using a sequential layout with the appropriate <MarshalAs> attribute works, but there are situations in which the example will fail. For example, on one test machine, the developer didn't provide a properly formatted name string, resulting in an error. See the example Visual Basic code on the CD for complete details.

The code for this example begins by determining the number of output wave devices. Notice that this is the waveOutGetNumDevs() function, so it won't return anything else. The number of devices is used to determine the number of times the code will call waveOutGet-DevCaps(). Each call to waveOutGetDevCaps() will use the current *Counter* value as the device identifier, as shown in the code.

As previously mentioned, the code doesn't spend a lot of time deciphering the various field values returned by the waveOutGetDevCaps() call. However, it does output the name and version as shown in Figure 11.7. Generally, you'll find that the wave device information will tell you basic device capabilities, device type, and device driver vendor name, but not much else. Any special device capabilities remain hidden unless you write code directly to the device or use other technology such as DirectX. However, this code will tell you enough to write code for simple games, most business applications, and even some multimedia applications.

FIGURE 11.7:

The example application outputs the device name and version number.

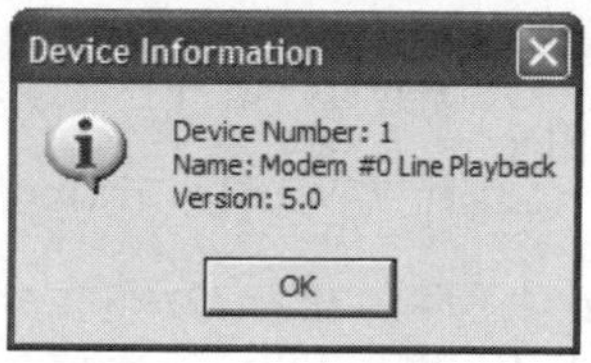

Device Information

Device Number: 1
Name: Modem #0 Line Playback
Version: 5.0

OK

Opening a File

Opening a multimedia file is actually one of the harder parts of using it. You'll find that once you've successfully opened and read the file, playing it and interacting with it in other ways is relatively easy. Part of the problem is the complexity of the file configuration—the file contains several components that you need to interact with as part of opening the data for use. Listing 11.3 shows the minimum code you'll need to open a multimedia file. Note that the listing doesn't include any of the function definitions, structures, or enumerations—we'll discuss these elements later in the chapter and you'll find the complete source code on the CD. You can find the source code for this example in the \Chapter 11\C#\PlayWave and \Chapter 11\VB\PlayWave folders of the CD.

Listing 11.3   **Opening a Multimedia File**

```
// This variable contains the name of the file to play.
private string File2Open;

// This variable contains a pointer to the wave device.
private HWAVEOUT WaveHandle;
```

```
// These variables contain the data format of the WAV file.
private WAVEFORMATEX WF;
private IntPtr WFPointer;

// This variable is a pointer to the actual WAV data.
private IntPtr WaveData;

// File bytes to read or the number of bytes previously read.
private Int32 BytesToRead;

private void btnOpen_Click(object sender, System.EventArgs e)
{
    OpenFileDialog Dlg = new OpenFileDialog();   // File Open Dialog
    Int32       Result;                          // Call result.
    IntPtr      MMIOHandle;                       // MMIO file handle.
    MMCKINFO    Parent;                           // Root node.
    MMCKINFO    Child;                            // Child node.

    // Set up the File Open Dialog
    Dlg.Filter = "Wave Format File (*.wav)|*.wav";
    Dlg.DefaultExt = ".wav";
    Dlg.Title = "Open WAV File Dialog";

    // Display the File Open Dialog and obtain the name of a file and
    // the file information.
    if (Dlg.ShowDialog() == DialogResult.OK)
    {
        // Set the file to open.
        File2Open = Dlg.FileName;

        // Open the requested file so we can determine the
        // data format.
        MMIOHandle = mmioOpen(File2Open,
                              IntPtr.Zero,
                              MMIOOpenFlag.MMIO_READ |
                              MMIOOpenFlag.MMIO_ALLOCBUF);

        // Check the results.
        if (MMIOHandle == IntPtr.Zero)
        {
            MessageBox.Show("Error opening file.",
                            "Application Error",
                            MessageBoxButtons.OK,
                            MessageBoxIcon.Error);
            return;
        }

        // Create a parent node. Verify that this is actually a
        // WAVE file.
        Parent = new MMCKINFO();
        Parent.fccType = mmioFOURCC('W', 'A', 'V', 'E');
        Result = mmioDescend(MMIOHandle,
```

```
                           ref Parent,
                           IntPtr.Zero,
                           MMIODescendFlags.MMIO_FINDRIFF);

// Check the results.
if (Result != MMSYSERR_NOERROR)
{
   // Display an error message.
   MessageBox.Show("This is not a real WAV file.",
                   "File Error",
                   MessageBoxButtons.OK,
                   MessageBoxIcon.Error);

   // Close the open MMIO file handle.
   mmioClose(MMIOHandle, 0);

   return;
}

// Create the Child node. Locate the formatting
// information within the file. This call will also
// fill both Parent and Child nodes with additional
// information.
Child = new MMCKINFO();
Child.ckid = mmioFOURCC('f', 'm', 't', ' ');
Result = mmioDescend(MMIOHandle,
                     ref Child,
                     ref Parent,
                     MMIODescendFlags.MMIO_FINDCHUNK);

// Check the results.
if (Result != MMSYSERR_NOERROR)
{
   // Display an error message.
   MessageBox.Show("Unable to find formatting data.",
                   "File Error",
                   MessageBoxButtons.OK,
                   MessageBoxIcon.Error);

   // Close the open MMIO file handle.
   mmioClose(MMIOHandle, 0);

   return;
}

// Read the data from the file.
BytesToRead = Child.cksize;
WF = new WAVEFORMATEX();
WFPointer = Marshal.AllocHGlobal(BytesToRead);
Marshal.StructureToPtr(WF, WFPointer, true);
if (mmioRead(MMIOHandle, WFPointer, BytesToRead) != BytesToRead)
{
```

```csharp
            // Display an error message.
            MessageBox.Show("File is truncated.",
                            "File Error",
                            MessageBoxButtons.OK,
                            MessageBoxIcon.Error);

            // Free the pointer memory.
            Marshal.FreeHGlobal(WFPointer);

            // Close the open MMIO file handle.
            mmioClose(MMIOHandle, 0);

            return;
        }

        // Convert the pointer to a structure.
        WF = (WAVEFORMATEX)Marshal.PtrToStructure(
            WFPointer,
            typeof(WAVEFORMATEX));
        Marshal.FreeHGlobal(WFPointer);

        // Open the wave device for use.
        Result = waveOutOpen(out WaveHandle,
                             WAVE_MAPPER,
                             ref WF,
                             0,
                             0,
                             0);

        // Check the result.
        if (Result != MMSYSERR_NOERROR)
        {
            // Display an error message.
            MessageBox.Show("Error opening wave device.",
                            "Application Error",
                            MessageBoxButtons.OK,
                            MessageBoxIcon.Error);

            // Close the open MMIO file handle.
            mmioClose(MMIOHandle, 0);

            return;
        }

        // Ascend from the format level of the file.
        Result = mmioAscend(MMIOHandle, ref Child, 0);

        // Locate the data area of the file.
        Child.ckid = mmioFOURCC('d', 'a', 't', 'a');
        Result = mmioDescend(MMIOHandle,
                             ref Child,
```

```
                           ref Parent,
                           MMIODescendFlags.MMIO_FINDCHUNK);

      // Check the results.
      if (Result != MMSYSERR_NOERROR)
      {
         // Display an error message.
         MessageBox.Show("Unable to find waveform data.",
                     "File Error",
                        MessageBoxButtons.OK,
                        MessageBoxIcon.Error);

         // Close the open MMIO file handle.
         mmioClose(MMIOHandle, 0);

         return;
      }

      // Read the data from the file.
      BytesToRead = Child.cksize;
      WaveData = Marshal.AllocHGlobal(BytesToRead);
      if (mmioRead(MMIOHandle, WaveData, BytesToRead) != BytesToRead)
      {
         // Display an error message.
         MessageBox.Show("File is truncated.",
                     "File Error",
                        MessageBoxButtons.OK,
                        MessageBoxIcon.Error);

         // Free the pointer memory.
         Marshal.FreeHGlobal(WaveData);

         // Close the open MMIO file handle.
         mmioClose(MMIOHandle, 0);

         return;
      }

      // Close the open MMIO file handle.
      mmioClose(MMIOHandle, 0);

      // Enable the Play button.
      btnPlay.Enabled = true;
   }
   else
   {
      // If the user didn't select anything, return.
      return;
   }
}
```

This example requires quite a bit of code just to open the file, but that's really the hardest part of the task. The code begins by creating several modulewide variables. Most of these variables provide general pointers to the data used by the rest of the application, so they're legitimately modulewide. I've attempted to keep the number of these variables small.

The btnOpen_Click() method begins by creating an Open WAV File Dialog that enables the user to select a file from the drive, as shown in Figure 11.8. This is one of the few standard pieces of code in the example, but a necessary piece in this case. If the user selects a file, then the rest of the code will open it. Otherwise, the btnOpen_Click() method exits without doing anything.

FIGURE 11.8:

The application provides a custom dialog box for selecting the WAV file.

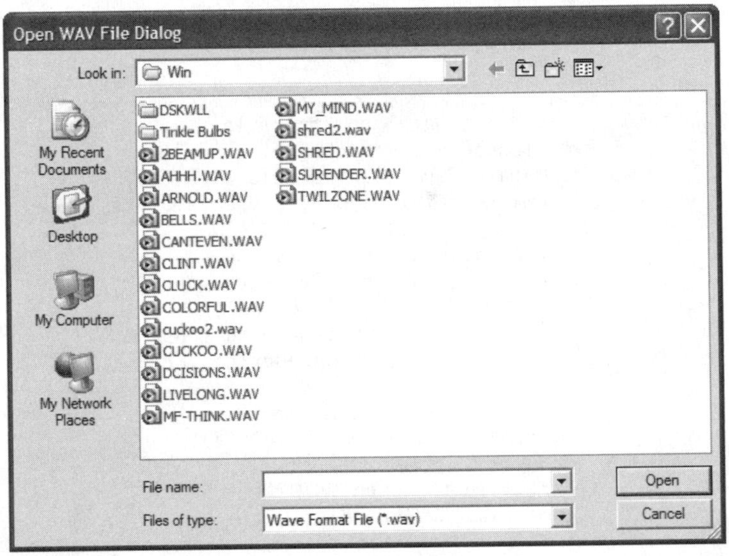

Once the code has a filename to use, it uses the mmioOpen() function to open the file. The multimedia input/output (mmio) functions enable you to open, read, write, and close files for use with multimedia functions. We'll see later in this listing that the mmio functions perform specific multimedia tasks. You should never use the handle returned by an mmio function for any purpose other than multimedia calls.

The next piece of code will look rather odd unless you know a little about WAV files. The multimedia chunk information data structure, MMCKINFO, contains information about the content of a multimedia file—a WAV file in this case. However, to gain access to this information, we need to overcome several hurdles. The first hurdle is the mmioFOURCC() function. In all actuality, the mmioFOURCC() function is a Visual C++ macro. Unless you want to write a special wrapper

DLL just for this macro, you'll need to translate it. The following code shows one example of how you can translate a bit-manipulation macro into something that C# can work with:

```
// This function mimics the Visual C++ macro of the same name.
public UInt32 mmioFOURCC(Char ch0, Char ch1, Char ch2, Char ch3)
{
    UInt32   Temp; // The temporary variable.

    // Convert each of the input characters and
    // bit shift as needed.
    Temp = Convert.ToUInt32(ch0);
    Temp = Temp + (Convert.ToUInt32(ch1) * 0x100);
    Temp = Temp + (Convert.ToUInt32(ch2) * 0x10000);
    Temp = Temp + (Convert.ToUInt32(ch3) * 0x1000000);

    return Temp;
}
```

As you can see, the code accepts four Char values as input and outputs them as a packed UInt32 value. The original macro bit shifts the four values using Visual C++ macro code, which won't work in C#. Of course, this begs the question of what a FOURCC value is. A FOURCC value stands for four-character code. Microsoft and other vendors used FOURCC values during the initial work in creating specifications for common files such as the WAV file. Figure 11.9 shows an example of the FOURCC values in a WAV file that I opened in the DEBUG.EXE application.

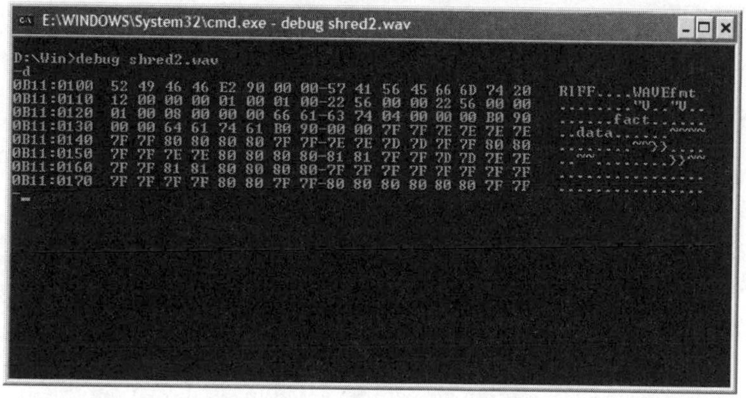

FIGURE 11.9:

WAV files differentiate file areas using a FOURCC entry.

Notice the key words RIFF, WAVE, fmt (with a space at the end), and data in the file. Each of these key words defines a data area with a particular type of data. The resource interchange file format (RIFF) heading tells any application opening the file that this is a standardized resource file. The WAVE entry tells what type of RIFF data the file contains—wave (digitized) audio. The fmt entry marks the beginning of the format data, while the data entry marks the beginning of the digitized sound. Understanding these key elements will make the code a lot easier to understand.

The code uses the MMCKINFO structure to tell the mmioDescend() function which part of the file to open. However, if you don't open the file in an organized manner, you'll quickly become lost. The mmioDescend() function can accept just a single MMCKINFO structure for a root node or two MMCKINFO structures for a child node. The root node for a WAVE file is the WAVE entry shown in Figure 11.8.

After the code finds the root entry, it needs to locate the fmt entry. The fmt entry contains information about the structure of the file. To open a wave device, you need to know that it can play the format the file is in. The second call to the mmioDescend() function fills out both the *Child* and *Parent* structures.

You'll remember that earlier I discussed wave functions, and we haven't seen any yet. The problem is that the wave functions require information about the WAV file and its format. The WAVEFORMATEX structure is the key to gaining that information. However, we can't access the information directly because the mmioRead() function used to read the data only works with unmanaged memory. As you can see in the listing, the code has to create the WAVEFORMA-TEX structure variable, *WF*, and then create a pointer to that structure named *WFPointer* by allocating memory using the Marshal.AllocHGlobal() method and creating an association using the Marshal.StructureToPtr() method. The code uses the mmioRead() function to access the required data. Of course, now we have to place the data pointed at by *WFPointer* into the *WF* structure using the Marshal.PtrToStructure() method. Finally, the code frees the memory used by *WFPointer*.

NOTE Visual Basic developers will need to use the GetType(WAVEFORMATEX) function in place of the typeof(WAVEFORMATEX) function shown in the listing for the Marshal.PtrTo-Structure() method. The two techniques normally produce functionally equivalent output. However, there is a chance of compatibility problems, so Visual Basic developers will need to exercise care when using the Marshal.PtrToStructure() method.

At this point, the code can finally open a wave device using the waveOutOpen() function. The code uses the WAVE_MAPPER constant instead of a standard device identifier so that Windows can choose the best multimedia device to play the sound based on the sound characteristics. Notice that the function doesn't initialize the *WaveHandle* argument—it's declared as an out rather than a ref. Unlike most of the handles we've used so far in the book, the *WaveHandle* is actually a data structure containing a single variable, as shown here:

```
// This structure takes the place of the DECLARE_HANDLE(HWAVEOUT)
// macro for Visual C++.
public struct HWAVEOUT
{
    public Int32   Unused;
}
```

NOTE Visual Basic developers will need to use <Out()> attribute rather than the out keyword used for C# with the waveOutOpen() function. In this case, the two techniques have the same effect. However, the two techniques aren't exactly the same, so Visual Basic developers will need to exercise care in the use of the <Out()> attribute. See the ms-help://MS.VSCC/MS.MSDNVS/cpref/html/frlrfSystemRuntimeInteropServicesOutAttributeClassTopic.htm help topic for additional details. See the ms-help://MS.VSCC/MS.MSDNVS/csref/html/vclrfOut.htm help topic for a comparison of the two keywords. The <Out()> attribute is only used with COM and P/Invoke scenarios, so Visual Basic developers can't use it with managed code as C# developers would use the out keyword.

Visual C++ uses the same data structure. However, it uses a macro to convert a generic data structure into the specific handle used for the call. We don't have that option in C#, so you'll need to create one data structure for each multimedia use. The *Unused* field will contain the handle on return from a successful call—a fact that you can verify by looking in the debugger. Never modify or use this value in any way—treat it as you would any other handle.

TIP If you specify any type of callback function option as part of the waveOutOpen() function call, you'll need to implement the callback function in your code. The management environment doesn't provide anything in the way of multimedia handling for you. The reason that this fact is important is that many of the Visual C++ examples show the code passing a handle to the current window for the callback function. Using this technique will always cause a .NET application to fail (the application might actually drop back to the Desktop without displaying any error information). Chapter 5 discusses the techniques for creating callback functions.

The code has now determined the format of the data within the WAV file and obtained a handle to a wave device. However, we still don't have any data to play. Remember that we're using a tree-like data structure, so the code has to move back from the fmt node to the root node. The mmioAscend() function performs this task by using the *Child* node as a reference point. The code then makes another call to the mmioDescend() function to obtain access to the data node of the WAV file.

NOTE The example application will only read small WAV files because it creates a single small buffer. Generally, if you want to read WAV files larger than 64KB, you need to create multiple buffers and link them together using the *lpNext* field of the WAVEHDR described in the next section, "Playing a File." Theoretically, .NET applications can handle larger files using a single buffer, but the wave functions tend to act strangely if you pass them a buffer larger than 64KB. Consequently, it's good to err on the side of caution in this situation.

At this point, the code creates an unmanaged buffer to hold the WAV data using the `Marshal` `.AllocHGlobal()` method. The `mmioRead()` function places the WAV file data within `WaveData`. The final steps are to close `MMIOHandle` and enable the Play button. We'll deallocate the memory held within `WaveData` later in the application.

Playing a File

Once you have the file open, the rest of the process is easy. The previous section showed how the application opened a WAV file, determined its format, opened a wave device, and finally read the data from the WAV file into memory. At this point, everything is ready to actually play the data contained in the WAV file. Listing 11.4 shows one method for playing the wave data. This source code appears in the same files as Listing 11.3.

Listing 11.4   Technique for Playing Wave Data

```
// This function prepares a WAVE header prior to
// playing the data.
[DllImport("WinMM.DLL", CharSet=CharSet.Auto, SetLastError=true)]
public static extern Int32 waveOutPrepareHeader(HWAVEOUT hwo,
                                                ref WAVEHDR pwh,
                                                Int32 cbwh);


// This structure contains the WAVE header data.
public struct WAVEHDR
{
    public IntPtr    lpData;
    public Int32     dwBufferLength;
    public Int32     dwBytesRecorded;
    public Int32     dwUser;
    public Int32     dwFlags;
    public Int32     dwLoops;
    public IntPtr    lpNext;
    public Int32     reserved;
}

// This function writes (plays) the WAVE data.
[DllImport("WinMM.DLL", CharSet=CharSet.Auto, SetLastError=true)]
public static extern Int32 waveOutWrite(HWAVEOUT hwo,
                                        ref WAVEHDR pwh,
                                        Int32 cbwh);

private void btnPlay_Click(object sender, System.EventArgs e)
{
    WAVEHDR  Header;  // The WAVE data header.
    Int32    Result;  // Results of the call.

    // Prepare the header.
    Header = new WAVEHDR();
```

```
Header.lpData = WaveData;
Header.dwBufferLength = BytesToRead;
Result = waveOutPrepareHeader(WaveHandle,
                              ref Header,
                              Marshal.SizeOf(Header));

// Check the results.
if (Result != MMSYSERR_NOERROR)
{
   // Display an error message.
   MessageBox.Show("Unable to create the WAVE data header.",
                   "Application Error",
                   MessageBoxButtons.OK,
                   MessageBoxIcon.Error);

   return;
}

// Play the data.
Result = waveOutWrite(WaveHandle,
                      ref Header,
                      Marshal.SizeOf(Header));

// Check the results.
if (Result != MMSYSERR_NOERROR)
{
   // Display an error message.
   MessageBox.Show("Unable to play the WAVE file.",
                   "Application Error",
                   MessageBoxButtons.OK,
                   MessageBoxIcon.Error);

   return;
}

// Enable the Pause and Stop buttons.
btnPause.Enabled = true;
btnStop.Enabled = true;
}
```

The waveOutPrepareHeader() function creates a header, the WAVEHDR data structure, for the wave device. Don't confuse this header with the formatting information data structure we created earlier. The WAVEHDR data structure contains the format of the data the wave device will play and the actual data in the *lpData* field. In addition, this data structure is buffer oriented. Notice the *lpNext* field. This field contains a pointer to the next WAVEHDR data structure in a group. As mentioned earlier, you should limit each header to 64KB of data and preferably less to ensure that the waveOutWrite() function handles it correctly.

Like the PlaySound() function we discussed in Chapter 1, the waveOutWrite() function also supports the concept of looping. However, you must specify the number of loops as part of the *dwLoops* field in the WAVEHDR data structure—there isn't any way to specify this value as part of the function call. Make sure you include the WHDR_BEGINLOOP and WHDR_ENDLOOP flags when using looping within your application. These flags tell Windows which block begins the loop and which block ends the loop.

The btnPlay_Click() function begins by creating the WAVEHDR data structure using the waveOutPrepareHeader() function. The only two values that the code must include are the number of bytes of data contained within the data buffer and a pointer to the data buffer itself. All of the other values provide amplifying information or are used for other purposes. For example, the *dwBytesRecorded* field is only used when writing the data to a file after recording it. This call can fail for a number of reasons. However, by the time you reach this point in the application, the two most common points of failure are corrupted data or a *cbwh* value that doesn't match the actual number of data bytes in the buffer. In some cases, the system could run out of memory, but this shouldn't happen when using a modern computer system. The application should check the validity of the device handle as part of the process of opening the file.

Using the waveOutWrite() function is simple. All you need to provide is the handle of the wave device, a reference to the header, and the number of bytes in the data buffer. Generally, this call can fail for the same reasons that the waveOutPrepareHeader() function will.

Pausing and Stopping a File

One of the main reasons to go through all of this work is to gain better control over the playback process. If you use the PlaySound() function, there isn't any way to pause the file and you can't control elements such as the volume. Listing 11.5 finally shows the benefit of using the techniques presented in this chapter. You'll find that most of the wave functions from this point on are as easy to use as the ones shown in the listing. In sum, creating all of the data required to use these functions is difficult, but performing tasks is relatively easy and you've gained a lot of flexibility.

Listing 11.5   Pausing and Stopping a File

```
// This function pauses the playback.
[DllImport("WinMM.DLL", CharSet=CharSet.Auto, SetLastError=true)]
public static extern Int32 waveOutPause(HWAVEOUT hwo);

// This function resumes the playback.
[DllImport("WinMM.DLL", CharSet=CharSet.Auto, SetLastError=true)]
public static extern Int32 waveOutRestart(HWAVEOUT hwo);
```

```csharp
private void btnPause_Click(object sender, System.EventArgs e)
{
    if (btnPause.Text == "Pause")
    {
        // Pause the current sound.
        waveOutPause(WaveHandle);

        // Set the button text.
        btnPause.Text = "Resume";
    }
    else
    {
        // Resume the current sound.
        waveOutRestart(WaveHandle);

        // Set the button text.
        btnPause.Text = "Pause";
    }
}

// This function stops the playback and resets the data pointer
// to zero (the start of the WAVE file).
[DllImport("WinMM.DLL", CharSet=CharSet.Auto, SetLastError=true)]
public static extern Int32 waveOutReset(HWAVEOUT hwo);

private void btnStop_Click(object sender, System.EventArgs e)
{
    // Stop the playback.
    waveOutReset(WaveHandle);

    // Disable the Pause and Stop buttons.
    btnPause.Enabled = false;
    btnStop.Enabled = false;
}
```

As you can see from the listing, a single call performs most tasks. It's important to note that there's a difference between pausing and resuming the sound. You must use the waveOutPause() function to pause the sound. However, calling this function a second time won't do anything. To resume the sound, you must use the waveOutRestart() function. The only value that either function needs is a handle to the wave device.

Stopping the playback means not only stopping the sound, but also moving the pointer back to the beginning of the data. When you play the sound again, Windows will begin at the front of the data area. Always use the waveOutReset() function to stop the playback. As with the other functions in this section, all you need to supply is a valid handle to the wave device to use this function.

Required Application Cleanup

Almost all of the variables we used in Listings 11.4 and 11.5 came from managed sources. However, there are two unmanaged variables in use in the application, and you must clean them up before the application exits. Otherwise, the application will definitely leak memory that Windows won't recover without a reboot. In addition, in rare cases, the user could also loose access to the wave device. Generally, it's a good idea to clean up the remaining unmanaged variables in the frmMain_Closing() method as shown in Listing 11.6.

Listing 11.6   Cleaning Up the Remaining Variables

```
// This function closes a wave device.
[DllImport("WinMM.DLL", CharSet=CharSet.Auto, SetLastError=true)]
public static extern Int32 waveOutClose(HWAVEOUT hwo);

private void frmMain_Closing(object sender,
                            System.ComponentModel.CancelEventArgs e)
{
   // Free the pointer memory.
   Marshal.FreeHGlobal(WaveData);

   // Close the open wave device.
   waveOutClose(WaveHandle);
}
```

As you can see, you need the Marshal.FreeHGlobal() function to free the data memory. Make sure you free the data memory before you close the wave device or the application might exit unexpectedly. The waveOutClose() function closes the handle to the wave device.

Using IconForge

I've used IconForge from CursorArts Company for quite a few of the examples in the book. After using it for a while and failing to exhaust the number of features it contains, I can say that it's probably the best special-purpose drawing program I've tried, especially for the low price ($37.95 plus shipping and handling at the time of writing). While you can create certain types of icons and cursors using the Visual Studio .NET IDE, you can't create all of the types that IconForge provides, and the tools feel cumbersome after you've tried this product. You can download an evaluation product at http://www.cursorarts.com/. There's also an evaluation copy of the current product in the \IconForge folder of the CD.

NOTE   I purposely used the evaluation version of the product for this section so that you could see what the version on the CD includes. The full version of the product provides more extensive features and also removes all of the evaluation reminder notices.

IconForge provides the features required to create both standard and animated icons, standard and animated cursors, multiple resolution icons, and icon libraries. You can also use a screen capture as a basis for creating a new cursor or icon. In short, IconForge provides everything you need to work with cursors and icons. Figure 11.10 shows the display for a typical 32×32-pixel icon. IconForge includes options for 16×16-, 24×24-, 32×32-, 48×48-, 64×64-, 72×72-pixel icons using 2, 16, 256, 24-bit (16.7 million), and 32-bit (16.7 million Windows XP) colors; you can also use custom sizes for your icons.

FIGURE 11.10:

IconForge helps you create both icons and cursors for your applications.

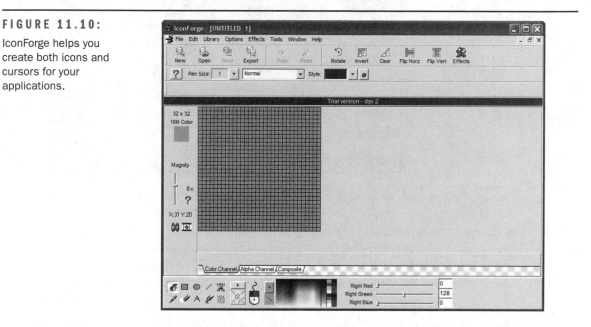

As you can see from the screen shot, IconForge provides a vast array of tools compared to the tools you'll find in the Visual Studio .NET IDE. Along the bottom you'll find all of the usual drawing tools, including one that draws a transparent color. A special Splatter tool draws splatters on the screen. You can use the Nudge tool to move an icon or cursor element a little at a time. Along the left side of the display are tools that magnify the icon, display it in preview mode, or add another frame to the icon window.

Some of the most interesting tools provided with IconForge are those that you don't see immediately. For example, click the Effects button on the toolbar and you'll see the wealth of effects shown in Figure 11.11. Each of the effects changes the set of controls presented in the middle of the display. Change these controls and you'll see a change in the appearance of your icon or cursor. The change doesn't take effect, however, until you click Apply. Even after you click Apply, clicking Undo will remove the change and return your icon to its previous state.

IconForge will undo an almost unlimited number of changes, so it's possible to return your icon or cursor to its original state if you feel the changes don't provide the impact you thought they would.

Many of the special effects supported by IconForge fall into the expected category. As with most drawing programs, you can modify the hue and saturation of your image. Some of the special effects are truly odd and also quite appealing. For example, the Whirlpool effect makes your icon or cursor appear as if the image elements had been whirled. There are also special effects called Mirror, Marbleize, and Mosaic that perform the functions their names imply. The Cloud effect is one of my favorites—it retains the original image but adds a cloud effect to it. The cloud effect tends to add interest to the image without making it impossible to figure out.

IconForge doesn't forget to provide all of the essential tools for cursor and icon drawing. For example, there's a hotspot editor you can use to create a hotspot on cursors. One of the more interesting tools is IconWrapper, shown in Figure 11.12. This tool enables you to add an icon to a file that normally doesn't accept an icon, such as a script. There's an example of a wrapped file in the \Chapter 11\IconForge folder of the CD.

To use the IconWrapper utility with a script, you need to provide the location of the script file, the location of the icon file, and the location of the WScript.EXE or CScript.EXE file (normally the \Windows\System32 folder). It's essential to provide the location of the scripting engine because, otherwise, the resulting executable will simply extract the script file and not execute it. You can also provide the name of an output EXE file. Click Create and Icon-Wrapper will generate an EXE file that contains the script and icon. The user will see your icon in Explorer. Whenever the user double-clicks the file, it will execute using the script engine as it normally does.

FIGURE 11.12:

The IconWrapper utility enables you to add an icon to a file that doesn't normally accept an icon.

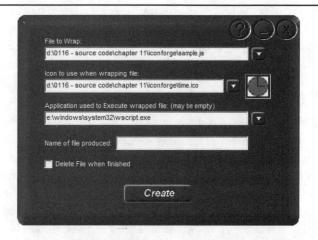

You can also use IconForge to extract bitmaps, icons, and cursors from other files. Simply use the File ➤ Acquire Icon from Resource command to display the Select an Executable dialog box. Choose the executable containing the bitmap, icon, or cursor that you want to extract (I'm using She1132.DLL as an example) and then click OK. You'll see the Extract Resource List from Executable File dialog box shown in Figure 11.13. In this case, the file contains all three categories of resources.

FIGURE 11.13:

Use IconForge to extract bitmaps, icons, or cursors from executable files.

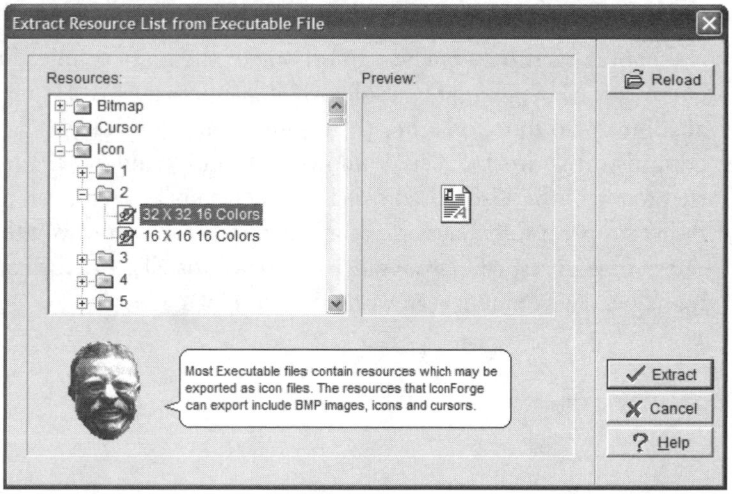

Notice the bodiless man in this screen shot. He spends plenty of time providing you with helpful advice on using the various application features. Sometimes the advice arrives a little late to use (as in this case), but it's always available. In general, you'll find that the developers of this application have made every attempt to create an easy-to-use environment. In some respects, the ease-of-use factor might be the best application feature of all.

Where Do You Go from Here?

This chapter has presented you with information about the Media Player. The first section of the chapter presented fun facts about the Media Player. Generally, it's useful to "play" with some of the features that Windows provides in order to gain a better understanding of what a user has to work with. The Media Player has gone from awkward utility to full-featured application in the years since Microsoft originally created it. The Media Player should present new opportunities for you to make your applications user friendly. Of course, playing with the Media Player for your own needs isn't a bad idea either. In fact, you'll probably want to spend some time learning more about the Media Player because we barely scratched the surface in this chapter.

This chapter has also demonstrated some new programming techniques for media that you might not have considered in the past. Windows development doesn't always have to present an austere environment—it's nice to have fun sometimes. The examples in this chapter have shown you both the practical and the fun aspects of the Media Player. Now it's up to you to determine if these new techniques fit somewhere in your organization. You might find that the help desk gets fewer calls when users like the applications they're using.

Chapter 12 shows you how to fill one of the biggest holes in the .NET Framework, Microsoft Management Console (MMC) support. MMC is a container application that has absolutely no function other than to host snap-ins. These snap-ins perform most of the administrative work under Windows 2000 and Windows XP. It might surprise you to know that many of the Visual Studio .NET beta testers asked for this particular feature but Microsoft didn't supply it for whatever reason. Chapter 12 will show you that creating an MMC snap-in doesn't mean resorting to an older version of Visual C++. You can create MMC snap-ins in the managed environment even without the use of a wizard.

CHAPTER 12

Working with Microsoft Management Console

- Using GUIDGen

- The Case for an MMC Snap-In

- Creating a Wrapper DLL

- Developing the MMC Snap-In Example

The Microsoft Management Console (MMC) is a container application that has no functionality outside of the snap-ins (COM controls) that it supports. Yet this particular application is the center of most of the management tools that Microsoft provides with Windows 2000 and Windows XP. In addition, it's one of the tools that you'll see used most often by third-party developers because the MMC environment is so flexible. As you'll see later, there's little doubt that MMC is one of Microsoft's better ideas because it can support a wide range of COM control snap-ins—anything you can imagine, in fact.

It's hardly surprising, then, that one of the most requested feature additions during the Visual Studio .NET beta test was support for the MMC snap-in. In fact, requests for this feature appeared on all of the newsgroups—language didn't seem to matter. Unfortunately, while support for the MMC snap-in appeared in early versions of the Visual C++ .NET beta, support was eventually dropped even for this language. None of the other .NET languages have ever supported the MMC snap-in directly. This omission is particularly difficult to understand considering that MMC is still a major part of Microsoft's strategy for Windows 2000 and Windows XP administrative tools.

NOTE One of the reasons that Microsoft support personnel offered for the omission of MMC support is the complexity of creating an MMC snap-in using the .NET Framework. Indeed, creating an MMC snap-in would be difficult in any environment without proper library and wizard support, but it can be done. Visual C++ 6 offered both library and wizard support for this task, making it relatively easy to write an MMC snap-in.

Writing an MMC snap-in means working intimately with COM. In fact, everything that MMC does is based on some type of COM interpretability. This chapter will show you how to create a basic MMC snap-in. This MMC snap-in demonstrates all of the principles you'll need to create an MMC snap-in of almost any complexity.

We'll also create an MMC wrapper DLL that you can use to create basic snap-ins and modify to meet your specific needs. The examples and the DLL should make it easier for most .NET developers to create an MMC snap-in as part of the application management strategy. In addition, these examples show how to work with COM using .NET—something that developers will have to do for the foreseeable future since there are so many components written for use with COM and most companies can't afford to throw away such a large investment.

NOTE None of the examples in this chapter work with Visual Basic and the CD lacks any Visual Basic source code for the examples. The main reason for this omission is that Visual Basic presents problems when you're working with pointers and some COM concepts. While Visual Basic developers can use most COM components, the purpose of this section is to provide an advanced COM example and the Visual Basic environment lacks the proper support.

Using GUIDGen

As with all COM objects, MMC snap-ins rely on registry entries to provide information about component configuration. The use of registry entries means that you need some way to uniquely identify your component, which means using a globally unique identifier (GUID). Because Visual Studio .NET doesn't provide this information automatically as the older, native code versions of the product did, you need to obtain the GUID manually. Fortunately, you can use a utility named GUIDGen to create the required GUIDs. You can access this utility using the Tools ➤ Create GUID command from within the Visual Studio .NET IDE or from within the \Program Files\Microsoft Visual Studio .NET\Common7\Tools folder. Figure 12.1 shows how this tool looks.

FIGURE 12.1:

The GUIDGen utility enables you to create GUIDs for your components.

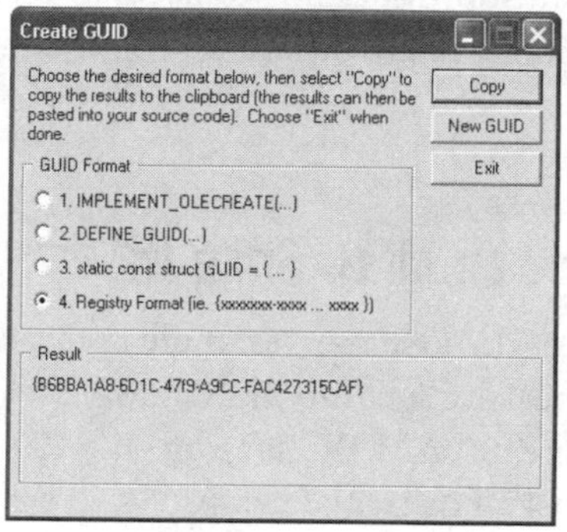

Notice that the figure shows option 4, Registry Format, selected. Make sure you always use this format for components created in C#. Click Copy to place the GUID on the Clipboard. You can then place it within the application using the following code:

```
[Guid("B6BBA1A8-6D1C-47f9-A9CC-FAC427315CAF")]
public class MySnapInData : IComponentData, IExtendPropertySheet
{
};
```

Of course, the class will contain other information. The important piece here is the placement of the [Guid] attribute. You need to provide GUIDs for both the component and the About dialog. The GUIDs also appear in the registry entry and serve to identify the snap-in to MMC. Here are the registry entries for the example MMC snap-in. Note that the entry wraps, in some cases, and that the actual entry would appear on a single line, as shown in the source code:

```
REGEDIT4

[HKEY_LOCAL_MACHINE\Software\Microsoft\MMC\Snapins\{B6BBA1A8-6D1C-47f9-
    A9CC-FAC427315CAF}]
```

```
"About" = "{BACD4F1D-8338-41ee-9D55-DDECE3D8BBCE}"
"NameString" = "An Example of an MMC Snap-In"
"Provider" = "DataCon Services"
"Version" = "1.0"

[HKEY_LOCAL_MACHINE\Software\Microsoft\MMC\Snapins\{B6BBA1A8-6D1C-47f9-
    A9CC-FAC427315CAF}\StandAlone]
```

There are a few notes about this part of the example. I began by adding a new text file to the project and simply renamed it with a .REG extension. The file must begin with REGEDIT4 as shown, and you need to add the main GUID key. Notice the use of curly brackets around the GUID entry (they don't appear in the [Guid] attribute entry). Only provide the About value if your snap-in has an About dialog. The NameString, Provider, and Version values are also optional. You must provide the StandAlone key, as shown, if you're following this example— snap-in extensions require different programming techniques from the ones shown for this example.

The Case for an MMC Snap-In

We'll work on a MMC snap-in example in this chapter because I consider it the most common example of a specialty application. A lot of developers on Microsoft's various newsgroups have asked how to create an MMC snap-in, and I'm sure that many more are wondering how to perform this task. The lack of any MMC projects in Visual Studio .NET and the changes to the MMC snap-in in Windows XP have led some developers to believe the MMC snap-in is going to become history very soon. That may be, but for today, the MMC snap-in still represents the best way of writing a configuration utility.

MMC is the application used by Windows 2000 and Windows XP to manage operating system functionality. You'll find it in the \System32 folder as MMC.EXE. MMC is a container application that hosts snap-ins—the container doesn't do much more than provide a place for the snap-in to perform its work. Of course, the container does lend a consistency to the user interface and ensures that each snap-in behaves in a certain way. Each configuration of snap-ins is called a console, and you'll find a list of these consoles in the Administrative Tools folder of the Control Panel. Figure 12.2 shows a typical example of a console—the Performance console.

In this case, the System Monitor and the Performance Logs and Alerts are actually two separate MMC snap-ins that appear together in this console. You can use the File ➢ Add/Remove Snap-in command to display the Add/Remove Snap-in dialog box, which contains a list of snap-ins used to create a particular console, as shown in Figure 12.3. Note that the folders beneath the Performance Logs and Alerts entry in Figure 12.2 are actually part of a single MMC snap-in.

FIGURE 12.2:

MMC consoles pair one or more MMC snap-ins with the MMC container application.

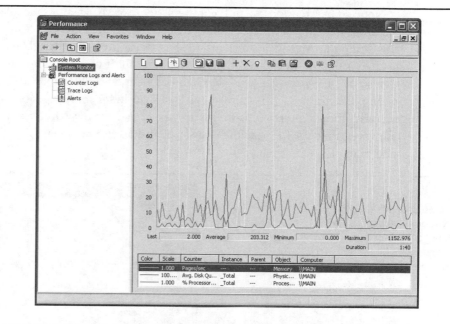

FIGURE 12.3:

Many consoles appear to contain just one control but are actually made of several controls.

You should also notice that the System Monitor is an ActiveX Control snap-in, not a standard MMC snap-in. You can always use standard ActiveX controls as MMC snap-ins, but most ActiveX controls lack the interfaces required to interact with the MMC container application. For example, I created a special type of pushbutton and inserted it in MMC (just to see what it would do). Yes, I could see the button and it reacted when I clicked it, but that's it. However, my pushbutton example does demonstrate that MMC is just another way to use COM, nothing more or less.

Notice the Extensions tab in Figure 12.3. Some MMC snap-ins include augmented features—additions that you can choose to include in the console. Figure 12.4 shows the extensions for the Computer Management snap-in. The extensions in this list add data views to a console created using the Computer Management snap-in. If you scroll through the list, you'll notice that some snap-ins are also used in stand-alone mode, which indicates the duality of their nature. Extension snap-ins rely on the host snap-in for some types of services and must implement additional interfaces as well as provide extra code for working with the host snap-in. However, they also provide the basic level of snap-in functionality that we'll discus in the first example in the chapter.

FIGURE 12.4:

Some snap-ins provide extended functionality for a stand-alone MMC snap-in.

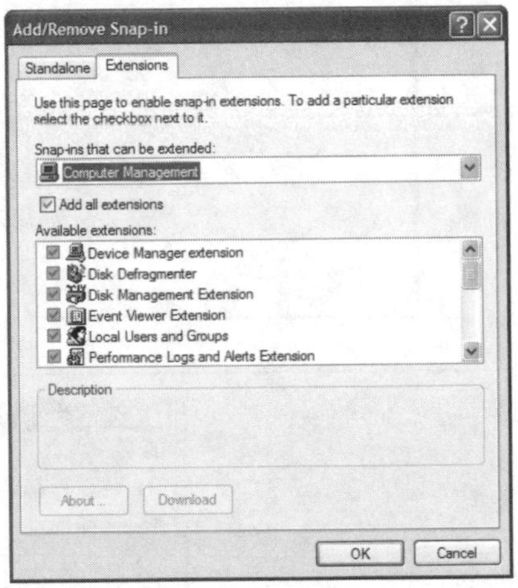

The "magic" for the MMC application is the MSC file. This file contains the information required to create a console. In fact, if you look in the \System32 folder, you'll find the PerfMon.MSC file that contains the information to create the Performance console. Interestingly enough, this file uses XML to store information and has used it long before XML was very popular on the Internet. Figure 12.5 shows a view of the MSC file using XML Notepad.

| TIP | XML is almost, but not quite, readable by the average human. Reading simple files is almost a trivial exercise, but once the data gets nested a few layers deep, reading it can become tiresome. That's why you should have a tool for reading XML in your developer toolkit. The only problem is that some of these tools cost quite a bit for the occasional user. Microsoft has remedied this problem a little with the introduction of XML Notepad (http://msdn.microsoft.com/library/default.asp?url=/library/en-us/dnxml/html/xmlpaddownload.asp). This utility is free for the price of a download and does a reasonable job of reading most XML files. |

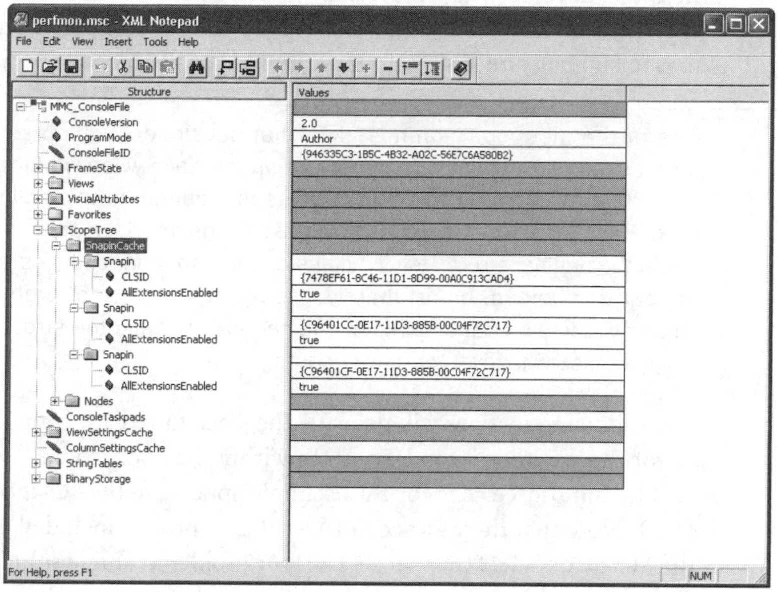

FIGURE 12.5:

MMC relies on MSC files that store configuration information in XML format.

Figure 12.5 shows an important bit of information about the MMC application. The first and third MMC snap-in globally unique identifier (GUID) entries correspond to the MMC snap-ins for the console. (You can validate this information by looking the GUIDs up in the registry using RegEdit.) The third entry actually points to the control responsible for handling ActiveX controls. If you look up the GUID for the second GUID entry, you'll notice that it's for a folder snap-in, the Console Root folder in Figure 12.2.

MMC does have quite a bit to offer in the way of control organization and presentation. While this chapter won't explore every MMC feature, you'll learn about quite a few of them. We'll explore the MMC application in more detail later as part of the example. For now, you have enough information to understand some MMC basics.

Creating a Wrapper DLL

There are many reasons to create a wrapper DLL for this example. However, there are two reasons that are more important than any other reason you might consider. The first reason is that MMC snap-ins are common and you'll probably create more than one during your career. Placing all of the common code in a wrapper DLL means that you don't have to cut and paste it later. The second reason is that no matter what you do, MMC requires access to some functions in the MMC.LIB file and this library is simply inaccessible from any .NET language.

Unless you develop your MMC snap-in in Visual C++ (in which case, you don't need this chapter), you'll have to write parts using C# and other parts using Visual C++. Using more than one language means creating multiple DLLs, which means using multiple files.

TIP	One of the most common mistakes that developers will make is attempting to use a struct in place of a class to implement an interface when working with C#. As a rule, you should never use a struct where a class is required. In this case, the struct is boxed by CLR, which means any changes you make to the interface are reflected in the boxed copy, not in the original struct. Using a class ensures that any changes you make in the interface appear as planned. Unfortunately, debugging this type of problem can be intimidating unless you know what to look for. You can always avoid the struct versus class conflict by using a class whenever you have doubts.

The following sections will describe the steps for creating an MMC wrapper DLL. The code for this example is too large to fit within the book, so we'll look at important segments of it. The full source code for this example appears in the \Chapter 12\MMCHelper folder of the CD. Note that there's a second Visual C++ project included with this DLL that appears in the \Chapter 12\MMCHelper\MMCHelper2 folder. A single solution file opens both projects because both projects form a single wrapper DLL in all reality.

Creating an Interface

There are a few problems you need to address when working with COM in a managed environment. The fact that the two environments are so different doesn't help matters much. COM uses an entirely different set of rules from the ones you've used with the .NET Framework.

One of the first problems that you'll need to consider is how to create a managed version of a COM interface. The best way to do this is to add three attributes to the interface description. These attributes tell the compiler to add information to the assembly that it wouldn't normally provide. The following list tells you about each of the attributes:

[ComImport]   This attribute tells the compiler that the interface is based on a COM interface with the same name. The .NET environment will actually import the COM definition for you. To use this attribute, the class in question must derive from Object, which means that many COM interfaces won't work with this attribute. Make sure you read the documentation for the interface completely. The [ComImport] attribute is always used with the [Guid] attribute—you must specify the GUID of the COM class that the interface will use. Finally, the class must not have any members—the .NET environment creates the required public constructor (without any parameters) automatically. In sum, this is a fast way to create an interface definition, but it's limited.

[InterfaceType]   This attribute describes the type of exposure to provide for the interface when exposed to COM. The acceptable values include *dual*, *IUnknown*, and *IDispatch*. Generally, implementing a *dual* interface is best because older versions of Visual Basic rely on *IDispatch* while older versions of Visual C++ rely on *IUnknown*. However, you can make the component slightly smaller by implementing one interface or the other if the component has a specific target environment.

[Guid]   This attribute assigns a globally unique identifier (GUID) to the interface. This must be the same GUID used by the COM unmanaged counterpart. If you aren't implementing an existing interface, then use GUIDGen (see the section entitled "Using GUIDGen" earlier in this chapter) to create a new GUID. Using the [Guid] attribute isn't mandatory, but it should be to ensure that the GUID for your component remains consistent.

Now that you know how to identify a COM interface substitute, let's look at a typical interface example. Here's the ISnapinHelp2 interface used to add help support to an MMC snap-in. The ISnapinHelp2 interface was introduced for MMC 1.1 and includes a second method for adding Web-based help to your snap-in:

```
[ComImport,
    InterfaceType(ComInterfaceType::InterfaceIsIUnknown),
    Guid("4861A010-20F9-11d2-A510-00C04FB6DD2C")]
public __gc __interface ISnapinHelp2
{
public:
    virtual /* [helpstring] */ HRESULT GetHelpTopic(
        /* [out] */ [Out]IntPtr *lpCompiledHelpFile) = 0;

    virtual /* [helpstring] */ HRESULT GetLinkedTopics(
        /* [out] */ [Out]IntPtr *lpCompiledHelpFiles) = 0;
};
```

NOTE   The example code is written in Visual C++ because that's what the Platform SDK documentation uses—we'll use C#, whenever possible, for the remaining examples in the book. The reason I'm using Visual C++ in this section is to make it easier to identify the components from the Platform SDK. In addition, you'll find some interfaces are actually easier to implement using Visual C++.

The first thing you need to notice about the interface is the __interface keyword. Visual C++ will compile an interface that uses the interface keyword without a single word of complaint until you attempt to use attributes with it. Because you won't always need to use attributes with interfaces, it's possible to create an interface that relies on the interface keyword instead of the __interface keyword. The interface version will never work properly in a managed environment.

If you're familiar with the ISnapinHelp2 declaration in MMC.H, you'll know that it derives from ISnapinHelp and lacks the GetHelpTopic() method declaration shown in the example code. It's impossible to derive a managed interface from an unmanaged interface. Consequently, it's often easier to create a combined managed interface, as shown in the example (that is, unless you expect someone to use the older interface for some reason, in which case you should implement both). Now that you've seen the Visual C++ implementation of the ISnapinHelp2 interface, let's look at the C# equivalent:

```
[ComImport,
 InterfaceType(ComInterfaceType.InterfaceIsIUnknown),
 Guid("4861A010-20F9-11d2-A510-00C04FB6DD2C")]
public interface ISnapinHelp2
{
    [PreserveSig()]
    int GetHelpTopic(out IntPtr lpCompiledHelpFile);
    [PreserveSig()]
    int GetLinkedTopics(out IntPtr lpCompiledHelpFiles);
}
```

While the Visual C++ code shares many similarities with the C# code, there are also some important differences (other than language-specific differences). Notice the use of the [PreserveSig()] attribute. Normally, the .NET environment converts interface method calls to an HRESULT format because that's what most of them use. The GetHelpTopic() function would actually appear as follows, without the [PreserveSig()] attribute:

```
HRESULT GetHelpTopic([out] IntPtr lpCompiledHelpFile,
                     [out, retval] int i);
```

In some cases, this conversion can cause odd application errors and even prevent the interface from working properly. The [PreserveSig()] attribute maintains the method signature you create for the interface as part of the interface definition. While using the [PreserveSig()] attribute is purely discretionary in Visual C++ because this language is able to use HRESULT values, C# developers should always use the [PreserveSig()] attribute unless they actually anticipate using the HRESULT value. The best idea is to look at the Platform SDK to see if the HRESULT value is used. In addition, look at a Visual C++ implementation of the same interface. Finally, if you have problems getting the interface to work in an application, try using the [PreserveSig()] attribute.

A second major difference in the two interface implementations is that the C# code relies on the out keyword while the Visual C++ counterpart uses the [out] attribute. Always use the out keyword, whenever possible, when writing interfaces using C#. Microsoft didn't spend a lot of time documenting the difference between the two, but you'll find that the out keyword works with fewer problems in C# code.

Because an MMC snap-in is normally an unmanaged COM object, your managed MMC snap-in will have to mimic its behavior. This means implementing at least the minimal subset of interfaces to create an operational MMC snap-in. The following list shows which interfaces the first example in the chapter will use:

- `IDataObject`
- `IComponent`
- `IComponentData`
- `ISnapinAbout`

NOTE   The smallest possible MMC snap-in implementation must contain four interfaces: `IDataObject`, `IComponent`, `IComponentData`, and `IClassFactory`. You don't need to implement `IClassFactory`, but the other three interfaces must appear within your code. However, the snap-in won't display correctly in the Add Standalone Snap-in dialog box (associated with the MMC application) without the `ISnapinAbout` interface. So, while you can get by without implementing it, the `ISnapinAbout` interface is actually a required interface.

A fully functional MMC snap-in will include several other interfaces. These interfaces aren't required to make the MMC snap-in work—you implement them to ensure the user can access features such as help and context menus. In other words, these are helpful user interface features. Generally, you'll want to implement the following list of interfaces to ensure the MMC snap-in will meet all users' needs:

- `ISnapinHelp2`
- `IDisplayHelp`
- `IExtendContextMenu`
- `IExtendControlbar`
- `IExtendPropertySheet`

There are a number of other interfaces you can implement as part of an MMC snap-in, all of which appear in the `MMC.H` file. MMC also implements a number of interfaces for you. While you can override these interfaces to provide special behavior, you don't need to create them for a simple MMC snap-in. These MMC-provided interfaces include the following:

- `IPropertySheetProvider`
- `IPropertySheetCallback`
- `IConsoleNamespace2`
- `IHeaderCtrl`

- IResultData
- IImageList
- IConsole2
- IContextMenuCallback
- IControlbar
- IToolbar
- IConsoleVerb

As you can see, creating a managed substitute for unmanaged COM is often a matter of knowing which interfaces to implement. Ultimately, the interfaces you implement affect the functionality of the resulting component and determine the utility of the component you create. For example, you don't have to implement the ISnapinAbout interface to create a functional MMC snap-in, but this interface is required if you want to provide at least some information to the user about the purpose of the MMC snap-in.

Even the optional interfaces will have a place in the wrapper DLL. For example, the IConsole2 interface provides the means to access the MMC environment. Therefore, even though you don't have to implement the IConsole2 interface, you'll need to include it in the DLL so that you can gain access to required MMC functionality. Another example is the IControlbar interface. This interface is used by the IExtendControlbar interface to add and remove toolbars and other controls to the MMC environment. Even though you don't need to implement the IControlbar interface, the IExtendControlbar interface requires access to it. These reference interfaces are clearly identified in the source code so you can see how they interact with the snap-in as a whole.

One of the best ways that I've found to learn about COM interfaces is to view implementations of similar controls using the OLE/COM Object Viewer utility. This utility shows which interfaces an existing control implements and therefore provides valuable clues when implementing similar controls when working with .NET. You'll also find clues in the various C/C++ header files because they normally define the interfaces for a particular type of control or component. The Microsoft documentation and online sources often point to the interface requirements for certain types of components as well. All it takes is a little detective work to learn which interfaces you must implement to create a basic component and which interfaces to add in order to gain some level of component functionality.

TIP Even though you don't have to create multiple files when working with Visual Studio .NET, it's often helpful to do so when working with moderate- to large-sized wrapper DLLs such as the one used in this example. Dividing code by type makes it easier to locate a specific piece of code. The example uses separate files for function implementations, structures, enumerations, and interfaces.

Writing the MMC Wrapper DLL

This section describes the portions of the MMCHelper.DLL that we'll use for every MMC snap-in that you create. You'll learn about some essential functions, the interface descriptions, enumerations, and structures. Each element of the MMCHelper.DLL will appear in a separate file to make it easier to view and modify the code later. This is a good practice to follow when you create large DLLs designed to act as helpers to components. Each file is named to reflect the content of one of the sections that follow.

Adding the MMC Functions

There are two types of functions that you'll need to access when writing an MMC snap-in. The first type is utility functions—the type of functions that convert data and perform other types of tasks required to marshal data between the managed and unmanaged environments. The second type is found in the MMC.LIB file. These functions perform MMC-specific tasks that you can't duplicate in any other way. A minimal MMC wrapper DLL will include property page support as a minimum, but there are other C library functions that you'll eventually need to add.

Now that you have some idea of what we're going to do in this section, let's discuss the functions. Listing 12.1 shows the data translation functions we'll need for this example. These functions help marshal the data from the managed environment to the unmanaged environment. Note that the source code contains additional documentation that doesn't appear as part of Listing 12.1. You'll find this source code in the Functions.CS file found in the \Chapter 12\MMCHelper folder.

Listing 12.1   An Overview of MMC Functions

```
public static Int32 RGB(Byte Blue, Byte Red, Byte Green)
{
    Int32 Temp; // The output value.

    // Bit shift the three values.
    Temp = Red;
    Temp = Temp + (Green * 0x100);
    Temp = Temp + (Blue * 0x10000);

    // Return the value.
    return Temp;
}

public static IntPtr TranslateBitmap(IntPtr InputBitmap)
{
    IntPtr      OutputBitmap;  // Handle for the translated bitmap.
    IntPtr      hdc;           // Handle to the current device context.
    DIBSECTION  ds;            // Device Independent Bitmap definition.
```

```
BITMAPINFO  bmi;            // Bitmap information structure.
IntPtr      Bits;           // Pointer to the bit values
UInt16      OldColorDepth;  // Original color depth of the bitmap.
Int32       BitmapLength;   // Size of the input bitmap.

// Initialize the structures.
ds = new DIBSECTION();
ds.dsBm = new BITMAP();
ds.dsBmih = new BITMAPINFOHEADER();
bmi = new BITMAPINFO();
bmi.bmiColors = new RGBQUAD();
bmi.bmiHeader = new BITMAPINFOHEADER();

// Obtain the device context for this display.
hdc = CreateCompatibleDC(IntPtr.Zero);

// Obtain the bitmap information passed from the snap-in.
BitmapLength = GetObject(InputBitmap,
                        Marshal.SizeOf(ds),
                        ref ds);

// Create a BITMAPINFO structure based on the DIBSECTION.
bmi.bmiHeader = ds.dsBmih;

// Change the color depth of the bitmap to match the screen
// color depth.
OldColorDepth = bmi.bmiHeader.biBitCount;
bmi.bmiHeader.biBitCount =
   (UInt16)GetDeviceCaps(hdc, DevCapParm.BITSPIXEL);

// Create a bitmap handle that uses the same color depth as
// the current screen.
OutputBitmap = CreateDIBSection(hdc,
                                ref bmi,
                                0,
                                out Bits,
                                IntPtr.Zero, 0);

// Return the bitmap's original color depth.
bmi.bmiHeader.biBitCount = OldColorDepth;

// Translate the bitmap into something the screen can display.
SetDIBits(hdc,
          OutputBitmap,
          0,
          bmi.bmiHeader.biHeight,
          ds.dsBm.bmBits,
          ref bmi,
          0);

// Delete the device context to free memory.
DeleteDC(hdc);
```

```
        return OutputBitmap;
    }

    public static Byte[] StringToByteArray(String Input)
    {
        Char  []CArray;     // Character array holding the string.
        Byte  []Output;     // Output data.
        Int32 CharCount;    // Character loop counter.
        Int32 UniCount;     // Unicode character loop counter.

        // Convert the input string to a character array.
        CArray = Input.ToCharArray();

        // Initialize the output array and counter.
        Output = new Byte[(Input.Length + 1) * 2];
        UniCount = 0;

        // Use a loop to place the character array values into the
        // Byte array.
        for (CharCount = 0; CharCount < Input.Length; CharCount++)
        {
            // MMC uses Unicode strings, so we need to convert each
            // single input character into a Unicode equivalent.
            Output[UniCount++] = (Byte)CArray[CharCount];
            Output[UniCount++] = 0;
        }

        // Add a null terminator.
        Output[UniCount++] = 0;
        Output[UniCount] = 0;

        // Return the result.
        return Output;
    }
```

The RGB() method is a conversion of yet another Visual C++ macro. In this case, the method accepts three color values as input, shifts the color values as needed to keep them separate within a single variable, and then returns that value. MMC often requires an application to provide a color mask for the icons it uses. This function helps create the value used to represent the color in the color mask.

One of the hidden issues of working with .NET is that it assumes that images should have certain features. Unfortunately, the assumptions it makes contrast with those required by MMC. One of the major issues is that .NET usually tries to use 32-bit color for all images while MMC requires that the color depth and other features of the bitmap match the operating system environment. The TranslateBitmap() method accepts a .NET bitmap as input and translates it into something that MMC can use.

Let's begin by looking at one of the variables used for this portion of the example. The example code requires access to a number of data structures—most of which are quite mundane. However, the DIBSECTION data structure is a little unusual and we'll want to discuss it as part of the TranslateBitmap() method. Here's the definition for the DIBSECTION data structure:

```
/// <summary>
/// This structure is used with the CreateDIBSection() function
/// to store information about the device independent bitmap (DIB).
/// </summary>
[StructLayout(LayoutKind.Sequential, Pack=1, CharSet=CharSet.Auto)]
private struct DIBSECTION
{
   BITMAP            dsBm;
   BITMAPINFOHEADER  dsBmih;

   // The original structure calls for an array of three
   // DWORD values.
   // DWORD              dsBitfields[3];
   // We can substitute three UInt32 values instead.
   UInt32            dsBitfields0;
   UInt32            dsBitfields1;
   UInt32            dsBitfields2;

   IntPtr            dshSection;
   UInt32            dsOffset;
}
```

Throughout the book, we've had to work hard to revolve certain data elements within structures. The DIBSECTION data structure contains one of those elements in the form of a DWORD array. Fortunately, it's easy to substitute three UInt32 fields in place of the DWORD array in this case. Don't get the idea that this solution is free. You must include the *Pack=1* argument in the [StructLayout] attribute for this solution to work. Otherwise, you'll see a wealth of strange and intermittent errors in your code. The rest of this data structure is relatively straightforward.

The TranslateBitmap() method code begins by initializing the data structures used to translate the bitmap. It then creates a compatible device context using the CreateCompatibleDC() function. The device context is normally used for drawing, but it also provides information about the current display environment. MMC requires a bitmap that has the same features as the current display environment, so learning what those features are is a logical first step. Notice that we pass a null pointer to the CreateCompatibleDC() function, which means it will return the drawing information for the Desktop rather than the current application.

Now that the code has an information source, it begins to create a BITMAPINFO data structure that contains the statistics for the current bitmap. Part of this process also creates the

DIBSECTION data structure discussed earlier using the GetObject() function. One of the entries in the BITMAPINFO data structure contains the color depth of the current bitmap, which the code saves in *OldColorDepth* for later use. The code obtains the correct color depth for the display setup using the GetDeviceCaps() function with the compatible device context handle obtained earlier and places it in the BITMAPINFO data structure. The final step is to use the CreateDIBSection() function to create a new bitmap based on the old bitmap data and new BITMAPINFO data structure content. The code returns the original color depth to the BITMAPINFO data structure for use in a final call.

At this point, the code has created a new bitmap, but the bitmap lacks data. All it has is a data structure that provides information about the format of the bitmap. The code uses the SetDIBits() function to move the data from the original bitmap to the new bitmap while taking the differences in bitmap structure into account. This means translating some colors to new values in order to make the new data compatible with the color depth information. The final step is to delete the compatible device context and output the modified bitmap.

The StringToByteArray() method fills in one of the few data translation gaps in the .NET arsenal. This function accepts a standard string as input and converts it to an array of bytes for use with MMC. The first step in this process is to create a character array from the string. The code then computes the length of the byte array by allowing two bytes for each character (for a Unicode representation) and adding two bytes for a terminating null character.

The code relies on a for loop to perform the actual conversion and data transfer. Each character consumes two bytes. The first byte is always a zero, while the second byte contains the current ANSI value of the individual characters in the character array. The final step is to add the null termination. The byte array will actually appear as a series of numbers that MMC will convert back to a string for display on screen. Interestingly enough, you only need to perform this conversion for some strings. For example, the strings for the About dialog box don't require conversion, but those displayed in the Scope pane do. Make sure you check the example code for the quirks in displaying strings in MMC.

As previously mentioned, we also require access to some of the functions found in the MMC.LIB file. The only problem with this requirement is that we'll need to use Visual C++ to create the required access. The use of two languages means that the wrapper DLL will actually have two DLL files. The use of two files further complicates things by creating a split in the MMCHelper namespace. It's enough to drive you mad, but there's an easy way to fix the problem. Let's begin by looking at the code for the two library calls. You'll find this source code in the MMCHelper2.H file found in the Chapter 12\MMCHelper\MMCHelper2 folder:

```
public __gc class HelperFunctions
{
public:
    // Allows the property sheet to notify the MMC snap-in component
```

```
// that the user has made a change to the object settings.
static HRESULT DoMMCPropertyChangeNotify(Int32 lNotifyHandle,
                                          LPARAM param)
{
    return MMCPropertyChangeNotify(lNotifyHandle, param);
}

// Frees the handle to an MMCN_PROPERTY_CHANGE message. This message
// is sent by the system as the result of a
// MMCPropertyChangeNotify()
// call by the property sheet.
static HRESULT DoMMCFreeNotifyHandle(Int32 lNotifyHandle)
{
    return MMCFreeNotifyHandle(lNotifyHandle);
}
};
```

As you can see, there's nothing unusual about this part of the wrapper. We use the Visual C++ HelperFunctions class to create a connection to the MMC.LIB functions. As previously mentioned, however, that access is in a separate file named MMCHelper2.DLL and somewhat inaccessible to the developer. To fix this section problem, we'll create another class in the C# portion of the code, as shown here. (Note that the source code file contains more documentation.) You'll find this source code in the MMCFunc.CS file found in the \Chapter 12\MMCHelper folder:

```
public class MMCImportedFuncs
{
    public static Int32 MMCPropertyChangeNotify(Int32 lNotifyHandle,
                                                 Int32 param)
    {
        return HelperFunctions.DoMMCPropertyChangeNotify(lNotifyHandle,
                                                          param);
    }

    public static Int32 MMCFreeNotifyHandle(Int32 lNotifyHandle)
    {
        return HelperFunctions.DoMMCFreeNotifyHandle(lNotifyHandle);
    }
}
```

This two-level approach does incur a small performance penalty, and there's no good way to overcome the problem. However, now the functions are easily accessible through the MMCImportedFuncs class to the developer using the MMCHelper.DLL file, and the function names are precisely the same as those found in the Visual C++ documentation for MMC. In short, sometimes you need to use multiple levels of declarations in order to achieve usability goals and the cost of a small hit in performance. However, it's important to at least try to find a solution that doesn't involve this approach whenever possible.

Defining the Interfaces

As previously mentioned, there are four essential interfaces you must define for an MMC snap-in: IComponent, IComponentData, IDataObject, and ISnapinAbout. Listing 12.2 shows the code for these four interfaces. Notice that working with interfaces in C# is similar to working with them in either the managed or unmanaged Visual C++ environment. Sure, there are some differences (and we'll discuss them all), but the essential coding technique is the same. Note that the listing doesn't include all of the comments that you'll find in the standard source code. You'll find this source code in the Interfaces.CS file found in the \Chapter 12\MMCHelper folder.

Listing 12.2   The Four Basic MMC Interfaces

```
[ComImport,
 InterfaceType(ComInterfaceType.InterfaceIsIUnknown),
 Guid("43136EB2-D36C-11CF-ADBC-00AA00A80033")]
public interface IComponent
{
    void Initialize(
        [MarshalAs(UnmanagedType.Interface)]Object lpConsole);
    [PreserveSig()]
    RESULT_VAL Notify(IntPtr lpDataObject,
                MMC_NOTIFY_TYPE aevent,
                Int32 arg,
                Int32 param);
    void Destroy(Int32 cookie);
    void QueryDataObject(Int32 cookie,
                        DATA_OBJECT_TYPES type,
                        out IDataObject ppDataObject);
    [PreserveSig()]
    RESULT_VAL GetResultViewType(Int32 cookie,
                        out IntPtr ppViewType,
                        out Int32 pViewOptions);
    void GetDisplayInfo(ref RESULTDATAITEM ResultDataItem);
    [PreserveSig()]
    RESULT_VAL CompareObjects(IDataObject lpDataObjectA,
                        IDataObject lpDataObjectB);
}

[ComImport,
 InterfaceType(ComInterfaceType.InterfaceIsIUnknown),
 Guid("955AB28A-5218-11D0-A985-00C04FD8D565")]
public interface IComponentData
{
    void Initialize(
        [MarshalAs(UnmanagedType.Interface)] Object pUnknown);
    void CreateComponent(out IComponent ppComponent);
    [PreserveSig()]
    RESULT_VAL Notify(IntPtr lpDataObject,
```

```
                        MMC_NOTIFY_TYPE aevent,
                        IntPtr arg,
                        IntPtr param);
    void Destroy();
    void QueryDataObject(Int32 cookie,
                        DATA_OBJECT_TYPES type,
                        out IDataObject ppDataObject);
    void GetDisplayInfo(ref SCOPEDATAITEM ResultDataItem);
    [PreserveSig()]
    RESULT_VAL CompareObjects(IDataObject lpDataObjectA,
                              IDataObject lpDataObjectB);
}

[ComImport,
 InterfaceType(ComInterfaceType.InterfaceIsIUnknown),
 Guid("0000010e-0000-0000-C000-000000000046")]
public interface IDataObject
{
    [PreserveSig()]
    RESULT_VAL GetData(ref FORMATETC pFormatEtc, ref STGMEDIUM pmedium);
    void GetDataHere(ref FORMATETC pFormatEtc, ref STGMEDIUM pmedium);
    [PreserveSig()]
    RESULT_VAL QueryGetData(ref FORMATETC pFormatetc);
    [PreserveSig()]
    RESULT_VAL GetCanonicalFormatEtc(ref FORMATETC pFormatetcIn,
                                     ref FORMATETC pFormatetcOut);

    [PreserveSig()]
    RESULT_VAL SetData(ref FORMATETC pFormatetc,
                       ref STGMEDIUM pmedium,
                       Boolean fRelease);
    [PreserveSig()]
    RESULT_VAL EnumFormatEtc(UInt32 dwDirection,
                             IntPtr ppenumFormatetc);
    [PreserveSig()]
    RESULT_VAL DAdvise(ref FORMATETC pFormatetc,
                       ADVF advf,
                       IntPtr pAdvSink,
                       ref UInt32 pdwConnection);
    [PreserveSig()]
    RESULT_VAL DUnadvise(UInt32 dwConnection);
    [PreserveSig()]
    RESULT_VAL EnumDAdvise(IntPtr ppenumAdvise);
}

[ComImport,
 InterfaceType(ComInterfaceType.InterfaceIsIUnknown),
 Guid("1245208C-A151-11D0-A7D7-00C04FD909DD")]
public interface ISnapinAbout
{
    void GetSnapinDescription(out IntPtr lpDescription);
    void GetProvider(out IntPtr pName);
```

```
    void GetSnapinVersion(out IntPtr lpVersion);
    void GetSnapinImage(out IntPtr hAppIcon);
    void GetStaticFolderImage(out IntPtr hSmallImage,
                              out IntPtr hSmallImageOpen,
                              out IntPtr hLargeImage,
                              out Int32 cMask);
}
```

As previously mentioned, every existing COM interface definition will include a few attributes to ensure that the managed environment provides the proper linkage to the unmanaged environment. In general, every MMC-related interface includes the [ComImport], [InterfaceType], and [Guid] attributes shown. Notice that the [InterfaceType] attribute uses the ComInterfaceType.InterfaceIsIUnknown enumeration value, which seems to contradict our previous discussion. Remember that we're working with MMC in this case, not creating a component for general use. MMC expects an IUnknown interface, so we can save some memory and improve performance slightly by implementing only an IUnknown interface.

The Initialize() method requires the *lpConsole* argument, which is a pointer to an interface. There are times when you have to pass an interface as part of the communication between MMC and the snap-in. You can perform this task using a number of techniques, but the technique that works best when you don't want to define and implement the interface in your component is to pass the interface as a specially marshaled object and use the [MarshalAs (UnmanagedType.Interface)] attribute. This technique ensures that the recipient will see the interface as an interface, even if it's operating in the unmanaged environment.

The next oddity is the MMC_NOTIFY_TYPE *aevent* argument of the Notify() method. The MMC_NOTIFY_TYPE enumeration contains a list of messages that the Notify() method can receive. The Platform SDK documentation shows the argument name as *event*, but we're using *aevent*. Remember that *event* is a keyword in C#, so we need to modify the name. The reason I chose *aevent* is that when you import a DLL that uses this same name from Visual C++, C# shows the argument as *@event* in the object browser.

Every message that your component receives from the Notify() function has different parameters. The IComponent::Notify help topic at ms-help://MS.VSCC/MS.MSDNVS/mmc/ mmc12ref01_97qx.htm contains a list of the messages. Click one of the associated links and you'll learn the particulars of that message, including the arguments that it requires. Looking through the list of messages, you'll notice that many of the arguments require pointer arguments. Consequently, determining the data type for the *arg* and *param* arguments is difficult. I chose to use Int32 values because that's what we've used for other messages and the example won't require many pointer values. You could also use an IntPtr for each of the two values. There are good arguments for both value types, so the choice of value type depends on how you plan to work with MMC.

The `QueryDataObject()` method is another method that works with an interface. In this case, the method receives an interface pointer from another object, so we have to handle the interface using a different technique than the `Initialize()` method discussed earlier. Notice that the `QueryDataObject()` method passes an object of type `IDataObject`. In addition, it uses out rather than `ref` as normal. A check of the Platform SDK documentation shows that this function receives the pointer from an outside source, which means you have to pass an uninitialized object. It's extremely important to determine how the argument is marked. The following list provides some general rules you can use based on the documentation:

[in]   Always initialize the object and fill it with data. The caller must provide data for `in` values.

[in, out]   Mark the object as `ref` and initialize it. You may also need to provide data for the object depending on the needs of the recipient. Generally, you'll receive data back from the call in the form of modified object properties or values.

[out]   Mark the object as `out`. Don't initialize the object or provide any data for it. You should always receive data from the call, even if the data is an error indicator.

The `CompareObjects()` method also works with interfaces in a manner similar to the `Initialize()` method. We'll actually provide these two interfaces as output. However, in this case, we've already defined the `IDataObject` interface for another call, so we don't need to use the specially marshaled object technique. This method shows you the direct method for passing interfaces that you've defined.

The `IComponentData` interface has many of the same methods as `IComponent`. Notice that there's a method for creating an instance of the component that receives a pointer to an `IComponent` interface. We'll see the importance of this method later while working with the example snap-in. The `GetDisplayInfo()` method is also important in that it's the first method that passes a structure. This data structure contains result data on return. Again, you'll see the importance of this method when we discuss the example snap-in.

The `IDataObject` interface includes methods for exchanging data between objects and creating data notifications. This interface requires use of more data structures than other interfaces we've viewed so far. In addition, you'll find that the use of these structures can become quite subtle, requiring careful coding on the part of the developer. Fortunately, MMC use of the `IDataObject` interface is relatively straightforward, so there won't be too many surprises for this example.

NOTE   There are a few special considerations when creating interface definitions. One of them is not to drive yourself crazy defining every potential interface element, especially if you'll never use it. One such example is the EnumFormatEtc() method of the IDataObject interface. The example code shows the *ppenumFormatetc* argument defined as an IntPtr. This argument is actually supposed to appear as an IEnumFORMATETC interface pointer. This interface is the COM version of the enumeration and it points to an array of FORMATETC data structures. It's unlikely you'll ever need the IEnumFORMATETC interface for your MMC snap-ins, so using an IntPtr doesn't present a problem in this case.

The ISnapinAbout interface is simultaneously the easiest and the hardest interface to implement. This interface enables your snap-in to provide identification information to MMC. It's the first interface used by MMC and could be the only interface used in a particular session. Three of the methods are exceptionally easy to implement because they only pass strings: GetSnapinDescription(), GetProvider(), and GetSnapinVersion(). The remaining two methods are more difficult to implement because they pass pointers to icons.

Passing a handle to an icon to MMC isn't the same as passing an icon to another managed application. MMC expects that the icon it receives is ready to display using the current system setup. Unfortunately, this means you'll normally have to manipulate that icon so it has the correct resolution and color depth. The TranslateBitmap() function described in the section entitled "Adding the MMC Functions" performs this task. MMC also requires a specially formatted bitmap so it knows which color to treat as transparent. The RGB() function creates the color mask as an Int32 value. We also discussed this function earlier, so we won't discuss it again here.

Defining the Enumerations

MMC snap-ins, like most of the interoperability scenarios we've discussed, require a number of enumerations to define acceptable data entry values and to make programming easier. You'll find the enumerations in the Enumerations.CS file found in the \Chapter 12\MMCHelper folder. All of the enumeration entries include full documentation on the purpose of the enumeration.

When you view the enumerations, you'll find that they provide varied input to the MMC snap-in. Some of the enumerations, such as RESULT_VAL, provide standard values. A few of the enumerations are MMC specific. For example, the MMC_NOTIFY_TYPE enumeration provides a list of standard notifications sent by the MMC container to the MMC snap-in, as shown here:

```
public enum MMC_NOTIFY_TYPE
{
    MMCN_ACTIVATE        = 0x8001,
    MMCN_ADD_IMAGES      = 0x8002,
    MMCN_BTN_CLICK       = 0x8003,
```

```
        MMCN_CLICK                = 0x8004,
        MMCN_COLUMN_CLICK         = 0x8005,
        MMCN_CONTEXTMENU          = 0x8006,
        MMCN_CUTORMOVE            = 0x8007,
        MMCN_DBLCLICK             = 0x8008,
        MMCN_DELETE               = 0x8009,
        MMCN_DESELECT_ALL         = 0x800A,
        MMCN_EXPAND               = 0x800B,
        MMCN_HELP                 = 0x800C,
        MMCN_MENU_BTNCLICK        = 0x800D,
        MMCN_MINIMIZED            = 0x800E,
        MMCN_PASTE                = 0x800F,
        MMCN_PROPERTY_CHANGE      = 0x8010,
        MMCN_QUERY_PASTE          = 0x8011,
        MMCN_REFRESH              = 0x8012,
        MMCN_REMOVE_CHILDREN      = 0x8013,
        MMCN_RENAME               = 0x8014,
        MMCN_SELECT               = 0x8015,
        MMCN_SHOW                 = 0x8016,
        MMCN_VIEW_CHANGE          = 0x8017,
        MMCN_SNAPINHELP           = 0x8018,
        MMCN_CONTEXTHELP          = 0x8019,
        MMCN_INITOCX              = 0x801A,
        MMCN_FILTER_CHANGE        = 0x801B,
        MMCN_FILTERBTN_CLICK      = 0x801C,
        MMCN_RESTORE_VIEW         = 0x801D,
        MMCN_PRINT                = 0x801E,
        MMCN_PRELOAD              = 0x801F,
        MMCN_LISTPAD              = 0x8020,
        MMCN_EXPANDSYNC           = 0x8021,
        MMCN_COLUMNS_CHANGED      = 0x8022,
        MMCN_CANPASTE_OUTOFPROC   = 0x8023
    }
```

The developer can use this list to determine which actions to act upon within the MMC snap-in. For example, if you want to provide refresh support, you'll need to implement the MMCN_REFRESH message. Likewise, if you want to provide support for printing, you'll need to implement the MMCN_PRINT message. If an MMC snap-in doesn't implement a particular message, the MMC container will provide either a default action or simply ignore the user request. You'll find that the container ignores the request more often than not.

Defining the Data Structures

Like many parts of Windows, you'll use a lot of data structures to create an MMC snap-in. For example, there are a number of private data structures used to create the data translation functions described earlier. However, there are two data structures that all MMC snap-ins use, and they appear in Listing 12.3. You'll find a complete list of the public data structures in the Structures.CS file found in the \Chapter 12\MMCHelper folder.

Listing 12.3   Structures Used by a Basic MMC Snap-In

```
[StructLayout(LayoutKind.Sequential)]
public struct RESULTDATAITEM
{
   public UInt32   mask;
   public Int32    bScopeItem;
   public Int32    itemID;
   public Int32    nIndex;
   public Int32    nCol;
   public IntPtr   str;
   public Int32    nImage;
   public UInt32   nState;
   public Int32    lParam;
   public Int32    iIndent;
}

[StructLayout(LayoutKind.Sequential)]
public struct SCOPEDATAITEM
{
   public UInt32   mask;
   public IntPtr   displayname;
   public Int32    nImage;
   public Int32    nOpenImage;
   public UInt32   nState;
   public Int32    cChildren;
   public Int32    lParam;
   public Int32    relativeID;
   public Int32    ID;
}
```

The code defines one data structure for the Result pane (the one on the right) and a second data structure for the Scope pane (the one on the left). Each of these structures defines a single item. In other words, it's quite likely that a single MMC snap-in will generate these data structures several times—once for each piece of information that the MMC snap-in needs to display on screen. The choice of data structure is obvious—use the one that fits the pane you want to populate with data.

As you can see, the SCOPEDATAITEM data structure contains entries that give it a name, several images, a state, a list of children, and several identifiers. Some of these items are set directly, while others are generated automatically for you by the MMC console. In some cases, such as the images, you have a choice of implementation techniques. If you don't set the image within the code, MMC will set the image using a default value.

The RESULTDATAITEM data structure contains entries that associate it with a particular scope data item, column, and row. Each result data item also has a name, image, and state associated with it. You can optionally set a data value and indent the result data item as needed. Like the scope data item, MMC will automatically assign values to some entries for you if you don't assign them within the code. For example, a result data item will have an image assigned to it even if you don't add one using the code.

Developing the MMC Snap-In Example

The MMC example we'll look at is basic—it includes just the essentials required to get MMC to recognize the component as a snap-in. This means implementing specific interfaces and ensuring that MMC will recognize the interfaces. We won't concentrate too hard on any serious content in this example because getting the snap-in to work is difficult enough for a first try. The example will show you how to use the wrapper DLL, create an About dialog box, display basic information about the snap-in in various places, and present some information on screen. We'll also discuss the use of nodes for presentation because this is a basic element of most snap-ins.

This example won't show you how to interact with other portions of Windows. In addition, this is a stand-alone snap-in. MMC supports various snap-in types and the stand-alone is the easiest type to create because it doesn't rely on the inner workings of any other snap-in. Another type of popular snap-in is the extension snap-in. An extension snap-in augments, modifies, or otherwise extends the functionality of an existing snap-in but can't run as a stand-alone entity. MMC also support combination snap-ins and other variants. Because of the number of varieties of MMC snap-ins, you should try this example first, then move on to more complex example, and finally, create precisely the type of snap-in needed for your application. You'll find the source code for this example in the \Chapter 12\MMCSample folder of the CD.

Developing an About Dialog

The About dialog is one of the easier parts of the MMC snap-in to create, and it's also the only part that works independently of the rest of the MMC snap-in. It helps to implement this part of the MMC snap-in first because you can quickly see that the MMC snap-in is registered correctly and has the ability to interact with MMC. Sometimes, creating the required interaction is harder than any other part of the development process because Microsoft doesn't make it easy to perform this task.

We'll explore the output of this example in the section entitled "Testing the Snap-In within MMC." For now, let's look at the code to create an About dialog. Listing 12.4 shows a complete implementation of the About dialog. The information might not be as complete as you'd like it to be, but every element of the About dialog is present and there's little reason to change it (except for content) in any MMC snap-in.

Listing 12.4   **Elements of a Standard About Dialog**

```
[Guid("BACD4F1D-8338-41ee-9D55-DDECE3D8BBCE")]
public class MySnapInAbout : ISnapinAbout
{
    // Define the icons for this snapin.
    IntPtr    MainIcon;    // Handle for the main icon.
    IntPtr    BMap16;      // Handle for the 16 X 16 bitmap.
    IntPtr    BMap32;      // Handle for the 32 X 32 bitmap.

    public MySnapInAbout()
    {
        try
        {
            // Retrieve an embedded bitmap from the current assembly.
            Assembly Asm = Assembly.GetExecutingAssembly();
            Stream    Strm =
                Asm.GetManifestResourceStream("MMCSample.Main.bmp");
            Bitmap    Temp = new Bitmap(Strm);

            // Place a handle for an icon based on the bitmap in MainIcon.
            MainIcon = Temp.GetHicon();

            // Create compatible bitmaps for the two bitmap images.
            IntPtr Translate = new Bitmap(Temp, 16, 16).GetHbitmap();
            BMap16 = MMCFunctions.TranslateBitmap(Translate);
            WindowsFunctions.DeleteObject(Translate);

            Translate = new Bitmap(Temp, 32, 32).GetHbitmap();
            BMap32 = MMCFunctions.TranslateBitmap(Translate);
            WindowsFunctions.DeleteObject(Translate);
        }
        catch (Exception e)
        {
            // Display a complete error message so the user knows what
            // went wrong.
            MessageBox.Show("About dialog failed to initialize.\r\n" +
                "\r\nSource: " + e.Source +
                "\r\nMessage: " + e.Message +
                "\r\nTarget Site: " + e.TargetSite +
                "\r\nStack Trace: " + e.StackTrace,
                "\r\nInitialization Error",
                MessageBoxButtons.OK,
                MessageBoxIcon.Error);
        }
    }
```

```
~MySnapInAbout()
{
    // Deallocate the memory used by the three images.
    if (MainIcon != IntPtr.Zero)
        WindowsFunctions.DestroyIcon(MainIcon);
    if (BMap16 != IntPtr.Zero)
        WindowsFunctions.DeleteObject(BMap16);
    if (BMap32 != IntPtr.Zero)
        WindowsFunctions.DeleteObject(BMap32);
}

public void GetSnapinDescription(out IntPtr lpDescription)
{
    // Output a description string.
    lpDescription =
        Marshal.StringToCoTaskMemUni("A Simple MMC Snap-In Example");
}

public void GetProvider(out IntPtr pName)
{
    // Output the name of the snap-in creator.
    pName = Marshal.StringToCoTaskMemUni("DataCon Services");
}

public void GetSnapinVersion(out IntPtr lpVersion)
{
    // Output a version number string.
    lpVersion = Marshal.StringToCoTaskMemUni("1.0");
}

public void GetSnapinImage(out IntPtr hAppIcon)
{
    // Output the main icon for the snap-in. This is the
    // icon that appears when a user adds the snap-in to the
    // console.
    hAppIcon = MainIcon;
}

public void GetStaticFolderImage(out IntPtr hSmallImage,
                                 out IntPtr hSmallImageOpen,
                                 out IntPtr hLargeImage,
                                 out int cMask)
{
    // Provide handles for each of the static image outputs.
    // You could provide separate bitmaps for the two small
    // image and the small open image.
    hSmallImage = BMap16;
    hSmallImageOpen = BMap16;
    hLargeImage = BMap32;
```

```
        // Provide a color mask for the images.
        cMask=0x00FFFFFF;
    }
}
```

The `MySnapInAbout` constructor creates the icons used for the MMC snap-in in general. The code obtains the required bitmap from the assembly using the `GetManifestResource-Stream()` method, modifies it for size using the `Bitmap()` constructor, and then calls the `TranslateBitmap()` method we discussed earlier to change the color depth. The resulting bitmaps are unmanaged resources that you must destroy before the MMC snap-in exits, as shown in the `MySnapInAbout` destructor.

The remaining methods for the interface all provide one kind of information. MMC polls each method as needed to populate dialog boxes. For example, if the user requests a description of the snap-in, MMC will call the `GetSnapinDescription()` method. Notice how the code marshals the strings in this case. We're creating the strings using the `StringToCoTask-MemUni()` in order to create an unmanaged resource for MMC. Because we're using standard .NET marshaling to perform the task, there's no reason to free the memory manually later.

Working with *IDataObject*

The `IDataObject` interface is the place where you can make the most mistakes in creating an MMC snap-in. In fact, implementing this interface with even slight errors can cause MMC to simply exit without an error message of any kind. Even if MMC does present an error message, it's likely that this message will fail to tell you anything that you can use to debug the MMC snap-in.

The `GetDataHere()` method is the one mandatory portion of the interface that you have to implement. In addition, this is the method that prevents Visual Basic developers from creating an MMC snap-in because it requires use of unsafe code. You must mark the method as `Unsafe` and diagnose any problems it creates with this condition in mind. Listing 12.5 shows a common approach to implementing the `GetDataHere()` method.

Listing 12.5   **Defining `GetDataHere()` for the `IDataObject` Interface**

```
public unsafe void GetDataHere(ref FORMATETC pFormatEtc, ref STGMEDIUM pMedium)
{
    IStream  DataStream;  // The data stream used to write data.
    Byte[]   DataBuffer;  // A data buffer.
    Int32    DataLength;  // Size of the data buffer.
    UInt32   DataSent;    // Number of bytes sent.
    Byte[]   Nothing;     // Data to send if there is nothing to send.
    UInt16   ClipFormat;  // Input clipboard format.
    GUID     TheGUID;     // Class ID for the node or this snap-in.
```

```csharp
// Initialize the data.
DataStream = null;
DataSent = 0;
Nothing = new Byte[2]{0x0, 0x0};
ClipFormat = (UInt16)pFormatEtc.cfFormat;
TheGUID = new GUID();

try
{
    // Open a global handle for the data stream.
    WindowsFunctions.CreateStreamOnHGlobal(pMedium.hGlobal,
                                           0,
                                           out DataStream );

    // Throw an exception if we couldn't open a global handle.
    if (DataStream == null)
    {
        throw new Exception("Unable to open a global memory handle " +
                            "for the datastream in " +
                            "MySnapInDO.GetDataHere() - " +
                            "CreateStreamOnHGlobal() method call " +
                            "failed.");
    }

    // Determine if we need to output a name string for this node.
    // The example doesn't support the zero deliminated node type, so
    // send nothing in that case.
    if (ClipFormat == CBDisplayName || ClipFormat == CBSZNodeType)
    {
        // Assign a value to the data buffer.
        if (ClipFormat == CBDisplayName)
            DataBuffer =
            MMCFunctions.StringToByteArray("MMC Example Display Name");
        else
            DataBuffer = Nothing;

        // Determine the data buffer length.
        DataLength = DataBuffer.Length;

        // Write the data to the data stream. Notice that you need to
        // create a fixed block in order to perform the write. This
        // ensures the snap-in writes the data without interference
        // from the garbage collector.
        fixed(byte* pData = DataBuffer)
        {
            DataStream.Write((IntPtr)pData,
                             (UInt32)DataLength,
                             out DataSent);
        }
```

```
      }
      // We need to send a GUID
      else if (ClipFormat == CBNodeType || ClipFormat == CBSnapinCLSID)
      {

          if (ClipFormat == CBNodeType)
          {
              TheGUID.Data1 = 0xB6BBA1A8;
              TheGUID.Data2 = 0x6D1C;
              TheGUID.Data3 = 0x47f9;
              TheGUID.Data4 =
           new byte[8] {0xA9, 0xCC, 0xFA, 0xC4, 0x27, 0x31, 0x5C, 0xAF};
          }

          else
          {
              // The GUID for this snapin
              TheGUID.Data1 = 0xB6BBA1A8;
              TheGUID.Data2 = 0x6D1C;
              TheGUID.Data3 = 0x47f9;
              TheGUID.Data4 =
           new byte[8] {0xA9, 0xCC, 0xFA, 0xC4, 0x27, 0x31, 0x5C, 0xAF};
          }

          // Create a memory structure to hold the Class ID.
          IntPtr pData = Marshal.AllocCoTaskMem(16);

          // We need to marshal this structure ourselves
          Marshal.WriteInt32(pData, 0, (Int32)TheGUID.Data1);
          Marshal.WriteInt16(pData, 4, (Int16)TheGUID.Data2);
          Marshal.WriteInt16(pData, 2, (Int16)TheGUID.Data3);
          for(Int32 Counter = 0; Counter < 8; Counter++)
              Marshal.WriteByte(pData,
                                Counter + 6,
                                TheGUID.Data4[Counter]);

          DataStream.Write(pData, 16, out DataSent);
          Marshal.FreeCoTaskMem(pData);
      }
  }
  catch(Exception Except)
  {
      // return a failure value.
      throw new Exception("Failure in MySnapInDO.GetDataHere()",
                          Except);
  }
}
```

The code begins by initializing the data structures. Notice that we create a special data structure containing a double null byte value to send if the code has nothing to send. This special data structure simulates a null Unicode value. Sending a single null value will have unpredictable results, so this is an important element to remember.

The first step in providing data for output is to create a new data stream. In many cases, you'll need to write data using this technique because the managed environment doesn't provide the required functionality. If the MMC snap-in can't allocate enough memory for the data stream, it throws an exception and exits because there's no way to continue without it.

After the code creates the data stream, it needs to check for the type of information that MMC is requesting by examining the *ClipFormat* value. If the requested type is CBDisplayName, the code uses the StringToByteArray() method we discussed earlier to create a Unicode byte array for output to MMC. In this case, the byte array will contain the name of the application. Notice the technique used to write this data to the data stream. We have to create a byte*, an unsafe type, pin it using fixed, and then write it using DataStream.Write(). Failure to use this technique will result in intermittent operation that you'll never resolve because the Garbage Collector is the source of the problem.

MMC can request other types of data, as shown in the listing. The second and third types, CBNodeType and CBSnapinCLSID, are essentially the same. The code creates what amounts to a GUID for the node or snap-in. Once the GUID is complete, the code sends it to MMC using the special write methods found in the Marshal class. Notice the technique used in this case writes the items individually, not as a single unit. We also have to allocate and free task memory for the data transfer.

Creating *IComponent* and *IComponentData*

The IComponent and IComponentData interfaces interact with the Scope and Result panes of the MMC snap-in display. Both interfaces include a number of methods, but the two essential methods are Initialize() and Notify(). The Initialize() method creates the data structures, images, and other data elements that Notify() will manipulate and present. The code for both of these methods can become long and tedious to write, but it's pleasantly easy to write after writing the IDataObject interface code.

The two interfaces are also the most free-form part of the MMC snap-in. You don't have to implement much to make the MMC snap-in work. Of course, if you want the MMC snap-in functional enough to perform work, then you need to implement the proper features, which is where the long coding sequences come into play. The basic MMC snap-in created for this example implements the MMCN_SHOW message, which means it must also implement the GetDisplayInfo() method. These two elements work together to display some data on screen. The following code shows a basic example of an MMCN_SHOW message implementation:

```
// The selected item needs to show something in the result pane
case MMC_NOTIFY_TYPE.MMCN_SHOW:
```

```
//Data.Node.onShow(m_Console, arg, param);
RESULTDATAITEM Item; // Result data variable.

// Create two headers.
MMCHeader.InsertColumn(0, "Name Type", 0, 250);
MMCHeader.InsertColumn(1, "Name Value", 0, 150);

// Initialize the result data variable.
Item = new RESULTDATAITEM();

// Create entries required for first item.  Include
// constants for relevant items in mask.  Make sure
// you use a callback for strings.  Set the image to
// the 16 X 16 pixel image.
Item.mask = (UInt32)(RDI.STR | RDI.IMAGE | RDI.PARAM);
Item.str = new IntPtr(-1); // MMC_CALLBACK
Item.nImage = 0;
Item.lParam = 0;
Item.nCol = 0;

// Display the first item.
MMCResultData.InsertItem(ref Item);

// Modify lParam member for second query.
Item.lParam = 1;

// Display the second item.
MMCResultData.InsertItem(ref Item);

// Perform the same two steps for subsequent items.
Item.lParam = 2;
MMCResultData.InsertItem(ref Item);
Item.lParam = 3;
MMCResultData.InsertItem(ref Item);
Item.lParam = 4;
MMCResultData.InsertItem(ref Item);
Item.lParam = 5;
MMCResultData.InsertItem(ref Item);
Item.lParam = 6;
MMCResultData.InsertItem(ref Item);
Item.lParam = 7;
MMCResultData.InsertItem(ref Item);

break;
```

The code begins by creating two columns and giving them the names Name Type and Name Value. It creates a new RESULTDATAITEM data structure because this information will appear in the Result pane. The RESULTDATAITEM data structure contains an item mask that indicates the type of information the result item will contain, the method of obtaining the information, the item image, and the item column number. The code then uses the Insert-Item() method to create eight columns worth of data on screen. The question is how MMC knows where to find this data because it obviously doesn't appear in this code. Look again at the *Item.str* value. It contains a value of –1, which means that MMC will call upon the Get-DisplayInfo() method for the data it needs.

The GetDisplayInfo() method contains a switch statement that creates a unique entry for each row of data inserted by the MMCN_SHOW message implementation. It uses the *Result-DataItem.lParam* value to determine which row to present on screen. Here's a sample of the presentation code:

```
case 0:

    // Display the NetBIOS name item.
    if (ResultDataItem.nCol == 0)
    {
        // Create the temporary data value, convert it
        // to a pointer, and then pass it to MMC.
        Temp = "NetBIOS Name";
        fixed (char* ResultData = Temp)
        {
            ResultDataItem.str = new IntPtr(ResultData);
        }
    }

    // The requester is asking for the second column.
    else
    {

        // See if there is a NetBIOS name for this item.
        if (WindowsFunctions.GetComputerNameEx(
            COMPUTER_NAME_FORMAT.ComputerNameNetBIOS,
            ComputerName,
            ref BufferSize))

            // Output the contents of the string buffer.
            fixed (char* ResultData = ComputerName.ToString())
            {
                ResultDataItem.str = new IntPtr(ResultData);
            }

        // If not, display a failure string.
        else
        {
```

```
        Temp = "Value Not Available";
        fixed (char* ResultData = Temp)
        {
            ResultDataItem.str = new IntPtr(ResultData);
        }
      }
    }
  }
  break;
```

MMC will call the GetDisplayInfo() method for each column of data that the MMCN_SHOW message implementation creates. Consequently, the first thing the code determines is which column MMC is requesting. If you have multiple columns of data and allow the user to select the columns arbitrarily, nesting another switch statement within the switch statement used for the row data will probably work best. In this case, the decision is relatively simple, so the code proceeds with an if statement.

If MMC requests the first column, the code outputs a simple string telling the type of data that will appear in the second column. When MMC requests the second column, the code calls GetComputerNameEx() to determine the requested computer name and then outputs that value. Notice that this is another situation in which the code must fix the memory used to hold the output string. However, instead of a byte*, we're using a char* for this portion of the example. MMC is full of such inconsistencies.

Testing the Snap-In within MMC

It's finally time to see the MMC snap-in we've created in action. Unfortunately, MMC still doesn't even know that the MMC snap-in exists. If you left things up to the .NET Framework, MMC would never know the MMC snap-in existed at all. We need one final piece of magic to make the MMC snap-in visible, and then we have to install the MMC snap-in for use.

Let's look at the magic first. MMC won't know your MMC snap-in exists until you create a special registry entry for it. This registry information appears in the \Chapter 12\MMCSample folder of the CD, along with the sample code. Here's what the registry entry looks like (the code will wrap in the book, so check the REG file as well):

```
REGEDIT4

[HKEY_LOCAL_MACHINE\Software\Microsoft\MMC\Snapins\{B6BBA1A8-6D1C-47f9-
    A9CC-FAC427315CAF}]
"About" = "{BACD4F1D-8338-41ee-9D55-DDECE3D8BBCE}"
"NameString" = "An MMC Snap-In"
"Provider" = "DataCon Services"
"Version" = "1.0"

[HKEY_LOCAL_MACHINE\Software\Microsoft\MMC\Snapins\{B6BBA1A8-6D1C-47f9-
    A9CC-FAC427315CAF}\StandAlone]
```

This registry entry tells MMC the GUID of the main MMC snap-in and the About dialog. It also gives the MMC snap-in a name that will appear in the Add Standalone Snap-in dialog box, the name of a provider, and the version number of the MMC snap-in. The StandAlone key tells MMC that this is a stand-alone snap-in and not an extension.

We're ready to install the MMC snap-in for use. The CD contains a compiled version of the MMC snap-in that you can test immediately, if desired. The following procedure tells how to install it:

1. Double-click the MySnapin.REG file in Windows Explorer. Windows will ask if you want to add the registry entries to your registry.

2. Click Yes. Windows will display a success message.

3. Locate the Register.bat file found in the \Chapter 12\MMCSample\bin\Debug folder. Double-click this file and you'll see a series of messages as the batch file registers the MMC snap-in. All that this batch file is doing is calling the RegAsm and GacUtil utilities to perform the required work.

WARNING   The number one point of failure for an MMC snap-in created with C# (once you get the code working) is a failure to register MMCHelper.DLL and MMCHelper2.DLL (the helper DLLs) in the GAC. It's best if you can use the copies of the files that appear in the directory with the MMC snap-in if you plan to create only one MMC snap-in or use the copies of the files that appear in a centralized location if you plan to create multiple MMC snap-ins. If you fail to register the helper DLLs, you'll normally see the snap-in in the MMC Add Standalone Snap-in dialog box, but you won't be able to obtain any help information about it. This is your sign that something is drastically wrong and you need to check the basics, including proper registration. Using an old version of the helper DLLs is something to consider if you receive a message that that MMC snap-in failed to initialize. You don't need to register the helper DLLs in the registry (and it's best if you don't). The example includes the Register.BAT and Unregister.BAT files in the \Chapter 12\MMCSample\bin\Debug folder on the CD as an example of how to create batch registration files for development. You must still add the registry file manually.

Once you get the MMC snap-in installed, you can test it. The following procedure shows a sample of what you should do to test a basic MMC snap-in:

1. Open MMC using the Start ➢ Run command. You'll see a blank MMC console.

2. Use the File ➢ Add/Remove Snap-in command to display the Add/Remove Snap-in dialog box. Click Add and you'll see a list of snap-ins. The example MMC snap-in appears in the list, as shown in Figure 12.6. If you don't see the example MMC snap-in, it isn't registered properly.

The Add Standalone
Snap-in dialog box will
contain the example
snap-in.

3. Highlight the example snap-in and click Add. The example MMC snap-in will appear in the Standalone tab of the Add/Remove Snap-in dialog box.

4. Click Close. You should test the About dialog at this point by highlighting the example MMC snap-in and clicking About. If the About dialog doesn't appear, there's something wrong with the code. The registry file is OK because the MMC snap-in would have never appeared otherwise. In addition, if there had been something wrong with the registration, you should have seen a message when you tried to add the MMC snap-in to the Add/Remove Snap-in dialog box.

5. Close the About Dialog box, if required. Click OK in the Add/Remove Snap-in dialog box. You should see the example MMC snap-in root node in the MMC console at this point. If you don't, there's probably something wrong with the `IDataObject` or `IComponent-Data` implementation. The `ISnapinAbout` and `IComponent` interfaces aren't in use at this point. The number one cause of problems is a bad `GetDataHere()` implementation.

6. Click the root node of the example MMC snap-in. You should see output similar to that shown in Figure 12.7. If you don't see proper output but the MMC snap-in doesn't fail, the problem is very likely in the message processing for the `Notify()` method of either the `IComponent` (Result pane) or `IComponentData` (Scope pane) interfaces. If the MMC snap-in does fail, begin checking for problems in the `Initialize()` method of the `IComponent` or `IComponentData` interfaces.

7. Close the MMC console without saving the settings. If the MMC snap-in registers a failure message, the problem is likely a memory or other resource leak. Unfortunately, there aren't any specific places this can occur, but it usually pays to check the `Notify()` method of the `IComponent` or `IComponentData` interfaces first.

FIGURE 12.7:

The final basic check
is to see if your
MMC snap-in
produces data.

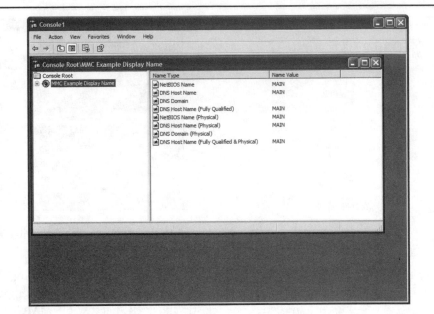

FIGURE 12.7:

The final basic check
is to see if your
MMC snap-in
produces data.

Where Do You Go from Here?

This chapter has provided you with three MMC snap-in examples. The task of writing an MMC snap-in using .NET is both easier and harder than writing one using the tools provided with Visual C++ 6. Certainly, the use of languages like C# and Visual Basic make the task easier because you don't have to worry about the low-level details that encumber Visual C++ developers. On the other hand, the lack of native support means you have to create everything by hand and from scratch—a difficult task to say the least. Hopefully, the tools provided in this chapter will make your task a lot easier—certainly the MMC helper DLL provided with the CD will make it easier to create the MMC snap-in code.

The only way to learn about COM development under Visual Studio .NET and MMC snap-in development in particular is to create some examples of your own. It's important to start out slowly. Don't try to create the management snap-in for your next database application on the first try—just displaying some simple data on screen for the first try is enough. Once you have the basic coding concepts down, try something more complex—creating a graphics application is a good second project. Next, move on to something that will actually perform useful work such as an MMC snap-in that modifies the registry or a database.

Chapter 13 begins the last part of the book. Another major omission in the .NET Framework lineup is support for DirectX. Microsoft may have actually underestimated the number of people using DirectX for business purposes, so support for it wasn't included in the initial version of the .NET Framework. At the time of this writing, there are rumors that Microsoft has started a beta for a DirectX add-on for the .NET Framework. Unfortunately, given the complexity of DirectX and Microsoft's current emphasis on security, you might not see this add-on for quite some time. Part IV of the book gives you the tools you need to work with DirectX today instead of waiting for Microsoft to deliver something tomorrow.

PART IV

Working with DirectX

CHAPTER 13

Creating DirectX Structures and Data Elements

- Using the DXDIAG Utility

- Working with the DirectX Structures

- Understanding DirectX Data Pitfalls in the Managed Environment

The drawing features provided by Microsoft's graphical device interface (GDI) and GDI+ are fine for simple applications, but if you want to perform any complex drawing, you need something like DirectX. Not only does DirectX help you create both two-dimensional (2D) and three-dimensional (3D) drawings, but it also helps you work with sound and other media technologies. In short, DirectX is the technology of choice when working with multimedia of any type, including both presentation graphics and games.

This chapter helps you understand the data structures and other data elements required by DirectX. Needless to say, these data structures are similar to those used by the Win32 API, but they're also more complex and require more precise definition in order to work. In addition, you'll find that DirectX is extremely math intensive, uses new data types, and generally requires a lot more work to use than the Win32 API.

> **NOTE**   There isn't any way that a few sections in a book can provide you with everything you need to know about DirectX. The purpose of the DirectX sections in this book is to show you how to work with DirectX in the managed environment. We'll discuss data conversions, function declarations, and other issues associated with using DirectX in the managed environment—just as we've discussed these issues for other types of development. Consequently, even though the examples are purposely kept simple for demonstration purposes, you might find that these chapters lack some information you need to use DirectX. If you've never used DirectX before, you'll probably need to add to your knowledge by looking through other books and Web sites.

We'll also discuss some of the pitfalls of working with DirectX. Microsoft has created a powerful API in DirectX—one that provides the developer with great access to the hardware. However, the flexibility and power of DirectX come at a price. A DirectX implementer needs to know more about how Windows and the hardware will react to specific changes in the environment. In addition, the DirectX implementer needs to understand how the managed environment will affect DirectX. For example, it's important to understand how the transitions required for the managed environment will affect performance and how using the managed environment changes programming techniques the developer might have used in the past. In sum, this chapter is an introduction to the main element of any application—we discuss data and how the environment interacts with that data.

Using the DXDIAG Utility

It might seem hard to believe, but some developers will attempt to develop applications for DirectX without testing their hardware for DirectX compatibility first. Of course, the fact that Microsoft often hides the utilities and other resources you need to perform such a check might contribute to the problem. Generally, you'll find that you need to perform a little investigative work to learn anything about DirectX—even small items, such as the capabilities of your machine, are often hidden.

The following sections provide you with a combination of a user and a developer view of the DXDIAG utility. This utility is an essential part of your DirectX programming experience because it tells you about your machine. At the most basic level, it tells you whether your machine is DirectX compatible. At a higher level, DXDIAG can tell you about the capabilities of your machine—whether it actually supports a DirectX feature you want to use in your application. Finally, developers can use this utility to learn about the DLLs and other components used for DirectX. It's important to remember that you need this information to create a link between the managed and unmanaged environments.

Learning More about DirectX

One of the best ways to learn about the new features of DirectX and the problems that you'll run into is to visit the Microsoft DirectX newsgroups. Besides providing you with the latest information, this dedicated group of users and developers can also help you locate and squash bugs in your DirectX application. In addition, these newsgroups can help you learn how users expect DirectX applications to react and the types of problems you can expect to see when using specific hardware or features.

The `microsoft.public.directx` newsgroups help you learn about DirectX features from a user perspective. For example, you can learn about the latest audio features in the `microsoft.public.directx.audio` newsgroup. The `microsoft.public.multimedia.directx` newsgroups will help you with the presentation aspects of this technology. You can even learn about multimedia programming in the `microsoft.public.multimedia.directx.danimation.programming` newsgroup.

There are two places to find developer information for DirectX on the Microsoft newsgroups. For general information about the Platform SDK functionality, look at the `microsoft.public.platformsdk.directx` and the `microsoft.public.platformsdk.graphics_mm.directx` newsgroups. The `microsoft.public.win32.programmer.directx` newsgroups contain particulars about various DirectX programming tasks. The `microsoft.public.win32.programmer.directx.ddk` newsgroup will even help you learn about driver development kit (DDK) issues.

You'll also want to spend some time learning about DirectX on Web sites. The DirectX Programming Faq (http://www.directxfaq.com/) contains a sorted knowledge base of information about DirectX. The DirectX Files site (http://www.thedirectxfiles.com/) contains information for both user and developer. For example, you can download DirectX plug-ins for your system. The developer resource section includes tips and techniques for writing audio synthesizers, among other examples. If code is what you mainly want to see, check the examples on Code Guru (http://www.codeguru.com/directx/index.shtml) and ActiveWin.com DirectX (http://www.activewin.com/directx/index.shtml). Both sites include a number of DirectX examples that should answer the most common developer questions.

The most important bits of information you can obtain from this section is the status of the drivers and DLLs installed on your machine. More than a few developers have reported problems on the various Microsoft DirectX newsgroups only to find that a DLL or driver on their machine was outdated. It's important to install and use the latest version of DirectX to obtain the best possible support for your application from the newsgroups. Generally, updates of DirectX fix more problems than they create (although it also seems that every new release also causes some new and not so exciting problems).

Learning about DirectX Compatibility

Developers generally have a good understanding of their system. However, it's still important to use the correct tool to check your system for compatibility concerns, yet the Microsoft documentation is a little light in this area. Fortunately, all you really need to know is where to look for the information and then understand what to do with the information you find.

The first step to check system compatibility is to start the DirectX diagnostic utility. You won't find it on your Start menu. Open the Run dialog box, type **DXDIAG**, and click OK. You'll see a DirectX Diagnostic Tool dialog box like the one shown in Figure 13.1. Note that the DirectX Diagnostic Tool will display a progress bar as it checks the capabilities of your system, the drives, and the version of DirectX installed.

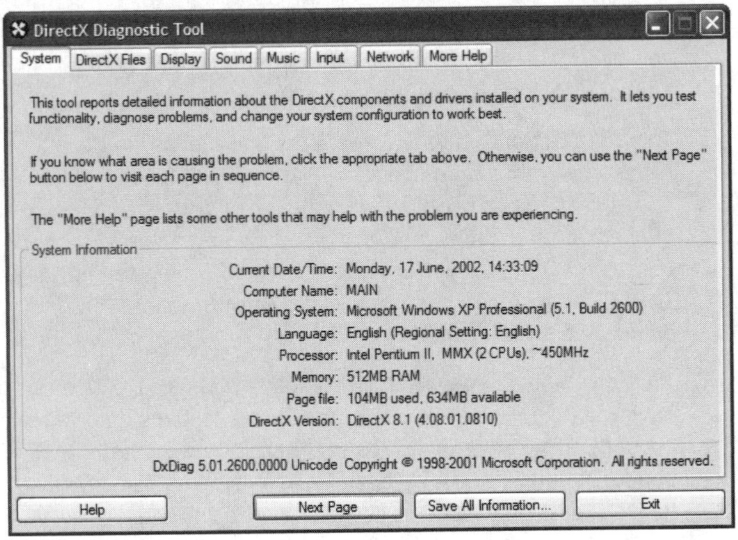

FIGURE 13.1:

The DirectX Diagnostic Tool checks your DirectX installation for problems.

The first setting I always check is the DirectX Version entry near the bottom of the dialog box. You need to go to the DirectX Web site (http://www.microsoft.com/directx/default .asp) to verify this version number against the current version that Microsoft supports. If you see that the Web site contains a newer version, download it, install it, and restart your machine. Using the most current version ensures that anything you develop will have the latest features. In addition, using the most current version generally ensures that you'll run into fewer bugs during your development experience.

NOTE The most current version of DirectX available as of this writing is version 8.1. However, this update concentrates on 3D drawing and many of you will still need to perform 2D drawing. Visual Studio .NET ships with DirectX 7 support, which excels at 2D drawing, so the examples in this chapter and Chapter 14 will use DirectX 7. I also tested these examples using DirectX 8.1. All of the 3D and extended examples in Chapters 15 and 16 were written and tested using DirectX 8.1 but should run on newer versions of DirectX as well. To use the examples in Chapters 15 and 16, you must download the latest DirectX SDK from http://www.microsoft.com/directx/default.asp.

Notice the Next Page button at the bottom of the screen in Figure 13.1. You'll find a button like that one on most of the DirectX tabs. What the button doesn't tell you is that clicking it runs a test on your system. Try clicking it now and you'll advance to the DirectX Files tab. If you see No Problems Found in the Notes section, you know that test passed.

Click Next Page again and you'll advance to the Display tab. The same success or failure message will appear in the Notes field again. However, this time you'll also see some diagnostic buttons, as shown in Figure 13.2. For example, you can disable Direct3D Acceleration by clicking the associated Disable button. Before you cripple your system, however, you'll want to test its compatibility with DirectX. Click Test DirectDraw and the DirectX Diagnostic Tool will perform extended tests on your system. If everything goes well, click Test Direct3D. These tests will verify that your display adapter can work with DirectX and therefore any application produced on your system. If you do run into problems, the DirectX Diagnostic Tool normally provides enough information for you to fix the problem yourself or ask intelligent questions of a support person. In some cases, you have to disable a hardware acceleration feature to gain true compatibility.

FIGURE 13.2:

Some of the DirectX tabs contain special test buttons you can use to check compatibility.

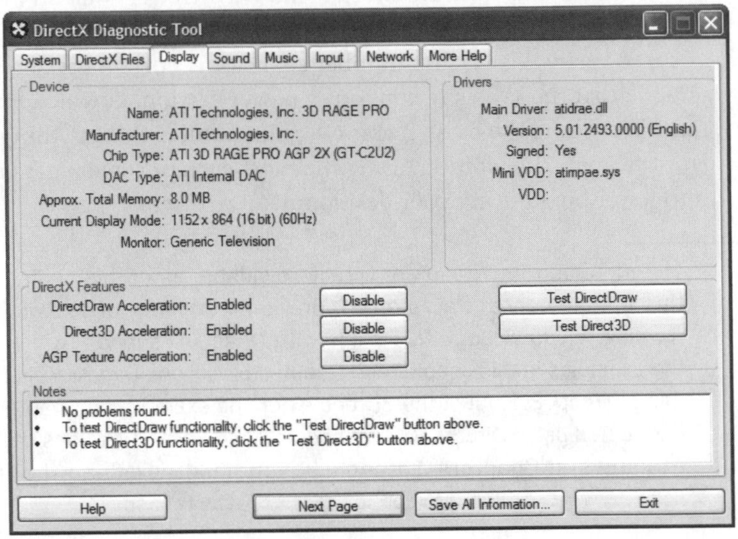

Follow the Next Page and testing process until you get to the More Help tab. If everything passes, at this point, your system is completely compatible with DirectX. Of course, there are differing levels of hardware capability, so you also need to consider how much DirectX support your system provides. For example, you might find that your sound card doesn't provide default port acceleration. If this feature is missing, you won't be able to use it in your application.

TIP   Sometimes you'll want to disable a hardware feature for reasons other than compatibility. For example, you might want to see how an application works with software emulation rather than the faster hardware support. Disabling the hardware support helps you to check the software emulation. In other cases, you might want to disable a hardware feature to see how a program will react on a less capable machine. Bugs might not show up until you have disabled some of the hardware functionality your machine provides. Some of the tabs also contain sliders that you can use to control features such as hardware acceleration. Choosing a lower amount of acceleration can often help in diagnosing subtle DirectX problems.

After you complete all of your tests, you can click the Save All Information button to display a Save As dialog box. The DirectX Diagnostic Tool can save all of the test results and other information about your system as a text file. Maintaining a copy of this text file helps you track your system in its ideal state and compare it to results you get during later tests. Performing a comparison can help you locate potential problems caused by system degradation.

Viewing the Drivers

Previous chapters have demonstrated that a knowledge of the files used to perform specific Win32 API tasks is essential if you want to use the functions those files contain in your applications. Working with DirectX is no different. However, DirectX does make it relatively easy for you to determine which files it uses and even the version numbers of those files. Figure 13.3 shows the DirectX Files tab of the DirectX Diagnostic Tool utility. Notice that this tab contains a complete list of the DirectX files.

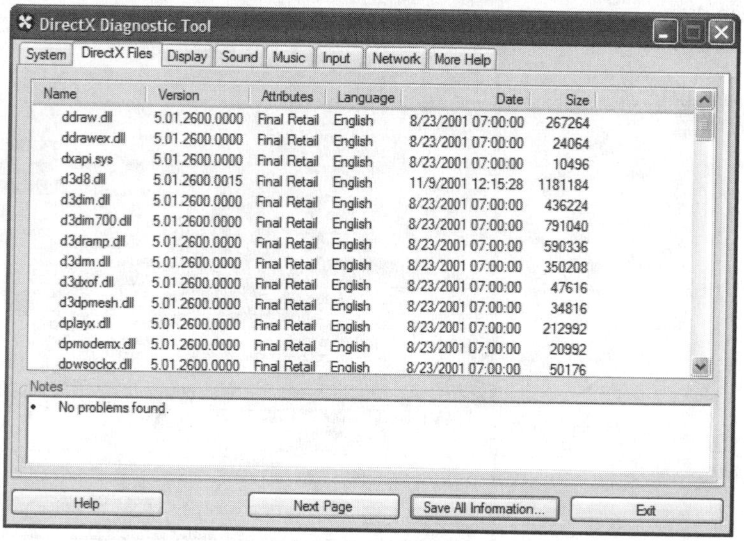

FIGURE 13.3:

The DirectX Files tab contains a list of the files used to implement DirectX on the host machine.

Unfortunately, all that this dialog shows you is the name of the file. There isn't any way to determine what the file does or the functions that it might contain. To learn more about the file, you need to investigate it. A first stop is to locate the file in the System32 folder and open the Properties dialog box for it. Generally, you'll find some descriptive information on the Version tab.

A second step is to look for the file in the Visual Studio .NET or Platform SDK help file. If you look for the DLL version of the file, you'll normally find support information and other helpful tips. However, if you want to learn how the file will affect your programming, look for the LIB file. For example, the first file in Figure 13.3 is DDraw.DLL. If you enter this name as DDraw.LIB in either of the two help files, you'll see various entries for interfaces, enumerations, functions, and programming tips.

Finally, you can use the Dependency Walker to view the file, just as we have for so many other DLLs in the book. Figure 13.4 shows the DDraw.DLL file. Notice the list of function names and file dependencies. Viewing a DLL in Dependency Walker normally provides clues that you won't find by just looking at the help files or performing a search online. However, you'll want to stick with the functions that are documented for public use, even if it takes a while to locate information about a function that looks interesting. Given that DirectX is a little less open than the Win32 API, you'll want to use this technique to ensure that you're gaining access to the full set of features the DLL has to offer.

FIGURE 13.4:

Always use the Dependency Walker to ferret out information about the DirectX DLLs.

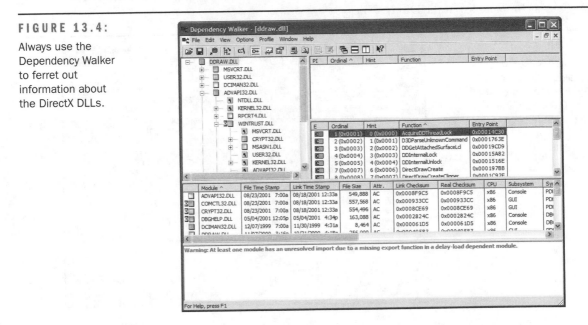

TIP

The DirectX DLLs also contain functions that are meant for internal use only. For example, a search through the help file didn't yield any information about the `AcquireDDThread-Lock()` function shown in Figure 13.4, yet this function exists. Other DirectX DLLs use this function and you should never call it in your application. Of course, it would help if Microsoft condescended to document this fact. One place to look for this type of information is the Clipcode.net-Knowledge Transfer Portal For Software Engineers (`http://www.clipcode.net/`) site. The `AcquireDDThreadLock()` function appears on the `http://www.clipcode.net/content/directdraw_direct3d_guide/03_developing_with_directx.htm` page.

Working with the DirectX Structures

Like the Win32 API and COM, DirectX uses a number of data structures to move data from one location to another. Unlike the Win32 API or COM, DirectX contains a relatively small number of structures, and they're actually organized the same way, so you'll experience fewer problems using them. However, the data structures tend to provide complex information because of the multimedia nature of DirectX. There are no small data structures that carry two or three items—many of these data structures contain huge amounts of information. This factor makes DirectX a lot harder to work with than either the Win32 API or COM.

The following sections will help you understand the DirectX data structures. We'll begin with an overview of the data structures. This section contains a short description of every data structure used in DirectX. You might be surprised at how few there really are. The next section begins looking at the techniques required to convert the data structures for managed environment use. Because the data structures are well defined and there are so few, you'll also find them as part of a DirectX DLL that we'll explore in this chapter and in the one that follows.

NOTE Visual Studio .NET comes with documentation for DirectX 7 and a preliminary version of DirectX 8.1. Most of this documentation also works fine for the released version DirectX 8.1, but there are a few changes that you'll want to know about. The best idea for DirectX 8.1 development is to download the current DirectX SDK from `http://msdn.microsoft.com/ library/default.asp?url=/nhp/Default.asp?contentid=28000410`. This MSDN site has a link that will help you download the current version of the SDK. Unfortunately, you'll still need to convert everything by hand. There are rumors that DirectX 9 will provide at least partial support for the .NET Framework, but don't expect to see complete support immediately. Be aware that a complete DirectX 8.1 download is 165.7MB. Fortunately, you can perform a component download. If you decide to perform a component download, you must download the DirectX Developer Runtime. In addition, you'll need one of the two language products. The Visual C++ product will prove the best choice because it contains the header files and other detailed information you'll need to perform managed application conversions.

An Overview of the Data Structures

DirectX uses a total of 19 specific data structures. Many of these data structures perform multiple tasks and the content depends on the task they're performing at the moment. Some of the data structures weren't used in the past, so the documentation Microsoft provides with Visual Studio .NET reflects this fact. Newer versions of DirectX do use more of the functions and data structures. The following list provides a short overview of these data structures:

DDBLTBATCH   DirectX uses this structure to pass blit information to the `IDirectDrawSurface7` `.BltBatch()` method. The structure includes both a source and destination rectangle for the blit, along with the address of a DirectDraw surface. Control flags determine the type of blit that occurs and there's a variable that holds the address of `DDBLTFX` structure containing additional blit effects.

NOTE A bit block transfer (blit) is the process of moving a bitmap from one device context to another. For example, a blit occurs when an application moves a bitmap from memory to the display. The blit occurs as a continuous operation. Some applications and function calls will also modify the bitmap during a blit. For example, a function could find all occurrences of the color red and change them to green during the blit. A blit could also change the bitmap's location on screen, providing an animation effect.

DDBLTFX DirectX uses this structure to pass raster operations (ROPs), effects, and override information to the `IDirectDrawSurface7.Blt()` method. This structure is also used as part of the `DDBLTBATCH` data structure. Essentially, this structure defines 2D drawing effects such as mirroring and rotating the image. The structure also contains entries for Z-buffering and alpha blending, but support for these entries is nearly non-existent in DirectX 7.

DDCAPS DirectX uses this structure to report the capabilities of the host machine using the `IDirectDraw7.GetCaps()` method. The output of this call includes the capabilities of both the hardware and the hardware emulation layer (HEL). The hardware and HEL capabilities appear in two difference copies of the `DDCAPS` data structure. This structure also contains the `DDSCAPS` and `DDSCAPS2` data structures, which are essentially sets of flags listing specific device capabilities.

DDCOLORCONTROL DirectX relies on this data structure to define the color controls used by a number of calls. The *dwFlags* member contains a list of the fields within the data structure that contain valid information. The `IDirectDrawColorControl.GetColorControls()` method also uses the *dwFlags* memory to indicate which controls a particular device supports.

DDCOLORKEY DirectX uses this structure to define a source color key, destination color key, or a color space. It's used with both the `IDirectDrawSurface7.GetColorKey()` and `IDirectDrawSurface7.SetColorKey()` methods. This data structure also appears as part of the `DDBLTFX` data structure. DirectX interprets the data structure as a color key when both the high and low range values contain the same data.

DDDEVICEIDENTIFIER2 DirectX uses this structure to obtain information about a device from a call to the `IDirectDraw7.GetDeviceIdentifier()` method. The return values include information such as the driver name and description, along with numeric data such as the driver version and the vendor identifier. You can use this structure with the associated `IDirectDraw7.GetDeviceIdentifier()` method to validate problem hardware prior to use with an application.

DDGAMMARAMP DirectX uses this data structure to pass red, green, and blue ramp data to the `IDirectDrawGammaControl.GetGammaRamp()` and `IDirectDrawGammaControl.SetGammaRamp()` methods. Each of the arrays in this data structure maps color values in the frame buffer to the color values passed to the digital-to-analog converter (DAC).

DDOVERLAYFX   DirectX uses this data structure to pass overlay information to the `IDirect-DrawSurface7.UpdateOverlay()` method. The `IDirectDrawSurface7.UpdateOverlay()` method modifies the appearance or position of an overlay. The overlay must have certain visual attributes as described in the Platform SDK documentation.

DDPIXELFORMAT   DirectX uses this structure to describe the pixel format of an `IDirect-DrawSurface` object for the `IDirectDrawSurface7.GetPixelFormat()` method. This is one of the few structures to rely on FOURCC data. It also accepts input in a number of formats under C/C++, which means that this structure is one that uses unions extensively. However, unlike other data structures with unions, converting these unions is quite easy.

DDSCAPS and DDSCAPS2   DirectX uses both of these structures to describe the capabilities of an `IDirectDrawSurface` object. The DDSCAPS2 data structure provides more information and requires four structure members. Both of these data structures appear as part of the DDCAPS data structure. The DDSCAPS data structure also appears as part of the DDSURFACEDESC data structure, while the DDSCAPS2 data structure appears as part of the DDSURFACEDESC2 data structure.

DDSURFACEDESC and DDSURFACEDESC2   DirectX uses both of these data structures to describe a surface. The DDSURFACEDESC data structure is still supported for old code but is superceded by the DDSURFACEDESC2 data structure for new code. The example code contains only the new version of the data structure. The `IDirectDraw7.CreateSurface()`, `IDirectDrawSurface7.SetSurfaceDesc()`, `IDirectDrawSurface7.Lock()`, and `IDirectDrawSurface7.GetSurface-Desc()` methods all rely on the DDSURFACEDESC2 data structure.

DDVIDEOPORTBANDWIDTH   DirectX uses this structure to describe the bandwidth characteristics of an overlay surface. The structure is used for output to a particular video-port and pixel-format configuration. The `IDirectDrawVideoPort.GetBandwidthInfo()` method relies on this data structure.

DDVIDEOPORTCAPS   DirectX relies on this data structure to define the capabilities and alignment restrictions of a video port. Developers normally use this structure with the `IDDVideoPortContainer.EnumVideoPorts()` method.

DDVIDEOPORTCONNECT   DirectX uses this data structure to describe a video-port connection. A developer can use this data structure with the `IDDVideoPortContainer.GetVideoPort-ConnectInfo()` method to open the video port and then obtain information about it. The information is retrieved in an array of DDVIDEOPORTCONNECT data structures.

DDVIDEOPORTDESC   DirectX uses this data structure to describe a video-port object that the developer wants to create. You'll normally use this data structure with the `IDDVideoPort-Container.CreateVideoPort()` method, which is used to create an `IDirectDrawVideoPort` object.

DDVIDEOPORTINFO DirectX uses this data structure to describe the transfer of video data to a surface. You'll normally use this data structure with the IDirectDrawVideoPort.StartVideo() method. This method enables the hardware video port and begins the transfer of data to the currently specified surface.

DDVIDEOPORTSTATUS DirectX uses this data structure to define the status of a video-port object. The status information tells whether the port is in use and includes a DDVIDEOPORTCONNECT data structure. There's also a flag that tells whether the port controls just the video or the Vertical Blanking Interval (VBI). You'll normally use this data structure with the IDDVideoPortContainer.QueryVideoPortStatus() method.

As you can see from the list, the data structures used by DirectX contain a wealth of information. The descriptions include the call information so that you know which methods require a certain data structure. The important concept to remember is that DirectX is a low-level API designed to make application code run faster and to provide developers with better access to the hardware. The cost of this access is the complex data structures we've just discussed.

Structure Conversion Essentials

DirectX is a data-intense technology in that the functions and interface methods require a lot of information to perform the simplest tasks. The data structure has to describe every operation in detail so that only the correct picture elements are affected by a given call. Unlike other types of computer tasks, working with graphics means working in the worlds of both math and art, so describing a picture element is difficult, even if you have the correct data structure to do it.

This section of this chapter discusses elements of the DirectXHelper.DLL found in the \Chapter 13\DirectXHelper folder of the source code CD. The source files actually contain a lot more code than appears in the chapter and we'll continue discussion of this DLL in Chapter 14. Although the example code is written in both C# and Visual Basic, the DirectXHelper.DLL code appears only in C# for ease of conversion. Make sure you review the source code files for full details on the DirectX implementation.

NOTE Just in case you think the whole experience with the FOURCC (four-character code) entries is limited to the Windows Media Player example in Chapter 11, you'll use them for DirectX too. You'll find a list of application FOURCC entries in the ms-help://MS.VSCC/MS.MSDNVS/dx8_vb/directx_vb/extras/DirectDraw7/vbddref_0uzm.htm help topic. Many of the media types you'll work with depend on the FOURCC entries for validation purposes, so it pays to become familiar with them.

Converting the *DDBLTFX* Data Structure

Some of the data structures aren't all that difficult to convert. For example, the DDBLTBATCH data structure is relatively straightforward. However, some of the data structures could give the average developer a nervous tick after a few hours of unsuccessful conversion. One of the most complex data structures is DDBLTFX. The structure contains five different unions, so converting it to something the managed environment can use is difficult to say the least. You can find the Visual C++ version of this data structure at ms-help://MS.VSCC/MS.MSDNVS/dx8_vb/ directx_vb/extras/directdraw7/ddref_0xmf.htm. Listing 13.1 shows the C# version of the data structure.

> **Listing 13.1   The Managed Version of the DDBLTFX Data Structure**

```
[StructLayout(LayoutKind.Sequential, Pack=1, CharSet=CharSet.Auto)]
public struct DDBLTFX
{
    public UInt32      dwSize;
    public DDFXType    dwDDFX;
    public UInt32      dwROP;
    public UInt32      dwDDROP;
    public UInt32      dwRotationAngle;
    public UInt32      dwZBufferOpCode;
    public UInt32      dwZBufferLow;
    public UInt32      dwZBufferHigh;
    public UInt32      dwZBufferBaseDest;
    public UInt32      dwZDestConstBitDepth;

    // This is the first of five unions.
    //union
    //{
    //    DWORD              dwZDestConst;
    //    LPDIRECTDRAWSURFACE lpDDSZBufferDest;
    //} DUMMYUNIONNAMEN(1);
    public UInt32      dwZDestConst;

    public UInt32      dwZSrcConstBitDepth;

    // This is the second of five unions.
    //union
    //{
    //    DWORD              dwZSrcConst;
    //    LPDIRECTDRAWSURFACE lpDDSZBufferSrc;
    //} DUMMYUNIONNAMEN(2);
    public UInt32      dwZSrcConst;

    public UInt32      dwAlphaEdgeBlendBitDepth;
    public UInt32      dwAlphaEdgeBlend;
    public UInt32      dwReserved;
    public UInt32      dwAlphaDestConstBitDepth;
```

```
// This is the third of five unions.
//union
//{
//    DWORD                 dwAlphaDestConst;
//    LPDIRECTDRAWSURFACE lpDDSAlphaDest;
//} DUMMYUNIONNAMEN(3);
public UInt32       dwAlphaDestConst;

public UInt32       dwAlphaSrcConstBitDepth;

// This is the forth of five unions.
//union
//{
//    DWORD                 dwAlphaSrcConst;
//    LPDIRECTDRAWSURFACE lpDDSAlphaSrc;
//} DUMMYUNIONNAMEN(4);
public UInt32       dwAlphaSrcConst;

// This is the fifth of five unions.
//union
//{
//    DWORD                 dwFillColor;
//    DWORD                 dwFillDepth;
//    DWORD                 dwFillPixel;
//    LPDIRECTDRAWSURFACE lpDDSPattern;
//} DUMMYUNIONNAMEN(5);
public UInt32       dwFillData;

public DDCOLORKEY ddckDestColorkey;
public DDCOLORKEY ddckSrcColorkey;
}
```

NOTE The reader will see the use of the term *blt* in sections of the code. The terms *blit* and *blt* are synonymous. Microsoft uses the two terms interchangeably for function calls and in their documentation. I chose *blit* as the more understandable term for use in the text of this book. However, the source code will contain a mix of both terms as appropriate.

As you can see, the data structure has five unions, all of which we convert to UInt32 values. Generally, you'll find that this form of the structure works well until you need to provide one of the IDirectDrawSurface data members. So, let's look at how this data structure is used. The key to the data structure is the *dwDDFX* member. This member describes what type of work the function will perform. The following enumeration shows the types of tasks that the structure can request the function perform:

```
public enum DDFXType
{
    //If stretching, use arithmetic stretching along the y-axis for this
```

```
    // blt.
    DDBLTFX_ARITHSTRETCHY   = 0x00000001,

    // Do this blt mirroring the surface left to right.  Spin the
    // surface around its y-axis.
    DDBLTFX_MIRRORLEFTRIGHT = 0x00000002,

    // Do this blt mirroring the surface up and down.  Spin the surface
    // around its x-axis.
    DDBLTFX_MIRRORUPDOWN    = 0x00000004,

    // Schedule this blt to avoid tearing.
    DDBLTFX_NOTEARING       = 0x00000008,

    // Do this blt rotating the surface one hundred and eighty degrees.
    DDBLTFX_ROTATE180       = 0x00000010,

    // Do this blt rotating the surface two hundred and seventy degrees.
    DDBLTFX_ROTATE270       = 0x00000020,

    // Do this blt rotating the surface ninety degrees.
    DDBLTFX_ROTATE90        = 0x00000040,

    // Do this z blt using dwZBufferLow and dwZBufferHigh as range
    // values specified to limit the bits copied from the source
    // surface.
    DDBLTFX_ZBUFFERRANGE    = 0x00000080,

    // Do this z blt adding the dwZBufferBaseDest to each of the sources
    // z values before comparing it with the destination z values.
    DDBLTFX_ZBUFFERBASEDEST = 0x00000100
    }
```

As you can see, the enumeration presents a series of standard graphic manipulation tasks, including rotation and mirroring. Consequently, the Z-buffering operations defined by the first two unions in the DDBLTFX data structure are only used for a subset of the tasks that the structure can request of the function. The alpha blending represented by the second two unions doesn't even have any tasks associated with it, so the function would need to support the task directly. There isn't any actual support for either Z-buffering or alpha blending in the IDirectDrawSurface7.Blt() method, so the value of these entries in the DDBLTFX data structure is minimal.

NOTE   Other data structures, such as DDOVERLAYFX, use the same union to allow use of either a constant or an IDirectDrawSurface object. In most cases, you can simply override the IDirectDrawSurface member entry and use a UInt32 to represent the value. Because the technique used is always the same, we won't look at other instances of this override in the chapter.

Eliminating Z-buffering and alpha blending leaves the fifth union in the DDBLTFX data structure—a problem because there's support for this feature. Listing 13.1 shows what you need to support the three fill options because they represent the options you'll use most often. If you decide to pass a pattern to the function, you can create an IntPtr to it and then convert the IntPtr to a number (which won't always work) or you can create a special version of the structure that includes the interface. The best idea is to try the three fill options first to see if they'll work for your application.

Converting the *DDCAPS* Data Structure

The DDCAPS data structure mostly contains members of types that we've already discussed at length, so for the most part, conversion is easy. However, the data structure contains a constant that we have to define because it's based on an equation that could change. The first bit of code for this conversion appears in the Functions class as follows:

```
public const int DD_ROP_SPACE = 256/32;
```

Now that we have the size of these arrays defined, we'll have to define the arrays. In previous chapters, we've looked at a number of ways to get around the whole problem of arrays, but this is a case where the option doesn't exist. Consequently, it's time to look at the rather thorny issue of defining an unmanaged array in the managed environment. Listing 13.2 shows the code we'll use to handle the arrays in this data structure (there are five of them).

Listing 13.2   **Converting the DDCAPS Data Structure Arrays**

```
//DWORD      dwRops[DD_ROP_SPACE];
[MarshalAs(UnmanagedType.ByValArray,
          ArraySubType=UnmanagedType.I4,
          SizeConst=Functions.DD_ROP_SPACE)]
public UInt32      []dwRops;
```

The magic of this solution is all in the [MarshalAs] attribute. However, it begins with a correct definition of the array type. The original array definition is commented out in the code. The new definition relied on a UInt32 array declaration. You must define it as UInt32 in this case or the code won't work. The [MarshalAs] attribute tells CLR that this is an array passed by value to the function. There are also ways to pass the array by reference. Notice the use of the new *ArraySubType* argument. It's essential to include this argument or CLR won't know how big to make the individual array members. Finally, we use the *SizeConst* argument to define the size of the array.

NOTE   Other DirectX data structures, such as the DDGAMMARAMP data structure, use the same array technique shown in this section. We'll only discuss one version of this array technique. However, you'll find it in use throughout the example code. DirectX relies heavily on array structures, all of which require some type of special handling.

If you define the array correctly, DirectX will at least recognize the resulting data structure. However, before you can use this data structure, you need to initialize the members, including the arrays. A sure sign that you've forgotten to perform this task is a null reference error message when you make the call. Listing 13.3 shows some typical initialization code for the DDCAPS data structure.

Listing 13.3   Initializing the DDCAPS Data Structure

```
DDCAPS   DevCaps; // A device capabilities data structure.

// Initialize the data structure.
DevCaps = new DDCAPS();

// Initialize the arrays.
DevCaps.dwRops = new UInt32[Functions.DD_ROP_SPACE];
DevCaps.dwSVBRops = new UInt32[Functions.DD_ROP_SPACE];
DevCaps.dwVSBRops = new UInt32[Functions.DD_ROP_SPACE];
DevCaps.dwSSBRops = new UInt32[Functions.DD_ROP_SPACE];
DevCaps.dwNLVBRops = new UInt32[Functions.DD_ROP_SPACE];

// Initialize the internal data structures.
DevCaps.ddsOldCaps = new DDSCAPS();
DevCaps.ddsCaps = new DDSCAPS2();

// Get the size of the data structure.
DevCaps.dwSize = (UInt32)Marshal.SizeOf(DevCaps);
```

As you can see from the example code, the initialization begins when the code creates a new instance of the DDCAPS data structure. The arrays are also initialized using the proper number of array elements. CLR is unlikely to detect problems in this area. It's theoretically possible to create array elements of the wrong type or size, even at this point in the application. Don't forget to initialize the data structures contained within the DDCAPS data structure. The code shows that both data structures are initialized using the proper data types. Finally, the code must set the size of the data structure. Figure 13.5 shows an initialized version of this data structure.

Previously, we had discussed a problem using the Marshal.SizeOf() function on structures containing arrays. The [MarshalAs] attribute defines the size of the array, so this problem no longer exists. However, we have a new problem. The [MarshalAs] attribute gives the developer a false sense of security because the compiler no longer complains about the arrays. Using arrays in a data structure is so error prone that you should only use them as a last resort, as we have in this instance. Always compare the final size of the data structure (using the value in the *DevCaps.dwSize* variable in this case) against an unmanaged equivalent (created in C/C++ in most cases) to ensure that the managed version is correct.

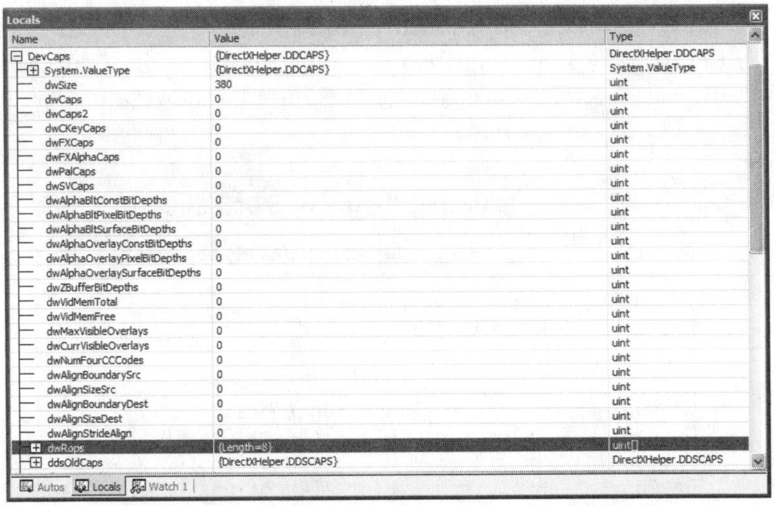

FIGURE 13.5:

It's important to initialize every member of the DDCAPS data structure.

Converting the *DDDEVICEIDENTIFIER2* Data Structure

The DDDEVICEIDENTIFIER2 data structure is relatively short, but it contains a number of odd conversions that will almost certainly cause trouble for some developers. The unmanaged version of this data structure appears at ms-help://MS.VSCC/MS.MSDNVS/dx8_vb/directx_vb/extras/directdraw7/ddref_4fg7.htm. Listing 13.4 shows the managed conversion of the data structure.

Listing 13.4   **The DDDEVICEIDENTIFIER2 Data Structure Is Short and Complex**

```
[StructLayout(LayoutKind.Sequential, Pack=1, CharSet=CharSet.Auto)]
public struct DDDEVICEIDENTIFIER2
{
   //char     szDriver[MAX_DDDEVICEID_STRING];
   [MarshalAs(UnmanagedType.ByValTStr,
            SizeConst=Functions.MAX_DDDEVICEID_STRING)]
   public String  szDriver;

   //char     szDescription[MAX_DDDEVICEID_STRING];
   [MarshalAs(UnmanagedType.ByValTStr,
            SizeConst=Functions.MAX_DDDEVICEID_STRING)]
   public String  szDescription;

   //LARGE_INTEGER  liDriverVersion;
   public Int64   liDriverVersion;

   public UInt32  dwVendorId;
   public UInt32  dwDeviceId;
```

```
    public UInt32   dwSubSysId;
    public UInt32   dwRevision;
    public GUID     guidDeviceIdentifier;
    public UInt32   dwWHQLLevel;
}
```

The first conversion problem in the DDDEVICEIDENTIFIER2 data structure is the two char arrays. We could create an array, use one of the techniques we used in previous chapters, or try the TCHAR method we used for the WaveCaps example in Chapter 11. It turns out that the TCHAR method works in this case. All you need to do is marshal the data as an UnmanagedType .ByValTStr type and declare a character array length using the *SizeConst* field. However, this method doesn't always work and you should use it with care.

One of the more interesting problem areas with the DDDEVICEIDENTIFIER2 data structure is the LARGE_INTEGER member, shown commented out in Listing 13.4. You might expect this member to convert directly to a managed type, but the declaration for this variable type tells a different story. Here's the C/C++ code for the LARGE_INTEGER data type:

```
#if defined(MIDL_PASS)
typedef struct _LARGE_INTEGER {
#else // MIDL_PASS
typedef union _LARGE_INTEGER {
    struct {
        DWORD LowPart;
        LONG HighPart;
    };
    struct {
        DWORD LowPart;
        LONG HighPart;
    } u;
#endif //MIDL_PASS
    LONGLONG QuadPart;
} LARGE_INTEGER;
```

This is a situation in which you could quickly become mired in detail by trying to emulate the precise details of the LARGE_INTEGER data type when it really isn't necessary to do so. The .NET Framework provides a suitable alternative for this data type that you can use without creating the strange-looking data structure shown in the example code. The clue for this conversion comes from the help file at ms-help://MS.VSCC/MS.MSDNVS/helplib/largeint_72lu.htm.

The key concept you need to consider is that this data type was created to help compilers without native 64-bit data types handle an integer of that size. Also notice that the description calls for a 64-bit signed integer, not an unsigned integer. You can't obtain these details by looking at the header file alone. Armed with this information, we can use a simple Int64 data type for the managed version of the data structure.

The final problem for this data structure is the use of a globally unique identifier (GUID) as one of the return types. A GUID contains a 128-bit numeric value with specific fields. Because there isn't any way to represent this value as a native type, we need to create a structure. Here's the data structure for a GUID used by this example:

```
[StructLayout(LayoutKind.Sequential, Pack=1, CharSet=CharSet.Auto)]
public struct GUID
{
    public UInt32  Data1;
    public UInt16  Data2;
    public UInt16  Data3;

    [MarshalAs(UnmanagedType.ByValArray,
               ArraySubType=UnmanagedType.I1,
               SizeConst=8)]
    public Byte     [] Data4;
}
```

As you can see, the first three fields are basic integer types. The fourth field is an array of eight byte values. There are a number of ways to represent this value, but using an array provides the best value in this case. One idea you might consider if you work with GUIDs a lot is to convert this structure into a class. The class would need functions to convert the GUID to a string and a string to a GUID. This exercise is left to the reader.

Defining *RECT*

There's one data structure that you'll see used as part of many of the DirectX data structures, RECT. Actually, this data structure is used with the Win32 API and COM as well, so it pays to place it in a common Windows library if you build one. The RECT data structure simply defines a rectangular area. It's normally used with graphic applications, but the actual location of the rectangle doesn't matter. Here's the definition of RECT that we'll use for DirectX purposes:

```
[StructLayout(LayoutKind.Sequential, Pack=1, CharSet=CharSet.Auto)]
public struct RECT
{
    public Int32   left;
    public Int32   top;
    public Int32   right;
    public Int32   bottom;
}
```

As you can see, there isn't anything complicated about this data structure. However, this particular data structure has actually caused some developers problems, mainly because of the data types used. Always use an Int32 data type for the RECT structure members.

Understanding DirectX Data Pitfalls in the Managed Environment

The DirectX programming environment presents a number of new challenges to the developer. Of course, working with DirectX itself can be a challenge because there are a number of issues to consider. However, the managed environment brings several new challenges and that's what we consider in this section.

One of the most important issues is performing the data conversions correctly. A DirectX application relies heavily on numeric data. It isn't always easy to tell when a data structure has returned the wrong information. When you convert a data structure that has at least some string data, the string serves as a means for detecting some types of errors. The pure numeric nature of many DirectX data structures makes this impossible. Consequently, you need to know the values of at least some of the numeric fields so that you can verify that the rest of the data structure contains good data. In sum, data validation is essential, but difficult.

We saw in the section "Converting the DDCAPS Data Structure" that DirectX also relies heavily on arrays that you can't dismiss, convert to something else, or define inline. This section shows one method for converting an array from a managed version to an unmanaged equivalent. However, the failure points in this conversion technique are many. For example, if you choose the wrong managed data type, the wrong *ArraySubType* argument value, or the wrong *SizeConst* argument value, the DirectX function will receive an array with incorrect data values. DirectX is very likely to go along with this error in most cases. The only error that it might detect is an incorrect *SizeConst* argument value. The result is that the display could act erratically, you might see data damage, or the application might not work at all.

Another problem is that you can actually overwork the data structures. One such example is the LARGE_INTEGER data type. The reason that the C/C++ headers create such a complex structure for this data type is that many C/C++ compilers don't support 64-bit integers natively. This concept is something you should keep in mind as you create data structures. For example, you might find the need to use a Currency data type in one of the structures. This is a data type that some C/C++ compilers don't support natively, yet the support is easily accessible from the .NET Framework. In sum, don't always re-create everything you find in the header files because you won't always need to do so.

Sometimes the data conversion problem isn't one of creating a managed version of an unmanaged data structure. For example, converting the elements in the DDPIXELFORMAT data structure is relatively easy. Coming up with a name for the new member is tough. Here are two examples of the unions that appear in this data structure:

```
//union
//{
//    DWORD dwRGBBitCount;
//    DWORD dwYUVBitCount;
```

```
//   DWORD dwZBufferBitDepth;
//   DWORD dwAlphaBitDepth;
//   DWORD dwLuminanceBitCount;
//   DWORD dwBumpBitCount;
//} DUMMYUNIONNAMEN(1);
public UInt32  dwCountDepthData;

//union
//{
//   DWORD dwRBitMask;
//   DWORD dwYBitMask;
//   DWORD dwStencilBitDepth;
//   DWORD dwLuminanceBitMask;
//   DWORD dwBumpDuBitMask;
//} DUMMYUNIONNAMEN(2);
public UInt32  dwMaskData1;
```

Needless to say, you can't use the same names as before because the union includes too many names to fit comfortably on a single line. Fortunately, all of the values are of the same type, which makes the conversion easy. In this case, I chose a generic name that appears to fit the functionality offered by each of the members. However, it's a less-than-perfect solution. Make sure you retain the original code as shown in the example when you rename a variable. Otherwise, other developers will have a difficult time reading your code.

A final area of concern for .NET developers who want to use DirectX is the use of pointers. It's important to remember how both .NET and the unmanaged environment work with pointers. In some cases, you might have to go back to a data structure and use an `IntPtr` type in place of the custom type you previously defined. When using any pointer, make sure you observe these rules:

- Allocate memory if the called function will write to a buffer or provide other feedback.

- Free any memory that you allocate.

- Pay close attention to the flow of pointers in a DirectX application because the function may provide you with a pointer into external memory.

- Use pinning when necessary to ensure that the Garbage Collector doesn't free memory it thinks is unused.

- Validate buffer sizes using test programs written in unmanaged Visual C++ whenever possible.

- Don't count on the documentation to provide accurate values of buffer size.

- Use the C/C++ headers to check pointers values whenever possible.

- Sometimes you'll need to use something other than an `IntPtr`, as in the case of some handle types used by the Win32 API.

Where Do You Go from Here?

We began this chapter by addressing a very simple issue, DirectX compatibility and functionality. Your hardware has to provide basic DirectX compatibility in order to create even a simple application. In addition, it must provide access to specific features if you want to use those features within your application. As you test your hardware, you begin to see which DLLs are in use and learn about DirectX features—it's a good first step to learning about DirectX. If you haven't already checked your hardware and learned which features it supports, now might be a good time to do so.

This chapter has also helped you understand the programming requirements for DirectX data structures and data elements. From our discussion, you learned that DirectX provides the developer with added flexibility but that this flexibility comes at the price of stricter programming requirements for the data structures and other data elements. In general, you'll find that the managed environment works well with DirectX as long as you take time to create the proper data structures first.

Besides checking your hardware, you'll want to perform a few other tasks before you move on to the next chapter. Make sure you check out all of the Web sites presented in this chapter because they contain helpful information you can use to make your DirectX programming experience better. In addition, fill in any gaps in your knowledge about DirectX (the essentials) by looking at a DirectX-specific reference. Most of these books are huge for good reason—DirectX is a complex topic.

Of course, understanding the data structures used by an API is only one step in learning to use it. DirectX is a complex programming environment that uses its own set of rules for working with both the Win32 API and the underlying hardware. Chapter 14 is going to show you how to use what you know now and combine it with some simple DirectX calls. In short, this is the first chapter where you'll really begin working with DirectX in any meaningful way.

Developing DirectX Access Routines

- Working with DirectX Functions

- Creating DirectX Callback Function Prototypes

- Working with the DirectX Interfaces and Classes

- Learning the DirectX Capabilities of the Host Machine Example

- A Simple 2D DirectDraw Example

B efore you can use DirectX, you need to know about the functions it provides and how to access them. Learning how to use DirectX in the managed environment will test most of the knowledge you've acquired throughout the book because it uses a variety of techniques to communicate with the client application. For example, many of the DirectX enumeration functions rely on callbacks, which is a technique we haven't used a lot for the Win32 API calls in the book. You'll also find some direct call functions, some functions that require complex structures, and even some Component Object Model (COM) functionality. DirectX uses all of the tricks we've learned so far.

NOTE   Most of the work you'll perform with DirectX involves COM. If you look at the data structure descriptions in Chapter 13, you'll notice that many of them discuss interface methods, not functions found within DLLs. However, DirectX isn't a pure COM environment, so we'll visit the non-COM elements first and then discuss the COM elements. Because this chapter focuses on managed application access to DirectX rather than on using DirectX in applications, it may seem that we're spending an excessive amount of time on areas you won't use very often. It's important to provide a complete picture of DirectX so you can use all of the features it provides within your managed application.

This chapter introduces you to DirectX version 7 programming—we'll discuss version 8.1 development in Chapter 15. We'll work with the DirectX functions, including the callback functions. The chapter will also help you understand the DirectX COM connection. In fact, this is the only connection that Visual Basic developers used to access DirectX in the past. The COM connection is important, and we'll look at the various interfaces used to implement it. Finally, you'll learn how to work with DirectX by creating several example programs. These examples aren't complex or awe inspiring, but they do show you how DirectX works in the managed environment.

TIP   Microsoft constantly updates the DirectX SDK. You can find the latest version, 8.1b (as of this writing), at http://www.microsoft.com/downloads/release.asp?ReleaseID= 40153&area=search&ordinal=2. The latest version includes mainly bug fixes, so there is no visible difference between it and original the 8.1 version. Consequently, this chapter will treat all 8.1 versions the same for discussion purposes.

Working with DirectX Functions

Unlike many parts of the Win32 API, the DirectX functions don't actually work with any data. The main purpose of these functions is to create objects and to request information about the DirectDraw-compatible hardware. Consequently, you'll use these functions once in each application. In fact, as we'll see in the section entitled "Working with the DirectX Interfaces and Classes," you can actually get by without using any of these functions at all if you take a pure COM approach to application development.

The following sections describe each of the DirectX functions, specifically those used for DirectDraw, in detail. Once you know about the functions, I'll show you the function declarations required to use them. The final section tells you about the special return values used by DirectX functions. You'll find all of the code for the listings in this section in the \Chapter 14\ DirectXHelper folder of the CD.

DirectDrawCreate() and *DirectDrawCreateEx()*

There are two functions you can use to create a DirectDraw object if you don't want to use the pure COM method: DirectDrawCreate() and DirectDrawCreateEx(). The latest version of the DirectX API supports both methods, but Microsoft recommends using the DirectDraw-CreateEx() function because it returns an object with full Direct3D support. The Direct-DrawCreate() function provides support for 2D drawing only.

Both functions require a globally unique identifier (GUID) as input for the first argument. The GUID points to a device driver—a requirement if the host system provides support for more than one display device. Setting this argument to null tells DirectX to use the active driver. You can also specify one of two constant values to place the system in a test mode: hardware (DDCREATE_HARDWAREONLY) or software (DDCREATE_EMULATIONONLY). Because you can supply more than one type of input for this argument, the example provides two overrides of each function.

The second argument is an IDirectDraw7 interface pointer. You'll need to provide this object reference as an Object or as an IntPtr. The example code uses an Object for ease of conversion.

The DirectDrawCreateEx() function includes a third argument not included with the DirectDrawCreate() function. The *iid* argument contains the Interface Identifier (IID) of the DirectDraw 7 object. Consequently, you must always use the IID_IDirectDraw7 constant defined in the library for this argument. The example defines this entry as a GUID structure, which is correct for the managed environment. However, the Platform SDK documentation describes the entry as a REFIID type. It isn't until you spend some time wandering through the C/C++ header files that you discover the two are equivalent in this case. Of course, creating a constant GUID value presents a problem for C# developers. Visual C++ developers have the DEFINE_GUID() macro they can use to create a constant GUID value, but C# doesn't define this mechanism. You can begin solving the problem by creating a special variable as shown here:

```
// This is a constant value substitute for the IID_IDirectDraw7
// iid value.
public static GUID IID_IDirectDraw7 =
    CreateIID.DEFINE_GUID(0x15e65ec0,0x3b9c,0x11d2,0xb9,
                          0x2f,0x00,0x60,0x97,0x97,0xea,0x5b);
```

As you can see, we make a static GUID variable equal to the output of a class function. There are a number of other ways to perform this task, but using a static class member function proves the best because you can hide the implementation details from the user. Listing 14.1 shows the class definition.

Listing 14.1   **Defining an IID Constant Value**

```
class CreateIID
{
   public static GUID DEFINE_GUID(UInt32 Data1In,
                                  UInt16 Data2In,
                                  UInt16 Data3In,
                                  Byte Data4_0In,
                                  Byte Data4_1In,
                                  Byte Data4_2In,
                                  Byte Data4_3In,
                                  Byte Data4_4In,
                                  Byte Data4_5In,
                                  Byte Data4_6In,
                                  Byte Data4_7In)
   {
      GUID  OutData = new GUID();   // Create the GUID.

      // Assign the IID_IDirectDraw7 values.
      OutData.Data1 = Data1In;
      OutData.Data2 = Data2In;
      OutData.Data3 = Data3In;

      // Remember to create the array and then assign
      // values to it.
      OutData.Data4 = new Byte[8];
      OutData.Data4[0] = Data4_0In;
      OutData.Data4[1] = Data4_1In;
      OutData.Data4[2] = Data4_2In;
      OutData.Data4[3] = Data4_3In;
      OutData.Data4[4] = Data4_4In;
      OutData.Data4[5] = Data4_5In;
      OutData.Data4[6] = Data4_6In;
      OutData.Data4[7] = Data4_7In;

      // Output the result.
      return OutData;
   }
}
```

Note that the class itself is hidden from view, but the DEFINE_GUID() method is visible internally. The DEFINE_GUID() method works precisely like the DEFINE_GUID() macro used by Visual C++, so you can transfer the data for IID calls to that macro directly to a C# application that incorporates this class. This is yet another way to create macro substitutes for the managed environment.

The DirectDrawCreate() and DirectDrawCreateEx() functions both include the same final argument and you must set it to null in all cases. The *pUnkOuter* argument is supposed to provide aggregation support for a future version of DirectX. The current version doesn't support this feature.

DirectDrawCreateClipper()

This function creates a DirectDrawClipper object, which describes a clipping area on the screen. DirectX supports two types of DirectDrawClipper objects: dependent and independent. Using this function creates an independent DirectDrawClipper object. A developer would use the IDirectDraw7.CreateClipper() method to create a dependent object.

The advantage of using an independent DirectDrawClipper object is that you can clip an area in any DirectDraw object. The disadvantage is that you have to manually release the object reference or wait until DirectX does it for you when the application terminates. When an application uses a dependent DirectDrawClipper object, the object is destroyed along with the DirectDraw object. There's less chance of a memory leak when you use this method of working with the DirectDrawClipper object, but this method could use more resources.

The Platform SDK documentation shows three arguments for the DirectDrawCreate-Clipper() function. However, only the second argument, *lplpDDClipper*, is actually used by the function. This argument contains a pointer to a DirectDrawClipper object. You must set the *dwFlags* argument to 0 and the *pUnkOuter* argument to null. The *dwFlags* argument could eventually modify the behavior of this function, much as using the special flag values for the DirectDrawCreate() and DirectDrawCreateEx() functions modifies their behavior. Likewise, the *pUnkOuter* argument will provide aggregation support in a future version of DirectX.

DirectDrawEnumerate() and DirectDrawEnumerateEx()

Both of these functions initiate an enumeration sequence similar to other enumerations we've discussed in the book. The enumeration provides information about the DirectX-capable devices that are installed on the host system. The DirectDrawEnumerate() function relies on the DDEnumCallback() function to handle the callback. Likewise, the DirectDrawEnumerateEx() function relies on the DDEnumCallbackEx() function to handle the callback. We discuss both callback functions in the section entitled "Creating DirectX Callback Function Prototypes" later in this chapter.

NOTE   The DirectDrawEnumerate() function is superceded by the DirectDrawEnumerateEx() function. Even though DirectX still supports the DirectDrawEnumerate() function, you should use the DirectDrawEnumerateEx() function in all new code. The example library contains a function declaration for only the DirectDrawEnumerateEx() function.

The DirectDrawEnumerateEx() function requires three arguments as input. The first is the address of a callback function. We'll create this callback as we did all of the examples in Chapter 5. This means creating a delegate and then a handler based on that delegate. The *lpContext* contains the address of an application-specific value that you can pass to the callback function each time DirectX calls it. Generally, you'll only use this argument if the callback function requires special data. Finally, you can pass flags in the *dwFlags* argument that changes the scope of the enumeration. The default value of 0 enumerates only the primary display device. The following list describes the other flag values:

DDENUM_ATTACHEDSECONDARYDEVICES   Lists any display devices that are part of the Windows Desktop. For example, it would list a second display adapter but not an inactive 3D accelerator.

DDENUM_DETACHEDSECONDARYDEVICES   Lists any display devices that are installed on the host system but aren't part of the Windows Desktop. For example, this flag would list an inactive 3D accelerator and other support hardware, but it won't list a second display adapter. To list all of the display devices, you must combine this flag with the DDENUM_ATTACHED-SECONDARYDEVICES flag.

DDENUM_NONDISPLAYDEVICES   Lists all non-display DirectX-capable devices, but it won't list any of the display devices. If you want to list all of the DirectX-capable devices on the host system, you must combine all three flags.

Function Declarations

At this point, you have a good idea of how the various DirectX functions work, so it's time to see how to declare them. Listing 14.2 shows typical DirectX function declarations. I say typical because some of the functions will require more than one implementation to satisfy some development needs. In fact, some functions require at least two declarations for a minimal implementation.

Listing 14.2   The DirectX Specific Function Declarations

```
/// <summary>
/// This function creates an instance of a DirectDraw object. The
/// object doesn't include Direct3D support.
/// </summary>
[DllImport("DDraw.DLL", CharSet=CharSet.Auto, SetLastError=true )]
public static extern Int32 DirectDrawCreate(GUID lpGUID,
                                            Object lplpDD,
                                            IntPtr pUnkOuter);

[DllImport("DDraw.DLL", CharSet=CharSet.Auto, SetLastError=true )]
public static extern Int32 DirectDrawCreate(IntPtr NO_GUID,
```

```
                                             Object lplpDD,
                                             IntPtr pUnkOuter);

/// <summary>
/// This function creates an instance of a DirectDraw object that
/// includes Direct3D support. Always used the IID_IDirectDraw7
/// constant for the third argument.
/// </summary>
[DllImport("DDraw.DLL", CharSet=CharSet.Auto, SetLastError=true )]
public static extern Int32 DirectDrawCreateEx(GUID lpGUID,
                                             Object lplpDD,
                                             GUID iid,
                                             IntPtr pUnkOuter);

[DllImport("DDraw.DLL", CharSet=CharSet.Auto, SetLastError=true )]
public static extern Int32 DirectDrawCreateEx(IntPtr NO_GUID,
                                             Object lplpDD,
                                             GUID iid,
                                             IntPtr pUnkOuter);

/// <summary>
/// This function creates a DirectDrawClipper object, which
/// describes a clipping area on the screen.
/// </summary>
[DllImport("DDraw.DLL", CharSet=CharSet.Auto, SetLastError=true )]
public static extern Int32 DirectDrawCreateClipper(
    UInt32 dwFlags,
    Object lplpDDClipper,
    IntPtr pUnkOuter);

/// <summary>
/// This function initiates an enumeration sequence that
/// provides information about the DirectX capable devices
/// that are installed on the host system.
/// </summary>
[DllImport("DDraw.DLL", CharSet=CharSet.Auto, SetLastError=true,
    EntryPoint="DirectDrawEnumerateExA" )]
public static extern Int32 DirectDrawEnumerateEx(
    Callbacks.DDEnumCallbackEx lpCallback,
    IntPtr lpContext,
    DDEnumType dwFlags);
```

All of these functions require some level of conversion. However, the DirectDrawCreate() and DirectDrawCreateEx() functions require multiple implementations because of the GUID pointer required as the first argument. We need some way to pass a null value to DirectX, and the best way to do that is to use an IntPtr. Remember to set the *pUnkOuter* argument to IntPtr.Zero in all cases because this feature isn't implemented. Also, you must use the IID_IDirectDraw7 constant for the *iid* argument for the DirectDrawCreateEx() function.

Many of the DirectX function calls aren't implemented as Unicode calls. The DDraw.DLL contains the proper Unicode function entry, but the function itself returns an error message. What this means is that you'll receive a return value of E_NOTIMPL (0x80004001) when you call the function—even if you provide the correct input values. This error number isn't registered as one of the errors that DirectX will return, which makes it even harder to troubleshoot. In fact, it's an error that you won't receive once your application is debugged and running. However, if you see this error during development, make sure you've added an *EntryPoint* argument to the [DllImport] attribute as shown for the DirectDrawEnumerateEx() function in Listing 14.2. This argument ensures that your application calls the correct function. Generally, you'll find that the error message goes away and you'll never see it again (at least not in this application).

The DDEnumCallbackEx() function contains more managed-code-specific changes than the other functions we have discussed. As previously mentioned, we're passing a pointer to a callback function delegate as the first argument. To make the code easier to read, use, and take apart for other uses, I decided to place the callback functions in a separate class (in a separate file). The Callbacks.DDEnumCallbackEx() member contains the definition of the DDEnum-CallbackEx() callback function. The example also uses a special enumeration to ensure that users of the library use the correct value for the third argument. Here's the definition of the DDEnumType enumeration:

```
public enum DDEnumType
{
    // Normally, this flag isn't required. Because we're using an
    // enumeration we need some way of listing only the primary display
    // device.
    DDENUM_NONE                         = 0x00000000,

    // This flag causes enumeration of any GDI display devices which are
    // part of the Windows Desktop
    DDENUM_ATTACHEDSECONDARYDEVICES     = 0x00000001,

    // This flag causes enumeration of any GDI display devices which are
    // not part of the Windows Desktop
    DDENUM_DETACHEDSECONDARYDEVICES     = 0x00000002,

    // This flag causes enumeration of non-display devices
    DDENUM_NONDISPLAYDEVICES            = 0x00000004,

    // This flag isn't part of the listing found in the C/C++ header,
    // but it makes working with the numeration easier.
    DDENUM_ALL_DEVICES                  = 0x00000007
}
```

Function Return Values

You might wonder why there's a separate section on return values in this chapter considering the amount of time we've spent looking at them in the past. DirectDraw relies on a common Visual C++ macro that we haven't discussed yet to create most of the error codes that it uses. I say most of the error codes, but some don't use the macro—they're based on something else. Confused yet? Don't be—we'll discuss the origins of the various error codes.

The first error code we'll discuss is DD_OK. This is the error code that you'll receive for successful completion of a function call. When you look for DD_OK in the DDraw.H file, you'll find that it's equal to S_OK, which isn't much help. The definition for S_OK appears in WinError.H. The definition is a cast to an HRESULT value of 0. Because C# doesn't support HRESULT and the value of S_OK is unlikely to change anytime soon, we can simply declare the value of DD_OK as 0. A few functions can return DD_FALSE. You'll follow essentially the same route we used for DD_OK to determine that DD_FALSE equals a value of 1. So much for the easy error codes.

The DDERR_GENERIC error code comes next on the list. When you look this error code up in DDraw.H, you'll find that it's equal to E_FAIL. The E_FAIL error result doesn't have a direct value either. It's the output of the _HRESULT_TYPEDEF_() macro with an input value of 0x80004005L. When you follow the _HRESULT_TYPEDEF_() macro to the WinError.H file, you'll find that it's another typecast to an HRESULT type. This same wild chase occurs when you want to learn the value of the DDERR_INVALIDPARAMS or DDERR_OUTOFMEMORY error code.

Some Win32 API function calls rely on a special Visual C++ macro to create an error value. The error value is composed of a severity level, a special offset, and the actual error number. However, DirectX doesn't rely on this macro directly; it follows a circuitous route to achieve the same goal. Let's begin by looking at the DDERR_DIRECTDRAWALREADYCREATED error code. If you look at the definition of this error code in the DDraw.H file, you'll see that it's defined as the output of a MAKE_DDHRESULT() macro value of 562. Here's the Visual C++ definition of the MAKE_DDHRESULT() macro:

```
#define _FACDD  0x876
#define MAKE_DDHRESULT( code )  MAKE_HRESULT( 1, _FACDD, code )
```

Notice the call to the MAKE_HRESULT(). This is the special Win32 API macro that I mentioned in the previous paragraph. Notice that it accepts a severity code of 1, a special constant value of _FACDD, and the actual error code. The MAKE_HRESULT() macro definition looks like this:

```
#define MAKE_HRESULT(sev,fac,code) \
    ((HRESULT) (((unsigned long)(sev)<<31) |
    ((unsigned long)(fac)<<16) |
    ((unsigned long)(code))) )
```

There are three ways to approach the problem presented by these error codes. You could simply define an enumeration that contains the output of the macros. Of course, Microsoft could decide to change the way the macro is calculated, which means that you'd have to make a lot of changes to your code later. You could create a custom function that combines the effects of the two macros. The problem with this approach is that it isn't very flexible and you'll still need to re-create the MAKE_HRESULT() macro for other Win32 API function calls. The third approach is the one used in the example. It creates functions the emulate both of the macros. Listing 14.3 shows the functions we'll use in this case.

Listing 14.3   Creating DirectX Error Codes

```
private const int _FACDD = 0x876;

public static Int32 MAKE_DDHRESULT(Int32 code)
{
    // Call the standard Windows API macro with the
    // correct error factors.
    return MAKE_HRESULT(1, _FACDD, code);
}

public static Int32 MAKE_HRESULT(Int32 sev, Int32 fac, Int32 code)
{
    Int64 Temp; // The temporary value of the error code.

    // Define the error code. Bit shift the severity
    // by 31 bits and the factor by 16.
    Temp = sev * 0x80000000;
    Temp += fac * 0x10000;
    Temp += code;

    // return the result.
    return (Int32)Temp;
}
```

As you can see, the functions match the macros pretty closely. Of course, there isn't much to the code found in the MAKE_DDHRESULT() function. All it does is call the MAKE_HRESULT() function to create the result (or error) value.

The MAKE_HRESULT() function might look a little odd at first. We need to provide a method for bit-shifting the three error values. Notice that *Temp* is an Int64 and not an Int32 as you might expect. The C# compiler won't allow use of an Int32 value for the type of bit-shifting that we're performing, so an Int64 value is the only alternative. The three values are shifted as appropriate and combined, just as they are in the macro. The result value is cast to an Int32 value and passed back to the MAKE_DDHRESULT() function, which helps create the error values used by the application developer.

Now that you have a better idea of how the managed environment creates the error codes, let's look at the error code listing. Listing 14.4 shows the error values and their associated groups.

Listing 14.4   DirectX Error Code Listing

```
// This is a list of the error codes used with the DirectX
// functions in this library.

// These are the general error codes used with most Windows calls.
public static Int32 DD_OK                        = 0x00000000;
public static Int32 DD_FALSE                     = 0x00000001;

// These error codes are based on existing Windows error codes such
// as E_FAIL.
private static UInt32 Temp1                      = 0x80004005;
public static Int32 DDERR_GENERIC                = (Int32)Temp1;
private static UInt32 Temp2                      = 0x8007000E;
public static Int32 DDERR_OUTOFMEMORY            = (Int32)Temp2;
private static UInt32 Temp3                      = 0x80070057;
public static Int32 DDERR_INVALIDPARAMS          = (Int32)Temp3;

// These error codes require a macro to create.
public static Int32 DDERR_INVALIDDIRECTDRAWGUID  = MAKE_DDHRESULT(561);
public static Int32 DDERR_DIRECTDRAWALREADYCREATED = MAKE_DDHRESULT(562);
public static Int32 DDERR_NODIRECTDRAWHW         = MAKE_DDHRESULT(563);
```

As you can see, the listing contains some error codes from each of the three groups that we discussed. The general error codes include DD_OK and DD_FALSE. The DD_OK return code is the only success indicator in the list. If you don't receive the DD_OK value, then an error has occurred. The DirectX equivalents of existing Windows error code groups signify failures such as an out-of-memory condition or invalid parameters. The DDERR_INVALIDPARAMS error value is the only failure condition that some functions indicate. Finally, the DirectX-specific error codes indicate some failure that's specific to DirectX, such as the lack of any DirectDraw hardware (DDERR_NODIRECTDRAWHW). In general, all DirectX error codes fall into one of these three groups.

Note the odd manner in which we create the second group of error values. The functions all output Int32 result values and the remaining error values are all Int32 values. Consequently, these error result values should also contain Int32 values. The C/C++ header contains the hexadecimal values shown, but C# won't allow the use of these values as input to an Int32. The easiest way to fix this problem is to create a temporary value to hold the UInt32 value and then cast that value it an Int32 as shown. This technique has the advantage of fully documenting the process and also retaining the original error value.

Creating DirectX Callback Function Prototypes

Like many newer parts of the Win32 API, DirectX relies on callback functions to return information to the calling application in an asynchronous manner. Using this technique ensures that the application will continue receiving information rather than get blocked waiting for the information to arrive in one chunk.

As you might imagine, all of these callback functions tell you something about DirectX. In fact, the DDEnumCallback() and DDEnumCallbackEx() functions are used with the Direct-DrawCreate() and DirectDrawCreateEx() functions to retrieve information about the hardware. We'll implement all of these callback functions as delegates, just as we did with the callback functions in Chapter 5. Many of the callback functions are called from COM interface methods rather than from standalone functions.

Now that you have a better idea of how the callback functions are used by DirectX, let's discuss them. In the following sections, I'll tell you about the callback functions. I'll also tell you which functions or methods will use the callback functions so you have a better idea of when to implement them. Look in the section entitled "Function Return Values" earlier in this chapter for the return values for these functions. You'll find all of the code for the listings in this section in the \Chapter 14\DirectXHelper folder of the CD.

DDEnumCallback() and DDEnumCallbackEx()

Both of these callback functions provide information about the DirectX-capable devices on the host system. The system calls these functions once for each device. The information includes the driver GUID, name, and description. The input also includes the context information passed to either the DirectDrawEnumerateEx() or DirectDrawEnumerateEx() function.

> **NOTE**   Because the DirectDrawEnumerate() function is superceded by the DirectDraw-EnumerateEx() function, the DDEnumCallback() function is essentially superceded as well. Even though DirectX still supports the DDEnumCallback() function, you should use the DDEnumCallbackEx() function in all new code. The example library contains function declarations for only the DirectDrawEnumerateEx() and the DDEnumCallbackEx() functions.

The DDEnumCallbackEx() function includes one additional piece of information—the handle to the monitor associated with the device. This value is null for the primary display device, non-display devices, and any device that lacks a Desktop connection. The monitor handle helps you discover information about the monitor so that any application you create can take the capabilities of the monitor into account as well.

EnumModesCallback() and EnumModesCallback2()

Both of these callback functions provide information about the display modes supported by a display device. The calling syntax for both functions is also the same. They both receive a structure containing surface description information and an object pointer containing context information. As usual, the context information is specific to the application and you don't need to provide it as part of the function call.

The EnumModesCallback2() function supercedes the EnumModesCallback() function. Even though DirectX still supports the EnumModesCallback() function, you should use the newer EnumModesCallback2() function and the associated IDirectDraw7.Enum-DisplayModes() method for application development.

The main difference between the two functions is that the EnumModesCallback2() function accepts a DDSURFACEDESC2 data structure as input. This data structure contains substantially more information than the DDSURFACEDESC data structure used by the EnumModesCallback() function. The additional information includes additional color references and texture information.

EnumSurfacesCallback(), EnumSurfacesCallback2(), and EnumSurfacesCallback7()

All three of these functions perform the same task—they enumerate the surfaces currently in use for a specific purpose on a display. Several methods call these functions, including the IDirectDrawSurface7.EnumAttachedSurfaces() and IDirectDrawSurface7.EnumOverlay-ZOrders() methods. All three callback functions are still supported, but you should use the correct call for the version of DirectX installed on the host system. In general, try to use the DirectX 7 calls when possible. Note that the example code contains support for only the EnumSurfacesCallback2() and EnumSurfacesCallback7() functions.

The callback functions accept three inputs. The first is the address of an IDirectDraw-Surface object. The nature of this object depends on the calling function and the version of DirectX in use at the time. The best capabilities come from a IDirectDrawSurface7 object (with IDirectDrawSurface and IDirectDrawSurface4 objects as the alternatives). Make sure you use only method calls supported by the calling interface.

The second argument is a DDSURFACEDESC or DDSURFACEDESC2 data structure. The two structures differ by the amount of surface description information they provide (as mentioned earlier). Both the EnumSurfacesCallback2() and EnumSurfacesCallback7() functions provide access to a DDSURFACEDESC2 data structure.

Finally, the third argument provides context information. This information is application specific, as usual.

EnumVideoCallback()

This callback function enumerates the video port capabilities of the selected display device. The IDDVideoPortContainer.EnumVideoPorts() method calls this function. The EnumVideo-Callback() function receives a DDVIDEOPORTCAPS data structure as input. It also receives the usual context information.

The DDVIDEOPORTCAPS data structure contains a wealth of information about the video port. Not all of the information is valid for every video port, so you need to check the status of the *dwFlags* field. Most video ports tell how large a display they accommodate and their port identification number. Ports also provide a series of flags that describe their capabilities, such as support for interlaced video.

Delegate Declarations

The previous sections discussed how you'd use the various callback functions in an application. It's time to look at the callback function declarations. Listing 14.5 shows the code we'll use in this portion of the example. Note that the documentation for each function has been removed—you can see the full documentation in the \Chapter 14\DirectXHelper folder on the CD.

Listing 14.5   **Callback Function Delegate Declarations**

```
public delegate Boolean DDEnumCallbackEx(IntPtr lpGUID,
                                         String lpDriverDescription,
                                         String lpDriverName,
                                         IntPtr lpContext,
                                         HMONITOR hm);

public delegate Int32 EnumModesCallback2(
   DDSURFACEDESC2 lpDDSurfaceDesc,
   IntPtr lpContext);

public delegate Int32 EnumSurfacesCallback2(
   Object lpDDSurface,
   DDSURFACEDESC2 lpDDSurfaceDesc,
   IntPtr lpContext);

public delegate Int32 EnumSurfacesCallback7(Object lpDDSurface,
   DDSURFACEDESC2 lpDDSurfaceDesc,
   IntPtr lpContext);

public delegate Int32 EnumVideoCallback(
   DDVIDEOPORTCAPS lpDDVideoPortCaps,
   IntPtr lpContext);
```

As you can see, there aren't any surprises in the delegate declarations. We're using the same techniques as before. The only argument you might want to change in each case is *lpContext*. The example uses an `IntPtr` in the interest of maximum flexibility. You could also use an `Int32` value or an `Object` if necessary.

Working with the DirectX Interfaces and Classes

As previously mentioned, DirectX relies heavily on COM to manipulate data and present it on an output device. Surprisingly, there aren't many DirectDraw-specific interfaces to learn about. The DirectX interfaces are targeted but contain quite a few methods. The following list won't provide you with an in-depth review of each interface, but it will provide you with enough information to begin using the interfaces to perform useful work. We'll also look at the interfaces in more detail in the example applications found in this chapter:

IDDVideoPortContainer   This interface contains methods that help you work with video ports. There are methods that open, close, and enumerate the ports, as well as determine their current status. The main use of this interface is gathering information about the DirectX environment.

IDirectDraw7   This is the main DirectDraw interface. You'll use it to create many of the other objects described in this section. It also has methods for information gathering (such as determining the number of display modes supported by the active device) and enumerating devices. You'll always create this interface before any other DirectDraw interface when creating a pure COM application.

IDirectDrawClipper   This interface helps you manage clip lists. A clipper controls the blitting of image data to a specific portion of a surface. Conversely, you can use it to crop an image that you want to blit to a surface. A clip list is a collection of clippers.

IDirectDrawColorControl   This interface controls the getting and setting of color objects in the DirectDraw environment. You'll use it whenever you want to change the color of all or part of a surface or drawing element.

IDirectDrawGammaControl   This interface enables you to adjust the red, green, and blue ramp values used on the primary surface in a DirectDraw application. The ramp values adjust the overall contrast and brightness of the image. Think of the ramp values as similar to a filter used on the front of a camera lens or the contrast and brightness controls on a television set.

IDirectDrawPalette   This interface controls the content and use of the DirectDraw palette. Just as an artist's palette contains only certain colors, DirectDraw limits your use of color to those found in the palette. In most cases, the default palette works fine. However, some images require special rendering, and therefore a special palette.

IDirectDrawSurface7   This is one of the essential interfaces for DirectDraw. You must create a surface on which to draw before you attempt to draw anything. DirectDraw supports (and often requires) the use of multiple surfaces. Each surface is a separate part of the drawing. Every application requires a primary surface as a minimum.

IDirectDrawVideoPort   This interface controls the actual interaction between DirectDraw and a display device. It includes methods for changing the color controls, modifying the synchronization settings, and performing other tasks related to display devices. As with many of the other interfaces, you can also use this interface to determine the status of selected software settings and devices.

Learning the DirectX Capabilities of the Host Machine Example

Sometimes you need to know how many display devices the host machine has available for drawing. In addition, you need to know the GUIDs of any ancillary devices so that you can access them as needed. The DirectDrawEnumerateEx() function we created for the DirectX-Helper library works perfectly for this purpose. The callback continues to receive input until DirectX has listed all of the devices.

Of course, this isn't the only method for checking out a host system. DirectX also comes with the DirectX Caps Viewer tool. This tool helps you learn more about a host system. Unfortunately, this second method works only if you have direct access the system, which is something that many developers won't have when creating applications.

No matter which method you use to learn about the host computer, you'll need to perform this task relatively often as you create DirectX applications. The following sections tell you more about the DirectDrawEnumerateEx() function and the DirectX Caps Viewer tool methods of learning the capabilities of a host system.

Using the *DirectDrawEnumerateEx()* Function

The DirectDrawEnumerateEx() function provides a programmatic method of determining the number and type of DirectX-compatible display devices on a given system. The advantage of using this function is that you can call it without creating any objects or performing any other tasks. The call is a straightforward use of standard Win32 API callback functionality. With this in mind, let's look at the example code found in Listing 14.6. You can find the source code for this example in the \Chapter 14\C#\DirectXCaps and \Chapter 14\VB\DirectXCaps folders of the CD.

Listing 14.6   **Enumerating Devices Using Code**

```csharp
private void btnTest_Click(object sender, System.EventArgs e)
{
    Int32 Result;   // The result of a call.

    // Create the callback function pointer.
    Callbacks.DDEnumCallbackEx DDCB =
        new Callbacks.DDEnumCallbackEx(DDCallback);

    // Clear the display area.
    txtDevices.Clear();

    // Call the function. This call will enumerate all of the devices.
    Result = Functions.DirectDrawEnumerateEx(
        DDCB,
        IntPtr.Zero,
        DDEnumType.DDENUM_ALL_DEVICES);

    // Check for errors.
    if (Result != Functions.DD_OK)
        MessageBox.Show("The following DirectX error occured: " +
                        Result.ToString("X"),
                        "Application Error",
                        MessageBoxButtons.OK,
                        MessageBoxIcon.Error);
}

public Boolean DDCallback(IntPtr lpGUID,
                          String lpDriverDescription,
                          String lpDriverName,
                          IntPtr lpContext,
                          HMONITOR hm)
{
    // Create a StringBuilder to hold the data.
    // Initialize it with the current display text.
    StringBuilder  SB = new StringBuilder(txtDevices.Text);

    // Display the string data on screen.
    SB.Append(lpDriverName + "\r\n");
    SB.Append(lpDriverDescription + "\r\n");

    // Display the GUID on screen.
    if (lpGUID != IntPtr.Zero)
    {
        GUID  DisplayGUID = new GUID();
        Marshal.PtrToStructure(lpGUID, DisplayGUID);
        SB.Append("Driver GUID: ");
        SB.Append(DisplayGUID.Data1.ToString() + "-");
```

```
        SB.Append(DisplayGUID.Data2.ToString() + "-");
        SB.Append(DisplayGUID.Data3.ToString() + "-");

        for (int Counter = 0;
            Counter < DisplayGUID.Data4.Length;
            Counter++)
        {
            SB.Append(DisplayGUID.Data4[Counter].ToString());
        }

        SB.Append("\r\n");
    }

    // Display the information on screen.
    SB.Append("\r\n");
    txtDevices.Text = SB.ToString();

    // Continue the enumeration.
    return true;
}
```

Because the DirectXHelper library contains all of the declarations needed to use this function, we don't have to add anything special to the application. Execution begins with a call to the btnTest_Click() method. The code creates a new DDEnumCallbackEx() delegate and assigns the DDCallback() method to it. This is the callback function pointer we'll pass to the DirectDrawEnumerateEx() function. Remember that the DirectDrawEnumerateEx() function also accepts a pointer to a context object and requires that you tell it which devices to enumerate. The btnTest_Click() method should end with a call to the DirectDrawEnumerateEx() function.

Notice that, unlike the callback function examples in Chapter 5, this example checks the *Result* value on return from the DirectDrawEnumerateEx() function call. You can always rely on Windows to support a call that enumerates windows using a standard Win32 API call. However, there's no guarantee that the client machine will provide the required support for DirectX. The developer must include code that checks the *Result* value to ensure that the machine provides the required support. If it doesn't, then the developer needs to provide code to exit the application with a suitable error code. This bit of code shows a second use for the DirectDrawEnumerateEx() function—validating a specific level of DirectX support. If this function fails, you know that the host machine lacks support for DirectX 6 or above.

The DirectDrawEnumerateEx() function will call the callback function DDCallback() for each DirectX compatible display device on the host system. Every device will return a driver name and description. However, the primary display adapter typically won't return a GUID or the handle of a display. Microsoft assumes that you already know this information and won't need additional input. Consequently, the DDCallback() function always checks the *lpGUID* entry to ensure that it actually contains data. In all other ways, the DDCallback() function is relatively simple and displays the data on screen. Figure 14.1 shows typical output from the example application.

The example application enumerates the DirectX-compatible display devices on the host system.

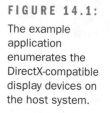

Using the DirectX Caps Viewer Tool

The DirectX Caps Viewer tool is one of the first utilities you should learn how to use after installing the DirectX SDK on your system. The data provided by this utility can save considerable time in locating hardware- and driver-related problems on your system. In fact, this is a tool that every administrator should learn how to use as well. The following sections discuss how you can use the DirectX Caps Viewer tool to improve the DirectX development experience.

An Overview of the DirectX Caps Viewer Tool

Before you can use this tool, you must install the DirectX SDK. You'll find the DirectX Caps Viewer tool in the \Start Menu\Programs\Microsoft DirectX 8.1 SDK\DirectX Utilities folder. The initial DirectX Caps Viewer tool display appears in Figure 14.2.

Notice that the DirectX Caps Viewer tool makes a distinction between devices and DirectX objects. There are separate entries for the display adapters on my system and the DirectDraw devices. The distinction is that the presence of a display adapter alone doesn't guarantee DirectDraw compatibility. Even if the display adapter would normally have all of the required hardware support for DirectX, the hardware still requires the proper driver. The important element for the DirectX developer is learning where to look for specific information about the host system. Generally, you'll want to use the DirectX-specific entries to learn what your application can actually do on the host system rather than what the hardware is capable of doing with the proper driver.

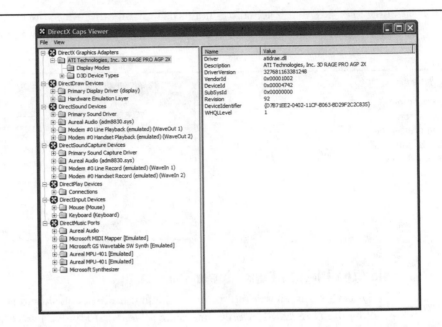

FIGURE 14.2:

The DirectX Caps
Viewer tool helps you
learn about the
DirectX capabilities of
your system.

Microsoft has improved DirectX capabilities over the years, mainly due to the input of game developers. The initial release of DirectX included visual elements and a few aural elements. The latest version of DirectX concentrates on four main areas of the multimedia experience:

- Visual
- Audio
- Data input
- Connectivity

The focus I chose for this book is the visual component of DirectX. This element shows up the best in books and it's what many business users will concentrate on learning first. However, it's important to consider the other DirectX components as well, because they do have an impact on the multimedia experience.

Converting the DirectX Caps Viewer Tool to a Data Structure

For DirectX application developers, there's a practical aspect in using this utility—it can provide validation of programming design decisions. You'll remember from Chapter 13 that DirectX relies on a wealth of data structures to communicate with the client application. Figure 14.3 shows a typical example of the output of one of these data structures.

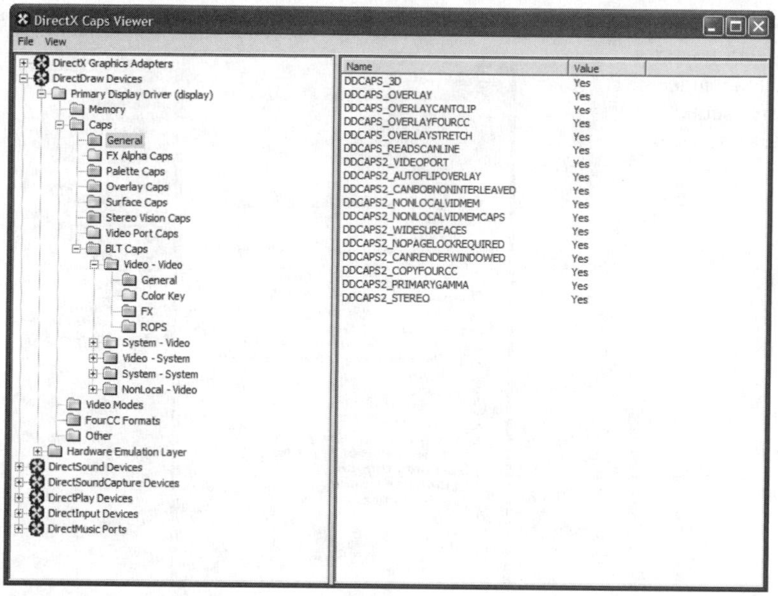

FIGURE 14.3:

Use the DirectX Caps Viewer tool to learn more about the content of various DirectX data structures.

For a comparison of the data shown in Figure 14.3 to a data structure, check the DDCAPS data structure explanation found at `ms-help://MS.VSCC/MS.MSDNVS/dx8_vb/directx_vb/extras/DirectDraw7/vbddref_89cy.htm`. (We also discussed this structure in the section entitled "Converting the DDCAPS Data Structure" in Chapter 13.) You'll find that the display in Figure 14.3 compares favorably to the DDCAPS data structure description. If you were developing an application that required information stored in this data structure, you could use the DirectX Caps Viewer tool to validate the results received by your application.

An Overview of the Sound Elements

Figure 14.4 shows the sound elements associated with DirectX. As you can see, the DirectX sound elements are divided into three areas: hardware, sound effects, and music. The element highlighted in Figure 14.4 is the hardware. Most machines will have several hardware sources that DirectSound will target, including the sound capability of the modem. However, notice in Figure 14.4 that the two modem entries include the term *emulated* in their description. This means that the modem doesn't provide any DirectSound-compatible hardware. DirectSound recognizes it as a valid device but will emulate the required functionality in software.

FIGURE 14.4:

The DirectX Sound
elements include
hardware, sound
effects, and music.

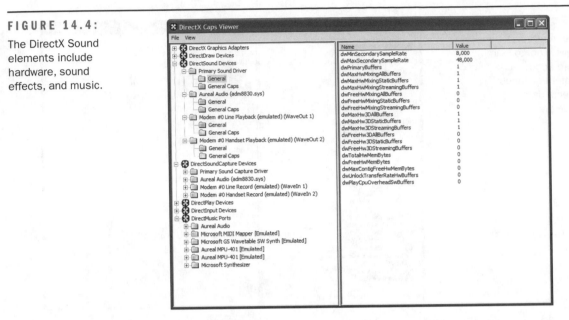

FIGURE 14.4: The DirectX Sound elements include hardware, sound effects, and music.

Moving on to the `DirectSoundCapture Devices` folder, you'll find the hardware that you saw in `DirectSound Devices` folder. The entries in the `DirectSoundCapture Devices` folder focus on sound effects. These entries describe the capabilities of the individual devices to record and play wave audio. The items of interest for developers in this situation are the entries in the `General Caps` folder for each device. This folder contains a list of the wave formats that each device can play and also tells you which formats you can use within your application.

Most systems contain a multitude of DirectMusic port entries. However, you'll usually find only one or perhaps two entries that rely on actual hardware. The remaining entries will reference emulated hardware. The most common emulated port is the Microsoft MIDI Mapper. The `Caps` folder for each device will tell you the type of device (input or output) and provide statistics such as the number of voices that the device supports.

An Overview of the Data Input Elements

The number and type of DirectInput devices that a system possesses varies based on the use of the system. Business systems normally contain the two DirectInput devices shown in Figure 14.5. In fact, the mouse and the keyboard the two devices you can count on for any system. If you want to create an application with general appeal, then target these two devices.

Every Windows
system will contain
a mouse and a key-
board.

The information found in the device folder depends on the device. As shown in Figure 14.5, the mouse folder contains information such as the number of buttons. In general, you can expect every device to provide type information. The type information tells you about the generic capabilities of the device.

Home and gaming systems will likely contain a number of additional devices such as joy-sticks. The information that DirectInput provides is a little sketchy in this area due, in part, to a lack of standardization. Although it's possible to categorize a joystick by the number of buttons it provides, it's difficult to provide standardized information about its programmability. This means the developer is still partially responsible for finding details about some input devices using direct hardware access.

An Overview of the Connectivity Elements

The term *DirectPlay* is somewhat misleading because you could use this feature for a number of purposes—many of which aren't related to playing games. Microsoft originally designed the feature for games, though, so the name stuck. The DirectPlay feature tracks DirectX connectivity, as shown in Figure 14.6.

Connectivity is a
requirement for
many multimedia
applications today.

As you can see, most systems will include support for a number of DirectPlay devices, including modem, serial port, network, and Internet. The Connections folder contains a list of these devices and each device folder will tell you about the sessions for that device. There's little in the way of capability information provided by DirectPlay because it's impossible to obtain that information until it establishes a connection.

A Simple 2D DirectDraw Example

As previously mentioned, there are two ways to access DirectX in the managed environment. You can use either the function call approach (as we did in the previous example) or the pure COM approach. This section shows how to work with DirectX using the pure COM approach. The example will demonstrate a simple 2D drawing. Of course, before we can use the COM approach, we'll need to import the DirectX COM object. The following sections show everything needed to create this example. You'll find the source code for this example in the \Chapter 14\C#\2DDraw and \Chapter 14\VB\2DDraw folders on the CD.

Importing the DirectX COM Library

One of the first steps you'll need to perform for any application that uses the COM method of accessing DirectX is to import the DirectX library into the application. The .NET environment will perform all of the work necessary to create a bridge between the managed environment and the COM library. If you've already worked with COM libraries in the past, you can import the library and skip the remainder of this section.

NOTE   It might be tempting to think that the DirectX COM library is complete. It's true that the library does provide access to all of the interfaces you need and most of the data structures. However, there are two sets of elements that are still missing. The first, and most important, are the function declarations you'll need to perform tasks such as enumerate the hardware on a host system. The second is the enumerated values used to detect error conditions. For this reason, you'll still want to include the DirectXHelper library (or an equivalent without the data structures) in your application.

It's important to remember that DirectX is unmanaged code. This means that some of the functionality you're used to seeing in the unmanaged environment may take on a different look in a .NET application. It also means that some COM libraries import better than others do. The DirectX library is one that imports with enough functionality that you can actually perform work with it. Unfortunately, other libraries aren't quite as useful when you import them (usually because they broke some of the rules for creating COM libraries), so you end up doing more work. The following steps show how to import the library:

1. Create a new project.
2. Right-click the References folder in Solution Explorer and choose Add Reference from the context menu. You'll see an Add Reference dialog box.

3. Select the COM tab and locate the DirectX 7 for Visual Basic Type Library entry shown in Figure 14.7.

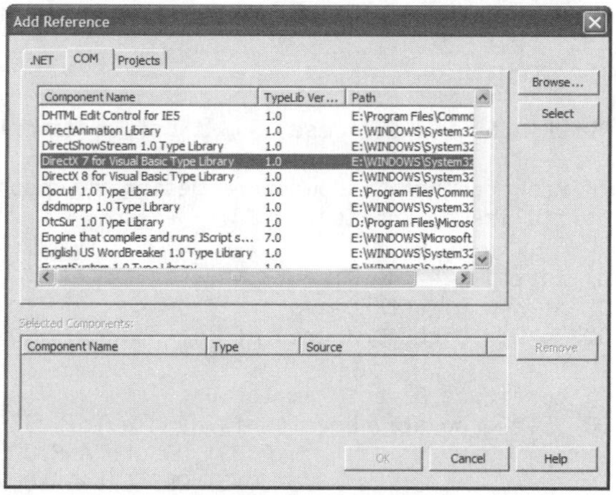

FIGURE 14.7:

Choose the DirectX 7 for Visual Basic Type Library for this example.

4. Click Select to place the library in the Selected Components list.

5. Click OK. Visual Studio will add the reference to the References folder in Solution Explorer.

Notice that the name doesn't match the entry in the Add Reference dialog box—it's listed as DxVBLib. This is the name you'll use to reference the library in your code. You'll also find the library listed as interop.dxvblib in the Object Browser. That's because we're using the interoperability functionality provided by Visual Studio .NET to access the COM library.

Writing the Code

This is an extremely simple 2D drawing example. All it does it read a file from disk and place it on screen. However, when running it, you'll notice some significant differences from performing the same task using native managed applications. Using DirectX begins by initializing the environment. Listing 14.7 shows how to perform this task.

Listing 14.7   **Initializing DirectX in the Managed Environment**

```
// These contants control the application configuration.
private const int SCREENWIDTH = 800;
private const int SCREENHEIGHT = 600;
private const int BITCOUNT = 32;
private const int BITMAPWIDTH = 100;
private const int BITMAPHEIGHT = 100;
private const String BITMAPPATH = "C:\\Colorblk2.bmp";
```

```csharp
      // These variables are used application wide.
      private DirectX7        DX7;    // DirectX 7 Object
      private DirectDraw7     DD7;    // DirectDraw 7 Object
      private DirectDrawSurface7 PSurf;    // Primary surface
      private DirectDrawSurface7 SSurf;    // Secondary surface

      public frmMain()
      {
         DDSURFACEDESC2 SurfDesc;    // Surface description.

         // Required for Windows Form Designer support
         InitializeComponent();

         // Initialize the DirectX environment.
         DX7 = new DirectX7Class();
         DD7 = DX7.DirectDrawCreate("");

         // Configure DirectDraw for use.
         DD7.SetCooperativeLevel(this.Handle.ToInt32(),
                            CONST_DDSCLFLAGS.DDSCL_FULLSCREEN |
                            CONST_DDSCLFLAGS.DDSCL_EXCLUSIVE);

         DD7.SetDisplayMode(SCREENWIDTH,
                            SCREENHEIGHT,
                            BITCOUNT,
                            0,
                            CONST_DDSDMFLAGS.DDSDM_DEFAULT);

         // Create the primary surface.
         SurfDesc = new DDSURFACEDESC2();
         SurfDesc.lFlags = CONST_DDSURFACEDESCFLAGS.DDSD_CAPS;
         SurfDesc.ddsCaps.lCaps =
            CONST_DDSURFACECAPSFLAGS.DDSCAPS_PRIMARYSURFACE;
         PSurf = DD7.CreateSurface(ref SurfDesc);

         // Create the secondary surface.
         SurfDesc = new DDSURFACEDESC2();
         SurfDesc.lFlags = CONST_DDSURFACEDESCFLAGS.DDSD_CAPS |
                           CONST_DDSURFACEDESCFLAGS.DDSD_HEIGHT |
                           CONST_DDSURFACEDESCFLAGS.DDSD_WIDTH;
         SurfDesc.ddsCaps.lCaps =
            CONST_DDSURFACECAPSFLAGS.DDSCAPS_OFFSCREENPLAIN;
         SurfDesc.lHeight = BITMAPHEIGHT;
         SurfDesc.lWidth = BITMAPWIDTH;
         SSurf = DD7.CreateSurfaceFromFile(BITMAPPATH, ref SurfDesc);

         // We're ready to begin drawing.
         StartDrawingLoop();
      }
```

The beginning of the listing contains constants you can change to meet the needs of your system. Make sure you change the location of the graphics file to match the image on your system. The \Chapter 14\Graphics folder contains the image shown later in the example. You'll also see four class-level objects: the object used to access DirectX, the DirectDraw object contained within DirectX, and the two surface objects used for drawing on screen.

The class constructor begins by initializing the application components as it normally does. Don't attempt to use DirectX until this process completes. Otherwise, your system may act abnormally.

Once the application configuration is complete, the code creates the DirectX object and then uses the DirectDrawCreate() method to create the DirectDraw object. The single argument for this method accepts a GUID. Because the application uses the active driver, there's no need to supply a GUID. Before the application can use the DirectDraw object, the code must configure it for use. Configuring the DirectDraw object means defining the display mode and cooperation level as a minimum, but you'll normally make other configuration changes as well.

DirectDraw applications rely on surfaces to present information. This application requires two surfaces. The first surface defines the client drawing area, while the second surface contains the image we want to display in the client drawing area. Most developers refer to this secondary image as the off screen image because you use it off screen until it's ready to present on screen. The next step the code takes is to configure these two drawing surfaces. In both cases, the code creates a surface description using a DDSURFACEDESC2 data structure and then calls a constructor function. The primary surface uses the CreateSurface() method, while the secondary surface uses the CreateSurfaceFromFile() method.

The final step is to call the StartDrawingLoop() method. The application is set up and ready to use. In fact, the display adapter has already changed modes and is ready to present any information the application creates. Listing 14.8 shows the code used to display an image on screen.

Listing 14.8   Displaying an Image On Screen

```
private void StartDrawingLoop()
{
   RECT  BMRect;      // Bitmap size.
   RECT  DrawRect;    // Drawing area size.
   Int32 DrawTop;     // Top of the drawing area.
   Int32 DrawLeft;    // Left side of the drawing area.

   // Result code from call.
   Int32 Result = (Int32)CONST_DDRAWERR.DD_OK;

   while (Result == (Int32)CONST_DDRAWERR.DD_OK)
   {
```

```csharp
            // Check for application events.
            Application.DoEvents();

            // Verify that DD7 is still valid.
            if (DD7 == null)
                break;

            // Make sure the application can display
            // the data.
            Result = DD7.TestCooperativeLevel();

            // If we can draw, begin displaying data.
            if (Result == (Int32)CONST_DDRAWERR.DD_OK)
            {
                // Create the bitmap sizing rectangle.
                BMRect.Top = 0;
                BMRect.Left = 0;
                BMRect.Right = BITMAPWIDTH;
                BMRect.Bottom = BITMAPHEIGHT;

                // Create the drawing area rectangle.
                DrawTop = frmMain.ActiveForm.Height -
                    frmMain.ActiveForm.ClientRectangle.Height;
                DrawLeft = frmMain.ActiveForm.Width -
                    frmMain.ActiveForm.ClientRectangle.Width;
                DrawRect.Top = DrawTop;
                DrawRect.Left = DrawLeft;
                DrawRect.Right = frmMain.ActiveForm.ClientRectangle.Right;
                DrawRect.Bottom = frmMain.ActiveForm.ClientRectangle.Bottom;

                // Display the drawing.
                Result = PSurf.Blt(ref DrawRect,
                                   SSurf,
                                   ref BMRect,
                                   CONST_DDBLTFLAGS.DDBLT_ASYNC);

                // Verify there were no errors. If so, recover.
                if (Result == (Int32)CONST_DDRAWERR.DDERR_SURFACELOST)
                {
                    DD7.RestoreAllSurfaces();
                    SSurf = null;
                    CreateOffscreenSurfaces();
                }
            }
        }
    }

    private void CreateOffscreenSurfaces()
    {
        DDSURFACEDESC2 SurfDesc;    // Surface description.
```

```
        SurfDesc = new DDSURFACEDESC2();
        SurfDesc.lFlags = CONST_DDSURFACEDESCFLAGS.DDSD_CAPS |
                          CONST_DDSURFACEDESCFLAGS.DDSD_HEIGHT |
                          CONST_DDSURFACEDESCFLAGS.DDSD_WIDTH;
        SurfDesc.ddsCaps.lCaps =
            CONST_DDSURFACECAPSFLAGS.DDSCAPS_OFFSCREENPLAIN;
        SurfDesc.lHeight = BITMAPHEIGHT;
        SurfDesc.lWidth = BITMAPWIDTH;
        SSurf = DD7.CreateSurfaceFromFile(BITMAPPATH, ref SurfDesc);
    }
```

The `StartDrawingLoop()` method begins by setting up a loop that will constantly refresh the image. Of course, setting up such as loop normally means that the application ignores all input. That's why the application includes a call to the `Application.DoEvents()` method. Using this method ensures that the application continues to respond to events.

There's a situation where the application could end in an odd part of the loop and cause a reference problem. The next step is to ensure that the DirectDraw object is still usable. If the code detects a condition where the object is no longer useable, it breaks out of the loop. In addition to checking the validity of the DirectDraw object, you must also verify that it can draw on screen. The `TestCooperativeLevel()` method performs this task.

Once the code determines that the DirectDraw object is valid and that it can draw on screen, it's time to prepare the drawing surface. The `BMRect` and `DrawRect` data structures contain the drawing coordinates for the application. Notice that both structures rely on the coordinate information supplied by the application for input. It's important to use the application data to ensure that you don't draw off the edge of the screen.

The `Blt()` method actually transfers the data from off screen to on screen. Notice that the code uses the two `RECT` structures and the secondary surface to accomplish this task. The application draws the image asynchronously. The final bit code ensures that the application doesn't lose the bitmap surface data and that the image on screen remains uncorrupted. If the bitmap surface data does become corrupted, the `CreateOffscreenSurfaces()` method performs the same initialization found in the class constructor.

The code must perform one additional task. When the user exits the application, the DirectX and DirectDraw objects still exist. These objects aren't under the purview of the Garbage Collector, so the application must release them manually. Listing 14.9 shows the code used for this purpose.

Listing 14.9   Cleaning Up on Application Exit

```
private void frmMain_Closing(object sender,
                        System.ComponentModel.CancelEventArgs e)
    {
```

```
    // Clean up the objects and DirectDraw setup.
    DD7.SetCooperativeLevel(this.Handle.ToInt32(),
                            CONST_DDSCLFLAGS.DDSCL_NORMAL);
    DD7.RestoreDisplayMode();
    DD7 = null;
    DX7 = null;
}
```

As you can see, the code needs to restore the display settings before the application exits using the SetCooperativeLevel() and RestoreDisplayMode() methods. Windows can also take care of this task, but there are situations when the display could become corrupted. It's better to handle this task as part of the exit code. Once the display is restored, setting the two objects to null (Nothing in Visual Basic) will free the memory. Figure 14.8 shows the output from this application.

FIGURE 14.8:

The sample application paints an image on screen within the client area.

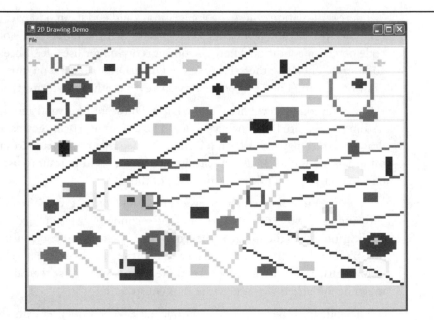

Using the GIF Construction Set

There are many different ways to add animated effects to applications. Some developers are under the impression that they must use DirectX or a technology like it to create good animation. The fact is that most business applications don't require animation and those that do can often present an acceptable appearance by using an animated GIF file. DirectX is a powerful technology that you can use to create everything from a simple business presentation to an advanced game; however, all of that power comes at a price—a fact that the example in this chapter demonstrated.

All that an animated GIF does is pack several pictures into one file. A browser plays these pictures back one at a time, which helps you to create the illusion of continuous animation. Because you can place a browser viewing area within standard .NET desktop applications, animation is freely available to anyone who wants it. You can also use special effects to create a slide show using a GIF by changing the interval between pictures.

NOTE   This section will show you how to create a GIF using the GIF Construction Set from Alchemy Mind Works. You can download it from several places. The best place is straight from the vendor at `http://www.mindworkshop.com/alchemy/gifcon.html`. This application also appears on the CD in the `\GIF Construction Set` folder.

We'll use the GIF Construction Set in this example for two reasons. First, since it's shareware, all of you can download it from the Internet and follow along with the examples. Second, it's a great program, and most people find that it works just fine for creating animated GIFs. At most, you'll notice the lack of an actual drawing program with this program, but Windows already supplies that in the form of Paintbrush or MS Paint.

You'll also need a graphics conversion utility if your drawing program doesn't support the GIF file format directly (neither Paintbrush nor MS Paint does). Both Graphics Workshop from Alchemy Mind Works (located in the `\Graphics Workshop` folder of the CD) and Paint Shop Pro by Jasc Software are excellent graphics conversion programs. Both vendors provide shareware versions of their product. You can find Alchemy Mind Works at the Internet site provided in the previous note. The JASC product appears at `http://www.jasc.com/`.

Start the GIF Construction Set program. Use the File ➤ Open command to view the contents of the `\Chapter 14\Animated Graphic` folder of the CD. Notice that the directory has several GIF files in it already. `Time0.GIF` is a base file—a blank used to create the animation effect. You can save a substantial amount of time by creating such a blank whenever you create an animation. In fact, cartoonists use this very technique. They draw the common elements of an animation once on separate sheets and then combine them to create the animation. Only unique items are drawn one at a time. `Time1.GIF` through `Time12.GIF` are the actual animation files—think of each one as an animation cel.

Let's create an animated GIF using these "cel" files. The following procedure isn't meant to lock you into a particular regimen, but it does show one way to use the GIF Construction Set to create one:

1. Use the File ➤ New command to create a new GIF. You'll see a blank GIF dialog. GIF Construction Set always assumes a standard background color of black. We'll need to change that value.

NOTE   Users familiar with older versions of the GIF Construction Set will be happy to hear that it automatically adjusts the size of the image now to match the figures in the GIF. Developers adjusted this value manually in the past with less than useable results in some cases.

2. Double-click the Header entry. You'll see the Edit Header dialog shown Figure 14.9. It helps you to change characteristics associated with the GIF—for example, the background color. Notice the Loop option on this dialog. If you keep this value set to 0, the GIF will continue looping indefinitely. This is a great idea, in most cases, but you might want to set this value to something else to save system resources when needed.

FIGURE 14.9:

Use the Edit Header dialog box to change the overall characteristics of the GIF.

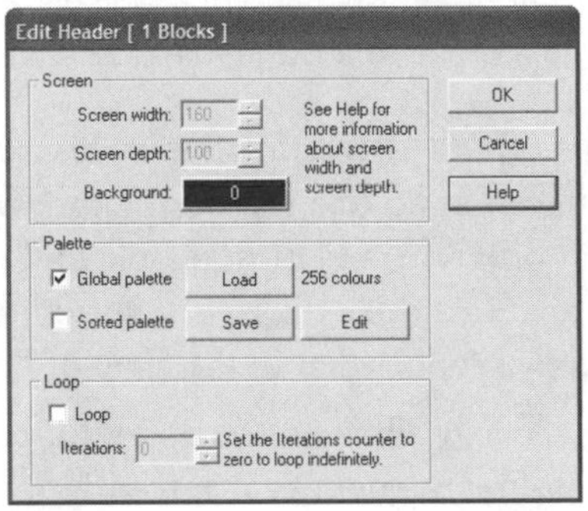

---

3. Set any header options. The example sets the number of loops to 10 for testing purposes, but you can set this value as you see fit. The example also sets the background color to white (color number 215). Click OK to make the change permanent.

4. Click the + button and select Image from the drop-down list (or use the Block ➢ Merge command). This command helps you to add an image to the GIF. You'll see a standard File ➢ Open dialog.

5. Double-click the first file you want to use in the animation. In this case, you'd double-click Time1.GIF. You'll see the Palette dialog shown in Figure 14.10. The palette for this graphic doesn't match the standard palette used by GIF Construction Set. Note that older versions of the GIF Construction set provided more options.

FIGURE 14.10:

Use the Palette dialog to modify the method used to handle color in imported graphics.

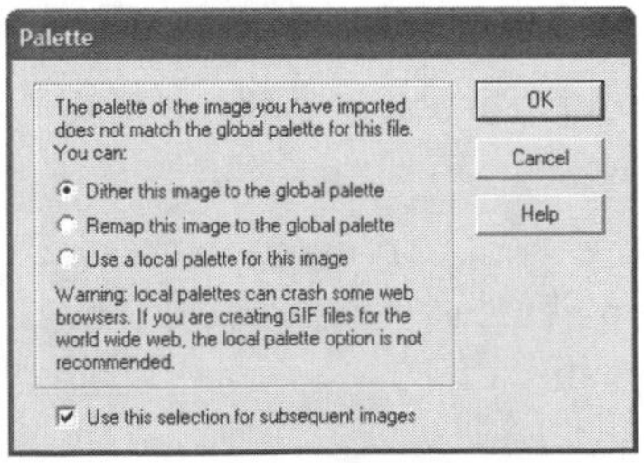

6. Select the Dither This Image to the Global Palette setting for compatibility reasons. Click OK to complete the process. GIF Construction Set will insert a new graphic into the GIF.

7. Click the + button and select Image from the drop-down list. You'll see the same File ➢ Open dialog as before.

8. Select the next image in the series and click OK. Click OK again if GIF Construction Set asks you about the palette setting. GIF Construction Set will automatically insert the image in the next position of the animation sequence.

9. Repeat steps 7 and 8 for the remaining GIFs in this animation (Time2.GIF, Time3.GIF, and so on). Now we have to insert some controls to make this image work properly.

10. Double-click Block 3 (the second image). You'll see an Edit Image dialog like the one shown in Figure 14.11. Notice that this dialog tells you about the image. You can also use this dialog to add control blocks between image elements. Control blocks allow you to modify the behavior of the animated GIF. For example, you can use a control block to set the time between pictures. Many browsers expect a control block between every image in your animated GIF, so you must add a control block starting with the second image.

FIGURE 14.11:

Use the Edit Image dialog box to change the characteristics of an individual cel.

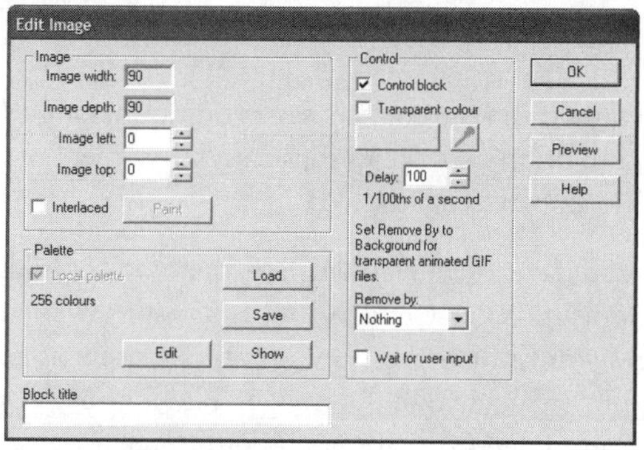

11. Check the Control Block option. Set the Delay field to 1. Click OK to add the control block. You won't see any difference in the main window.

12. Click the next Image entry.

13. Repeat steps 11 and 12 for each of the images. You'll end up with a series of images, as shown in Figure 14.12. (Make sure you add a Control object to the last image, since the animated GIF will automatically loop back to the first image.)

FIGURE 14.12:

The end result is a series of images with control settings.

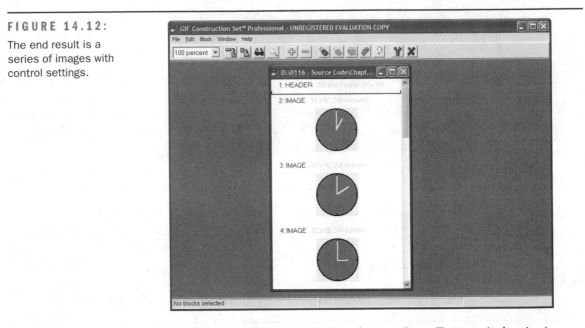

14. To view the completed animation, click the View button. Press Esc to exit the viewing area.

15. The only thing left to do is save your animated GIF file. Use the File ➤ Save As command to do that. You could use any filename, but for the purposes of this example, save the file as AnimatedTime.GIF.

Now you have an animated image that you could display using a number of techniques, including using a browser window. Interestingly enough, the animated GIF is simply a series of images—nothing more. So you can also use it as an image list within a DirectX application by clipping offsets within the image. The number of ways to use the stacked image technique found in animated GIFs are nearly unlimited.

TIP   You can find a demonstration of how to use an animated GIF within a desktop application in the \Extras\AniDisplay folder of the CD. The example folder contains complete source code and documentation, plus a test file you can use with the example. You can also use this example to test other animated GIFs downloaded from sources such as the Internet.

Where Do You Go from Here?

This chapter has shown you the basics of using DirectX functions and interfaces. You learned about both standard function calls and callback functions. In general, you'll find that this chapter provides all of the basics you need to construct any DirectX application. In fact, we've already looked at what you'll need to do to put a 2D application together.

Although you have all of the basics you need to know, this chapter hasn't even begun to explore the 2D features of DirectX. This is a good time to explore the 2D capabilities more and spend more time working with the data structures we discussed in the previous chapter. DirectX is a technology best learned one step at a time. For example, you should learn more about the math required for 2D drawing—something we haven't discussed much in this chapter.

At this point, you know how to work with a basic 2D application. Now you need to know how to put a 3D application together and how to apply more advanced programming techniques. The use of 3D drawing is increasing, so knowing how to work with the 3D functionality that DirectX provides is important. Chapter 15 will show you the basics of working with 3D applications. We won't do anything fancy, but you'll learn enough to perform the required conversions for the managed environment.

Creating Applications with DirectX 8.1

- An Overview of DirectX 7 and DirectX 8.1 Differences

- Using the DirectX Control Panel Application

- Using the DMO Test Utility

- A Simple 3D Display Example

- Using the Force Feedback Editor

- A Simple DirectInput Example

- Using the DirectX Texture Tool

The past two chapters have helped you understand the data structures, functions, and other elements that make up DirectX in general and DirectX 7 specifically. This chapter moves from DirectX 7 to DirectX 8.1. Both versions of this technology are still in common use, so it's important to know about the feature sets of both products. The first section of the chapter will provide an overview of these differences so you can write applications that use the full functionality that each version can provide.

In general, most developers currently write 2D drawing applications to the DirectX 7 standard but use DirectX 8.1 for 3D drawing. I say in general because you'll find exceptions to the rule. This chapter includes some 3D drawing examples so that you can see how this technology works with DirectX 8.1.

The final piece of the puzzle for this chapter is to look at some of the other tools that the DirectX SDK provides. It's important to know what tools you have at your disposal when you install the SDK because creating a 3D drawing is difficult (perhaps impossible) without them. This chapter will discuss the DMO Test utility, the Force Feedback Editor, and the DirectX Texture Tool. The DirectX Texture Tool is actually the most important of the three because it helps you create realistic drawings with less work than drawing every surface individually.

NOTE As with the other DirectX chapters in this book, the goal of this chapter is to help you understand DirectX use within the managed environment. The examples aren't meant to make you a DirectX programming wizard, nor are they meant to show you every feature of DirectX—that would require another book. The examples will help you understand how DirectX fits within the managed environment and alerts you to any oddities that you might encounter making the various interfaces work. Our point of concentration in this chapter is what makes DirectX 8.1 different from DirectX 7, which means we'll also discuss differences in working with the interfaces in the managed environment.

An Overview of DirectX 7 and DirectX 8.1 Differences

DirectX has been an example of continuous evolution. There are a number of reasons that Microsoft created DirectX 8.1. Obviously, the hardware capabilities addressed by DirectX 7 are now common and ordinary—DirectX 8.1 addresses the capabilities of the new hardware on the market. Of course, Microsoft has to add the usual number of new capabilities to the product. Finally, there are the usual bug and performance fixes to consider, as well as features that make the product easier to use.

The following sections discuss the differences between DirectX 7 and DirectX 8.1 in greater detail. The features aren't necessarily discussed in light of the "gee whiz" factor they provide or in the order that Microsoft marketing thought important. The focus of these sections is features that make life easier for the developer and improve performance. I've paid particular attention to features that might cause developers to have problems in the managed environment.

Consolidated Objects

One of the issues that Microsoft addressed in DirectX 8.1 was "object creep." In DirectX 7, it seems that you have an object for everything and that each of those objects requires a separate creation step. If you want to create a DirectDraw and a Direct3D object in DirectX 7, you'll likely have to perform two separate steps and create two separate objects. The problem with this approach is that it's hard getting the two objects to work together, so you end up writing some odd code to do it. DirectX 8.1 consolidates DirectDraw and Direct3D into a single DirectX Graphics module with the name of Direct3D. Now you can create 2D and 3D graphics on the same surface without the problems introduced by separate objects.

Consolidation is good from the usability viewpoint. Using one object to create both 2D and 3D elements makes life easier for the developer because now you don't have as many objects to worry about. However, consolidation can also become problematic in the managed environment. It's important to remember two essential points about DirectX. First, it was and still is optimized for use by Visual C++ developers (despite the kludges added to support Visual Basic). Second, Visual C++ offers flexibility that the managed environment can't easily provide. In this case, consolidation could mean subtle errors in your application. These objects require data in data structures. Set a data structure up incorrectly and you might find that the application doesn't work as anticipated. The data might be correct for a 2D object but not for the 3D object that you're trying to create.

TIP　　Visual Basic developers who want and need more than the basic DirectX SDK can provide will want to look at the Phantom Reality site at `http://www.phantomreality.com/`. This vendor produces an assortment of 2D and 3D multimedia tools.

Sometimes the objects are still separate, but Microsoft has introduced an additional level of cooperation. That's the case with DirectMusic and DirectSound. A DirectMusic object can now load sounds found in WAV files. Even though the DirectSound object still exists and most developers will use it when they play sounds alone, the DirectMusic object is the focal point for DirectX 8. You can place both sounds and music using a single DirectMusic object. Of course, this introduces another confusion factor for managed environment developers— it's possible to create subtle data errors that DirectX won't catch because of the additional flexibility it provides.

Updated Objects and Features

One of the best new features for developers who work in the unmanaged environment is the addition of a debug build. This debug build helps you learn what's going on inside DirectX. It works the same as the debug builds you create for your application. The only problem is that the DirectX libraries are unmanaged code applications, which means that Visual Studio .NET might stumble a bit when viewing them. You'll find that you can generally find what you need, but not always. Sometimes the debugger just won't work with the unmanaged code. You can switch between debug and released versions of DLLs using the DirectX Control Panel Application described later in this chapter.

You'll find that Microsoft spent a lot more time working on the Direct3D library than the DirectDraw library in DirectX 8.1 for good reason. Most, if not all, game programming now uses 3D drawing techniques. CAD and other engineering and scientific disciplines also rely on 3D drawing techniques. About the only area where 2D still reigns supreme is business graphics and only because many business graphics still have to appear in print. Eventually, business graphics will also use 3D drawing techniques. The following list provides a quick overview of some of the 3D drawing additions for DirectX 8:

Special Effects   The special effects now include strings and you can add comments. You can still use special effects that are limited by the FOURCC designations, but Microsoft no longer requires that you use them. This means you have access to more types of special effect files. The problem for the managed environment developer, however, is ensuring that those files will actually work in the managed environment with the target hardware. Generally, you'll still find that using files with the FOURCC designations is the safe bet.

Pixel Shaders   DirectX 8.1 comes with better support for pixel shaders. The developer has access to additional instructions, modifiers, and registers. This particular feature won't present any more problems in the managed environment than it does for developers in the unmanaged environment.

Texture Library   The biggest change for the texture library is support for dynamic textures. This feature enables you to create a basic texture that morphs to create what appears as multiple textures to the end user. This version also uses a higher-quality encoding algorithm and allows you to obtain information about the texture without loading it into memory first. A new constant, CONST_D3DPOOL.D3DPOOL_SCRATCH, enables you to load textures that the physical devices can't support. The library provides methods to transform the texture into a form that the physical devices can support.

Math Library   DirectX is math intensive. The developer must compute the exact location and form of each object during an animation sequence. Consequently, any help that the math library can provide will only speed the coding of an application. The library adds support for most important functions for 3D-Now!, Streaming SIMD Extensions (SSE), and SSE2. It also adds support for 16-byte aligned matrices.

> **NOTE** If you haven't worked long with DirectX, you might not know about 3D-Now! and SSE/SSE2. 3D-Now! is AMD's built-in processor support for graphics. It purportedly provides better graphics execution times than Intel's Multimedia Extensions (MMX) technology. Read more about this technology at http://www.amd.com/us-en/Processors/TechnicalResources/0,,30_182_857_992,00.html. Intel, not to be outdone by AMD, has introduced SSE and SEE2 technologies that reduce the overall number of instructions to perform an application task. SSE2 provides 144 more instructions than the SSE variant. You can read more about this product at http://www.intel.com/design/Pentium4/prodbref/index.htm.

Drawing Features   DirectX 8 improves the 3D drawing capabilities of DirectX in general. The new features include multisampling rendering support, point sprites, 3D volumetric textures, and higher order primitives. I won't cover these updates in any depth in the book, but it's important to know they exist. None of these new features will cause problems for managed environment developers except that performance might not be what you expect.

DirectInput features a number of new input device changes. A game-specific feature is support for additional pedal data. Even though some developers might associate the joystick with games, others use the joystick with other application types, especially those in the scientific arena. The updates for joystick support include better recognition of joystick slider data. Precision measurements make both scientific and game applications work better. Finally, DirectInput has added support for action mapping. This feature makes it possible to map a physical input device element to an action in the application. For example, clicking the button on a joystick could fire a machine gun or retrieve a sample using the robotic arm of a remotely operated vehicle (ROV).

Some developers felt that DirectPlay support in DirectX 7 was a joke, and a very bad one at that. DirectPlay has improved in DirectX 8.1 in so many ways that it might not be possible to discuss them all here. The feature that will definitely matter most includes better security. Developers will find that DirectPlay now provides good support for firewalls and also network address translation (NAT). Even though security is important, most gamers are looking for performance. Microsoft has completely rewritten the objects for DirectPlay so that it performs better. You'll also find that DirectPlay now uses easy-to-understand URLs instead of GUIDs for destination information. Finally, DirectPlay now includes support for voice transmission so you can talk to other people while using a network connection to transmit other forms of DirectX data.

An Overview of the Tools

One of the newest tools provided with DirectX 8 is the MeshView Tool. This tool loads, displays, manipulates, and stores meshes used to display 3D data on screen. You can view the mesh information in wireframe, edge, crease, strip, adjacency, or normal form (or any combination thereof). The utility will provide a skin for the mesh, and you can choose the form of that skin along with the technique used for skinning. The MeshView Tool includes a number of shapes, including cylinder, sphere, torus, square, and teapot. We'll discuss this tool in greater detail in the section titled "Using the MeshView Tool" in Chapter 16.

Another tool that's been around, but is greatly improved for DirectX 8, is the DirectX Control Panel Application. Unlike the DirectX Diagnostic Tool, this utility is designed specifically for developer use. It enables a developer to modify the way DirectX reacts to an application during critical stages of debugging. We'll examine the DirectX Control Panel Application in more detail later in this chapter.

Previous versions of DirectX left the DirectPlay developer out in the cold—there weren't any tools for testing a connection. Consequently, developers had to rely on trial and error to get connections correct and they often failed. The DirectPlay Network Simulator makes it possible to test your DirectPlay applications in greater depth before you actually begin testing them on an actual network. This means that you'll spend less time debugging and also end up with a better application in the long run. We'll discuss this tool in greater detail in the section titled "Using the DirectPlay Network Simulator" in Chapter 16.

Using the DirectX Control Panel Application

You'll find the DirectX Control Panel Application in the Control Panel after installing the DirectX SDK. This applet has the usual DirectX icon. What it does for developers is nothing less than amazing. Once you begin using this tool, you'll wonder why Microsoft didn't include it in previous versions of the product.

NOTE For whatever reason, the DirectX Control Panel Application doesn't seem to install properly into the Windows XP System32 folder. If this problem occurs on your system, simply copy the DirectX.CPL file from the \DXSDK\bin\DXUtils folder to the \WINDOWS\system32 folder of your system. Restart your machine and the DirectX Control Panel Application should appear in the Control Panel. If all else fails, you can double-click the DirectX.CPL file from within Windows Explorer to start it.

When you initially open the DirectX Control Panel Application, you'll see the DirectX tab of the DirectX Properties dialog box. This tab tells you which version of DirectX your system is running and also provides access to a button found on every other tag—DxDiag. The DxDiag button will open the DirectX Diagnostic Tool that we discussed in section titled "Using the DXDIAG Utility" in Chapter 13.

The Direct3D tab contains the first developer-related information for this utility. Figure 15.1 shows the features of this tab. As you can see, it contains a lot of developer-oriented controls. The first control that you should become familiar with is the Debug Output Level slider. Interestingly enough, you can tell DirectX to tell you every woe it has or to shut up and process information. Most developers will want to turn off the output unless they're actually creating an application because it can become quite annoying. This slider appears on every tab so you can control the debug output of each DirectX feature individually.

FIGURE 15.1:

The Direct3D tab controls operation of 3D drawing on your system.

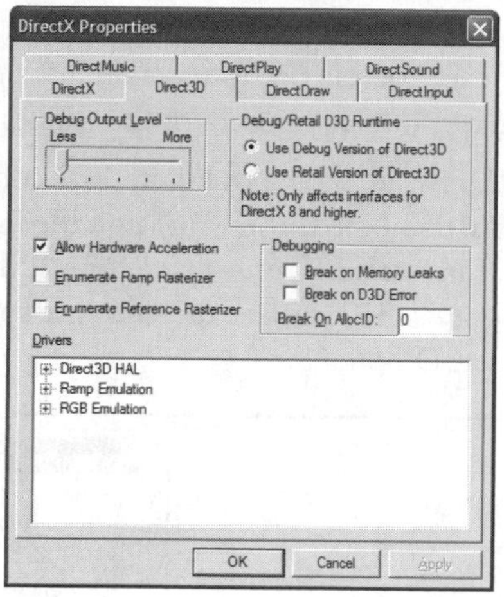

NOTE   Don't confuse the Direct3D tab with the DirectDraw tab. Use the Direct3D tab to control 3D drawing data and the DirectDraw tab to control 2D drawing data. In some cases, you'll want to change the settings on both tabs to ensure that you have the system set up correctly for the current task.

The next point of interest is the Debug/Retail settings. Every tab also has this feature. It enables you to switch between the debug and retail versions of DirectX so that you can test your application in both environments. Previous versions of DirectX forced the developer to use either the debug or the retail version of the product and didn't offer any means of tuning the debug output. As you can see, DirectX 8.1 is a vast improvement from the developer's perspective. Note that this feature only affects DirectX 8.0 and DirectX 8.1 libraries—it won't affect older libraries installed on your system.

The middle portion on the left side of the dialog box contains three check boxes that enable you to control performance. You'll use the Allow Hardware Acceleration feature most often.

Clearing this option will force DirectX to use software emulation, even if hardware acceleration is available, so that you can measure worst-case performance for a system setup. These options might appear grayed out if your system doesn't provide support for the required feature.

The two debugging check boxes on the right side of the dialog box enable you to control how DirectX breaks within the debugger. Sometimes it's useful to see how your application affects DirectX so that you can change the way your application makes function calls and performs other tasks. This is one of the most useful features for developers who are trying to get DirectX to work in the managed environment because it can also help you tune your function, structure, and interface declarations.

The final area of interest on the Direct3D tab is the Drivers list box. This area contains a list of the drivers that affect Direct3D. However, unlike most driver lists, this one is formatted for developer use. You can use it to obtain information such as the GUID for the driver—a handy feature we could have used for the applications in previous chapters.

The DirectDraw tab shown in Figure 15.2 comes next. Remember that Direct3D and DirectDraw are combined. You won't find the usual Debug Output slider on this tab. However, some features are the same. For example, there's a Use Hardware Acceleration check box that you can use to force the driver to use software emulation. This option is separate from the Direct3D option.

FIGURE 15.2:

The DirectDraw tab augments the information found in the Direct3D tab.

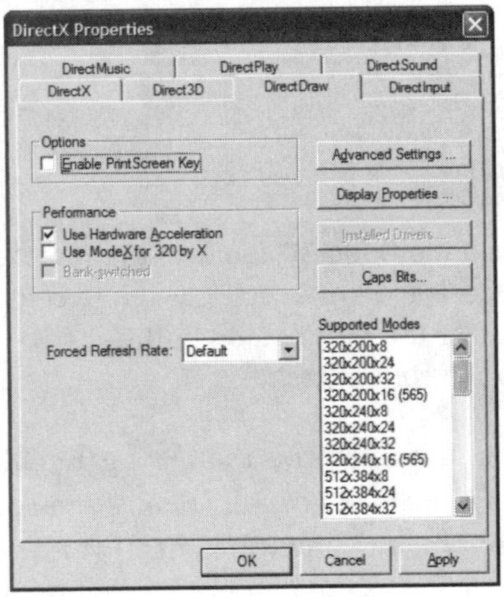

Some of the options are answers to developer requests of the past. For example, you couldn't use the Print Screen key to output screen data in the past. DirectX 8 provides this option so developers can grab screen shots with little trouble with the understanding that the Print Screen key can affect application execution.

Click Advanced Settings and you'll see a DirectDraw Advanced Settings dialog box that allows you to modify the normal operation of DirectX. For example, you can disable MMX or Accelerated Graphics Port (AGP) support to emulate certain system setups. You can also simulate a system lock failure and fine-tune emulation support.

The last three buttons display standard dialog boxes. For example, click Display Properties and you'll see the standard Display Properties dialog box. The last two options on this dialog tab display the modes that the display adapter supports and allow you to change the default refresh rate.

The DirectInput tab shown in Figure 15.3 contains the usual slider and Debug/Retail option. As you can see, this tab contains check boxes that determine which DirectInput features generate debug information. This is an important option because you might be interested in only one DirectInput area in your application. Getting debug information from all of the devices would prove confusing to say the least. In addition, an application might not even use the mouse or the joystick. Some developers might want to eliminate the keyboard if they're using it for debugging purposes. In short, these four options help you control the debugging environment with greater accuracy.

FIGURE 15.3:

The DirectInput tab provides options for controlling which devices generate debug information.

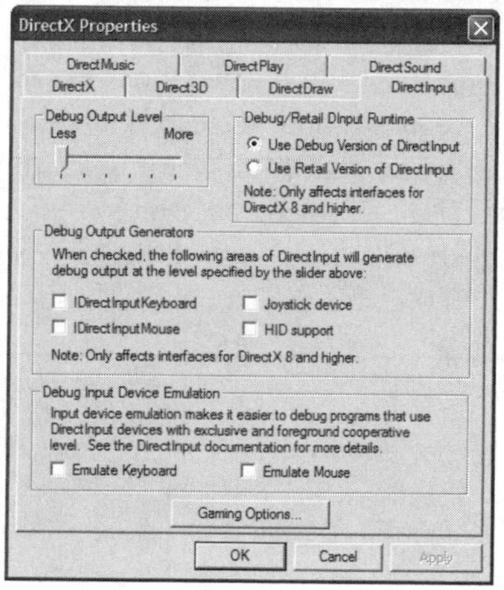

NOTE   The HID Support check box located on the DirectInput tab is for devices that provide this special form of support. Many mouse vendors provide this support and it's normally an option for game controllers. Look in the Human Interface Devices folder of the Device Manager to determine if your system has human interface device (HID) support. Generally, a HID provides additional input about the support it provides and could include special functionality, but you'll normally use it as a standard device in DirectX programming.

DirectX 8.1 also provides the means for emulating the keyboard or mouse. You might wonder why this feature is important at first, only to discover how essential it is when you're attempting to debug the application. The emulation feature helps you keep the application environment separate from the debugging environment. The act of separating the two environments reduces a noticeable delay when stepping through an application in debug mode.

Click Gaming Options and you'll see the Game Controllers dialog box. This dialog box contains settings for adding, removing, and configuring game controllers on your system. The four controller types include joystick, game pad, flight yoke or stick, and racecar controller. You can also choose the number of controller axes and buttons, add support for a point-of-view (POV) control, and include rudders or pedals. If the controller fails to work as anticipated, you can troubleshoot it. There are also options for calibrating the device.

The DirectMusic tab is pretty mundane compared to the other tabs we've discussed so far. It contains the usual Debug Output Level slider and the Debug/Retail options. The main portion of this tab is filled with a list of music ports. However, unlike the Drivers list on the Direct3D tab, this one doesn't provide you with any driver information. In sum, this tab provides quick information and debugging selections but not much else.

The DirectPlay tab shown in Figure 15.4 is unusual in that it doesn't provide a Debug/Retail selection. Notice that this tab does provide a Break on Assert option that controls whether the application debugger will stop when it detects an assert error in the DirectPlay modules. Most developers will keep this option cleared unless the application is failing every time there's a network dialog. In general, you'll want to set the Debug Output Level slider to its maximum level first to see if the problem is found in the debugging messages that the module outputs. Breaking on assert can cause odd problems in the managed environment. In fact, you might find that it leaves the system in an unstable state that requires an eventual reboot.

FIGURE 15.4:

The DirectPlay tab lacks some of the features found on the other tabs.

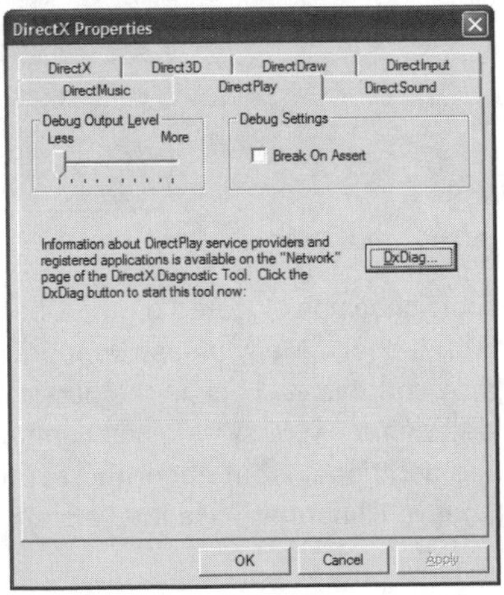

The DirectSound tab also lacks the Debug/Retail option. However, it does contain the Debug Output Level slider. The Media Properties pushbutton displays the standard Sounds and Audio Devices Properties dialog box. The Sound Playback and Sound Recording list boxes contain a list of sound devices you can use for debugging. If you choose a specific device rather than the primary device option, the dialog box will also show the driver module information for the selected sound device.

Using the DMO Test Utility

A DirectX Media Object (DMO) is a COM object that processes data located in a client-supplied buffer. DirectX commonly uses a DMO for special effects. For example, a DMO could add a reverberation effect to sound data. Of course, before a DMO can add reverberation effects to a sound file, it must provide the proper COM support. The DMO Test utility can check a DMO for proper COM operation in both the streaming and API levels. In short, it's a form of ActiveX Control Test Container for DirectX. This tool can check the DMO for correct COM support, but it can't test the DMO for correct operation. In other words, a DMO can provide all of the correct support and still not create a reverberation effect.

Testing a DMO, even one that you haven't created, means creating a test file, selecting some test sources, determining which tests you want to run, and finally running the tests. It sounds like a lot to do, but you can actually perform the task with little effort because many of the tools you need are graphical—just point and click. We actually need the services of another utility to create the test file and select a test source. The first section that follows shows how to create the test file using the GraphEdit utility described in more detail in Chapter 16. After we create a test file, you'll see how to use the DMO Test utility.

Creating a Test File Using GraphEdit

The GraphEdit utility is extremely versatile, and this section shows only one use for this utility. We need to create a test file for the WavesReverb DMO tested in the next section of the chapter. Because this is a sound source, we'll need to begin with a WAV file. The following steps show how to create a suitable test file:

1. Use the File ➢ Render Media File command to open a WAV file. GraphEdit will automatically create a standard rendering sequence similar to the one shown in Figure 15.5. This image shows the sequence that a standard WAV file goes through during the playing process. However, we want to test a DMO, so this sequence won't work for the example. We need to add a DMO filter to the mix.

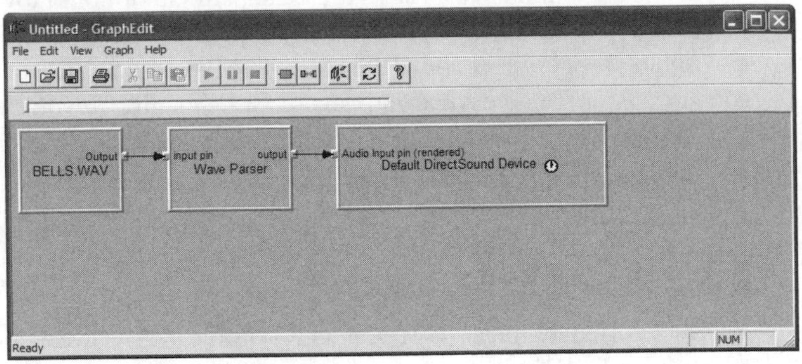

FIGURE 15.5:

GraphEdit begins by creating a standard rendering sequence for your WAV source file.

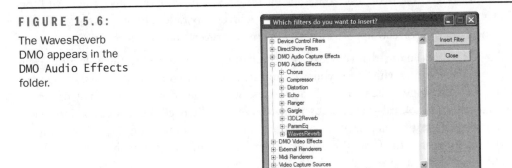

2. Use the Graph ➤ Insert Filters command to display the list of filters available to the GraphEdit utility. Figure 15.6 highlights the DMO filters and focuses on the Waves-Reverb option. This is the DMO we want to test.

FIGURE 15.6:

The WavesReverb DMO appears in the `DMO Audio Effects` folder.

3. Select the WavesReverb option and then click Insert Filter. The filter will appear in the GraphEdit diagram. It isn't connected to anything yet, so you won't notice any difference in the sound if you play it.

4. Select the arrow connecting the Wave Parser to the Default Sound Device object and delete the arrow.

5. Create a connection between the output of the Wave Parser to the input of the Waves-Reverb object. GraphEdit will automatically add an ACM Wrapper object to the series of objects.

6. Create a connection between the output of the WavesReverb object to the Default Sound Device. Click Play. You should hear the reverberated sound. We don't need the Default Sound Device object for the test file, but it's always a good idea to run a test to ensure that you have the right series of objects connected together.

7. Delete the Default Sound Device object. At this point, clicking Play will result in hearing nothing at all. There's no output. We need an output, but not the one originally provided. The DMO utility requires the output of the DMO Data Dump filter.

8. Insert the DMO Data Dump filter using steps 2 and 3. You'll find the DMO Data Dump filter in the `DirectShow Filters` folder. When you insert the DMO Data Dump filer, it will ask for the name of an output file. Type **MyTest** and click Open.

NOTE Windows XP often fails to register the DMO Data Dump filter, so you wont' find it in the `DirectShow Filters` folder. If this happens, open a command window. Locate the `\DXSDK\bin\DXUtils` folder on your system. Type **RegSvr32 DMODump.DLL** and press Enter. You'll see a message that the DLL is properly registered.

9. Connect the DMO Data Dump filter to the WavesReverb output. Your diagram should look like the one shown in Figure 15.7.

FIGURE 15.7:

The final setup for the test source

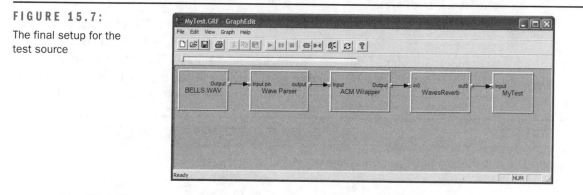

10. Click Play. The file will play and the Play button will highlight again. The test file is complete.

Testing the WavesReverb DMO

It's finally time to perform a test on the WavesReverb DMO. You'll find the test files for this example in the `\Chapter 15\DMOTest` folder of the CD (including the files that we created in the previous section). The example will show how to run all of the available tests. Your DMO test might be more selective or your might create custom tests. The following steps show how to set up the DMO test:

1. Use the Tests ➤ Select Tests command to display the Select Tests dialog box shown in Figure 15.8. This dialog contains the standard set of tests that Microsoft suggests you run on a DMO. You can also use these tests to check the performance of an existing DMO in a new test scenario, such as after installing updated DLLs or new hardware. Of course, there's nothing to stop you from testing multiple DMOs.

2. Click Add All to add all of the standard tests as shown in Figure 15.8. Click OK to close the Select Tests dialog box. At this point, we know which tests will run but haven't selected a test DMO yet.

3. Use the Tests ➤ Choose DMOs command to display the Select DMOs for Test dialog box shown in Figure 15.9. Notice that this dialog box shows the WavesReverb DMO checked. You could test any of the DMOs in this list, but the example will check only the Waves-Reverb DMO. We still need to add the test file for this DMO. If you run the tests without adding at least one test file (you can always add more), at least some of the tests will fail.

4. Right-click the WavesReverb DMO entry and choose Select Test File from the context menu. You'll see a Select Test Files dialog box.

5. Click Add. You'll see an Open a File dialog box.

6. Locate the test file we created using GraphEdit. Highlight the file and click Open. You'll see the file added to the Select Test Files dialog box.

7. Click OK. The Number of Test Files column entry for the WavesReverb DMO will show that you have one test file selected. We're ready to run the selected tests on the Waves-Reverb DMO.

8. Click OK to close the Select DMOs for Test dialog box. Use the Tests ➤ Run All Tests command to begin the testing process. It will take a while for DMO Test to check all of the test conditions. When the test series completes, you should see output similar to that shown in Figure 15.10.

FIGURE 15.10:

The output screen will show whether the DMO passed or failed the tests.

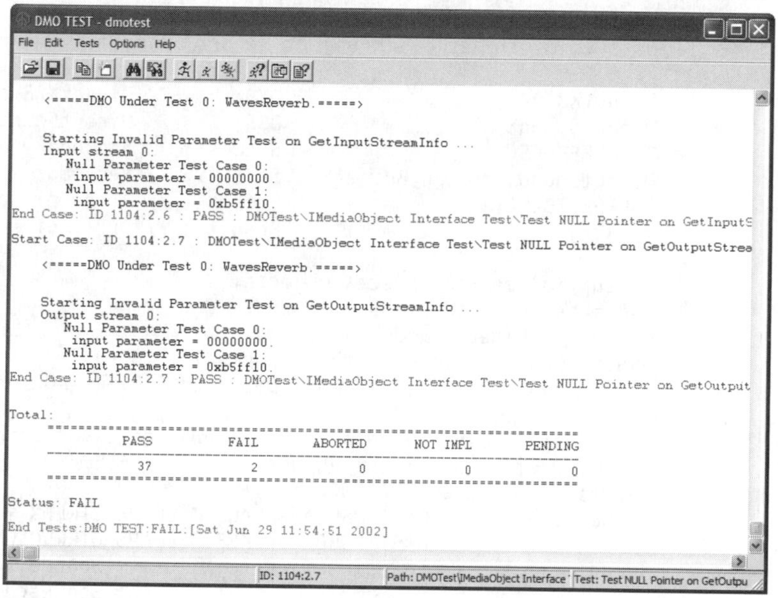

It might disturb you to see that this built-in DMO failed two tests. I ran the same DMO with several input files and it failed on some but not on others. The example file was specifically selected to show a failure condition. When you do test a DMO, it's important to use more than one test file so you can see how the DMO reacts to a variety of media types. In addition, it's important to run the tests more than one time—this DMO doesn't fail with the same data file every time the test is run. The data and environment you choose for testing is just as important as the test scenarios.

NOTE The MyTest.PRO file is a text file that you can easily edit with Notepad. You'll need to edit this file to change the location of the MyTest file used for testing purposes.

A Simple DirectSound Example

We saw in the previous section that DirectSound supports a number of DMOs that can add effects to sound files. In this section, we see how one of those DMOs works in practice. Listing 15.1 shows the code for a basic DirectSound example. You'll find the source for this example in the \Chapter 15\C#\DirectSound and \Chapter 15\VB\DirectSound folders of the CD.

Listing 15.1   **Playing a Sound Using DirectSound**

```
private void btnPlay_Click(object sender, System.EventArgs e)
{
    DirectX8               DX8;      // DirectX 8 object
    DirectSound8           DS8;      // DirectSound 8 object
    DSBUFFERDESC           SecDesc;  // Secondary sound buff desc.
    DirectSoundSecondaryBuffer8  SecBuff;  // Secondary sound buffer.
    DSEFFECTDESC[]         Effects;  // Array of sound effects.
    Int32[]                Results;  // Array of result values.

    // Initialize the DirectX objects.
    DX8 = new DirectX8Class();
    DS8 = DX8.DirectSoundCreate("");
    DS8.SetCooperativeLevel(this.Handle.ToInt32(),
                      CONST_DSSCLFLAGS.DSSCL_NORMAL);

    // Initialize the sound buffer. Allow control of both the
    // sound effects and the volume.
    SecDesc = new DSBUFFERDESC();
    SecDesc.lFlags = CONST_DSBCAPSFLAGS.DSBCAPS_CTRLFX |
                  CONST_DSBCAPSFLAGS.DSBCAPS_CTRLVOLUME;
    SecBuff = DS8.CreateSoundBufferFromFile(@txtSource.Text,
                                     ref SecDesc);

    // Check for special effects.
    if (cbReverb.Checked)
    {
        // Create a special effect.
        Effects = new DSEFFECTDESC[1];
        Effects[0].guidDSFXClass =
            AUDIOCONSTANTS.DSFX_STANDARD_WAVES_REVERB;
        Effects[0].lSize = Marshal.SizeOf(Effects[0]);
        Effects[0].lFlags = 0;
        Results = new Int32[1];

        // Perform a cast on the two arrays.
        Array Effects2 = (Array)Effects;
        Array Results2 = (Array)Results;

        try
        {
```

```
            // Set the special effects.
            SecBuff.SetFX(1, ref Effects2, ref Results2);
        }
        catch (COMException COMErr)
        {
            // Display the error code and exit.
            MessageBox.Show("Error Code: 0x" +
                        COMErr.ErrorCode.ToString("X") +
                        "\r\n" + COMErr.Message,
                        "COM Error",
                        MessageBoxButtons.OK,
                        MessageBoxIcon.Error);
            return;
        }
    }

    // Play the sound.
    if (cbLooping.Checked)
    {
        // Play with looping enabled.
        SecBuff.Play(CONST_DSBPLAYFLAGS.DSBPLAY_DEFAULT |
                    CONST_DSBPLAYFLAGS.DSBPLAY_LOOPING);

        // Display a quit message.
        MessageBox.Show("Click OK to Stop Looping",
                    "Loop Stop Message",
                    MessageBoxButtons.OK,
                    MessageBoxIcon.Information);

        // Stop the sound.
        SecBuff.Stop();
    }
    else
        // Play just once.
        SecBuff.Play(CONST_DSBPLAYFLAGS.DSBPLAY_DEFAULT);

    // Clean up the objects.
    SecBuff = null;
    DS8 = null;
    DX8 = null;
}
```

The code begins by creating the DirectX 8.1 object and associated DirectSound object. You must set the level of cooperation for the DirectSound object using the `SetCooperativeLevel()` method or DirectSound won't play anything at all. In most cases, you want to set the level of cooperation to normal.

Notice that we're using a secondary buffer in this example. The `DirectSoundSecondary-Buffer8` object, *SecBuff*, will act as the conduit for playing sounds. To create a secondary buffer, you need to create a description using the `DSBUFFERDESC` structure. Buffers can also use a number of flags. It's important that you specify the correct flags or the buffer won't work as anticipated. In this case, the code provides flags for both sound effect and volume control. The buffer is actually created by the `CreateSoundBufferFromFile()` method. There are also ways to create the buffer from scratch, to use an alternate sound path, and to use a resource, so you don't have many limitations when using DirectSound.

Adding a sound effect is relatively easy. All you need to do is create a `DSEFFECTDESC` array and an array of `Int32` values. The `DSEFFECTDESC` array holds the GUID for each of the effects that you want to add to a buffer. The `Int32` array contains the result values from adding the sound effects to the buffer. The `SetFX()` method performs the actual addition.

The `SetFX()` method represents the first DirectX problem for the book. The default import specifies a numeric input as the first argument, the effects array, and the results array. There's no override for a situation where you don't want to provide any new effects but want to remove the existing effects. The DirectX SDK documentation specifies that you must provide a value of 0 and two `null` values for the arrays, but this is impossible with the current interoperability layer. There are only two ways around this problem. First, you can create your own interface implementations. Second, you can create a new object each time you want to remove the effects added to an existing object.

The final bit of code shows how to implement looping in the example. When you add looping to a sound, it continues to play over and over again until stopped. The example shows a quick method for starting and stopping the sound. Of course, you can also play the sound once and exit the application.

Notice that the example ends by cleaning up the objects. Make sure you always clean up your DirectX objects. In this case, you must clean them up in the opposite order of creation. Otherwise, you'll see an error message as the application exits.

Using the Force Feedback Editor

Most input devices do just what their name implies—they provide an application with some type of user input. The user experience is one of sitting in place playing a game. However, as computer graphics and sounds have helped gamers become more immersed in their games, some vendors thought it would be a good idea to add some sense of feel to the input device. After all, a pilot actually feels the effect of the air rushing against the skin of the plane and the engine pulsing with power. That's the reasoning behind force feedback—it provides a joystick with instructions that enable it to simulate the feel of the yoke on a real plane. The user experience becomes more realistic because now sights, sounds, and even sensations that are modeled after the real-world experience (or someone's interpretation of that experience) surround the user.

The Force Feedback Editor creates standard resource interchange file format (RIFF) files that contain instructions to create a feel within a joystick, yoke, gamepad, or other input device designed to provide tactile output. You can start the application and even create files with it even if you don't have a force feedback device attached to the system. However, if you want to test the files, you'll need an input device with force feedback capability. Generally, it's better if you use the same type of device that the game user will employ to play the game because different devices will react differently to the force feedback instructions. The sensation of touch is also highly subjective, which means you should have several developers test the file. Figure 15.11 shows the initial Force Feedback Editor window.

FIGURE 15.11:

The Force Feedback Editor helps you create tactile feedback for users of your application.

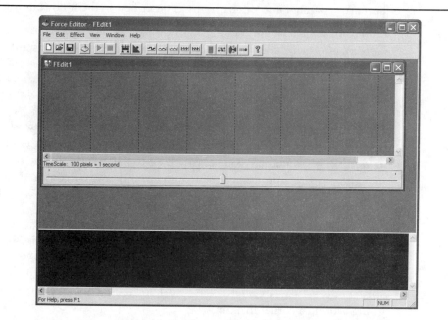

NOTE This section isn't implying that the only use of force feedback is game design, but that's the most common way that force feedback is used today. Force feedback is also useful in any simulation. For example, a driving school simulator could employ force feedback within the car steering wheel to reproduce the effects of the road. In some cases, force feedback would be useful (and was even used before it appeared on personal computers), but these simulations rely on complex and proprietary machines. For example, pilots commonly train in simulators that offer a variety of tactile feedback. It's unlikely that these huge training systems will be replaced with a personal computer any time soon. Consequently, the main focus of force feedback development today is the game.

You can create force feedback files of almost any length using the Force Feedback Editor. The application begins by showing you about 10 seconds worth of force feedback. Some sequences, such as machine gun fire, might require less time, while others, such as a flight sequence, might require more. In general, tactile feedback sequences are repeated throughout the application as needed. In some cases, such as road effects for a car, the same sequence is repeated over and over again. You can control the time interval displayed on screen by changing the position of the Time Scale slider at the bottom of the display.

The application provides the full list of effects, all of which are accessible from the Force Feedback Editor toolbar. You can also select an effect from the Effect ➤ Insert menu. The effects are separated into three groups as described in the following list:

General   A general effect is one that normally applies over the range of the effect sequence. General effects include constant force and ramped effects. A constant force effect changes the amount of force required to perform a task and maintains that level of force throughout the effect. A ramp effect either starts at a high level and decreases or starts at a low level and increases.

Wave   Wave effects are short and choppy. Imagine a bumpy road for a driving simulation or the effect of machine gun fire. The effect of each wave effect is a tad difficult to describe in words—it's something you actually have to feel. Wave effects come in several varieties, including square, sine, triangle, sawtooth up, and sawtooth down. The sine wave effect tends to be rolling, while the square wave is bumpy and the triangle wave is sharp. Of course, your perception will likely vary from mine.

Condition   Some tactile feedback falls into well-known sensations based on the user's interaction with their environment. For example, most people know the feeling of bouncing up and down on something like a trampoline quite well from childhood. This is the spring effect. Likewise, inertia has well-known effects. For example, you feel inertia when going around a corner in a car.

Let's look at this tool in more practical terms. Say you wanted to create an effect that felt like a car going around a corner a little too quickly. Figure 15.12 shows that you might combine a triangle effect, an inertia effect, and two ramps. You'll find this example in the \Chapter 15\ ForceFeedback folder of the CD.

As you can see, each effect is placed within a particular time sequence. You can move the effects around and change their length. Of course, this only defines when the effect will happen and how long it will happen. True tactile feedback requires more input than time and duration, and this input is often of a complex nature.

Creating an effect
sequence means
combining different
effects over time.

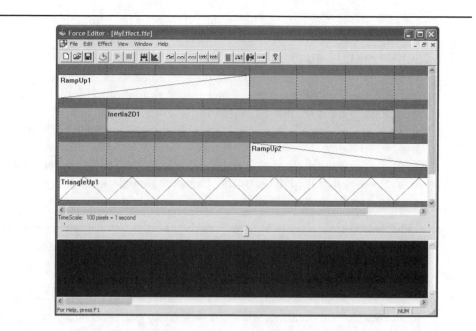

Each effect also comes with a set of properties you can adjust. We're not going to visit every effect and its associated properties—that's a topic for another book. However, we can look at one effect. Right-click RampUp1 and choose Properties from the context menu. Figure 15.13 shows the tabs for this effect. You might be surprised at just how many things you can change about a simple ramp, but they all make a difference in how the effect feels to the end user.

Even simple ramp
effects have several
properties that
modify the tactile
feedback the user
receives.

The Ramp tab controls how the effect varies over time. In this case, we're telling the ramp effect to begin at a low level and then increase to the maximum effect level over time. The envelope varies the manner in which the effect changes. The ramp begins as a straight line, but you can modify the effect so it uses a logarithmic, sine, or other envelope. The Axes tab determines which axes of the input device are affected by the ramp. The Timing tab tells how long the effect lasts and determines if there's a delay in starting it. Finally, the General tab contains a field for changing the name of the effect on screen. As you can see, there are many ways to change what the user feels even within a single effect.

This section hasn't really explored the Force Feedback Editor completely, but you should have a better idea of how it can change the user's application experience. As mentioned earlier, even though force feedback is currently the domain of game players, it does have many practical applications outside that arena. Given the rate of computer hardware development, it may not be too long before all kinds of input devices employ some form of tactile feedback. For example, imagine a garment design application where the designer could actually feel the fabric as they designed the garment. The same thought holds true for many other scientific, engineering, and art applications.

DirectX, the Managed Environment, and Performance

The question of DirectX compatibility and availability has consumed more than a few message threads in the various Microsoft newsgroups. The DirectX API is substantial, and Microsoft designed it long before the managed environment was even a concept, much less an implementation as it is today. Anything this complex and designed so far outside of the conventions of the managed environment is bound to cause some level of concern and controversy.

As you've learned throughout the three DirectX chapters so far, the support you can expect to receive from the DirectX COM interface is less than complete. We had to create the `DirectXHelper.DLL` to overcome certain problems with DirectX COM support. What you might not know is that parts of the DirectX COM support were added for Visual Basic developers and never fully integrated into DirectX. For example, the initial DirectX libraries created an object using standard function calls—not a special call that's part of the DirectX interfaces. Using DirectX as we have means adding a kludge to a kludge—a poor idea at best.

We've gotten around most of the problems in using DirectX in the managed environment. You've seen a number of example applications that use DirectX, and you'll see more as the book runs to completion. However, there's a question of performance to answer. Adding a kludge to a kludge can make a platform unstable. You might run across problems we haven't discussed in this chapter because of the way that DirectX is put together. However, adding even one kludge to a system will result in a performance hit. Adding multiple kludges together to create a coherent system makes the performance problem even worse.

The jury is still out on just how bad the performance problems are when using DirectX in a managed environment. A few hard-core developers are saying that DirectX is completely unworkable in the managed environment, but you've already seen that that viewpoint is a little extreme. However, it's very likely that complex applications might prove too much for the managed environment until DirectX 9 appears on the scene. Even a moderately complex application will suffer some level of performance degradation.

Continued on next page

The real issue is one of deciding whether the developer productivity and other gains offered by the managed environment outweigh the performance and reliability concerns of using DirectX 7 or DirectX 8.1 in the managed environment. For a simple application, the answer is relatively easy—use the managed because it has too much to offer to ignore. When working with a moderately complex application, the answer might be harder to come by, but most developers will probably choose the managed environment when performance isn't the main issue. Complex applications will probably require old techniques and the unmanaged environment for right now, but be prepared to switch when DirectX 9 appears.

A Simple DirectInput Example

DirectInput works with a number of devices. However, one element is true for all of them. Generally, you'll want to know the device's current status. The example application for this section deals in part with that scenario. However, before you can work with the device, you need to know that it exists. The code shown in Listing 15.2 shows how to collect the Direct-Input device information for your system. It also contains some of the initialization code for this example. You'll find the source code for this example in the \Chapter 15\C#\DirectInput and \Chapter 15\VB\DirectInput folders of the CD.

Listing 15.2 **Enumerating the DirectInput Devices**

```
private DirectX8      DX8;    // DirectX 8 object
private DirectInput8 DI8;     // DirectInput 8 object

public frmMain()
{
   // Required for Windows Form Designer support
   InitializeComponent();

   DirectInputEnumDevices8   Devs;    // DirectInput enumeration.
   DirectInputDeviceInstance8 DevInst; // A single device instance.
   StringBuilder             Output;  // The output string.

   // Initialize the DirectX objects.
   DX8 = new DirectX8Class();
   DI8 = DX8.DirectInputCreate();

   // Display a list of DirectInput 8 devices.
   // Create a list of devices for this machine.
   Devs = DI8.GetDIDevices(CONST_DI8DEVICETYPE.DI8DEVCLASS_ALL,
      CONST_DIENUMDEVICESFLAGS.DIEDFL_ATTACHEDONLY);

   // Display the device list. Remember to start the
   // Counter at 1 for VB.
```

```
Output = new StringBuilder();
for (int Counter = 1; Counter <= Devs.GetCount(); Counter++)
{
   // Get a device instance.
   DevInst = Devs.GetItem(Counter);

   // Addend the device information.
   Output.Append(DevInst.GetProductName());
   Output.Append("\r\n" + DevInst.GetInstanceName());
   Output.Append("\r\n" + DevInst.GetDevType());
   Output.Append("\r\n" + DevInst.GetGuidInstance());
   Output.Append("\r\n" + DevInst.GetGuidProduct());
   Output.Append("\r\n" + DevInst.GetGuidFFDriver());
   Output.Append("\r\n\r\n");
}

txtDevices.Text = Output.ToString();
}
```

As you can see from the code, the example begins by creating the appropriate DirectX objects. The code then creates a device enumeration using the GetDIDevices() method. The flags you supply for this method determine the type of output you receive. Normally, it pays to select the smallest subset of information possible so that you only have to search through a limited number of devices. In this case, the example limits the output to the attached devices.

NOTE   Notice that the code in Listing 15.2 contains an odd setup for the for loop. You must initialize *Counter* to 1 because that's what Visual Basic 6 would use. This is a common problem when working with DirectX. The error message you receive when this problem occurs won't match the error seen in Visual Basic 6 because it's an interoperability problem now. If you see the infamous "The parameter is incorrect" error message, this is one place to look.

After the code creates a device enumeration, it creates an instance of each device using the GetItem() method in a loop. Remember that DirectX is unmanaged, so it doesn't support enumerators. As you can see from the source listing, the device instance data includes information such as the device name, its instance name, a type, and the GUIDs used to identify the device. Figure 15.14 shows the initial screen with the device enumeration for my system.

Now that you know how to enumerate the devices, it's time to do something with them. Listing 15.3 shows the method used to list the mouse status. The keyboard status information is gathered in the same way, so the listing doesn't show this code.

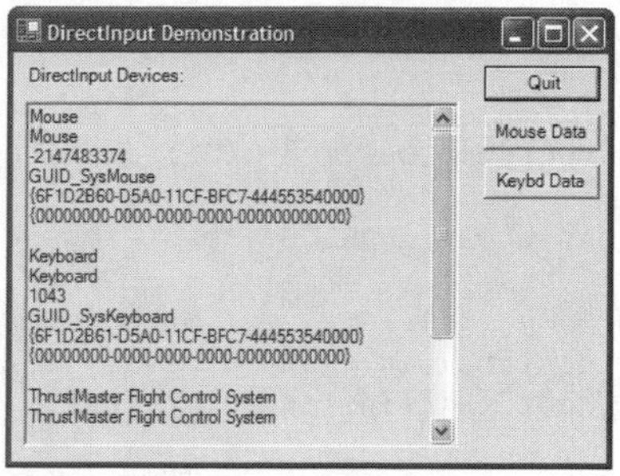

FIGURE 15.14:

A typical device
enumeration

FIGURE 15.14:

A typical device
enumeration

Listing 15.3   Displaying the Mouse Status

```csharp
private void btnMouseData_Click(object sender, System.EventArgs e)
{
    DIMOUSESTATE2  State;   // DirectInput device state.

    // Make sure the DirectInput 8 Device is empty.
    if (DID8 != null)
        DID8 = null;

    // Get the device information.
    CreateInputDevice("Mouse");

    // Get and display the device data.
    State = new DIMOUSESTATE2();
    try
    {
        DID8.GetDeviceStateMouse2(ref State);
    }
    catch (FileNotFoundException FNFE)
    {
        MessageBox.Show("Message: " + FNFE.Message +
                        "\r\nSource: " + FNFE.Source +
                        "\r\nTarget Site: " + FNFE.TargetSite +
                        "\r\nStack Trace: " + FNFE.StackTrace,
                        "Application Error",
                        MessageBoxButtons.OK,
                        MessageBoxIcon.Error);
        return;
    }

    // Display the status information.
    MessageBox.Show("Buttons: " + State.Buttons.ToString() +
                    "X Axis: " + State.lX.ToString() +
                    "\r\nY Axis: " + State.lY.ToString() +
                    "\r\nZ Axis (Wheel): " + State.lZ.ToString(),
                    "Mouse Information",
```

```csharp
                    MessageBoxButtons.OK,
                    MessageBoxIcon.Information);
}

private DirectInputDevice8 DID8; // DirectInput 8 device

private void CreateInputDevice(String DeviceName)
{
    String                   StrGuid; // String version of GUID.
    DirectInputEnumDevices8     Devs;    // DirectInput enumeration.
    DirectInputDeviceInstance8 DevInst; // A single device instance.

    // Create a list of devices for this machine.
    Devs = DI8.GetDIDevices(CONST_DI8DEVICETYPE.DI8DEVCLASS_ALL,
        CONST_DIENUMDEVICESFLAGS.DIEDFL_ATTACHEDONLY);

    // Search for the correct GUID. Remember to start the
    // Counter at 1 for VB.
    StrGuid = "";
    for (int Counter = 1; Counter <= Devs.GetCount(); Counter++)
    {
        // Get a device instance.
        DevInst = Devs.GetItem(Counter);

        if (DevInst.GetProductName().ToUpper() == DeviceName.ToUpper())
        {
            StrGuid = DevInst.GetGuidInstance();
            break;
        }
    }

    // Verify we've found a GUID.
    if (StrGuid == "")
    {
        MessageBox.Show("Device Not Found",
                        "Application Error",
                        MessageBoxButtons.OK,
                        MessageBoxIcon.Error);
        return;
    }

    // Create the DirectInputDevice.
    DID8 = DI8.CreateDevice(StrGuid);
    DID8.SetCooperativeLevel(this.Handle.ToInt32(),
                            CONST_DISCLFLAGS.DISCL_NONEXCLUSIVE |
                            CONST_DISCLFLAGS.DISCL_BACKGROUND);

}
```

As you can see, determining the device status is a two-step process. The first step is to obtain the device-independent information. The `CreateInputDevice()` method performs this task. The code passes this function a string that describes the device, and the function creates a `DirectInputDevice8` object for it. The second step is to fill a device-specific data structure with information about the device.

The `btnMouseData_Click()` method begins by calling the `CreateInputDevice()` method with a "Mouse" string. When the `CreateInputDevice()` method returns, the `btnMouseData_Click()` method can use the `GetDeviceStateMouse2()` method to fill the `DIMOUSESTATE2` data structure, *State*, with mouse-specific information. You must place the call to `GetDeviceState-Mouse2()` in a `try...catch` statement because this method call can fail for a number of reasons. The code ends by displaying the current mouse data.

When you look at the `CreateInputDevice()` method code, you'll notice that it begins with an enumeration similar to the one we used earlier. In this case, the code looks for a specific string within the enumeration. When the code finds this string, it places the associated instance GUID into *StrGuid* using the `GetGuidInstance()` method. The GUID you use is important because it determines which device DirectInput will create for you.

The `CreateDevice()` method creates the `DirectInputDevice8` object. You must set the cooperative level to one of the recognized combinations before doing anything else with the object. The best combination for determining the device status is `CONST_DISCLFLAGS.DISCL_NONEXCLUSIVE` or-ed with `CONST_DISCLFLAGS.DISCL_BACKGROUND`.

Using the DirectX Texture Tool

If a development team were to create every aspect of the art that goes into many applications today, it would take substantially longer to create them. The race to create a better way to draw computer images began almost as soon as there were computers that could display graphical data. The earliest computers came with nothing more than ways to position a cursor and draw a dot. The next generation of computers came with a set of functions that created graphics primitives that a developer could use to speed the drawing of common graphic elements. These graphics primitives improved over the years, and we have substantial drawing libraries today. The ability to create textures to place within areas of an image represents a new twist to an ongoing struggle. The DirectX Texture Tool is a utility that helps the developer create textures to use in drawings.

This isn't a drawing tool. You need to create the texture as a separate file. The DirectX Texture Tool prepares the drawing you create for use as a texture. A texture map uses the DXT compression format. The blit functions provided with DirectX can also create these texture maps, but it's often easier to create them in advance.

When you initially start the DirectX Texture Tool, you'll see a blank display. Click the New Texture button and you'll see the New Texture dialog box shown in Figure 15.15.

The DirectX Texture Tool defines images by texture type, size, and color depth.

As you can see, there are several settings that you must make before you can create a texture map. The first setting is the type of texture map you want to create. The following list tells you about the options:

Standard Texture   A standard texture is one in which there's one texture and possibly one alpha (opacity) file.

Cubemap Texture   The cubemap texture consists of multiple textures, each of which is placed on specific axes of the texture map.

Volume Texture   The volume texture uses 3D collections of pixels (known as texels) to paint 2D representations of 3D objects such as cones and spheres.

The Dimensions group includes the width and height of the texture map. The width and height normally matches the width and height of the images you want to use. The MipMap Levels field determines the number of levels of texture maps within the file. Each level uses a lower resolution than the one before it. This helps in situations where the user display might not support the desired resolution, the image is in the distance (and therefore doesn't require high resolution), or the designer is trying to create a special effect. The Volume Depth setting is only used with volume texture maps. This value represents the z-axis of the texel.

The Surface/Volume Format options determine the color depth of your texture map, including the alpha (opacity) value. These settings are based on the number of bits used for each color setting. An 8×8×8 setting uses 32-bit color. Notice that there are some settings that don't include the alpha setting and others that are based on standard texture compression formats.

Once you decide on a format for your texture map, you'll need to import the graphic. This task is relatively easy when working with a standard texture. All you need to do is use the File ➢ Open Onto This Surface command to display the Open dialog box. Select the texture you want to import (any DDS, BMP, JPG, TGA, PNG, or DIB file) and then click Open.

If you're working with other formats, you'll need to make some selections first. For example, when working with a cube texture, you need to select the cube face using the options on the View ➢ Cube Map Face menu. After you select the cube face, add an image to it using the File ➢ Open Onto This Surface command. Likewise, if you chose to include several mipmap levels in your texture map, you'll need to use the View ➢ Smaller Mip Level or the View ➢ Larger Mip Level command to choose the correct mipmap level before you import the image.

Remember that this is a data conversion tool, so there isn't much in the way of special features. You can zoom in and out by using the plus and minus keys. The Page Up and Page Down keys help you select a mipmap level. The Format menu has most of the tools on it. Look at this menu and you'll see that you can convert a standard texture map into either a cube or volume texture map. The program will also create additional mipmap levels for you based on the content of the current image. Finally, you can change the surface format if you've made a mistake. When you complete the data conversion tasks for the texture map, save it to disk using the File ➢ Save command. (You'll find a sample texture and texture map file in the `\Chapter 15\TextureTool` folder of the CD.)

Where Do You Go from Here?

This chapter has told you several new things about DirectX. You now know the major differences between DirectX 7 and DirectX 8.1. The chapter has also shown you how to use several more of the assortment of tools that the DirectX SDK provides. Finally, we've discussed some of the problems you'll experience using DirectX in the managed environment through several application programs. While this chapter hasn't made you a DirectX expert, you do know enough to create simple programs in the managed environment, which is something that many developers have discussed on Microsoft's .NET newsgroups.

The problem now is figuring out where to go from here. You have the basics of working with DirectX in a managed environment, but you don't know some of the advanced techniques. Now that you know the pitfalls of working in the managed environment, it's time to look at online resources, newsgroups, and other books to learn more. This chapter's focus is getting you started, but you actually have a long way to go before you can develop applications that rely on DirectX with any level of proficiency. Use this opportunity to experiment—you might find that DirectX actually works better in the managed environment than it does in its native unmanaged environment.

We've explored several utility programs in this chapter. However, it's important to become proficient in their use if you want to create truly usable DirectX applications. To do this, try using them for some other sample tasks. For example, you may want to check the other DMOs. Testing other DMOs will help you learn both DMO Test and GraphEdit because other DMOs will require other types of test files.

To help you along with the goal of building proficiency with DirectX in the managed environment, Chapter 16 is going to look at some more advanced examples. You still won't be able to create the graphics for the next animated movie that Hollywood produces, but this chapter will take you one step closer to realizing your objective of developing great applications in DirectX. We'll also look at a few more of the utilities provided with the DirectX SDK. These tools, like the examples, are a little more advanced, so they'll fit right in with our other goals.

CHAPTER 16

Extended DirectX Programming Examples

- Using the GraphEdit Utility

- Using the DirectPlay Network Simulator

- Using the MeshView Tool

- Using a Mesh Example

We've spent a lot of time looking at what DirectX can do and how to make it perform tasks within the managed environment. This chapter helps you put together all of the skills you've learned so far to create more complex applications. We'll also begin using some of the extended features that DirectX can provide.

The chapter will combine tools with examples. There are three tools that we'll explore: the GraphEdit utility, DirectPlay Network Simulator, and the MeshView Tool. You'll learn about each tool first and then see an example of how to use it with your code. This is perhaps the best way to demonstrate the extended capabilities of DirectX 8.1.

NOTE   As with the other DirectX chapters in this book, the goal of this chapter is to help you understand the extended features that DirectX provides for use within the managed environment. Our discussion of the tools will provide you with an overview of their capabilities—there's still more to learn about them. The examples aren't meant to make you a DirectX programming wizard, nor are they meant to show you every feature of DirectX—that would require another book. The examples will help you understand how DirectX fits within the managed environment and alerts you to any oddities that you might encounter making the various interfaces work.

Using the GraphEdit Utility

Working with media is a process—learning to work with media is not something that happens all at once or even as part of a short procedure. The GraphEdit utility helps you match data sources, data parsers, filters, and outputs. We discussed one use for the GraphEdit utility in the creation of test files in the section titled "Creating a Test File Using GraphEdit" in Chapter 15. In that case, we created a special sequence of a WAV file, a wave parser, the reverberation filter, and a special output device for creating test files. That's just one of a myriad of uses for the GraphEdit utility.

In the following sections, we'll look at the GraphEdit utility in some detail because it's one of the more important tools in the DirectX SDK. Not only can you use it in standalone mode, you can use it with other applications (as we already have in Chapter 15). In addition, we'll discuss some of the special features of this product and how you'd combine them to gain access to some types of media functionality. Of course, in the interim, we'll discuss the main purpose of this tool—a means for testing various object combinations before you place them in your code. You'll find the sample files used in this section in the \Chapter 16\GraphEdit folder of the CD.

Creating a Connection

The process of building a file with the GraphEdit utility is called rendering. That's why you don't open a WAV file; you render it using the File ➤ Render Media File command. Of course, if the data source you want to use is on the Internet, you can always use the File ➤ Render URL command. Unlike rendering a local file, however, rendering a file on the Internet means waiting for it to download and knowing the precise URL (there's no browse function).

Another way to render a media file is to connect to it remotely. You add a Running Object Table (ROT) entry to your application for the filter that you want to monitor. Run the application. Use the File ➤ Connect to Remote Graph option to create a connection between the GraphEdit utility and your application. The GraphEdit utility now becomes part modeling tool, part monitor, and part debugger. Unfortunately, this option doesn't work with Microsoft's Media Player because it doesn't include the requisite ROT entry for performance reasons (keeping the ROT entry out tends to make the application slightly more secure, as well, because a third party can't monitor what's going on inside).

The GraphEdit utility also points to two potential problems for managed environment developers. The first is that you're reliant on unmanaged code to create the connection in the first place. We've already dealt with the problem for a significant portion of the book, so I won't discuss the ramifications again here. The second problem, creating a ROT entry, is the one that you do need to address from a fresh perspective.

Creating a ROT entry means calling a Win32 API function, so you'll need to use PInvoke and COM interoperability as a minimum to get around the problem. It turns out that ROT functionality actually appears in the Win32 API as the `IRunningObjectTable` interface. You need to use the `Register()` method to add your application to the list. To verify that your application actually made it to the ROT table, you need to check for it using the IROTVIEW Windows Application located in the `\Program Files\Microsoft Visual Studio .NET\Common7\Tools\Bin` folder of your hard drive. Figure 16.1 shows the output of this application. Note that most applications are listed by their GUID, not by a human-readable name. You can modify this behavior by providing a moniker as one of the `Register()` method parameters.

However, in this case, many developers who've tried to work with DirectX in the managed environment say that writing a wrapper DLL is your best choice because it gets around several DirectX problems as well. As we've seen in past chapters, some areas of DirectX simply don't behave well even if you rely on the COM interoperability features for Visual Studio .NET. In short, if you need to use the GraphEdit utility to monitor or debug your application through a remote connection that relies on a ROT entry, try using a wrapper DLL to perform the task.

FIGURE 16.1:

Use the IROTVIEW Windows Application to verify that your application is properly registered.

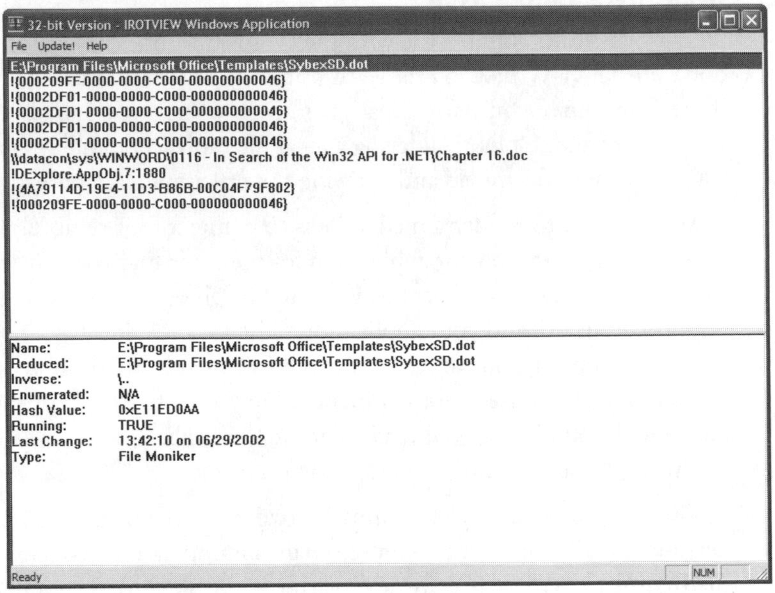

Working with Multiple Streams

Media works with the concept of streams. Some files, such as WAV files, include just one stream, so viewing them is straightforward—as we saw in Chapter 15. Other types of media include multiple streams. For example, a movie file will contain a minimum of two media streams: one for video and a second for audio, as shown in Figure 16.2. The file will contain two output connectors, and each stream follows a course to a combined or a separate output device. In the case of a movie file with two streams, the output devices are obviously separate.

FIGURE 16.2:

Many media files contain two or more data streams, each of which requires separate processing.

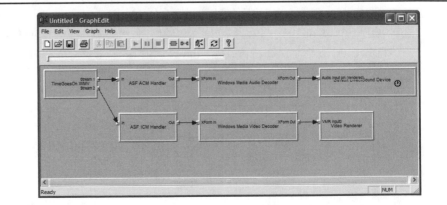

If you compare this figure with a typical WAV file rendering such as the one shown in Figure 16.3, you'll notice an interesting difference. The WAV file requires a single decompression (parsing) step, while the multiple stream ASF (movie) file requires two steps. In fact, multiple stream files can require more than two processing steps per stream in order to separate and decompress the data.

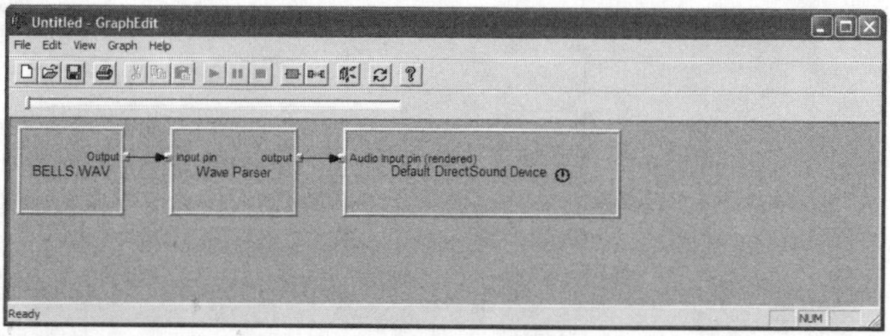

FIGURE 16.3:

Single-stream WAV files require less processing than multiple-stream ASF files.

The splitting of the multiple data streams requires some management functionality in the form of an Audio Compression Manager (ACM) and an Image Color Manager (ICM). The managers do more than sort through the information looking for the right type of data; they also help regulate data flow and manage data synchronization.

Each of these managers feeds its output into some type of data parser. The parser could have any of a number of names, depending on vendor whims and the actual functionality included within the parser. Both of the streams in Figure 16.4 rely on decoders from the Windows Media Player. However, the player doesn't necessarily support older formats.

Figure 16.4 shows a file in an older format. Notice that the same two managers separate and synchronize the data streams. However, in this case, the video stream is parsed using the Microsoft MPEG-4 Video Decompressor, which is an older technology employed by previous versions of Windows. The point is that we've now looked at two ways of rendering the video stream and there are still other methods. The filters you choose to render a video stream modify the way the system interprets it and finally presents it to the end user.

What are the lessons learned for the managed environment from this section? The first, and most important, lesson is that you can run into situations in which a managed adaptation will work fine with one file type but not another. The unmanaged environment has an advantage in easier access to filters. Managed applications will need to control the file types selected by users with greater care and ensure that the selected filters will actually work from the managed environment. If you need to access a large number of file types, it might be easier to write a wrapper DLL to perform many (if not most) processing tasks.

The second lesson is that the performance issues that plague managed applications when working with a single stream will become progressively worse when working with multiple streams. Not only do you have more filters to consider, but there are also multiple streams of data to manage. Many developers who've tried to work with multiple-stream files have noted synchronization problems between the data streams. It's difficult to muster the processing power required to keep all of the data streams in synchronization because of the number of layers the data must traverse.

FIGURE 16.4:

Data management is separate from data parsing in all multimedia files.

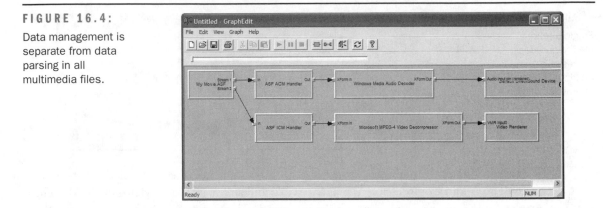

Working with Filters

We saw in Chapter 15 that you can add filters to a data stream to modify the output in some way. In that chapter, we added a reverberation filter to an audio stream in order to test the filter using the DMO Test utility. However, that chapter focused on the filter as a black box, and there really is more to filters than that. Generally, you'll find that filters not only add some type of functionality to data stream processing, they also add some level of control to the effect that the filter produces. In some cases, the control added by the filter is actually more than the associated Windows controls would lead you to believe.

> **TIP**
> Microsoft provides a lot of information about working with CODECs and filters—most of it incomprehensible unless you already know something about them. Fortunately, there's a basic article entitled "CODECs 101 for Microsoft Windows Media Technologies" that tells about working with these low-level components. You can find this article at `http://msdn` `.microsoft.com/library/default.asp?url=/library/en-us/dnwmt/html/codecs` `.asp`. This article explains the essentials of CODECs, tells about the codecs provided with Windows and DirectX, and includes limited usage information.

Look again at the processing stream presented in Figure 16.2. Each of the blocks in that diagram is a filter, and every filter has settings that you can control. For example, consider the Windows Media Audio Decoder filter. Figure 16.5 shows that this filter includes an equalizer that you can use to polish the sound. Of course, GraphEdit helps you judge the result of changes to the filter properties used to modify a data stream by playing the new configuration immediately. This interactive filtering experience helps a developer create applications with better sound, even if the original sound source is found lacking.

FIGURE 16.5:

The Windows Media Audio Decoder filter can help you polish the sound output of an audio stream.

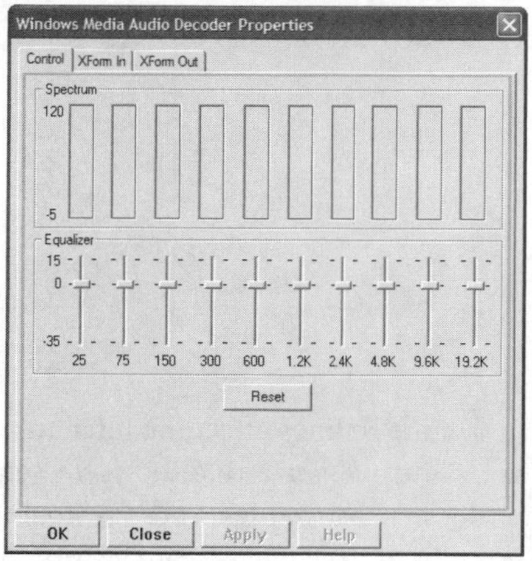

Notice that this dialog box also provides you with information about the input to and output from the filter on separate tabs. In most cases, these tabs don't contain any configurable settings, but they do contain information about the connection. The connection information can be extremely helpful to developers attempting to re-create a series of connections programmatically. For the managed developer, the information can also prove helpful in troubleshooting connections. As we've seen in several sections of the DirectX portion of this book, working with DirectX in the managed environment is hardly straightforward because of the changes required to make DirectX work.

TIP

The GraphEdit toolbar includes several filter-oriented buttons to speed your use of the application. The Insert Filters button displays the Which Filters Do You Want to Insert dialog box. Use the entries in this dialog box to add new filters to the display. The Disconnect All Pins button removes the connections between all of the filters. This option makes it easier to add new filters to the display and then create the required connections later. Finally, the Refresh button repaints all of the filters on the display. This feature helps ensure that any changes you make to the filter settings actually appear on the display.

A data stream is stored in files, manipulated by filters, and then output to a device for presentation. Without an output device, there's no reason to perform any other part of the data manipulation. The final filter in a data stream is less of a presentation of the device's capabilities than it is a view of how the data stream sees the device. In addition, some device filters include data stream–specific adjustments, as shown in Figure 16.6.

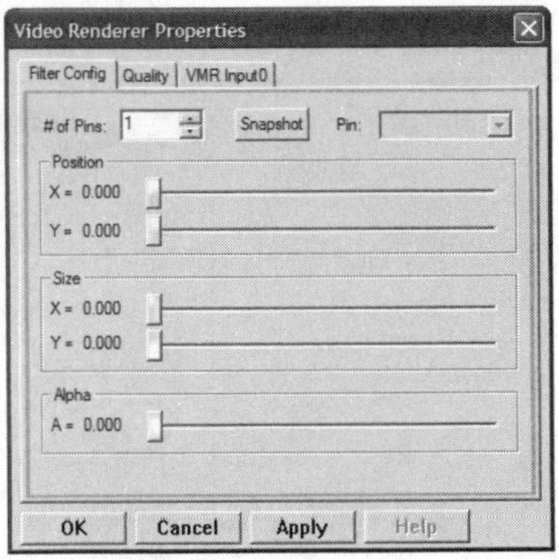

FIGURE 16.6:
Device filters view the device from the data stream perspective.

As you can see, the settings affect the filter, not the device itself. The device settings are still under user control. Figure 16.6 shows the settings in their default state, which means that the filter doesn't change these settings from the user configuration. The other tabs in this dialog box describe the data stream view of the device. However, many of the statistics aren't available until after you play the data stream. For example, the entries on the Quality tab remain at 0 until DirectX has determined the actual quality achieved using this data stream. Quality can't be judged until the data stream is played because each set of filters affects performance in a different way. This leads us to the discussion found in the next section—performance tuning.

Performance Tuning

The GraphEdit utility can do more than simply help you select and configure filters (along with creating debugging information for them). It can also help you consider the performance aspects of your application—an important consideration in a managed environment where every performance setting is important. For example, consider the TimeGoesOn.WMV file filter shown in Figure 16.2. You might not think that a simple file filter could contain much of interest for performance tuning, but it does. Figure 16.7 shows that this filter contains a buffer setting. Using a higher setting ensures that playback runs smoothly, but at the cost of memory. You need to consider the cost of the memory against the performance benefit. In some cases, the tuning process might involve checking performance on several machine categories to ensure that the buffer size is optimal.

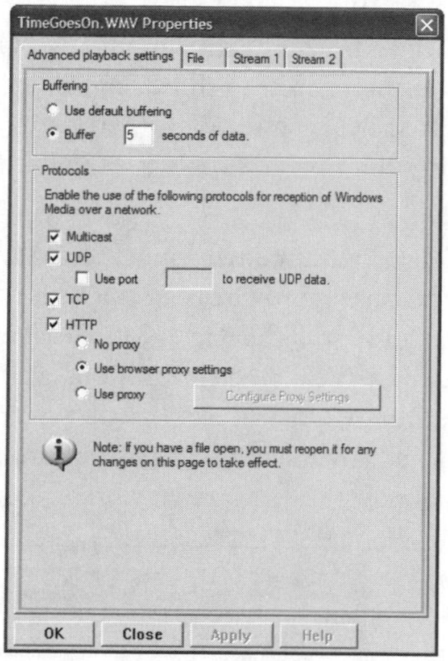

FIGURE 16.7:

Even a file filter has settings that you can use to tune the performance of a data stream.

Sometimes a performance tuning opportunity isn't obvious. Look again at Figure 16.7 and you'll notice that it includes the option to select protocols for the file. Each of these protocols requires memory and also uses some number of processing cycles. If you remove unneeded protocols from the list, you can free memory for use in buffers as well as a few processing cycles. This small change could make the difference between a file that plays smoothly and one that has the jitters.

GraphEdit helps you measure the effects of performance tuning in several ways. The most important method is using your own ears and eyes. You can usually see or hear the same differences that the user will see or hear. However, sometimes a change is more difficult to quantify, and that's when you need a second GraphEdit feature.

Each of the filters in a data stream can include performance data. In fact, the output filter usually does include performance data. This performance data can help you determine if a particular change is worthwhile. For example, you might want to improve the frame rate for a video data stream. Checking the Quality tab of the output filter will normally tell you if a performance change in a downstream filter improves the frame rate. You can also check for issues such as the error rate experienced by the output filter. In some cases, these statistics point out flaws in an otherwise good setup.

Saving the Result

One way to save your GraphEdit design is as a GRF file. In fact, you'll find GRF files for the two examples in this chapter in the \Chapter 16\GraphEdit folder of the CD. However, for developers of managed applications, there's a more exciting alternative in the form of XML output. To select this option, simply use the File ➤ Save as XML option instead of the normal File ➤ Save option.

The .NET development environment actually provides a significant advantage when using XML output because it provides extremely good XML data handling. Figure 16.8 shows an XML Notepad view of the data. Notice that every filter appears in the list, along with every connection used by the filters. In addition, every setting you make within the filters is also stored within the XML hierarchy. In other words, GraphEdit becomes a significant time-saver for managed environment developers who need to access DirectX without a lot of trial and error. You know the data stream works because you've already tested it.

FIGURE 16.8:

XML Notepad shows that you can save all of your GraphEdit data in XML format.

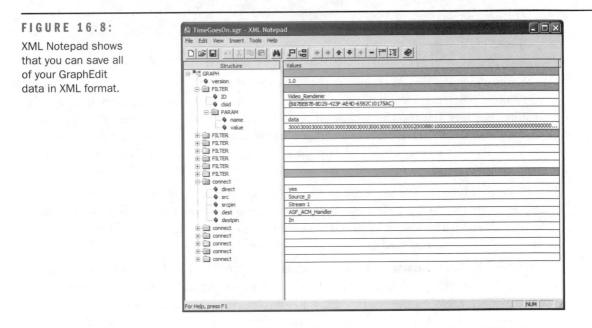

All that a .NET developer need do to make use of the output of GraphEdit is import the XGR file containing the XML version of the GraphEdit data. Once imported, the file provides everything the developer needs to re-create a data stream configured within GraphEdit. This technique greatly reduces the chance for errors in configuring a DirectX data stream within the managed environment.

NOTE   XML is almost, but not quite, readable by the average human. Reading simple files is almost a trivial exercise, but once the data gets nested a few layers deep, reading it can become tiresome. That's why you should have a tool for reading XML in your developer toolkit. The only problem is that some of these tools cost quite a bit for the occasional user. Microsoft has remedied this problem a little with the introduction of XML Notepad (`http://msdn.microsoft.com/library/default.asp?url=/library/en-us/dnxml/html/xmlpaddownload.asp`). This utility is free for the price of a download and does a reasonable job of reading most XML files. (Microsoft hasn't bothered to update the date for this site, but be assured that XML Notepad runs fine under both Windows 2000 and Windows XP.)

Using the DirectPlay Network Simulator

The main use for DirectPlay today is games. Two people who want to play a game together (either as allies or enemies) make a connection between their computers. The copies of the games on both computers synchronize so that the two players can see each other. Of course, the technology works for more than two players, but the principle is the same no matter how many players you add. The two major considerations are the number of players that a developer thinks the game should support and the availability of resources such as memory and network bandwidth to support the player data.

TIP   There are situations in which an application crash can leave DirectX in an unstable state. One of the most common causes of problems in Windows 9x occurs when the DDHelp process remains active after an application using DirectX crashes. The active process prevents the application from restarting and prevents any other applications that rely on DirectX from starting. A developer can resolve this problem by running the Kill Help utility. Most .NET developers will never need to use the Kill Help utility, but it helps to know that it exists. This utility doesn't display any text on screen, any prompts, or even a success message, but it does stop the DDHelp process from running so that the developer doesn't have to reboot the text system.

In the future, developers will likely use DirectPlay for other purposes. For example, a developer could create a modeling application that allows interaction by more than one person. DirectPlay would help two or more people interact with the modeling program in a way that all of the participants could see. In some respects, the application would work just as a game does today, but it would use real data in a real-world scenario. The technique is essentially the same.

No matter what type of application you create to use DirectPlay, the need to test the network connection between participants is important. However, you can't always tell how the participants will create a connection when you design the application. A game player might decide to create a connection to a friend across a dial-up connection rather than use a standard network. So you must also test the connection using various connection types and speeds. The DirectPlay8 Network Simulator shown in Figure 16.9 offers such choices.

FIGURE 16.9:

The DirectPlay8 Network Simulator creates specific test conditions for an application.

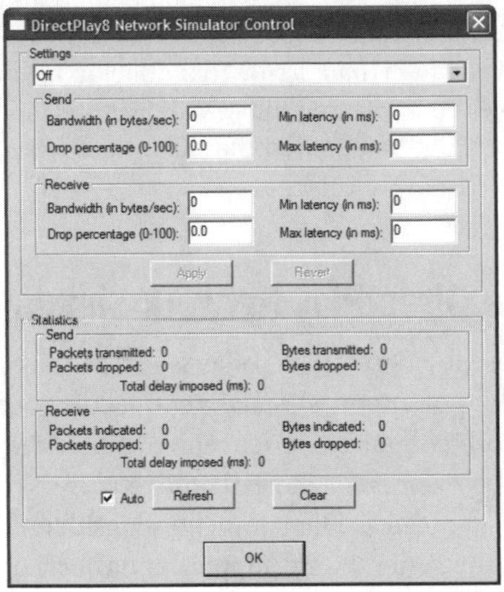

As you can see from Figure 16.9, the application begins in the Off position. You can start the application by selecting a network connection type and speed in the Settings field. Figure 16.10 shows the choice of settings available. Notice especially the Custom setting, which helps you create your own test settings.

FIGURE 16.10:

You can use the standard or custom settings for test purposes.

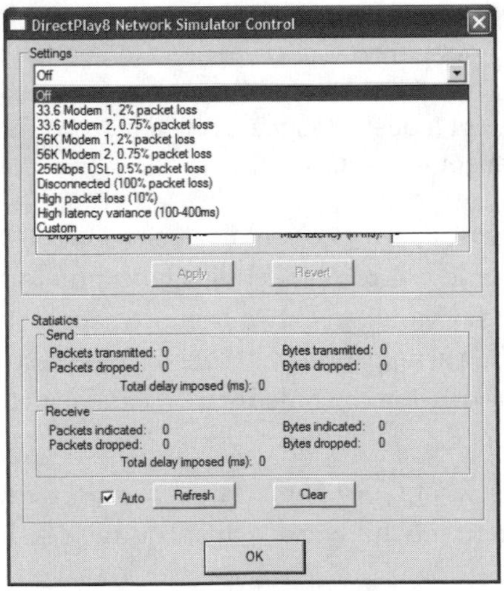

When you select a particular entry in the Settings field, the DirectPlay8 Network Simulator automatically fills in the values required in the Send and Receive groups. You can tweak these settings as needed to define specific network connections. The moment you change one of the fields in either group, however, the DirectPlay8 Network Simulator selects the Custom entry in the Settings field. Note that a change you make won't take effect until you click Apply. Clicking Revert automatically changes the settings back to the previous values.

The Statistics group that makes up the bottom half of the dialog box tells you how well an application performs given the settings that you've chosen. You can use these statistics to determine when an application is operating at less than peak performance. In some cases, modifying an application slightly will improve the performance. However, it all comes down to the amount of data you need to transmit between two copies of an application. The DirectPlay8 Network Simulator can also help you determine the minimum bandwidth requirements for the application. Publishing these statistics ensures that the user's experience will always match what you've simulated in the testing environment.

Using the MeshView Tool

A mesh is a description of a 3D object. The description relies on a series of triangles that are expressed using vertices (the angles in the object) and faces (the flat surfaces). The mesh also includes ancillary information in the form of materials and textures that determine how DirectDraw will skin the 3D object. All of this information is stored in memory when used to draw an image on screen. The information can also appear in an X or an M file for permanent storage. (You'll find the X files used for this section in the \Chapter 16\MeshView folder of the CD.) The MeshView Tool performs five essential tasks in relation to these files and the meshes they describe:

- Open and view existing mesh files
- Create new meshes based on graphics primitives
- Convert meshes to progressive meshes
- View the animations contained within mesh files
- Manipulate mesh and progressive mesh data, but not content

NOTE The MeshView Tool is a complex utility from both a usage and conceptual perspective. This section tells you about some of the basics of the tool, but it doesn't delve into the intricacies of using it. For example, we won't discuss the animation feature. The point of this section is to discuss how the tool works and then show how you can use it for managed applications.

One of the most important features of the MeshView Tool for the managed environment developer isn't even on this list. The MeshView Tool can validate the output of your application. Simply output the data you've created to an X file. If the MeshView Tool can read the file, then you know the file is essentially correct. You can further validate the mesh using the MeshOps ➢ Validate Mesh command. This command only becomes available after you choose one of the selection tools (such as Vertex Selection) and rotate the object.

Another important reason to use the MeshView Tool is to gain an understanding of how meshes work. To do this, you'll need to create a simple image, change it, and view the effects. In fact, the following sections will take you through the process of creating a mesh, adding color to it, and then distorting it. This set of tasks will help you understand meshes better, teach you to use the MeshView Tool, and help you learn about the various elements of an X file so you can sight-validate the output of your managed application.

Creating a Mesh

The MeshView Tool comes with a variety of built-in graphics primitives. We aren't going to create a fancy image in this example. In fact, starting simply is the best way to go because the math for complex images can quickly make even simple manipulations too difficult. The example will begin with a simple cube. The following steps will show you how to create, view, and save the cube mesh:

1. Use the File ➢ Create Shape ➢ Create Box command. Notice that you can create a variety of other shapes including a sphere, torus, and even a teapot. Of course, these are simply primitives for experimentation—a real application would likely use more complex shapes.

2. Click the Edge Mode button on the toolbar. This button displays the edges of the triangles used to create the cube. You don't have to perform this step to save the file, but it's important to see how the cube is constructed before we add color to it. Notice that each face consists of two triangles. This information will become important in the sections that follow.

3. Rotate the image by dragging one of the faces. Figure 16.11 shows what you might see at this stage. (The figure also contains labels so you know the name of each button since the utility doesn't provide balloon help to identify them.) Notice that the shading of each face changes as you move the cube. This shading is automatic—you don't add it as part of the X file data. Each triangle used to create the cube has separate color and texture information—an important feature when you create oddly formed shapes as we will later in this section.

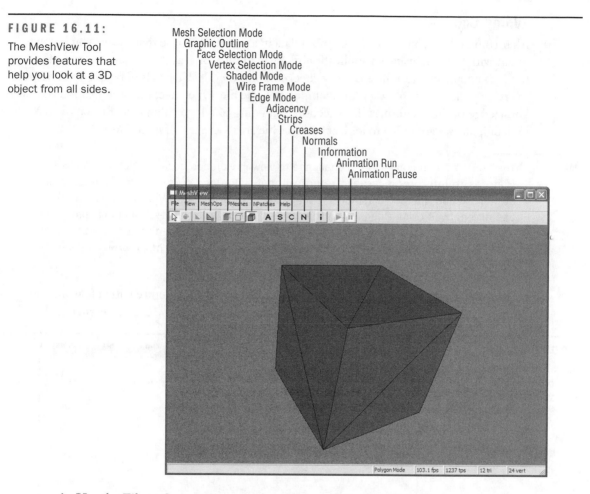

FIGURE 16.11:

The MeshView Tool provides features that help you look at a 3D object from all sides.

4. Use the File ➤ Save As command to display the Save As dialog box.

5. Verify that the Save Hierarchy check box is checked. Select Text for the X File Format option.

6. Type a name for the file. The name of the file in this example is Box1.X. Make sure you type the file extension because the utility won't add it for you.

7. Click Save. You now have a text file containing the settings for a basic cube. If you opened this X file using the File ➤ Open Mesh File command, you'd see the same cube that we just created.

Adding Color

It's fortunate that you can store the mesh data in a text file because that means you can experiment with the data using an application that you know works at the outset. Any modifications you make to a test file are easily checked using the MeshView Tool before you attempt to create your own application for manipulating the file. Of course, file modifications require knowledge of the file format. This section isn't going to tell you about the format of an X file in detail, but we are going to look at one specific area—the use of materials in an X file.

> **TIP**
>
> The Box1.X file is going to be a challenge to view in Notepad because Notepad lacks the features to interpret a carriage return without a linefeed correctly. You can certainly attempt to use Notepad to modify the X file produced by the MeshView Tool, but easier-to-use alternatives exist. One product that you should try is Notepad+. This utility produces plain-text files, just as Notepad will, but it includes a wealth of additional features that make the developer's life easier. You can download Notepad+ at http://www.mypeecee.org/rogsoft/.

The data storage in an X file looks very much like a C data structure with a few bits and pieces of information added. Figure 16.12 shows the Box1.X file we created earlier.

FIGURE 16.12:

The text form of the X file looks just like C data structure code.

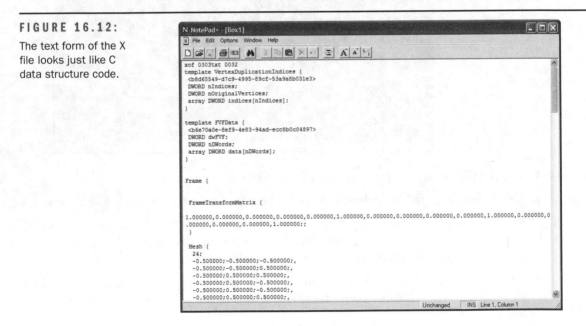

The part that we're actually interested in changing appears in the `Frame` data structure. The X file currently holds a single material that defines the color of all of the faces. Here's what the code looks like.

```
MeshMaterialList {
1;
12;
0,
0,
0,
0,
0,
0,
0,
0,
0,
0,
0;

    Material {
     0.500000;0.500000;0.500000;0.000000;;
     0.000000;
     0.500000;0.500000;0.500000;;
     0.000000;0.000000;0.000000;;
    }
}
```

The first number in the `MeshMaterialList` data structure determines the number of materials in the list and the second number determines the number of faces. The numbers that follow contain the number of the materials to use to display the individual triangles used to create a face. There are 6 sides to a cube and 2 triangles used to create each of the sides, so the structure contains a total of 12 faces.

The `Material` data structure contains a series of numbers. The numbers we're most interested in are the first four. They reflect the initial color of the material in red, green, blue, and alpha blending level (the amount of transparency that a pixel has). The four sets of numbers determine the face color, power level, specular color, and emissive color. You can learn more about the various color values in the article entitled "Mathematics of Lighting" at `ms-help://MS.VSCC/MS.MSDNVS/dx8_vb/directx_vb/Graphics/ProgrammersGuide/UsingDirect3D/LightsAndMaterials/MathematicsOfLights/MathematicsOfLights.htm`.

Let's say that you want each face of the cube to have a different color. The first task you need to perform is to define additional materials and remove the current material. A material definition should appear at the beginning of the `Frame` data structure before the `Mesh` data structure. The `Material` data structure requires a name so you can reference it later. Here's a typical Material definition for a face color (you can see the entire list of six colors in the `Box2.X` file):

```
Material RedMaterial {
1.000000;0.000000;0.000000;1.000000;;
0.000000;
0.000000;0.000000;0.000000;;
0.000000;0.000000;0.000000;;
}
```

As you can see, the first value, red, is set to the highest level possible. You can use any value between 0 and 1 to represent the intensity of any color. It's helpful to experiment with the other color values once you understand how the face color works. The other color values help you achieve special effects.

Once you define the required colors, you need to add them to your 3D object by modifying the `MeshMaterialList` data structure. The following code shows how you'd make each face of a cube contain a different color:

```
MeshMaterialList {
  6;
  12;
  0,
  0,
  1,
  1,
  2,
  2,
  3,
  3,
  4,
  4,
  5,
  5;;

  {RedMaterial}
  {GreenMaterial}
  {BlueMaterial}
  {YellowMaterial}
  {TealMaterial}
  {PurpleMaterial}
}
```

As you can see, the data structure defines 6 materials now. It still has 12 faces and each face pair uses a different material. Consequently, each face pair (or face of the cube) will have a different color. Load the Box2.X file into the MeshView Tool and see for yourself how DirectX would render this object.

Making Other Changes

There are a number of other changes you can make to the initial image we created. One such change is to modify the appearance of the image. To do this, you need to modify the intersection of all of the vertices that make up a particular picture element. Of course, this means accurately selecting the vertices you need to change. Click the Face Selection Mode and Vertex Selection Mode buttons to display the highlighted vertex on screen as shown in Figure 16.13. The selected vertex has a red dot over it, while the selected face is outlined in yellow.

FIGURE 16.13:

The MeshView Tool makes it easy to accurately select a vertex and face.

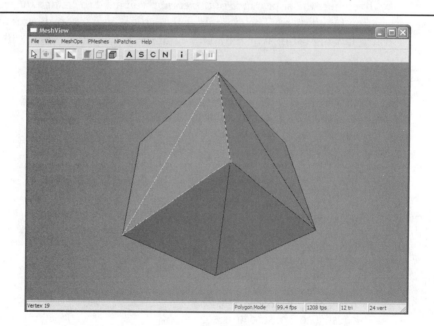

Once you select a vertex and face, you can click the Information button to display the dialog shown in Figure 16.14. As you can see, the vertex number for this face is 19. We need two other vertex numbers in order to change this corner of the figure. It turns out that the other two faces are vertex numbers 2 and 5.

This Face Information
dialog box tells you
about the selected
vertex and face
combination.

To change the appearance of this corner, you need to change the Mesh data structure information for all three. The example changes the x- and y-coordinates to 0.300000 as shown in
the following listing (you'll find the complete listing in the Box4.X file on the CD):

```
Mesh {
    24;
    -0.500000;-0.500000;-0.500000;,
    -0.500000;-0.500000;0.500000;,
    0.300000;0.300000;0.500000;,
    -0.500000;0.500000;-0.500000;,
    -0.500000;0.500000;-0.500000;,
    0.300000;0.300000;0.500000;,
    0.500000;0.500000;0.500000;,
    0.500000;0.500000;-0.500000;,
    0.500000;0.500000;-0.500000;,
    0.500000;0.500000;0.500000;,
    0.500000;-0.500000;0.500000;,
    0.500000;-0.500000;-0.500000;,
    -0.500000;-0.500000;0.500000;,
    -0.500000;-0.500000;-0.500000;,
    0.500000;-0.500000;-0.500000;,
    0.500000;-0.500000;0.500000;,
    -0.500000;-0.500000;0.500000;,
    0.500000;-0.500000;0.500000;,
    0.500000;0.500000;0.500000;,
    0.300000;0.300000;0.500000;,
    -0.500000;-0.500000;-0.500000;,
    -0.500000;0.500000;-0.500000;,
    0.500000;0.500000;-0.500000;,
    0.500000;-0.500000;-0.500000;;
```

The vertex numbers begin at 0 and progress to 23. As you can see, we've changed the values for vertex numbers 2, 5, and 19. Figure 16.15 shows the results of the changes.

Modifying the three vertices gives the cube a new appearance.

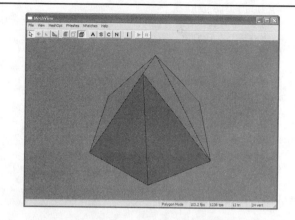

The final change we'll look at is applying a texture to a cube. In section titled "Using the DirectX Texture Tool" in Chapter 15, we discussed how you could create a texture for use in a DirectX application. It's time to look at one way to apply a texture to an existing X file. The first step is to update the Material data structure so it contains a texture description in the form of a TextureFilename data structure. Here's the modification for the *RedMaterial* reference (you'll find the complete source code in the Box4.X file on the CD):

```
Material RedMaterial {
1.000000;0.000000;0.000000;0.000000;;
0.000000;
0.000000;0.000000;0.000000;;
1.000000;0.000000;0.000000;;
TextureFilename {"bricks.dds";}
}
```

The second step is to define how you want the texture to appear on the screen. This means defining a value for each vertex in the object. To do this, you use the MeshTextureCoords data structure as shown here:

```
MeshTextureCoords {
    24;
    1.000000;0.000000;
    0.000000;-1.000000;
    -1.000000;0.000000;
    0.000000;-1.000000;
    1.000000;0.000000;
    0.000000;-1.000000;
    -1.000000;0.000000;
```

```
0.000000;-1.000000;
1.000000;0.000000;
0.000000;-1.000000;
-1.000000;0.000000;
0.000000;-1.000000;
1.000000;0.000000;
0.000000;-1.000000;
-1.000000;0.000000;
0.000000;-1.000000;
1.000000;0.000000;
0.000000;-1.000000;
-1.000000;0.000000;
0.000000;-1.000000;
1.000000;0.000000;
0.000000;-1.000000;
-1.000000;0.000000;
0.000000;-1.000000;
}
```

Each entry defines a single vertex in the object. Figure 16.16 shows the results of these changes when applied to the colored cube. As you can see, the brick texture we created in Chapter 15 takes on the color of each face and the shape of the cube. The MeshView Tool uses all three of these elements to produce a specific effect on the original cube.

FIGURE 16.16:

The final output of our sample shows the effects of color and texture on a cube.

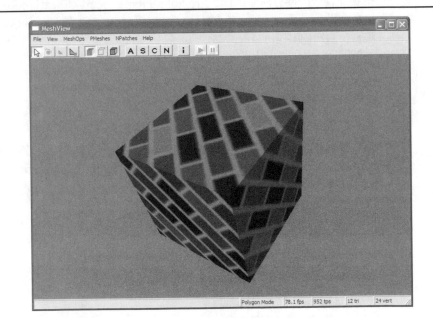

Using a Mesh Example

Now that you've seen how a mesh is constructed and how to test the content of an X file, it's time to see what you've learned in action. The example in this section performs the simple task of loading an X file and rendering it. The example code will demonstrate that some of the DirectX code is the same as you've used in the past but other code is different because of the managed environment. In fact, this example contains a few surprises that you might not have expected.

Initializing the Application

Let's begin with application initialization. Listing 16.1 contains the constructor for the form. You'll find this code in the \Chapter 16\C#\MeshView and \Chapter 16\VB\MeshView folders of the CD.

Listing 16.1   **Mesh Example Initialization**

```
// DirectX objects.
private DirectX8       DX8;      // DirectX 8 object.
private Direct3D8      D3D8;     // Direct 3D object.
private Direct3DDevice8 Device;   // Display device.

public frmMain()
{
   D3DDISPLAYMODE        Mode;      // Display mode.
   D3DPRESENT_PARAMETERS  Params;    // Display parameters.

   // Required for Windows Form Designer support
   InitializeComponent();

   // Initialize the DirectX objects.
   DX8 = new DirectX8Class();
   D3D8 = DX8.Direct3DCreate();

   // Create a device to use for drawing. Begin by obtaining the
   // current display mode. Set the display parameters. Finally,
```

```
// create the device.
Mode = new D3DDISPLAYMODE();
D3D8.GetAdapterDisplayMode((int)CONST_D3DCONST.D3DADAPTER_DEFAULT,
                                ref Mode);
Params = new D3DPRESENT_PARAMETERS();
Params.Windowed = 1;
Params.SwapEffect = CONST_D3DSWAPEFFECT.D3DSWAPEFFECT_COPY_VSYNC;
Params.BackBufferFormat = Mode.Format;
Params.BackBufferCount = 1;
Params.EnableAutoDepthStencil = 1;
Params.AutoDepthStencilFormat = CONST_D3DFORMAT.D3DFMT_D16;
Device = D3D8.CreateDevice(
    (int)CONST_D3DCONST.D3DADAPTER_DEFAULT,
    CONST_D3DDEVTYPE.D3DDEVTYPE_HAL,
    pnlDisplay.Handle.ToInt32(),
    CONST_D3DCREATEFLAGS.D3DCREATE_SOFTWARE_VERTEXPROCESSING,
    ref Params);

// Set the device state.
// Turn off culling.
Device.SetRenderState(CONST_D3DRENDERSTATETYPE.D3DRS_CULLMODE,
                        (int)CONST_D3DCULL.D3DCULL_NONE);
// Turn on the Z buffer.
Device.SetRenderState(CONST_D3DRENDERSTATETYPE.D3DRS_ZENABLE, 1);
// Turn on lighting.
//Device.SetRenderState(CONST_D3DRENDERSTATETYPE.D3DRS_LIGHTING, 0);
// Set the ambient lighting color.
Device.SetRenderState(CONST_D3DRENDERSTATETYPE.D3DRS_AMBIENT,
                        -1);

}
```

The example begins like many of the DirectX examples so far: by creating the DirectX and Direct3D objects. Working with a mesh also means creating a device—essentially a virtual display adapter and monitor combination on which you display the data. To create a device, the code needs to obtain the real display information using the GetAdapterDisplayMode() method. Once the code has this information, it can fill out a D3DPRESENT_PARAMETERS data structure (Params) that contains the information used to create the device. The Direct3D parameters control the operations the device can perform.

The code uses the D3D8.CreateDevice() method to create the device. This method accepts the parameters, a device type, the handle to the current window, and some creation flags as input. We'll use a default adapter type for the example. In addition, the example relies on hardware support. If your system only provides support for software emulation, you'll need to change the CONST_D3DDEVTYPE.D3DDEVTYPE_HAL enumeration value to CONST_D3DDEVTYPE .D3DDEVTYPE_SW. If the code attempts to create a device for a system that doesn't support the request device type, the call will fail, so it's important to check for a `null` return value in your production code and make an alternative device creation call (or exit from the application).

When the `D3D8.CreateDevice()` method returns, *Device* is in a default state that doesn't work for anything. Microsoft is assuming that you'll configure the device for your needs. The final four lines of code configure *Device* for the needs of this application by setting the render state using the `Device.SetRenderState()` method. The code controls the device setting using the `CONST_D3DRENDERSTATETYPE` enumeration members. In this case, the code sets the culling state, Z buffer, lighting, and ambient lighting color. Notice that I've actually commented the ambient color setting out. We'll see later in this example why this setting can cause problems or fix them, depending on the situation.

Loading a Mesh File

At this point, the main DirectX objects are set up. However, we can't do any more until the user opens the application. Listing 16.2 shows the code to open an X file and process it for use. This code demonstrates the prerequisites for preparing to render (display) the file, but we won't display it yet.

Listing 16.2   Loading the X File

```
// These are the global file-related objects.
private string          File2Open;  // The file we want to render.
private D3DXMesh         Mesh;       // The Mesh Object.
private D3DMATERIAL8[]   Materials;  // Array of materials.
private Direct3DTexture8[] Textures; // Array of textures.

private void mnuFileOpen_Click(object sender, System.EventArgs e)
{
    OpenFileDialog Dlg;      // File Open Dialog
    D3DX8          Worker;   // A worker object.
    D3DXBuffer     Adjacency;// Adjacency data buffer.
    D3DXBuffer     MatBuffer;// Materials buffer.
    Int32          MatCount; // Number of materials.
    String         TextName; // Name of the texture file.
    String         FilePath; // Path to the texture file.

    // Set up the File Open Dialog
    Dlg = new OpenFileDialog();
    Dlg.Filter = "X Format File (*.x)|*.x";
    Dlg.DefaultExt = ".x";
    Dlg.Title = "Open X File Dialog";

    // Display the File Open Dialog and obtain the name of a file and
    // the file information.
    if (Dlg.ShowDialog() == DialogResult.OK)
    {
```

```
// Set the name of the file.
File2Open = Dlg.FileName;

// Load the X file.
Worker = new D3DX8();
Adjacency = Worker.CreateBuffer(0);
MatBuffer = Worker.CreateBuffer(0);
MatCount = 0;
Mesh = Worker.LoadMeshFromX(File2Open,
                            (int)CONST_D3DXMESH.D3DXMESH_MANAGED,
                            Device,
                            ref Adjacency,
                            ref MatBuffer,
                            ref MatCount);

// Obtain a list of materials and textures.
Materials = new D3DMATERIAL8[MatCount];
Textures = new Direct3DTexture8[MatCount];
FilePath = File2Open.Substring(0,
                               File2Open.LastIndexOf("\\") + 1);
for (int Counter = 0; Counter < MatCount; Counter++)
{
    // Get a material from the buffer.
    Worker.BufferGetMaterial(MatBuffer,
                             Counter,
                             out Materials[Counter]);

    // Set the material ambient color.
    Materials[Counter].ambient = Materials[Counter].diffuse;

    // Determine if there is a texture to process.
    TextName = Worker.BufferGetTextureName(MatBuffer, Counter);
    if (TextName != null)
    {
        // Obtain the texture.
        Textures[Counter] =
            Worker.CreateTextureFromFile(Device,
                                         FilePath + TextName);
    }
}

// Tell DirectX that we're done with the materials buffer.
MatBuffer = null;

// Render the object.
Render();

// Start the timer.
RenderTimer.Start();
```

```
        // Enable the timer setting menu.
        mnuTimerSet.Enabled = true;
        mnuTimerSet.Text = "Stop";
    }
}
```

The first task the code performs is to create more fields that the entire class can use. Unlike the DirectX objects the code created earlier, these objects are file specific and enable other parts of the application to interact with the file. The *File2Open* variable contains the path and name of the file. You should always create such a variable because your code is likely to need it. The *Mesh* variable contains the mesh object, which includes the display data. The *Materials* and *Textures* arrays contain the colors and textures used to render the image on screen. The last three variables are all that application requires in the form of file objects to render the image on screen.

The mnuFileOpen_Click() method begins as any file opening code would: by creating the dialog box and waiting for user input. If *Dlg* returns DialogResult.OK, the application begins processing the resulting filename. Otherwise, the application exits to the main form and waits for the user to stop clicking Cancel (or exit the application).

The code begins by creating an instance of the D3DX8 worker class (Worker). The Worker object provides access to a wealth of methods that you can use to manipulate graphics files of all types, including mesh files. The code then creates two temporary buffers, *Adjacency* and *MatBuffer*, that the application will use to hold data from the X file. The LoadMeshFromX() method loads data from the X file that the user selected into the two buffers and the device. The *MatCount* variable holds the number of materials retrieved from the X file and stored in *MatBuffer*. *Device* now contains the data required to render the image, but we still need to perform other tasks on the buffers.

TIP   Listing 16.2 contains the *Adjacency* buffer for the LoadMeshFromX() method even though the application will never use the data contained within the buffer. C# doesn't provide a method to leave out optional parameters, so we're forced to use this technique to keep the compiler happy even when the application doesn't need the data. You can get around the optional parameter problem, in some cases, by using either the Type.Missing or Missing.Value value. Of course, other options include using null or IntPtr.Zero as needed.

The next step in the process is to create *Materials* and *Textures* arrays. The code sizes these two arrays to hold the number of items specified by *MatCount*. Given the way that an X file stores the texture information, the *Textures* array will never include more items than the *Materials* array, so using this technique is safe. The code uses a for loop for processing. It begins by obtaining the current material from *MatBuffer* using the BufferGetMaterial() method. The code must call this method once for each material in the buffer. We've set the device to display the ambient color, so the next step is to transfer the *diffuse* color value to the *ambient* color value in the *Materials* array.

Getting the texture comes next. The code checks for a texture attached to the current *MatBuffer* entry using the BufferGetTextureName() method. If *TextName* is null on return, then the material doesn't include a texture. Otherwise, the code combines the *FilePath* contents with *TextName* to create a filename and path. It uses the CreateTextureFromFile() method to place the texture within the Textures array.

The code has to perform some cleanup at this point. Because we don't need *MatBuffer* anymore, the code sets this object to null. Remember that we're still working with unmanaged code. You'll create a memory leak if you don't perform this step. The code calls Render() to render the image on screen, starts the timer used to update the image, and enables the Timer ➤ Stop menu item. At this point, the first image is displayed on screen and the display will receive regular updates.

Displaying the Image On Screen

It's finally time to discuss the rendering process. Listing 16.3 shows one way to render an image on screen. This is probably the least-code-intensive method for displaying a rotating image on screen. Once you get past these basics, the coding can become quite intense because you start working with the mathematics required to render images precisely.

Listing 16.3   Rendering the Image

```
// Define the D3DXMatrixRotationY() function.
[DllImport("DX8VB.DLL", CharSet=CharSet.Auto, SetLastError=true,
    EntryPoint="VB_D3DXMatrixRotationY")]
public static extern void D3DXMatrixRotationY(out D3DMATRIX MOut,
                                              float angle);

// Define the D3DXMatrixLookAtLH() function.
[DllImport("DX8VB.DLL", CharSet=CharSet.Auto, SetLastError=true,
    EntryPoint="VB_D3DXMatrixLookAtLH")]
public static extern void D3DXMatrixLookAtLH(out D3DMATRIX MOut,
                                             ref D3DVECTOR VEye,
                                             ref D3DVECTOR VAt,
                                             ref D3DVECTOR VUp);

// Define the D3DXMatrixPerspectiveFovLH() function.
[DllImport("DX8VB.DLL", CharSet=CharSet.Auto, SetLastError=true,
    EntryPoint="VB_D3DXMatrixPerspectiveFovLH")]
public static extern void D3DXMatrixPerspectiveFovLH(
    out D3DMATRIX MOut,
```

```
            float fovy,
            float aspect,
            float zn,
            float zf);

// We need to use pi for some of the values.
public const float pi = 3.1415F;

private void Render()
{
    D3DMATRIX               WorldView;   // Drawing matrices world view.
    D3DMATRIX               Camera;      // Drawing matrices camera view.
    D3DMATRIX               Projection;  // Drawing matrices projection.
    D3DVECTOR               Vect1;       // Matrix vectors.
    D3DVECTOR               Vect2;       // Matrix vectors.
    D3DVECTOR               Vect3;       // Matrix vectors.

    // Clear the display area.
    Device.Clear(0,
                IntPtr.Zero,
                CONST_D3DCLEARFLAGS.D3DCLEAR_TARGET |
                CONST_D3DCLEARFLAGS.D3DCLEAR_ZBUFFER,
                0xFFFFFF,
                (float)1.0,
                0);

    // Begin the scene.
    Device.BeginScene();

    // Set up the world view.
    D3DXMatrixRotationY(out WorldView, DateTime.Now.Millisecond);
    Device.SetTransform(CONST_D3DTRANSFORMSTATETYPE.D3DTS_WORLD,
                        ref WorldView);

    // Set up the camera view.
    Vect1 = new D3DVECTOR();
    Vect2 = new D3DVECTOR();
    Vect3 = new D3DVECTOR();
    Vect1.x = 0;
    Vect1.y = 3;
    Vect1.z = -5;
    Vect2.x = 0;
    Vect2.y = 0;
    Vect2.z = 0;
    Vect3.x = 0;
    Vect3.y = 1;
    Vect3.z = 0;
    D3DXMatrixLookAtLH(out Camera, ref Vect1, ref Vect2, ref Vect3);
    Device.SetTransform(CONST_D3DTRANSFORMSTATETYPE.D3DTS_VIEW,
                        ref Camera);
```

```
// Set up the projection view.
D3DXMatrixPerspectiveFovLH(out Projection, pi / 4, 1, 1, 1000);
Device.SetTransform(CONST_D3DTRANSFORMSTATETYPE.D3DTS_PROJECTION,
                    ref Projection);

// Render the mesh. Set the materials and textures, and then draw
// the mesh subset.
for (int Counter = 0; Counter < Materials.Length; Counter ++)
{
   Device.SetMaterial(ref Materials[Counter]);
   Device.SetTexture(0, (Direct3DBaseTexture8)Textures[Counter]);
   Mesh.DrawSubset(Counter);
}

// End the scene.
Device.EndScene();

// Present the scene on screen.
Device.Present(IntPtr.Zero, IntPtr.Zero, 0, IntPtr.Zero);
}
```

Notice that the code begins by using [DllImport] to access some functions in the DX8VB.DLL, which is surprising considering that this is the same DLL used for the COM library. It turns out that the .NET interoperability layer doesn't always do a good job of importing everything you need into the IDE. DirectX provides an extensive math library (among other functions) that's totally inaccessible because the math functions aren't imported.

You should see another surprise in the code at this point. This is the first time we've had to use the EntryPoint property. As shown in Figure 16.17, the function names listed in the DirectX help files don't match the function names that actually appear in the DLL. Microsoft had to write a Visual Basic compatibility layer to make DirectX work properly with this language. Consequently, the developers at Microsoft had to give the Visual Basic specific functions special names, with the result shown in Figure 16.17. This use of alternative names is another problem to look out for when working with DLLs, especially those used to support COM.

There's one additional surprise in this DLL. Notice that the function declarations define *MOut* as an out value rather than a ref. In addition, the other arguments are defined as ref values. The reason that this is a surprising turn of events is that the Visual Basic would lead you to believe that you can pass these arguments by value. Even the Visual C++ documentation only passes the *MOut* argument as a pointer (by reference), so there's apparently no reason to set the declarations up as we have. This is one of those odd declarations that you discover by trial and error rather than by observation. Try changing the function calls to the Visual Basic or Visual C++ documented format and you'll find that they no longer work properly (or perhaps at all).

FIGURE 16.17:

Exercise care when importing COM libraries because you might leave the functions behind.

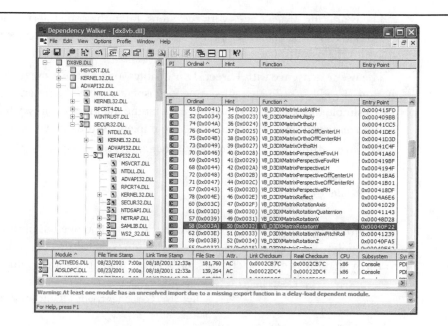

It's time to look at the Render() method. The code begins as you might expect. It clears the display. Make sure you clear both the target area and the Z buffer as shown in the code or you'll have unpleasant results (mainly data corruption). The Clear() method also accepts a background color (white, in this case), the Z buffer depth (where 1.0 is farthest away and 0.0 is closest), and a stencil buffer setting.

Drawing the image begins by a call to the BeginScene() method. The code then sets various matrices for display purposes. Notice that this is where we use the math functions declared earlier in Listing 16.3. This book isn't about the math behind DirectX, so I'll leave a complete discussion of the intricacies of matrix code to someone else. The important issue is that you need to set up a world view, camera view, and projection view in order to see the image. One item of note is that you need to provide some value in radians for the D3DXMatrixRotationY() function. The example uses the current time in milliseconds (DateTime.Now.Millisecond), which produces acceptable results if you synchronize this value with the timer interval.

After the code sets up the various matrices, it begins to render the image. Direct3D requires that the code render the image on a material-by-material basis. Consequently, the code uses a for loop to process each material and texture in turn. The application relies on the SetMaterial() and SetTexture() methods to perform the processing. Once the code has applied the current color and texture, it uses the Mesh.DrawSubset() to display image components that use that material on screen.

The rendering process ends with two steps. First, the code tells the device that the scene has ended using the EndScene() method. Second, the Direct3D device presents the rendered image to the real display using the Present() method. At this point, the user sees the image.

The user experience with Direct3D probably won't be the same without some form of animation. To add an animated effect to your display, you need a timer. The example application uses a simple timer to render the image each time the timer expires, which hopefully produces smooth animation. Here's the code used to implement the timer:

```
private void timer1_Tick(object sender, System.EventArgs e)
{
   // Render the object.
   Render();
}
```

As with every other DirectX example in the book, you need to perform some cleanup when you complete the application. Here's the cleanup code for this example. Notice that we need to verify that the Mesh object exists. Otherwise, the application could exit with an error:

```
private void frmMain_Closing(object sender,
                           System.ComponentModel.CancelEventArgs e)
{
   // Clean up the DirectX objects.
   if (Mesh != null)
      Mesh = null;
   Device = null;
   D3D8 = null;
   DX8 = null;
}
```

A Few Words about Output

Let's look at the output of the application as it exists now. Figure 16.18 shows the standard output with color. Notice that the colors interact with the texture just as they did in the MeshView Tool.

I mentioned earlier in the section that you need to exercise care in setting up your device. In some cases, you might discover to your horror that the X file loads and displays but the image lacks color. This normally occurs because you've turned off lighting effects. Likewise, if you add lighting when all you need is a texture, the image might not appear as anticipated—it might have odd interactions in the texture.

Let's see an example of a device setup change. Remove the comments from this line of code in Listing 16.1:

```
Device.SetRenderState(CONST_D3DRENDERSTATETYPE.D3DRS_LIGHTING, 0);
```

Recompile the code and run it. Load the Box4.X file and your output should look similar to that shown in Figure 16.19. This is the texture-only version of that X file. If you load any of the other X files that we created with the MeshView Tool, you'll notice that they all display without color (you can only see them if you change the background color of the application).

FIGURE 16.18:

The standard output from the application allows color and texture to interact.

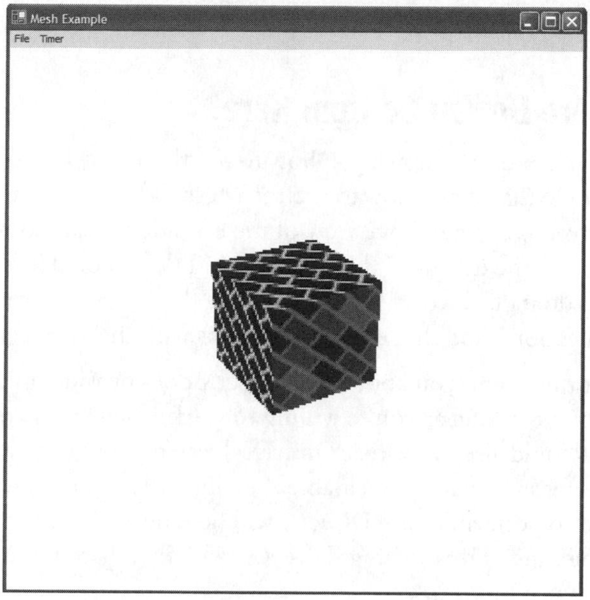

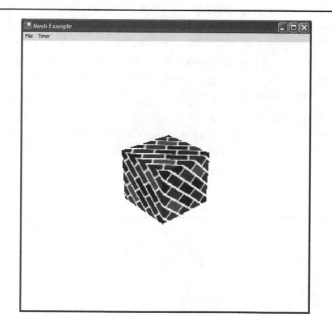

FIGURE 16.19:

A texture-only form of the Box4.X file

The moral behind this particular piece of coding is that you need to verify that your DirectX settings are correct before you blame the managed environment for some oddity in your code. The fact is that DirectX is complex even without the vagaries of managed code to worry about—using managed code only adds to the developer's burden.

Where Do You Go from Here?

This chapter has shown you how to use three new DirectX tools. You've also seen a coding example that shows how to use the MeshView utility with your application. What you've received is a general overview of the extended capabilities of DirectX—we haven't really explored the depths of this complex API. You should leave this chapter knowing that the tools do indeed work, that they reduce the effort required to code certain types of DirectX applications, and that everything works with the managed environment—at least partially.

At this point, you know that DirectX does provide full functionality in the managed environment as long as you're willing to work around some problem areas. From the examples, you should also know that DirectX doesn't work nearly as fast in the managed environment as it does in a native executable. Finally, you should understand that the amount of work you need to perform to use DirectX will be reduced by the introduction of DirectX 9. However, at the time of this writing, DirectX 9 is still in beta and Microsoft hasn't provided a release date for it.

If you plan on working with DirectX in your applications, it's time to explore further. This book hasn't covered a lot of areas that you'll need to learn before you can write professional-quality DirectX applications. For example, we haven't discussed much of the math behind DirectX even though DirectX is a math-intensive development environment. We also haven't discussed the art that goes into DirectX development—three chapters in a book aren't enough to cover such broad issues. You need to learn more about the general use of DirectX.

Congratulations, you've finished the chapters in the book. However, you're not finished yet. There are still two appendices to view, a glossary to use, and an Extras folder on the CD to exploit. In short, even though the text is finished, there are still more avenues to explore before you can say that you've learned everything this book has to offer.

PART V

Appendices

Appendix A

Fifty-Two Tips for Error-Free Win32 API Access

We all like the little bits of information that say a lot in a short space, especially when working with complex ideas or concepts. These tips are especially worthwhile because they often represent hours of work. They will help you create a better environment in which to access the Win32 API. Many of them are significant and show the hours of work required for discovery; others are subtle suggestions exposed in a moment of clear thinking. A few of the tips simply consist of good-to-know information of the common-sense variety. No matter the source, there's one tip for each week of the year. The tips are presented in no apparent order and you can skip around when reading them if you like.

1. When working with enumerations, it's usually best to create a single enumeration that contains all possible values for a situation rather than create many custom enumerations for each call that requires a portion of the entire enumeration. The use of custom enumerations leads to confusion on the part of other developers and increases the work required to use the Win32 API, without much benefit to the originator.

2. Verify the type of variable that a handle or other pointer requires. In most cases, you'll use an `IntPtr` to represent a handle or other pointer. However, some pointers (especially handles) use a structure instead. In this case, use the data structure. The biggest clue to look for is the use of macros when declaring the handle or other pointer. Macros generally signal the use of a data structure or other non-`IntPtr` form of variable.

3. Always free unmanaged memory that you allocate using any of the methods we have discussed throughout the book. This includes memory allocated using the `Marshal` `.AllocHGlobal()` function. Failure to free memory that you allocate outside of Garbage Collector control will create a memory leak because the Garbage Collector only works with managed resources.

4. The `[MarshalAs]` attribute represents one of the most flexible ways to create an interface between managed and unmanaged data. Generally, you'll use the `[MarshalAs]` attribute more often with Visual Basic than you will with C#, but both languages require this feature for certain types of data transmission such as COM interfaces and `Char` arrays.

5. Sometimes the specific name of a Win32 API function will remain elusive—you remember what the function does but can't quite remember the function name so you can look it up in the Platform SDK documentation. When this happens, you can use the Search feature of the Platform SDK documentation to look up the function name. Unfortunately, Microsoft's search mechanism isn't known for it's ability to locate all of the information pertaining to a subject, so it often pays to perform the same search using a search engine like Google (http://www.google.com/advanced_search). In addition, you can perform searches using specific keywords in the Platform SDK documentation index. For example, many functions come in a Get or a Write form. Looking through the list of entries in these areas of the documentation might help you locate a function that eludes other forms of search.

6. You can use either an enumeration or a class as a container for a list of variable values. When using a class, declare the individual members as `public const` with a variable type. The class method offers better control over the enumeration member types; an enumeration is more memory efficient.

7. Use .NET Framework data types whenever possible. This technique avoids conflicts with native language data types and makes the code more portable. In addition, some languages, such as Visual Basic, benefit from using the .NET Framework data types.

8. Make sure you perform the correct bit-level manipulations when working with flags. In most cases, you'll want to create an enumeration that contains the various flag bit locations and then and the flag with the enumeration value. Flags generally require use of an if statement to ensure that the application reacts to them properly.

9. Avoid excessive data-manipulation-oriented Win32 API code by using built-in .NET Framework functionality. For example, you can obtain the handle for the current object by using the *this.Handle* property.

10. Spy++ can provide you with valuable information about the manner in which Windows interacts with an application. For example, you can use Spy++ to determine the actual value for a window handle and use this value to check the output of any functions used by your application. Spy++ also helps you with message handling needs and can tell you about the threads used by your application.

11. Visual Basic doesn't provide support for pointers. Consequently, when you need to use pointers in your application, the best option is to use Visual C++ to write a wrapper DLL. When speed and use of a single language is most important, find a way around using the point (such as an `IntPtr`) or rely on C# as your development language.

12. Watch out for the variable in disguise. Some variables look like one type in the Platform SDK when they're really another type in the C/C++ header files. If you're unfamiliar with a variable type listed in the documentation, it always pays to research it and verify that it actually is a specific variable type.

13. Normally, there's no way to implement a union within managed data structures. Generally, you have to create one version of the data structure for each member of the union. However, you can get around this requirement by ensuring that you understand which form of the data structure your application will use—implementing only the form of the data structure that your application needs will help avoid confusion on the part of other developers.

14. Make sure you understand all features of the `[DllImport]` attribute. This is a versatile attribute that is the main tool used to create linkage between the managed environment and any unmanaged DLLs that you want to use. It's also important to understand the limitations for the current `[DllImport]` attribute implementation. For example, you can't use it to make calls to a DLL that uses the `FastCall` calling convention.

15. Always rely on vendor documentation when working with hardware DLLs. In many cases, the vendor will provide special functions to access special hardware features. The vendor might also require data in a format different from the standard Windows input for that call or provide multiple forms of the same function.

16. Look for inconsistencies in the Win32 API call syntax when debugging your application. For example, some calls return an HRESULT value, some a Boolean value, others a numeric value, and still others an object such as a handle. Failure to detect these differences can cause errors in your application code, even if the Win32 API call succeeds.

17. Some functionality requires clever programming techniques rather than difficult programming techniques. For example, you can give your applications a Windows XP appearance by creating a manifest file rather than writing the drawing code directly. Of course, there's no free lunch. Many clever programming techniques have limitations that you need to consider. In the case of a manifest file, it affects only the Windows-drawn controls and won't affect owner-drawn controls.

18. Spend time learning about the System.Runtime.InteropServices namespace. This namespace contains a wealth of classes and attributes you can use to make access to both the Win32 API and COM much easier.

19. You can use the Win32 API FormatMessage() function to interpret the numeric output of the Marshal.GetHRForLastWin32Error() method, the Marshal.GetLastWin32Error() method, or the GetLastError() function.

20. Use the PostMessage() function when you want to send a message and have the call return immediately. Likewise, use the SendMessage() function when you want the message to complete before the function returns.

21. Windows always creates a set of environmental strings for your application. In most cases, the strings will include path information. The strings could also include information about the user and the computer system. Reading and adding to these strings is always acceptable, but avoid modifying the strings if possible.

22. Always use events to handle Windows messages and delegates to provide support for callback functions. The main reason you want to use events to handle Windows messages is to allow someone inheriting from your code to access the message without worrying about the details of the Windows message.

23. Use the .NET Framework to implement required functionality whenever possible, even when the method for accessing the required .NET Framework function is arcane. For example, many developers will forget that they can access all of the features of other .NET languages using the Interaction class. Making Win32 API calls is error prone and causes performance degradation, but it's the only way to accomplish some tasks.

24. One alternative to using the `FormatMessage()` function to interpret an error code is to use the Error Lookup utility. This utility accepts a number as input and an optional DLL where the associated error messages are found and outputs the human-readable error message.

25. Beware of threading problems when working with the Win32 API. Always be sure that any modifications to the data in the main window are made by functions in the main thread. The same holds true for any other graphic element—always make sure that your application handles them in a thread-safe manner.

26. The `WM_SYSCOMMAND` message is one of the more flexible messages offered by the Win32 API. It helps the developer to perform tasks such as manipulate windows and turn on the screensaver.

27. Make sure you check the version of Windows running on the host system whenever you attempt to use version-specific features. Older versions of Windows don't support the rich set of features found in newer versions. In many cases, they don't support essentials, such as full security, either. When in doubt, check the Windows version of the host to ensure that you have full access to the desired feature.

28. To provide cues for other developers when a Win32 API function argument will accept an enumeration value, use the `enum` name as the argument type. In this case, however, you'll need to ensure that the enumeration provides the correct data type for the Win32 API call or the function may fail to work as anticipated.

29. Always implement data structures fully. Even if a shortened form of the data structure will work for the current project, it's likely that you'll need the data structure in the future. In addition, you can't be sure of side effects that will occur when using an incomplete version of the data structure. Sometimes Windows will use reserved or unused data members for specific purposes (such as the storage of pointers and handles).

30. Don't assume that all undefined flag values constitute an error. There are four possible reasons for an undefined flag value. First, the flag value could be incorrect, in which case you should display an error message. Second, the host could support an undocumented flag value that's designed for that version of Windows. Third, the undefined value could mean that the call failed. Fourth, an undefined flag value could be the correct output given some environmental or application condition. The call might produce multiple outputs, one or more of which include an undefined flag value.

31. Windows provides a means for creating your own custom messages. Always use the `RegisterWindowMessage()` function to register a unique name for your custom message.

32. Make sure you use role-based and token-based security appropriately in your applications. Each form of security has a specific purpose in the Windows environment. Role-based security is better suited to distributed applications and situations in which you need to

know what type of user is accessing an application and associated data. Token-based security works better in situations in which you need to maintain strict control and information about the user.

33. Avoid using unsafe code whenever possible. Any code that relies on the use of manual pointers (* symbol) or addresses (& symbol) is unsafe code. Only C# supports this method of working with the Win32 API. Unsafe code blocks double the potential for problems with the Win32 API call because the compiler and runtime both reduce the number of checks they make. Of course, there are situations in which you can't avoid using pointers unless you want to create a wrapper DLL using Visual C++ (an effort that comes with its own set of problems). Generally, you can avoid using pointers by relying on the out and ref keywords and using IntPtr variables.

34. Use the in and out designations in the Platform SDK documentation to determine the flow of data between your application and the unmanaged environment. Variables marked as [in] are normally passed by value. You'll use a reference (the ref keyword in C#) for variables marked as [in, out]. Finally, variables marked as [out] are normally passed in an uninitialized state using the out keyword or the [out] attribute.

35. The Platform SDK generally lists a C/C++ library as the source of a Win32 API call. In most cases, there's a corresponding DLL that the .NET developer will rely on to access the function. However, in some cases, the function only appears in the C/C++ library. Whenever this problem occurs, you'll need to use a wrapper DLL to access the function.

36. The serial and parallel ports are examples of hardware that provide standardized access under Windows. However, if you want to access specific devices, you'll need access to a third-party library and its accompanying documentation.

37. Use multiple overrides of the same Win32 API function to create certain effects. For example, if you want the ability to assign a null value to a structure, you need one version of the function call with the structure in place and a second version with an IntPtr substituted for the structure.

38. Make sure you understand the use of special-purpose messaging functions. For example, it's essential to know the purpose of the PostThreadMessage() function if you want to manipulate threads directly.

39. Windows uses a message pump to deliver and process messages. There are literally thousands of Windows messages that you can use to communicate with your own application as well as other applications executing on the system. Make sure you spend time learning about the various messages and message classes that the Win32 API provides.

40. Most developers consider the GetLastError() function unsafe for use in the managed environment because CLR could have made another Win32 API call in the interim. Always

use the `Marshal.GetHRForLastWin32Error()` method or the `Marshal.GetLastWin32Error()` method for maximum compatibility.

41. Always use a `String` for one-way text data transfers. Using a `String` is more efficient than creating a `StringBuilder` object. In addition, CLR has to perform less marshaling of the data value.

42. Always use a `StringBuilder` object when the Win32 API call is expecting a text buffer into which it will write data. A `StringBuilder` is more resource and processor intensive, but CLR can change the value of a `StringBuilder`, while the value in a `String` remains constant.

43. At least a few of the Win32 API calls you want to make will require the use of a Visual C++ wrapper DLL. Make sure you include `Windows.H` as part of `STDAFX.H` to make sure the Visual C++ wrapper DLL will work correctly. In addition, you must include certain `#defines` to ensure that the compiler will enable advanced Windows features.

44. Always verify that the message function you want to use is still viable. For example, the `PostAppMessage()` function has been replaced by the `PostThreadMessage()` function. Using the wrong function in your application can cause errors if newer versions of Windows don't support the replaced function.

45. Look for hidden .NET Framework functions to help resolve Win32 API call problems. For example, one of the most common graphics calls is `GetDC()`. This function will work in most, but not all, cases with a .NET application. In many cases, you can use the .NET Framework `CreateGraphics()` function to obtain the graphical presentation for the object in question and then use the `GetHdc()` function to obtain a handle to the device context.

46. One reason to use a Win32 API call instead of the built-in .NET Framework functionality is that the Win32 API provides extended functionality. For example, the .NET Framework emulates the functionality provided by the `MessageBox()` function. Using the `Message-BoxEx()` function provide access to the Help button, among other features.

47. If you're unsure about the name of a function within a DLL, use the Dependency Walker utility to check it. The Dependency Walker utility can also help you determine the ordinal number of a function and the number of functions with similar names. In many cases, a DLL will contain multiple versions of the same function to handle data in different ways. The most common difference between functions is that some use Unicode characters and some use ANSI characters.

48. Not all flags are single-bit values. Some flags consume two or more bits within the variable returned by a Win32 API call. In this case, you'll need to set up special handling for the flag value and could find that transferring the flag value to another variable is well worth the effort. The most important task is to determine the proper reaction to each flag value and to ignore undefined flag values.

49. Although there's no requirement to use the [StructLayout] attribute, using it can help you obtain better results when creating data structures. The LayoutKind enumeration helps determine the final data presentation to the Win32 API call. In addition, you can use the CharSet, Pack, and Size fields to ensure that the output of the structure is acceptable. The Size field is especially useful when you want to ensure that the Win32 API sees a structure of a specific size.

50. Never use your old Visual Basic Win32 API function declarations within the managed environment. Microsoft has changed how Visual Basic works. Consequently, the older code will cause problems in the newer .NET applications.

51. Macros present one of the harder elements of the Win32 API to convert to the managed environment. In many cases, you can use a constant value to represent the macro. Some macros will require the construction of bit-manipulating functions. Finally, a few macros actually create other data elements, such as structures. When you find such a macro, determine what type of data element it creates and then define the data element directly.

52. When all else fails, read the Platform SDK documentation. Reading about the function now saves a considerable amount of debugging time later.

Appendix B

Fixes for Common API Access Errors

- Resolving Data Corruption in Data Structures

- The [DllImport] Attribute Works Improperly

- Data Transfer Problems

- .NET Implementation of COM Interface Doesn't Work

- Handling Memory Leaks and Other Resource Problems

- Windows Doesn't Appear to Handle Messages Correctly

I t's always going to be hard to create applications that use more than one system for making calls, obtaining system resources, and performing other tasks. No matter how well you build the bridge between the two technologies, there are going to be problems in translating calls and data from one technology to the other. For this reason, there is some risk in using the interoperability techniques found in this book. No matter how closely you follow the examples, there are going to be times where the Win32 API throws a monkey wrench in your plans and makes it difficult to obtain a desired effect in your application.

This appendix provides some fixes for the most common Win32 API access errors based on personal experience and the experiences of other developers on the various .NET newsgroups. While these sections may not fix every error that you have accessing the Win32 API, they'll at least give you some ideas of where to look for answers. Even a hint of where to look when you're scratching your head late at night is better than no information at all. However, I'd also like to provide updates to this appendix on my Web site. If you see a problem that doesn't appear in this appendix (or anywhere else in the book) and you think that other developers are also seeing this problem, feel free to write me about it at JMueller@mwt.net. When you write, please include a short description of the problem, some sample code if possible, and your suggested fix for the problem.

Resolving Data Corruption in Data Structures

Several areas of the book have mentioned the fact that managed data and unmanaged data are essentially incompatible. Whenever you pass data from the managed environment to the unmanaged environment, the Common Language Runtime (CLR) marshals the data for you—it converts the data as needed for the two technologies. Generally, CLR does a good job of translating the data for you assuming you provide the correct data as input. In some cases, CLR needs a little help translating the data, so you can use the [MarshalAs] attribute to tell CLR how to marshal the data. For example, you might need to tell CLR to marshal data as a wide (Unicode) string instead of an ANSI string in some cases.

Most developers figure out how to use the [MarshalAs] attribute with functions because the feedback is immediate. In fact, Windows will often tell you that the data is in the incorrect format as an error code. However, Windows doesn't provide such feedback with data structures. In many cases, the developer has no idea that the data is in the wrong format or suffers corruption during transit. Consequently, debugging this problem can be particularly troublesome.

The first place to look for errors is the structure header definition. Make sure you include the required arguments in the [StructLayout] attribute. Many developers forget to tell CLR which character set to use or how to pack the data structure. Both of these omissions can cause serious damage to your data because CLR makes certain assumptions about the data based on the call you make and the host operating system.

The second place to look is the data fields within the structure. This is where the [MarshalAs] attribute comes into play. Read the Platform SDK documentation carefully to look for clues about the data in the structure. Remember that in many examples in the book you discovered inconsistencies in the Win32 API implementation and how to learn about those inconsistencies in the documentation. If the Platform SDK documentation doesn't provide the required information, try looking through the C/C++ header files. Often the header files contain fixes that don't appear in the documentation. Finally, look online for example code, advice from fellow newsgroup members, and Microsoft Knowledge Base articles about the topic. All of these sources can help you track down a need to marshal data in a certain way when using data structures.

The *[DllImport]* Attribute Works Improperly

Most of the Win32 API calls that you'll make use standard calling conventions. In many situations, you can use the [DllImport] attribute with just the name of the DLL you want to use—the compiler will find the rest of the required information based on your function declaration. However, as you've seen in many of the examples in the book, you sometimes need to specify the proper character set using the CharSet field because the DLL in question has more than one implementation of the same function. We've also seen how to use the SetLastError field to retrieve any error information the DLL can provide.

Unfortunately, sometimes using the basic fields won't make the function work properly. For example, older C DLLs often use alternative calling conventions. You can get around this problem by using the CallingConvention field. This field tells CLR which calling convention to use. An associated enumeration contains options for the following calling conventions:

- CDECL
- FastCall
- StdCall
- ThisCall
- WinApi

This WinApi option is the default setting and the one you should use in most cases. It tells CLR to use the StdCall convention when an application runs on standard Windows (the callee cleans the stack) and CDECL when the application runs on Windows CE (the caller cleans the stack). Even though the enumeration contains an option for the FastCall convention, this version of the .NET Framework doesn't support it. In other words, you might be out of luck calling certain types of DLLs using the [DllImport] attribute for now, but Microsoft is planning on resolving this issue in the future.

In at least a few cases, you'll need to specify an entry point to the DLL using the EntryPoint field. This field helps resolve problems with DLL versus common naming of functions. It also helps you choose a specific function when Windows might choose another form of the function based on the platform (ANSI versus Unicode character support is one instance). Sometimes you'll need to use an ordinal value in place of a string to ensure that you get the correct function number. One of the mistakes that developers make is forgetting to add a pound sign to the ordinal value. For example, you'd need to specify an ordinal value as shown here:

```
[DllImport("WinMM.DLL", EntryPoint="#188")]
public static extern Int32 waveOutGetDevCaps(IntPtr uDeviceID,
                                             ref WAVEOUTCAPS pwoc,
                                             UInt32 cbwoc);
```

This form of the [DllImport] attribute ensures that the function calls the waveOutGetDevCapsW() function and not the waveOutGetDevCapsA() function. The first form is the Unicode version normally used on Windows NT, Windows 2000, and Windows XP. The second form is normally used on Windows 9x machines. The important thing to remember is that without the # sign, CLR would look for the 188() function, which doesn't exist in WinMM.DLL.

Data Transfer Problems

Transferring data between the managed and unmanaged environment is problematic because you're essentially working with two different data management systems. Most developers will find that the .NET Framework provides great variable support for common values such as integers, but that things get a little weird when you start working with arrays and handles. COM presents more than a few challenges because you need to work with interfaces, function pointers, and objects. In sum, it's amazing that data transfer works at all between the managed and unmanaged environments because there are so many differences between them. Fortunately, the [MarshalAs] attribute can handle most of the problems—at least if you know how to use the various attribute features correctly.

Throughout the book, we've looked at various [MarshalAs] attribute features. The most common feature is using the UnmanagedType enumeration to select the correct unmanaged data type. However, this enumeration contains more than a few data types and it's easy to choose the wrong one. In many cases, the compiler will happily compile the application to use a data type that's obviously incompatible with the function or method that the application wants to call. Consequently, the first place to look for problems in your code when data transfer problems occur is the data type selected for marshaling purposes. For example, if you're working with a COM interface and are passing an interface pointer using an `IntPtr` variable, you need to marshal the interface using the `UnmanagedType.Interface` enumeration member. Of course, you might also need to choose a specific type of COM pointer, such as the `UnmanagedType.IDispatch` or `UnmanagedType.IUnknown` enumeration member.

It's also important to look at the various fields you can add to the `[MarshalAs]` attribute. For example, we've used the `SizeConst` field to help marshal `Char` array variables. Using this field saves untold grief in getting the managed environment to work with the unmanaged array. Of course, it's not always correct to even pass an array. In more than one situation, we created the effect of a fixed length array by passing the correct number of variables of the anticipated type. No, it doesn't look as clean as using an array, but the technique still works.

One of the more interesting field values is `MarshalCookie`. This field isn't strictly necessary. For example, we passed cookies in the MMC example for the book without using it. However, adding the `MarshalCookie` field does provide additional information to the marshaler and can reduce problems in a multithreaded environment, where the need to obtain a particular instance of the object is important.

Despite the power of the `[MarshalAs]` attribute, there are times when you'll need to construct a Visual C++ wrapper DLL to perform the required conversion or at least create a conversion routine of your own. Looking again at the MMC example, there isn't any way to marshal an icon so that it's the correct size and color depth. This is the type of data conversion that you need to perform using a custom routine. The fact that the need for the data routine is essentially hidden makes it even more important to research the data requirements of the recipient first. Nowhere in the documentation does it tell you that you'll need to translate .NET icons to use them with MMC. The MMC documentation was created long before .NET appeared on the scene, and MMC is one of the features that Microsoft decided not to support, so there isn't any documentation on the topic. If you try the `[MarshalAs]` attribute and find the support lacking, it's time to don your detective hat and perform a little research on the data requirements for your application. In many cases, you'll find that you overlooked a `[MarshalAs]` attribute feature or need to write a custom translation routine.

Sometimes a data transfer problem is one of misinterpretation. The .NET documentation isn't clear about when you should use a `String` versus a `StringBuilder`, so it's easy to create a variable of the wrong type and attempt to pass it to the Win32 API function. In some cases, even running the application won't produce any type of error message that you can use as a starting point for your detective work. When this occurs, you need to look at the data requirements for the Win32 API call closely and then match those requirements to the .NET Framework variable types. A `String` cannot change, so it's not a good candidate for use as a buffer. On the other hand, a `StringBuilder` can change, and developers often use it to improve application performance for that reason. Consequently, a `StringBuilder` is the correct choice when you need to pass a buffer to a Win32 API call rather than to a constant text value.

It's also important to use the [StructLayout] attribute as needed in your applications. Sometimes the managed environment will experience problems in creating a structure that matches the Win32 API function or COM method requirements. In this case, you can use the Size field to ensure that the structure is an appropriate size. Using the CharSet field ensures that the function will receive string variables of the correct size. You can also use the LayoutKind.Explicit setting to set the size and location of individual fields within the data structure.

.NET Implementation of COM Interface Doesn't Work

We discussed this particular problem lightly in the COM areas of the book, but it requires a second look. Many developers will look at the .NET Framework documentation and see that it supports an interface such as IDataObject. Because many COM applications rely on the IDataObject interface, many developers will fall into this particular trap. The general rule of thumb to follow is that the .NET Framework has a complete lack of COM interface support. If you see an interface with a name you need in the .NET Framework, it's likely that the interface simply has the same name, not the same support as the COM counterpart. In general, you'll need to research the interface to see if the COM and the .NET Framework version are the same.

This brings up another potential problem—which is one of creating classes derived from the interface. Some developers have also experienced a problem where they described an interface implementation, derived from the interface, and created all of the required methods within the class only to find that the class doesn't work as anticipated (or even compile in some situations). In some cases, the compiler might become confused when it sees two interfaces with the same name and use the wrong one to compile the application. Generally, use full name qualification in the class definition when there's a potential for confusion.

Sometimes a developer can become fixated on the anticipated solution to a problem and overlook an obvious answer—I certainly know that I have. There's a chance that you'll implement an interface that also appears in the .NET Framework, find that it doesn't work, and try a number of solutions to resolve the problem—all of which are based on the idea that the problem is one of .NET versus COM implementation. In some cases, the problem is one of implementation. If you've tried every other method of resolving the conflict with COM, look again at the interface definition to ensure that you've created it correctly. Pay particular attention to data types because many developers run into this problem. Make sure you use the [MarshalAs] attribute as needed to ensure that the interface reflects the COM version. (See the section "Data Transfer Problems" for more details.)

Handling Memory Leaks and Other Resource Problems

Some developers are under the impression that .NET applications can't leak memory and will never have problems with resources because the Garbage Collector handles all of these problems. The fact is that management of unmanaged memory or resources always falls on the developer. The Garbage Collector will only manage memory and resources that it knows about—that it was involved in allocating on behalf of the application. Because of the amount of misinformation on various Web sites and newsgroups, many developers will fall into this trap. The result is that you might see more memory and resource problems, not less—at least until developers fully understand how .NET memory management works.

Of course, the main .NET Framework class for working with unmanaged memory and other resources is `Marshal`. The `AllocCoTaskMem()` and `AllocHGlobal()` functions are the main methods for allocating memory. Any memory you allocate within your application requires deallocation by the appropriate function, which is `FreeCoTaskMem()` and `FreeHGlobal()` in most cases. The only exception to this rule is if the Win32 API call frees the memory for you. The clue that the Win32 API function frees the memory for you is that you'll see an exception from CLR when the application tries to free the memory. If you see an error message, check the Platform SDK documentation to ensure that the function you called frees the memory—the documentation normally contains this information.

The same process that you use for memory is also used for resources. Any resource that you access using a .NET Framework call must also be freed using a .NET Framework call. However, in this case, you must always free the resource. None of the Win32 API calls will free the resource for you. If you see an error message when you attempt to free the resource, it usually means that there's some problem with your code or that you never gained access to the resource in the first place (in which case, you'll see other errors).

Make sure you always use the proper pointer functions for moving data between environments. For example, the `PtrToStructure()` function will create a structure based on the date pointed at by a pointer. Likewise, the `StructureToPtr()` function accepts a structure as input and creates a pointer to it. You must allocate the unmanaged memory to create the pointer before calling the `StructureToPtr()` function and deallocate the memory when the application is done using it.

The problem with memory and resource leaks is subtler than many developers realize. For example, any time a Win32 API function or a COM method returns data that your application doesn't allocate, you need to consider whether your application will have to free the memory used by that data. Visual C++ developers will remember using the `LocalFree()` function to free memory allocated by applications. If you use a function call that requires use of `LocalFree()`, then you'll need to gain access to that function through the Win32 API because the .NET Framework doesn't provide support for it. The same holds true for any resources that you allocate using a Win32 API call. Make sure you use the proper Win32 API call to free the resource when the application is done using it.

Windows Doesn't Appear to Handle Messages Correctly

Above all, Windows relies on messages to perform a multitude of tasks. There's a message for just about every task you can imagine. The problem is the overwhelming number of messages that developers have to consider when creating an application. In some cases, several messages have similar functionality, making it difficult to locate just the right message to accomplish a given task. For example, when you read the descriptions of the WM_ACTIVATE and WM_ACTIVATEAPP messages, it might be hard to figure out which message to use.

Some messages are meant to work in a sequence, so you must send more than one message to complete the task. For example, the WM_LBUTTONDOWN is always followed by the WM_LBUTTONUP message. Otherwise, Windows assumes that the user always has the left mouse button down and will perform a continuous drag operation. Of course, one cycle of a WM_LBUTTONDOWN and WM_LBUTTONUP message is a click. Some developers might think that they should use a double sequence for a double-click, but Windows requires use of the special WM_LBUTTONDBLCLK message instead.

Another point of confusion is the message itself. The documentation for many messages discusses an LPARAM and a WPARAM value. Some developers will attempt to send numeric information for these two arguments in all cases, but that won't work in either the managed or the unmanaged environment. Sometimes these arguments contain pointers to other objects, such as a data structure. To send the message, you must create the data structure and fill it with information first. In short, make sure you understand the requirements for using the message—especially the content of the two parameters associated with the message.

Choosing the correct message function is also a concern. Many of the message functions are easy to identify, but many developers have a problem figuring out when to use the Send-Message() function versus the PostMessage() function. The SendMessage() function waits until an action initiated by a message completes. It's important to use this function when your application has to wait for the task to complete before it begins the next task. Timing and synchronization are important no matter what application environment you use. The Win32 API provides the various message functions to help synchronize application activities.

A final concern for message processing is ensuring that your application actually handles the message in question. Managed applications don't handle many of the Windows messages, which means you'll have to provide code for handling them. Remember to override the WndProc() function to add your own message handling code to the application. In addition, remember to call the base.WndProc() function to ensure that your application handles all of the default messages as well.

Glossary

A

Accelerated Graphics Port (AGP) A special PC bus used specifically for display adapters. An AGP-based display adapter can operate at much higher speeds than the normal ISA or PCI bus will allow. What this means to the user is that display speeds are much higher. In addition to making the display adapter faster, AGP also allows the adapter to directly access main memory as if it were part of the adapter's private memory storage. This in turn allows the display adapter to store more complex objects like textures, which are used to improve display appearance.

access control entry (ACE) Defines the object rights for a single user or group. Every ACE has a header that defines its type, size, and flags. Next comes an access mask that defines the rights a user or group has to the object. Finally, there's an entry for the user's or group's security identifier (SID).

access control list (ACL) Part of the Windows NT security API used to determine both access and monitoring properties for an object. Each ACL contains one or more ACEs (access control entries) that define the security properties for an individual or group. There are two major ACL groups: SACL (Security Access Control List) and DACL (Discretionary Access Control List). The SACL controls the Windows NT auditing feature. The DACL controls access to the object.

access token A definition of the rights that a service or resource requestor has to the operating system. This is the data structure that tells the security system what rights a user has to access a particular object. The object's access requirements are contained in a security descriptor. In short, the security descriptor is the lock and the access token is the key.

ACE See *access control entry.*

ACL See *access control list.*

ACM See *Audio Compression Manager.*

Adaptive Differential Pulse Code Modulation (ADPCM) A data encoding technique used for sound systems. Unlike some encoding techniques, ADPCM supports compression. Sound cards normally provide encoding and compression functionality in hardware. In most cases, the sound card will support several standardized compression levels and a few custom compression levels. In addition, the sound card can usually perform data encoding and decoding without compression.

ADPCM See *Adaptive Differential Pulse Code Modulation.*

AGP See *Accelerated Graphics Port.*

American National Standards Institute (ANSI) An organization dedicated to creating standard implementations of common technologies. For example, this group created the American Standard Code for Information Interchange (ASCII) character standard commonly used for application development.

American Standard Code for Information Interchange (ASCII) A standard method of equating the numeric representations available in a computer to human-readable form. The number 32 represents a space, for example. The standard ASCII code contains 128 characters (7 bits). The extended ASCII code uses 8 bits for 256 characters. Display adapters from the same machine type usually use the same upper 128 characters.

Printers, however, might reserve these upper 128 characters for nonstandard characters. Many Epson printers use them for the italic representations of the lower 128 characters, however.

ANSI   See *American National Standards Institute.*

API   See *application programming interface.*

application programming interface (API)   A method of defining a standard set of function calls and other interface elements. It usually defines the interface between a high-level language and the lower-level elements used by a device driver or operating system. The ultimate goal is to provide some type of service to an application that requires access to the operating system or device feature set.

argument   A value you pass to a procedure or function. The procedure or function recognizes the value as a parameter. Values can include objects, pointers, and data structures as well as standard data.

array   A free-form structure that acts much like a database with a single field. An array lets you randomly or sequentially access each element by number.

ASCII   See *American Standard Code for Information Interchange.*

asynchronous message handling   A method of sending a message in which the message handler acts upon the message data in the background and the calling thread proceeds immediately to the next processing step.

AT command   The text representation of an interactive request sent to the firmware of a modem using application software. Many of these commands are standardized. For example, the ATDT command tells the modem to dial the number that follows the command when it detects a dial tone. The AT command set also includes instructions for testing and configuring the modem. Most modems also include specialized instructions that work only with that vendor's hardware and firmware.

Audio Compression Manager (ACM)   The Windows element that provides mapping between audio devices and the drivers that support them. For example, this is the element that would intercept device open function calls and determine which device to access. The ACM also controls CODECs, format converters, and filters.

B

Background Intelligent Transfer Service (BITS)   A specialized background data transfer technology that enables an application to continue transferring data without restarting even if the system experiences a loss of connection or reboots. The transfer continues wherever it left off before the disruption.

bit block transfer (blit)   The process of moving a bitmap from one device context to another. For example, a blit occurs when an application moves a bitmap from memory to the display. The blit occurs as a continuous operation. Some applications and function calls will also modify the bitmap during a blit. For example, a function could find all occurrences of the color red and change them to green during the blit. A blit could also change the bitmap's location on screen, providing an animation effect. Some sources use the shorter blt version of this term.

bitmap   A file or OLE object containing the binary representation of a graphic image in raster format. Each pixel on the display is represented as one entry in the file. The size of the entry depends on the number of colors the image supports. Common sizes include monochrome (1 bit), VGA (4 bits), SVGA (8 bits), and true color (24 bits).

BITS   See *Background Intelligent Transfer Service*.

blit   See *bit block transfer*.

buffer   The area in memory where program variables or other data is stored. For example, applications will normally read more than one page from a word-processed document to improve performance. The applications store pages in addition to the one currently viewed by the user in the buffer until needed.

C

callback function   A specialized piece of code that handles data requested by another thread in the same application from an external source, such as the operating system. For example, when an application requests a list of processes from Windows, Windows returns the data to a predefined callback function in the background. The address of the callback function is supplied by the requestor to the external source as part of the request.

CLR   See *Common Language Runtime*.

CODEC   See *coder/decoder* and *compression/ decompression*.

coder/decoder (CODEC)   A driver, hardware device, or application that encodes and decodes data of various types. The encoding process places the data in standard packages that allow easier and faster transmission. The decoding process returns the data to its original format for presentation. This term most often refers to a hardware CODEC. It is also associated with telecommunications or the transmission of data rather than localized handling and storage of data.

COM   See *Component Object Model*.

Common Language Runtime (CLR)   The engine used to interpret managed applications within the .NET Framework. All Visual Studio .NET languages that produce managed applications can use the same runtime engine. The major advantages of this approach include extensibility (you can add other languages) and reduced code size (you don't need a separate runtime for each language).

Component Object Model (COM)   A Microsoft specification for an object-oriented code and data encapsulation method and transference technique. It's the basis for technologies such as OLE (object linking and embedding) and ActiveX (the replacement name for OCXs—an object-oriented code library technology). COM is limited to local connections. DCOM (Distributed Component Object Model) is the technology used to allow data transfers and the use of OCXs within the Internet environment.

compression/decompression (CODEC)   An application, device driver, or piece of hardware used to compress or decompress data in various formats. This term is most often associated with media data such as sound or video. In general, this term refers to software more often than it does hardware. Most hardware CODECs are used for coding/decoding, not compression/decompression, although some hardware has both functions built into one unit.

console   The generic term for a workstation used to monitor server status information. In most cases, the workstation and server are the same device. Most people associate consoles with a character mode interface, but this isn't a requirement.

cookie   One or more special files used by an Internet browser to store site-specific settings or other information specific to Web pages. The purpose of this file is to store the value of one or more variables so that the Web page can restore them the next time the user visits a site. A web-master always saves and restores the cookie as part of some Web page programming task using a programming language such as JavaScript, Java, VBScript, or CGI. In most cases, this is the only file that a webmaster can access on the client site's hard drive. The cookie could appear in one or more files anywhere on the hard drive, depending on the browser currently in use. Microsoft Internet Explorer uses one file for each site storing a cookie and places them in the Cookies folder that normally appears under the main Windows directory. Netscape Navigator uses a single file named COOKIE.TXT to store all of the cookies from all sites. This file normally appears in the main Navigator folder.

cracker   A hacker (computer expert) who uses their skills for misdeeds on computer systems where they have little or no authorized access. A cracker normally possesses specialty software that allows easier access to the target network. In most cases, crackers require extensive amounts of time to break the security for a system before they can enter it.

D

DAC   See *digital-to-analog converter.*

DACL   See *Discretionary Access Control List.*

data structure   A specialized development object that contains one or more data elements in a particular format and order. A data structure can mix data types and can rely on a specific memory layout for use. Data structures can contain other data structures or objects in a nested format. Some data structures allow use of multiple data types to represent a single data element. For example, C developers will see unions within a data structure that allow the data structure to accept multiple data types for that element. Some data structures also allow unnamed sub-structures. Many application languages view data structures as a specialized form of class with specific limitations. In general, a data structure contains variables only and never contains code.

database management system (DBMS)   A method for storing and retrieving data based on tables, forms, queries, reports, fields, and other data elements. Each field represents a specific piece of data, such as an employee's last name. Records are made up of one or more fields. Each record is one complete entry in a table. A table contains one type of data, such as the names and addresses of all the employees in a company. It's composed of records (rows) and fields (columns), just like the tables you see in books. A database may contain one or more related tables. It may include a list of employees in one table, for example, and the pay records for each of those employees in a second table.

DBCS   See *Double-Byte Character Set.*

DBMS   See *database management system.*

DCB   See *Device Control Block.*

DDK   See *driver development kit.*

Device Control Block (DCB)   A structure used to create an interface between an application and a device. In most cases, the DCB contains pointers to configuration information in the application's data area. DCBs allow the programmer to request information about the device or to change its current status. Some devices also provide a method for retrieving data using a DCB.

digital-to-analog converter (DAC)   The element of a display adapter responsible for converting the digital representation of a picture element (pixel) into a voltage used to present the pixel on a display device. The continuous conversion of digital pixels to voltages creates a wave representative of the analog signal.

DirectX Media Object (DMO)   A COM object that processes data located in a client-supplied buffer. DirectX commonly uses a DMO for special effects. For example, a DMO could add a reverberation effect to sound data.

Discretionary Access Control List (DACL)   A Windows security component. The DACL controls access to an object. You can assign both groups and individual users to a specific object.

DLL   See *dynamic link library.*

DMO   See *DirectX Media Object.*

Double-Byte Character Set (DBCS)   A non-ASCII method of formatting characters that requires two bytes for each character instead of one. The DBCS allows an application to display words using character sets from non-English-speaking countries.

driver   A special operating system file that allows some presentation graphic programs to send data to an output device. (See also *device driver.*)

driver development kit (DDK)   A special set of libraries, include files, source code, and utility programs designed to augment the native capabilities of a programming language product. A programmer normally writes driver software to allow applications or the operating system to communicate with the underlying hardware in some way. A DDK is designed to make the development of such software easier. You'll find that most drivers are written to run at the operating system level, so the associated DDK provides utility programs that also operate at that level.

dynamic link library (DLL)   A specific form of application code loaded into memory by request. It's not executable by itself. A DLL does contain one or more discrete routines that an application may use to provide specific features. For example, a DLL could provide a common set of file dialogs used to access information on the hard drive. More than one application can use the functions provided by a DLL, reducing overall memory requirements when more than one application is running.

E

EIDE drive   See *extended integrated device electronics drive.*

enumeration   (1) The act of listing the content of a list, data structure, array, or other object containing multiple data elements. (2) A special data structure that contains a list of recognized data element values that an application can use for verification purposes. (3) A list of acceptable data element values that appears within an integrated development environment (IDE) or other application in the form of help.

event handler   A special method or function that reacts to specific system or user events such as clicking a button on a form or the loss of focus for a textbox.

extended integrated device electronics drive (EIDE drive)   A hard disk drive that uses the extended integrated device electronics (EIDE) interface. All the components needed to use and access the drive are located on the drive itself. A cable connects the drive to a host adapter, which connects the drive to the PC bus. The main difference between the IDE and EIDE interface is that the EIDE interface uses a wider data bus and provides more bandwidth. The EIDE interface also includes reliability and other specialized features not found in the IDE interface.

F

filter   An application, piece of hardware, or driver that accepts raw data as input, processes it in some way, and then outputs it as a finished product. Filters perform a variety of tasks, including data translation, enhancement, and reduction. For example, a sound filter that changes PCM data into ADPCM data performs data translation. Another sound filter could perform data enhancement by adding a reverberation effect. A third sound filter could control the intensity of the sound by performing data reduction.

G

GDI   See *graphical device interface.*

GIF   See *Graphics Interchange Format.*

graphical user interface (GUI)   (1) A method of displaying information where presentation and content both depend on the hardware capabilities and software instructions provided by the underlying system. A GUI uses the graphics capability of a display adapter to improve communication between the computer and its user. Using a GUI involves a large investment in both programming and hardware resources. (2) A system of icons and graphic images that replace the character mode menu system used by many machines. The GUI can ride on top of another operating system (like DOS and Unix) or reside as part of the operating system itself (like OS/2 and Windows). Advantages of a GUI are ease of use and high-resolution graphics. Disadvantages consist of higher workstation hardware requirements and lower performance over a similar system using a character mode interface.

graphical device interface (GDI)   One of several components in the Windows operating system. The GDI controls the way artistic graphic elements are presented on screen. Every application must use the API provided by this component to draw or perform other graphics-related tasks.

Graphics Interchange Format (GIF)   One of two standard file formats used to transfer graphics over the Internet (JPEG is the other). There are several different standards for this file format, the latest of which is the GIF89a standard you'll find used on most Internet sites. CompuServe originally introduced the GIF standard as a method for reducing the time required to download a graphic and the impact of any single-bit errors that might occur. A secondary form of the GIF is the animated GIF. It allows the developer to store several images within one file. Between each file are one or more control blocks that determine block boundaries, the display location of the next image in relation to the display area, and other display features. A browser or other specially designed application will display the graphic images one at a time in the order in which they appear within the file to create animation effects.

GUI   See *graphical user interface*.

H

handle   A pointer to a resource allocation. The handle provides a method for the application to "grasp" and use the resource. Handles are used for a variety of tasks, including gaining access to a window. If an application wants to allow an external function to manipulate a resource it owns, it usually passes the resource handle to allow the external function access.

hardware emulation layer (HEL)   The portion of the software that represents all or part of a physical device. The HEL commonly replaces missing functionality for a display or audio device so that the application can continue to render the information that relies on the missing device functionality. In most cases, the HEL will use multiple steps to send data to existing hardware elements in order to create an effect similar to the actual hardware effect. Generally, using a HEL is slower than using the actual hardware.

HEL   See *hardware emulation layer*.

HID   See *human interface device*.

hierarchical   (1) A method of arranging data within a database. Hierarchical databases rely on a node structure rather than a relational structure. (2) A method of displaying information on screen that relies on an indeterminate number of nodes connected to a root node. (3) A chart or graph in which the elements are arranged in ranks. The ranks usually follow an order of simple to complex or higher to lower.

human interface device (HID)   A term that refers to the ergonomic functionality provided by a device or the ability of the device to create a human-to-computer interface. Generally, a HID provides additional input about the support it provides and could include special functionality. An application must provide special programming to make use of the HID features. General technologies such as DirectX normally treat all devices equally. For example, a mouse is always a mouse when used with DirectX, even if it does include HID features.

I

ICM   See *Image Color Manager.*

IDE   See *integrated development environment.*

IDE drive   See *integrated device electronics drive.*

ILDASM   See *Intermediate Language Disassembler.*

IMA   See *Interactive Multimedia Association.*

Image Color Manager (ICM)   A special graphics subsystem component that converts the colors produced by one device so that they're compatible with those available on another device. The result is that the output of both devices doesn't show the normal variations in color that some program applications currently produce.

integrated development environment (IDE)   A programming language front end that provides all the tools you need to write an application through a single editor. Older DOS programming language products provided several utilities, one for each of the main programming tasks. Most (if not all) Windows programming languages provide some kind of IDE support.

integrated device electronics drive (IDE drive)   A hard disk drive that uses the integrated device electronics (IDE) interface. All the components needed to use and access the drive are located on the drive itself. A cable connects the drive to a host adapter, which connects the drive to the PC bus. Early IDE devices included hard drives only. Newer IDE devices include tape and CD-ROM drives as well.

Intermediate Language Disassembler   (ILDASM) A utility that enables a developer to examine code within a .NET assembly. The disassembler shows the intermediate language (IL) code created by a compiler and interpreted by the Common Language Runtime (CLR). A developer can also use this utility to create a text file containing the IL code within the assembly.

Interactive Multimedia Association (IMA)   A standards body responsible for defining multimedia standards on the Internet. One of the more important efforts of this standards body is the Adaptive Differential Pulse Code Modulation (ADPCM) standard, which is used for the serial wave driver in Windows 95.

L

LCD   See *liquid crystal display.*

liquid crystal display (LCD)   The electronic presentation device used by most laptop computers, handheld devices, cellular telephones, and other portable electronics. The LCD is flat and doesn't rely on tube technology in the way that many desktop display devices do. The LCD comes in many different forms and uses various technologies for presentation. There are both black-and-white and color versions of the LCD. In most cases, the LCD is a shutter-type technology where the shutters are electronically controlled and allow light from a source to pass through when open.

locally unique identifier (LUID)   Essentially a pointer to an object, the LUID identifies each process and resources for security purposes. In other words, even if a user has two copies of precisely the same resource option (like a document), both copies would have a unique LUID. This method of identification prevents some types of security access violation under Windows NT.

LUID   See *locally unique identifier.*

M

managed code   A .NET programming term that infers that the code runs under the Common Language Runtime (CLR) and relies on an intermediate language (IL) rather than native code. A managed application requires less programming effort on the part of the developer and reduces the amount of resource management the application must perform because the CLR performs the required management automatically. Many applications do run slower in a managed environment than they would in an unmanaged environment.

marshal   The act of making data created by one object accessible and acceptable to another object. The act of marshaling usually includes moving the data from one memory space to another memory space. The act could also include some type of data conversion. The type of data conversion depends upon the requirements of both objects and the data types that they support.

marshaler   The application, object, or other entity that performs marshaling between two objects. (See *marshal* for an explanation of

marshaling.) Many applications define the marshaler by the type of memory it uses or the threading model it requires. For example, many developers rely on the Visual C++ free threaded marshaler to perform many data management tasks.

MDI   See *multiple document interface.*

message handler   A specialized piece of code that accepts input from the message pump for a given message. The message handler is normally registered with the application so the message pump knows where to direct the message content. A message handler must accept a specific number of arguments and a given order as defined by the message. The arguments normally contain message-specific data required to process the message. Some message handlers can also accept user-defined data in order to perform specialized data processing.

Microsoft Installer (MSI)   (1) A technique for installing applications within Windows that allows later removal even if the system configuration has changed. This technique also provides support for additional vendor information, partial installations, multiple configurations, and installation recovery. (2) A file format containing instructions for installing Windows applications. The file is actually a database that contains specialized instructions and data in a specific format that's read by the Microsoft Installer application.

Microsoft Management Console (MMC)   A special application that acts as an object container for Windows management objects like Component Services and Computer Management. The management objects are actually special components that provide interfaces that allow the user to access them within MMC to maintain and control the operation of Windows. A developer can create special versions of these objects for application management or other tasks. Using a single application like MMC helps maintain the same user interface across all management applications.

Microsoft ZIP (MSZIP)   The specialized file compression technology used by Windows and other Microsoft applications. The technology relies on functions found in the `SetupAPI.DLL` file. This new file compression technology replaces the Lempel-Ziv algorithm used in older versions of Windows.

MIDI   See *musical instrument digital interface.*

MMC   See *Microsoft Management Console.*

mmio   See *multimedia input/output.*

MMX   See *Multimedia Extensions Processor.*

modality   The measure of a resource's responsiveness to external manipulation. For example, the term *modality* is applied to windows to indicate whether the window waits for user input before it returns to the calling application. Most dialog boxes are modal because they wait for a user response before they allow the user access to the window that created the dialog box. On the other hand, a child window in a multiple document interface (MDI) application is modeless because it doesn't wait for specific user input to end.

Motion Picture Experts Group (MPEG)   A standards group that provides file formats and other specifications in regard to full-motion video and other types of graphic displays.

MPEG   See *Motion Picture Experts Group.*

MSI   See *Microsoft Installer.*

MSZIP   See *Microsoft ZIP.*

Multimedia Extensions Processor (MMX)   The latest edition of the Intel family of processors includes multimedia-specific commands within the chip. Instead of multiple commands to perform a multimedia-related task, one command will do. This version of the chip should boost overall system performance. It should also allow vendors to produce less-expensive PCs by using less-complex parts in construction.

multimedia input/output (mmio)   Win32 API functions that enable the developer to open, read, write, and close files for use with multimedia.

multiple document interface (MDI)   A method for displaying more than one document at a time within a parent window. The Program Manager interface is an example of MDI. You see multiple groups within the Program Manager window.

multithreaded application   An application that relies on more than one thread of execution to perform a given task. (See *multithreading* and *thread* for additional details.)

multithreading   An operating-system-specific technique for breaking one or more application tasks into multiple threads of execution. Using this technique allows the operating system to devote more resources to higher priority tasks, increasing perceived system performance. The programmer must write the application to take advantage of this operating system feature when available.

musical instrument digital interface (MIDI)   A method for allowing musical instruments to interact with a computer system. There are two components to MIDI. The hardware component provides a physical connection between a computer and a musical instrument. The software component provides the means to represent music in digital format. This includes storage of the information in either an RMI or MID file.

N

NAT   See *network address translation*.

network address translation (NAT)   The process of converting a local friendly name for a resource into a global resource identifier. For example, Windows uses this feature to convert local resource requests into Internet addresses.

NTFS   See *Windows NT File System*.

P

PDA   See *personal digital assistant*.

personal digital assistant (PDA)   A very small PC normally used for personal tasks such as taking notes and maintaining an itinerary during business trips. PDAs normally rely on special operating systems and lack any standard application support.

PID   See *Process Identifier*.

pointer   (1) An arrow-shaped object used to show the currently selected menu item. (2) An arrow-shaped graphic used to show the viewer which object a label identifies.

point-of-view (POV) control   The control found on some joysticks; enables the user to change the perspective of the scene displayed on screen without using keyboard controls.

POV   See *point-of-view (POV) control*.

Process Identifier (PID)   A numeric value associated with a process running on a specific machine. Every process has a unique PID, making it possible to locate a specific process even if there are multiple copies of a single application running on the machine. The PID is used by a wide variety of monitoring applications. It's also used to access an application or as a means of identification when terminating an errant application.

R

raster operation (ROP)   A description of a scan drawing technique that uses lines to present a graphic element on a device such as a monitor. Such a device uses scanning techniques for display. The effect of scanning left to right and top to bottom while drawing lines that create a visual effect is called raster. A raster operation describes picture slices so the device can present the completed graphic on screen.

resource interchange file format (RIFF)   A specialized FOURCC. This heading tells any application opening the file that this is a standardized resource file. For example, a WAV file would contain this entry if it used the standard wave file format.

RIFF   See *resource interchange file format*.

role-based security   A method for controlling access to an object based on the requestor's job function within an organization. In other words, if the requestor has a specific job function (or role), then they're allowed to access the object. This method of maintaining security is an extension of groups. However, unlike groups, a requestor must perform a specific job function before access is granted. This security methodology is normally used with COM+ applications.

ROP   See *raster operation*.

ROT   See *Running Object Table*.

ROV   A remotely operated vehicle.

Running Object Table (ROT)   A special Component Object Model (COM) table maintained by the operating system. Components that will allow a client to create a connection to a running instance need to register themselves in the ROT. There are two levels of registration: strong and weak. The main difference between strong and weak ROT registrations is that a strong registration will prevent an object from shutting down until all of the connected clients have also shut down. A weak reference will get shut down automatically once all strong references to the object are cleared. In most cases, you'll want to use the default registration level of weak.

S

SACL   See *Security Access Control List*.

scalability   A definition of an object's ability to sustain increases in load. For example, companies often rate networking systems by their ability to scale from one to many users. Software scalability determines the ability of the software to run on more than one machine when needed without making it appear that more than one machine is in use.

SCSI adapter controller   See *Small Computer System Interface (SCSI) adapter controller*.

SDK   See *software development kit*.

Security Access Control List (SACL)   One of several specialized access control lists (ACLs) used to maintain object integrity. This list controls Windows's auditing feature. Every time a user or group accesses an object and the auditing feature for that object is turned on, Windows makes an entry in the audit log.

security descriptor   A reference to the level of security assigned to an object. This is the data structure that tells the security system what rights a user needs to access the object. The user's rights are contained within an access token. In short, the security descriptor is the lock and the access token is the key.

security identifier (SID)   The part of a user's access token that identifies the user throughout the network—it's like having an account number. The user token that the SID identifies tells what groups the user belongs to and what privileges the user has. Each group also has a SID, so the user's SID contains references to the various group SIDs that they belongs to, not a complete set of group access rights. You'd normally use the User Manager utility under Windows NT to change the contents of this access token. You'll use the Active Directory Users and Computers console when working with Windows 2000.

serial stream A method of data transfer where each bit is transmitted using a single bit path. Instead of transmitting the data in packets, the sender transmits the data continuously. This technique works well in applications such as multimedia where the recipient must receive a single continuous data stream and the size of the stream is unknown or too large for local memory.

SID See *security identifier*.

single-threaded application An application that contains just one thread of execution that begins at the start of the process and ends with the process. (See *thread* for additional information.)

Small Computer System Interface (SCSI) adapter controller A computer interface card that allows you to connect up to seven devices to the computer system. The current SCSI standard is SCSI-2. Typical SCSI devices include tape drives, hard disk drives, and CD-ROM drives. SCSI devices typically provide high-transfer rates (10–15MB/s) and access times (device type dependent).

snap-ins Component technologies allow one application to serve as a container for multiple subapplications. A snap-in refers to a component that's designed to reside within another application. The snap-in performs one specific task out of all of the tasks that the application as a whole can perform. The Microsoft Management Console (MMC) is an example of a host application. Network administrators perform all Windows 2000/XP management tasks using snap-ins designed to work with MMC.

software development kit (SDK) A special add-on to an operating system or an application that describes how to access its internal features. For example, an SDK for Windows would show how to create a File Open dialog box. Programmers use an SDK to learn how to access special Windows components such as OLE.

Sound Retrieval System (SRS) A fancy term for a sound card and associated circuitry. The SRS interprets digital input and outputs it as analog sound. It can also accept analog sound and translate it into digital data that the system can manipulate and store on disk.

spool The act of placing data in a temporary buffer for processing at a later time. The buffer often appears in a specific place on a hard drive. In many cases, the application that originates the data doesn't process it—a secondary application performs this task in the background. One of the most common examples of spooling is the data sent by an application to a buffer on disk for processing by a printer application.

SRS See *Sound Retrieval System*.

synchronous message handling A method of sending a message in which the calling thread waits for the message handler to complete processing of the message data before allowing the calling thread to resume. The calling thread is blocked until the message hander returns, which means the application can appear to stop executing.

T

thread One executable unit within an application. Running an application creates a main thread. One of the things the main thread does is display a window with a menu. The main thread can also create other threads. Background printing may appear as a thread, for example. Only 32-bit applications support threads.

token   The representation of data, an object, database element, programming syntax, or other information using a code word, phrase, number, or object. For example, in programming, a token could represent a statement, punctuation mark, argument, or other syntactical element. Users often receive tokens describing their rights as part of the security features of an operating system. Networks also use tokens to control data flow and perform other tasks.

U

Unicode character   A double-byte character used to represent more than the character set used by the English language. Unicode character sets are standardized by international convention. Advanced operating systems normally rely on Unicode for enhanced language support and consistent data handling. (Contrast this character support with that provided by ANSI using the ASCII character set.)

Uniform Resource Locator (URL)   A text representation of a specific location on the Internet. URLs normally include the protocol (`http://`, for example), the target location (World Wide Web, or `www`), the domain or server name (`mycompany`), and a domain type (`com` for commercial). It can also include a hierarchical location within that Web site. The URL usually specifies a particular file on the Web server,

although there are some situations in which a Web server will use a default filename. For example, asking the browser to find `http://www.mycompany.com` would probably display the `DEFAULT.HTM` file at that location.

uninterruptible power source (UPS)   Usually a combination of an inverter and a battery used to provide power to one or more electrical devices during a power outage. A UPS normally contains power-sensing circuitry and surge-suppression modules. Some UPSs provide standby power and a direct connection between the power source and the protected equipment. Other UPSs use the power source to charge the battery constantly. The protected equipment always derives its power from the inverter, effectively isolating the equipment from the power source.

Universal Plug and Play (UPnP)   A specialized form of device communication wherein the device provides information that allows an operating system to install support for it even if the device isn't physically attached to the system. UPnP supports any intelligent device using any network connection. Theoretically, you could write an application that enables the user's furnace to send a message to the user stating that the temperature has dropped below prescribed limits.

Universal Serial Bus (USB)   A form of serial bus that allows multiple external devices to share a single port. This technique reduces the number of interrupts and port addresses required to service the needs of devices such as mice and modems.

unmanaged application environment   A native code platform that lacks support for memory management and other features such as a

Garbage Collector. The .NET initiative has made it necessary to differentiate between applications that support the Win32 API and native code directly from those that use the .NET Framework. An unmanaged application allocates and deallocates memory itself and doesn't rely on the Garbage Collector to perform this task. The advantage is that the developer gains full access to the Win32 API. The disadvantage is that the approach is error prone and can result in memory allocation errors (among other problems).

unmanaged code   A .NET programming term for natively compiled code that runs directly under DOS or Windows. Native code executes without the benefit of the Common Language Runtime (CLR).

UPnP   See *Universal Plug and Play.*

UPS   See *uninterruptible power source.*

URL   See *Uniform Resource Locator.*

USB   See *Universal Serial Bus.*

V

variable   An identifier used to point to an area of memory containing a value.

VBI   See *Vertical Blanking Interval.*

Vertical Blanking Interval (VBI)   The time during which the display doesn't present any information on screen because the scan line is moving from the lower right corner to the upper left corner of the display.

VFAT   See *Virtual File Allocation Table.*

Virtual File Allocation Table (VFAT)   An enhanced method of disk formatting based on the FAT system. It allows for additional functionality such as long filenames.

W

WAV file   A type of file used to store sound data. The file can hold data in different formats, which include stereo or monaural, sampling frequency, and sampling size. In addition to data, the file contains descriptive information that the calling application uses to reconstruct the stored sound.

Web Distributed Authoring and Versioning (WebDAV) protocol   A protocol that allows a developer to publish files or folders to any Web service that provides the required support. This protocol provides automatic encryption and decryption to keep the data secure, which also makes the data transfer process transparent.

WebDAV protocol   See *Web Distributed Authoring and Versioning protocol.*

Windows NT File System (NTFS)   The method of formatting a hard disk drive used by Windows NT/2000/XP. While it provides significant speed advantages over other formatting techniques, only the Windows NT/2000/XP operating system and applications designed to work with that operating system can access a drive formatted using this technique. Windows 2000 uses NTFS5, a version of this file system designed to provide additional features, like enhanced security. Windows XP uses a newer version of NTFS than Windows 2000 uses; it provides other improvements such as encrypted file sharing.

Windows Scripting Host (WSH)   The Windows capability to write and execute scripts at the system level. This allows the user to reduce the number of repetitive tasks required to get applications to work together. A user can use a script, for example, that scans their hard drive for errors, backs it up, then optimizes it—all without any work on the user's part except for the initial script execution. The user may have to perform additional work if the script encounters an error, but nothing more than the user would normally do. Scripts can employ one of two default languages, JavaScript or VBScript. The user can also create scripts via languages like REXX and Perl when working with a third-party add-in product.

wrapper DLL   A dynamic link library that provides access to Windows or C library functionality that's inaccessible from the managed environment. For example, you need a wrapper DLL to create an interface to the functions found in the MMC.LIB file used by C/C++ applications for MMC snap-in development.

WSH   See *Windows Scripting Host.*

Index

Note to the Reader: Page numbers in **bold** indicate the principle discussion of a topic or the definition of a term. Page numbers in *italic* indicate illustrations.

M

O

P

TELL US WHAT YOU THINK!

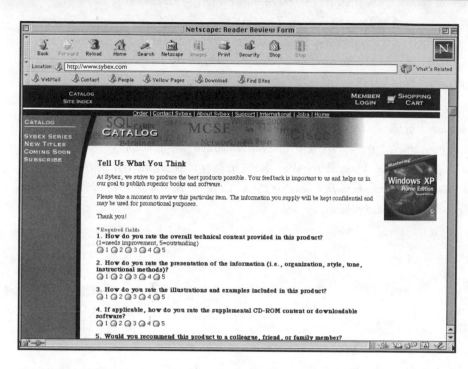

Your feedback is critical to our efforts to provide you with the best books and software on the market. Tell us what you think about the products you've purchased. It's simple:

1. Go to the Sybex website.
2. Find your book by typing the ISBN number or title into the Search field.
3. Click on the book title when it appears.
4. Click **Submit a Review.**
5. Fill out the questionnaire and comments.
6. Click **Submit.**

With your feedback, we can continue to publish the highest quality computer books and software products that today's busy IT professionals deserve.

www.sybex.com

SYBEX Inc. • 1151 Marina Village Parkway, Alameda, CA 94501 • 510-523-8233

SYBEX®

The quotation on the bottom of the front cover is taken from the forty-first chapter of Lao Tzu's Tao Te Ching, the classic work of Taoist philosophy. This particular verse is from the translation by D. C. Lau (copyright 1963) and communicates the idea that true experience is not the end result, but the journey getting there. The verse at the end of this passage says: "It is the way alone that excels in bestowing and in accomplishing."

It is traditionally held that Lao Tzu lived in the fifth century B.C. in China, during the Chou dynasty, but it is unclear whether he was actually a historical figure. It is said that he was a teacher of Confucius. The concepts embodied in the Tao Te Ching influenced religious thinking in the Far East, including Zen Buddhism in Japan. Many in the West, however, have wrongly understood the Tao Te Ching to be primarily a mystical work; in fact, much of the advice in the book is grounded in a practical moral philosophy governing personal conduct.